INTERNATIONAL HANDBOOK ON WHISTLEBLOWING RESEARCH

International Handbook on Whistleblowing Research

Edited by

A.J. Brown

Professor of Public Policy and Law and Program Leader, Public Integrity and Anti-corruption, Centre for Governance and Public Policy, Griffith University, Australia

David Lewis

Professor of Employment Law, Middlesex University, UK

Richard Moberly

Associate Dean for Faculty and Professor of Law, University of Nebraska College of Law, USA

Wim Vandekerckhove

Senior Lecturer in Organizational Behaviour, University of Greenwich Business School, London, UK

Edward Elgar

Cheltenham, UK • Northampton, MA, USA

Published by
Edward Elgar Publishing Limited
The Lypiatts
15 Lansdown Road
Cheltenham
Glos GL50 2JA
UK

Edward Elgar Publishing, Inc.
William Pratt House
9 Dewey Court
Northampton
Massachusetts 01060
USA

A catalogue record for this book
is available from the British Library

Library of Congress Control Number: 2014932513

This book is available electronically in the ElgarOnline.com Law Subject Collection, E-ISBN 978 1 78100 679 5

MIX
Paper from
responsible sources
FSC® C013056
FSC
www.fsc.org

ISBN 978 1 78100 678 8

Typeset by Columns Design XML Ltd, Reading
Printed and bound in Great Britain by T.J. International Ltd, Padstow

Contents

Contributors

Brita Bjørkelo is a licensed Clinical Psychologist and has written a Ph.D on 'Whistleblowing at Work: Antecedents and Consequences'. She has also contributed to papers and book chapters about whistleblowing, bullying, workaholism and sexual harassment and published in journals such as *Journal of Managerial Psychology*, *Psychology and Society*, *Journal of Occupational and Organizational Psychology* and *European Journal of Work and Organizational Psychology*. Dr Bjørkelo works as an Associate Professor at the Police Leadership and Management Program, Department of Post-Graduate Studies, Norwegian Police University College, Oslo, Norway, and is also project manager of a research project on Ethics, Social Media and Teacher Education.

Rachelle Bosua is a lecturer in the Department of Computing and Information Systems in the School of Engineering at the University of Melbourne, Australia. She received her Ph.D in 2008 and since then her research interests include a number of areas that involve the supportive and enabling role of information and communications technologies (ICT) in different organizational contexts. In particular, she is interested in the role of social networks and social media in the creation, sharing and dissemination of knowledge within and across teams and organizations. She is also working in the areas of secure information and knowledge management, knowledge strategy and knowledge retention. More recently she has started exploring the area of flexible work and aspects of ICT that facilitate and enable the many facets of a new mobile workforce.

A.J. Brown is Professor of public policy and law, and program leader, public integrity and anti-corruption, in the Centre for Governance and Public Policy, Griffith University, Australia. He is a former senior investigator for Australia's Commonwealth Ombudsman and has worked in all branches and at all levels of government, as well as researching and consulting in other areas of complex governance reform. He is a member of the board of directors of Transparency International Australia. He has been project leader on major national and international studies into whistleblowing, including the 'Whistling While They Work' project, and was editor and co-author of *Whistleblowing in the Australian Public Sector* (2008) and *Whistling While They Work* (2011), published by the

Australia and New Zealand School of Government and ANU E-Press. He has been a major advisor to Australian governments on whistleblowing law reform, including the Public Interest Disclosure Act 2013 (Commonwealth of Australia).

Hege Høivik Bye is a social psychologist whose main research interests are discrimination, workplace diversity and acculturation processes, cultural differences in self-presentation, and recruitment and selection. The current chapter is her first publication on whistleblowing. Dr Bye works as an associate professor at the Department of Psychosocial Science at the Faculty of Psychology, University of Bergen, Norway.

Kim Crow is a Research Associate of the College of Law, Australian National University. Kim has a BA and LLB (hons) from the University of Melbourne. She is an Australian Olympic Rower (Olympic Silver Medalist, Double Sculls, 2012; Bronze Medalist, Single Sculls 2012) and was captain of the Australian Rowing Team in 2009. She has worked in private legal firms specializing in commercial and intellectual property law.

Tom Devine is legal director of the Government Accountability Project (GAP), Washington DC, USA, where he has worked since January 1979. GAP is a non-profit, non-partisan public interest organization that champions the rights of whistleblowers, those employees who exercise freedom of speech to challenge abuses of power that betray the public trust. During his 33 years at GAP he has represented or informally helped over 6,000 whistleblowers to defend themselves against retaliation or make a difference, and has been a leader in the campaigns to pass or defend 25 major domestic or international whistleblower laws enacted over the last two decades. He has been an 'Ambassador of Whistleblowing' for the State Department in over a dozen nations on speaking tours to advocate whistleblower rights as a cornerstone transparency reform for globalization. Tom has authored or co-authored numerous newspaper and law review articles and books, including *The Corporate Whistleblower Survival Guide: A Handbook for Committing the Truth*, which won the award as 'International Business Book of the Year' at the 2011 Frankfurt Book Fair.

Suelette Dreyfus is a Research Fellow at the Department of Computing and Information Systems at the University of Melbourne, Australia. Her research interests include the impact of digital technologies on whistleblowing, institutional accountability and the role of the media. She also works in the e-health and e-education areas, where her work has appeared in academic journals such as *Nursing Outlook* and *Emergency*

Medicine Australasia. Prior to working as an academic researcher, she worked as a professional journalist on Australia's largest selling daily newspaper, where she trained and worked as a staff reporter. She is the author of a well-known book about computer hacking, *Underground*, which has been translated into seven other languages and made into two films.

Terry Morehead Dworkin is Scholar in Residence at the Seattle University Law School and is the Jack R. Wentworth Emerita Professor, Business Law, of the Kelley School of Business at Indiana University, USA. She has served as President of the Academy of Legal Studies in Business and been Resident Director of the Center for European Studies in the Netherlands; a scholar at the Institute for Advanced Legal Studies in London, England, and a law teacher at the Friedrich-Schiller University in Germany. She has received many research awards including four Holmes-Cardozo and Hoeber research awards from the Academy of Legal Studies in Business, who in 2008 also awarded her the Senior Faculty Award of Excellence.

Bea Edwards is the Executive Director and International Program Director at the Government Accountability Project (GAP), a US non-profit organization that promotes accountability by protecting whistle-blowers, advancing occupational free speech and empowering citizen activists. Ms Edwards holds a MA in Latin American Studies from the University of Texas and a Ph.D in Sociology from the American University. Before joining GAP, she monitored loans and projects of the World Bank and the Inter-American Development Bank for Public Services International, a global labor federation of public sector unions. She has also served as a Senior Specialist for Social and Economic Affairs at the Organization of American States, designing vocational training programs for post-conflict settings.

Björn Fasterling is a professor of law and business ethics at EDHEC Business School in Lille, France. He teaches legal management, international commercial law, European law, corporate governance and corporate social responsibility. He researches and publishes in the fields of business ethics, compliance and legal management. Prior to joining EDHEC, Prof. Fasterling practiced as a German lawyer in the Berlin office of the US law firm Wilmer Hale. Björn Fasterling holds both German Law degrees (1. state exam 1997, 2. state exam 2001), a Ph.D in Law (Dr. iur.) from the University of Osnabrück (2001) and an LLM degree from the University of Stockholm (1998). He is a German national and, in addition to German, speaks English, French and some Swedish.

Tom Faunce BA/LLB (Hons) (ANU) BMed (Newcastle) Ph.D (ANU-Crawford Prize) is an Australian Research Council (ARC) Future Fellow. He is a Professor jointly in the ANU College of Law and College of Medicine, Biology and the Environment. He is team leader of an ARC Discovery Grant focused on developing a conceptual framework for implementing aspects of the US False Claims Act in Australia and has published widely in this area.

Paul Harpur is a Lecturer at T.C. Beirne School of Law, the University of Queensland, Australia. Dr Paul Harpur's research and teaching expertise are in the areas of anti-discrimination laws, work health and safety laws and corporate social responsibility; he has published on these topics in international law journals. Dr Harpur has a mixture of practice and research experience, having formerly practiced as a lawyer and held research posts, including research fellowships at the University of Queensland, Griffith Law School and on an Australian Research Council Grant with Griffith University, the Queensland University of Technology, the United Nations University, New York University and the Centre for International Governance (Canada).

Reeva Lederman is a well-known academic in the area of Health Informatics. She has published in esteemed journals such as the *European Journal of Health Informatics* and *ACM Transactions on CHI* and was the 2012 recipient of the Stafford Beer Medal in Information Systems Research. She has had an academic posting at the Department of Computing and Information Systems, University of Melbourne, Australia, since 2000.

David Lewis is Professor of Employment Law at Middlesex University, London, United Kingdom. He has considerable experience as a consultant and is an ACAS arbitrator. David has jointly authored three general books on employment law and has contributed to and edited three specialist works on whistleblowing. He has been researching the subject of employment protection for whistleblowers since 1994 and recent empirical studies have been funded by the British Academy and the Nuffield Foundation as well as SAI Global. David has published internationally in law, business ethics, information technology and human resource management journals. He is currently convenor of the International Whistleblowing Research Network.

Jos Leys worked as a financial professional before joining the Center for Ethics and Value Inquiry (CEVI) at Ghent University, Belgium, where he is currently rounding off his Ph.D research. He holds Master degrees in economics and in philosophy, and has published on business ethics, professional ethics and socially responsible investment.

Kim Loyens studied Criminology and Public Administration at the KU Leuven, Belgium. She holds a Ph.D in Criminology. For her doctoral study at the KU Leuven, she conducted ethnographic research on ethical decision-making in the Belgian labor inspection and federal police. She currently works at the Utrecht University (Netherlands) as an assistant professor and at the Leuven Institute of Criminology (Belgium) as a lecturer. Her publications include work on peer reporting, rule-bending, integrity systems and whistleblowing policies in *Administration and Society*, *Journal of Business Ethics*, *Police Practice and Research*, *Policing* and *Innovation*. She has provided advisory services on ethics management for the Belgian police and on anti-corruption for the European Commission.

Jeroen Maesschalck studied Public Administration and Philosophy at the University of Ghent (Belgium) and at the London School of Economics and Political Science (UK). He holds a Ph.D in Social Sciences from the KU Leuven (Belgium). He is currently associate professor at the Leuven Institute of Criminology of the KU Leuven, where he is the vice-dean of research of the Faculty of Law. His research and teaching focus on public administration ethics and on management and policy making in the criminal justice system. His publications include contributions in *Journal of Business Ethics*, *Administration and Society*, *Public Administration* and *Public Integrity*. He has consulted on ethics management both within Belgium (local, regional and federal government) and internationally (e.g., OECD).

Brian Martin is Professor of Social Sciences at the University of Wollongong, Australia. He is the author of a dozen books and hundreds of articles on dissent, non-violent action, scientific controversies, democracy and other topics. He has served as president of Whistleblowers Australia and is currently vice-president and editor of the organization's newsletter, *The Whistle*. He hosts a large website on suppression of dissent.

Daniel P. Meyer is Executive Director for Intelligence Community Whistleblowing and Source Protection (ED-ICW&SP), serving as a direct-report to the US Government's Inspector General of the Intelligence Community. From 2004 to 2010 Mr Meyer served the Inspector General of the US Department of Defense first as Director, Civilian Reprisal Investigations and then as Director, Whistleblowing and Transparency. In these positions, Mr Meyer either investigated or had oversight of cases regarding disclosures on the 9/11 attacks; the use of security-clearance decision-making as a tool for reprisal and discrimination; and the treatment of both soldiers and their remains after injury or death during the Global War on Terror. Prior to 2004, Mr Meyer was General Counsel for Public Employees for Environmental Responsibility (PEER) where he appeared before the US Court of Appeals for the First Circuit on the question of state sovereign immunity under Federal whistle-blowing statutes. Mr Meyer is a survivor of the 1989 explosion onboard the battleship *Iowa* (BB-61), which took the lives of 47 of his shipmates. He took his Bachelor's degree at Cornell University (1987); juris doctorate at Indiana University School of Law, Bloomington (1995); and has professional certificates as a National Security Studies Fellow from Maxwell School, Syracuse University (Leadership Course, 2004; Decision-Making Course, 2005).

Marcia P. Miceli is Professor of Management at the McDonough School of Business, Georgetown University, Washington DC, USA. Her research concerns whistleblowing and employee voice in organizations. She also studies compensation systems. Together with Janet Near and Terry Dworkin, she has published two books on whistleblowing. Her earlier articles have appeared in journals such as *Academy of Management Journal*, *Academy of Management Review*, *Administrative Science Quarterly*, *Business Ethics Quarterly*, *Human Relations*, *Industrial and Labor Relations Review*, *Industrial Relations*, *Journal of Applied Psychology*, *Journal of Business Ethics*, *Journal of Management*, *Organization Science* and *Personnel Psychology*.

Simon Milton received his Ph.D from the University of Tasmania reporting the first comprehensive analysis of data modelling languages using a common-sense realistic ontology. Dr Milton continues his interests in the ontological foundations of information and the implications of top-level ontological commitments in information modelling. His work extends to the value and use of information in business, science and society. He is an Associate Professor in the Department of Computing and Information Systems at the University of Melbourne, Australia, and director of Melbourne School of Information.

Richard Moberly is Associate Dean for Faculty and a Professor of Law at the University of Nebraska College of Law, USA. He graduated *magna cum laude* from Harvard Law School and served as an editor of the *Harvard Law Review*. Professor Moberly has published numerous articles on whistleblowing, including an empirical study of Sarbanes-Oxley claims published in the *William and Mary Law Review*. He has also testified before the US House of Representatives on whistleblower protection in the United States and spoken internationally on the Sarbanes-Oxley Act and also on whether corporate codes of ethics provide protection to whistleblowers.

Frederick M. Morgan, Jr is a partner in the US Qui Tam/FCA firm Morgan Verkamp. He has 29 years' experience in complex federal litigation at the trial and appellate levels bringing FCA cases against pharmaceutical and medical device companies, defense contractors, Medicare providers, and others who provide goods or services to the United States. Rick was one of Taxpayers Against Fraud's 'Whistleblower Lawyers of the Year' in 2010. After graduating from the University of Cincinnati College of Law in 1983, Rick served for two years as Law Clerk to United States District Judge David S. Porter. He then was selected through the Attorney-General's Honors Program as a Trial Attorney in the Civil Division of the United States Department of Justice in Washington DC, routinely appearing in courts throughout the country on behalf of the United States. He returned to Cincinnati in 1990 and has represented whistleblowers since 1996. Rick has served or is serving as lead or co-lead counsel in cases against Boeing, HCA, Blackstone Medical/Orthofix, General Electric, General Dynamics, Lockheed Martin, Dyncorp, Solvay Pharmaceuticals, Novartis Pharmaceuticals, Pfizer, and others. Settlements include Blackstone/Orthofix, US$30 million; Novartis, US$20 million; Novartis, US$422 million; Boeing, US$61.5 million; Diabetes Treatment Centers, US$30 million, and many others. In addition to his duties to Morgan Verkamp's clients, Rick is an active speaker and author regarding the False Claims Act. Rick also has drafted 'friend of the Court' briefs in three Supreme Court cases involving the False Claims Act, one of which was filed on behalf of Senator Charles Grassly, the Act's principal sponsor. He is regularly consulted by practitioners, academicians and journalists seeking knowledge about the False Claims Act.

Janet P. Near is a professor and the Dale M. Coleman Chair of Management in the Department of Management and Entrepreneurship at the Kelley School of Business, Indiana University, USA, where she teaches organizational theory and design. Her research concerns whistleblowing in organizations and organizational dissent. She also studies the effects of job satisfaction on life satisfaction and implications of this relationship for job performance. She has published two books (most recently, Miceli, Near and Dworkin, *Whistle-blowing in Organizations*, 2008) and over 60 articles in journals such as *Academy of Management Journal*, *Academy of Management Review*, *Administrative Science Quarterly*, *American Business Law Journal*, *Human Relations*, *Industrial*

Labor Relations Review, *Journal of Applied Psychology*, *Journal of Business Ethics*, *Journal of Organization Behavior*, *Journal of Management, Organization Science,* and *Personnel Psychology*. She has served previously as department chairperson and as chairperson of Doctoral Programs in Business.

Tony Nikolic is a Research Associate at the Australian National University College of Law. He has an Honors Degree in Social Science Criminology, Bachelor of Law from the University of Western Sydney and Diploma of Business Management. He currently resides in Sydney, Australia, and enjoys spending time with his children. After working most of his career as a tradesman in telecommunications, he moved towards writing in academia after a life-changing accident. Following his graduation from University he worked with the Australian Institute of Criminology on the Drug Use and Monitoring Project (DUMA) before progressing into academic writing where his passion has turned to writing about *(qui tam)* public/private laws. He is a keen musician and sports fan and prospective Ph.D candidate.

Jane Olsen is a Senior Researcher/Analyst, Public Interest Disclosures Unit, NSW Ombudsman, in the New South Wales (NSW) public sector, Sydney, Australia. She is a former Research Officer, Research and Prevention Unit, Crime and Misconduct Commission (Queensland), and Senior Research Assistant in the Socio-Legal Research Centre, Griffith University, Australia. She has researched, published and provided extensive policy advice to government agencies on the practicalities of whistleblowing.

Michael T. Rehg is an associate professor of management at California State University, Chico, USA. He holds a Ph.D from Indiana University in strategic management. His research has been published in academic journals including *Human Relations*, *Organization Science*, *Human Resource Management*, *Business Ethics Quarterly*, *Journal of Business Ethics* and *Cross Cultural Management: An International Journal*. His research focuses on the whistleblowing process, the influence of culture on whistleblowing, and retaliation against whistleblowers.

Peter Roberts was until recently Senior Lecturer in the Australian Graduate School of Policing and Security at Charles Sturt University, Canberra. He teaches a number of subjects at the graduate level and has worked on Australian Research Council-funded research projects examining national integrity systems and public sector whistleblowing, publishing in both areas. Peter was principal author of the final report of the whistleblowing research project 'Whistling While They Work', *A Good*

Practice Guide for Managing Internal Reporting of Wrongdoing in Public Sector Organizations. Before going to CSU, Peter was a Senior Executive with the Commonwealth Attorney-General's Department and the National Crime Authority.

Marit Skivenes is a professor at the Department of Administration and organization theory, University of Bergen, Norway. Her research is about whistleblowing, publicity, the welfare state and child welfare systems. She has authored several articles, book chapters and books with S.C. Trygstad on topics that include disclosure legislation and whistleblowing in the Norwegian labor market.

Rodney Smith is Associate Professor in the Department of Government and International Relations at the University of Sydney, Australia. His research interests include public sector integrity and corruption. He was a chief investigator on the Australian Research Council-funded 'Whistling While They Work' project that resulted in the first systematic studies of Australian public sector whistleblowing.

John Spencer is a barrister and former Chief Reporter with the Incorporated Council of Law Reporting for England and Wales. He is a visiting lecturer at Middlesex University, UK.

Maureen Spencer is a Principal Lecturer in Law at Middlesex University, United Kingdom. Her teaching and research interests include criminal evidence, public law, labor law and legal education. She has published widely in these areas in journals including *Journal of Law and Society*, *Legal Studies* and *Northern Ireland Legal Quarterly*. She is currently writing a monograph on the history of trial secrecy in common law jurisdictions. The book will draw on policy as well as trial papers to trace the use of public interest immunity certificates and, more recently, specific legislation to deny to defendants and claimants access to evidence which is available to state authorities.

Sissel C. Trygstad is a research director at Fafo, Institute for Labour and Social Research, in Oslo, Norway. Her research is about participation, workplace democracy, work organization and whistleblowing. She has published a number of articles and book chapters with M. Skivenes as well as a book entitled *Public Information, Freedom of Speech and Whistleblowers in Norwegian Municipalities* (2012).

Eva Tsahuridu is the Professional Standards and Governance Policy Adviser of CPA Australia. She oversees the policy, guidance and resource development in professional and ethical standards and governance. She participates in a number of forums on ethics and governance and is a technical adviser at the International Ethics Standards Board for Accountants (IESBA) of the International Federation of Accountants (IFAC). She contributes to CPA Australia's publications *INTHEBLACK, INPRACTICE* and *Real Business*. Before she joined CPA Australia, Eva was an academic in Australian and European universities developing and teaching business ethics and governance courses and managing undergraduate and post-graduate programs. Eva publishes in the areas of business ethics, governance and management and contributes to academic journals as a member of editorial boards and as a reviewer.

Tina Uys is Professor of Sociology at the University of Johannesburg, South Africa, and was the head of department for 12 years. She is the Vice-President (National Associations) of the International Sociological Association (ISA) for the term 2010–2014 as well as the Vice-President (Programme) of Research Committee 46 on Clinical Sociology. She is also a member of the Editorial Collective responsible for *South African Review of Sociology*, the official journal of SASA. Tina is a past president of the South African Sociological Association (SASA) and of the Research Committee on Social Psychology (RC42), as well as a past member of the ISA's Executive Committee (2006–2010). She specializes in clinical sociology, focusing on whistleblowing, contested identities in student communities and South African sociology. She has also published on HIV/AIDS, relative deprivation and developments in higher education.

Wim Vandekerckhove is Senior Lecturer in Organizational Behavior at the University of Greenwich Business School, United Kingdom. He is the coordinator of the special interest group on Teaching Business Ethics within the European Business Ethics Network. He has published widely on whistleblowing, business ethics and global ethics.

Shelley Walden was until recently the International Program Officer for the Government Accountability Project (GAP), where she monitored whistleblower protections at numerous international governmental organizations (IGOs). She has co-authored several GAP studies including 'Tipping the Scales: Is the United Nations Justice System Promoting Accountability in the Peacekeeping Missions or Undermining it?' and has spoken about whistleblower protections at labor events organized by the Federation of International Civil Servants' Associations and the World Food Programme Staff Association. Her analysis of the shortcomings in the United Nations' justice system was published in the book *A Global Agenda: Issues Before the United Nations 2009–2010*. Before joining GAP in 2004, Ms Walden worked as a freelance journalist and as a Foundation for Sustainable Development fellow with Save the Children in Bolivia, where she helped launch a housekeepers' rights campaign.

She holds a BA in Journalism and International Studies from the University of North Carolina at Chapel Hill.

Chris Wheeler is the Deputy NSW Ombudsman, in Sydney, Australia. He has close to 30 years' experience in complaint handling and investigations, as well as extensive experience in management and public administration. Among other things, Chris is responsible for the work of the Public Administration Division of the Ombudsman and direct oversight of the responsibilities conferred on the Ombudsman under the Public Interest Disclosures Act. He also has responsibility to lead and coordinate the preparation of publications issued by the NSW Ombudsman to guide and improve the performance by public officials of their duties. Chris is also a town planner and lawyer who previously worked in a variety of positions in state and local government in NSW and Victoria. He also worked for some years as a solicitor in the private sector.

Jason Zuckerman is Senior Legal Advisor to the Special Counsel at the US Office of Special Counsel (OSC), Washington DC, USA. Prior to joining the OSC, Zuckerman litigated whistleblower retaliation, discrimination and *qui tam* cases, including cases setting precedent on the scope of whistleblower protections for private and public sector employees. In addition, Zuckerman worked with public interest organizations to draft and secure passage of whistleblower protection laws. Zuckerman has written more than 20 articles on whistleblower laws and co-authored a chapter on litigating whistleblower cases for the 2004 volume *Whistleblowing: The Law of Retaliatory Discharge* (BNA Books), and drafted a chapter on the DC Whistleblower Protection Act for the *DC Practice Manual*. Zuckerman graduated *magna cum laude* from Georgetown University and received his law degree from the University of Virginia. In law school, he received the University of Virginia School of Law's Pro Bono Award for his advocacy on behalf of prison inmates and mentally disabled individuals.

Foreword

Whistleblowing, and whistleblowing research, have come a long way, and fast. I can still remember how in 2001, after several years of research on whistleblowing laws, and collaboration with Professor Janet Near on a study of their effectiveness, I approached her about helping to sponsor an international conference on whistleblowing. It had become evident that state whistleblowing statutes in the United States, passed to protect whistleblowers and encourage reporting, were not very effective. It seemed to me that we could benefit from an exchange of experiences, findings and ideas with researchers from other countries. The result was the world's first International Whistleblowing Conference, held at Indiana University's Bloomington campus in April 2002. It was an exciting time because the field was so new and rapidly developing, and it was a unique opportunity to discuss our interests and results with others. That event seems so very recent – only a little over a decade ago.

How could it only be so recently that the first international research meeting dedicated to whistleblowing was held? Perceived wrongdoing and individuals who report it to others to try and get it stopped have been around as long as humanity. So why is research into such a vital, ubiquitous phenomenon in social and political life so relatively young? Of course, research into whistleblowing has been going on longer than since 2002. In modern times, the first major gatherings and publications dealing with the increasingly important roles of organizational insiders who report wrongdoing began to emerge in the United States in the 1970s, spurred by Ralph Nader's encouragement of whistleblowing to help control government employees' wrongdoing. The importance of whistleblowing seems to have grown in line with the scale and complexity of institutions since the 1950s and 1960s, with the growth of ever more powerful government agencies and corporations, and with globalization. However, the first published studies of whistleblowing tended to be qualitative, case study or anecdotal accounts of different individual whistleblowers and their struggles to uncover wrongdoing in powerful institutions, as well as what happened to them. Unsurprisingly, these were usually prominent and public cases, and somewhat heroic but chilling tales.

How typical were these experiences? From the 1970s and 1980s on, governments began investigating changes to try and outlaw retaliation against whistleblowers who 'did the right thing' and reported breaches of law and other organizational wrongdoing. This created a new focus for legal researchers, but how could we know, especially from those chilling tales, whether this new recognition of whistleblowing was working or not? Research was ad hoc, fragmented and under-valued. Whistleblowing may have become a recognized topic in the media, politics and law-making, but in research terms it was so recent and cut across so many areas of the social sciences that it seemed marginal to all of them.

All this began to change somewhat by accident, or good fortune, when Marcia Miceli and Janet Near recognized the potential of the data contained in the 1980 US Merit System Protection Board survey, and started on their now recognized analyses. Using the first large-scale survey data on the perception and reporting of wrongdoing in institutions, a more systematic way of studying whistleblowing as an element of organizational behavior was born. When Janet and I wrote our first whistleblowing article in 1987, there was little published research. Finding a journal that recognized whistleblowing as a legitimate area of scholarly endeavor was difficult. But that, too, began to change as more whistleblowing laws were passed, and more studies emerged. In 1992, publication of the Miceli and Near groundbreaking book, *Blowing the Whistle*, significantly changed the research landscape. It also gave me the chance to continue my collaboration by contributing the chapter on the law of whistleblowing.

By 2002, those who gathered in Indiana were in no doubt as to whistleblowing's potential and importance, and it seemed as if the rest of the world, too, was finally catching on. At the end of that year, *Time Magazine* listed three female US whistleblowers – Cynthia Cooper, Colleen Rowley and Sherron Watkins – as its Persons of the Year. The global consequences, if people inside organizations knew of major failures of integrity and governance but did not speak up, were becoming ever more obvious and more dire. Today, many countries embrace whistleblowing as an important tool in fighting corruption, enforcing laws, protecting public safety and helping ensure good governance. Laws designed to encourage whistleblowers and protect those who report wrongdoing have accelerated. For example, Australia has just adopted a federal whistleblowing statute, and in the United States, the recent Dodd-Frank legislation, passed to help prevent future financial crises, incorporates whistleblower sections to encourage the reporting of financial misdeeds. International anti-corruption treaties give priority to whistleblowing.

This book demonstrates how whistleblowing researchers, too, have been continuing to rise to this challenge, and how they should do so into the future. It provides the world's most comprehensive and authoritative guide to whistleblowing research, to date. Responding to the wider awakening, researchers have banded together since 2009 through the International Whistleblowing Research Network, whose meetings that year and each year since 2011, at Middlesex University, London, and Seattle University show that the pace is picking up. In this book we see the work and forward plans of an unprecedented diversity of researchers and practitioners from different disciplines, as well as different parts of the globe. The sophistication of the chapters confirms how much has changed. Now, social scientists from all corners of the world are interested to follow the path blazed by Janet Near and Marcia Miceli and engage in far more systematic, empirical research. The Australian 'Whistling While They Work' research, which features prominently in this book, is just one further groundbreaking example.

The definition of whistleblowing developed by Professors Miceli and Near three decades ago has become the standard one used by most researchers. Perhaps even more important, though, is their influence on the recognition that whistleblowing is a process composed of multiple steps: noticing the wrongdoing, deciding to act, getting some managerial response to the evidence of wrongdoing, and dealing with actual or potential retaliation against the whistleblower. Depending on the organizational or governmental response, the whistleblower may decide to report externally, with different effects on both the whistleblower and the organization. By structuring research in this manner, social scientists have been able to paint a picture that sometimes challenges media stereotypes, and provides pointers that can be useful to legislators and agencies in addressing problems.

The research presented in this book utilizes and builds on this systematic approach. The editors have assembled a team of authors who, step by step, demonstrate what knowledge we have worldwide, and what knowledge we need, to achieve more effective whistleblowing and greater protection for whistleblowers, as well as the public policy steps that can and should be taken. For example, researchers examine what types of wrongdoing should be reported, and importantly, various factors that motivate and could induce observers of wrongdoing to report it. Relevant to this is the question of whether rewards, which are heavily relied upon in the United States but seldom used elsewhere, should be used as an incentive to report. A chapter on role-prescribed whistleblowing offers a different perspective on inducements. Other research focuses on the complaint recipients, their reactions and how to better protect whistleblowers from retaliation. Equally important are recommendations for new research into the real purpose of whistleblowing: how to protect society when decision-makers and organizations do not respond adequately to allegations of wrongdoing. Related to this is research on whistleblowing in the new media, how whistleblowers react to detriments suffered and criminal penalties for retaliation or making knowingly false allegations. Crucial to understanding these questions is research that examines cultural influences on whistleblowing and theories that can support more nuanced and complex future studies. Throughout these topics, there is conceptual and practical advice on how the research should be done. In some ways, this handbook comes full circle with the chapter by Miceli, Dreyfus and Near who re-examine definitional questions and whether there is a need for a new or expanded reporting terminology.

This book is also set to become the standard reference on whistleblowing research for many years, because it not only takes stock of existing research, but sets out the questions that are yet to be answered. These are inclusive of all the key topics, from basic definitional questions about what whistleblowing is, to extremely complex questions about how organizations and governments are responding to it, and whether they are doing enough to sufficiently maximize it. Recent events emphasize how timely this is, because public policy and legislative responses to whistleblowing continue to show how difficult these processes can be, and how selectively the principles of whistleblower protection may be embraced. The revelations of Edward Snowden and Private Manning have been met with condemnation and criminal prosecution by the US government, as well as praise and support from other quarters as the repercussions of the revelations continue internationally. Their actions have also generated much discussion centered on what is legitimate whistleblowing, and whether, or when, whistleblowing deserves praise and protection. Countries and organizations are struggling to find the best way to recognize the role of whistleblowing in their governance systems. There is real demand for evidence as to how the different values associated with whistleblowing can be reconciled and how effective whistleblowing can be made to work.

While the pursuit of systematic, empirical research is a common thread throughout this book, its implications for the real world are never lost. As many examples show, whistleblowing remains fundamentally about the people who make up organizations and institutions: the individuals who speak up, and those who must decide what to do in response. Giving voice and meaning to the humanity of these people, and the challenges they face, continues to lie at the heart of whistleblowing research. However, with the disciplined approaches suggested here, focused on new questions, and through comparative research conducted more consistently across more organizations and more countries, whistleblowing research stands to provide many more insights into how our institutions should respond.

The publication of this book presents a tremendous opportunity to reflect on the progress and acceptance of whistleblowing research. It was pure fortune that Professors Near, Miceli and I were at the Indiana University Business School at the same time and recognized a mutual interest in whistleblowing – their's from a social science perspective and mine from a legal one. I have greatly benefited from having the opportunity to work with them, as have many students and scholars. This book not only documents the growing body of interdisciplinary research that stands as testament to their careers, but sets out clear questions and challenges for a whole new generation of researchers to follow in their distinguished footsteps. The book provides a welcome invitation to scholars and practitioners from every branch of social science, including law and government, to engage with one of the most challenging but important fields of research of our time.

TERRY MOREHEAD DWORKIN
Seattle, November 2013

Acknowledgements

This book would not have been possible without the dedicated support of Dr Daniela di Piramo of Griffith University's Centre for Governance and Public Policy, who supported the editors with copy-editing, reference checking and endless other editorial coordination. Her professionalism and attention to detail were tireless, and the book is testimony to her careful eye as well as her dedication to the content.

We would also like to thank the editorial team at Edward Elgar for the invitation to compile the handbook, their patience and support through to completion.

We all also wish to thank our institutions for their support, and our family and friends who also understand, and help bear the burden, of the fact that whistleblowing research is much more than just a 'day job'.

Our greatest thanks go to our authors for agreeing to participate and providing such high-quality contributions to this vital field. We also wish to thank the broader membership of the International Whistleblowing Research Network for their very active participation in research and other debates in the brief years since the Network's establishment in 2009. Their involvement in conferences and correspondence has suggested many avenues for academic exploration, including many of the issues that have been raised and analyzed in this handbook.

Any active researchers with an interest in the highest quality interdisciplinary research into whistleblowing are welcome to join the Network by emailing its convenor, David Lewis at d.b.lewis@mdx.ac.uk.

A.J. BROWN
Griffith University

DAVID LEWIS
Middlesex University

RICHARD MOBERLY
University of Nebraska

WIM VANDEKERCKHOVE
University of Greenwich

1. Whistleblowing, its importance and the state of the research

David Lewis, A.J. Brown and Richard Moberly

WHY WHISTLEBLOWING?

To the uninitiated or the foolish, 'whistleblowing' may readily seem like a niche, almost boutique issue for research and policy making. The 'disclosure by organization members (former or current) of illegal, immoral or illegitimate practices under the control of their employers, to persons or organizations that may be able to effect action' (Near and Miceli 1985: 4), sounds like a very specific, perhaps even narrow or technical field of study. And yet, in the modern age of institutions, whistleblowing is now established as one of the most important processes – if not *the* single most important process – by which governments and corporations are kept accountable to the societies they are meant to serve and service. The ability for organizational 'insiders' to speak up about wrongdoing, and what happens afterwards in terms of corrective responses and treatment of the people involved, lies at the very heart of the health of all institutions and modern regulatory processes, right across society. In many ways, therefore, the subject could also not be broader, nor more far-reaching in terms of its complexities and consequences.

This Handbook provides researchers and policy makers from around the world with a comprehensive overview of the state of our knowledge regarding this vital process, in light of the last 30 years of progressively more systematic research into whistleblowing. As well, it provides cutting-edge analysis of the conceptual and practical challenges that researchers should confront in the next decade, if our knowledge is to develop so as to better inform the way that whistleblowing is understood and responded to by organizations, regulatory authorities and governments. The Handbook follows and draws upon some important previous stocktakes of coverage and gaps in existing research (e.g., Mesmer-Magnus and Viswesvaran 2005; Miceli *et al.* 2008), and observations on the limitations of inconsistent and uncoordinated research (Miceli and Near 2013) as well as closely related fields like employee voice (Burke and Cooper 2013). The book also comes at a time when the reform of institutions, policies and laws to better recognize whistleblowing, and protect whistleblowers, has evolved into a global policy issue, supported by commitments from governments through international instruments from the United Nations Convention Against Corruption (UNCAC) to the G20 Anti-Corruption Action Plans (see, for instance, Calland and Dehn 2004a, 2004b; Lewis 2010).

But for all its importance, whistleblowing is no simple issue. Its implications are felt from the micro to the macro levels of our institutions; from the coalface of frontline human resource management and organizational justice, to the complex politics of modern regulation aimed at ensuring integrity and responsibility in the behavior of particular institutions and industries, to the high politics of accountability and corruption affecting entire governments. To meet modern reform needs, research must therefore be both theoretically grounded and applied. Above all, it must be interdisciplinary, which is why this Handbook brings together scholars and policy practitioners not from any single field, but from sociology, political science, psychology, information systems, media studies, business, management, criminology, public policy and several branches of law. As will be seen, research into whistleblowing is becoming increasingly 'mainstream' in all these disciplines, which only increases the challenge of maintaining the relationships between them.

In all these fields and on almost every major topic reviewed in the book, the approach to researching whistleblowing also faces a significant 'fork in the road'. We reflect further on the outlook for whistleblowing research in the concluding chapter, drawing together these shifts and departures; but as we will see through the rest of this Introduction, there is almost no aspect of current knowledge which is free from policy or theoretical contention, or which does not cry out for a more sophisticated empirical approach. This makes whistleblowing a fertile field for a new generation of researchers. Moreover, although they contain plenty of conceptual meat, the problems are not just theoretical and academic. They reflect a real demand from institutions and regulators for better, more reliable evidence regarding the value of whistleblowing and the options for recognizing and maximizing that value. As a result, not only is there both scope and likelihood for expansions in applied empirical research, but every major new research project has the potential to help break new ground.

This Handbook is structured so as to provide something of a road-map, both to these fields of research and to these new opportunities and challenges. While many chapters focus on research conducted in a particular country, or undertake comparison between a number of studies and countries, there is no geographic structure to the book. Nor is the book divided according to the different types of whistleblowing or whistleblowing policies that might be found in the public and private sectors. It is clear that in most of its aspects, whistleblowing does vary between countries, sectors and even industries or policy areas, whether this is in terms of basic understandings, attitudes to wrongdoing, the desirability and methods of reporting it or legal protection obligations or the machinery for regulatory oversight. However, existing research suggests these differences represent important variations on more consistent themes, based on the reality that corruption and malpractice can arise in any institutional setting, as can the reporting of it. Instead, the Handbook is concerned with the overall need to better understand the complex inter-relationships between the different elements of the whistleblowing process, in any or all settings, including not only the nature of the whistleblower and the form of wrongdoing, but the method of reporting, the likelihood of wrongdoing being rectified, the incidence of retaliation, and the cultural, organizational and institutional arrangements that influence management and regulatory responses.

As a result, the three parts of the Handbook each contain six chapters devoted to major topics which are central to whistleblowing research and policy making, anywhere and everywhere. Part I deals with 'Research Fundamentals', a set of essential issues regarding how the phenomenon of whistleblowing is defined and understood for the purposes of all research and policy making. Part II is a step more applied, dealing with 'Organizational Culture and Responsiveness'. These chapters show how when it comes to actually undertaking research into whistleblowing, on each major element or dimension of the whistleblowing process, there are serious design issues to be confronted and solutions found for the new and better ways that more insightful data can be gathered. Part III is more applied again, dealing with 'Research in Action', by looking at what we know about legal and policy responses of societies to whistleblowing. These chapters emphasize how little policy making has been informed, to date, by good research and evidence about what works or what does not at institutional levels. These chapters reinforce not only the academic, but practical importance of research which addresses the challenges set out in Parts I and II.

We begin by introducing these topics, beginning with the fundamental question, 'what is whistleblowing?' and demonstrating, along the way, why it is important. In the course of painting this landscape, we introduce each chapter in turn, showing how each topic fits with these basic questions. As Terry Dworkin reminds us in the Foreword to this book, while good whistleblowing research involves many disciplines and technicalities, it is all also fundamentally about people. Accordingly, we will include some prominent examples of whistleblowing incidents and individuals, before turning to final reflections on how the Handbook should be used.

WHAT IS WHISTLEBLOWING?

A whistleblower is fundamentally an organizational or institutional 'insider' who reveals wrongdoing within or by that organization or institution, to someone else, with the intention or effect that action should then be taken to address it. This definition is essentially a paraphrase of the most widely used definition in whistleblowing research, cited at the beginning of this chapter (Near and Miceli 1985: 4). Tried and tested over many years, it is the departure point for most chapters in this book. However, the variety of definitions in different policy settings, public discussion and legislation reflect the different approaches that can be taken to this topic.

In some cases, other definitions may be narrow. Few doubt that employees who disclose wrongdoing about their employing organization fit the definition; hence, the International Labour Organization simply describes whistleblowing as 'the reporting by employees or former employees of illegal, irregular, dangerous or unethical practices by employers' (*ILO Thesaurus* 2005). However, at the heart of the Near and Miceli definition, 'organization members' can plainly fill broader categories of 'insiders', with these and even broader categories occupying a serious debate when it comes to policy making and law reform (see, e.g., Brown 2013: 160–5; see also Figure 1.1). In much public debate, the term 'whistleblower' is easily applied to *anyone* who discloses wrongdoing and who may require (on someone's account) support or protection for having done so. The Parliamentary Assembly of the Council of Europe's Committee on Legal Affairs and Human Rights (COER 2010) regarded 'whistleblowing' as: 'concerned individuals sounding the alarm in order to stop wrongdoings that place fellow human beings at risk'. The US Government Accountability Project defines whistleblowers as 'individuals who use free-speech rights to challenge abuses of power that betray the public trust' (see Devine and Massarani 2011: 4). Transparency International takes a middle path of a slightly broader basic definition based on Near and Miceli ('the disclosure of information related to corrupt, illegal, fraudulent or hazardous activities being committed in or by public or private sector organizations – which are of concern to or threaten the public interest – to individuals or entities believed to be able to effect action'), but also goes on to make clear its view that a whistleblower is an insider for whom the organization has responsibility:

> a whistleblower is any public or private sector employee or worker who discloses information [as defined above] … and who is at risk of retribution. This includes individuals who are outside the traditional employee-employer relationship, such as consultants, contractors, trainees/interns, volunteers, student workers, temporary workers, and former employees. (Worth 2013: 87; see also Osterhaus and Fagan 2009: 44–5)

These definitional variations show that debate is alive and well regarding the reasons for, and nature of, the recognition that societies are giving to the role of individual citizens in reporting wrongdoing by or within their organizations and institutions. Underpinning these debates are two issues: a growing recognition that individuals are in need of support and protection for playing this role; and the value of the information that they can provide, as the trigger for institutional, regulatory and societal responses to deal with wrongdoing. The focus on 'insiders', especially but not limited to employees, reinforces these issues. As will be seen throughout the book, it is insiders who often possess the most crucial such information – but they may not be the only ones. It is also insiders who, due to their position within and dependency on the institution concerned, are seen as requiring assistance, incentives or even compulsion to speak up, and who may face the worst kinds of reprisals and consequences – but again, they may not be the only ones.

The research fundamentals dealt with by the first chapters in the book revolve around these basic issues. The recognition of whistleblowing as a topic for public policy, management and law reform stems from the consequences of the conflicting values, judgments and reactions that attach to individuals who report wrongdoing. Any such process of disclosure may provoke these conflicts, if it comes as a challenge to the power, authority or interests of others. And these conflicts in values and judgment will necessarily vary depending not only on those battling interests, but the particular cultural context: whether we are talking about organizational, industrial, professional or societal culture. It is for this reason that, even in an employment context but also more broadly, debate around whistleblowing often plays out in terms of issues of loyalty. Another presumption shared by most whistleblowing research, and most if not all authors in this book, is that higher social and public interests trump this debate, because whistleblowing can and should be understood as a 'pro-social' process (Dozier and Miceli 1985; Brief and Motowidlo 1986). This means behavior that is 'defined by some significant segment of society and/or one's social group as generally beneficial to other people' (Penner *et al.* 2005: 366), irrespective of what particular objectives were intended or outcomes caused in the individual case. But even in societies where this diagnosis now has strong support in policy and law, not all commentators have approved of whistleblowing. In 1971, in the United States, the Chairman of General Motors, James Roche, stated:

> Some of the enemies of business now encourage an employee to be disloyal to the enterprise. They want to create suspicion and disharmony and pry into the proprietary interests of the business. However this is labelled – industrial espionage, whistleblowing or professional responsibility – it is another tactic for spreading disunity and creating conflict. (Walters 1975: 27)

Subsequently, such views have been criticized for placing silent loyalty to organizations who engage in wrongdoing above any ethical or social duty. It is a positive sign that many today would view whistleblowing as an act of loyalty, rather than disloyalty to an employer. For example, where an organization has stated that its staff are expected to report suspected wrongdoing, the failure to do so may be regarded as disloyal. Indeed, if workers have a legal obligation to raise concerns, not doing so may be treated as misconduct (Lewis 2011a). In carrying out research on whistleblowing, we need to be conscious that individuals may well have conflicting loyalties within the organization. In some situations, loyalty to an employer may not be perceived as consistent with that owed to others, for example, the family, work colleagues, a supervisor, a union or wider society – with the impacts of these conflicting loyalties on a person's willingness to report wrongdoing, or how they do so, or the consequences that follow, representing important topics for research.

From country to country, not only may these perceptions of loyalty differ, but it may be difficult to locate *any* term or concept that equates to the positive, pro-social concept of whistleblowing introduced above. Even in the United States, the management guru Peter Drucker was of the opinion that whistleblowing was simply another word for 'informing' (cited in Benson 1992). Indeed, most whistleblowing laws avoid using the word 'whistleblower' in their actual text, instead describing the circumstances in which people are entitled or encouraged to expose wrongdoing and be protected for doing so. One reason for not using the expression 'whistleblower' is its negative historical connotations, in many settings, alongside or overwhelming any positive ones, particularly in countries where oppressive governments have encouraged citizens to denounce the activities of political opponents.

For all these reasons, this Handbook does not propose any new universal definition of whistleblowing, but encourages research that works with existing definitions; is explicit about the assumptions in those definitions; and tests out their practical implications and boundaries. We begin with two chapters setting out key elements of this definitional landscape in greater detail. In Chapter 2, 'Understandings of Whistleblowing: Dilemmas of Societal Culture', Wim Vandekerckhove, Tina Uys, Michael T. Rehg and A.J. Brown explore the complexity of researching the impact of culture on whistleblowing, giving specifics on how various cultures view the act of reporting wrongdoing through a variety of perspectives and preconceptions. They present a review of prior cross-cultural whistleblowing studies, as well as a guide to improving the foundations of future studies. The chapter notes that most cultural studies of whistleblowing use a single framework, developed by Hofstede, to examine cultural dimensions, but argues that by itself, Hofstede's framework is too limited to give a powerful explanation of the interaction between culture and whistleblowing, because it focuses on a mythical, omnipresent national culture that either does or does not lead to whistleblowing behavior. Instead, after presenting results from a new study comparing public attitudes towards whistleblowing in the United Kingdom and Australia, Chapter 2 asserts that a better approach may be required and outlines newer cultural theories that could support more nuanced future study. It also contains important practical advice on the conduct of cross-cultural research.

In any given cultural context, however, we still have the challenge of being clear on *who it is* whose reporting behavior is being analyzed. In Chapter 3, 'Outsider "Whistleblowers": Conceptualizing and Distinguishing "Bell-Ringing Behavior"', Marcia P. Miceli, Suelette Dreyfus and Janet P. Near tackle the problem thrown up by the apparently increasing application of the term 'whistleblower' to persons who are not members of the organization responsible for the wrongdoing, and thus fall outside the traditional definition. They posit that rather than subsuming all reporting behavior under the term whistleblowing, there are distinctions between 'insider' and 'outsider' reporting that can lead to variations between the two groups and require different if related research approaches. In particular, the chapter discusses potential differences based on how the disclosers acquire information; the channels they use; whether they demand anonymity; and their motivations for reporting wrongdoing. As a result, the authors suggest a different label for 'outsider' reporters: 'bell-ringers' (see also Figure 1.1). They provide real world examples of bell-ringers, such as Harry Markopolos, who made public attempts to have the US Securities and Exchange Commission deal with the alleged Ponzi scheme of Bernard Madoff, which saw thousands of investors defrauded of US$65 billion. Despite often being called a whistleblower, Markopolos

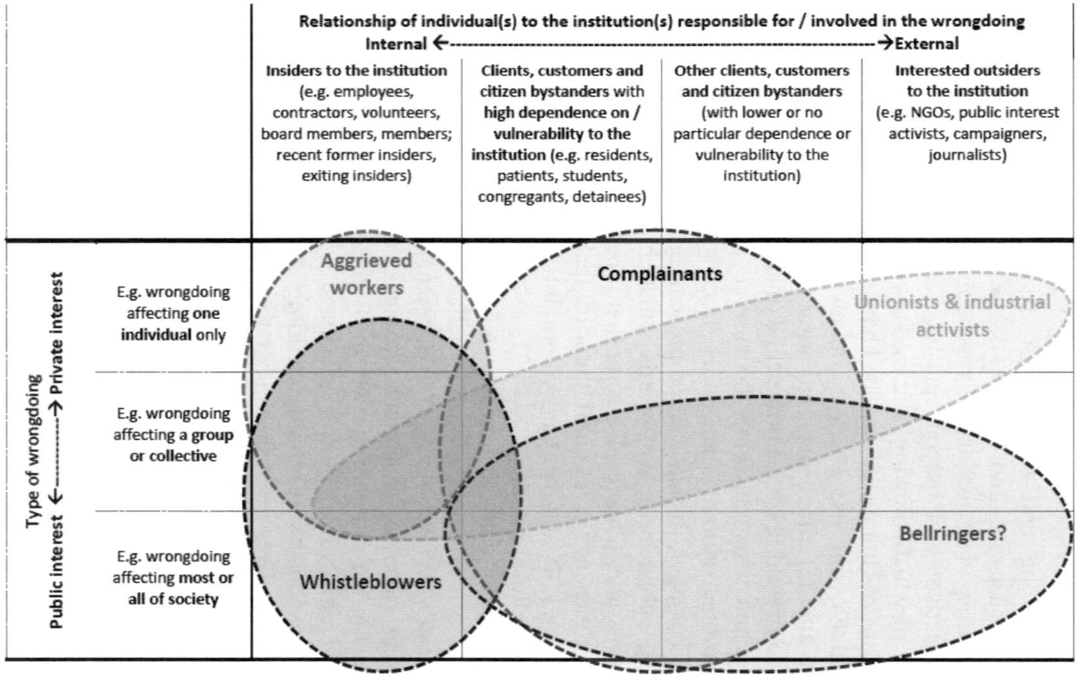

Source: Brown 2013: 162

Figure 1.1 An indicative guide to classifying whistleblowers, complainants, witnesses and victims of organizational wrongdoing

was not a member of staff and thus could not raise his concerns within Bernard Madoff's organization, nor did he have that status when he approached regulators. This important chapter will influence the way future researchers think about the differences between various types of reporters, and support new parallel research into bell-ringing, to develop a 'better understanding of incidents and processes that may seem similar to whistleblowing, but which are actually different, and about which currently much less is known'.

WHAT IS WHISTLEBLOWING ABOUT?

The next most fundamental element of whistleblowing is the subjects that it concerns – the wrongdoing that whistleblowers perceive and reveal. Arguably, this is the most important element since it defines the key benefits of whistleblowing for society. It is because whistleblowers disclose suspected wrongdoing that the pro-social value of the process becomes clear, and their treatment by organizations and society becomes so important. No matter how complex, the benefits of whistleblowing to democratic societies are increasingly recognized. It has been argued that whistleblowing laws can be used as a measure of 'the democratic maturity as well as the humaneness of a country' (Vinten 1994: 4). Governments are encouraging the reporting of wrongdoing because it advances the interests of openness, transparency and public integrity generally. Wrongdoing may be fraud or maladministration by public agencies, or it may be illegalities that have not been dealt with internally by private organizations. It may be corruption, the global cost of which was estimated by the World Bank in 2004 at US$1 trillion, and which is a major obstacle in the world fight against poverty. Less corruption would enable monies meant for infrastructure and capacity-building in developing countries to be spent on what it was meant for, rather than lining the pockets of politicians, civil servants and contractors (Carr and Lewis 2010). Because corruption is notoriously difficult to detect and address through formal channels, especially in developing countries, whistleblowing is an important means by which it can be exposed.

Whistleblowing may also be about other types of wrongdoing, such as the health and safety of the general public, for example, in relation to hazardous industries or terrorist activity. Indeed, it may be about any breaches of law, morals or accepted institutional practice where the impacts on others can be seen to be 'wrong'. Part of the growing utility of whistleblowing stems from moves away from state regulation to self-regulation in most countries, leaving organizations and industries free to monitor their own compliance with regulatory requirements, but also giving whistleblowers a key role as 'internal antennae' for problems (Pemberton *et al.* 2012). As Figure 1.1 shows, perceived wrongdoing can theoretically be spread on a continuum between wrongdoing that only affects individual, private or personal interests and 'wrongdoing that threatens wider organizational and/or public integrity, above and beyond any outcomes for affected individuals (public interest)' (Brown and Donkin 2008: 9). Such distinctions may be important for the different complaint avenues, institutional and regulatory responses and protections that can or should be triggered by whistleblowing. However, as recognized throughout this book, such distinctions can be difficult to operationalize in practice and also difficult to research (see also Brown and Donkin 2008: 15). In some cases, a personal grievance about bullying, harassment or favoritism may be entirely that, or it may indicate more general problems in a workplace, or be so serious that it represents a breach of criminal law, or be so systemic that it affects the integrity and performance of the entire institution.

Nevertheless, a stronger focus on the wrongdoing revealed by whistleblowers, and what is done about it, has become a major research shift, supported by this Handbook. Almost 20 years ago, Near and Miceli (1995: 681) defined 'effective whistleblowing' as 'the extent to which the questionable or wrongful practice (or omission) is terminated at least partly because of whistleblowing and within a reasonable time frame' – and noted the surprising lack of systematic research on this basic measure of the impact, and therefore the value, of whistleblowing. This may be because, once upon a time, it was hard to find prominent examples of where institutions or regulators were actually listening to whistleblowers. More recently, apparently in line with changing social and official attitudes, this is changing. For example, Cynthia Cooper, a vice-president of internal audit at US company WorldCom, took her evidence of suspicious activities to the company's board of directors, leading to corrective action to deal with the corporate fraud. She was one of three US whistleblowers recognized by *Time Magazine* as its 2002 Persons of the Year. In the United Kingdom, Gary Brown was a marketing executive at Abbey National, who suspected that his director, Michael Doyle, was defrauding the bank of hundreds of thousands of pounds. Brown found another job before taking his concerns to the board of Abbey National, leading to internal and police investigations which saw Doyle sentenced to eight years in jail, in 1997, for fraud totalling about UK£1 million. Brown received a UK£25,000 reward from the bank for the stress he had been through and returned to Abbey National in a more senior role.

There are other examples. In Europe, Paul van Buitenen was a Dutch assistant auditor in the European Commission's Financial Control Directorate who, in 1998, drew the attention of a member of the European Parliament to fraud and mismanagement within the Commission. Although he was suspended and had his salary cut, van Buitenen's revelations together with the public reaction to his treatment ultimately led to the resignation of the entire Commission, and he eventually returned to the European Commission in a different capacity. In Australia, nurse manager Toni Hoffman raised doubts about the competence of a surgeon, Jayant Patel, at Bundaberg Hospital. After she brought the matter to the attention of her local MP as a last resort, who made it public, it emerged that Patel had faced disciplinary action for medical negligence in the United States. A 2005 Commission of Inquiry commended Hoffman for her professionalism, senior managers were sacked, major institutional changes followed, and Patel was prosecuted for manslaughter over a number of patient deaths. Back in the United Kingdom, Stephen Bolsin, a consultant anaesthetist at the Bristol Royal Infirmary, established that too many babies were dying during heart surgery. His six years of effort to improve the service led to a dramatic fall in mortality rates, but also led to confrontation with paediatric cardiac surgeons; it was only after he eventually took his concerns to the media that a major government inquiry made wide-ranging recommendations about reform of clinical governance in hospitals in the United Kingdom (see Bristol Royal Infirmary Inquiry 2001).

Empirical research has also finally begun to turn towards more systematic evidence of the primary outcomes of whistleblowing. In 2006, the major Australian study, 'Whistling While They Work', surveyed 7,763 employees from 118 public sector organizations. Due to its scope and scale, this research is mentioned in many chapters of this book. Two-thirds (63 per cent) of all those who reported wrongdoing, including 56 per cent of public interest whistleblowers, believed their report was investigated; and about half (31 per cent of all whistleblowers) considered that things became 'better' as a result (Brown, Mazurski and Olsen 2008: 42; Smith and Brown 2008: 111–12). Whether this is a high result or a low one will depend on further comparative and longitudinal research; but it is now clearer that whistleblowing can be, and often is, highly effective in addressing wrongdoing.

To properly measure whistleblowing and its impacts, decisions have to be made about how wrongdoing itself is defined. In Chapter 4, 'Wrongdoing: Definitions, Identification and Categorizations', Marit Skivenes and Sissel C. Trygstad provide an essential overview of this important and necessary definitional prerequisite to any whistleblowing behavior.

While our basic definition of whistleblowing refers to 'illegal, illegitimate, or immoral' conduct (Near and Miceli 1985: 4), this chapter examines the concept in detail by exploring the cultural, organizational, social, legal and personal contexts that impact whether a potential whistleblower recognizes wrongdoing as such. Skivenes and Trygstad identify six dimensions that influence the definition of wrongdoing across these contexts and evaluate the numerous legal definitions of the types of wrongdoing required by law to be reported in order for a whistleblower to receive protection from reprisal. They also examine the costs and benefits of a narrow versus a broad definition of wrongdoing and explore the impact that labor norms may have on the types of wrongdoing that organizations and the law encourage to be reported. Ultimately, they demonstrate why researchers should pay more attention to the essential concept of defining the types of misconduct society wants insiders to report.

Recognizing the organizational and social value of whistleblowing, through the wrongdoing uncovered, also raises other fundamental definitional problems. Once, whistleblowing was regarded as an entirely voluntary process, with concepts of support and protection geared towards those who 'went out of their way' to report wrongdoing when others did not. Increasingly, the value of whistleblowing is being recognized not only by new encouragements, but new expectations that insiders will report wrongdoing. In Chapter 5, 'Whistleblowing Duties', Jos Leys and Wim Vandekerckhove explore the implications of the growing categories of individuals who have a 'role-prescribed' duty to blow the whistle, as opposed to acting voluntarily. Although this mandatory obligation may arise ostensibly from company codes of conduct, statutes, regulations or societal norms and expectations, Vandekerckhove and Leys develop a detailed taxonomy of wrongdoing and of various roles within an organization to argue that determining one's duty to blow the whistle depends upon a combination of these factors. Their in-depth analysis adds significant theoretical depth to the ways that different types of whistleblowing should be defined for research purposes, as well as assisting with the design and evaluation of whistleblowing policies that purport to create whistleblowing duties.

HOW TO FRAME WHISTLEBLOWING RESEARCH

The trend towards more systematic research into whistleblowing also raises fundamental questions about what should be the focus of whistleblowing studies, with important lessons for past studies that should not be lost. When systematic, survey-based research into whistleblowing began to expand in Western countries in the 1990s, it often focused on levels of employee awareness of whistleblowing laws and policies, and on employee intention or 'propensity' to blow the whistle, with fewer studies into how many employees actually did so, and the nature of the outcomes. Just as public attitude research is showing a higher-than-anticipated level of public sympathy for whistleblowing, research has long indicated that a majority of employees consider that they should and would report wrongdoing, if they observed it; but whether they actually perceive it, and what they then do, may be a different matter.

In Chapter 6, 'On the Appropriateness of Research Design: Intended and Actual Whistleblowing', Brita Bjørkelo and Hege Høivik Bye discuss the difference between studies that focus on actual whistleblowing and those that focus on intended whistleblowing. They re-examine conclusions from Mesmer-Magnus and Viswesvaran's meta-study (2005: 288–9) that many variables used in whistleblowing studies were stronger correlates of intent to blow the whistle rather than actual whistleblowing, and whistleblowing intent and actual whistleblowing may even be unrelated phenomena. Bjørkelo and Bye assert that the differences Mesmer-Magnus and Viswesvaran found can be traced more to methodological differences between studies, rather than to substantive differences between the two concepts. After reviewing more recent literature, they conclude that the 'intended–actual whistleblowing relationship is under-investigated … and the research that exists is likely to underestimate the relationship due to the timing of measurement' of key variables. They suggest future research should focus on this relationship by using the 'reasoned action' approach promoted by Fishbein and Ajzen (2010), which Bjørkelo and Bye believe can show the relationship between salient beliefs about a variety of factors (such as individual, social and organizational norms) and better link evidence of intended whistleblowing with actual whistleblowing.

A final fundamental issue which is central to all whistleblowing research is the role of power. In systematic social-scientific research, as opposed to case study and anecdotal accounts, the qualitative dimensions of whistleblowing incidents and experiences easily become submerged under a sea of statistics. Surprising statistical results, such as that a majority of whistleblowers are not ignored, or that not all whistleblowers necessarily suffer, may obscure the great risks, conflicts and tensions that remain intrinsic to whistleblowing, depending on who and what interests stand to be challenged by revelations of wrongdoing, how they are made and the power of whistleblowers relative to those responding to, or affected by, their disclosures. Were it not so, whistleblowing would not remain such a vexed policy issue.

The conundrums have always been most visible in the outcomes that can befall whistleblowers who expose serious political wrongdoing, especially in areas where the politics is 'high stakes' and information is normally tightly controlled, such as national security. These are not new issues. For example, one of the world's most famous, modern whistleblowers was Daniel Ellsberg who, in 1969, secretly made copies of classified US government documents to which he had access as an employee of the RAND Corporation. The 'Pentagon Papers', as they became known, demonstrated that the Johnson Government had lied to both Congress and the public about the likely outcome and effects of the Vietnam War. In 1971, after Ellsberg leaked the documents to the *Washington Post* and other newspapers, attracting charges under the Espionage Act 1917 as well as of theft and conspiracy, US National Security Advisor Henry Kissinger labelled him 'the most dangerous man in America'. In 1984, Clive Ponting was a senior civil servant at the UK Ministry of Defence who sent documents to an MP relating to the sinking of an Argentine warship during the Falklands War, demonstrating that the ship had been sighted a day earlier than officially reported and was outside the naval exclusion zone when attacked. Charged with a criminal breach of the Official Secrets Act 1911, Ponting claimed by way of defense that he acted in the public interest and that his disclosure was protected by parliamentary privilege, and was acquitted by the jury – but this was despite the judge's direction that 'the public interest is what the government of the day says it is'.[1]

In 1986, Israeli nuclear technician Mordechai Vanunu was sentenced to 18 years' imprisonment for revealing details of Israel's secret nuclear weapons programme to British newspapers. However, such treatment is not simply a Cold War phenomenon. Even since his release in 2004, Vanunu has continued to suffer restrictions of liberty and other official repercussions. In 2003, Katharine Gun, a former translator at the UK Government Communications Headquarters (GCHQ), leaked an email to a newspaper which contained top secret information about illegal activities by the United States in relation to obtaining UN approval for the invasion of Iraq. Her employment was terminated and she was charged with an offense under the Official Secrets Act 1989, although the case was dropped after her lawyers sought evidence of the UK Government's advice about the legality of the invasion. In July 2013, former US Army Private Bradley (now Chelsea) Manning was sentenced to 35 years' imprisonment by a military court for theft, espionage and other military offenses, after providing WikiLeaks with large volumes of classified information, including wrongdoing in the conduct of the Iraq and Afghanistan wars (O'Brien 2013; Hartmann 2013). At the time of writing, US security contractor Edward Snowden is in hiding in Russia, after revealing details of extensive and intrusive surveillance activity by the National Security Agency.

These high profile examples are not typical of all whistleblowing activity, and all involve public rather than internal whistleblowing – an issue discussed further below. However, they highlight a key element of what is true about all whistleblowing circumstances or situations where we might have wished for the whistle to be blown, even if only internally or to regulatory agencies. For example, in the United Kingdom, after 167 lives were lost in the North Sea's 1988 Piper Alpha oil platform disaster, the Cullen Inquiry (1990) found that the disaster could have been averted, but 'workers did not want to put their continued employment in jeopardy through raising a safety issue that might embarrass management'. The staff had short fixed-term contracts and there was a lack of alternative employment in the region. In other words, the fundamental issue was one of power.

In Chapter 7, 'Whistleblowing and Power', Kim Loyens and Jeroen Maesschalck show how this issue needs to be remembered in all empirical research, by re-examining the traditional relationship between power and whistleblowing. They call for a robust, new examination of the complex factors affecting the decision to blow the whistle, including the need to supplement the classic 'reporting-silence' dichotomy used in most whistleblowing studies with alternative responses to organizational misconduct, including sabotage, secret sharing and confrontation of the wrongdoer. They also argue that a context-specific approach should be used to examine the decision to blow the whistle, rather than the 'locus of control' approach used in most current research. They conclude with specific methodological suggestions to strengthen the depth and complexity of research related to the connection between whistleblowing and power.

RESEARCHING WHISTLEBLOWING IN CONTEXT

From the discussion so far, it is clear that research into whistleblowing is important, but has faced many challenges and continues to do so. From understandings to date, nevertheless, the shift from broad stereotypes towards a more context-specific approach to research is not only possible, but underway. Each of the last two chapters of Part I highlight the need to move beyond over-simplistic conceptual dichotomies in the way research is approached. It is also now clearer that applied research into whistleblowing, as a process, raises as many or more questions about the culture and responsiveness of institutions to whistleblowing, as it does about the behavior and experience of whistleblowers themselves.

Part II of the book thus moves to a range of issues that are central to understanding whistleblowing, and its outcomes, in its organizational and institutional context, beginning with three further areas in which simplistic dichotomies are starting to be broken down. Following on from the last chapter, a road-map for moving beyond the 'reporting-silence' dichotomy is provided by Jane Olsen in Chapter 8, 'Reporting Versus Inaction: How Much is There, What Explains the Differences and What to Measure'. She highlights the growing body of empirical research on the incidence of whistleblowing in and about organizations, but also its limitations, including the difficulties of interpreting different results gained through different research methods. While there are broad similarities between large-scale studies in comparable contexts, greater precision about the reality and significance of similarities and differences, as well as any longitudinal changes, depends on a more consistent research approach. For example, studies by the US Merit Systems Protection Board suggest that half or more of federal public servants have observed organizational wrongdoing and about 30 per cent reported it (Miceli *et al.* 2008; MSPB 2011). However, surveys of US private sector employees indicate that while about 50 per cent similarly observed wrongdoing, as few as 40 per cent acted on that knowledge (ERC 2010a). Using different methods again, the Australian 'Whistling While They Work' surveys recorded 71 per cent of respondents as having observed serious wrongdoing, and 28 per cent as having reported (Brown, Mazurski and Olsen 2008: 38).

Just as importantly, while such research may start out as seeking to understand levels of whistleblowing, it rapidly becomes obvious that the underlying need is just as much to understand why many people who observe wrongdoing do *not* blow the whistle – or 'inactive observation' (Miceli and Near 1988). Time and again, political recognition of the value of whistleblowing comes in the wake of revelations that people in organizations knew about wrongdoing which subsequently exploded, but did not reveal it. The United Kingdom's Piper Alpha oil platform disaster has just been mentioned. More recently in the United Kingdom, after it was uncovered that Harold Shipman, a general medical practitioner, had murdered over 250 of his patients, the inquiry report highlighted the perennial problem of junior clinical staff being unwilling to raise concerns about senior colleagues, for fear of blighting their careers (Fifth

Report of the Shipman Inquiry 2004: para. 11.79). In Australia, whistleblowing law reform was spawned by the extent of revelations by the Fitzgerald Inquiry into official corruption in Queensland (1987–1989), that honest police personnel had observed corruption but felt powerless to act. In 2002, the Sarbanes-Oxley whistleblower provisions in the United States were in direct response to Congress's concern about the 'corporate code of silence' that encouraged insiders to remain silent in the face of massive corporate fraud (Moberly 2012a: 3). Therefore, as Olsen shows, an increasingly important task for researchers is to examine not only why people blow the whistle, but why those who observe wrongdoing choose not to disclose it.

Moreover, as Loyens and Maesschalck emphasize, the options faced and taken up by observers of wrongdoing are more than simply formal reporting and silent inaction. As documented in the literature on 'employee voice', there is at least one other path routinely taken up by insiders with concerns: exit. A typical example where exit should itself have triggered reform was the case of Joy Cawthorne, who resigned as an instructor at a UK outdoor activity centre in protest over its safety standards. This was not enough to prevent the deaths of four children in a canoeing accident in Lyme Bay, England; subsequently, Cawthorne gave evidence against her former employer, who was convicted of manslaughter and sentenced to three years' imprisonment. In Chapter 8, Olsen describes how the Australian 'Whistling While They Work' research took a first major step towards more effective measurement of organizational responsiveness to wrongdoing, by focusing not only on rates of whistleblowing or reporting in an organization, but also on 'inaction rates', defined as the proportion of employees who observed wrongdoing they considered serious, but who did not report it, nor took any other action, in circumstances where no one else had reported it.

Secondly, simplistic impressions are also being broken down by research into the motivations for whistleblowing. On one level, research has moved away from diagnosis of motives, because contrary to many stereotypes and some legal regimes, a discloser's motive is simply not relevant to the core issue raised by the reporting of wrongdoing, which is whether that wrongdoing should be investigated and dealt with. Moreover, focusing on motives can encourage unhelpful stereotypes of whistleblowers as either generally altruistic and heroic, or as predominantly disgruntled employees with a vengeance or an 'axe to grind' – when neither is accurate or useful as a general description. Apart from the problem of ascertaining a person's motive at any particular time, research suggests that many whistleblowers intend to benefit both themselves and others, and that their motives do not substantially influence the decision to report (Miceli and Near 2010: 77). Indeed, the increasing diversity of obligations on individuals to blow the whistle, discussed earlier, are intended to trigger self-interested motives (such as avoiding disciplinary action) as well as encourage altruistic ones. Whistleblowers who do not exhaust internal channels may be regarded as irresponsible. As we will see below, the book also discusses the success of financial incentives for whistleblowing. Under the model of whistleblowing as a pro-social activity, motives become a secondary consideration.

At the same time, the specific mix of motives – real or perceived – for blowing the whistle in the individual case will necessarily impact on the process, in terms of how managers and others in the organization will respond, the level and nature of potential retaliation, and the complexity of the management responses. Different motives may emerge at, and impact on, different stages of the process: a personal grievance about bullying or harassment may be mixed with more public interest reasons for reporting it, where the harassment is systemic or serious or affects others; or it may be the real reason for raising other unrelated wrongdoing; or it may only arise after other wrongdoing has been reported and the organization fails to respond properly (Brown, Mazurski and Olsen 2008: 36). In Chapter 9, 'Motivations for Whistleblowing: Personal, Private and Public Interests', Peter Roberts presents data from surveys and interviews conducted as part of the 'Whistling While They Work' project to demonstrate the complex spectrum of mixed motivations that is evident in whistleblowing in practice, as against theory. Although motivations can be roughly divided between altruistic and self-interested motives, he presents a taxonomy of various motivations in either category and notes that these may also overlap to some degree, frequently causing the line between these categories to blur. This complex array of motives is often not easily captured through the past survey mechanisms, but has important implications for researchers, organizational leaders and policy makers, especially with respect to how support or protection are provided, and workplace relationships managed.

Thirdly, much public debate about whistleblowing has been dominated by the evidence of the retaliation and adverse outcomes that can befall those who report wrongdoing, to the extent that some researchers argue that whistleblowing is synonymous with suffering. Certainly, repercussions for whistleblowers can be dire, as already seen from some of the examples above. In South Africa, Wendy Addison was an accountant at LeisureNet Ltd who alleged that the top management had participated in corruption. Rather than taking remedial action, her employer dismissed her. In addition to becoming unemployable due to the notoriety of her case, Addison lost the support of family and friends and received death threats that caused her to leave the country. This was notwithstanding that she was vindicated: LeisureNet became arguably the biggest corporate disaster in South African history, with jail terms imposed on the wrong-doers in 2007 and upheld on appeal in April 2011. Other examples will be referred to below. At the same time, however, we have already cited more successful examples; and empirical studies support a somewhat surprising conclusion that not all, nor even most, whistleblowers necessarily suffer in these kinds of ways.

One problem is that current measures tend to be simplistic, allowing analyses according to whether whistleblowers have suffered direct retaliation or they haven't, without recognizing a wider range of factors that may influence good and bad outcomes, including indirect and subjective factors, as well as the relative seriousness of different factors. In Chapter 10, 'Whistleblowers and suffering', Rodney Smith examines research on the suffering endured by whistleblowers, explaining that suffering is such an important part of the whistleblower narrative that it is important to understand exactly how much and what kind of suffering occurs and its effects on individuals and organizations. Further, the lesson from existing empirical research that many whistleblowers do not suffer begs further questions, such as what distinguishes whistleblowers who suffer from those who do not? And, do some types of suffering occur more frequently than others? Smith calls for a new generation of studies to delve deeper into the complex questions surrounding the full range of adverse outcomes, what causes them, and what may help limit or prevent them.

WHISTLEBLOWING RECIPIENTS AND RESPONSES

The vast bulk of whistleblowing research to date has focused on whistleblowers: what makes them report, what they report, how many and how often whistleblowers come forward, and what happens to them. But to understand whistleblowing in context, and especially how whistleblowing can be made more effective, it must be recognized that whistleblower and non-whistleblower behavior, characteristics and outcomes are only one part of the puzzle. Increasingly important is the behavior of those who receive whistleblowing disclosures, and what they do about them. Indeed, while the study of whistleblower behavior and outcomes may remain a necessary and often fascinating focus, from a public policy perspective it is the response to disclosures which is actually the more important field of study – but which is in its relative infancy.

Most of the prominent examples of whistleblowing referred to so far involve disclosures about wrongdoing that have made it into the media, and played out in the public domain. In fact, systematic research has confirmed that this type of disclosure represents a small minority of whistleblowing. Studies routinely show that at least in developed countries, less than 10 per cent of disclosures about wrongdoing are ever made to persons outside the organization, with the bulk of internal disclosures not even made to hotlines or auditors, but rather directly to the whistleblower's supervisor or immediate managers (see e.g., Donkin *et al.* 2008; ERC 2010a: 5; PCaW 2013). Accordingly, most researchers now reject the view that the raising of a concern only amounts to whistleblowing if there is an external or public disclosure (cf. Jubb 1999; Truelson 2001). None of the definitions referred to above draws a distinction between internal and external whistleblowing. To do so would ignore the reality that public disclosures are usually made as a last resort, after having been first raised internally and/or with regulators (Near *et al.* 2004). Not surprisingly, therefore, research suggests that internal and external whistleblowers have similar characteristics (Dworkin and Baucus 1998), with 'few substantial differences in antecedents or outcomes of whistleblowing as a function of type of channel used' (Miceli *et al.* 2008: 7). The processes are also related by the fact that risk of external disclosure, if protected or made easy, puts pressure on employers to have policies and procedures which encourage internal reporting in order to avoid that outcome.

All the same, despite being only the public tip of the whistleblowing iceberg, disclosures to the media play an important role in defining social and political responses to whistleblowing and often represent whistleblowing at its highest-stake stage. The protections available to disclosers under common law and statute vary massively for public as opposed to internal or regulatory disclosures. Increasingly, as discussed in Part III of the book, public disclosure is being built into countries' whistleblowing regimes, as a third 'tier' of disclosure if internal or regulatory disclosures fail or are impractical (Vandekerckhove 2010; Brown 2011b). However, often there is no legal recognition for public whistleblowing, leaving it undistinguishable from other 'leaking' or unauthorized disclosure of confidential or unpublished information. This includes political and commercial leaks in order to manipulate media coverage, not simply disclosures intended to expose wrongdoing. While some countries provide legal protection for public whistleblowing in specified circumstances, leaking is frequently still tortious and sometimes criminal. It has also been a common feature of leaking that disclosers are anonymous or insist on secrecy, whereas the identity of whistleblowers is often known or revealed – although this has changed with the arrival of the Internet, which provides a speedy and efficient way to disseminate information while preserving anonymity. This can be done in isolation, for example, via blogs and Twitter, as well as through platforms like WikiLeaks or GlobalLeaks, which facilitate the uploading of documents.

Studying when and how whistleblowers access the media, and how the media respond to and use whistleblowing disclosures, is therefore important. Yet despite the dominance of disclosures to the media in anecdotal and narrative research about whistleblowing, systematic research on the relationship between whistleblowers and the media is surprisingly rare. There are obvious questions to be pursued about the role that the media plays in supporting whistleblowers, given the tension between assumptions that the media should be a whistleblower's best friend, and normal commercial news-gathering imperatives. Contrary to a belief that journalists naturally understand whistleblowers, the fact is that the media is ignorant about much whistleblowing because it is being satisfactorily dealt with internally or by regulators. Effective whistleblowing is plainly less newsworthy. The media may also be more interested in the activities and fate of the messenger, than in the message. A content analysis of newspaper coverage in the United Kingdom between 1997 and 2009 found that whistleblowers were mainly covered positively (54 per cent) or neutrally (41 per cent), but such positive representations may be motivated by journalists' self-interest in creating 'narratives of whistleblowers as heroic, selfless individuals to establish the legitimacy of their claims of systemic wrongdoing in the public interest' (Wahl-Jorgensen and Hunt 2012: 1, 9). In other circumstances, the media may contribute to negative public impressions of whistleblowing, as documented by the Shipman Inquiry in the United Kingdom (Fifth Report of the Shipman Inquiry 2004: paras 11.7 and 11.12).

In Chapter 11, 'Going Public: Researching External Whistleblowing in a New Media Age', Rachelle Bosua, Simon Milton, Suelette Dreyfus and Reeva Lederman examine these complex relationships between whistleblowers and the media. The authors focus especially on the way that new information technology is altering the traditional relationship, both in how information is delivered between the two as well as the amount and type of information able to be disclosed. Of course, this raises significant problems, such as whether new technology will sufficiently protect the security of the information and the anonymity of the whistleblower. To explore these issues, the authors present new research on the experiences of a group of investigative journalists and whistleblowers in various countries, highlighting many of the key elements of the relationship which stand out for further study.

Even more important is research into what happens when whistleblowers try to disclose internally or through official channels, as remains the case for the vast bulk of the time. History is full of examples of employees who raised internal concerns about wrongful practices, only to find that the organization had no proper process for recognizing the disclosure. In 1984, the world's worst industrial disaster in Bhopal, India, saw thousands die as a result of gas escaping the Union Carbide plant. Detailed investigations revealed that cost cutting measures had adversely affected work conditions and the maintenance of safety systems, but warnings and the concerns of workers were disregarded, both by the company and the local authority. Another disastrous case was the sinking of the ferry *Herald of Free Enterprise* at Zeebrugge in 1987, causing the death of 193 people. The investigation found that employees had aired their concerns on five previous occasions about the ship sailing with its bow doors open, but those sensible suggestions which may have prevented the disaster had not received the 'serious consideration' they deserved (Sheen 1987). In 2003, an Australian Customs Officer, Alan Kessing, wrote two reports about lax security at Sydney airport. These included information about drug trafficking and security passes which had been issued to illegal immigrants as well as people with criminal convictions. The reports were buried, but after they were leaked to *The Australian* newspaper in 2005, an inquiry resulted in an AU$200 million security upgrade. Kessing was prosecuted for the leak, despite denying being the source.

Similarly, in May 2008, at the onset of the global financial crisis, Matthew Lee, a vice president at Lehman Brothers, warned senior management about accounting irregularities. An investigation by the company's auditor, Ernst & Young, declared Lee's allegations to be without foundation and he lost his job, even though his suspicions were eventually confirmed in a subsequent bankruptcy examiner's report. Such cases also raise questions not only about how organizations do or do not recognize disclosures, but also the readiness and accessibility of regulatory agencies as conduits for whistleblowing. There are many cases where internal reporting proved ineffective, and external reporting would clearly have been desirable but did not occur. For example, in the United States, employee Sherron Watkins wrote to the chief executive of Enron about questionable accounting, but the company management sought to remove her rather than confront the issues raised (Sterling 2002). She was subsequently criticized for not raising her concerns externally. But such criticisms hinge on assumptions that regulators are also good at recognizing and acting on disclosures, when this may be variable. In

Australia, Note Printing Australia company secretary Brian Hood questioned payments that turned out to be an extensive system of foreign bribery and was forced out of the government-owned banknote company. Perhaps he too could have been criticized for not taking it further; but when James Shelton, a sales executive in a sister company, Securrency, took even firmer information to the Australian Federal Police, they also initially declined to investigate for lack of evidence. It was only when Shelton became an anonymous media source that effective investigation followed, leading to criminal trials in which both whistleblowers gave evidence and successful convictions (ABC 2013).

Such failures and tardiness can nevertheless obscure the reality that organizations and institutions are also becoming increasingly *better* at recognizing and receiving disclosures. Research is beginning to reinforce the societal importance of whistleblowing, with evidence of the benefits that accrue to organizations and regulators by facilitating and responding well to whistleblowing. In the Australian public sector, research suggests that employee reporting is the 'single most important trigger for the uncovering of wrongdoing' within the integrity and corporate governance systems of organizations (Brown, Mazurski and Olsen 2008: 43–4). While the benefits of early identification of workplace problems may apply across the board, they are increasingly well documented when it comes to controlling fraud. A Price Waterhouse crime survey of more than 5,400 companies in 40 countries found that the average loss from fraud per company was US$3.2 million in 2007, but whistleblower 'hotlines' as well as internal and external sources were the initial method of detection in 43 per cent of cases, and 'tipsters' (i.e., whistleblowers) were the single most effective source of information in detecting corporate crime (Price Waterhouse Coopers 2007). In 2008, the Association of Certified Fraud Examiners (ACFE) similarly reported that 46 per cent of the 959 fraud cases under review were exposed by whistleblowers, with 58 per cent of the tips coming from employees (ACFE 2008). However, financial wrongdoing is just the most easily quantifiable area in which whistleblowing pays off; employee reporting can be critical to quality control, risk management and good governance in almost any area. Coming full circle, timely detection of problems through internal disclosures may prevent or reduce the need for regulatory action and help to avoid embarrassing external disclosures in the media.

In Chapter 12, '"To Persons or Organizations that May be Able to Effect Action": Whistleblowing Recipients', Richard Moberly presents a comprehensive examination of the last two decades of research about official complaint recipients. Over 20 years ago, Miceli and Near (1992: 73) declared that no research addressed the role of the person who receives a whistleblower complaint. Moberly notes that this conclusion is no longer accurate, given studies demonstrating that people who contact their line manager about wrongdoing give them the chance to deal with it before the matter escalates, and that organizations are increasingly recognizing the value of establishing effective internal whistleblowing policies and procedures. Nevertheless, Moberly argues that, despite these studies, the role of the recipient remains under-studied relative to its importance in the whistleblower process. He points out numerous new areas of research that could be conducted to advance our knowledge of how recipients react to whistleblower disclosures and might better protect whistleblowers and ensure the wrongdoing they identify is properly remedied.

In Chapter 13, 'Managerial Responsiveness to Whistleblowing: Expanding the Research Horizon', Wim Vandekerckhove, A.J. Brown and Eva Tsahuridu continue this examination of players other than the whistleblower, focusing especially on substantive as opposed to procedural action in response to whistleblowing. The chapter highlights the important shift occurring after 30 years of research, from thinking about how to protect whistleblowers from organizations, to how to protect society from organizations that do not respond effectively to whistleblower warnings. This shift is predicated on the overwhelming evidence that whistleblowers will report internally before blowing the whistle externally – a process which perhaps requires a fundamental rethinking of whistleblower research to examine 'how the management processes of organizations and whistleblowing interact and interrelate'. Chapter 13 begins this new conversation by discussing two types of organizational response: 'hearer action' which addresses the misconduct exposed by the whistleblower, and 'protector action' which describes organizational responses that protect a whistleblower from unfair detrimental outcomes. The chapter includes new findings from the Australian 'Whistling While They Work' study demonstrating that research can effectively examine managerial responses to whistleblowers, if only the right questions are asked, and concludes by presenting a new theory to study the courage of managers, individually and collectively, to listen to and to protect whistleblowers.

RESEARCH, REGULATION AND REALITY

At the outset, we said these research problems were not just theoretical and academic. They also reflect a real demand from institutions and regulators for better, more reliable evidence regarding the value of whistleblowing, and the options for recognizing and maximizing that value. It is because whistleblowing is increasingly recognized as being in the public interest that researchers have focused attention on measures that facilitate the raising and investigation of concerns and the protection of disclosers. From the discussion so far, it is also clear why organizations and institutions support this research, for directly and indirectly detecting and controlling wrongdoing, preventing clashes with regulators and boosting corporate governance.

How research can best support improved regulatory and institutional practice, however, remains an important global challenge. Over the last 30 years, most regulatory and institutional reform, and changes to organizational governance, have been reflected in or driven by legislative reforms aimed at recognizing and protecting whistleblowers. Such legal measures are motivated by a range of objectives, ranging from the utilitarian concerns of detecting and correcting wrongdoing, to justice concerns about the unfair outcomes so often experienced by insiders who report wrongdoing. However in most countries, they also interlace with other pre-existing social norms and legal regimes, going to the same objectives, such as witness protection in criminal justice systems, and legal defenses, exemptions and protections for employees or others whose disclosures about wrongdoing would otherwise breach discipline or confidentiality. Indeed, these conjunctions of policy and legal objectives highlight that the management of whistleblowing involves the juggling of a range of sometimes competing values, interests and objectives, sometimes in general, sometimes in the individual case. While the contributors to this Handbook are clear on the pro-social objectives and value of whistleblowing, all are also well aware that the whistleblowing process can involve these conflicting values. For example, allowing anonymous disclosures and providing assurances about confidentiality may be regarded as consistent with a whistleblower's rights to privacy and freedom of expression, but be inconsistent with data protection arrangements and an alleged wrongdoer's right to information. It is possible to reconcile these principles, but it requires clear legal and procedural hierarchies of obligations and rights, capable of being translated into organizational practice.

Similarly, the potential usefulness of public interest disclosures for remedying societal problems, on the one hand, and the vulnerability of the discloser, on the other, has motivated some to elevate whistleblowing to a fundamental right in employment (Lewis 2008). Although this demand has not yet been successful, the expansion of laws which promote public interest disclosures by organizational insiders are moving in this direction; as is growing support for regimes which offer financial inducements to whistleblowers in certain circumstances. Yet all these trends need to recognize the complexity of circumstances and issues raised by whistleblowing, rather than simply being designed as 'symbolic' laws and procedures which state broad objectives that are not implementable, or are only triggered in situations which amount to unrealistic or even fictitious stereotypes. For example, it has been suggested that whistleblowers should be recognized in the British honors system for their good citizenship (Stonefrost 1990). Such suggestions have obvious merit, but the fact is that regimes for encouraging and managing whistleblowing, including protecting whistleblowers from unfair outcomes, simply do not work if only triggered in circumstances where everyone is satisfied that the only motives for whistleblowing were altruism and good faith.

Research that shows how these different values can and should be resolved, in practical ways by managers, regulators and policy makers, is now in hot demand. Internationally, however, there has been a deficit of research which even effectively maps the different legal models that societies are using to recognize whistleblowing. Only recently, Vaughn (2012) has drawn on his experience to make sense of four different perspectives that often inform whistleblowing laws and lead to different, often uncoordinated, legal strategies: employment, open government, market or regulatory perspectives, and human rights (see Figure 1.2). Some of these reflect a greater concern with individual rights, and others with institutional reform; while some are more likely to be pitched at the public rather than at the private sector. Already this model is proving useful to make sense of different legal efforts, and in attempting to explain why many seem so misaligned, misdirected or ineffective. For example, Dworkin and Brown (2013; see also Brown 2013) note that provisions dealing with public or media disclosure are closely related to Vaughn's human rights and open government perspectives, while institutional or structural approaches to whistleblowing align with Vaughn's institutional reform dimension, and anti-retaliation approaches can be seen as an aspect of individual rights, including but not limited to employment law perspectives. As Dworkin and Brown acknowledge, the task for researchers is not to reconcile these perspectives and models, but to help policy makers understand that they contain different elements which need to be accommodated if legislation is to be successful both in encouraging whistleblowing and protecting disclosers.

When it comes to translating research into action, therefore, we begin with Chapter 14, 'Whistleblower Protection: A Comparative Law Perspective'. Björn Fasterling picks up these debates by describing important considerations for scholars engaging in comparative legislative research.

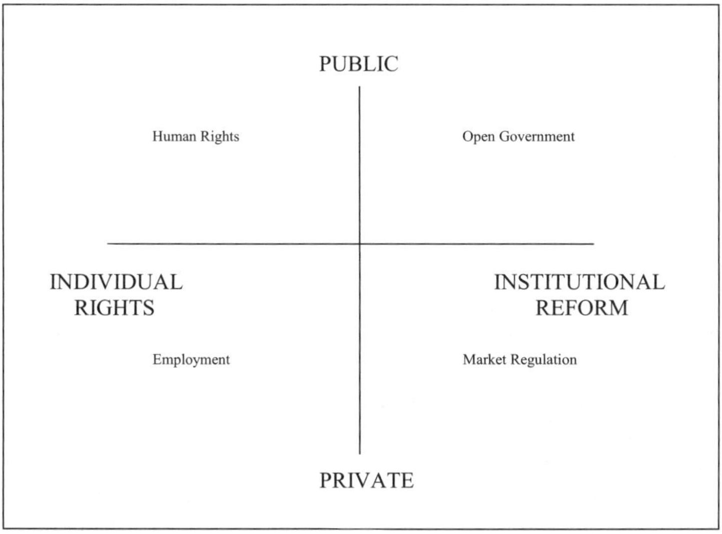

Source: Vaughn 2012: ch. 15

Figure 1.2 A matrix of perspectives on the nature of whistleblowing provisions

He notes that legislation can also be conveniently separated or mapped using the two dimensions noted earlier: justice and utilitarian dimensions. In other words, laws that recognize and protect whistleblowers' freedom of expression, and those that aim at increasing the effectiveness of preventing and detecting dangers to wrongdoing and violations of law. Of course, these two categories are themselves interrelated and have some overlap, and Fasterling provides useful analysis of how they may relate to the pictures provided by Vaughn, and Dworkin and Brown. Further, he emphasizes the challenging reality that effective legislative research must look not only to 'special purpose' or 'stand alone' whistleblower protection laws typical of some English-descended common law countries, but also to whistleblower protections embedded in other laws, ostensibly dealing with other subjects. Fasterling's analysis provides important guidance for any research that attempts to compare lessons from different legal regimes.

Across the world, nevertheless, there are three bodies of legal responses which are particularly important to analyze for their different effects. The first and arguably most important of these are civil and employment remedies, intended to increase organizational responsiveness to whistleblowing, and deliver justice to whistleblowers who suffer unfair outcomes, by providing them with access to compensation and other remedies. The importance of these responses is obvious. Early in the chapter, we gave five examples of high profile, effective whistleblowing which was wholly or largely acted on, sooner or later with major positive effects (Cynthia Cooper; Gary Brown; Paul van Buitenen; Toni Hoffman; and Stephen Bolsin). However, only the first three of these can also be seen as successful in the sense that the information was acted on without permanent employment consequences for the discloser. Even then, there were many other costs and consequences. Toni Hoffman was neither sacked, demoted nor disciplined, but received compensation for stress and other impacts of the process, together with a stalled career and the impacts of the wrongdoing itself.

Stephen Bolsin fared less well again: as a result of his efforts, he was unable to obtain work in the United Kingdom and emigrated to Australia. There are many other examples for why a diverse range of civil and employment remedies need to be considered. In the United Kingdom, Kate Schroder blew the whistle on a fraud on a government-funded training scheme, providing evidence of serious contractual non-compliance to her managers, and then to an appropriate external agency when she suspected a cover-up was under way. However, her employer then dismissed her for breach of confidentiality, and in the subsequent press coverage, issued a statement which inferred that she herself was involved in fraud. Schroder settled a libel action for UK£25,000 plus costs. While protection and remedies are all the more important in 'David versus Goliath' situations, organizational liability for failing to respond properly can become very large where, as is often the case, it is senior managers who blow the whistle. In Japan, Michael Woodford, chief executive of Olympus, had worked for the company for 30 years, but was dismissed in 2011 after issuing warnings about corruption at the top management level and questioning dubious payments. Olympus initially denied the allegations but eventually admitted that it had hidden UK£1.1 billion of losses over 20 years. Woodford initially sought reinstatement but ultimately accepted UK£10 million in settlement of his unfair dismissal claim, which incidentally, he brought not in Japan, but in the United Kingdom.

In Chapter 15, 'The Key to Protection: Civil and Employment Law Remedies', David Lewis, Tom Devine and Paul Harpur review the different legal systems intended to make these types of remedies real in the United States, United Kingdom, Australia, Canada and New Zealand. Even in countries with such similar legal traditions, and where 'special purpose' whistleblower protection laws are often in place, there is great variation and a mixed track record. This gives plenty of scope for further and better research on basic issues about the interface between whistleblower protection and employment law, workplace health and safety law, formality of dispute resolution mechanisms, and burdens of proof. The authors note the general problem that it is exceedingly rare for governments to adopt or reform their laws based on any actual empirical research into what types of protections are needed, or are currently provided but not working; the Australian public sector being the most notable recent exception. Such research is, however, increasingly possible.

One of the topics thrown up by Chapter 15 is the apparent success of the reward or bounty model for compensating whistleblowers in the United States, relative to other strategies (see also Dworkin and Brown 2013). In Chapter 16, 'Because They Have Evidence: Globalizing Financial Incentives for Corporate Fraud Whistleblowers', Tom Faunce, Kim Crow, Tony Nikolic and Frederick M. Morgan, Jr continue this focus with a global survey of such laws, intended to encourage whistleblowers to report misconduct by providing them with monetary rewards calculated as a percentage of the fraud or financial loss associated with the wrongdoing, or the penalties for wrongdoing imposed through regulatory action. Arguing that the False Claims Act (FCA) in the United States provides the most comprehensive and successful example of such provisions, the authors assert that the FCA could serve as a model for an international system of rewards based on multilateral trade agreements. This chapter is an important new look at whether and how this US version of the bounty model could be expanded to promote whistleblowing about fraud worldwide.

By contrast, in Chapter 17, 'When It All Goes Bad: Criminal Remedies', Maureen Spencer and John Spencer discuss an under-studied, under-recognized, and more problematic aspect of how whistleblowing is dealt with in law: the use of criminal law. They do so from two perspectives. First, many countries and jurisdictions have criminal provisions that punish retaliation against whistleblowers specifically, or witnesses to wrongdoing more generally. Spencer and Spencer argue that not much is known about these provisions, but that there are indications the laws are not utilized much to punish retaliators, raising many research questions about their utility or what might be needed to make them more effective. This contrasts with criminal provisions that are used *against* whistleblowers, such as those prohibiting whistleblowers from disclosing certain information, especially national security matters. Unlike the anti-retaliation criminal provisions, these laws seem to be enforced frequently against whistleblowers, especially in recent years. Chapter 17 ultimately argues that the criminal law has a complex and perhaps contradictory relationship with the act of whistleblowing, and that scholars should examine the relationship in more depth.

Civil, employment, reward-based and criminal law responses to whistleblowing are all important. Like other elements of legal responses, they are crucial topics for more in-depth research, to better inform policy making. However, in seeking to establish how to better recognize and protect whistleblowing in practice, the focus of research and policy making alike has been on what makes for an effective national legal response. In addition to this vital question, there are two major areas in which even less research has been done.

The first is the need for a greater transnational and international focus on whistleblowing, in the era of ever-intensifying globalization. This has already been hinted at, in the potential application of reward and *qui tam* laws to transnational companies; and the fact that whistleblowers may already be able to achieve more effective protection under the laws of a jurisdiction other than the one in which either wrongdoing or retaliation occurred, depending on the structure and ownership of the employing corporation. The need for effective whistleblowing regulations and policies in international governmental organizations and programs are perhaps an even more burning priority. The challenge was demonstrated by the case of Kathryn Bolkovac, made famous by the confronting 2010 movie, *The Whistleblower*. Bolkovac was a former Nebraskan (US) police officer who in 1999 joined the UN Police Task Force in post-war Bosnia, employed by DynCorp, a private military contractor. As a human rights investigator, she was shocked to discover that people from her mission were engaged in human trafficking and sexual slavery; but when individuals were implicated, investigations were brought to an end by sending the suspects to another mission or returning them to their country, while surviving victims were repatriated or transported elsewhere so they would not be available for interview. Bolkovac raised the issue with about 50 United Nations staff and officials, as well as DynCorp managers, but was demoted and eventually sacked for allegedly falsifying time sheets. She was vindicated when her whistleblowing was found to be the real reason for her dismissal, but not through any United Nations response; rather, once again, by a UK employment tribunal.

In Chapter 18, 'Whistleblower Protection in International Governmental Organizations', Shelley Walden and Bea Edwards explore the complexities of this pressing issue. International governmental organizations (IGOs) exist outside the legal regulations of individual countries and often operate in extreme secrecy, raising the spectre of fraud and abuse. Yet, protections for insiders who come forward with information about

IGO misconduct face uncertain and often insufficient protections. Relying on their extensive experience studying IGOs, the authors examine the numerous flaws in ad hoc IGO whistleblower protection systems and suggest several avenues for further research and evidence-based policy reform in this area.

Secondly, flowing from this, there is surprisingly little research into the nature and effectiveness of *practical* efforts and strategies aimed at whistleblower protection, more generally within organizations, even where national or subnational laws mean that such strategies are now legally required. Most researchers, policy makers and managers know that legislation, in and of itself, is a blunt instrument for influencing organizational and behavioral change. The question of whether such legislative objectives are being implemented, or what strategies for whistleblower support and protection would be best supported and promoted by legal regimes, depends on knowledge of what actions are actually being taken by organizations and regulators to support whistleblowers in practice. Moreover, these questions depend on how whistleblowers are supported by managers and regulators in a proactive sense, once the disclosure is made, and not simply in reaction to any detrimental outcomes they may begin to suffer. Directly or indirectly, the thrust of whistleblower protection laws relies on organizations learning to embed at least a 'compliance' approach, but preferably a 'beyond compliance' approach to whistleblowing within their own management culture and systems.

In many circumstances, the benefits to the organization itself are now clear, because without such an approach, any moral or legal obligation to report wrongdoing will continue to be in conflict with, and overtaken by, a worker's self-interest in keeping their head down, in order to retain his or her job. Thus, without intervention, whistleblowing can be seen as a public and organizational good that will continue to be under-produced, unless the economics for the individual whistleblower are rebalanced towards speaking up, rather than staying silent. It can also be argued that employers have an interest in internal disclosure procedures being made mandatory, as this may help to ensure that competitors do not get an unfair advantage through improper behavior that goes undetected for longer. At the same time, the practicalities of whistleblower protection will often also rely on the roles of regulators or oversight agencies. There will always be situations where the problems or challenges raised by a whistleblower may be too great, or too ingrained in the management culture or operations of an organization, for that organization to see the whistleblowing for what it is, in which case they will still deny support. Examples include another whistleblower made famous by the 1999 movie, *The Insider*. Dr Jeffrey Wigand was sacked as vice-president for research and development at Brown and Williams Tobacco Corporation after objecting to his employer's attempts to conceal the addictive and toxic nature of its product (Devine and Massarani 2011: xiii). Such concealment was such an endemic part not only of that company's operations, but the entire tobacco industry, that it was unrealistic to expect the company to support or protect him; the question then becomes, who else will do so?

Chapter 19, 'Whistleblower Support in Practice: Towards an Integrated Research Model', highlights the need for, and potential shape of, greater empirical research into the content and operations of disclosure procedures and systems, with a focus on how better whistleblower support strategies might be institutionalized. A.J. Brown, Dan Meyer, Chris Wheeler and Jason Zuckerman (three of them policy practitioners rather than researchers) present a comparison of how whistleblower protection is pursued in the US federal government and the Australian public sector. These are jurisdictions with related, long-standing and recently amended whistleblowing regimes, but quite different institutional approaches. The study highlights that it is only by collecting information regarding what is going on inside organizations that any systematic picture of the effectiveness of whistleblowing regimes can be formed, reinforcing the importance of questions raised in Chapter 13. So far, this research has been at best 'one off' rather than ongoing, with official longitudinal data gathering generally limited to levels of perceived wrongdoing and reporting rather than more comprehensive data on the effectiveness of whistleblower protection. The chapter identifies five particular challenges to drive the development of a more integrated research model, beginning with the need for agreed, efficiently gathered, comparable indicators of organizational success, and concluding with the need for performance information which supports more meaningful regulatory oversight. The feasibility of meeting these challenges is also demonstrated, making this chapter a further departure point for a new generation of research.

CONCLUSION

From this range of topics and the chapters that deal with them, it can be seen that the Handbook sets out a rich international stocktake of empirical research, and existing and potential research methods. Our purpose is to equip policy makers, institutional managers and other stakeholders in good governance with better tools for understanding, measuring, managing and harnessing whistleblowing as an organizational and political process. As a result, many chapters point to significant shifts in focus or research method, especially towards understanding how managers and institutions respond to whistleblowing, rather than simply whistleblowers themselves.

Nevertheless, there would be no such thing as whistleblowing, were it not for whistleblowers. Before concluding the book, Brian Martin therefore returns us to important issues of research focus, design and ethics, in Chapter 20, 'Research that Whistleblowers Want – and What They Need'. Drawing on decades of personal experience with research, advocacy and support for whistleblowers, Martin sets out the need for research focused on providing practical advice to individuals as they contemplate whether and how to blow the whistle. He gives numerous examples of the type of studies that would be beneficial, particularly focusing on the political and communication skills necessary to bring about organizational change. Martin argues that whistleblowers need 'practical skills and insights into the ways organizations and society operate' so that they can navigate the dangerous waters of bureaucratic cultures that easily turn hostile to whistleblowing. His potential research agenda presents an important call to arms for research geared towards helping insiders increase the effectiveness of their own whistleblowing, both in terms of achieving changes that stop and prevent wrongful practices, and their own survival.

Finally, in Chapter 21, 'Strategic Issues in Whistleblowing Research', led by Wim Vandekerckhove, we pool key lessons from all the chapters in this book, emphasizing how research into whistleblowing is shifting, and likely to shift further. Throughout, the objectives of our authors have been to interpret and reinforce the importance of whistleblowing, but also to advance debate on key contextual and definitional questions in whistleblowing research, which underpin how research into whistleblowing is currently conducted and might be best conducted in the future. Irrespective of geography or sector, we give an overview of how research is being and can be used to improve organizational, regulatory and political systems. We have also sought to provide current and new researchers with practical insights into how research might be focused to provide new knowledge, as well as reinforce existing findings. And we have sought to demonstrate how and why the best research will be conducted in collaboration with regulators and organizations who want to understand how whistleblowing is working, how it could be managed better, and how whistleblowing laws and policies could be better designed to 'fit their purpose'. Obviously, we also hope that whistleblowing's practical importance will see well-designed research win greater support from funding bodies.

We began by asserting that 'whistleblowing' may seem like a niche, almost boutique issue for research and policy making – but only to the uninitiated or the foolish. Any researcher or policy maker who has read this introduction, let alone the rest of this Handbook, is no longer in the realm of the uninitiated. But it is in the *realpolitik* of employment relationships, organizational life and volatile public affairs that greater knowledge about whistleblowing really matters. We hope that an understanding of the current research issues and challenges demonstrates that it is only the foolish manager or decision maker who, having spent any time in their role, could still consider that their response to those who report institutional wrongdoing is either simple or of only passing importance. We hope that the next generation of research into whistleblowing will continue to fill these needs, and strengthen the management and political cultures of our societies, by helping ensure that questions of how to respond to whistleblowing are given the care and attention they deserve.

NOTE

1. *R v Ponting* [1985] CLR 318 (UK).

PART I

RESEARCH FUNDAMENTALS

2. Understandings of whistleblowing: Dilemmas of societal culture

Wim Vandekerckhove, Tina Uys, Michael T. Rehg and A.J. Brown

INTRODUCTION

Is research into whistleblowing the same all over the world? Can we even say that 'whistleblowing' occurs all over the world, in every country or every society, in a way that is so similar that it can be researched everywhere the same way? The answer to these broad questions is almost certainly 'no'. As discussed in Chapter 1, the term 'whistleblowing' itself has its own origins in particular societies and particular cultures, where there are many ways of understanding it, even before trying to cross into other languages and cultures. How the concept is perceived in different cultures is a crucial threshold question.

Yet, at the same time there is good reason to believe that everywhere, in all societies, humanity functions using conceptions of right and wrong conduct. As social animals, humanity everywhere organizes itself in groups, and increasingly, in organizations and institutions, albeit in a myriad of ways and for different social, economic and political purposes. Whatever the mode of human organization, we know that the processes by which perceived wrongdoing comes to light and is dealt with are inherently important (for a definition of wrongdoing see Skivenes and Trygstad, Chapter 4). And so, we search for research approaches which acknowledge and explain the different ways that this occurs, in order to know whether or how the reporting or disclosure of wrongdoing is manifested, how it compares, what its implications are, and how it is best understood, encouraged or managed. Given that societal cultures do vary, what does this mean for the phenomenon of whistleblowing? What does it imply for international organizations operating in societies with different cultures, that create whistleblowing policies and seek to manage reactions to the reporting of wrongdoing? How do corporate subsidiaries implement policies in societal cultures different from their home base in ways that are effective in the host country culture? Can policies and legislation about whistleblowing developed in one society ever transplant effectively into another, depending on the extent of social differences? There are many practical reasons why we want to understand the role of culture in whistleblowing, and vice versa.

To date, research has not effectively isolated the effect of societal culture on whistleblowing, but this is an understandable outcome. Culture and whistleblowing are each very complex concepts to measure, making their interaction even more so. While we are increasingly living in a global village, this only underlines the importance of conducting comparative research between different cultures and societies which can accurately identify both similarities and differences. Gael McDonald (2000) argues that the principal methodological concern when conducting cross-cultural research is one of equivalence: 'are the meanings of key concepts defined equivalently and has the research been designed such that the samples, instrumentation, administration, analysis, and interpretation are equivalent with reference to the cultures in the study' (McDonald 2000: 89).

In this chapter, we demonstrate that for cross-cultural research into whistleblowing to date, this has proved a substantial challenge. So far, while the research record is important, it is relatively shallow. Overall, we argue it is time to develop a revised model (or models) for investigating and comparing how whistleblowing manifests in different societies, and the implications of cultural difference for how it is understood and managed. In the next section we sketch some of the basic implications of how concepts of whistleblowing have developed, followed by a basic overview of how the study of culture has interfaced with whistleblowing research to date – chiefly through the model of culture's influences on organizational life developed by Hofstede (1980, 1991, 2002). In the third section we review the empirical record of this research since it began in the early 1990s, and which, despite the dominance of Hofstede's model, gives very mixed results. The fourth section then highlights some further limitations of the research based on that model. We review other research raising questions about the model and present findings from our own research on the acceptability of whistleblowing in the United Kingdom and Australia, illustrating the limited explanatory (and even predictive) power of Hofstede's model. In the fifth section, we discuss what kind of adapted or alternative research model might provide greater cross-cultural insights into whistleblowing. In particular, we suggest further examination of Schwartz's approach (Schwartz 1994, Schwartz and Bardi 2001) as a possible research perspective, one that would allow for cultural shift and universals. The final section discusses some key practical and methodological problems faced by researchers who wish to research whistleblowing cross-culturally, before conclusions are drawn.

DEFINITIONS AND CONSTRUCTS

'Whistleblowing' and Culture

The history of research into culture and whistleblowing, for the purposes of this discussion, begins in the 1970s, when the modern organizational conceptions of these constructs began to take shape. As discussed in Chapter 1, widespread use of the term 'whistleblowing' in public policy dates from the famous US 1972 report on professional responsibility (Nader *et al.* 1972; also see Vandekerckhove 2006: 7–17). In 1982, Parmerlee *et al.* published an article entitled 'Correlates of Whistle-blowers' Perceptions of Organizational Reprisals', the first systematic analysis of empirical evidence regarding whistleblowing, using the US Merit Systems Protection Board survey data from 1980.

The mostly positive or 'pro-social' concept of whistleblowing defined by Bjørkelo and Høivik Bye in Chapter 6 can thus be seen as originating substantially in the United States, where it has since continued to strongly resonate; as it also has, arguably, in other English-speaking countries. However, operationalizing the same concept in other languages and contexts is far from automatic or easy. In our own experience, the challenges of translating the concept in different cultural contexts – let alone researching it – is reinforced by impressions conjured up by such efforts. These range from an interpreter being unable to find a Portuguese translation in Brazil, as the idea was unknown, to bemusement on the faces of an audience of sociologists in Taiwan, to outrage from an audience of state officials meeting in Uganda that any subordinate could even consider being so disloyal. Civil society organizations or policy advocates seeking to foster a positive local language equivalent of 'whistleblowing' may adopt particular terms with this objective in mind. For example, whistleblowing is translated in French as *droit d'alerte*, meaning the 'right to raise the alarm' (Dussuyer *et al.* 2011: n. 12). In Dutch, a whistleblower is called a *klokkenluider* or bell-ringer which refers to a historical practice of a person ringing the church bell to warn of impending danger – a concept to be discussed further by Miceli, Dreyfus and Near in Chapter 3.

However, the concepts used in different languages also create, or may be attempts to respond to, different images of how the activities of whistleblowers should be judged. According to Aaron Levine (2011: 69),

Jewish law simply prohibits whistleblowing, as one is not allowed to be a 'talebearer' through '(1) reporting wrongdoing that someone is planning to do, or has already done, to the listener, and (2) reporting misconduct planned for someone other than the listener'. In Israel, the introduction of whistleblower protection legislation failed because the then prime minister and chief of staff were against supporting or rewarding so-called 'squealers' (Ben-Yehuda 2001: 53), emphasizing the power of this negative element:

> The organization sees whistle-blowing as betraying of the interests of the organization, violating the rules of hierarchy, bypassing authority, squealing, damaging the reputation of the organization, acting in a hostile manner toward the organization, poisoning the atmosphere, and supplanting cooperation with suspicion. Whistle-blowers, on the other hand, tend to justify their activities in such terms as doing one's job, being faithful to the community, revealing the truth, and doing something that is in the best interests of the organization. (Ben-Yehuda 2001: 79)

In Afrikaans, a whistleblower is also sometimes referred to as a *verklikker* or squealer, with the same negative connotation. However, the South African experience also emphasizes another complicating cultural dimension. As an example of a country with an authoritarian past, the concept of whistleblowing becomes even more negative if associated with past political history involving 'informing'. During the apartheid years, informers to the South African police and security structures were called *impimpis*, and their betrayal of the struggle against apartheid was often punished by death through 'necklacing' (a tyre filled with fuel was placed around their necks and set alight; see Uys 2010: 122–3). In Germany, the Gestapo and the Stasi's reliance on denunciations by friends and colleagues to bolster their reign of terror may still lead to dismissal of any discussion of protection for whistleblowers, as they can be tarred with the same brush as these earlier informers (Strack 2011: 109). Similarly, in China attempts to promote anonymous whistleblowing hotlines are often met with abhorrence because of the link with the Cultural Revolution, when children were encouraged to inform on their parents, neighbors on their neighbors and students on their teachers (Martens and Crowell 2006: 104).

Similarly, a study on curbing public sector corruption in post-Communist Europe (Ukraine, Bulgaria, Slovakia and the Czech Republic) found that 19 per cent of the general public and 34 per cent of street-level officials considered the encouragement of officials to expose wrongdoing to be 'unnecessary' or 'actually harmful'. Especially high resistance to whistleblowing in the Czech Republic (26 per cent for the general public and 51 per cent for street-level officials) was interpreted as reflecting 'the bitter experience of "informing" under an externally imposed communist regime' (Miller *et al.* 2001: 315).

When researching whistleblowing in cross-cultural contexts, it is thus essential to distinguish when the respondents are talking about the disclosure of information about perceived wrongdoing where disclosure is in the interests of the powerful (informing), or where it serves to curb the abuse of power, in which case it is whistleblowing (Orr 1981). The line may not always be distinct. In some cultural contexts, the interests of the powerful and other interests (e.g., those of the powerless) may actually align, in which case some reporting that would otherwise simply be 'informing' may have increased social acceptability, because even though it involves reporting colleagues or peers, it also constitutes a curbing of abuse of power. How it will be perceived, on balance, may nevertheless vary depending on the context and political history; and may vary depending on the views and values of sub-groups, even within the same society. Even within societies or cultures where an overall more positive conception of whistleblowing has evolved, the concept can involve conflicting and negative values. In general, the disclosure of perceived wrongdoing by members of the group or organization involved tends to bring issues of conflicting loyalties or even betrayal to the fore. In Australia, for example, the dictionary definition of 'to blow the whistle on' was until recently: '*Colloq.* to betray, esp. to the authorities' (*Macquarie Dictionary* 1982: 1488). Legislative committees have recommended the need for a general 'culture change' in order to effect 'a fundamental shift in Australian values and ethics' to overcome the social stigma associated with whistleblowing (Senate (Australia) 1994: xiii), or what has been described as a 'well-documented anti-dobbing culture which is contrary to whistleblowing' (Sawyer 2004). Journalists who strongly maintain that whistleblowers are vitally important to the public interest also believe that this is 'probably not the generally held community view' (Oakes 2010: 296). Such evidence tends to suggest that, even if accentuated by particular political histories in some cultures, informing is viewed in a negative light in most cultures.

At the same time, the *perception* that whistleblowing is culturally unacceptable in any given society, for whatever reasons, may not accord with the *reality* of how whistleblowing is actually viewed by that society. In 2012, research into public attitudes to whistleblowing was undertaken by Griffith University and the University of Greenwich, through online public omnibus surveys of stratified, random samples of Australian adults (n = 1,211) and UK adults (n = 2,000) (see Brown *et al.* 2012; Vandekerckhove 2012; Brown, Dreyfus and Vandekerckhove 2014).[1] In both countries, only around half of respondents (Australia, 53 per cent; United Kingdom, 47 per cent) felt that in their society, it was 'generally acceptable for people to speak up about serious wrongdoing, even if means revealing inside information', even though a much higher proportion of the same samples (81 per cent, in both countries) felt that 'people should be supported' for revealing wrongdoing, even if it meant revealing inside information, as against being punished. This highlights that perceptions of cultural acceptability may depend on a wider range of factors than what it is that the population of that society actually think. Further results from this study will be discussed below.

Studies show that at least some of the assumptions that may confound cross-cultural research can be reduced, or managed, by using survey or interview questions which use neutral, descriptive language to describe whistleblowing, rather than using the term 'whistleblowing' or equivalent terminology. At the same time, definitions of whistleblowing used, and dependent variables measured, have naturally varied among researchers. The most common type of whistleblowing used as a dependent variable has been the likelihood of blowing the whistle (LBW), measured as expressed likelihood using scenarios for which respondents indicated whether or not they would blow the whistle (e.g., Sims and Keenan 1999). Some culture-related studies have separated internal whistleblowing and external whistleblowing, an important distinction due to the implications for the whistleblower and organization of going to an external outlet.

For the dependent variable, some studies have used internal and external whistleblowing, the moral perception of whistleblowing, intention or likelihood to blow the whistle, personal propensity, organizational propensity to blow the whistle, voice or internal reporting (and this is not a complete list!). An important difference between whistleblowing and voice appears to be what the reporting is uncovering. Voice includes raising or drawing attention to any problems, whereas whistleblowing has always been defined as targeting wrongdoing, and therefore may involve a higher range of risks. As MacNab *et al.* (2007a) point out, similarly, internal reporting is an authorized, internal action, which is not the case with all types of whistleblowing (although it may apply to some types of actions, such as those of an internal auditor). Many chapters in this volume (e.g., Chapters 4, 6, 7, 8, 12, 13) highlight the many different characteristics of whistleblowing which can lead to significant differences in the research, depending on which are operationalized, and how.

What Concepts of 'Culture'?

If anything, an even more complex array of choices confronts the conceptualization of culture for the purposes of this research. This is the chief concern of the remainder of this chapter. Anthropologists, naturally, have been studying culture for a long time. However, the study of cross-cultural differences and similarities with respect to whistleblowing has generally taken place through the prism of cross-cultural business and management research, due to the extent to which whistleblowing is defined as a form of organizational behavior (employees reporting wrongdoing within or under the control of their organization, whether internally, to regulatory authorities, or externally to the public). While cross-cultural 'comparative management' had been studied in the 1970s (Negandhi 1974; Kelley and Worthley 1981), it was only after publication of Hofstede's first *Culture's Consequences* book (1980) that cross-cultural business research started to appear more frequently (Child 1981; Adler 1983; Negandhi 1983).

Since that time, the effect of culture on whistleblowing, or how whistleblowing takes place in different cultural contexts, have been the subject of approximately 16–20 empirical research articles, depending on what is accepted as whistleblowing behavior. Chiefly, these have sought to use Hofstede's model to test for any relationships. The first such study to specifically examine culture and whistleblowing appeared in an accounting context using employees from France, Norway and the United States (Schultz *et al.* 1993). Comparative studies like this have dominated the research. When single country studies are included, a total of 17 such studies have been published in academic journals since 1993.

To be sure, all whistleblowing takes place within a specific national cultural context, so in a sense all whistleblowing publications can be said to have a cultural aspect. For instance, we could take all of the studies from the United States and attribute the whistleblowing behavior to the highly individualistic and/or low 'Power Distance' dimensions of US culture, being key dimensions of Hofstede's model, as will be discussed. Many studies purporting to study the link between national culture and whistleblowing have simply measured employee whistleblowing intentions using samples from two or more nations, and then compared the results. A constant methodological challenge is the simple problem of different measures being used in different nations, preventing direct comparisons. Thus, studies need to have cross-national or cross-cultural comparison as a goal at the start, before results across national cultures can begin to be effectively compared.

While Hofstede's model has been pervasive, and deploys particular dimensions as discussed in the next section, the fact is that defining culture is not a simple matter. Operationalizing it for the purposes of research is even less so. It requires the identification of structural dimensions of culture that have specific relevance when researching whistleblowing. Lim and Firkola (2000: 138–40) stress the importance of defining culture when conducting cross-cultural studies, especially in the absence of a generally accepted definition and theory of culture. Culture is particularly problematic to define because of its conceptual complexity, on the one hand, and the absence of a 'commonly accepted language to describe it' (Yeganeh *et al.* 2004: 71–2).

Earley (2006: 925) argues that researchers should distinguish between culture as a value or set of values, and culture as the meaning people assign to aspects of the world they live in. This distinction could be viewed as reflecting the difference between a realist approach aimed at explaining, and a social constructivist approach aimed at understanding, the constructions or interpretations of actors (Yeganeh *et al.* 2004: 67–70). It could also be argued that knowledge of cultures requires considering both 'the real manifestations of cultures and the reflexive processes where the actors make sense of their cultures' (Yeganeh *et al.* 2004: 70), as emphasized by the Australian and the UK results already cited. In conducting cross-cultural research, it is therefore important to indicate whether culture is studied as 'real systems of beliefs and values' or as the interpretations that actors give to these, or both.

Various researchers have identified weaknesses in the operationalization of culture when conducting cross-cultural research. In a review of 15 years of cross-cultural research in the field of management control systems, Harrison and McKinnon (1999) identified a tendency to view culture in a simplistic way, not only with regard to the range of the dimensions that are considered but also in terms of universality, uniformity, weight and intensity. According to McDonald (2000: 90–3), the first of such over-simplifications is the tendency of cross-cultural researchers to compare nations, rather than cultures. However, whereas 'nation' can be defined as 'people inhabiting one country under the same leadership and administration', 'culture' refers to 'the shared beliefs and symbols of a group of individuals' (McDonald 2000: 91). More than one culture can therefore be present among the people living in a particular country (the nation), and a particular culture can be located in more than one nation.

For similar reasons, Schaffer and Riordan (2003: 178) suggest that the use of other markers of culture besides country should be explored. Yeganeh *et al.* (2004: 75–6) distinguish between monolithic cultures with a high degree of homogeneity and pluralistic cultures which are heterogeneous and contain a number of subcultures. They argue that the nation should only be used as the cultural unit of analysis if the researchers can demonstrate that the countries under study are internally homogenous while differing meaningfully from each other with regard to the variables being studied. Doran (2001: 240) tries to resolve this issue by identifying so-called 'mainstream' respondents in North America, defined as 'native English-speakers who were born in North America and whose parents were born in North America'. While this may be valid for some purposes, it raises the question of whether all second-generation English-speakers in the United States and Canada can really be considered one culture. This question is also raised squarely by the further results from the Australia–United Kingdom study, presented below. Secondly, studies of populations within a particular country should take into account the extent to which these populations are culturally homogenous, especially where high levels of ethnic diversity and/or population movements are present. Whether such variations relate to ethnic, religious or other similar dimensions of culture, or to other factors, however, is not straightforward. Socio-economic factors can also be either determinative or descriptive of different cultural groups. In South Africa, for example, perceptions with regard to whistleblowing have also been identified as influenced at least as much by social class, which while inter-related with issues of race or ethnicity, may also function independently:

> [W]histleblowing is a predominantly middle-class phenomenon in South Africa, done by those with self-confidence and an understanding of the system, and, perhaps, who also perceive themselves as able to find other employment should they be punished for whistleblowing. (Irish-Qhobosheane 2007: 174)

Given that whistleblowing specifically concerns the relationships between individuals and particular groups to which they belong, within communities or societies, the particular cultures of those sub-groups becomes obviously important. In some cultures a high value is placed on loyalty to the organization you work for. Martens and Crowell (2006: 104) indicate the high premium placed on organizational loyalty in Japan and Korea. However, within societies, and even within specific industries and sectors, organizational cultures themselves vary. Whether organizations foster a culture of loyalty, and how this impacts on whistleblowing and its outcomes, is clearly dependent on more than simply generalized understandings of how values of loyalty feature in the culture of the society as a whole. Similarly, whistleblowing often involves questions of power, and the role of individuals or groups in a process increasingly recognized as important for the curbing of abuses of power. Accordingly, understanding how whistleblowing manifests or is perceived in different social contexts might be more usefully explored by investigating the 'political culture' of that group – meaning a citizenry's body of 'collective assumptions' about governing institutions and processes, embedded in wider power relationships and woven into their assumptions about life (Smith 2001) – as opposed to trying to investigate culture in a more generalized, ethnic or racial sense.

Finally, McDonald (2000) also stresses the importance of indicating whether variations in perceiving culture are employed as a causal, intervening or residual variable. When using culture as an independent variable it should be made clear whether reference is made to the dominant culture, a subculture or the culture of origin. Comparative researchers should also consider which behavior can be considered culturally specific or universal. Last, the possible presence of cultural bias should be explored, either through the way in which data is collected, or whether the researcher could have given some indication of preferred outcomes or even the possible impact of the cultural origin of the researcher.

Overall, the complexity of the concept means that researchers must carefully consider whether the way in which they employ culture is appropriate for the research questions at hand. Once the specific purposes for investigating issues of culture are made explicit, along with the nature and dimensions of the particular constructs of culture that are relevant to those purposes, it then becomes possible to integrate culture into the theoretical framework for the research project.

APPLYING HOFSTEDE: RESEARCH RESULTS TO DATE

To date, the bulk of research into culture's effect on whistleblowing has answered these questions by looking at the cultural dimensions developed by Hofstede. On one hand, that is helpful, as it builds depth of findings regarding the dimensions and their effect on whistleblowing. On the other hand, as will be discussed, it means we do not know much about other conceptions of culture regarding whistleblowing. Further, the bulk of research using Hofstede's dimensions of culture is limited to just three dimensions: Individualism-Collectivism (IC), Power Distance (PD) and Uncertainty Avoidance (UA). Two further dimensions have featured in the research, but only to a more limited extent, so the record does not contain much on these dimensions. Masculinity-Femininity (MAS) refers to the distinction between a high value placed on financial success and advancement (masculine) as opposed to an appreciation for relationships, cooperation and security (feminine). Organizations with a feminine culture therefore resolve conflicts through compromise and negotiation, while those with a masculine culture resolve conflicts through a struggle between the conflicting parties (Sims and Keenan 1999: 140). MAS has been included in three studies, one of which found a positive relationship with whistleblowing (Tavakoli *et al.* 2003), while the other two did not find a significant relationship (Brody *et al.* 1999; Zhuang *et al.* 2005). Long-Term Orientation (LTO) was included in one study, that found a positive relationship with whistleblowing intent (Zhuang *et al.* 2005). LTO was only established by Hofstede in his 1991 book and was originally named 'Confucian Dynamism'. Other dimensions are still emerging, such as Indulgence versus Restraint (Hofstede *et al.* 2010).

Before further considering the best ways to approach culture in whistleblowing research, it is useful to form an overview of the lessons derived from the application of Hofstede's approach thus far, in terms of each of the main dimensions studied: Individualism-Collectivism (IC), Power Distance (PD) and Uncertainty Avoidance (UA). Of the 17 empirical studies using Hofstede's culture dimensions and whistle-blowing as a dependent variable found to date, 12 included samples from the United States. Of those, eight compared the United States with one other country, while three included the United States and two other countries, and one with three other countries. Only eight countries have been represented more than once: United States (12); Canada (4); China, Mexico and Taiwan (3); Japan, Turkey and India (2); and the rest only once: Australia, Columbia, Croatia, France, Jamaica, Malaysia, Norway, France and South Korea.

Individualism-Collectivism (IC)

While in an individualistic culture the focus is on self-expression and independence from the organization, collectivism emphasizes the import-ance of employees acting in ways to benefit their in-group through shared beliefs, views, needs, norms, duties and the maintenance of stable and long-term membership. The studies using this dimension are summarized below. Most found a positive relationship between Individualism-Collectivism (IC) and whistleblowing of various kinds. However, a significant number of studies did not find a relationship and a few found the opposite relationship. One study by Sims and Keenan (1999) found positive, negative and no relationship, depending on the type of wrongdoing or different aspects of the process. This study used samples from the United States and Jamaica with fairly low sample sizes, 44 and 42 individuals respectively, and used the country level as the measure of culture. The two nations do have a fairly large difference in IC, while the other dimensions are very similar with the exception of UA. Zhuang *et al.* (2005) found that a Chinese sample was more likely to report peers than a sample of more individualistic Canadians, which results in a negative relationship between IC and peer reporting. This was not found for supervisor reporting, however, and the results were attributed to PD rather than IC or LTO, which had greater differences across the nationalities than PD.

Thus, the issue is more complex than simply blowing the whistle or not blowing the whistle, even though five of the studies listed below did find positive relations between LBW and IC. For instance, both Keenan (2007) and Zhuang *et al.* (2005) used samples from China and compared those to Western samples (US and Canadian, respectively), yet came up with somewhat different results. Samples from these studies were almost the same (70/75 and 77/82), however Keenan (2007) used mid-level managers in large companies, while Zhuang *et al.* (2005) used accounting students. Perhaps that is the difference, except that other studies using students found positive relationships. The issue of sampling, and how confidently any differences can be put down to dimensions of culture as opposed to other factors, will be returned to below.

Four other studies comparing Eastern and Western samples found similar positive results: Brody *et al.* (1998) compared the United States with Japan; Brody *et al.* (1999) and Su *et al.* (2010) compared the United States and Taiwan; and Patel (2003) compared Chinese-Malaysian and Australian samples. Since all of these studies found a positive relationship between IC and LWB and three used student samples, this garners more support for an overall positive conclusion between these two variables.

Power Distance (PD)

Power Distance is the degree to which employees feel comfortable approaching and/or contradicting their supervisors. Patel (2003) found PD to be negatively related to the likelihood to blow the whistle (LBW) and the acceptance of whistleblowing. These findings on LBW were replicated by Su *et al.* (2010), while Tavakoli *et al.* (2003) found it negatively related with both LBW on major fraud and personal and organizational propensity to blow the whistle. MacNab *et al.* (2007a)

Table 2.1 Overview of the literature: Relationship with IC

Positive relationship with IC	*Whistleblowing variable*
Brody *et al.* 1999	WB intentions or likelihood of WB
Brody *et al.* 1998	WB intentions or likelihood of WB
Su *et al.* 2010	WB intentions or likelihood of WB
Patel 2003	Likelihood of WB and acceptance of WB
Sims and Keenan 1999	Organizational propensity
Keenan 2007	Likelihood of WB (major fraud, minor fraud, harm to others); personal and organizational propensity
Negative relationship with IC	*Whistleblowing variable*
Sims and Keenan 1999	Likelihood of WB – major fraud
Zhuang *et al.* 2005	Likelihood of peer reporting
No relationship with IC	*Whistleblowing variable*
Sims and Keenan 1999	Individual propensity, likelihood of BW of minor fraud and harm to others
Peek *et al.* 2007	Individual propensity
MacNab *et al.* 2007a	Internal reporting or external WB
MacNab *et al.* 2007b	Individual propensity for WB
Keenan 2002a	Likelihood of WB; personal propensity

found PD to be negatively related to internal reporting, but positively related to external whistleblowing. However, Keenan (2002a), Peek *et al.* (2007) and Schultz *et al.* (1993) did not find a relationship between PD and propensity (or likelihood) to blow the whistle. To sum up, there are four studies that found a negative relationship between PD and whistleblowing, while three of them did not find a relationship.

Let us first look at the three studies that did not find a relationship. In Keenan (2002a), Indian managers were expected to have 'less positive perceptions about whistleblowing' than American managers, but the results, although in the expected direction, were not significant (Keenan 2002a: 81). The lack of significance could have been due to the sample size of 31 Indian managers and 45 US managers. Even with the low sample sizes, they did find personal propensity to blow the whistle to be significantly lower among the Indian managers. Personal propensity was defined essentially as whether whistleblowing was an acceptable practice. Peek *et al.* (2007) used 37 US, 24 Canadian and 17 Mexican accounting students, so their results are also based on a low sample size and non-significance is not surprising. They focused on sexual harassment, which is a more specific case of wrongdoing that may be affected by different cultural norms. Type of wrongdoing has been found to be an important element of the process in a US sample (Near *et al.* 2004), and may also have affected the results of the study by Peek *et al.* (2007). Schultz *et al.* (1993) also found no differences comparing French to US and French to Norwegian samples, but samples ranged from only 32 to 50 individuals.

Table 2.2 Overview of the literature: Relationship with PD

Positive relationship with PD	*Whistleblowing variable*
MacNab 2007a	Propensity for external whistleblowing
Negative relationship with PD	*Whistleblowing variable*
Botero and Van Dyne 2009	Voice
Keenan 2002a	Personal propensity for WB
MacNab 2007a	Internal reporting
Patel 2003	Likelihood of BW, acceptance of WB
Su *et al.* 2010	Likelihood of BW
Tavakoli *et al.* 2003	Likelihood of BW on major fraud, personal and organizational propensity to blow the whistle
Zhuang *et al.* 2005	Supervisor reporting
No relationship with PD	*Whistleblowing variable*
Keenan 2002a	Organizational propensity, LBW
Peek *et al.* 2007	Victim or observer blowing the whistle
Schultz *et al.* 1993	Likelihood of reporting

Of the seven studies that did find a negative relationship, Patel (2003) and MacNab *et al.* (2007a) measured culture at the individual level and used working adults rather than student samples. They also had larger sample sizes, with Patel (2003) ranging from 72 to 92 in the three country samples while MacNab *et al.* (2007a) samples were 248, 463 and 476. Patel (2003) found Australians to be more likely to engage in whistleblowing and more accepting of whistleblowing as an action than either Indians or Chinese-Malaysians. These results were attributed to the low PD/high Individualism of Australian culture compared to its Indian or Chinese-Malaysian counterpart. MacNab *et al.* (2007a) found that for US and Canadian samples, PD was negatively related to internal reporting, but positively related to external whistleblowing for US, Canadian and Mexican samples. Another study by Zhuang *et al.* (2005) based on a Chinese sample found that reporting wrongdoing of peers was more likely than the reporting of wrongdoing of supervisors and attributed this to the high PD of the Chinese culture, whereas a Canadian sample did not show that effect (China is also a low Individualism/high LTO culture, so which one of these is really responsible for the result?). Based on these findings, then, it is important to separate out the different channels available, as the effects of culture on their use could vary.

Uncertainty Avoidance (UA)

Uncertainty Avoidance is the degree to which employees feel threatened by unknown or uncertain situations and therefore pursue predictability through an emphasis on rules and procedures. There were three positive, zero negative and five no relationship findings among the studies including UA. Again, low sample sizes likely affected the results in several of the studies that found no relationship, while two studies finding positive relationships contained 476 (MacNab *et al.* 2007a) and over 1,000 total subjects (MacNab *et al.* 2007b). This is interesting in that the subjects came from countries that are relatively low in UA (Canada and the United States), and one that is relatively high in UA (Mexico). However, the data were collected at the individual level, so national comparisons may not be appropriate. Thus it may be fair to conclude that UA has a positive effect on whistleblowing intentions based on these studies.

Table 2.3 Overview of the literature: Relationship with UA

Positive relationship with UA	*Whistleblowing variable*
MacNab 2007a	Internal reporting and external WB
MacNab 2007b	Propensity for BW
Sims and Keenan 1999	Likelihood of BW
No relationship with PD	*Whistleblowing variable*
Brody *et al.* 1998	WB intentions
Brody *et al.* 1999	WB intentions
Peek *et al.* 2007	Propensity for WB
Schultz *et al.* 1993	Likelihood of reporting
Sims and Keenan 1999	Individual propensity

Summary

As can be seen, the two most studied dimensions from the Hofstede model, IC and PD, do show somewhat consistent findings regarding their effects on whistleblowing. If we ignore studies which found no relationship between whistleblowing intentions and IC or PD, then eight of 11 studies found a positive relationship between IC and whistleblowing intentions, while only one of six studies found PD to be positively related to whistleblowing. Since PD and IC are negatively related, these findings reinforce each other as to their effects on whistleblowing. However, this conclusion ignores the studies that found no relationship between whistleblowing and IC (seven studies) or PD (four studies).

The next most researched dimension was UA, which showed a positive relationship to whistleblowing intentions in four studies, a negative relationship in one study and three studies which found no relationship. As already mentioned, only limited research has been conducted involving other dimensions. Tavakoli *et al.* (2003) found a positive relationship between the masculinity-femininity dimension and LBW for major fraud, personal propensity and organizational propensity; while Zhuang *et al.* (2005) found a positive relationship between long-term orientation and likelihood of peer reporting.

In general, the research using Hofstede's dimensions suggests that whistleblowing is more likely to take place in societal cultures that are low in Power Distance, high in Individualism, and high in Uncertainty Avoidance. However, these generalizations do not hold true for all types of situations. We also do not know much else about other dimensions due to the scarcity of research on those areas.

All of these findings are somewhat tempered by the choice of nations, which in most cases does not isolate one dimension of societal culture from at least one other dimension. This is a problem for the ten studies that used nation as a proxy for Hofstede's cultural dimensions. For example, in Brody *et al.* (1998), the countries used were the United States and Japan. There is almost an equal difference between those two nations in IC and UA, but an even greater difference exists in the LTO dimension, which was not the focus of the study.

Another conclusion to be drawn, reinforcing our earlier observations of the multi-faceted nature of whistleblowing, is that the reporting type and channels used to report wrongdoing have an impact that is different across cultures. Merely asking respondents whether they would blow the whistle is not detailed enough to observe these differences. Researchers also need to ask whether whistleblowers would use internal or external channels. The same is true of types of wrongdoing. Several studies asked respondents what they would blow the whistle about; for instance, major fraud, minor fraud or acts that caused harm to others. Other studies used specific types of wrongdoing such as sexual harassment. Differences can be seen across societal cultures depending on these details. These nuances thus have to be built into the research design, or at least borne in mind, to better understand how the process unfolds in different contexts.

UNANSWERED QUESTIONS: THE LIMITS OF THE HOFSTEDE MODEL

In their own review of cross-cultural research in cross-national contexts, Tsui *et al.* (2007) write that such research is more complex than domestic cross-cultural studies, not only because matching samples can be hard to attain, but because cross-level (individual, organizational, national) theorizing is required. National level characteristics need to be related to individual level or team level responses. One of the reasons why the Hofstede model is so dominant in cross-cultural whistleblowing research may be because it does provide such linking, and some backing for using nation as a proxy for culture.

However, in addition to results to date being very mixed, as shown above, this model has also been heavily contested; the reasons include the fact that it fails to adequately address some of the challenges noted earlier in the chapter. In order to establish how the Hofstede model might be best used in future whistleblowing research, or other models developed or deployed, it is useful to further explore its limitations. Some of these are theoretical and methodological; others are suggested by different results obtained using other approaches; finally, some are reinforced by our own research.

Theoretical and Methodological Challenges

McSweeney (2002) argues that Hofstede's model is fundamentally flawed because its methodological assumptions simply do not hold. First, Hofstede used IBM employee surveys to generalize national populations, raising the question of how representative IBM employees were in the 1970s for entire national populations. Secondly, there is again an issue of sample sizes, which in some countries were less than 200. Another deeper problem is that in Hofstede's model, the uniformity of a national culture (i.e., everyone in a particular nation shares that national culture) is concluded from an average tendency, even though surveys using Hofstede's measurement tool show considerable intra-country differences in individuals' responses: 'Highly varied responses were converted into single national IBM responses and those averaged responses … were then labeled the respective national cultural differences' (McSweeney 2002: 100).

Hofstede has acknowledged such limitations and provided further validation of his first findings published in 1980 (Hofstede 2002). There are also other strengths to his research design: by keeping organizational culture constant, and only using responses from marketing and sales employees within a single company, across different nations, it remains plausible that any difference between national samples can be attributed to actual national differences. However, whether these differences pertain to 'national culture' as opposed to other forms of culture remains problematic. McSweeney (2002) argues that the three cultures – organizational, occupational, national – are not as independent as Hofstede assumes. Even though IBM was noted in the 1970s as having a strong organizational culture, it seems implausible there would be only one IBM culture. According to McSweeney (2002: 95–6), Hofstede requires us to accept that:

> every German 'laboratory clerk' … had the same laboratory clerks' culture as every other German laboratory clerk which was also the same occupational culture as that of every Bangladeshi laboratory clerk, and so forth.

Hofstede's claim that it is national culture which is most pervasive and causal to practices means that the social and the institutional are seen as consequences of national culture. As McSweeney (2002: 99) also argues, this creates a paradox: 'National cultures are said to influence occupational contexts and practices, but somehow that national diversity is not assumed to create national differences in occupational or organizational cultures'.

Others argue that if these three levels of culture were not distinguishable, there would be 'no need to control for organization and occupation as extraneous variables' (Williamson 2002: 1377). However, it is a pertinent critique for whistleblowing research. As observed earlier, whistleblowing relates so inherently to organizational context and relationships (usually professional or employment relationships) that it is questionable whether it is ever truly possible, or even desirable, to minimize or remove these forms of culture from the equation. Further, whistleblowing has also been researched as a form of resistance or dissent, which implies the existence of other organizational cultures besides the official one.

Alternative Conceptions of Individualism/Collectivism

Other conflicting results have been found using measures of culture, different from Hofstede's. Nayir and Herzig (2012) measured Individualism separate from Collectivism and found both to be positively related to whistleblowing intentions, using a sample from Turkey. Trongmateerut and Sweeney (2013) found that collectivist Thai subjects showed a significantly higher effect of subjective norms on WB intention than individualistic US subjects. Such results are important because they challenge fundamental assumptions that whistleblowing is necessarily an individualistic process, in which 'lone wolf' dissenters assert their rights or values against a collective or institution. Instead, they permit circumstances where whistleblowing involves giving voice to collective concerns or activating collective interests. They also support a more nuanced approach to the different conceptions of social, group or organizational loyalty that may operate in any whistleblowing situation, including conflicting loyalties, and different ways that group and societal culture together influence how these conflicts are managed.

Partly in compensation for the structuralist or functionalist nature of the dimensions of culture used by Hofstede, some attention has been given to Confucian teaching, as noted earlier. The fifth of Hofstede's dimensions, added in 1991, was originally named 'Confucian Dynamism' but was renamed in the 2001 edition of *Culture's Consequences* as

'Long-Term Orientation' (Fang 2003). Noting the considerable continuity in the conceptualization of this fifth dimension, namely, the Chinese Value Survey, Fang (2003) offers a profound critique of this conceptualization by tracing how it attempts to simplify 40 different Chinese values. As noted earlier, the one whistleblowing study to use it (Zhuang *et al.* 2005) found a positive relationship between this dimension and likelihood of peer reporting.

Two further studies have also examined Confucianism: Hwang *et al.* (2008), and Park *et al.* (2005). While Hwang *et al.* (2008) found that Confucian teaching would not suppress the intention to blow the whistle, it did not explore the many dimensions of Confucianism. The study did include the concept of *guanxi*, a Chinese understanding of reciprocating obligation and loyalty that is layered depending on the nature of the relationship, and found it to be negatively related to whistleblowing intentions. However, Park *et al.* (2005) break down Confucian teaching into five components, as the complexity of the construct indicated potentially different relationships between its dimensions and whistleblowing intentions. They examined to what extent Confucianism and Collectivism influenced whistleblowing intentions in South Korea. Discussing how Confucianism has been used to derive opposite hypotheses on whistleblowing intentions, they go on to develop two hypotheses deriving predictions from five Confucian ethics traits: Father-Son (FS), Old-Young (OY) and Trust-Friends (TF) negatively relate to whistleblowing intentions, while Sovereign-Subject (SS) and Husband-Wife (HW) relate positively. They find significant positive correlations between SS, HW and internal whistleblowing.

Importantly, Park *et al.* (2005) also apply a more sophisticated understanding to the roles that cultural values of Individualism and Collectivism play in whistleblowing, by recognizing that these each have horizontal and vertical dimensions, as developed by Triandis (1995; 1996) and Triandis and Gelfland (1998). 'Horizontal Individualism' stands for individuals who perceive themselves as self-reliant, unique and distinctive from groups, but also see themselves as equal to all others. 'Vertical Individualism', on the other hand, refers to a desire to move up in a hierarchy in competition with others. 'Horizontal Collectivism' means one sees oneself not only as equal to others, but also emphasizes common goals, sociability and interdependence. 'Vertical Collectivism' then stresses loyalty to one group and hierarchical relationships, both implying a willingness to sacrifice one's own goals for those of a group and to submit to authority.

Park *et al.* (2005: 400) found that 'employees' responses differed depending on whether Collectivism was horizontal or vertical, casting doubt on the general belief that the more collectivistic an employee is, the more negative his or her intentions for whistleblowing will be. In contrast to the pattern of the majority of the studies using Hofstede's dimension, Horizontal Individualism was not related to any type of whistleblowing. Vertical Individualism did correlate positively with internal whistleblowing; but so did Horizontal Collectivism which also correlated with external whistleblowing. Only Vertical Collectivism did not correlate with either form of whistleblowing.

Park *et al.* (2008) then used the same four types of cultural orientation in a cross-cultural comparison of whistleblowing attitudes in the United Kingdom, Turkey and South Korea. They also looked at further types of whistleblowing: anonymous, internal, formal and informal. Naturally results were conflicting: Individualism on the horizontal dimension was positively related to internal, formal and informal whistleblowing, while Vertical Individualism was negatively related to internal whistleblowing, but positively related to anonymous and informal whistleblowing. Although we cannot directly compare these results with studies that used Hofstede's dimensions, we do see a difference depending on type of whistleblowing. They found differences with regard to how nationalities score against cultural orientation, but interestingly they also found that individuals from all three nations prefer formal, internal and anonymous reporting over informal, external or identified whistleblowing. By finding measures of culture that are more nuanced, and appropriate to the different particularities of whistleblowing sought to be studied, these studies appear to be offering significantly greater promise.

An Empirical Challenge: United Kingdom and Australia

Finally, the limitations of Hofstede's model for whistleblowing research are reinforced by some of our own more recent research. As introduced earlier, research into public attitudes to whistleblowing was undertaken in 2012 by Griffith University and the University of Greenwich, through online public omnibus surveys of stratified, random samples of Australian adults (valid responses n = 1,163) and UK adults (valid responses n = 1,532). Table 2.4 shows aggregate findings for another of the eight questions asked.

Table 2.4 How acceptable is reporting wrongdoing in the United Kingdom and Australia?

		UK	Australia
Year of Data Collection		2012	2012
Population (n)		(1,532)	(1,211)
Q4. How acceptable do you personally think it is for someone to reveal inside information about serious wrongdoing by each of these different types of people?			
Q4A. Serious wrongdoing by people in charge of an organization			
	Acceptable	74.0	85.6
	Neither	8.3	10.2
	Unacceptable	17.7	4.2
TOTAL		100.00	100.00
Q4B. Serious wrongdoing by other staff or workers in an organization			
	Acceptable	72.7	81.4
	Neither	9.2	12.9
	Unacceptable	18.1	5.7
TOTAL		100.00	100.00
Q4C. Serious wrongdoing by a family member or personal friend working in the organization			
	Acceptable	62.7	64.3
	Neither	16.8	22.1
	Unacceptable	20.5	13.6
TOTAL		100.00	100.00

Sources: Brown *et al.* 2012; Vandekerckhove 2012; Brown, Dreyfus and Vandekerckhove 2014

These differences showed to be significant ($p<.001$), at a low to moderate level ($V = .238$ for Q4A; $V = .201$ for Q4B; $V = .129$ for Q4C).

Looking at the Power Distance and the Individualism index, from the bulk of the studies conducted to date using Hofstede, we would expect a high acceptance in both countries for whistleblowing. The findings in Table 2.4 confirm these expectations. However, there are also differences between the UK and the Australian results for which Power Distance and Individualism, at least as conceptualized by Hofstede (see Figure 2.1), simply do not account.

In Table 2.4, the percentage of respondents from the United Kingdom indicating it is *unacceptable* to report wrongdoing is higher than in Australia, irrespective of whether the wrongdoing is by people in charge

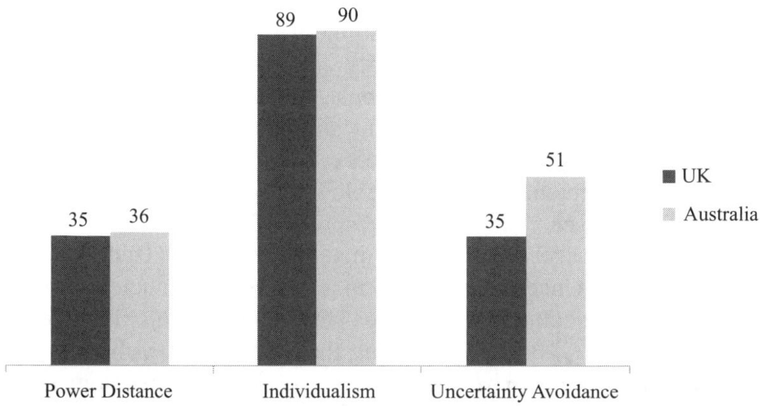

Source: geert-hofstede.com

Figure 2.1 Hofstede's power distance, individualism and uncertainty avoidance scores for United Kingdom and Australia

(A), colleagues (B) or family or (C) friends. Assuming that Individualism is positively related to whistleblowing, the marginally higher score for Individualism for Australia (90 compared to 89 for the United Kingdom) cannot explain a 10 per cent or more difference in our findings. The same applies to the close Power Distance score (36 for Australia compared to 35 for the United Kingdom). If Power Distance as measured by Hofstede is truly so similar in these countries, and is negatively related to acceptance of whistleblowing, then why is the reporting of wrongdoing significantly more unacceptable in the United Kingdom?

This challenge is reinforced by the shrinking difference in acceptability of whistleblowing with regard to who the wrongdoer is. Both the United Kingdom and Australia show a similar pattern: reporting wrongdoing by people in charge, such as supervisors, (A), is found to be more acceptable than reporting wrongdoing by colleagues or peers (B), and the latter is more acceptable than reporting wrongdoing by family or friends (C). The important finding, however, is that whereas for wrongdoing by people in charge the difference is 11.6 per cent (Australia > United Kingdom), the difference for wrongdoing by colleagues is 8.7 per cent (Australia > United Kingdom), and further collapses to only 1.6 per cent (Australia > United Kingdom) for wrongdoing by family or friends.

Figure 2.1 shows more difference between the United Kingdom and Australia on Uncertainty Avoidance (UA) (35 compared to 51), which is the other dimension from Hofstede's model used in at least some whistleblowing studies. Hence our findings might be a case where one dimension is isolated. There is also some difference between the United Kingdom and Australia on Masculinity and on LTO, but nothing to the extent of the difference in UA. Thus, to find any national cultural explanation for these differences (and similarities) between the United Kingdom and Australia using Hofstede, we would have to explain the differences on acceptability of whistleblowing solely through Uncertainty Avoidance. However, what we measured with Q1 comes close to 'individual propensity' for which Sims and Keenan (1999) found no relationship with Uncertainty Avoidance. It is also unclear how one would explain the declining differences between the United Kingdom and Australia on Q4A, Q4B and Q4C using that dimension, without resorting to ad hoc explanations. The Uncertainty Avoidance dimension might at best be used to explain or predict overall acceptance, or acceptance of internal versus external whistleblowing, but not instances where the wrongdoer is the independent variable. For that, Power Distance or perhaps Individualism still seem most appropriate.

As a result, culture as measured by Hofstede seems insufficiently sensitive not only to the complexity of dimensions such as Individualism/Collectivism, relevant to whistleblowing research, but also to the dimensions of political culture which are most pertinent to understanding the different ways in which different groups relate to the power structures of their institutions. In many respects, the ethnologies, economic and employment systems and formal political systems of the United Kingdom and Australia could not be more similar, Australia being almost entirely an immigrant, colonial society descended from Britain. Yet partly because of that history, their underlying political culture is also often recognized as quite different, with democratic and egalitarian values seen as having taken root especially strongly, and developed more strongly, in Australia, supported by often favorable economic circumstances (Patapan *et al.* 2005).

Together with the mixed results shown in the previous section, the fact that Hofstede's model could not have predicted, and cannot be used to explain these findings, seems to confirm that cross-cultural whistleblowing research is in need of a research model that is different from the dominant model in cross-cultural management studies (i.e., Hofstede's model). In particular, unless dimensions of culture more relevant to the dynamics of whistleblowing are used, then any such model seems likely to remain limited; these might include dimensions that recognize rather than try to exclude the effects of organizational and occupational cultures, more nuanced dimensions of social values such as Individualism and Collectivism, and dimensions of political culture.

AN EXTENDED OR ALTERNATIVE MODEL OF CULTURE?

The question becomes, what might be more promising research models for cross-cultural research on whistleblowing? Some departure points are already suggested by the critiques and alternative approaches touched on above. A key one is plainly the problem of a 'national culture' being presumed from national averages of results on particular measures, when it may be the distance or distribution between results within countries, or other particular groups, which provide more pertinent indicators of cultural difference. For whistleblowing research, the variance in individual responses to the perception of wrongdoing may well be more pertinent than simply a national average. Whistleblowing has been an important issue in business ethics and organizational behavior research, precisely because not everyone is doing it. Moreover, the proportions of organization members doing it varies massively between organizations, even within the same nation or specific jurisdiction or economic and social sectors, again reinforcing that there may simply be no value in explanations of national culture that do not take account of these dimensions. Following this criticism through, Tsui *et al.* (2007: 460–1) instead recommend a 'configural approach':

> a group construct can have one of three types of properties: global, shared, or configural. A global property is a relatively objective, easily observable characteristic that does not emerge or originate from the perceptions of individual group members [an example is GDP]. A shared property originates in the common experiences, perceptions, cognitions, or behaviors of the individuals within a group. … Culture as it is currently used in the literature assumes a shared property of a nation. A configural property captures the variability of the individual characteristics of individual group members. However, these properties, unlike shared properties, are not expected to have a consensual element. Examples of configural property are income disparity or value differences between people in different ethnical groups or regions within a country.

Finding it strange that we continue to treat culture as a global property (nation as a proxy) or a shared property (mean scores of culture values), Tsui *et al.* (2007: 461) suggest that instead, the 'idea of tightness or looseness of a culture … may be relevant for considering the configural property of culture'. For predicting the occurrence or success of whistleblowing, the configural property of a culture might be more useful than a simple mean score on cultural values. This is in line with Williamson (2002: 1379), who states that an assumption of cultural uniformity 'can lead to the ecological fallacy of predicting an individual's values from his or her national culture'.

To apply such a configurative approach, we thus first suggest altering the strength of national culture as an independent variable. In Hofstede's model, national culture is treated as situationally non-specific (McSweeney 2002). It has the status of a causal independent factor, pervasive in all spheres of life. The configurative approach suggested by Tsui *et al.* (2007) would take us away from a causal model towards models where national culture is either a mediating or a moderating variable. In a mediating model, one would examine the process by which national culture influences whistleblowing. A moderating model then would suit research that aims at gaining insight into the conditions under which national culture influences whistleblowing.

The configurative approach thus would need a mediating model of national culture. It would, for example, allow us to extend country-specific whistleblowing research into cross-national comparison. There is a growing consensus that contextual factors more than personality traits influence the decisions of whistleblowers. However, this consensus emerges from one-country studies (mainly US, but also Australian and increasingly elsewhere). To our knowledge, there are no cross-national studies that test national differences in which contextual factors influence whistleblowing decisions. In that sense, cross-cultural studies have so far done little to extend our insight into whistleblowing decisions or attitudes, to a cross-cultural level.

An example of whistleblowing research where a moderating approach could be helpful relates to the (in)stability of cultural values. Because Hofstede's model is a causal one, it cannot reconcile the fact that whistleblower protection is becoming widespread across the world, as discussed in Chapter 1, and later chapters of this volume (see particularly Walden and Edwards, Chapter 18, on whistleblower protection in international government organisations), even in countries that score dramatically differently on the dimensions of the model. Hofstede's model assumes cultural values do not change, or at least not within the scope of one or two generations. Hence, this is why we may still regard his data from the 1970s and mid-1990s as valid measures of today's cultural values.

Assuming this is correct, a moderating approach may allow those of Hofstede's dimensions used to date to derive cross-cultural hypotheses on whistleblowing decisions, such as Power Distance (PD) and Individualism/Collectivism (I/C), to still play a useful role. In Hofstede, PD is negatively correlated with I/C. If Individualism refers to the emotional independence of a person from groups or organizations, then this is opposite to PD, which we can understand as the acceptance of hierarchy and ascribed social inequality (Gouveia and Ros 2000: 26). Now, we also know I/C correlates with gross national product (GNP), in the sense that greater wealth is also associated with more Individualism (Gouveia and Ros 2000 name Japan as an exception). Hence we would expect that countries with rapid GNP increases, such as the BRIC countries (Brazil, Russia, India and China), would also develop, or reflect, more individualist values. By using Hofstede's I/C dimension in a moderating model, we could infer that rapidly developing collectivist economies would be more accepting of whistleblowing than would slowly growing collectivist economies. This could then be tested in research.

Further ways to use Hofstede's measures in a moderating model might include the question of whether the existence of legislation in a country cuts through national cultural values against whistleblowing (such as HP difference or low Individualism). If so, this would suggest legislation is a condition under which those national cultural values lose influence, but the answer may depend on the nature of the legislation and evidence of its effects, as also discussed in later chapters. Also relevant may be any elements of culture, including political culture, which explain how the policy change was achieved. Comparing differences between sectors or industries across countries would also allow us to test the hypothesis that the type of sector or industry functions as a condition which national cultures cannot influence. Other whistleblowing research within the functionalist paradigm, but using other conceptualizations of the I/C dimension, shed a different light on the relation between Hofstede's PD and I/C, as seen above through the work of Park *et al.* (2005) and Park *et al.* (2008).

While Williamson (2002) offers arguments in defense of Hofstede's research, he also points out that research within an 'interpretivist' paradigm, complementing Hofstede's functionalist research, would be welcome for three reasons. The first is that an interpretivist paradigm assumes voluntarism of people who are able to respond to, and participate in the construction of their social environment. In that sense it stands in contrast to the determinism suggested by Hofstede's functionalist model, in which people are 'cultural dopes' (McSweeney 2002). The second reason is that interpretivist research can cope with people's ability to hold opinions that appear incompatible for someone from a different culture. Williamson (2002) argues that identifying incompatibility is problematic within the functionalist paradigm, but that ideographic research methods can do this. The third reason Williamson (2002: 1388) gives for using interpretivist methods is that 'culture is a construct, and as such has no direct measure'. However, as outlined early in the chapter, construct validity is a problem of all nomothetic research of culture (that is, research aiming to generalize) not just Hofstede's model.

Finally, some of the alternative whistleblowing research noted above points the way to a whole new avenue for cross-cultural whistleblowing research: research aimed at identifying and testing what may be universal dimensions of whistleblowing, instead of assuming and trying to confirm cultural differences. The finding of Park *et al.* (2008) that individuals from three very different nations all prefer formal, internal and anonymous reporting over informal, external or identified whistleblowing, is such a departure point. The Australian and UK comparison also points to the rich possibilities: on one measure (acceptability of reporting family or friends) the relative unacceptability of whistleblowing seems universal, even when on another (acceptability of reporting people in power), significant differences emerge. This is where we gain particular insight from the work of Schwartz and Bardi (2001: 24–5):

> Clearly, a difference perspective provides significant insights. When we shift our focus to similarities, however, we achieve new insights.
>
> 1. There is a common pan-cultural baseline of value priorities: there is a striking level of agreement across societies regarding the relative importance of different types of values …
> 2. The observed pan-cultural value hierarchy can tentatively be understood as reflecting adaptive functions of values in meeting three basic requirements of successful functioning, ordered by importance: cooperative and supportive primary relations; productive and innovative task performance; gratification of self-oriented needs and desires.
> 3. It is only against the background of the pan-cultural normative baseline that we can accurately discern what is distinctive and therefore informative regarding the value priorities of the members of a particular group … To gain a full understanding of human value priorities, we must take note of the interplay of both differences and similarities.

In his own approach, Schwartz (1994) lists ten values for study, and which of the three basic requirements these source from. These values are power, achievement, hedonism, stimulation, self-direction, universalism, benevolence, tradition, conformity and security. Rather than the bipolar dimensions in Hofstede's model, these values form a continuum. Schwartz orders them as a circular structure in which adjacent value types share a motivational emphasis (Schwartz 1994: 24). Each two or three values share a higher order value: self-enhancement (power, achievement, hedonism), openness to change (hedonism, stimulation, self-direction), self-transcendence (universalism, benevolence), conservation (security, conformity, tradition). Schwartz (1994: 42) finds that:

> there is support for the near universality of the four higher order value types and of their organization into two dimensions that structure value systems. Moreover, there is considerable evidence that, when they think about the importance of their values, many people, across contemporary societies, implicitly recognize the ten value types and the postulated conflicts and compatibilities among them.

We speculate that Schwartz's model could be usefully applied to a new generation of research on whistleblowing and culture. Schwartz's model does not suggest that every culture would have similar attitudes to whistleblowing. What it does open up, however, is the possibility that whistleblowing might be supported in different cultures as a manifestation of, or behavior which follows, different values. Schwartz gives an example of a research project he did on readiness of Israeli Jews to make contact with Israeli Arabs. He formulates hypotheses that self-transcendence values (universalism and benevolence) correlate positively with readiness for contact, and uses his model to show how the hypotheses can be tested, namely, that correlations should 'peak at universalism and become progressively less positive in both directions around the circle to tradition' (Schwartz 1994: 41).

To give a final example of how this might be useful in whistleblowing research, we return to Park *et al.* (2005). Some of their Confucian and Collectivism types correlated with 'non-action', meaning that someone did not report the wrongdoing they observed. They note that this non-reporting is not necessarily the opposite of whistleblowing, because it could be that employees remain silent when they observe wrongdoing, but 'would intend to respond later in some fashion. For example, they might prefer to personally ask the wrongdoer to take responsibility for his or her wrongdoing so that he or she could save one's face' (Park *et al.* 2005: 399). The need to transcend this dichotomy also emerges in other chapters, for a range of reasons (see especially Olsen, Chapter 8). We believe Schwartz's model offers scope to derive a hypothesis for the future research Park *et al.* (2005) call for. Moreover, finding out what the preferred routes are for the correction of perceived wrongdoing in organizations in various cultures would also shed light on how this 'behavioral core' of whistleblowing plays out in more varieties than the whistleblowing/silence dichotomy (see Chapters 3, 7, 8, 10, 13).

RESEARCHING WHISTLEBLOWING IN CROSS-CULTURAL CONTEXTS

Irrespective of what model is used, there are also general lessons of which cross-cultural researchers need to remain aware, in the whistle-blowing context. As already mentioned, for example, a constant methodological challenge is the simple problem of different measures being used in different nations, preventing direct comparisons. Thus, studies need to have cross-national or cross-cultural comparison as a goal at the start, before results across national cultures can begin to be effectively compared. In cross-cultural research, it is especially important that measure equivalence is achieved across cultures. The first factor related to measure equivalence is linguistic and conceptual equivalence, which is achieved via the conceptualization and operationalization of core concepts, such as discussed at the start. Larkin *et al.* (2007) argue that successful multilingual translation in qualitative research requires a mutual consultation process in translation that goes beyond the traditional forward-backward translation. During the consultation the role of the four dimensions of cohesion, congruence, clarity and courtesy in the translation process should be explored. Cohesion entails that the translator should reflect on the context of the translation, in particular the partnership between the translator and the researcher, on the one hand, and the relationship between the researcher, the translator and the respondent, on the other. Congruence requires equivalence and agreement between the concepts employed in the different languages.

Conceptual clarity should also be accompanied by a consideration of the level of politeness in the language used that would be appropriate in different contexts. Where respondents from different cultures share a common language a decision should be taken whether to administer the questionnaire in English to all the respondents or whether to translate it into the applicable native languages. The advantage of item equivalence should be weighed up against the possible influence this might have on response patterns, such as the tendency for non-American respondents to provide more extreme responses when they are completing a questionnaire in English rather than in their native language (Schaffer and Riordan 2003: 189–90).

In the second place, scale and score equivalence is related to the use of multiple regression and multivariate analysis that entails the use of techniques such as factor analysis, cluster analysis and multi-dimensional analysis. In the case of score analysis it is especially important to take cultural differences in the answering of questions into account, for example, the inclination of Japanese respondents towards average or non-committal answers as compared to the Anglo-American inclination to be more extreme in their answers (McDonald 2000: 95). Cultures can also differ with regard to the extent to which they are likely to agree on an item even if it does not reflect their true feelings (Schaffer and Riordan 2003: 192). Furthermore, the discussion of models above reinforces the importance of considering to what extent survey data measured at an individual level can be viewed as capturing constructs at a collective level (Earley 2006: 926).

A third factor in measure equivalence is sample equivalence, which is achieved through the selection of country locations on a theoretical basis followed by the identification of representative samples of the location's population that 'best reflect the nation's central tendencies' (McDonald 2000: 99). Yeganeh *et al.* (2004: 77–9) compare convenience, systematic and random sampling as approaches to sampling cultures. While convenience sampling necessitates the development of post hoc explanations as the sampling of cultures is not theoretically based, random sampling has traditionally required huge resources. This is increasingly less the case in industrialized countries, or countries where technological take-up is otherwise high, because computer-assisted telephone and Internet surveying can become very cost competitive. However, these advantages cannot be assumed everywhere – certainly not everywhere that cross-cultural research may wish to go.

Systematic sampling, where the selection of cultures is done based on their variation on a theoretical continuum, requires that the cultures should differ significantly with regard to the relevant theoretical dimensions. When deciding on the number of cultures to be included, care should be taken that the research design cannot be accused of an ethnocentric bias. Careful consideration of a possible lack of representativeness of the selection of subjects and the possible dependence of samples as a result of the global village we live in, could demonstrate the possible impact of these factors on the quality of the comparisons done and the conclusions drawn.

When interpreting and analyzing data, it is of particular importance to assess the extent to which two forms of bias – social desirability response and non-response – threaten the validity of the research. Zeller (1993: 103) defines social desirability as 'a situation in which respondents say what they think the researcher wants to hear rather than what they believe [or what they have done]'. According to Chung and Monroe (2003: 291), this tendency leads to respondents over-reporting actions and behaviors that are socially desirable and under-reporting those that are not. Social desirability is linked to the possibility of a self-presentation bias, where respondents could massage their stories or adapt their replies in terms of how socially desirable they perceive those answers to be. They are therefore more likely to give an answer that they perceive to be socially desirable than one that is not (Bryman 2001: 123).

The occurrence of social desirability responses does not mean that respondents are consciously lying. Various issues are at stake. Alford (2001: 8) expresses it very well when he talks about the inability of whistleblowers to remain loyal to their story:

> For the whistleblower to be loyal to his or her story, he or she would have to know and accept some terrible truths about the world, above all that his sacrifice will not be redeemed. No one will be saved by his suffering, not even himself. The organization he worked for will not be made better, and those who worked with him will not have become more moral by virtue of his example.

In their study on the public service ethic of whistleblowers, Brewer and Selden (1998: 427–8) employed a number of techniques in order to diminish the possible bias introduced by self-reporting. They used a large survey that did not focus on whistleblowing exclusively but phrased questions in general, hypothetical terms that would not trigger attempts at justification. These questions were alternated by questions that required reports on concrete events which generally tend to be more accurate and objective. Anonymity was also ensured which reduces the danger of social desirability responses.

Comparisons of qualitative and quantitative studies demonstrated a greater vulnerability to self-presentation bias in qualitative studies. During interviews and focus groups, respondents are afforded little privacy and the degree of anonymity they can reasonably expect to receive is dramatically reduced. This tends to strengthen the likelihood of self-deception and impression management occurring and leads to an increased social desirability bias (Randall and Fernandes 1991). Self-presentation bias is also influenced by the extent to which respondents are convinced of the seriousness of the scientific endeavor and the importance of their contribution to it (Catania *et al.* 1993: 151; Uys 2002).

The use of multiple methods could enhance the credibility of the findings, especially where qualitative methods are employed (Doran 2001: 242). Rossouw (2004: 29) argues for the use of methods that would enable the researcher to uncover the moral attitudes and intentions of individuals, for example, by means of self-report surveys, as well as their actual moral behavior, which would require more phenomenological strategies in a naturalistic setting. Documentary studies can also assist in accessing the institutionalization of moral behavior in the organizational context. Jo *et al.* (1997) recommend the use of both direct and indirect questioning in order to reduce social desirability bias, especially in the case of sensitive constructs. A variety of research methodologies is therefore required to capture the full complexity of cultural embedment in organizations.

A technique that is particularly appropriate for conducting sensitive research is the narrative interview as it 'envisages a setting which encourages and stimulates interviewees to tell a story about some significant event in the informants' life' (Bauer 1996: 2). This technique entails the interviewer's presentation of the initial central topic to the respondent. The respondent is invited to tell his or her story. The narration is then followed by a questioning phase during which clarifications of the story are sought in a non-threatening manner.

While sensitive research can possibly result in the appearance of a social desirability bias, this kind of research also tends to be vulnerable to non-response. In some respects, interviewing whistleblowers does not seem to present a serious obstacle. Many whistleblowers seem to have a deeply felt need to communicate their story to the world as part of the process of dealing with their experiences. However, whistleblowers who have not suffered significantly, or at all, may be less interested in participating, especially if part of the reason for their lesser suffering is that they have not been prominently identified (or self-identified) as whistleblowers in the first place. Non-response can also be more of an issue when trying to get access to employers to get their side of the story, or especially to convince employers to allow access to their employees.

Finally, most whistleblowing research raises special issues of confidentiality, security and ethical conduct of research. Employees are typically hesitant to participate in interviews if they suspect that their employers might get access to the data. On the other hand, self-administered surveys are probably less susceptible to non-response bias as the respondents are able to remain anonymous. Yeganeh *et al.* (2004: 77) argue that equivalence of response rates across cultures is almost impossible to achieve. Particular attention should therefore be given to assessing the possible impact of non-equivalent response rates on the accuracy of the data collected.

CONCLUSIONS

In this chapter, we have discussed how whistleblowing has been and could be researched from a societal culture perspective. First, there are many basic questions of research method that are raised by cross-cultural research into whistleblowing. Sample size and representativeness are perhaps the most critical ones.

Secondly, our review suggests that there is a need for careful development of the constructs involved in whistleblowing that are under study. Propensity or stated intention or likelihood are not enough. Developing a real understanding of how attitudes and experiences might differ between groups requires attention to what kinds of whistleblowing are being discussed (e.g., what channels, including internal, regulatory or public); what types of wrongdoing; and most importantly, wrongdoing by whom, in relation to the whistleblower. Issues widely presumed to be influenced by national or cultural context, such as differing degrees of group loyalty or preparedness/ability to challenge authority, cannot be properly measured unless these constructs are detailed and incorporated.

Thirdly, the choice of dimensions of culture that are being tested is important. We need to be clear on national, organizational, professional culture; political culture; elements of culture that relate to ethnicity or religion, by virtue of particular values associated with membership of social groups that may or not be associated with economic or political institutions (be they religious, family, community), and so on. Superficially, dimensions such as I/C and PD in Hofstede appear relevant to whistleblowing, but require development and articulation.

Fourthly, and in connection to that, particular dimensions of culture (and indeed whistleblowing) can be measured in different ways. We need to tread research paths that lead beyond the Hofstede model.

Finally, whistleblowing is in need of a coherent model or models of cultures which would ideally package the relevant dimensions and test for relevant factors in a coherent and reliable way.

NOTE

1. We thank colleagues from the University of Melbourne, Dr Suelette Dreyfus, Dr Simon Milton, Dr Rachelle Bosua and Dr Reeva Lederman, for their input into the design of these survey questions, which were common with the first World Online Whistleblowing Survey conducted in 2012–2013 under a joint project between Griffith University and the University of Melbourne. Thanks also to the Australian Research Council for funding support to that project under DP1095696. Other results from the first stages of that project are discussed by Bosua, Milton, Dreyfus and Lederman, Chapter 11.

3. Outsider 'whistleblowers': Conceptualizing and distinguishing 'bell-ringing' behavior

Marcia P. Miceli, Suelette Dreyfus and Janet P. Near

INTRODUCTION

Precision is important in definitions of human behaviors, for practical reasons and also to allow careful empirical research comparing and contrasting these behaviors. Empirical research on whistleblowers typically relies on a widely used definition (King 1997), namely, that 'whistle-blowers are organization members (including former members and job applicants) who disclose illegal, immoral, or illegitimate practices (including omissions) under the control of their employers, to persons or organizations who may be able to effect action' (Near and Miceli 1985: 4). The use of a standard definition by most researchers has allowed empirical investigation of differences between whistleblowers and others reporting wrongdoing and also among different types of whistleblowers. Whistleblowing has been previously defined by researchers as involving several specific characteristics; however, the distinctions between whistleblowers and other individuals disclosing organizational wrongdoing can be subtle or ambiguous, often causing the media and other stakeholders to refer to all as 'whistleblowers'.

In this chapter we propose that when perceived organizational wrongdoing is reported by individuals who are not now and never were members of that organization (i.e., the focal organization), especially if seeking widespread dissemination of information about the perceived wrongdoing, then the antecedents of reporting, the process for reporting and the outcomes of reporting may be different than for whistleblowers. We propose the term 'bell-ringers', to distinguish these individuals from whistleblowers. To explore this, we propose: (1) to identify and define an important set of behaviors that may be labeled as 'whistleblowing', but that are in fact distinct from whistleblowing, and which we will call 'bell-ringing'; (2) to describe the definitional elements of bell-ringing and the rationale for them; (3) to illustrate differences between bell-ringing and whistleblowing (and other incidents) using some examples recently reported in the media; and (4) to identify three dimensions on which bell-ringing incidents may differ: information acquisition, channels and anonymity, and motivations of the bell-ringer.

Our primary goal is to encourage careful research about differences and similarities between bell-ringers and whistleblowers, which is possible only when the distinctions between the two types of reporters are acknowledged and understood. We believe this will assist readers with scholarly or practical interests in whistleblowing and related types of incidents to identify and consistently distinguish among them, in order ultimately to better understand why these events occur and what processes they may set in place. We aim to stimulate investigation and, ultimately, better understanding of incidents and processes that may seem similar to whistleblowing, but which are actually different, and about which currently much less is known. We do not address any legal issues, for instance, whether laws do or should distinguish these parties, as that is outside our scope. Certainly, some whistleblowing legislation in different countries may work either by design or accident to encompass disclosures by individuals who fall outside the above definition of whistleblowing, as well as those within it (for legal issues see Chapters 14 to 17). One benefit of a clearer distinction between whistleblowing and similar but different behavior may be in supporting better studies of how well such legislation works. In the meanwhile, we hope our chapter will be helpful to researchers, journalists, managers and policy makers who might be the recipients of complaints or expressions of concerns. We begin by offering a definition of bell-ringing and specifying how it is similar to and different from whistleblowing.

DEFINING BELL-RINGING

The definition of whistleblowing cited above has been extensively debated and discussed and, as noted above, widely utilized in empirical research (Miceli *et al.* 2008). So we will not undertake further debate; instead we will rely on that definition. In this section we define a similar behavior we call 'bell-ringing', which differs from whistleblowing in important ways. We define 'bell-ringing' as having four key elements:

(1) the disclosure by individuals who are not journalists or publishers (generally voluntarily and at their own initiative) of information about

(2) perceived wrongdoing (including omissions) under the control of organizations
(3) of which they are *not* members (including former members or job applicants), to
(4) parties or entities that disclosers reasonably believe can stop the wrongdoing or can disseminate the information widely.

Because each of these elements may be controversial, below we have considered each in depth, and have described our rationale and the evidence for it. Indeed, the choice of the term itself may be controversial, or a better term might potentially be found for describing behavior that meets these criteria. For example, in Dutch, the term most widely used for whistleblower is already *klokkenluider*, which translates into English as 'bell-ringer', meaning that in Dutch, at least, this choice of term may not be useful.[1] Nevertheless, even if there is debate over the best term, the key issue is the apparent need for a more precise descriptor for people in distinctive and different positions. Given the lack of such a descriptor so far in the English language, in this chapter we will persist with the term 'bell-ringer'.

To begin this exploration, we offer an example of a bell-ringer who has been incorrectly labeled as a whistleblower. We are referring to Harry Markopolos, a former securities industry executive, who reported Bernie Madoff's Ponzi scheme to the US Securities and Exchange Commission (SEC). Markopolos, who did not work for Madoff, said he had tried to get regulators to probe Mr Madoff from 2000 and called SEC officials 'too slow, too young and too under-educated' to catch the alleged fraud (BBC News 2009). He spent many hours documenting the suspected Ponzi scheme and provided the documentation to the SEC, but they failed to stop the fraud. Subsequent events show that Markopolos was correct about serious wrongdoing taking place, that the failure to correct it cost many Madoff clients millions of dollars of savings and retirement income, and that the scheme and its collapse had ripple effects on many other investors (BBC News 2009). Markopolos is thus the classic 'bell-ringer' as we define the term, rather than a whistleblower, both with respect to his initial report to the SEC about Madoff's firm's wrongdoing and, later, in his public statements (e.g., in a Congressional hearing) with respect to the errors of omission or commission by the SEC. Below we describe each of the four elements of the definition of 'bell-ringing' in more detail.

Element One: Disclosure at One's Initiative by Non-Journalists

The first element of our definition emphasizes that bell-ringing, like whistleblowing, constitutes disclosure. Disclosure is defined as 'the act or an instance of disclosing; exposure; or, something disclosed: revelation'.[2] Therefore, an act that does not involve disclosure cannot be bell-ringing. For example, a customer who expressed her outrage about bad treatment by her cable service provider by taking a hammer to the company's offices and damaging a customer service representative's computer (Tucker 2007) is neither a bell-ringer nor a whistleblower, because this action is not disclosure. In general, most consumer or customer complaints aimed simply at rectifying problems with a service or entitlement, even when made more conventionally to the organization involved, do not constitute disclosure. Had the customer instead (or in addition) gone to her local TV station's consumer affairs reporter, provided evidence, and asked for an investigation into perceived cable company wrongdoing, she would be a bell-ringer. Likewise, an individual who hacks into company websites in order to make service unavailable to customers, i.e., distributed denial of service attacks (DDoS)[3] is not a bell-ringer, unless he or she has *also* disclosed information about perceived wrongdoing and meets other elements of the bell-ringer definition.

In this element of the definition, we have expressly excluded media journalists, whose purpose is the dissemination of news and information. The media journalist represents or is an agent of a media organization which, with a publisher as its head, disseminates information more widely. So while a newspaper may, for example, run a public campaign on a matter to influence decision makers in City Hall, it also distributes information to many people who have no direct power to stop the wrongdoing (average readers). Similarly, when WikiLeaks publishes information in order to reach a wide audience, it serves a media role, just as the *New York Times* or the *Guardian* does. Thus, the individuals involved in WikiLeaks, such as Julian Assange, would not be considered bell-ringers but rather media journalists and publishers, with respect to many incidents reported to them. As such, journalists and publishers are more appropriately viewed as (communication) channels that can receive information from bell-ringers (discussed later, with regard to the fourth element). Some sources for media organizations may be bell-ringers, but in many cases, it is not possible to know definitively. For example, sources for WikiLeaks are anonymous, providing information via a digital drop box that shields their identities, and more traditional channels often provide similar options to remain anonymous.

Having said this, we recognize that this is one of many grey areas that need further analysis and empirical investigation. For example, in some legal contexts, the risks of retaliation against journalists or even publishers for pursuing politically controversial stories about wrongdoing may be very real, and may be just as important as, or a more important policy issue than, protecting original sources (be they whistleblowers or bell-ringers, as we have defined them). Accordingly, a schematic representation developed by Brown (2013; see also Chapter 1), suggests the term bell-ringer might usefully apply to disclosures by *any* organizational non-members (that is, that it might hinge mainly on our third element below), even if they are a communication channel rather the original source. At this time, we do not include journalists in our definition of bell-ringers because they differ in several ways from reporters who are not journalists, including perhaps the types of retaliation they might experience but also their motivation for reporting, which might not be considered voluntary. But we recognize that potential differences between journalists and bell-ringers should be examined empirically; research might in fact show that they are more similar than different.

Disclosure is typically voluntary and initiated by the observer of perceived wrongdoing. Although this point was not addressed explicitly in the whistleblowing definition we cited, there has been some discussion in the whistleblowing literature about it. For example, some scholars have discussed jobs or roles that require reporting wrongdoing (see Brown 2008; Mazerolle and Cassematis 2010; Miceli and Near 1992; Miceli *et al.* 2008). Whistleblowing researchers have differentiated 'role reporting' or 'role-prescribed whistleblowing' from other types of whistleblowing, although these terms have been defined in different ways (see Brown 2008; Miceli and Near 1992; Miceli *et al.* 2008; Miceli *et al.* 2012).

Because by definition bell-ringers do not report wrongdoing within the organizations in which wrongdoing is believed to occur (i.e., the focal organization) and of which they are members, they cannot be said to hold roles that require internal reporting with respect to what they observe. Further, they cannot receive and take action on information from others about wrongdoing of certain types within their organizations, as in role reporter whistleblowing (Brown 2008). Therefore, this distinction is not relevant to bell-ringing.

At an extreme, the voluntarily initiated standard for bell-ringing may be difficult to meet. For example, laws may require citizens to report suspicious activity to law enforcement, which may imply that reporting crimes is not voluntary. Hence, citizens who initiate these reports may not be viewed as acting voluntarily. But discretion is generally exercised even in these instances; therefore, we would consider the actions towards the left end of a continuum ranging from purely voluntary to purely obligatory. In the case of organizational wrongdoing, the degree of voluntariness may get muddied; for example, there are cases where reluctant witnesses called by courts or regulators to testify have been retaliated against by the organizations that employed them (Meinert 2012), implying that the retaliators viewed the witnesses' acts as voluntary, even where the witnesses did not wish to testify and where ostensible legal protection from retaliation existed. This raises many issues regarding duties to whistleblow, discussed elsewhere (see Leys and Vandekerckhove, Chapter 5). These subpoenaed witnesses could be considered reluctant whistleblowers. Likewise, we generally consider non-employee witnesses who are subpoenaed to be reluctant bell-ringers.

Similarly, if a journalist investigates some tips and, seeking confirmation, contacts a witness who did not provide the tips, at this point, we would not view the witness to be a bell-ringer, even if he or she confirms the tip information (nor is the journalist). Confirmation could be viewed as voluntary, but the witness did not initiate the disclosure and may not have intended to be involved. On the other hand, perhaps under some circumstances, some of these witnesses could be considered to be reluctant bell-ringers. One implication is that research is needed to sort out what types of distinctions are helpful; the predictors and consequences of one type of behavior may or may not differ from those of another.

Element Two: Organizational Wrongdoing

The second element of the definition is that bell-ringers, like whistleblowers, report wrongdoing they perceive to be under the control of at least one organization. The definition incorporates the same conditions for defining perceived wrongdoing as the whistleblowing definition, i.e., illegal, immoral or illegitimate activity or omissions. Individuals who report clearly individual wrongdoing, not conducted within the context of an organization, are neither whistleblowers nor bell-ringers. Two examples are reporting someone breaking into a neighbor's house to the police, or reporting a neighbor who is suspected of cheating on his or her income taxes to the tax authorities. Although these are important behaviors, examining them is outside the scope and focus of this chapter, because they do not involve organizational wrongdoing. Incidents involving non-victims' reactions to burglaries, assaults or other individual crimes have been the focus of other areas of research, such as the extensive social psychological literature on bystander intervention (see Latané and Darley 1970; Manning *et al.* 2008).

It is only when the wrongdoing being reported is one for which organizations or institutions are responsible that a disclosure about it would constitute either whistleblowing or bell-ringing as per the cited definitions. This would also include wrongdoing where the organization itself could be a victim, such as employee theft, because the wrongdoing is occurring within an organizational context.

Element Three: Non-Member Status

The third element is that bell-ringers are *not* employed by and are *not* members of the focal organization. Prior whistleblowing research in the management literature (e.g., Miceli *et al.* 2008) typically uses the term 'organizational member' to refer to an employee-employer relationship, broadly defined to include former members, who might have been fired or driven to quit after reporting wrongdoing. The term also includes job applicants who believe they witnessed wrongdoing as applicants, e.g., they were denied a job opportunity due to unfair discrimination, and who blew the whistle on it. Applicants and former members could be blacklisted in the industry and thus could experience some negative outcomes.

The traditional usage of the term 'organizational member' in the organization theory literature would also include volunteers (e.g., non-paid workers for an organization) and students in an educational institution, though their membership may be viewed on a continuum based on their level of organizational commitment (Pfeffer and Salancik 1978). However, in the whistleblowing literature, volunteers and students typically were not considered '(focal) organizational members' or potential whistleblowers. For example, surveys typically did not include these groups. Therefore, for the most part and for the purposes of defining whistleblowing and bell-ringing, members of organizations are employees or office-bearers or office-holders and are part of the authority structure of the organization, meaning that the organization has substantial power over them or their career opportunities. We return to this point when discussing volunteers, students and others, below.

We recognize that the above definition of organizational membership may not necessarily square with legal definitions of it, which may vary in different countries. Organizational scholars are concerned with understanding the motivations of people who report organizational wrongdoing; the constraints that may keep them from acting; the extent to which they are dependent on organizations; how organizational responses (or non-responses, e.g., to allow the wrongdoing to continue) may affect them; how they can influence organizations; and other variables. Legal scholars or policy makers may have different goals in mind, and may tailor definitions to serve those goals. For example, they may argue for extensions of protections and obligations to many people whom organization scholars would separate into different categories or view as having different motivations, different power or dependency relationships, and so forth. Of course, scholars in both groups, as well as journalists, managers, citizens, policy makers and other parties, may share some goals, such as improving the wellbeing of members or the larger society.

In contrast to whistleblowers, who must be members, bell-ringers by definition are not member of focal organizations, even if they are in another relationship with them, such as clients, customers, consumers or competitors. For example, Markopolos, a competitor and not an employee of Madoff, reported the Madoff Ponzi scheme to the SEC because he wanted it investigated. Clearly, people who have never had direct access to 'insider' information, or who are never in a position of dependency on a focal organization, such as Markopolos, would not be considered members. But competitors, clients and customers may have enough information to report as bell-ringers. Of course, many people who are far removed from an organization would be unlikely to obtain sufficient information of wrongdoing to raise concerns.

But two questions come to mind. First, what about people somewhere in the middle, namely, 'outsider' non-employees who have some connection that might give them access to important information, such as strategic partners like contractors or sub-contractors? Secondly, what about other people who may in some sense be considered 'insiders', at least temporarily, and become aware of organizational wrongdoing, for example, as a volunteer, a patient or an inmate within a residential facility, or a student within an educational institution, a temporary employee who actually is paid by an employment firm, or a family member of someone in these categories? We prefer to consider them as non-members and thus potential bell-ringers, rather than as members (and thus potential whistleblowers), and we will consider these two questions in more depth to explain our rationale.

Concerning both questions, as noted earlier, whistleblowing research published in management journals generally has not treated such individuals as 'members', although they could be, for the purposes of applying legal protections. A focal organization may have direct or indirect responsibility for certain non-employees, and some non-employees may owe or feel some degree of loyalty or obligation to the focal organization. However, in most instances, their relationships with the focal organization are fundamentally different from those of employees, for the reasons noted above, and for several additional reasons that may be relevant to wrongdoing observation and reporting.

Regarding the first question, contractors and sub-contractors may have fleeting relationships with many organizations, each of which may have less power over contractor employees' actions than those organizations have over their own employees. For example, take the case of a small electrical business that does contracted work for many companies. The electricians may not feel a sense of loyalty to any of the companies that use their employer's services (i.e., the focal organizations), other than to simply perform their short-term jobs competently, and they may be more directly guided by their own boss's views, rules, and so on, as well as by the professional standards of their occupation. Further, they typically would have less familiarity with the members of the focal organization and more than likely would not have access to or knowledge about a focal organization's internal channels for whistleblowing, particularly formal ones, other than their own. They typically would have fewer long-standing relationships with co-workers in the focal organization and would be less affected by the workplace dynamics and interdependencies.

Indeed, what would 'internal channels' mean, for these individuals? This is an important question, because research is consistent in showing that the vast majority of whistleblowers begin the process by reporting it to someone within their organizations, and most never report it outside their organizations; the small minority who later report it to an external party, such as the media, typically have been thwarted or ignored by their organizations and have chosen to persist (Rehg *et al.* 2008). A recent study focusing primarily on private sector employees in the United States shows that only 2 per cent of whistleblowers reported perceived wrongdoing exclusively through channels external to the organization (ERC 2012a). In many instances it is difficult to clearly conceive of parallel channels for non-employees.

Our second question asked whether volunteers, patients in hospitals, inmates in correctional facilities, students in educational institutions, or family members of someone in these categories should be considered organizational members. Like some contractors, these individuals typically expect to have limited-term relationships with the focal organization, in contrast to employees who may hope to make careers with organizations. We propose that this affects their likelihood of seeing wrongdoing, of taking action, and other outcomes. For example, volunteers typically can quit at any time without losing income and thus are far less dependent on an organization for income, benefits or other rewards than are many employees; they are often part-time workers. Compared to employees, they may be less invested in and embedded in the organization where wrongdoing is perceived to be occurring. They may be less influenced by work group dynamics within that organization. Volunteers, like employees, may choose an option other than voice, e.g., loyalty, neglect or exit, when they are dissatisfied (see Farrell 1983). But, compared to employees, they may be more likely to exit and find another organization or form their own, than to challenge practices or feel compelled to stay and endure them.

Nevertheless, volunteers and some other groups mentioned have 'insider' status in some important ways, while not being considered members. Thus, they are potential bell-ringers, who may also be subject to risks of retaliation or other consequences that could be comparable to those confronted by potential whistleblowers. These factors make them deserving of study, but this does not mean that bell-ringing is the same as whistleblowing. Instead, one implication is that, because of potentially higher risks of negative outcomes for certain contractors, volunteers, students and others compared to those for other types of potential bell-ringers, such as competitors, the factors affecting the process for deciding whether to ring the bell, and the consequences, may differ.

Thus, we view non-employees like those identified above not as members, and because of this, they are potential 'bell-ringers' but not whistleblowers. In any event, given the lack of research on this point, we believe it is best to distinguish non-employees, such as volunteers, students, contractors or sub-contractors, from employees or officers of a company – at least until empirical research has been completed to assess potential differences between employees and non-employees, and possibly among different sub-groups of non-employees. Further, future empirical research may show that some of the distinctions we now see are not particularly meaningful, or that the conceptualization should vary by country or culture, for example. But this is an issue that cannot be addressed with empirical research without precise, though preliminary, distinctions among categories of reporters of wrongdoing, i.e., whistleblowers versus bell-ringers, and perhaps among bell-ringers, who may vary in the extent to which they are 'outsiders'.

Element Four: Parties or Entities to Whom Disclosures are Made

The fourth element of the definition is that bell-ringers report perceived wrongdoing to parties or entities that they reasonably believe can stop the wrongdoing or can disseminate the information widely (bell-ringing channels). Whistleblowers, by definition, report wrongdoing to parties or entities they believe could stop wrongdoing; thus, they generally have pro-social motives, wishing to benefit others, even if they may also have other motivations (Dozier and Miceli 1985; Miceli *et al.* 2008; see also Roberts, Chapter 9).

Bell-ringers *may* have this motivation but need not necessarily have it; they could instead provide information to an entity or party that could disseminate the information widely. For example, bell-ringers may or may not believe that a governmental agency, the *New York Times* or WikiLeaks could directly cause an organization to correct wrongdoing. They may instead be outraged that wrongdoing is being cloaked in secrecy and want the cloak removed so that as many people as possible know about it. They could also want credit for being right about something that occurred, or have other motives for wanting others to know about some practice. We speculate that in many cases, where bell-ringers give information to journalists, they do ultimately hope that wrongdoing will be corrected, in addition to wanting information disseminated widely and possibly having other motivations. However, we believe that restricting bell-ringing to cases where the parties or entities to whom disclosure is made are those who could reasonably be believed to have power to bring about wrongdoing cessation would exclude many cases that should be considered bell-ringing. In a later section of this chapter, we will return to this fourth element, with a more in-depth discussion of several recent incidents.

OTHER DEFINITIONAL ISSUES

We want to clarify four more points regarding definitions and terminology. First, rather than 'bell-ringers' we could instead use terms such as 'leakers' or 'informants'. However, 'leaked' may imply that the disclosed information is understood to be confidential or to involve secrets, for instance, involving national security. But in some instances that we call bell-ringing, information given to the media, unions or governmental officials may not be confidential, but rather, the discloser believes that some organization is harming others and that authorities or the media are not aware of the harm. The information may be sourced from public documents, but the analysis of that information may show a pattern that reveals wrongdoing. 'Informant' may have connotations not intended here; for example, informants may provide police officers with information on the criminal activities of others, while themselves being criminals; they may be known pejoratively as 'snitches'. Therefore, we have chosen what we believe to be a term without these connotations.

Secondly, we exclude from further consideration cases where parties clearly are neither bell-ringers nor whistleblowers. For example, an observer of perceived organizational wrongdoing may first confront the perceived wrongdoer(s), and such confrontation may or may not successfully resolve the issues (Kaplan *et al.* 2010). Therefore, individuals who take no action beyond confrontation are neither whistleblowers nor bell-ringers.

Thirdly, as noted above, organizations such as media outlets cannot be bell-ringers or whistleblowers because they do not fit the definitions of bell-ringing or whistleblowing. Those who receive tips, reports or other types of disclosures may instead serve as bell-ringing (or whistleblowing) channels or complaint recipients. Because some readers may believe that the term 'complaint recipient' (used in the whistleblowing literature) would not apply in some instances of bell-ringing, the term 'channels' (as in communication channels) may be more appropriate. For example, a tip or set of documents given to WikiLeaks or a newspaper may not represent a complaint in the same sense that filing a complaint of unfair discrimination with one's employer's human resources office would.

Channels may attempt to encourage disclosures because they have the responsibility for stopping wrongdoing (e.g., internal auditors, regulatory organizations), because such matters may be of public or reader interest, thus potentially increasing profitability of media outlets (e.g., newspapers, television news shows), or because disclosures may help reduce their costs (e.g., a private health insurance company whose managers want to reduce fraudulent claims by insured members or health care providers). How channels respond to these disclosures is very important, but this topic is beyond the scope of this chapter (for more on the recipients of complaints, see Moberly, Chapter 12).

Fourthly, both whistleblowers and bell-ringers may experience negative outcomes after acting. For example, former members (whistleblowers) may have been driven out of their employing organizations by hostility or other acts of retaliation. Either they or bell-ringers may find that the 'small world' network of other employers in the industry may blacklist them from obtaining jobs at other firms. Friends or community members may reject or avoid either bell-ringers or whistleblowers. However, as already noted, the experience or avoidance of negative outcomes is not part of the definition of either construct. Before these outcomes can occur, the act of whistleblowing or bell-ringing must have occurred. The observer of wrongdoing therefore cannot know before acting whether negative outcomes will occur, although she or he may make judgments about what might happen. Moreover, whistleblowing and bell-ringing are actions taken by individuals; negative outcomes directed towards them comprise actions not taken by these same individuals but rather, actions taken by others. Therefore, these must be viewed as separate phenomena. This perspective is consistent with that proposed by some researchers interested in employee performance, the definition of which includes only employee behaviors, and not the results or outcomes of those behaviors (Aguinis 2013). To further illustrate and clarify these definitional issues, we next consider some public incidents that may qualify as 'bell-ringing'.

SOME AMBIGUOUS INCIDENTS: BELL-RINGING OR WHISTLEBLOWING?

Consider the following events that have been described in the media recently. Although the case of Harry Markopolos is probably one of the best known and clearest cases of bell-ringing, what about other incidents: do they involve bell-ringing, whistleblowing or something else? To address the question we will describe each briefly, and then take each in turn. All of the incidents have been called 'whistleblowing' by at least one journalist or media outlet, but we believe that at least some of them involve bell-ringers, as with the Markopolos case. We have selected cases that are well documented, rather than other recent cases on which important details are not yet available. In some cases we temper our conclusions by indicating what appears to be true at this time, rather than making more definitive statements. As these incidents are recent, more information may be forthcoming that could confirm or clarify the issues at a later time. We also include some cases where media, or sources quoted by journalists, differed as to whether the individuals involved should be considered whistleblowers, and we attempt to sort out the controversy; our purpose is to illustrate how the term 'whistleblowing' may be used differently by different people and how media usage could be improved if the term was used consistently. We provide a few examples to illustrate the concept of bell-ringing and contrast it with whistleblowing, and do not attempt to provide a comprehensive list of interesting cases, because there are too many for us to do so in one chapter. The cases we include are:

(1) some actions of the International Association of Whistle Blowers and other patient advocacy groups that work for improvement in health care (International Association of Whistle Blowers 2011);
(2) the actions of Bronwyn Pullar, an Accident Compensation Corporation of New Zealand (ACC) claimant, who called attention to

privacy breaches and other problems within the ACC, after it failed to approve her claims for payment (Parker 2012);[4]

(3) allegations by parents and by other parties that a former coach abused children on the campus of Pennsylvania State University (US) and elsewhere (e.g., Armour 2011);

(4) citizens' reporting of perceived tax fraud or other violations of tax law to the US Internal Revenue Service (IRS), charged with ensuring federal tax law compliance (Dale 2010; Internal Revenue Service 2012);

(5) the alleged leaking of secret military documents to WikiLeaks by intelligence analyst Bradley (now Chelsea) Manning, who was a soldier in the US Army at the time (Edmonds and Rowley 2011; Marshall 2012);

(6) the actions of the 'pink slime reluctant whistleblower', a scientist concerned about tainted meat (Avila 2012; Gillam 2012);

(7) 'anonymous' hacking of websites and release of documents regarding practices to which the hackers objected (*Sydney Morning Herald* 2013; Coleman 2011; Maslin 2012; Stableford 2011).

Patient Advocacy Groups

Patients, their friends, their family members and others who are concerned about medical errors or other problems within a health care system that harm patients have formed advocacy groups to try to remedy the problems and alert others, and have sometimes been called 'whistleblowers' (International Association of Whistle Blowers 2011). Participants in such groups may go to the media to call attention to their concerns. Where group participants also are members of the focal organization, such as a hospital nurse who believes that surgeons in his or her hospital are engaging in risky procedures, their actions would meet the requirements of the definition of whistleblowing. However, patients, friends and others who are *not* members of the perceived organization would instead meet our definition of bell-ringers, where they voluntarily disclose information about perceived wrongdoing (including omissions) under the control of organizations of which they are *not* members (including former members or job applicants), to parties or entities that they reasonably believe can stop the wrongdoing or can disseminate the information widely.

Bronwyn Pullar and the Accident Compensation Corporation of New Zealand

In New Zealand, the ACC alone provides accident insurance for all work and non-work injuries. An accident victim, Bronwyn Pullar, filed a set of claims for compensation entitlements with the ACC. When the claims were not processed, Pullar and another party, a national politician (Michelle Boag), met with officials of the ACC. In the interim, someone had emailed Pullar the private names and details of more than 6,500 ACC claimants (*New Zealand Herald* 2012). Pullar revealed the privacy breach to the media. The ACC then alleged that she 'tried to use that information as leverage against the corporation' during the meeting, to extort action; however, a police investigation concluded that nothing criminal had occurred (Parker 2012).

Pullar has been called a 'whistleblower' (e.g., *New Zealand Herald* 2012). Pullar disclosed her concerns about the ACC to Boag and to the media, but she was not a member of the ACC. Therefore, she qualifies as a bell-ringer rather than a whistleblower.

The Penn State Scandal

Until he was fired (Hall 2013), Mike McQueary was an assistant coach of the American football (gridiron) team at Pennsylvania State University. According to media reports and grand jury testimony (Armour 2011), in 2002 he allegedly witnessed a retired Penn State coach, Jerry Sandusky, sexually assaulting a child in a university locker room. After discussing the matter with his father, McQueary reported the incident to his supervisor, the head coach, Joe Paterno, the following day. Paterno, now deceased, was a successful coach at Penn State for nearly five decades and a very powerful figure at the university, because in the United States successful college football programs produce substantial revenue from ticket sales, television coverage and many other sources, at 'powerhouse' schools like Penn State. Further, alumni often give more money when the team does well, and the community outside the university is often affected, for instance, restaurants and hotels do more business when the team is playing at home. Aside from the financial significance of the team, many members of the university community are throughout their lives emotionally invested in supporting their teams, just as fans of professional cricket, football (soccer), basketball or other teams may be around the world.

Paterno and McQueary discussed the matter with other university officials, but they did not notify the police other than the university's internal police force. Parents had made other allegations against Sandusky in 1998 and later, in 2005–2006, leading to a grand jury investigation (Gowen 2011). Only after the grand jury released the results of its investigation were the incidents widely publicized, leading to public outcry and to the firing of Paterno and the university president. Sandusky was ultimately convicted of some crimes, and the university president and other officials face charges that they conspired in a cover up (Hall 2013).

The parents in this case appear to meet all elements of the definition of bell-ringers. They initiated disclosure of information about perceived wrongdoing (including omissions) under the control of organizations of which they were *not* members (including former members or job applicants), to parties or entities that they reasonably believed could stop the wrongdoing or could disseminate the information widely.

McQueary appears not to be a bell-ringer, but he could be a whistleblower. The ambiguity about classifying McQueary centers on two questions: (1) was Sandusky's behavior 'organizational wrongdoing' on the part of the same organization that employed McQueary? and (2) given that teachers and certain others are legally mandated to report suspected child abuse, was McQueary voluntarily reporting the perceived wrongdoing?

Regarding (1), the definition of wrongdoing within the definition of whistleblowing is quite broad, and it includes practices under the control of McQueary's employer. Because (a) the incident McQueary allegedly witnessed occurred on campus; (b) the university was alerted to prior incidents involving Sandusky; and (c) Sandusky could have been banned from the campus and the incidents reported to legal authorities outside the university, which might have led to earlier wrongdoing cessation, prosecution and conviction, this incident would constitute a practice under the control of McQueary's employer. Regarding (2), as noted earlier, 'purely' discretionary or voluntary action is not required for whistleblowing, and discretion often is exercised even where whistleblowing is ostensibly role-prescribed, for instance, a faculty may not report suspected cheating to designated university bodies, even where it is required to do so. Further, there was considerable ambiguity in 2002 about whether coaches were among those required by Pennsylvania to report suspected child abuse (Shapiro 2011). McQueary clearly took the initiative.

Therefore, McQueary is a whistleblower, and in fact might be entitled to protection under whistleblowing laws in Pennsylvania (Armour 2011). Thus, while others were fired after the incidents came to public light in 2011 for not taking sufficient action against Sandusky, and some parties have criticized McQueary for not doing more, McQueary may be protected from retaliation and has filed suit over his firing (Hall 2013). In summary, this case involved both a whistleblower (McQueary), and bell-ringers (parents).

Tax Fraud Reporters

The IRS offers an incentive program for 'whistleblowers', using the term in a specific way. The IRS 'may pay awards to people who provide specific and credible information to the IRS if the information results in the collection of taxes, penalties, interest or other amounts from the noncompliant taxpayer' (IRS 2012). Noncompliant taxpayers may be individuals or companies. The agency encourages citizens to report 'solid information, not an "educated guess" or unsupported speculation. We are also looking for a significant federal tax issue – this is not a program for resolving personal problems or disputes about a business relationship' (IRS 2012). The IRS provides different sets of procedures depending on the magnitude of potential revenue involved and other factors.

A citizen who provides evidence that a taxpayer has significant unreported income could *not* satisfy our definition of bell-ringer, unless that taxpayer (or non-payer) was an organization or an individual acting in his or her role as an organization member (e.g., a business contact), rather than an individual acting on his or her own. The citizen could not be a whistleblower if not employed by that focal organization. Thus, the IRS program is actually for varying types of cases; probably most commonly for reporting non-organizational wrongdoing and, occasionally, for bell-ringing or for whistleblowing.

The IRS has a separate program for anyone who wants to report 'misconduct, waste, fraud or abuse by an IRS employee or a Tax Professional' (IRS 2012). Tax Professionals are non-IRS employee private individuals or companies who prepare tax returns that are submitted on behalf of a taxpayer to the IRS. Thus, this program could also encourage internal whistleblowing by IRS employees, or external whistleblowing by non-IRS employees about their employers, as well as bell-ringing, for instance, by a taxpayer who was solicited for a bribe while an IRS employee audited him or her, or by a taxpayer whose preparer misrepresented his or her qualifications or engaged in other misconduct. In these examples, the behavior occurred in the context of an organization.

Bradley Manning and WikiLeaks

In May 2010, US Army Private Bradley (now Chelsea) Manning was arrested in Iraq on suspicion of releasing large volumes of classified military and foreign affairs information to WikiLeaks – the largest known unauthorized release of such information in history (Marshall 2012). In the course of that year, WikiLeaks published the information itself and provided the information, including classified documents, to other media outlets for coordinated joint publishing activity. These media partners included the *New York Times*, the (UK) *Guardian* (Calderone 2011), and the German magazine *Der Spiegel*, among others. The documents 'contained numerous revelations, from the extent of civilian casualties and allegations of torture in Iraq to the intricacies of US foreign policy' (Calderone 2010). In July 2013, Manning was convicted by a US military court and sentenced to 35 years' imprisonment for theft, espionage and other military offenses. In the course of the trial, she admitted to supplying the information to WikiLeaks, but maintained that she did so 'to show the true cost of war' (see O'Brien 2013) and that at the time, she believed release of the information 'was going to help people, not hurt people' (see Hartmann 2013).

Because Manning was employed by the Army and thus a member of the alleged wrongdoer organization, she is not a bell-ringer. However, there is disagreement about whether she is a whistleblower. For example, Sledge (2012) argues that '[a]t the heart of the controversy over Manning is whether [her] alleged actions represented those of a whistleblower uncovering serious government misdeeds – or of a soldier who was breaking the law'. Using our definition, Manning is an external whistleblower, because she said she believed that providing information to WikiLeaks could lead to wrongdoing cessation.

We want to emphasize, however, that our labeling Manning (or any other party) as a whistleblower does not imply a judgment of her actions as 'good' or 'bad'. Some journalists or their organizations have proposed that 'whistleblower' now has positive connotations and thus they are hesitant to label Manning as such, if disapproving of some or all of her actions (Calderone 2010). However, the definition cited here was devised for the purposes of investigating whistleblowing theoretically and empirically; it does not evaluate the action in normative terms, but merely describes it. Thus, we do not enter that debate.

Obviously, the Manning case raises many serious and complex questions, for instance, about addressing what may be conflicting goals (e.g., protecting national security, respecting authority, maintaining humane treatment of persons, avoiding the cover up of possible war crimes, maintaining integrity and transparency), or about the ethical obligations that might have led Manning to take alternative actions, that is, whether she was an internal whistleblower who was thwarted and ignored. However, these questions are beyond the scope of this chapter, which focuses on providing definitional clarity for the purposes of investigating and ultimately gaining better understanding of certain phenomena, and their causes and consequences.

We should note that the labelling of WikiLeaks a 'whistleblower website' by some news organizations and others (*Sydney Morning Herald* 2013; Maslin 2012) is problematic (Calderone 2010). WikiLeaks is an online document clearinghouse, news and publishing site. Its obtaining and revealing emails owned by Stratfor, a private intelligence firm in the United States (Weber and Satter 2012), has again drawn attention to the complex issues involved in perceived organizational wrongdoing and the sharing of information about it. WikiLeaks is not a person, and therefore it cannot be an organization member, and consequently it is not a whistleblower (Clairmont 2011). Further, it is not a website exclusively for whistleblowers, in that the people who deliver documents to it may not necessarily be members of the organizations to whom the information relates; and some may be disclosing information about matters other than perceived organizational wrongdoing. Therefore, calling WikiLeaks (and other websites with similar missions) a 'whistleblower website' may confuse some very distinct types of events, each with different causes, dynamics and consequences. Neither is WikiLeaks a bell-ringer. In any event, it is important to understand WikiLeaks as a general news media site or channel, publishing news stories and related documents that may have come from different types of places.

The 'Pink Slime Reluctant Whistleblower'

Gerald Zirnstein worked as a microbiologist at the US Department of Agriculture (USDA). In 2009, in what he thought was a private email to a co-worker, he objected to the approval by USDA of 'the unlabeled and unappetizing bits of cartilage and other chemically-treated scrap meat going into US ground beef', which he called 'pink slime' (Gillam 2012). He later left the agency. His email was released to the *New York Times*, as part of a Freedom of Information Act request (Gillam 2012). As a (former) member of the alleged wrongdoing organization reporting inside information, Zirnstein is not a bell-ringer.

Despite his now being called a whistleblower and reluctantly accepting the label (Gillam 2012), Zirnstein was *not* an internal whistleblower at the time of the email, unless he believed that the fellow scientist to whom he expressed concerns had the power to stop it, or unless he also expressed concerns to another party who did. He also was *not* an external whistleblower in relation to the *Times*, because he did not initiate sending the email to them, and 'never intended to publicize the issue' although 'he does hope the furor will bring about change' (Gillam 2012). However, in 2012, Zirnstein and his fellow scientist, now retired, pursued the issue with ABC News (Avila 2012), and thus now could be considered to be external whistleblowers.

'Anonymous'

One final example of recent events reported in the media that could qualify as bell-ringing concerns the actions of 'Anonymous' (Stableford 2011). Members of a group known as Anonymous, who are cloaked in secrecy, have claimed responsibility for attacking and shutting down commercial or governmental websites (often via DDoS), in response to actions they find objectionable (Coleman 2011). For example, several members of Anonymous have been sentenced to jail for shutting down PayPal, the bill-paying website, and other sites (*Sydney Morning Herald* 2013). These hackers acted after PayPal prevented its customers from donating to WikiLeaks, following WikiLeaks' release of US State Department internal messages (Maslin 2012). Anonymous has also released large amounts of information relating to different organizations as a deliberate part of their activities (Coleman 2011).

Clearly, Anonymous does not constitute a whistleblower as per our cited definition, given that individuals who are part of Anonymous are not members of the organization in which wrongdoing is allegedly occurring. Further, in interviews, some members of Anonymous or groups that may be similar have suggested that stopping wrongdoing (as required for whistleblowing) is not among their motivations (Maslin 2012). However, some of Anonymous' members' actions *could* constitute bell-ringing.

The first issue is whether Anonymous, a cluster of individuals or smaller groups of hackers, social activists, artists, programmers, system administrators, security researchers and others, constitutes an organization itself, or whether its members operate as individuals. To the extent that we can view members of other groups, such as patient advocacy groups, as constituting individuals, we need not be overly concerned with this question. Further, Anonymous 'purports to have no leaders, no hierarchical structure, nor any geographical epicenter' (Coleman 2011). Therefore, our focus shifts to a second issue concerning the actions that members of Anonymous might take. Some might constitute 'disclosure'; others might not; and only the former can be eligible to be considered 'bell-ringing.' For example, the hacking of the PayPal website alone does not appear to involve disclosure. However, other Anonymous projects, such as OpTunisia, which involved technically funneling videos of street violence out of Tunisia in early 2011 (Coleman 2011), *would* fit our definition of bell-ringing. OpTunisia was designed to release information about a well-known corrupt government's crackdown on its own people, with a view to either stopping that government's wrongdoing or disseminating information about the crackdown around the globe.

DIMENSIONS OF BELL-RINGING INCIDENTS

These examples illustrate that there is a need for conceptual clarity and consistency in the use of the terms 'bell-ringer' and 'whistleblower'. They also imply that bell-ringing incidents can vary across several dimensions. For example, just as whistleblowers can choose to disclose information to a variety of potential complaint channels, potential bell-ringers may consider several different potential recipients of the information they have, such as a regulator or a journalist. We next identify three primary dimensions on which these incidents may vary.

Earlier, we discussed how bell-ringers may be rather far 'outside' the focal organization, or in some ways considered 'insiders', or at some point in between. Consideration of events reported in the media reveals at least three dimensions on which bell-ringing incidents may vary: (1) how bell-ringers acquire information; (2) the channels, or parties to whom bell-ringers provide information, and whether bell-ringers seek to remain anonymous; and (3) the motivations of bell-ringers. We will again use the term 'focal organization' to refer to the perceived wrongdoer(s), about which the information is provided. Below, we discuss each of these, in turn.

Information Acquisition

Interesting questions can be raised around the issue of how information comes into the hands of bell-ringers and whether this affects later stages of the bell-ringing process. As outsiders (unlike whistleblowers), they may not encounter information about the focal organization as a part of their working role. Do some seek the information actively? For others, does information come to them through serendipity? Does it matter how the information arrives on the bell-ringer's doorstep at all? These questions remain for future research.

Related to this is the question of whether the information provided by bell-ringers is as compelling as that provided by whistleblowers. If the goal is to create change, it may be that 'insiders' are able to provide stronger evidence of wrongdoing than are 'outsiders'. For example, in the Penn State case cited above, we do not know whether evidence from the whistleblower or evidence from the multiple bell-ringers had greater impact in persuading authorities to indict and ultimately to convict Sandusky. To address this question systematically will require thoughtful empirical studies and legal analysis.

Channels and Anonymity

As noted earlier, many potential channels may solicit or receive tips, documents or other information from prospective bell-ringers. Any organization that the prospective bell-ringer considers to have the ability to stop the wrongdoing or to disseminate information widely may qualify. Some examples include:

(1) a political party, a group of Members of Parliament or a parliamentary committee;
(2) an existing regulatory or criminal justice channel formally designated by law (e.g., the police, the SEC);
(3) an organization that may be victimized by wrongdoing or whose constituents may be victimized (e.g., a health insurance company to which a care provider organization may be submitting fraudulent claims);
(4) a traditional news organization, e.g., the *Sydney Morning Herald*, the news division or a tipster line of a local or network television station;
(5) a non-traditional news publisher or online outlet that requests and/or publishes disclosures, e.g., WikiLeaks, or a hybrid outlet, such as MurdochLeaks, established to encourage both employees of Murdoch news media enterprises or outsiders to provide tips about concerns within Murdoch-affiliated institutions (Stableford 2011);
(6) authorized non-profit organizations, such as Taxpayers Against Fraud.

Many research questions could be examined with respect to the choice of channels. For example, do individuals who have decided to share information with the media provide it to external channels with whose missions they feel the most sympathy (Calderone 2011)? Do the prospective bell-ringer's perceptions of the vetting process the channel will use affect the choice of media channels (Calderone 2011)? Do prospective bell-ringers consider protections for anonymity and confidentiality, including the level of encryption in the case of online sites? Some of these questions may also be relevant to predicting external whistleblowing as well. Researchers are encouraged to draw on theory on whistleblowing, communication channels, information technology and other topics to devise hypotheses that can be tested.

Motivations of the Bell-ringer

As noted earlier, by definition, bell-ringers disclose information about focal organizations to channels that can stop wrongdoing or disseminate information widely. This implies that, although they may have multiple and mixed motivations, at a minimum, they must wish either to stop wrongdoing or to get the word out about their concerns (or both), perhaps because of a general belief in transparency or, more specifically, a belief that others have the right to know about something that currently is secret.

In addition, they may have other motivations. For example, some may have participated in wrongdoing but decided to stop and perhaps to seek a 'deal' for coming forward to a regulatory channel. Others may have revenge motives; they may believe that they were personally harmed, and want to get even by embarrassing the focal organization. Some may have other reasons for wanting to see the focal organization hurt. Still others may be primarily interested in monetary or other valuable rewards offered as incentives to provide information.

Because bell-ringers are not required by definition to want to stop wrongdoing (as whistleblowers are), conceivably a larger proportion may have more anti-social motives than do whistleblowers. It is easier to imagine how one who merely wants others to know about questionable activity (and not to stop it) might also want to cause harm, particularly given that such a bell-ringer's job is not controlled by the focal organization and so she or he is less at risk than is a whistleblower. The factors that affect whether bell-ringers come forward could differ depending on which motivations were present. These speculations also suggest another empirical question: that channel representatives, such as journalists, may face particularly tricky challenges in attempting to determine the credibility of the bell-ringer. These and other empirical questions should be investigated in future research.

CONCLUSION

Whistleblowers have become increasingly important in alerting society to organizational wrongdoing, in part because organizational members often have access to more sensitive information than do outsiders. As social media, new technologies and other information-sharing mechanisms become stronger, we might expect that non-members will also learn more about organizational wrongdoing and be willing to report it. There are most certainly differences between reporters who are members (whistleblowers) and those who are not. We have proposed that non-members who report organizational wrongdoing should be termed bell-ringers and that they be distinguished from whistleblowers, so that differences between the two types of reporters may be carefully and empirically investigated in future research. We also offered a preliminary proposal of some ways in which bell-ringing incidents may differ.

Certainly there may be similarities in the processes and reactions that whistleblowers and bell-ringers encounter, but any real differences that exist will not be fully appreciated unless researchers attempt to carefully delineate those differences and their effects. Similarly, the fact that bell-ringing behavior and organizational responses to it are important areas of study, and may even be growing in importance, should neither detract from nor be allowed to obscure the distinctive characteristics of whistleblowing.

NOTES

1. See the terminology used by the Netherlands' Whistleblower Advice Centre, available at www.adviespuntklokkenluiders.nl, as well as online dictionaries (e.g., http://en.wiktionary.org/wiki/klokkenluider.
2. 'Definition of "Disclosure"', *Merriam-Webster* 2012, available at www.merriam-webster.com/dictionary/disclosure.
3. 'Denial-of-Service Attack', Wikipedia. 2012, available at http://en.wikipedia.org/wiki/Denial-of-service_attack.
4. See 'Accident Compensation Corporation', Wikipedia. 2013, available at http://en.wikipedia.org/wiki/Minister_of_ACC.

4. Wrongdoing: Definitions, identification and categorizations

*Marit Skivenes and Sissel C. Trygstad**

INTRODUCTION

This chapter discusses the many aspects and dimensions of organizational wrongdoing that underpin and give rise to whistleblowing processes. Our aim is to examine the conceptual understanding of acts of wrongdoing and the factors that may influence perceptions of the distinction between acts of wrongdoing and non-wrongdoing by organization members: employees, managers, board members, workers and so forth. For simplicity, we include in the term 'wrongdoing' concepts such as 'misconduct', and behavior, whether it be 'illegal', 'illegitimate' or 'immoral'. Consider the following situation: an employee observes what she believes is the harassment of another employee. Should she report this event? This depends on the context of the organization, society, sector, industry and country in which the worker is embedded. It is impossible to identify all conceivable organizational wrongdoings, but we can attempt to identify the main structural dimensions and factors that determine whether an action within an organization is considered 'wrongdoing' with regard to a potential whistleblowing process.

There is a set of variables at the individual and contextual levels that may impact considerations of whether an event involves wrongdoing, what can rightfully be reported and what is protected. Such variables include legislation, the labor market model and country context, local and global norms, the type of organization, the role and obligations of organizational members and so forth. All legislation that sets standards for illegal and legal actions is important to the definition and understanding of wrongdoing in an organization. Some countries define the scope of whistleblowing narrowly, whereas other countries include a broad range of issues that may be regarded as wrongdoing in a whistleblowing process. Furthermore, whether an organization is part of the private or public sector provides some restraints concerning what may be legitimate to report and to whom. Different industries and different enterprises may have demands and standards that affect what is considered right or wrong, and these standards are often regulated in formal and informal guidelines and codes of conduct that are expected to be followed by workers. Individual factors are also important in assessing and interpreting an act.

In this chapter, we begin with definitions of wrongdoing, including a set of dimensions that are important for assessments of possible acts of wrongdoing. Thereafter, we outline two labor market models and relate them to wrongdoing and the whistleblowing processes. In the following section, we discuss how wrongdoing increasingly seems to involve a duty to report and consider the importance of employee participation and communication. Finally, in our concluding remarks, we present a model that shows the major structures and factors for understanding definitions of wrongdoing, and we discuss the need for comparative research.

WRONGDOING: WHAT IS IT?

An act of whistleblowing implies that an act of wrongdoing has happened, is ongoing or is about to happen. Furthermore, someone must report the observed wrongdoing. However, a perception or suspicion of wrongdoing may also create a whistleblowing situation. For example, Norwegian legislation states that if there is reason to believe that an act of wrongdoing is occurring or that an individual is planning an act of wrongdoing, it is correct to blow the whistle (Ministry of Labor and Inclusion (Norway) 2006).

The most frequently used definition of whistleblowing in empirical research describes wrongdoing as 'illegitimate, illegal or immoral actions or practices' (Near and Miceli 1985: 4; Miceli *et al.* 2008; Near *et al.* 2004). Based on this broad definition, it is obvious that what is considered wrongdoing may be contested because this definition covers all types of sins and licentious actions. Illegal acts are perhaps the simplest type of wrongdoing because they involve all actions that are considered an offence by the law in a state or country. For example, the Norwegian Working Environment Act (WEA) 2005, which covers almost all workers in the public as well as the private sector, states that it is illegal to harass a worker. This is so strongly stated that both co-workers and managers have an *obligation* to blow the whistle if they detect harassment. However, complications occur regarding what types of actions qualify as acts of harassment (Skivenes and Trygstad 2010a). In a comparative setting, we find that harassment is illegal in Norway but not in other countries, such as the United States (Miceli *et al.* 2008). It is even more difficult to determine a definition of the concept of immoral wrongdoing, which concerns what is good and right for people and society. For example, in a Norwegian context, some (perhaps many) people would find it immoral if a priest who no longer believed in God and the Christian message maintained his job as a priest. Furthermore, the concept of illegitimacy also poses a challenge because it involves fairness, such as in a process toward an outcome or in a game situation. For example, if an employer tells employee A and employee B that a promotion will be given to one of them depending on the effort they put into a new project, it would be illegitimate to have already given the promotion to B and to let A work hard in the belief that the promotion might be the reward. This would be deception. However, within some industries and countries, this situation may not be illegitimate; it may be a way of testing employees' commitment and loyalty. We will return to the contextual factors below.

Six Intrinsic Dimensions which Influence the Assessment of Wrongdoing

When a worker, manager or organization member assesses a potential act of wrongdoing, there are at least six dimensions that are important. An act or perception of wrongdoing can be highly subjective and is a well-known challenge in whistleblowing research (Miceli *et al.* 2008). A subjective perception of wrongdoing occurs when there is a lack of intersubjectivity regarding the perception, such as when others do not have the same perceptions of and reactions to the incident or when the matter is private. For example, Norwegian legislation on whistleblowing states that acts that may violate one's political or ethical convictions are not covered by the WEA 2005 (Ministry of Labor and Inclusion (Norway) 2006: 50). The other end of this spectrum involves acts that have an objective character in that there is an explicit statement or agreement that the act involves wrongdoing or a commonly accepted norm, such as stealing. Wrongdoing may be related to facts, such as the level of radiation, or it may be related to values and norms, such as the respectful treatment of a patient. The former is often easier to agree upon than the latter. It may also be a consideration whether wrongdoing is intentional. Wrongdoing may also be measured by frequency (e.g., if it happens often, occasionally or only once), and it may be important for the consideration of an act of wrongdoing if it affects vulnerable persons (or groups) versus non-vulnerable groups. Thus, there are six dimensions that potentially affect the assessment of an alleged act or practice of wrongdoing and the degree of importance (or seriousness) of an act of wrongdoing. Figure 4.1 presents these dimensions.

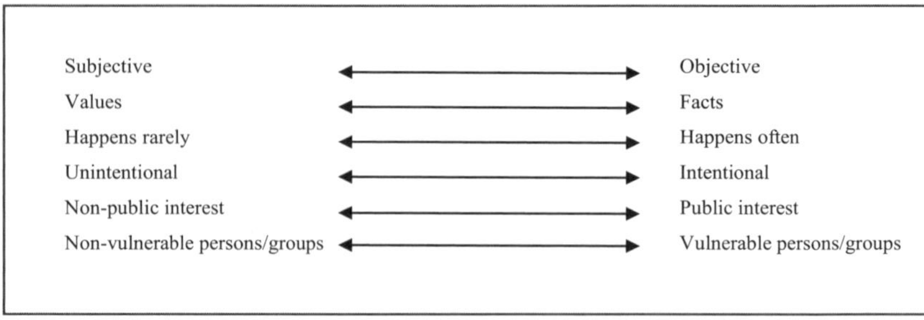

Figure 4.1 Wrongdoing and assessment dimensions

On a general level, it is expected that subjective perceptions and issues about values are more difficult to agree upon than incidents that are objective and fact based. In his broad definition of wrongdoing, Warren (2003) includes an intersubjective element. 'Employee deviance' is defined as 'behavioral departures from norms of a reference group [that] illustrate how one person's behavior has the potential to cause disastrous consequences for not only organizations but also entire industries and society' (Warren 2003: 622). Similarly, if wrongdoing occurs frequently, is intentional and harms vulnerable persons, it is regarded as more severe than when it occurs rarely, is unintentional and harms non-vulnerable persons or groups. Finally, wrongdoing incidents that concern non-public interests have a much narrower set of considerations and, as such, have fewer stakeholders. For example, Norwegian legislation draws the line between non-public and public interests by referring to interests the public may have. When employees notify the public, the criterion of general interest has an impact on whether notification is to be regarded as acceptable. For example, the public has an interest in circumstances involving threats to life or health and the misuse or corruption of public resources. In certain cases, internal character, such as personal conflicts, also has general interest, but this depends on the type of business. A famous Norwegian case illustrates this situation. In 2006, the head of the Norwegian Confederation of Trade Unions (LO), the most influential trade union organization in Norway, was voted by the press as the most powerful woman in Norway. In January 2007, an employee printed her resignation letter in Norway's largest newspaper, claiming that the head of LO had harassed her and other employees. The head of LO argued that the case was an internal personnel conflict regarding an incompetent employee. The case received enormous publicity, and the employee who resigned was labeled a whistleblower. In March 2007, the head of LO resigned as a direct result of the whistleblowing.

Discussions related to acceptable and unacceptable actions and what should be regarded as illegal, illegitimate or immoral may have huge effects on the dimensions of subjective versus objective and private versus public interests. The perception of management style is not necessarily a subjective and non-public issue. On the contrary, and as the case above illustrates, it may be an objective matter for the public. The six intrinsic dimensions in Figure 4.1 present some potential reactions to and perceptions of observations of wrongdoing. The importance and impact of these dimensions are expected to differ in different contexts, as will be shown in the remainder of the chapter.

Wrongdoing Definitions in Research and Legislation

Defining wrongdoing as illegal, immoral and illegitimate acts is problematic because it is such a wide definition. An Australian-led research group (Brown *et al.* 2012; Brown, Vandekerckhove and Dreyfus 2014) has suggested a somewhat stricter definition of wrongdoing. They point to stakeholders in the wider society and define serious wrongdoing as:

> when a person or organisation does things that are unlawful, unjust, dangerous or dishonest enough to harm the interests of individuals, the organization or wider society.[1]

A decisive criterion in this definition is that the act '*harm[s] the interests* of someone or something'. As such, the assessment of an act of wrongdoing relates to the criterion of harm. The implication is that an act may be illegal, but if it does not cause harm to anyone's interests, it is not an act of organizational wrongdoing.

In the United Kingdom, the relevant statutory provisions derive from the Public Interest Disclosure Act (PIDA) 1998, which inserted a new Part IVA into the Employment Rights Act (ERA) 1996. A 'qualifying disclosure' is (ERA 1996, section 43B(1)):

any disclosure of information which includes one or more of the following:

(i) a criminal offense;
(ii) a failure to comply with any legal obligation;
(iii) a miscarriage of justice;
(iv) danger to the health and safety of any individual [i.e., not necessarily a worker];
(v) damage to the environment;
(vi) the deliberate concealment of information tending to show any of the matters listed above.

(Cf. Lewis and Trygstad 2009).

The UK definition combines a wide definition of wrongdoing with a criterion that an act causes harm, for example, to the environment.

Another way of introducing a qualifier is to raise the threshold for wrongdoing by demanding that a certain procedure is followed. In Norway, the definition of wrongdoing is broad, and the threshold for reporting is low. However, to ensure order, a whistleblower is asked to report within the organization or to use established procedures.[2] However, reporting wrongdoing to union representatives and/or the health and safety inspectors and to supervisory authorities, such as the Norwegian Directorate of Labor Inspection, is always appropriate. An employee's right to disclose is also regulated in section 100 of the Norwegian Constitution. This section stipulates as a general principle that 'Everyone shall be free to speak his mind frankly on the administration of the State and on any other subject whatsoever'. In other words, grounds must be given for *restrictions* on the employee's right to disclose, not the other way around.

Another type of qualifying criterion involves the legislator establishing a threshold for reporting organizational wrongdoing. According to the UK legislation, a worker must reasonably believe that the information and any allegations contained in this information are substantially true (cf. Lewis and Trygstad 2009). Disclosures are protected provided that the whistleblower can establish that he/she reasonably believed that the information reflects one of the categories of malpractice listed in the Act (see above). Several countries including the UK and Norway also require or promote reporting that is done 'in good faith', although this can be controversial (see for example, Lewis, Devine and Harpur, Chapter 15).[3] Irrespective, the consequence is that many incidents can be reported.

Many of the professional codes of conduct, such as the American Psychiatric Association's Principles of Medical Ethics (2010), the American Medical Association's Code of Medical Ethics (2001) and the Australian Association of Social Workers' Ethical Guidelines (2010), have broad definitions of wrongdoing that usually include immoral and illegitimate behavior and refer to patients' or service users' best interests and welfare. One way of determining that a report of wrongdoing is not subjective or overly inclusive can be found in the following guideline from the Australian Association of Social Workers (AASW 2010):

> Any criticism of colleagues' practice or behaviour must be defensible and should be dealt with in a professional manner. Social workers will not make trivial and vexatious complaints about colleagues.

The professional codes of conduct and legislation in Norway and the United Kingdom may be considered relatively wide in terms of the definition of wrongdoing. At the other end of the spectrum, we find, for example, France, which has promulgated a law on the protection of whistleblowers in the public and private sectors that is only applicable in the context of corruption, such as fiscal or financial matters, accounting or suspected bribery offenses. The legislation in the EU organization is also an example of a narrow definition of wrongdoing. The European Union institutions regulate whistleblowing about serious wrongdoing in the Staff Regulations of Officials of the European Communities, articles 22a and 22b (EC 2004). The incidents of wrongdoing that can or should be reported are illegal activities that are 'detrimental to the interests of the communities' (distinguished from the 'public interest') or 'the seriously irregular professional conduct of a colleague'. For some issues, employees at the EU institutions have an obligation to report to the nearest manager or director, and for other issues, they have the right to report to a given set of units (Rohde-Liebenau 2006: 43).

As illustrated above, the legislation in different countries varies regarding whether an act qualifies as wrongdoing and, as such, whether it should be regulated by law. The right to disclose also differs by sector. In some countries, such as the Netherlands and Germany, the right to report wrongdoing is restricted to employees in the public sector (Vandekerckhove 2010).

The research literature includes frequently used lists of wrongdoing incidents to determine what is reported and how these reports are handled. Examples of operational lists are given by Near *et al.* (2004: 231; cf. Miceli *et al.* 2008: 20) and Brown and Donkin (2008: 14) and are presented in Table 4.1.

Table 4.1 List of wrongdoing incidents

Near *et al.* 2004	Brown 2008
Stealing	Misconduct for material gain
Waste	Conflict of interest
Mismanagement	Defective administration
Safety problems	Waste or mismanagement of resources
Sexual harassment	Improper or unprofessional behavior
Unfair discrimination	Personnel or workplace grievances
Other violation of law	Perverting justice or accountability

Sources: Near *et al.* 2004: 231; Brown and Donkin 2008: 14

Both lists include wrongdoing related to acts that harm an enterprise and its employees. The list by Brown and Donkin (2008) also includes wrongdoing that may harm the wider society. One reason for this larger scope might be that the list was developed for research in the public sector, whereas the list developed by Near and her co-authors was developed on the basis of studies in larger organizations across many sectors (Miceli *et al.* 2008: 20). In Table 4.2, we combine these lists. We also take into account that specific professions in some countries impose a duty to report violations of professional codes of conduct.

An organization's ability and willingness to discuss questions such as what is good quality, what is ethically acceptable, and what is a good work environment are dependent on many factors. As Kaptein (2011: 516) points out, ethical culture represents part of the informal organizational context, whereas policies, processes and programs represent aspects of the formal organizational context. Our point of departure is that an organization has formal and informal codes that are written and unwritten. The type of labor market model in which an organization participates also determines whether violations of such codes are regarded as wrongdoing.

Table 4.2 Issues that influence definitions of wrongdoing

	National legislation	Professional standards	Enterprise's code of conduct
For whom?	Entire labor market or just public sector?	For all in the profession or just some?	For all or just for special groups?
About what?	Specific types of wrongdoing or a wide definition?	What kind of wrongdoing?	Specific types of wrongdoing or a wide definition?
Right or duty to report?	Does one have a duty to report and, if so, about what?	Does a professional have a duty to report or just a right?	Does one have a duty to report and, if so, about what?
Sanctioned?	Is the employee sanctioned if not reporting?	Is the professional sanctioned if not reporting?	Is the employee sanctioned if not reporting?
Whistleblowing procedures?	Are enterprises obliged to have routines or procedures?	Where should a professional report?	Does the enterprise have routines or procedures, and who designed them?

INDUSTRIAL RELATIONS AND LABOR MARKET REGIMES

Thus far, we have discussed how culture and formal and informal institutions affect perceptions of acceptable and unacceptable actions. First, individuals are influenced by the organization in which they work. As Near *et al.* argue, the 'kind of wrongdoing prevalent in an organization may vary with organizational type' (2004: 237). Secondly, what is considered wrongdoing differs across industries, sectors and countries. A relevant example is the 'battle' between Samsung and Apple and the role of a Samsung employee (Michael) who was hired at a new job in Samsung, Korea. This case shows how context may play a decisive role in considerations of wrongdoing. The 'Free Press Release Distribution Service' presents the following excerpt from the case:

> Samsung made a generous offer of employment and Michael began work in the summer of 2008. During his first six months on the job, Michael 'kept his nose down and was largely in observation mode', making sure to work hard and impress his bosses, a VP and an SVP. In early 2009, Michael earned a commendation for his work performance, a rare feat so early in one's tenure at Samsung.
>
> With those early victories in hand, Michael felt it was time to report on his observations to senior management, per the CEO's instructions. So Michael met with his bosses, HR, and both in-house and outside counsel for Samsung, reporting instances of intellectual property theft, bribery, accounting fraud, and an overall culture of non-compliance and corruption.
>
> What came next was an utter shock for this Silicon Valley trained professional. He was asked not to come to the office. When pressed, Samsung's HR told Michael that he was being transferred to another Samsung office. When the transfer never materialized, he was ultimately asked to resign from his position at the company. In a state of total disbelief, Michael contacted the anti-corruption authorities in Korea and was told that they have no jurisdiction over Samsung.
>
> So Michael returned to the US and after many months of deliberation and with the help of an old business school professor, contacted Apple's Steve Jobs in February of 2011 regarding intellectual property issues that affected Apple products. Mr. Jobs immediately put Michael in touch with Apple's attorneys and the first of Apple's lawsuits against Samsung was filed a few months later. (PRLOG 2012)

The case illustrates that wrongdoing, reported or not, happens within a society and an organizational context that sets the standard for the types of practices and actions that are considered wrongdoing. It also points to the crucial questions of who has the authority to decide what wrongdoing is and the responsibility to stop it. For example, when wrongdoing is defined only as illegal matters or actions (which is a narrow definition, cf. Warren 2003: 625), it still depends on the types of circumstances that are regulated by law.

Labor market institutions, industrial relations and work organizations may create contexts that formally and informally frame the concept of right and wrong as well as the norms and values outside and inside an organization. The labor market model may influence what is regarded as an appropriate form of action (Scott 1995) when considering whether an incident should be regarded as wrongdoing. According to Appelbaum and Schmitt (2009) and Mahoney and Thelen (2010), different regimes have different approaches to work design, human resource practices and collective representation. In a cross-national study of low wage occupations in five industries[4] in six countries (Denmark, France, Germany, Netherlands, United Kingdom and United States), Appelbaum and Schmitt argue that institutions (and their deterioration) play a large role in explaining differences between countries, and they distinguish between *market employment regimes* and *inclusive employment regimes*. It is important to highlight that the two regimes differ in a systematic way in the extent of workers' involvement in decision-making, ranging from strongly institutionalized participation in inclusive systems to the exclusion of labor as a significant player in decision-making in market regimes (Gallie 2007: 17–19). These differences influence who has the authority to define an act as wrongdoing. Furthermore, they are likely to affect whistleblowing procedures (if present) and to directly influence considerations of non-public or public interests.

In market employment regimes, the primary question is how to ensure that management governs the company in line with the owners' interests (principal-agent theory). According to mainstream corporate governance theory, the owners' legal interests (claims, ownership) are considered superior to all other stakeholders, and proprietary rights provide the owners with the exclusive right to submit a claim to those who manage the company. From this perspective, whistleblowing can be regarded as an instrument for increased efficiency. People who report wrongdoing can assist their employers by offering solutions to work problems. Thus, whistleblowing can be viewed as part of a strategy to maintain and improve the quality of production processes. Examples of wrongdoing could be the waste of corporate assets and poor job performance. Wrongdoing may also include more serious events, such as theft, embezzlement and corruption. Notification of these and related types of wrongdoing assists employers in rectifying errors and potentially in proposing measures to resolve problems related to manufacturing or customer or user management (Miceli *et al.* 2008). Hence, whistle-blowing is connected to corporate governance (CG) and corporate social responsibility (CSR).

At this time, Norway is the only one of the Nordic countries that has regulated the right to report wrongdoing. Norway has what Vandekerckhove (2010) defines as a three-tiered model, which allows an employee to report (1) inside the organization, (2) to a proxy of society, and (3) to society (if specific criteria are fulfilled, see Lewis and Trygstad 2009). Norway can be considered an inclusive employment regime. The industrial relations system is characterized by high union density and a high level of collective agreement coverage, which gives trade unions, health and safety representatives and employees important roles as stakeholders. At a general level, there are well established channels for representative and individual voices. In contrast, the United Kingdom and the United States are generally considered to be 'archetypical example[s] of a liberal market economy' (Brewster *et al.* 2007: 246). These countries have a relatively low level of union density and coverage of collective bargaining, especially in the private sector.[5] Genuine industrial partnerships are rare, workplace relationships are often adversarial and low on trust, and many workers rely on individual legal rights rather than union or safety representatives[6] to provide employment protection. Further, protection against arbitrary dismissal is scarce, and the power distance between employers and employees is enormous. It is reasonable to assume that the two different regimes may affect the issue of wrongdoing. For instance, the legal frameworks in which workers in the United States and Norway operate are quite different. As noted by Miceli *et al.* (2008: 4–5):

> an employee may consider acts such as manager firing employees arbitrarily, bullying employees … to be immoral or illegitimate in the Weberian sense (Weber 1947). These actions are typically not illegal in the United States, but they can be considered triggering events for whistleblowing.

As mentioned above, in Norway, harassment is a type of incident that the WEA 2005 requires employees to report. It is also illegal to fire employees arbitrarily. Dismissals are regulated in collective agreements and in the WEA 2005.[7] According to Norwegian legislation, these issues are considered wrongdoing under the term 'illegal', whereas in the United States this is not the case.

Narrow or Wide Definitions of Wrongdoing

In inclusive employment regimes, the company is seen as a social institution that is intertwined in various coordinating mechanisms that regulate its relationship to its environment (Hall and Soskice 2001). A company that is viewed as a social institution implies that society has both rights and obligations to regulate the company's relationship to the world. The purpose of business should therefore extend beyond the maximization of efficiency and profit. Society and various stakeholders, such as trade union representatives and health and safety delegates, have a legitimate right to influence these regulatory mechanisms, as demonstrated by the manner in which the different parties responsible for a collective agreement regulate the company's relationship with its employees. This may widen the scope of what is considered wrongdoing.

We argue that in a market employment regime it is much more likely that wrongdoing is defined narrowly, such as by connecting wrongdoing to illegal matters or actions. This may have negative effects because it may limit the scope of wrongdoing. In labor market models characterized by a shareholder perspective, such a definition may exclude issues such as mismanagement, harassment, unfair treatment of employees and unfair dismissals outside the scope of what is considered wrongdoing because these actions do not necessarily violate the law. On the contrary, issues like this may be regarded as a matter of subjective consideration and non-public interest. Di Lorenzo (2007) illustrates the dilemma of a narrow definition by referring to the pharmaceutical industry, which may claim that it attempted to comply with the law but that its 'wrongdoing' arose inadvertently because of the vagueness of the law. Contemporary corporate social responsibility (CSR) emphasizes that it stands for the set of obligations that extend beyond what is required by the law (Carroll 1979; Hagen and Trygstad 2008; Hagen 2010). In other words, a company that takes responsibility should also consider matters that are immoral and/or illegitimate. An example of this is the Norwegian oil and gas company Statoil, which has an all-encompassing definition of wrongdoing. This broad approach may not be surprising because the Norwegian state owns 67 per cent of the company. The company's 'ethical code of conduct' aims to outline in a clear and unambiguous way the ethical standards and requirements that apply to business practice and personal conduct for all persons working for the company, including members of the board of directors and the subsidiaries of Statoil (Statoil 2011: 5). The aspects of wrongdoing listed in the document include corruption, equality and diversity issues, personal conduct and the work environment. An example of the work environment is the following:

> The individual must refrain from all conduct that can have a negative effect on colleagues, the working environment or Statoil. This includes any form of harassment, discrimination or other behavior that colleagues or business associates may regard as threatening or degrading. The individual must not behave in a manner that can offend local customs or culture. (Statoil 2011: 21–2)

A narrow definition in a business environment characterized by a strict shareholder perspective may offer little room for reporting incidents that have negative impacts on actors other than shareholders. Furthermore, the definition of wrongdoing may be colored by what the owners consider damaging for the company's reputation in the short term. A narrow definition may also hinder public discussions of the types of matters that *should* be a question of legal regulation. Brown and Donkin (2008: 14) argue:

> A wide definitional approach was necessitated not only by the imprecision of existing categories, but by the inherent dangers of taking too restrictive an approach, whether in research or in legislation. For example, restricting whistleblowing to only 'serious' examples of public interest wrongdoing begs the question of in whose judgment the wrongdoing meets that threshold.

There may also be challenges in relation to a wide definition of wrongdoing, as we see in the Norwegian model of inclusive employment. In a recent labor dispute handled by the Norwegian District Court, an employee argued that he had blown the whistle on organizational wrongdoing.[8] The court considered a list of 11 reported wrongdoings, mostly related to employees' roles and ranging from the illegitimate use of the enterprise's car for private purposes to employees who worked fewer hours than required. All but one of the incidents was defined by the court as legitimate reporting of wrongdoing. Although the employee was fully within his rights to blow the whistle and report the incidents, the case material from the court shows that the employee was perceived as an annoyance at the workplace. Rather than choosing his battles, he reported any incident, resulting in a negative impact on the work environment.

WRONGDOING IN ACTION

In our research, we discovered that the threshold for the seriousness of wrongdoing might differ within an organization, not only between the management and employees but also within both groups. By using vignettes to illustrate a whistleblowing event, Skivenes and Trygstad (2010b, 2012) documented that the willingness to act is closely related to the perceived seriousness of an incident. One of their vignettes described a case in which an employee reported several times to her immediate supervisor that economic issues and claims concerning efficiency reduced the opportunity to provide service users (children in need, elderly in care and pupils) with the service and help they needed and should receive according to the law. Finally, the employee reported the incident to a journalist (Skivenes and Trygstad 2010b). The wrongdoing described pointed to a violation of WEA 2005 and guidelines regulating professionals. Half of the respondents from the municipal sector regarded the case so seriously that they considered whistleblowing to the reporter the correct thing to do. The other half did not support the whistleblowing action and found it unacceptable. According to professional guidelines and the law, the described vignette was an example of illegal wrongdoing. In summary, the seriousness of the incident and the whistleblowing act were controversial in the example.

Hence, a narrow definition of wrongdoing may refer not only to the incident in question but also to the degree of seriousness. Vandekerckhove (2006) suggests a similar problem when he examines how the process of policy formulation through successive parliamentary bills and position statements from lobbying groups has limited the types of wrongdoing that qualify as protected disclosures. He considers this narrowing to be an ethical risk. A recent study by Vandekerckhove and Lewis (2012) examines guidelines on whistleblowing in five major institutions.[9] One of these elements is 'about what' (i.e., the type of wrongdoing), which varies from a broad definition to the narrower definition that the 'issue must be serious enough' (Vandekerckhove and Lewis 2012: 7). This brings us back to the question raised above by Brown and Donkin (2008: 14), regarding in whose judgment the wrongdoing meets that threshold.

Given the asymmetrical power relations within the work organization, it may be difficult for an employee to argue that an act, incident or matter involves wrongdoing. There is evidence from Norwegian court cases in which acts of wrongdoing and whistleblowing are disputed.

A Duty to Report?

As explored in more detail by Leys and Vandekerckhove (Chapter 5) organizational members increasingly have a duty to report wrongdoing. For many, this has long been a part of their job description, such as when working in an audit unit. In the Norwegian context, there are several issues related to wrongdoing that are mandatory for workers to report. WEA 2005, section 2–3(1) imposes a general duty on employees to 'actively co-operate on implementation of measures to create a satisfactory and safe working environment'. Specific obligations are found in WEA 2005, section 2–3(2), including the requirements to:

(b) immediately notify the employer and the health and safety delegate and to the extent necessary other employees when employees become aware of faults or defects that may involve danger to life or health and they themselves are unable to remedy the fault or defect; …
(d) ensure that the employer or safety representative is notified as soon as employees become aware of harassment or discrimination at the workplace.

These duties are matched by 'a right to notify concerning censurable conditions at the undertaking' (WEA 2005, section 2–4(1)) and protection against retaliation (WEA 2005, section 2–5). In addition, Helsepersonelloven, the law concerning employees in the health sector, states that workers have a duty to report incidents that involve danger to the life or health of patients or other users of the service (section 17; this is also outlined in Lewis and Trygstad 2009).

Discussions of Wrongdoing Standards

We have argued that the number of stakeholders involved may influence the definition of wrongdoing. We also believe that discussions within an organization may raise awareness of what should be considered an act of wrongdoing. Near *et al.* (2004: 237) find in their study of a large military base that members who attended a training session aimed at increasing awareness of unlawful discrimination and sexual harassment were more likely to indicate awareness of such incidents (that is, they observed more wrongdoing than others) than their co-workers who did not attend the training session. Employees in an organizational culture characterized by openness and communication are likely to have a more consensual view of what may be regarded as illegal, immoral and illegitimate. However, an organization characterized by openness and communication requires time and space to discuss issues, such as what types of activities will be considered wrongdoing.

In the Nordic countries, local trade unions are important stakeholders in organizations. According to the WEA 2005, it is always legitimate to report wrongdoing to trade union representatives and health and safety delegates. A relevant question is whether unions participate in negotiating whistleblowing procedures. We lack cross-national studies that examine the role of trade union representatives in whistleblowing processes. However, we have some data from a study conducted in Norway in 2010 that suggests that 36 per cent of respondents reported that there were whistleblowing procedures in their workplace, and 5 per cent responded that these procedures were in progress. The presence of whistleblowing procedures was highly correlated with the presence of trade union representatives in the workplace (Trygstad 2010).[10] We also found that almost seven out of ten companies with whistleblowing procedures in the workplace reported that trade unions at the local level contributed to the development of these procedures, and 30 per cent responded that employees were involved; 14 per cent answered that the whistleblowing procedures were designed by external consultants or counsellors. These findings differ from a study of confidential reporting/whistleblowing procedures in the top 250 FTSE firms (Lewis and Kender 2010). In Lewis and Kender's study, only 11 (17 per cent) respondents consulted unions about the introduction of these procedures.

An interesting question is whether involvement makes a difference. In the Norwegian study, the majority (78 per cent) responded that notification procedures could be used in all situations, which is highly consistent with the wide definition of wrongdoing in Norwegian legislation. Eight per cent said that the procedures were reserved for special cases, whereas 14 per cent did not know. Of those who responded that procedures were reserved for certain types of issues, the three top issues were (1) violations of health and safety regulations (including harassment); (2) financial fraud, bribery or theft; and (3) neglect, abuse or improper handling of the user or customer. In other words, although the procedures were restricted, wrongdoing that may harm the employees was at the top.

Whether trade union representatives are involved in designing whistleblowing procedures depends on the industrial relations in a specific country, sector, industry *and* enterprise. This situation may affect the definition of wrongdoing as well as the potential duty to report. From a European point of view, labor lawyer Daugareilh discusses the increasing growth of whistleblowing procedures and how these procedures have been included in company structures in the name of corporate governance (Daugareilh 2008). In the wake of the US Sarbanes-Oxley Act of 2002, transnational companies have increasingly introduced whistleblowing schemes, often with a duty to report as part of the policy: 'In the name of ethics, individual workers are called upon to step in and report anyone who is likely to damage the interests of the firm'. Vandekerckhove (2006, 2010) seems to share some of Daugareilh's concerns when he points to the tendency to impose a duty both in the legislation regarding notification and in whistleblowing procedures. He argues that there are clear attempts to institute a liability in which the employee becomes the guardian of legitimacy. British Petroleum's (BP) code of conduct could be interpreted in such a way. It states, 'All of us at BP, without exception, are duty bound to follow and uphold our Code of Conduct – and we must all remember that failure to do so can put BP and ourselves at risk' (BP 2012: 7). Further, 'Failure to follow this code is misconduct, which could result in disciplinary action and even dismissal' (BP 2012: 8). In 2011, 550 persons were dismissed due to non-compliance and unethical behavior.

We do not know whether trade union representatives or other employee representatives have been involved in developing the codes of conduct. According to Daugareilh (2008), however, they are seldom involved. The procedures are largely shaped by management or others within or outside the company, such as external law firms or consulting agencies. Such an approach fits mainstream corporate governance theory, as mentioned above. From a Nordic perspective, it is paradoxical to impose a duty for three main reasons. First, it is a paradox simply because employees or their representatives are not involved in designing the procedures. Secondly, employees or employee representatives have no impact on the content of the procedures, the subjects that must be reported, and how the notifications to responsible persons should be handled. Thirdly, the whistleblowing literature clearly shows that in several countries, whistleblowing is often a hazardous act.

We lack data to determine the impact of employees, trade union representatives and other employee representatives on the design of whistleblowing procedures, which affect perceptions of wrongdoing and provide information about appropriate actions. Nonetheless, the findings from Norway provide some indications. As mentioned, trade union representatives participate in the development of whistleblowing procedures in many companies, including transnational companies (e.g., Aker Solutions, Veritas, Telenor, Statoil). Our findings show that the presence of whistleblowing procedures in the workplace has a positive effect on the whistleblowing process. Employees who work in companies that have procedures in place are more likely to report wrongdoing, have greater success and receive more positive feedback than those without. These findings demonstrate that the presence of procedures can make the whistleblowing process more predictable and less arbitrary. However, in our view, this requires the involvement of actors within and outside the company other than management. This form of involvement will lead to better knowledge about the existence of such procedures, and it may expand the issues that are considered wrongdoing.

CONCLUDING REMARKS

In this chapter, we have argued that organizational, national, supranational and industrial relations and labor models affect understandings and formal definitions of wrongdoing. But there is also a set of intrinsic dimensions involved in an assessment and perception of a potential wrongdoing act: whether, for example, a case involves values as best interests versus facts (such as the level of radiation in the soil). Further, there are local and global cultures and norms. Increasingly, there are global rights and norms that seem to have some universal standing, for example, the ban on child labor and workers' rights to have a pollution-free work environment. In Figure 4.2 we show how these understandings play out.

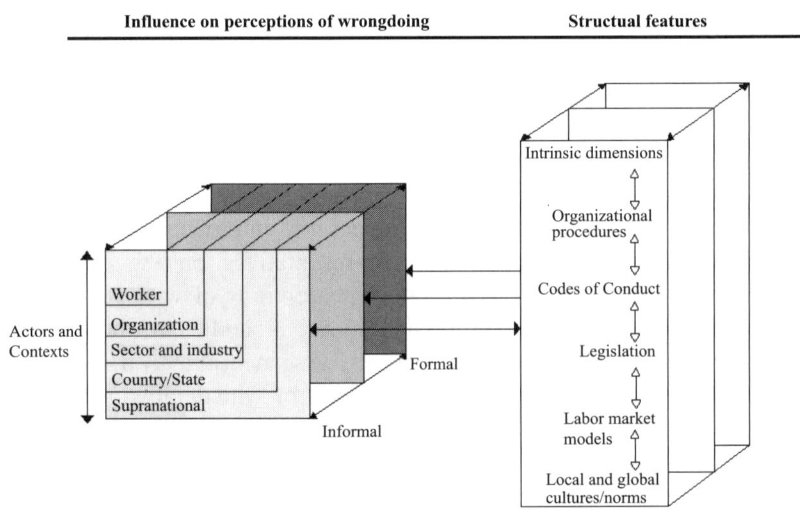

Source: This figure is modeled after a figure in Wulczyn *et al.* 2010: 22 on child protection systems

Figure 4.2 Framework for definitions and perceptions of wrongdoing

There is an ongoing discussion about broad or narrow definitions of wrongdoing. These definitions depend on context, as we have shown. We argue, along with most researchers in the field (Brown 2008; Miceli *et al.* 2008), that wrongdoing should be defined broadly so that it can be reported and so that reporters are protected. For research purposes and cross-national studies, a broad approach to wrongdoing is necessary because a range of factors (as illustrated in Figure 4.2) determines the scope of possible wrongdoing. However, what may be regarded as a serious act of wrongdoing in one country may be considered a minor violation in another country, as the Samsung case (United States–Korea) illustrates. As researchers, we must be sensitive to cultural and institutional differences. Further, it is important not just to look at definitions in legislation or in codes of conduct, but also at how different definitions are interpreted and translated in different organizations, industries, sectors and countries. We do think that the processes of interpreting and translating are related to the stakeholders involved and the degree and level of discussion inside each organization. In these processes, a presumed subjective opinion of wrongdoing may be objective and a presumed private matter can turn in to a public issue. The participation in this kind of processes will be related to the distribution of power in the organization. It is about 'Who shall decide?'. We do think it is important to include questions concerning who has had any impact on designing whistleblowing procedures: do trade union representatives, health and safety officers and/or employees have any role in defining appropriate and inappropriate actions? Are trade union representatives and/or health and safety officers given any role to play in a whistleblowing process? This calls for comparative studies of wrongdoing and whistleblowing, especially comparative studies conducted under different labor market models.

NOTES

* We are grateful for the insightful comments from the editors of this book. We also want to thank Berit Crosby for assistance.

1. See https://whistleblowingsurvey.org/english/survey.html#a3.
2. Norwegian Working Environment Act (WEA) 2005, s. 2–4(2).
3. See www.europarl.europa.eu/committees/en/cont/studiesdownload.html?language Document=EN&file=60152.
4. Nursing assistants and cleaners in hospitals, cashiers and stock/sales clerks in food and electronics retail trade, process operatives in meat processing and confectionary, housekeepers in hotels, and incoming sales/service operators in call centers.
5. According to the Department for Business, Innovation and Skills in the United Kingdom, in 2007 overall union density was 28 per cent. In the public sector, it was 59 per cent, but it was only 16 per cent in the private sector. For 34 per cent of UK employees, pay was covered by a collective agreement.
6. The Safety Representatives and Safety Committee Regulations of 1977 allow recognized trade unions to appoint safety representatives, and the Health and Safety (Consultation with Employees) Regulations 1996 give similar rights to employees without union representation.

7. In the WEA 2005, the term of notice is at least one month. The dismissal must be sent to the employee by post, and the employee has the right to require negotiations and to take legal action (WEA 2005, s. 15–4).
8. Court of Appeal, 2011–05–02. LB–2010–40623, Borgarting Court.
9. Council of Europe Resolution (COER)1729; Transparency International (TI), Recommended Principles for Whistleblowing Legislation; European Union Article 29 Data Protection Working Party (EUWP) Opinion; International Chamber of Commerce (ICC), Guidelines on Whistleblowing; and British Standards Institute (BSI), Whistleblowing Arrangements Code of Practice 2008.
10. In February 2010, we conducted a whistleblowing survey of 6,000 Norwegian employees and managers across sectors and industries. The response rate was 47 per cent.

5. Whistleblowing duties

Jos Leys and Wim Vandekerckhove

INTRODUCTION

Recent research suggests that whistleblowing is increasingly framed as a duty, or as mandatory, rather than as a right. Hassink *et al.* (2007) use a sample of European-listed companies, showing that 66 per cent frame internal whistleblowing as an employee obligation. Moberly and Wylie (2011) analyze a US sample showing that 96 per cent of codes of conduct adopted by companies phrase internal whistleblowing as an employment obligation. We have come a very long way, then, since whistleblowing was formerly portrayed either as the heroic assumption of the upright individual or as a treacherous, subversive breach of loyalty.

The recent trend applies to various members of organizations, with different types of contracts and different types of professional status. However, the discharging of these duties is not evident, as the risk of retaliation is always on the cards. Vandekerckhove and Tsahuridu (2010) argue that the discursive evolution on whistleblowing during the past 30 years makes it conceptually possible for organizations to impose a duty on their employees to report suspected wrongdoing internally, to shed off (or pass on) their duties towards society. However, they warn that the hazardous practicalities of erroneous reporting and the lack of safe organizational cultures pose serious questions to this conceptual possibility. Tsahuridu and Vandekerckhove (2008) point out that there is a blurred line between whistleblowing rights and whistleblowing duties. Their philosophical analysis has concrete iterations in policy making, where legislation and guidelines on how to design and implement whistleblowing policies often take opposing positions on the issue (Vandekerckhove and Lewis 2012). Furthermore, it is not because someone simply claims that you have a duty that this is indeed the case, nor is it the case that you might not have other, more compelling duties.

It must be clear to the reader that we do not offer a legalistic analysis of whistleblowing duties. Rather, our aim in this chapter is to offer an analytical tool that is both conceptually sound as well as useful for practitioners. The chapter develops the argument that whether someone, in their role as a member of an organization, has a duty to blow the whistle or not depends on the type of wrongdoing one is witnessing in combination with the role one has assumed. We hope that our philosophical analysis of the duty question can help to clarify where most of our confusion about this question arises. We do not answer the question of whether an individual actually has to blow the whistle – that decision is with the individual who has to take into account the risks and other particularities – but we purport to give univocal guidance on whether the individual has a duty given that she finds herself in a certain role. We aim to cover all roles that come with organizational conduct and we aim to cover all types of organizations.

This contribution is structured as follows. First, we elucidate upon the concept of duty we will be using. Then, we present and apply a typology of occasions to blow the whistle, a typology of wrongdoing that is exhaustive. These first two sections constitute the conceptual framework for answering the duty question. They stipulate the abstract understandings of what we mean and the organization which we will be using in this chapter. The third section deals with the duties of an employee blowing the whistle on comportment by co-employees. The fourth section considers whether particular employees have different duties. The fifth section analyses the situations in which an employee of one organization has the duty to blow the whistle on practices by employees of a hosting organization. The sixth section answers the question of whether professionals, in the strict sense of the word, differ from employees in having duties to blow the whistle. The final section covers the role of any other witness of wrongdoing, subsumed under the role of citizen.

DUTY

'Duty' has at least a twofold sense. At the personal level, duty is something the individual feels she must do; she senses a moral urge, an obligation or a strong invitation to commit herself to a course of action or other. The origin and the nature of this feeling need not concern us here; it might be the result of religious beliefs, a good upbringing, animal instincts or whatever. This feeling might conflict with other feelings, such as loyalty (Vandekerckhove and Commers 2004) or fear (Mesmer-Magnus and Viswesvaran 2005). And the duty felt might also conflict with other duties equally felt. For our purposes here, this feeling of duty is of no concern, except for the fact that we aim to help those who feel a duty to blow the whistle by handing them a tool to discern whether this feeling is justified.

Besides a feeling, duty is also something that comes with a position, a role. In this sense, it is not a mere feeling, indeed, it need not be accompanied by a feeling of duty; rather, it is something that is open to rational discussion and common understanding. The duties that concern us in this chapter are obligations that pertain to a role and thus to a particular situation, to a particular constellation. In this, they differ from norms that also contain obligations but apply universally, that apply to all rational beings as in Kantian philosophy. If there are such norms and what their content might be need not concern us here. Whistleblowing always occurs within an organizational setting and, therefore, by definition, the individuals involved always have a particular role. They act in a professional capacity, as members of an organization, just like those who commit the alleged wrongdoing and those who receive the information about it, or those who carry another particular role. All roles other than those explicitly discussed in the following sections have been subsumed under 'citizen' as a kind of ultimate role. If there are any Kantian norms, they might be found in that section.

Duties might conflict because the individual may carry more roles than one – in fact, we nearly all do: we are employees, but also members of a family and citizens of a state. One's civic duty consists in obeying the laws that apply, to the letter and in spirit. One's duty as a parent, or more generally, as a ward, consists in fostering the development of the child. These two examples illustrate two different types of duty: the first are duties one incurs as a member, the second are fiduciary duties that are intrinsic to a particular role. The fiduciary relationship, on the part of the ward, entails the duty to decide on every course of action in view of the development of the child – in fact, to be a ward is exactly that. Typically, in a relationship that entails fiduciary duties, the strength of both parties is quite unequal. The child is nearly helpless regarding nocuous behavior on the part of the ward.[1]

A third type of duty goes with the role of a professional; the most well-known example is the Hippocratic Oath. The physician solemnly pledges to put the body of knowledge he came to acquire solely to use in order to serve one overriding end: the health of the patient. It should be noted that the relationship between a physician and her patients entails fiduciary duties and there might be some doubts whether this really is a separate type of duty. The strength in the relationship between patient and physician is all on the part of the latter, because of the radically unequal distribution of medicinal knowledge. But engineers make vows comparable to those of physicians and it is less clear where the fiduciary aspect comes in. For the sake of keeping things simple, in what follows we will understand any professional status as entailing some particular kind of duty, related to the purpose of the profession at hand, whether this be medicine or engineering or something else.

An important aspect of the typology of whistleblowing duties we will develop are a number of stipulations. We take the role of an employee of an organization to entail duties of the second type, fiduciary duties, whether she is employed as a member of the board, as a high-ranking executive, a technical specialist or a humble worker.[2] Hence we regard as an employee anyone who is employed in an organization by those who fund the organization. Employees are then agents who act on behalf (hence their fiduciary duty) of the funders who are the principals. Employees of a business organization have the fiduciary duty to foster the cause of the corporation: to maximize the net present value for the owners while producing goods or rendering services for customers in a market. Likewise, employees of a governmental agency have the fiduciary duty to foster the cause of the agency: to render a service or to produce goods at a minimal cost for the taxpayer. Likewise, employees of a charity have the fiduciary duty to foster the purpose of the organization: to maximize the set cause within the rules of the game and with minimal leakage of donors' money. This goes to say that our analysis covers all types of organizations that are set up with the purpose to accomplish some economic goal, to produce or to render a service.[3]

As in the example of the ward and the physician, the strengths of both parties are quite unequal: the financing party is at the lower end of the information asymmetry on two counts. First, the financing party, whether this is a shareholder, the taxpayer or a donor, is simply not present when the money is put to use. In this sense, this party is an outsider of the organization. As the patient and the child, the financing party has no alternative but to put her trust in the stronger party.[4] Secondly, the activity at hand is likely to be one on which the financing party has no particular expertise, simply because one cannot be an expert in every domain, whereas organizations are by definition specialized. These two informational weaknesses are at the root of the fiduciary duties entailed in the employee-funder relationship.

Even when this is clear and quite uncontroversial, it does not tell us whether and when an employee has a fiduciary duty to blow the whistle. Alas, this cannot be answered in abstracto, i.e., without having a clear view on the alleged wrongdoing that is occurring or has occurred. We will turn to this in the next section, but first we have to say something on possible conflicts.

Besides being an employee, one is also a citizen and most of the time also a contributing member of a household, a provider. It is important to note that conflicts of roles might arise. For instance, the duty to blow the whistle one possibly incurs in the capacity of an employee, does not sit easily or might be to be at odds with the duty as a provider for a family household. Frequent consequences of blowing the whistle are retaliation, loss of job, loss of health, loss of financial assets – hence, one has to think twice before blowing the whistle even if it is one's duty. Nearly always, there are other duties that might conflict or whose performance might be hampered. This being said, we provide no guidance on how to solve these conflicts or how to live with them; that is something the individual must decide for herself.

WRONGDOINGS

While acting in their organizational role, employees of all three types of organizations might engage in a panoply of wrongdoings. First, we should distinguish wrongdoings from activities one despises or rejects from a religious, political, aesthetic or otherwise value-driven assessment. These valuations are not of an ethical type.[5] From an ethical perspective, wrongdoings consist either of (1) a transgression of applicable norms; in (2) neglect of purpose or pursuit of wrong purpose; or in (3) the negligent or intentional causing of unpermitted consequences (or several of these at the same time).

All of these wrongdoings or instances of unethical conduct show a lack of integrity on the part of the perpetrators-employees, who are expected not to violate norms, only to pursue legitimate goals and not to cause harm while going about their job. So, the question will be on what breaches of integrity is there a duty to blow the whistle. However, this general ethical typology of wrongdoings does not exhaust the perspectives; most pertinent for our purpose here is to relate the unethical conduct to the purpose of the organization.

The potential whistleblower might discern three relationships: (A) wrongdoing that is intended to foster the material or financial purpose of the organization; (B) wrongdoing that is unrelated to the purpose of the organization; (C) wrongdoing that goes against the purpose of the organization.

Typical instances of (A) are the violations of anti-trust regulations or untruthful external communications, whether in advertising for sales or in campaigning for collection of funds.

Typical instances of (B) are the occurrence of sexual abuse, moral harassment or mobbing but also using one's position to win converts to some religious or political ideas. These wrongdoings occur within the organization but their intent is not at all related to the purpose of the organization. Rather, it is an intrusion of the private or the communal realm in the functioning of the organization. As a matter of fact, this is where the diseases of the community (racism, mobbing, ostracism, and the like) or the diseases of the individual (sadism, narcissism, despotism, and the like) infect the organization. To be clear, we do not mean to say that the occurrence of such wrongdoings does not affect the organizational purpose. To the contrary, if the social construct of the organization is to be understood as a dedicated organ of society, which it quite literally is, or a piece of machinery, we would say it is being infected or starts to rust or to corrode due to the local sociopathology or psychopathology. But as to intent, the wrongdoing is completely unrelated to the purpose of the organization or the sub-organization where it occurs.

Typical instances of (C) are theft, either massive and spectacular, as in Enron, or more common as in taking stationery at the beginning of a school term, but also sneaky mission creep, such as empire building, or simply gross neglect of fiduciary duty.

This combination of salient ethical features yields what we will refer to as a matrix of wrongdoings (Table 5.1).

Table 5.1 Matrix of wrongdoings

Wrongdoing by employees	For the purpose of the organization (A)	Besides the purpose of the organization (B)	Against the purpose of the organization (C)
(1) Transgression of norms	Breaches of consumer protection regulation and anti-trust law, active bribery	Pedophilia by priests; moral harassment; mobbing; stealing from colleagues	Stealing from the organization; passive bribery; industrial espionage
(2) Teleopathic action	Mission creep, financial myopia, usurpation	Recruiting or lobbying for political, religious, cultural, ideological and organizational purposes	Nepotism in recruiting, empire building, gross inefficiency or ineffectiveness, taking bribes
(3) Causing unwanted consequences	Imposing excessive material risks; causing collateral damages	Negatively affecting the social climate	Causing imputable damages

Most of the business ethics literature is consciously or unconsciously preoccupied with type (A) cases.[6] To take an example close at hand: where Vandekerckhove and Tsahuridu (2010: 365) write that '[m]any whistleblowers suffer severe retaliation for disclosing misconduct of their organization' and that the knowledge concerns 'organizational activities that in some way harm society', they have type (A) cases in mind. The organization (rather than individuals, employees) is the perpetrator and society (rather than some particular outside or inside party to the organization) is the victim. In this type of situations, the (illegitimate) pursuit of the organizational purpose is hampered by the whistleblower and hence it is the organization (rather than employees within the organization) that retaliates. It is in this frame of mind that they 'reject a positive duty for potential whistleblowers'.

In contrast, the sexual abuse of children by priests (type (B)) most certainly is not an organizational activity nor was it caused by organizational functioning. The practice did occur within the frame of professional activities, but it was individual priests who abused their position, without consent of the authorities within the organization. Even if some condone it, it is hard to image them doing so because they believe the abuse to be somehow contributing to the cause of the organization. The practices were 'under the control of the employers' in the sense of the definition by Near and Miceli (1985) and hence eligible for whistleblowing. Likewise, employees who suffer moral harassment are not victims of organizational activity, despite the practice occurring within the organization, and the practice being remediable by the employer.

Ethical failures of type (C) are also covered by the definition in Near and Miceli (1985). For instance, the alleged industrial espionage with Renault was signaled by a whistleblower. Yet, it is not society at large or some external interest that is victimized by organizational functioning. To the contrary, it is the financing party of the organization that is victimized by some of its employees.

We have now established a more elaborate scheme for framing misbehavior within an organizational context, whether this is in businesses, not-for-profit organizations or government agencies. With this in mind, we can now turn to the questions about duties.

DUTY OF AN EMPLOYEE TO BLOW THE WHISTLE ON CO-EMPLOYEES

Based on the above, we maintain that each and every employee of an organization has a fiduciary duty to blow the whistle on breaches of integrity of type (C) committed by co-employees of his organization. This fiduciary duty is owed to the financing party of the organization. It is owed, whether or not it is in the organization's policy or code of conduct (and hence explicitly part of the employment contract). It is owed, whether or not the financing party has taken due care to facilitate the fulfillment of the duty, i.e., whether or not the financing party has taken due care to set up a whistleblowing system. In this context, it is important to reiterate that the employee is a fiduciary agent of the organization's funder and not of her colleagues, her superior officer, the head of her department, the Human Resources Department, her CEO or even the board. Feelings of loyalty towards the perpetrators might conflict with this (feeling of) duty, but they are ethically speaking irrelevant and even inadequate. Loyalty is owed to the funder: the shareholder, the donor or the taxpayer.

This is different for types (A) and (B). If the organization has no stated policy on wrongdoings of type (A) or (B), the employee does not have a duty to blow the whistle *qualitate qua*. It might be that for type (A) civic duties are in force, but this depends on the jurisdiction. The same goes for wrongdoings of type (B). Irrespective of whether or not these are conceived as duties in the context that surrounds the organization, it is not the case that such duties arise from one's employment contract for wrongdoings of type (A) or (B).

However, when the code of conduct or the stated policy of the organization includes a section on employees blowing the whistle ('report' or 'raise concern') on wrongdoings of type (A) or (B), then this is part of their fiduciary duty to the funder of the organization. Whether or not this policy is explicitly endorsed by the financing party, it simply is a duty that comes with the employment contract. Hence, for types (A) or (B) wrongdoing, the whistleblower has a duty only if there is an explicit policy; for type (C) wrongdoing the whistleblower always has a duty, regardless of whether or not there is an explicit policy.

We do not take the presence of a duty to imply that this duty overrides all other considerations. For instance, a solid procedure and adequate protection should be in place to make the disclosing of information comfortable or at least less hazardous. It would be wise for the potential whistleblower to have a look at precedents and how they have been treated. If previous whistleblowers were retaliated against, suffered job loss or have become social outcasts, it also would be wise to consider finding a new job first before disclosing the information.[7]

EMPLOYEES: SPECIAL CASES

A first further question is whether temporary employees also have the duty to blow the whistle. The answer is, quite obviously, that the employee with a temporary contract incurs the same duties as the employee with an 'ongoing', 'rolling' or 'tenured' contract. While the person is in the employ of the organization, everything that has been said in the previous section applies.

A second case is that of the volunteer, i.e., the employee who is not paid and is not bound by a classical employment contract. Of course, this *cas de figure* occurs only exceptionally with business organizations, rather seldom with governmental organizations, but more frequently with charities. Yet, the above reasoning applies in full even if the employee is neither paid nor bound by an employment contract. She at least accepts fiduciary duty towards the funder of the activities in which she formally partakes. When volunteering in a fire brigade and observing the paid employees committing wrongdoings of type (C), there is a duty to blow the whistle. It does not need to be explained that a volunteer much more easily than an employee can terminate the relationship with the organization and is comparatively more immune to adverse consequences of blowing the whistle.

Within an organization, several functions are explicitly concerned with deviations from good practice. The purpose of their very function is to look for, identify and signal wrongdoings or the risk thereof. Thus, making up our third special case of employees are auditors, compliance officers, quality managers, safety managers, controllers, and the like. Of course, it is their very duty to perform the function they have taken up.

The task they perform and their function makes them a possible target for obstruction and retaliation. Hence, most often, compensatory measures are installed; for instance, they report to the highest authorities within the organization or the person that occupies the role is protected against dismissal by law. The individuals who perform these functions are employees. Hence they incur the same duties as any other employee. However, given the specific nature of their function, we do not say that they 'blow the whistle' while going about their job. Rather, they just perform what is asked from them by the employer. If they do stumble upon wrongdoing that is outside the scope of their assignment, their position is identical to that of any other employee.

A fourth special case is that of the CEO and perhaps other members of the highest executive rank. They have the same fiduciary and other duties as any other employee. Yet, their position empowers them to put a halt to wrongdoings committed by subordinate employees. Hence, their duty is to blow the whistle in all cases of our wrongdoing matrix (Table 5.1), but in the other sense of the expression: they have to blow the whistle as a referee does when observing the players committing transgressions. If and when they are confronted with wrongdoing committed by equals and not empowered to put a halt to the wrongdoing, they should address the board to which they have ready and direct access by virtue of their position. Even then, to blow the whistle is not without its hazards.[8]

EXTERNAL EMPLOYEES

While going about performing their tasks, organizations often recur to the services of outsiders. These individuals are not in the employ of the organization whilst doing what they do. Either they are self-employed or they are in the employ of an organization that is in the business of rendering services. It goes without saying that those external employees might stumble upon wrongdoing committed by employees of the client organization. Does their duty equal that of an employee-member of the client? To answer this question requires some additional nuances.

First, they have a duty to signal wrongdoing if this is stipulated in the contract, either directly or indirectly. It is directly in the contract when this contains a clause that says something along these lines: 'when in the course of working in our organization, the contractor takes notice of "wrongdoings", the contractor should relay this information to …'. By signing the contract, the duty is accepted. It is indirectly implied by the contract when the external employee is made to report to an officer of the client organization and it is part of the instructions she receives. For instance, when an external engineer is participating in the production process of the hosting organization, she will be instructed to observe the same safety measures as the employees of the hosting organization. In the same breath, she will be instructed to pass information about employees neglecting those safety measures. Here, she incurs the duty because the contract entails that the external employee is reporting to the customer. It stands to reason that the instruction to blow the whistle in these cases is closely related to the task at hand and to the material processes the employee is actually involved in. The *cas de figure* applies to safety measures, good manufacturing practices, government regulations pertaining to process or output, such as US Food and Drug Administration (FDA) prescriptions, and the like. This is to say that the duty to blow the whistle will usually be restricted to wrongdoings of type

(A) of our wrongdoing matrix (Table 5.1) and, more specifically, (1) and (3) restricted to some technical fields.

If and where the contract is silent on whistleblowing, the duties of the external employee are not that clear-cut if the organization of employment does not provide explicit instructions. In accordance with the reasoning above, the external employee has a fiduciary duty towards her own employer and she bears no fiduciary duties towards the employer or the financing party of the client organization in which she performs tasks. Hence, if she observes wrongdoing by the employees of the hosting organization, she has no duty to report this to the funder of that organization; this is especially salient for wrongdoings type (C) row (3) of the wrongdoing matrix (Table 5.1). To blow the whistle on those or any other type in the matrix would impact the interests of her own employer, mostly in a negative way. Hence, bringing information about wrongdoing out in the open would very likely amount to a violation of fiduciary duty towards her own employer. By contrast, it would be fully within her fiduciary duty to relay the information to her superior officer in the organization of employ, especially when she deems the wrongdoing to be material for either the client organization or for the service-providing organization. This might be the case, for instance, if reputation penalties would be high or the solvency of the customer organization is implied, which would rule out wrongdoings of type (B). The authorities of the service-providing organization are then enabled to decide on a course of action: terminate the contract, abstain from further contracting, transmitting the information to the authorities of the client organization or even go public with it. Unless explicitly foreseen, employees that perform in hosting organizations are not empowered to decide and consecutively act upon the situation themselves. To do so would hurt the legitimate interest of one's employer. If there is a duty here, it consists in reporting instances deemed relevant to the officers at home. In turn, their duty is first and foremost to the funder of their organization to whom they owe a fiduciary duty.

By nature, wrongdoings observed will pertain to the task one is performing in the hosting organization. An external payroll administrator might observe breaches of labor regulation; an external software engineer might observe flawed and dangerous software constructs. The latter observing transgressions of labor regulation and the former identifying corrupt software are much less likely to occur. If such observations are made, they are made accidentally. Indeed, to serve in a professional capacity entails that one does not occupy herself with what is not being asked and with what is outside the scope of the task at hand. A software engineer is not concerned with the finer details of labor regulation; a payroll administrator is not an authority on software design. The scope for possible whistleblowing by external employees is therefore restricted if they go about their work in a professional manner, even if their occupation is not a profession in the strict sense.[9] It is towards that role, that of the professional in the strict sense, that we now turn.

A SPECIFIC DUTY FOR PROFESSIONALS?

We will not on this occasion discuss at length what exactly constitutes a profession and what occupations are eligible for the status of a profession. Uncontroversial is, first, that in order to qualify as a profession, an occupation requires a considerable body of knowledge and practice to be executed well; that knowledge is unequally distributed within society, hence the necessity to trust professionals. The case of the medical profession comes readily to mind. Secondly, a profession has a clear purpose towards the body of knowledge that is to be put to use. In the case of medicine, this is health (rather than pain, disease or death) and the pursuit of this purpose cannot be corrupted by other purposes (such as financial gain, becoming popular or distributing justice). The individuals who share that knowledge and purpose form a profession, an institution. This institution manages the standards and condition for membership (hence occupational practice) and it guards the behavior of its members. It develops standards of behavior and ethical codes. It might or it might not be the case that those codes entail clauses that deal with whistleblowing, although they are very unlikely to use that term.

What are the duties of a professional when she witnesses wrongdoing? Most, if not all, professional codes refer to confidentiality. The professional is to treat information obtained in the course of rendering professional services as confidential. The outspoken presence of this duty is constitutive for the trust conferred by the client and is a condition for the performance of the profession in the first place. When you invite a physician into your home and entrust her with private matters in the course of diagnosing, the physician is bound to treat this information as confidential and is barred from divulging it to any other party whatsoever. This also applies when the information contains positive knowledge about wrongdoing. The image of the physician treating gangsters pursued by the law comes to mind. The duty of the physician is to look after the health of the wounded gangster. She is not to divulge the gangster's whereabouts to any outside party. Hence, the duty of the professional is not to blow the whistle and to remain silent in all circumstances. In contrast to employees who have a right even if they do not have a duty to blow the whistle, professionals have a duty *not* to blow the whistle; unless, of course, the code of ethics that rules professional behavior mentions exceptions. Before turning to that possibility, we should consider a particular case of wrongdoing.

Suppose a doctor observes wrongdoing that is likely to cause a detrimental impact on health, for instance, the non-observance of hygienic regulation in a food producing plant. Suppose the engineer observes that some building is being constructed in such a sloppy manner that it causes clear and present danger to those who go near it. Cases like these fall in row (3) of the wrongdoing matrix (Table 5.1) and pertain to a very particular set of unwanted consequences. Indeed, it is the very purposes of the professions, health and public safety, which are at stake. Hence, it is the duty of the said professionals to blow the whistle on the nocuous practices. This is so in the twofold meaning of the term: they have to put a stop to these malpractices by virtue of their own authority, blow the whistle as a referee, and, if that is not a given possibility, they should pass the information to a party who has the authority to do so.

The duty of confidentiality is a necessary concomitant of professionalism but is a mere secondary to the main purpose of the profession, which overrides it. It is quite imaginable that a member is barred from the profession and from professional practice if she is seen to violate the confidentiality clause in the charter of the profession. Yet in contrast, it would be absurd to strike off a member who is seen to foster the very purpose of the profession, even if she has to breach the standard confidentiality that is owned even to perpetrators. Confidentiality is not an absolute for professionals; they have the duty to blow the whistle on practices that harm the very purpose the profession pursues.

One might comment that our choosing of the medical and the engineering professions as examples is biased and does not exhaust the issue. Indeed, it is very easy to go along with the reasoning in the preceding paragraph if it concerns lofty purposes such as (public) health and (public) safety. Other purposes might not provoke as much sympathy or might seem to weigh a lot less. Moreover, the list of possible professions is open and not well delineated. Consider, for instance the financial advisor who might or might not be organized or recognized as a professional in the strict sense, who has taken a vow of confidentiality but who is likely to stumble upon transgressions of fiscal norms by her clients sooner or later; or the accountant who might or might not fit the muster of the classic profession, but who has taken a vow of confidentiality and is likely to stumble upon substandard accounting practices sooner or later. Here, duties are not that easy to discern. When witnessing wrongdoings of all kinds, members of the profession at hand might nurture quite different opinions on the courses of action and the duties involved.

At this point two avenues of establishing duties can be taken. The first is that government issues laws that regulate these predicaments; the second is that the profession issues regulations. An instance of the former is the obligation for financial intermediaries, lawyers and notaries to inform upon cases of money laundering they might happen to witness in the course of rendering professional services. Thus, for well-delineated cases, the default of confidentiality is overruled and the duty to blow the whistle is imposed by law. Of course, practitioners of the profession are fully aware of this duty as it is a condition of professionalism to be knowledgeable about the rules of the profession. Not to perform the duty to blow the whistle in cases prescribed by the law would equal corruption, as would ignorance about the duty. Their clients have the same information, so they are not taken by surprise and cannot reproach a breach of confidentiality.

The second avenue is that professional bodies issue prescriptions for their members. An instance of these is the regulation issued by the International Federation of Accountants (IFAC 2012). As in the case of law issued by government, the prescriptions are known to practitioners and their customers. The latter cannot be reproached for, and the former cannot be accused of, breaching confidentiality. As in the law, confidentiality is the default; the duty to inform on wrongdoings is restricted to specific cases. The IFAC restricts the duty to report on wrongdoings by applying it solely to (alleged) illegal acts, i.e., transgression of norms (row 1 of the wrongdoing matrix, Table 5.1), inasmuch as those norms are positive law;[10] also excluded are illegal acts that are 'personal', i.e., that are committed by employees of the organization but are unrelated to the business activities of the organization (IFAC 2012: 6): this is type (B) of the wrongdoing matrix. The motivation brought forward by the IFAC fits with what we wrote about professional attitude in the preceding section: such information is merely accidental.[11] As the information acquired does not pertain to the performance of the professional role, it is not a professional duty to blow the whistle. If the professional person has a duty to blow the whistle, it is not a professional duty but a duty embedded in some other role, most likely that of a citizen. Furthermore, the norm transgressions on which the accountant has the duty to blow the whistle pertain solely to accounting matters (IFAC 2012: 8).[12] Indeed, only on issues that pertain to the accounting expertise does the role of the accountant differ from that of the citizen. It is to the role of the citizen that we now turn.

CIVIC DUTIES TO BLOW THE WHISTLE

Whether a citizen has a duty to blow the whistle and on what wrongdoings is in the law of the jurisdiction. All citizens are supposed to be knowledgeable about the laws that apply. With these two simple sentences, the matter is ethically exhausted. What remains is a panoply of jurisdictions, laws and wrongdoings. Indeed, it goes without saying that jurisdictions differ in imposing duties. In some, the citizens have the duty to prevent harm being done to fellow citizens; by keeping silent and not blowing the whistle, they are liable to be found in breach of the duty to lend assistance to persons in need. In other jurisdictions, this duty is not in positive law and whether a witness has the duty to speak up and is to be held liable for damages incurred is an issue that is determined case by case.

We consider our enumeration of roles to be exhaustive. That is to say, all possible roles not treated explicitly above are to be included under the role of 'citizen'. For instance, a customer, a neighbor, a competitor, someone who is merely passing by, has no particular duties attached to this temporary, ephemeral and accidental capacity. Whether she has any duty has to be answered by answering the very question of the citizen, without regard to the particularities of the witnessing.

CONCLUSION AND FURTHER RESEARCH AVENUES

A duty to blow the whistle comes with a role. Employees have the fiduciary duty to signal wrongdoing that goes against the purpose of the organization and they have the duty to signal any wrongdoing if and when they are asked to do so.

What we have presented in this chapter is a series of duties to blow the whistle as they pertain to different roles within an organization. We had to develop a typology of wrongdoings in relation to the purpose of the organization in order to render a nuanced answer to the question 'does the employee have a duty to blow the whistle?'. Whether one has a duty to blow the whistle depends on the type of wrongdoing one is witnessing in combination with the role one has assumed.

Although we approached the task of developing these typologies with techniques of analytical philosophy, we strongly believe that the distinctions we make and the inferences we draw from these do matter in practice. Hence, we believe the typologies developed in this chapter can be of aid when designing, analyzing, critiquing or evaluating whistleblowing policies.

However, we must acknowledge that what we have provided here is not a fully equipped toolbox. We have not shed light on the process of whistleblowing. This process includes two dimensions into which further intelligence needs to be put to work. The first of these dimensions concerns the *how* of whistleblowing. If there is a duty to blow the whistle for a particular role, *how* should this be done: anonymously, confidentially, in an identified form, as an allegation or a reasonable suspicion, and so forth? The second dimension relates to the *recipient* of whistleblowing. If there is a duty to blow the whistle, to whom must this be done? (For whistleblowing and recipients see Bosua *et al.*, Chapter 11, and Moberly, Chapter 12). We have argued here that a duty to blow the whistle stems from the fiduciary duty between agent and principal. For public sector agencies the principal is the taxpayer. But does that duty imply blowing the whistle immediately to the citizenry, in public? We are inclined to suggest that any duty to blow the whistle would entail a duty to follow a tiered approach. It would be useful if further research would link the typology of wrongdoing and the series of role-dependent duties to the question of how far whistleblowing should escalate. We refer to the three-tiered model presented in Vandekerckhove (2010): internal/proxy-for-society/public. If there is a duty to blow the whistle, must all tiers be used successively? Do duties to blow the whistle require the whistleblower to take it to the public tier if the other two are not responding or are corrupt? Does that depend on the type of funder (principal), i.e., does that differ for public sector agencies, businesses and charities? Or does that depend on the type of agent, i.e., does that differ for professionals or according to the hierarchical position of the employee or the volunteer?

A final suggestion for further research building on our typologies developed here relates to clusters of duties and clusters of rights and duties. If an employee has a duty to blow the whistle, what are the implied (or required for practical feasibility) duties on fellow employees, funders and legislators (the state which has the duty to protect the human rights of its citizens)? There is ample work available on these matters, but for research to more effectively shed light on their implications, it seems necessary to relate or reorder it to the typologies developed here.

NOTES

1. 'Ward' in this context refers to guardianship over a minor, rather than to the minor himself or herself.
2. Hereby, we radically extend the scope of the position argued for more extensively and more eloquently by Marcoux (2003), who envisages stakeholder discourses that are mainly targeting privately owned corporations and usually keep silent on

charities and government sponsored agencies. We also like to draw attention to the work in Lewis (2011a) which offers comments on some case law in England and Wales on fiduciary duties of employees. He resists the notion that all employees have fiduciary duties, understood as the duty to act solely in the interests of their employers. He submits that there are important legal distinctions between fiduciary obligations, on the one hand, and the employee's duty of fidelity, on the other. As examples of exceptions to the employee's duty of fidelity, Lewis mentions situations where an organization's activities conflict with the public interest. He further argues that legislation acknowledges that employees have loyalties to their dependants (e.g., a right to paid leave) and the general public (e.g., whistleblower legislation such as the UK Public Interest Disclosure Act (PIDA) 1998). We believe our analysis in this chapter integrates Lewis' comments and concerns, in the sense that it allows for the concrete phenomena Lewis raises whilst maintaining the model of fiduciary duty. Crucial to this is that we understand the fiduciary duty of the employee to be to the funder of the organization, rather than the manager (CEO or departmental manager, or even board). We believe that the reader of both this chapter and Lewis (2011a) might mistakenly see the views in these papers as contradictory, if this distinction is not understood. We trust we are in line with the thrust of Lewis (2011a) as he alludes to Vandekerckhove and Commers (2004) notion of 'rational loyalty' to assert that internal whistleblowing should be seen as an act of loyalty because it draws the attention of the employer to wrongdoing. We concur with Lewis' reading of Flanagan (2008, cited in Lewis 2011a: 74–5), 'Flanagan observes that in reality the duty of fidelity is not distinct from a fiduciary obligation or duty of confidence but is merely another description of it'.

3. Implicitly excluded are clubs and all types of leisurely organizations, the purpose of which is not external and also political organizations such as political parties. Families and states are not organizations.
4. Of course, this is mitigated by a host of arrangements to alleviate the information asymmetry, such as accounting regulation, obligatory external audits, whistleblowing policies, and the like, but all of these together do not do away with the information asymmetry and therefore the necessity to entrust one's interests or one's finances.
5. They occur in the business context, however. An example is the ex-Goldman Sachs officer who published on the culture of bad taste in internal customer attitude by the said financial institution. He reported no hard facts or ethical faults.
6. Note that Alford (2001) only envisages this type of wrongdoing and only very restrictedly so, namely, related to the highly abstract notion of 'public good'. This perspective does not include wrongdoings in columns (B) and (C).
7. Paradoxically, when one is no longer in the employ of the organization, there is no longer a duty to disclose the information. That is to say that if there remains a duty, it is as a citizen, not as an employee.
8. Cf. the Olympus whistleblower.
9. For this rather myopic aspect of the professional attitude, we refer to the eloquent exposé on professionalism by Seabright (2010: ch 9: 'Professionalism and Fulfillment in Work and War').
10. As the document clearly states, it does not cover all wrongdoing: unethical acts that are not also potentially illegal are not envisaged by the proposed duty to blow the whistle (IFAC 2012: 6).
11. Information about such acts would not be considered to be 'acquired as a result of professional and business relationships'. A professional accountant's rights and responsibilities with respect to disclosing such acts would be the same as for any other member of society (IFAC 2012: 6–7).
12. Also of note is that the ethics code for the accountant allows for exceptional circumstances that free her from her duty, for instance, threats to the physical safety

of the professional accountant or others (IFAC 2012: 10). This clause refers to the hazards that go with blowing the whistle (IFAC 2012: section 1). Circumstances of a commercial nature, such as the loss of a client or income, would, however, not constitute exceptional circumstances (IFAC 2012: section 1).

6. On the appropriateness of research design: Intended and actual whistleblowing

Brita Bjørkelo and Hege Høivik Bye

INTRODUCTION

The act of trying to stop wrongdoing goes way back in time (cf. Park *et al.* 2005; Vinten 1994). However, whistleblowing research is commonly depicted as related to civil and worker initiatives in the United States in the 1960s and 1970s (Bok 1981). In those times, one of the first efforts to create a body of research consisted of compilations of case stories of the experiences of whistleblowers (for instance, see Nader *et al.* 1972; Peters and Branch 1972). This period also included books and movies based on experiences from whole organizations and actual cases (for instance, see Anderson *et al.* 1980; Maas 1973). Later, theoretical papers and empirical research of the act of reporting wrongdoing at work became more common (Miceli and Near 1989; Parmerlee *et al.* 1982). While the first compiled versions of whistleblowing cases were important for getting attention to the topic, theoretical and empirical research was and is crucial to gaining systematic knowledge about whistleblowing at work.

The act of whistleblowing is commonly defined as 'the disclosure by organization members (former or current) of illegal, immoral or illegitimate practices under the control of their employers, to persons or organizations that may be able to effect action' (Near and Miceli 1985: 5). Studying real-life whistleblowing is hard due to several factors. It is a sensitive topic, so gaining entry into organizations and ensuring participants that their anonymity will be kept can be challenging. Moreover, in quantitative research designs large samples are necessary to get sufficient numbers of silent observers and actual whistleblowers for statistical analysis. Difficulties such as these make it challenging to answer the key question 'What makes observers of wrongdoing decide to blow the whistle?'. As a result, some researchers have turned to the study of intentions to report. Focusing on intentions has many advantages. It is less sensitive and anyone, not just actual observers or whistleblowers, can report their willingness to report various types of wrongdoing. Moreover, in experimental designs contextual factors can be manipulated and their causal impact on intentions to report can be observed. The problem is that results from studies on actual and intended whistleblowing often point in different directions. In this chapter we will argue that many of the apparent inconsistencies and lack of coherence in findings are due to methodological rather than substantial factors. We will also outline how the reasoned action approach (Fishbein and Ajzen 2010) can serve as an integrating theoretical framework for research on actual and intended whistleblowing. Finally, we will make some practical recommendations for future research on whistleblowing. In the next two sections we will first present the two research lines, actual and intended whistleblowing, and then we will present some of the measures that seem to be most widely applied in the investigation of these two types of whistleblowing.

TWO RESEARCH LINES: INTENDED AND ACTUAL WHISTLEBLOWING

Empirical research on whistleblowing has often focused either on which factors predict whistleblowing when people are faced with scenarios describing wrongdoing (intended hypothetical reporting), or on what employees who have *actually* reported wrongdoing are characterized by and have experienced. Unfortunately, these two strands of research have seldom intertwined. In their 2005 meta-analysis of the whistleblowing field, Mesmer-Magnus and Viswesvaran reported that they had located only two studies linking intent to blow the whistle with actual reporting. An overview of studies since their review (identified by a cited reference search in the ISI Web of Science database, August 2012) showed that intentions to report and actual reporting have not been linked in more recent research either (see Table 6.1).

Our minor pilot review (Table 6.1) shows that there is a tendency towards more focus being directed at intended and other aspects of whistleblowing; more so than studies of actual whistleblowing or studies of the relationship between intended and actual whistleblowing. One way to approach this situation is simply to state that the number of studies that address the relationship between intended and actual whistleblowing should be increased. Another is to aim at bringing these two lines of research closer together through theory, that is, by applying a theoretical perspective that can provide a language for these two lines to talk to each other.

Table 6.1 Whistleblowing studies after 2005 citing Mesmer-Magnus and Viswesvaran's (2005) meta-analysis

Authors	Year	Intended	Actual	Relationship between intended and actual	Other
1. Avery, McKay and Hunter	2012				X
2. Bashir, Khattak, Hanif and Chohan	2011		X		
3. Calderon-Cuadrado, Alvarez-Arce, Rodriguez-Tejedo and Salvatierra	2009				X
4. Casal and Bogui	2008	X			
5. de Graaf	2010				X
6. Decker and Calo	2007				X
7. Fredin	2011				X
8. Hassink, de Vries and Bollen	2007				X
9. Hedin and Mansson	2012		X		
10. Jackson	2008				X
11. Jetten, Hornsey, Spears, Haslam and Cowell	2010				X
12. Kaplan, Pany, Samuels and Zhang	2009	X			
13. Kaplan, Pope and Samuels	2011	X			
14. Kaptein	2011	X			
15. Kish-Gephart, Detert, Trevino and Edmondson	2009				X
16. Klaas, Olson-Buchanan and Ward	2012				X
17. Kölbel and Herold	2010				X
18. Liyanarachchi and Newdick	2009	X			
19. Liyanarachchi and Adler	2011	X			
20. Miceli, Near and Dworkin	2009				X
21. Nayir and Herzig	2012	X			
22. Nielsen and Einarsen	2008		X		

Authors	Year	Intended	Actual	Relationship between intended and actual	Other
23. Oh and Teo	2010	X			
24. Ohnishi, Hayama, Asai and Kosugi	2008		X		
25. Park and Blenkinsopp	2009	X			
26. Pauksztat, Steglich and Wittek	2011	X			
27. Pemberton, Tombs, Chan and Seal	2012				X
28. Pillay and Dorasamy	2011				X
29. Richardson and McGlynn	2011		X		
30. Robinson, Robertson and Curtis	2012	X			
31. Rothwell and Baldwin	2007b	X	X		
32. Seifert, Sweeney, Joireman and Thornton	2010	X			
33. Skivenes and Trygstad	2010		X		
34. Stansbury and Victor	2009		X		
35. Taylor and Curtis	2010	X			
36. Teo and Caspersz	2011				X
37. Trevino, Weaver and Reynolds	2006				X
38. Vadera, Aguilera and Caza	2009				X
39. Zhang, Chiu and Wei	2009	X			
40. Zyglidopoulos and Fleming	2008				X
Total number of studies		15	8	0	17

Another issue raised by the meta-analysis by Mesmer-Magnus and Viswesvaran (2005) is that there are variations in the correlates of intended and actual whistleblowing, which at a first glance seem to indicate that there is little value in the intent approach for understanding actual whistleblowing.

Measuring Actual Whistleblowing

Research on actual whistleblowing has been conducted in several ways, although there are (as of now) no standard cross-nationally validated instruments for measuring whistleblowing at work. However, a dominant tradition in the measurement of actual whistleblowing has been the different versions of questionnaires applied in the large-scale studies conducted by the Merit System Protection Board (MSPB) in the United States since the 1980s (Brown 2008; Near and Miceli 2008). In this tradition, respondents are first asked whether they had 'personally observed or obtained direct evidence of' one or more of 18 types of wrongdoing (for instance, accepting bribes or kickbacks and/or unwelcome sexual advances or requests for sexual favors that are made a condition of employment or are used as a basis for employment or career decisions) during the last 12 months (Miceli *et al.* 2012: 933). After this, respondents are asked to select 'the one activity that represents the most serious problem you observed or obtained direct evidence of'. Whistleblowing is further measured as the proportion of respondents who have observed wrongdoing and have reported it to a valid complaint recipient. In addition to yielding information about types of wrongdoing and whistleblowers, this approach gives information about whether respondents are aware or unaware of a wrongdoing, coded as observers and non-observers, respectively, as well as respondents who do not report the misconduct they have witnessed, namely, inactive or silent observers (for a detailed and thorough description of the questions applied, see Miceli *et al.* 2012: 933–4).

The approach employed in the MSPB studies may be labeled a *behavioral approach*. Whistleblowing is measured by asking questions about the observation and reporting of wrongdoing and afterwards respondents are categorized into groups such as non-observers, observers and whistleblowers (Miceli and Near 1984). The behavioral approach yields overall information about how much wrongdoing is observed and how many blow the whistle. This approach also assumes that the listed wrongdoings, which according to the definition should be illegal, unethical or illegitimate acts, are not interpreted differently across countries of application. A behavioral approach can have limitations when applied as an operational definition across national settings (see, for instance, Jubb 1999, as well as Vandekerckhove *et al.*, Chapter 2).

An alternative is the operational definition approach (Bjørkelo 2010). In this tradition, respondents are presented with an operational definition of whistleblowing (based on the state-of-the-art definition by Near and Miceli, in Bjørkelo *et al.* 2010: 378):

> Whistleblowing is when an employee (former or current) that is witnessing or has *witnessed* an unethical, illegal or illegitimate practice at work openly (not anonymous) reports about it to a person or a body that has the ability to change the practice. Whistleblowing is not when the reporting is done in order to gain personal profit. The person or body that receives the report may be internal to the organization (for example: a leader, safety deputy, elected employee representative), but may also be an external body or group of influence (for example: the police or other public authorities, media, or an environmental organization). Reporting about one's own exposure to workplace bullying, is NOT regarded as whistleblowing.

Respondents are *then* asked whether they would describe themselves as whistleblowers or not. Thus, the evaluation of whether the act that is reported is considered illegal, unethical and illegitimate is left to respondents in the respective countries where a study is conducted. Only thereafter is a list of specific wrongdoing types presented. The operational definition approach potentially improves the link between the theoretical definition and cultural perceptions of types of wrongdoing (on the difficulty of defining the type of wrongdoing that should be reported for one to consider a disclosure an act of whistleblowing, see Skivenes and Trygstad, Chapter 4). The drawback of this approach is that it is not clear whether respondents who do not label themselves as 'whistleblowers' are silent observers or non-observers. In order to calculate the prevalence of whistleblowing it is therefore important to include a measure of the total amount of wrongdoing observations made before the operational definition is presented.

Applying operational definitions across nations without any consideration or adjustment poses a threat to validity. If no adjustment is made (i.e., an etic approach), the underlying assumption is that the same operational definition can be applied universally, regardless of national or cultural context (Ryan *et al.* 1999). When culture is taken into consideration (i.e., an emic approach), Ryan and colleagues argue that the underlying assumption is that taking into account relevant characteristics of the national culture at the place of application is a prerequisite for achieving culture-appropriate measurement. However, this is *not* to say that the development of a new measure in each nation of application is recommended. What *is* recommended is to ensure that the measure intended for use is evaluated and found helpful in the nation of application before data are collected.

Measuring Intended Whistleblowing

Research on intended whistleblowing has applied a number of measures. One is the Whistleblowing Propensity Inventory (WPI). The WPI was developed by Keenan (1990), based on the questionnaires applied in the MSPB studies. In the WPI, respondents are asked whether they would 'feel personally obliged to report it' if they 'were to observe a dishonest or fraudulent activity' (Keenan 1995: 576). Examples of the ten types of fraudulent and wrongful activities provided are stealing funds or property, bribes and sexual harassment (Keenan 2000). Changes in terminology from the MSPB studies, which concerned federal employees, were made in order to 'reflect work environments of managers within the private sector' (Keenan 1990: 227). Items are introduced as measuring 'opinions and perceptions about organizational practices in regards to whistleblowing' and respondents are asked to indicate their intention to report on a scale from 1 (definitely no) to 5 (definitely yes) for each of the ten types of wrongdoing (Keenan 1995: 575–6).

Another way of measuring whistleblowing intent has been applied by Park and Blenkinsopp (2009). They measured whistleblowing intention by asking the question: 'If you found wrongdoing in your workplace, how hard would you try to do the following?' (Park and Blenkinsopp 2009: 549). This question was followed by eight items describing possible complaint recipients inside and outside the organization such as 'Report it to the appropriate authorities outside of the organization' (external whistleblowing) and 'Report it to the appropriate persons within the organization' (internal whistleblowing). For each of these items, participants were asked to indicate how hard they would try to report on a scale ranging from (1) 'not at all' to (5) 'very hard'.

Ellis and Arieli (1999) measured whistleblowing intent by presenting participants with three improper situations or scenarios. An example of the situation was the following: 'An officer in your brigade, above you in rank, gave a false report of amount of engine running-time during drills' (Ellis and Arieli 1999: 954). Participants were then asked about their whistleblowing intention, measured by the questions 'If you encountered this situation, would you report it?'. Intentions were to be indicated on a seven-point scale (–3 through 0 to +3).

Similarly, in a study of certified accountants, Liyanarachchi and Adler (2011) measured whistleblowing intent with the use of the propensity to blow the whistle instrument (PBW). In PBW, participants were first presented with three whistleblowing scenarios and subsequently asked how likely it was that the 'individual in each of the scenarios would blow the whistle' (Liyanarachchi and Adler 2011: 172). The response categories were on a seven-point Likert-type scale for each scenario. The authors then made a composite score of the participants' responses from the three scenarios. In contrast to the other measures of intentions described above which are focused on what the respondents themselves would do, Liyanarachchi and Adler's (2011) approach focused on what the respondents believed a third person (described in the scenarios) would do.

In a study by Brabeck (1984), 32 undergraduates first filled out the defining issues test (DIT).[1] Participants were told that the administrator, a graduate student, was collecting data for a study he was conducting. The task was to read an article, authored by a professor-investigator, and answer questions about it in a later test. Participants were then presented with different articles that contained errors. After a month, participants responded to the whistleblowing questions. Intended whistleblowing was measured by the amount of participants who reported on the designed errors in the article to the investigator in the trial. In another scenario study, Miceli, Dozier and Near (1991) measured intended whistleblowing by asking participants whether, during the study, they were asked to do anything they would consider objectionable. This question followed a staged situation where students had 'witnessed apparent wrongdoing by a research assistant' (Miceli, Dozier and Near 1991: 271).

In addition to either actual or intended whistleblowing, the World Online Whistleblowing Survey[2] investigates *public views* about whistleblowing, and among other things, asks participants who are members of an organization whether they would feel 'personally obliged to report it to someone' in their organization if they observed wrongdoing. Participants are asked to respond on a five-point scale ranging from (1) 'strongly disagree' to (5) 'strongly agree'.

To summarize, actual whistleblowing is typically measured by either the behavioral approach where the respondents indicate whether they have observed and reported various types of wrongdoing, or by the operational definition approach where respondents read a definition of whistleblowing and label themselves as whistleblowers or not. Intentions to blow the whistle have been measured by questions of whether the respondents would report specific types of wrongdoing (Keenan 1990; 2000) or report wrongdoing in general (Park and Blenkinsopp 2009), as well as by asking respondents to indicate how they themselves or a third person would behave in a hypothetical scenario (Ellis and Arieli 1999; Liyanarachchi and Adler 2011). In addition, it can also sometimes be difficult to categorize a study as focusing on *either* purely intended *or* actual reporting.

CORRELATES OF INTENDED AND ACTUAL WHISTLEBLOWING

Due to the variety of ways to approach whistleblowing in research, Mesmer-Magnus and Viswesvaran (2005) compared results from studies focusing on intentions with results from studies on actual reporting. One of the main findings from their meta-analysis was that 'the predictors of the intent to blow the whistle are not the same as those of actual whistleblowing' (Mesmer-Magnus and Viswesvaran 2005: 288). Moreover, the authors stated that many of the variables 'measured in studies of whistleblowing are stronger correlates of whistleblowing intent than of whistleblowing action' (2005: 288–9). Finally, they found that the very limited research on the relationship between intended and actual whistleblowing suggests that whistleblowing intentions are unrelated to actual whistleblowing. What do these findings imply? Are intended and actual whistleblowing different things? Are studies on intentions to blow the whistle uninformative when the goal is to understand whistleblowing in natural contexts? Before drawing such conclusions, we will take a closer look at methodological factors that may be central to understanding the divergent results.

To our knowledge, there are no published prospective field studies of whistleblowing, that is, studies in which the hypothesized predictors of blowing the whistle are measured at one point in time and actual whistleblowing is measured at a later time. Rather, field studies of whistleblowing have been cross-sectional and focused on asking managers and employees about their experiences (Miceli *et al.* 2008). In scenario studies, on the other hand, the hypothesized predictors are typically measured before the respondents engage with the scenario, or predictors are experimentally manipulated. In a simplified fashion, we can say that in existing field studies the predictors of whistleblowing are measured *after* the respondents have blown the whistle (or decided to remain silent) and in scenario studies the predictors are measured *before* the decision is made. We believe that this is crucial in interpreting the discrepancy between the correlates of intended and actual whistleblowing that Mesmer-Magnus and Viswesvaran (2005) described.

For some variables, the timing of measurement is not essential in interpretation. For example, demographics (sex, age, tenure, education, etc.) and basic personality traits that are quite stable in adulthood are not likely to change substantially during the whistleblowing process. When whistleblowers are found to be extroverted and report that they perceive themselves to be domineering in interpersonal interaction, more so than non-reporters (Bjørkelo *et al.* 2010), is it reasonable to believe that these traits predispose individuals to be proactive in the face of wrongdoing. It is unlikely that going through a whistleblowing process would make someone not previously extroverted, extroverted, or someone who perceives himself or herself as submissive, domineering in interpersonal interaction. It *is* however possible that the shape and composition of a person's 'normal profile' can stay the same but become elevated in stressful situations. Hypothetically, a person that has a profile characterized by extroversion and interpersonal dominance can, for instance, develop a more *peaked* profile (i.e., higher scores on these two dimensions) if they have been exposed to retaliation after they reported wrongdoing at work. Although *some* studies have investigated the relationship between individual whistleblowing and validated measures of personality (i.e., Bjørkelo *et al.* 2008), few if any have, to our knowledge until now, measured personality profiles with validated measures before and after a whistleblowing *and* a subsequent retaliatory process over time.

For other variables, the timing of measurement is essential in interpretation. For example, Mesmer-Magnus and Viswesvaran's meta-analysis suggests that threats of retaliation negatively impact on observers' intentions to blow the whistle, but that it is not related to actual whistleblowing. How can this be explained?

In Miceli and Near's (1984) study (which is included in the Mesmer-Magnus and Viswesvaran meta-study), respondents were asked (1) how confident they were that they would not be retaliated against if they were to report illegal or wasteful activities; and (2) how well the federal government protected employees who reported illegal or wasteful activities. The respondents were next asked to report (3) whether they had observed and reported such activities in the last year. This resulted in a classification of the respondents into groups of non-observers, inactive observers, internal whistleblowers (internal reporting exclusively) and external whistleblowers (predominately combined internal and external reporting). These four groups differed in their perceptions of whether they would be retaliated against, with externals perceiving the highest risk of retaliation, followed by inactive observers, internals and non-observers. Based on these findings, Miceli and Near (1984: 701) conclude that 'whistle-blowers were not more likely to perceive that a retaliatory climate existed than were inactive observers'.

Does this mean that threat of retaliation does *not* influence actual whistleblowers' decision to report? What the data *do* show is that peoples' experiences of having observed (or not observed) and reported (or not reported) *in the past* influence their *present* estimates of likely retaliation for hypothetical reporting. This does not necessarily inform us of how perceived likelihood of retaliation *weighed in on* the whistle-blowers' and inactive observers' decision at the time they decided to report or not. This implies that it is premature to conclude that a threat of retaliation is only a predictor of intentions to blow the whistle and not of actual whistleblowing.

Similarly, Mesmer-Magnus and Viswesvaran (2005) found differences in the relationship between job satisfaction and intended and actual whistleblowing. Whereas job satisfaction was unrelated to intentions to report, it was positively correlated with actual reporting (intent $r = -0.01$; actual $r = 0.19$). This finding implies that people's level of job satisfaction is not related to their evaluation of what they would do when faced with hypothetical wrongdoing. However, people who *have* blown the whistle (and remain with their organization) seem to be a bit more satisfied at work than those who did not blow the whistle. Because job satisfaction fluctuates in response to important events at work, these results are uninformative when it comes to understanding *how* a person's level of job satisfaction at the time when wrongdoing was observed and prior to making the decision to report/not report actually influenced their decision. As these examples illustrate, some of the apparent inconsistencies in the correlates of intent to report and actual reporting may be due to methodological rather than substantive issues.

FACTORS INFLUENCING THE PREDICTIVE VALIDITY OF INTENTIONS TO BLOW THE WHISTLE

The second issue raised by Mesmer-Magnus and Viswesvaran (2005) is that very few studies have linked intentions to blow the whistle with actual reporting. Mesmer-Magnus and Viswesvaran (2005) report that they found only two studies that included both a measure of intended and actual whistleblowing. The observed mean of the correlation between whistleblowing intent and actual whistleblowing was 0.05. Does this signify that whistleblowing intentions are unrelated to actual reporting? The empirical data are at this point too sparse to draw definite conclusions, but as intentions tend to be good predictors of behavior (Fishbein and Ajzen 2010), we believe it would be wise to consider some of the factors that may lead to an under-estimation of the relationship between whistleblowing intentions and behavior.

Although conceptually researchers are interested in predicting future behavior from intentions, it is not uncommon that a measure of intention is presented simultaneously with a measure of current or past behavior

(Fishbein and Ajzen 2010). For example, in a field study in a fast food restaurant setting, Victor *et al.* (1993) assessed an employee's intentions to report on peers who took or gave away an order of French fries, *and* at the same time asked respondents to indicate whether they had reported on this type of theft in the past year. This was one of the studies included in Mesmer-Magnus and Viswesvaran's (2005) analysis. The observed correlation between intentions to report and past reporting was $r = .18$ ($p < .05$). Aside from the possibility that this correlation may be attenuated due to the categorical nature of the whistleblowing variable, it is also possible that some of the respondents had experienced retaliation after previous reporting and thus would be less willing to report peer theft in the future. In fact, Zhang *et al.* (2009a) found, in a scenario study among bank employees, that those with previous personal experience with whistleblowing tended to have lower scores ($r = -.20$) on (hypothetical) intentions to report afterwards. We have not been able to locate any studies that have investigated the relationship between intentions to report (whether hypothetical or actual intentions) and *subsequent* actual reporting.

It is also important to consider differences between hypothetical and real situations (Fishbein and Ajzen 2010). Other cognitions (e.g., risk assessments) and emotions (e.g., fear, doubt) may become psychologically salient in real situations and change the intentions a person formed when contemplating a hypothetical situation. Being asked about one's general intentions to report wrongdoing, for instance, 'If you found wrongdoing in your workplace, how hard would you try to [report to different recipients]?' (Park and Blenkinsopp 2009: 549) is therefore likely less predictive of people's actual reporting at a later time, than intentions formed when one has actually observed wrongdoing and consider reporting in real life. For instance, MacNab and colleagues (2007a: 23) would argue that studies on whistleblowing intent are not assumed to evoke 'the type of real-world pressure faced by someone in an actual situation'.

Intentions may also change over time, and temporally unstable intentions are less likely to predict behavior (Fishbein and Ajzen 2010). At this point, the stability of observers' intentions to report, between when the initial intentions are formed and when the act of blowing the whistle is performed or the decision to remain silent is made, is not known. These factors pose a challenge in terms of deciding on an optimal time lag between the measurement of intentions to report and actual reporting. On the one hand, one could expect intentions to remain fairly stable over weeks or months after the decision to blow the whistle is made, if the observer is determined to report the wrongdoing and is just waiting for the right time and opportunity. On the other hand, one could argue that intentions to blow the whistle are likely to be unstable and change quickly in response to certain situations and external events (e.g., threat of retaliation and job loss). A decision-making process predominantly characterized as a 'choice-less choice' and a feeling of being 'compelled to act' has, for instance, previously been described by Alford (2001, 2007).

It seems clear that the intended–actual whistleblowing relationship is under-investigated in whistleblowing research and the research that exists is likely to under-estimate the relationship due to the timing of measurement (i.e., measuring intentions after reporting). In addition to an increased focus on methodological issues when trying to integrate research on whistleblowing intentions and behavior, we would like to propose that the reasoned action approach (Fishbein and Ajzen 2010) can serve as a useful integrative framework. The reasoned action approach has a long history from Fishbein's expectancy–value model, to the theory of reasoned action and the theory of planned behavior. We focus on Fishbein and Ajzen's most recent conceptualization as described in their 2010 book *Predicting and Changing Behavior: The Reasoned Action Approach.*

REASONED ACTION APPROACH

The central idea in the reasoned action approach is that human social behavior can be predicted by a set of core factors, namely, attitudes, perceived norms, perceived and actual behavioral control, and intentions.[3] *Attitudes* have their basis in behavioral beliefs, which are beliefs about the positive or negative consequences (i.e., costs and benefits) of performing the behavior in question. An attitude towards a specific behavior is the person's positive or negative evaluation of *personally* performing the behavior. *Perceived norms* have their basis in normative beliefs, which are people's beliefs about whether individuals or groups who are important to them (i.e., *referents*) would approve of their performing the behavior and whether these referents (would) perform the behavior themselves. Together, these normative beliefs create a perception of the normative pressures to perform or not perform the behavior in question. A person's *perceived behavioral control* finds its basis in control beliefs, which are beliefs about factors in the environment or personal factors that can help or impede performance of the behavior.

Together, a person's attitude towards a specific behavior, perceived norms regarding the behavior, and perceived control over the behavior inform the person's *intention* or readiness to perform the behavior. Actual performance of the behavior becomes more likely as the intention to perform it becomes stronger. However, this hinges on the condition that the person's perceived behavioral control accurately reflects his/her *actual control* (i.e., relevant skills and abilities, barriers and facilitating factors) over the behavior. Actual behavioral control therefore moderates the relationship between intentions and behavior. When perceived behavioral control matches actual behavioral control it also acts as a moderator between intentions and behavior (Fishbein and Ajzen 2010). In addition to these core components, a host of background factors can be incorporated into a reasoned action model to explain individual and contextual origins of the different beliefs underlying the behavior.

Interpretation of Whistleblowing Studies within the Reasoned Action Approach

The model of whistleblowing as pro-social organizational behavior proposes that when someone has identified an activity as wrongful (phase 1), experiences that it is not being corrected (phase 2), and decides that they have a responsibility to report and that whistleblowing is an available option (phase 3), the person weighs the potential cost and benefits of blowing the whistle as well as other options for action (see Miceli *et al.* 2008: 38 for an illustration of the model). It is primarily in this final stage of decision-making that the processes described by the reasoned action approach take place.

Some researchers have already employed a version of the reasoned action approach in the study of whistleblowing (Ellis and Arieli 1999; Oh and Teo 2010; Park and Blenkinsopp 2009). In a questionnaire study of South Korean police officers, Park and Blenkinsopp (2009) asked their respondents to indicate their (hypothetical) intentions to blow the whistle internally and externally if they were to observe wrongdoing at work. General attitudes to whistleblowing and subjective norms correlated with intentions to report both internally ($r = .37$ and $r = .42$, respectively), and externally ($r = .25$ and $r = .33$, respectively), and perceived behavioral control predicted intentions to report internally ($r = .28$).

Similarly, Ellis and Arieli (1999) asked general officers in the Israeli Defence Forces to report their (hypothetical) intentions to blow the whistle in three different scenarios and measured their general attitudes and subjective norms regarding reporting. They found that attitudes and norms correlated with intentions to report across scenarios ($r = .47$ to $.64$ and $r = .48$ to $.58$, respectively), but norms were the stronger predictor of intentions. What these studies demonstrate is that the reasoned action approach can be applied to intended whistleblowing. However, because they were focused on hypothetical scenarios they did not include a behavioral component (i.e., actual whistleblowing). This is a valuable point of entry for future research. In the following section we will describe the core constructs in the reasoned action approach in more detail and outline how existing whistleblowing research that did not have this theoretical starting point can be interpreted in light of the reasoned action model.

Behavioral Beliefs and Attitudes to Whistleblowing

An attitude to an object is determined by the strength of beliefs that the object has certain attributes and the positive/negative evaluation of those attributes (Fishbein and Ajzen 2010). In our context the object is the behavior of blowing the whistle, and the attributes can be, for example, ethicality ('whistleblowing is the right thing to do'), expected efficacy ('whistleblowing will terminate the wrongdoing'), and potential for retaliation ('whistleblowing is punished'). Beliefs regarding these and other attributes of whistleblowing may be held with varying strength. An observer of wrongdoing may strongly believe that blowing the whistle is the ethically right thing to do, but be less certain in her belief that it will be effective. Moreover, each attribute may be evaluated differently; stopping wrongdoing may have a strong positive evaluation, and being retaliated against a strong negative evaluation. This means that two observers of wrongdoing may hold an equally favorable attitude to reporting, but for different reasons.

Some of the predictors included in prior whistleblowing research constitute behavioral beliefs. For example, Chiu (2003) focused on the belief that whistleblowing is ethical. Others have included beliefs such as likelihood of protection from retaliation (Miceli and Near 1984); anticipated regret associated with whistleblowing versus remaining silent (Fredin 2011); and beliefs that reporting ethical concerns (whistleblowing) would result in being seen as a trouble-maker and snitch (Stansbury and Victor 2009).

In research where the reasoned action approach has been employed, a wider set of behavioral beliefs have been investigated. Ellis and Arieli (1999) listed between 15 and 21 behavioral outcomes for each of their scenarios. The beliefs were centered around organizational revenge or positive responses (e.g., 'My report will stand out as an educational example' and 'My periodical evaluation will be hurt'); the negative or positive influence of reporting on the opinions of others ('My status with my commanders will rise' and 'The brigade's soldiers and commanders will plot against me'); and positive and negative implications directly related to the job (e.g., 'The armoured military vehicle will be serviced according to its running time'). Similarly, Park and Blenkinsopp (2009) included behavioral beliefs such as that whistleblowing prevents harm to the organization and can lead to control of corruption.

Thus, organizational members tend to hold both positive and negative beliefs about reporting organizational wrongdoing. This could be a contributing factor to the rather weak relationships between separate behavioral beliefs and actual whistleblowing (see Mesmer-Magnus and Viswesvaran 2005; Miceli and Near 1984; Stansbury and Victor 2009). We propose that, in accordance with the reasoned action approach, the combination of *salient* beliefs regarding whistleblowing will be a better predictor of attitudes to whistleblowing, and subsequently intentions to blow the whistle and actual reporting, than *single* beliefs. This is consistent with the idea put forth by Miceli *et al.* (2008), that the final step in the decision-making process leading up to whistleblowing is an evaluation of the ratio of benefits versus costs of reporting, which is also described in actual whistleblowing cases (e.g., Bjørkelo 2010).

Normative Beliefs and Perceived Norms

Beyond beliefs about the pros and cons of blowing the whistle, an observer of organizational wrongdoing will also have normative beliefs pertaining to whistleblowing. In the reasoned action framework, norms are the 'perceived social pressure to perform (or not perform) a given behavior' (Fishbein and Ajzen 2010: 130). More specifically, there are two types of perceived norms: perceptions of what important others think one should do (injunctive norms) and perceptions of what others actually do (descriptive norms). Injunctive normative beliefs pertaining to whistleblowing can be based on what other organizational members such as colleagues and supervisors would expect (e.g., 'My boss would expect me to report this') whereas descriptive normative beliefs can be based on what similar others do (e.g., 'I know that my colleagues have reported previously in similar situations'). Beyond giving information about what others do, descriptive norms inform us what is likely to be an effective and adaptive action. Referring to work by Cialdini, Fishbein and Ajzen (2010: 132) state that:

> [I]n addition to the direct effect of descriptive norms on intentions described earlier, descriptive norms can also have indirect effects. We often have information about the behavior of others that goes beyond simply registering what they are doing. First, we may note that their behavior is rewarded or

> punished by others, and this information can influence attitudes toward the behavior as well as lead to the inference that the behavior is prescribed or proscribed (injunctive norm). Second, we may learn that the behavior leads to other positive or negative outcomes, again affecting attitudes, and third, we may learn that certain resources are required and certain barriers have to be overcome to perform the behavior. The latter would influence perceptions of behavioral control.

The normative perspective has been included in existing whistleblowing research mainly by the focus on organizational climate for whistleblowing which has been found to be related to both whistleblowing intentions and actual reporting (Mesmer-Magnus and Viswesvaran 2005). Rothwell and Baldwin (2007b) looked at whistleblowing in the police, ethical climate and five forms of misconduct. Team climate was measured with Victor and Cullen's (1988) typology of ethical climates and consists of 'self-interest, company profit or efficiency, friendship or team interest, social responsibility, personal morality, rules or standard operating procedures, and law and professional code' (Rothwell and Baldwin 2007b: 343). The results indicate that a friendship or team climate (a type of perceived norms) generally explains the willingness to report wrongdoing at work, but not actual whistleblowing frequency.

In a study of 6,000 workers, Trygstad (2010) found that organizational climate influences whether employees dare to report wrongdoing at work and experience protection against retaliation. Therefore whistleblowing is 'not purely an individual-level phenomenon' but depends on the level of ethical culture at the workplace (Zhang *et al.* 2009a: 643). A healthy organizational culture is also found to be associated with a greater *willingness* to report wrongdoing at work (Kaptein 2011). Thus, in relation to the reasoned action approach, we would propose that organizational cultures or climates are background factors that influence employees' perceived norms regarding whistleblowing.

Control Beliefs and Perceived Behavioral Control

Similar to the way behavioral beliefs inform attitudes to whistleblowing, beliefs about internal and external factors that may help or hinder performance of a behavior inform a person's perceived control over the behavior. Control beliefs may be based on previous personal experiences, second-hand information (e.g., observations of co-workers' experiences) as well as other factors that influence one's perceived ability to perform the behavior. More specifically, perceived behavioral control is a function of the strength of salient beliefs about control factors combined with the perceived power of each factor in helping or impeding performance

(Fishbein and Ajzen 2010). For example, an observer of wrongdoing may believe that information about the correct procedure for internal reporting is readily available to him, and that this makes reporting somewhat easier. At the same time, he may be convinced that blowing the whistle requires him to present the evidence in an assertive manner and that this makes reporting difficult. Descriptions of actual whistleblowing cases have shown that the existence and awareness of reporting procedures is not necessarily associated with an effective whistleblowing experience (e.g., one that stops wrongdoing) or whistleblower protection (e.g., Monsen 2008).

Various variables have been included that measure characteristics thought to reflect control or power in the whistleblowing situation, such as tenure, age, job level, pay grade and supervisor status (Miceli *et al.* 2008; Skivenes and Trygstad 2010a). When relationships between these variables and intended or actual whistleblowing are found to be significant, they suggest that whistleblowers are more powerful than those who did not blow the whistle (Miceli *et al.* 2008). For example, Mesmer-Magnus and Viswesvaran (2005) found that job level was positively related to both intended and actual whistleblowing. These findings are replicated in recent research: Bjørkelo and colleagues found that respondents holding a leadership position or who were union or Health, Safety and Environment (HSE) representatives were more likely to report wrongdoing at work (Bjørkelo *et al.* 2011). In Norway, for instance, all organizations must have HSE representatives and employ HSE reporting systems to report general mistakes or deviation from established standards of operation (Bull, Riise and Moen 2002). Similarly, Rothwell and Baldwin (2007b) found that supervisory status was a consistent predictor of both willingness and frequency of whistleblowing. With respect to age and tenure, Stansbury and Victor (2009) found that young and short-tenured employees were less likely to have blown the whistle. From a reasoned action perspective this makes sense, because employees' job level and similar variables should be related to their control beliefs as well as reflect their actual behavioral control.

Also, many of the personality or individual difference variables investigated in prior whistleblowing research are related to control, such as internal locus of control, self-esteem, proactive personality, extrovert character and interpersonal dominance (Bjørkelo *et al.* 2010; Miceli *et al.* 2008; Miceli *et al.* 2012). There is evidence that whistleblowers are more extroverted, dominant and disposed to be proactive than their non-whistleblowing colleagues (Bjørkelo *et al.* 2010; Miceli *et al.* 2012). What is interesting to note is that in the study by Miceli and colleagues (2012), a more direct measure of perceived control in the whistleblowing situation (perceived leverage in the situation) was a stronger predictor of actual whistleblowing (odds ratio 2.34, 95% CI = [1.89, 2.90]) than the dispositional variable of proactive personality (odds ratio 1.43, 95% CI = [1.18, 1.74]). Interpreted in light of the reasoned action framework, this could suggest that *dispositional* aspects of control (e.g., proactive personality) can be thought of as distal background factors influencing employees' control beliefs and perceived behavioral control in the specific whistleblowing situation; these in turn are more *proximal* antecedents of actual whistleblowing. The same argument can be applied to power-related demographical variables.

FUTURE DIRECTIONS

Ideally, the methods used for providing knowledge should depend on the research aims. In this way, aims of study would determine whether to study intended or actual whistleblowing. Studies of factors that influence intentions (through attitudes, norms, control and underlying beliefs) are informative; however, when the situation changes, so do attitudes and norms. It is therefore important to include attitudinal, normative and control variables along with intent, actual, contextual and other individual difference variables.

An ideal design would be to survey a very large sample of employees and identify those who are witnessing (or have recently witnessed) wrongdoing at work, but have not yet decided whether or not to act. These observers could be asked to indicate their attitudes towards reporting the wrongdoing, their subjective norms regarding reporting, perceived control over reporting, and intentions to report. After a period of time, the observers would be surveyed again at one or more occasions to assess actual whistleblowing. It is commonly argued that it is extremely difficult to collect longitudinal data from the same set of individuals on whistleblowing because of issues related to anonymity (Mesmer-Magnus and Viswesvaran 2005; Miceli *et al.* 2008). We agree that it is difficult; however, it is not impossible.

The Bergen Bullying Research Group at the University of Bergen, Norway, has conducted a three-wave longitudinal survey that included questions about whistleblowing along with other sensitive topics such as bullying, workplace conflict, sexual harassment and health.[4] The data collection was managed by Statistics Norway, the Norwegian National Bureau of Statistics. Statistics Norway has access to all inhabitants' personal identification numbers (NO), which correspond to peoples' national insurance number (UK) or social security number (US). The respondents were informed that (1) the survey was performed in accordance with Norwegian laws and regulations; (2) Statistics Norway was subject to the control of the Norwegian Data Protection Authority as well as their own Ombudsman for the protection of privacy in research; (3) the survey was approved by the Regional Ethics Committee for research; (4) it would not be known outside Statistics Norway what individuals had responded to the survey and that staff at Statistics Norway were bound by legal confidentiality; (5) the researchers would receive anonymous data; and (6) the identifying information would be completely deleted after the final wave. The response rate was 56.4 per cent in the first wave and 70 per cent in the second wave (Berthelsen *et al.* 2008; Nielsen *et al.* 2012). A third wave has also been conducted but has not been described in a public report as yet.[5] These numbers suggest that it is not unlikely that participants in some situations and nations will be willing to respond, even when the topic is sensitive and remaining completely anonymous is not possible. In order to conduct such a research design anonymity is crucial, particularly when responses need to be matched across time. This can be solved with a unique respondent-generated code. Further, there are available guidelines for constructing questionnaires to measure the components of the reasoned action approach.

CONCLUSIONS

One of the main recommendations from the 1996 review of the whistleblowing field was the importance of 'scholars in all fields to acknowledge the existence of the whistle-blowing myths and the misinformation that perpetuates them, as well as opportunities for interdisciplinary cooperation in investigating the whistle-blowing phenomenon' (Near and Miceli 1996: 523). We would also like to draw attention to the recommendation from the review by Mesmer-Magnus and Viswesvaran (2005: 295): 'To advance our understanding of this field, we need to explore and enumerate the processes that occur between the time wrongdoing is witnessed and when actual whistleblowing occurs'. We would like to join these recommendations and contribute to the way whistleblowing is investigated globally. Developing measures that can be applied across countries is one important task for future research, as it will allow for comparisons across cultural contexts and ease interpretation of findings. Furthermore, research on intended and actual whistleblowing needs to be integrated in order to understand when and how intentions to report wrongdoing turn into whistleblowing (action). As we have argued, one way to do this is by applying the theoretical framework of reasoned action. This framework specifically addresses the link between intent and actual behavior and has documented well the predictive effect of intentions on behavior (Augoustinos and Walker 1999). A reasoned action approach can also serve to integrate our understanding of more distal antecedents of whistleblowing, such as organizational climates and individual differences, into a coherent theoretical framework.

NOTES

1. The DIT was developed by Rest based on the work by Kohlberg on moral reasoning (Rest *et al.* 2000). The aim of the DIT is to understand and predict moral behavior (Marnburg 2001). The regular version of the DIT consists of six ethical dilemmas that are followed by 12 items that represent issues that can be considered in the decision-making process (Rest *et al.* 1997). The participant is then asked to rate 'each item in terms of how important it is, and then rank the most important items (the top four ranks)' (Rest *et al.* 1997: 500).
2. See https://whistleblowingsurvey.org (Brown *et al.* 2012; Brown, Vandekerckhove and Dreyfus 2014).
3. For a model and illustration of the theory see http://people.umass.edu/aizen/tpb.diag.html.
4. See Berthelsen *et al.* (2008) and www.uib.no/rg/bbrg/.
5. Personal communication, S. Einarsen, September 2012.

7. Whistleblowing and power

Kim Loyens and Jeroen Maesschalck

INTRODUCTION

Whistleblowing is a complex phenomenon that is inextricably linked to power relations within organizations. This results from organizational power relationships often being asymmetric and dynamic (Pfeffer and Salancik 1978). Staff members who decide to blow the whistle mostly lack the authority to change organizational misbehavior in any other way and therefore have to rely on informal bases of power (Elliston 1982; Weinstein 1979; Near and Miceli 1985).

This informal power should, however, not be under-estimated. Whistleblowers who are not heard within their organization might turn to external reporting channels, possibly leading to bad publicity and other damage for the organization (Parmerlee *et al.* 1982). Moreover, whistleblowers who decide to exit the organization take with them knowledge and experience that are valuable for the organization. The latter can be linked to the resource dependence theory, which states that resources are controlled by some parties and that other parties depend on these resources (Pfeffer and Salancik 1978). Miceli and Near (2002: 458) explain that whistleblowers who possess 'unique skills, secrets, or other resources the organization needs and cannot easily replace' can more effectively blow the whistle because the organization is dependent on them. In that sense, whistleblowing has also been called a political action (Farrell and Petersen 1982) in which dependent actors in an organization reverse their dependency by challenging actors with authority to deal with organizational misbehavior (Near and Miceli 1985). Dependent actors then aim at a redistribution of power or benefits within the organization (Farrell and Petersen 1982; Cavanagh *et al.* 1981).

Actors with authority, however, partly counteract this reversal or redistribution of power by (threatening) retaliations against whistleblowers, such as deliberately depriving them of their credibility or finding ways to make them leave the organization. Staff members can, however, sometimes also rely on formal sources of power, such as labor unions. Skivenes and Trygstad (2010a: 1080) argue that employee representation is an important power resource in organizations. Union representatives can influence decision-making, help employees to deal with internal conflicts and even stop illegal behavior. Linked to whistle-blowing, labor unions can raise matters of concern and protect whistle-blowers against reprisals.

Research on the link between whistleblowing and power has mostly focused on 'power games' or 'power shifts' between those who blow the whistle and those against whom the whistle is blown. Both individual (often informal) power and collective power (e.g., through labor unions) of whistleblowers are then addressed. Several authors have applied power theories to whistleblowing and tested numerous hypotheses that result from it.

First, Miceli and Near (2002) found evidence in three quantitative studies of the impact of position power on the effectiveness of whistle-blowing. Particularly, their analysis led to the conclusion that when whistleblowing is role-prescribed – or is, in other words, part of the formal job description of the whistleblower – the reporting act is more effective. This results from the fact that these whistleblowers 'are ostensibly acting within their authority' (Miceli and Near 2002: 458). They link this finding to the minority influence theory (Moscovici 1976), which states that individuals with an opinion that deviates from the majority will be more influential when they are considered 'more credible, confident, competent and objective' (Miceli and Near 2002: 458). Role-prescribed whistleblowers have more credibility than persons whose job descriptions do not include whistleblowing and will thus be more influential. Along the same lines, Miceli and Near (2002) found that using internal reporting channels is more effective when staff members blow the whistle by informing complaint recipients who are officially designated to receive reports of wrongdoing. This can be explained by the fact that the latter often have a high status in the organization as a result of their legitimate authority or expert power (French and Raven 1959). This finding can be linked to the official role of union representatives as recipients of concerns (Skivenes and Trygstad 2010a).

Secondly, Hopman and van Leeuwen (2009) studied inter-group whistleblowing, in which misbehavior of another group is reported within or outside one's own group. In two experiments, they learned that negative information about another group can enhance the standing of one's own group. However, this was only the case when one's own group had a lower status than the other group. Reporting the misbehavior that had occurred in the other group was then considered a means to put one's own group in a better light. However, when part of a higher status group, it was considered more beneficial to reprimand the other (lower status) group, because by doing so one's own higher status was reinforced.

This chapter aims at broadening the perspective of the current whistleblowing literature by opening the lens to other types of research opportunities into the power aspect of whistleblowing. It proposes three ways in which the research agenda of whistleblowing studies can be extended and enriched. For this, inspiration will be drawn from other disciplines and theoretical traditions. The first part of the chapter discusses the idea of considering whistleblowing decision-making a dichotomy, in which organizational members can choose between reporting or keeping silent, that is typical for most whistleblowing studies (Teo and Caspersz 2011). Broadening this perspective could lead to identifying other types of responses to reporting dilemmas, thus enriching the whistleblowing literature, as also argued elsewhere in this book (for example Olsen, Chapter 8, on the measurement of 'inaction' as against silence).

The second part looks at the theme of 'locus of control', which has been given much attention in whistleblowing studies that deal with the role of power. The variable 'locus of control' is said to have strong explanatory power in the sense that it often plays a crucial role in decision-making processes in reporting dilemmas. However, research seems to have neglected the impact of context in 'locus of control' explanations for whistleblowing. We will argue that this issue can, at least partly, be solved by integrating the classic whistleblowing literature with what will be described as the 'causal mechanism' approach. Arguably, certain causal mechanisms could provide insight into the relationship between context and 'locus of control'.

The third part addresses the lack of explanatory complexity in whistleblowing studies. This can be illustrated with at least two examples. First, whistleblowing studies often overlook the fact that the decision to report cannot be explained by simply reversing the explanations for the decision to keep silent. This can be illustrated by referring to the common explanation for keeping silent, which is the fact that observers of wrongdoing consider the risks of retaliation by the organization to be too high (Miceli *et al.* 1999). This finding leads some researchers to argue that whistleblower protection might encourage reporting, because it removes the main motive for keeping silent. This is, however, not necessarily the case, because explanations for the occurrence of behavior are not just the reverse of explanations for the non-occurrence of behavior. Hence, researchers should look for asymmetrical explanations for decision-making in reporting dilemmas. Secondly, most studies aim at finding a single model to explain reporting decisions, while in reality different causal pathways could lead to the decision to report and different causal pathways could lead to the decision to keep silent. Therefore, more research is needed that identifies these various (and often incompatible) causal pathways.

MOVING BEYOND THE CLASSIC WHISTLEBLOWING/SILENCE DICHOTOMY

Most whistleblowing studies attempt to explain why staff members decide to blow the whistle on organizational misbehavior, or why they do not. This approach seems to imply a dichotomy in whistleblowing decision-making of 'reporting' versus 'keeping silent'. This dichotomous approach can, at least partly, be explained by the dominance of quantitative methods in whistleblowing studies, and particularly surveys, in which variables are often dichotomized. Moreover, these studies typically focus on (antecedents of) reporting or the lack thereof, and not on (antecedents of) other types of responses to reporting dilemmas (Teo and Caspersz 2011). In practice, however, responses to whistleblowing dilemmas are more varied. Staff members who observe misbehavior in their organization could, for example, also decide to reprimand misbehaving colleagues or to gossip about it with other staff members. Because reality is thus more complex than the classic dichotomy, research is needed to describe and explain these alternative responses to observed misbehavior. Arguably, this could be achieved by using qualitative methods like in-depth interviews (Vandekerckhove 2006) and ethnographic techniques (Loyens 2012a) that seem particularly useful to study the wide array of possible responses to observed misconduct and thus enable the study of real-life behavior.

Whistleblowing can be considered a form of resistance in the workplace, next to other forms of resistance, such as sabotage, foot-dragging and work-avoidance strategies (Mansbach 2011; Elliston 1982). However, researchers rarely focus on these other forms of resistance to organizational misbehavior in empirical studies. Miceli and Near (1992: 33) acknowledge that whistleblowing is only one possible response to observed misbehavior in the array of many alternatives. Inspired by Graham's typology of responses to organizational decline (1986), they refer to responses such as sabotage, strike, secret sharing and confrontation with the wrongdoer. However, most of their empirical work does not incorporate these alternatives, but rather bundles them under the general category of 'silence', as opposed to 'whistleblowing' (Miceli and Near 1992).

Only a few attempts have been made to address these other responses to organizational misbehavior in empirical research. Teo and Caspersz (2011) start from the observation that the dichotomous perspective is central in academic research as well as in whistleblowing policies and legislation. They argue that the whistleblowing/silence dichotomy can be considered a social construction that controls staff members as a form of 'discourse' in the Foucauldian meaning. Foucault (1980) defines 'discourse' as the point of intersection between bodies of knowledge and disciplinary practices in which the latter refer to instruments of social control. The whistleblowing/silence dichotomy is then an instrument of social control that 'limits the possibilities of alternative employee pro-social behavior that may present and rectify organizational wrongdoing' (Teo and Caspersz 2011: 240). In other words, powerful actors in an organization formulate the top-down expectation that staff members who observe wrongdoing should either report it or keep silent. Because the act of whistleblowing is risky (Miceli *et al.* 1999), many staff members choose the 'silence' option, which is often in the best interest of powerful actors in the organization.

Teo and Caspersz (2011) add that staff members who feel restrained by the whistleblowing/silence dichotomy sometimes try to resist it by looking for alternative responses that are considered less risky than reporting, but nevertheless enable them to show their disapproval for the misbehavior. Their qualitative study leads to the identification of four types of resistance against misbehavior beyond the classic dichotomy: the use of code names, sarcasm, jokes and gossip (Teo and Caspersz 2011: 244–6), all of which are ways to try to impact organizational misbehavior with a reduced risk of retaliation. The results show that, although these informal types of conversation on the surface often serve the purpose of keeping mutual relations light-hearted and creating a fun atmosphere, they could be rather effective in impacting organizational misbehavior. This is illustrated in the following quote expressed by a middle-level seniority employee in a small financial services organization (Teo and Caspersz 2011: 245):

> I have had problems with someone coming in consistently late in the past, and it's affected morning procedures … After a while, I'd just start looking at my watch and say, 'did you forget to set the alarm then?'. She realized that I had been noticing when she was coming in late, and it stopped almost straight away.

Similarly, Teo and Caspersz (2011: 246) argue that gossiping about co-workers' lack of work discipline could be an effective form of resistance to organizational misbehavior, in the sense that it makes other staff members comply with the organizational procedures, because they are aware that next time the gossip could as well be about them. Hence, while the whistleblowing/silence dichotomy reinforces top-down control of supervisors, these informal responses to organizational wrongdoing seem to encourage informal control among co-workers.

Increasingly, not only management and co-workers, but also citizens and customers control staff members' behavior. This becomes clear in the 'glass cage' metaphor that has, at least partly, replaced the Weberian 'iron cage' metaphor (Gabriel 2008). Weber's 'iron cage' (1922) refers to a bureaucracy that controls everything through rational procedures, rules and processes. Several authors have argued that this idea of a rigid, rational and predictable organization is no longer sustainable, as a result of the current emphasis on consumer power.[1] Gabriel (2008: 310–11) proposes the 'glass cage' as an alternative, by which he refers to 'the consumer as the measure of all things, ... who seeks not merely the useful and the functional, but the magical, the fantastic, and the alluring'. This 'glass cage' shares characteristics of Foucault's Panopticon (1977) in the sense that surveillance is omnipresent in different forms, such as electronic, spatial, psychological and cultural control measures. The latter is related to the notion of 'ideal control' in which managers try to change organizational cultures by encouraging staff members to internalize organizational values, views and ideas as their own (Cobb *et al.* 2001). Because of an obsession for transparency in 'glass cage' organizations, staff members are constantly exposed to the 'customer's critical gaze' (Gabriel 2008: 313), whose demands for good customer service, quality and customer friendliness are internalized as 'a force of self-control and self-policing'.

Moreover, this customer as critical observer puts staff members in a powerful position. Because in a 'glass cage' everything staff members do is transparent for the critical customer, staff members can embarrass managers in the presence of the public, just like children can embarrass their parents in the presence of strangers (Fleming 2005). Hence, the 'glass cage' puts staff members into a position in which they can restrict managers' power to control them. This type of organization is, for example, extremely vulnerable to whistleblowing, because this act reveals weaknesses and shortcomings of the organization which highly depends on the positive assessment of consumers (Gabriel 2008). However, there are also other ways in which staff members in 'glass cage' organizations can express resistance, such as responding to managerial ideas with cynicism or amusement (Jermier *et al.* 1994; Sturdy 1998; Gabriel 1999). This has been referred to as 'resistance through distance', because it aims at sidestepping managerial control instead of confronting it (Collinson 1994). A more direct form of engaging with managerial ideas are verbal subversions of management control (Kunda 1991), which has been referred to as a means of resistance to ideal control (Cobb *et al.* 2001). Thus, while the intrusive 'glass cage' control measures seem to succeed better than the 'iron cage' in limiting individuals' privacy in organizations, their pervasive and invasive character offers various new options for staff members to exercise resistance against managerial control. Because these can be highly effective in putting managerial discourses in a bad light, disagreeing staff members who threaten to use them might regain some power.

In ethnographic research by Loyens (2013) on ethical decision-making in labor inspections and police agencies, alternative ways of dealing with whistleblowing dilemmas were also explicitly looked for. This study identified two ways in which labor inspectors and police officers reacted to organizational misbehavior. First, respondents sometimes openly discussed unethical behavior of co-workers in the presence of other team members and of the co-worker in question as a form of resistance to the highly individualistic culture in the organization. This culture was particularly linked to the system of 'case officer' in which each inspector or detective is responsible for his/her own investigations, and therefore does not accept criticism from co-workers. Secondly, respondents sometimes decided to reprimand their colleague to try and change their behavior, which is a less drastic option than the former one. These findings show the importance of informal control in whistleblowing dilemmas, as has also been found by Teo and Caspersz (2011).

Alternative responses to organizational wrongdoing have also been studied in the 'Whistling While They Work' project in Australian public sector agencies (Brown 2008). In a quantitative survey among 7,663 public officials from 118 public agencies across four Australian jurisdictions (i.e., Commonwealth, New South Wales, Queensland and Western Australia), not only the reporting and non-reporting rates were examined, but also the 'middle solution' in which staff members decided not to report the misbehavior because other action was taken (Brown, Mazurski and Olsen 2008: 47). The latter includes alternative formal or informal responses to organizational wrongdoing. The average reporting rate in each of the four jurisdictions varied from 49.7 per cent to 54.8 per cent, but as many as 15.2 per cent to 19.8 per cent decided to deal with the matter themselves in an alternative way. Discussion of the significance of this for measuring 'inaction rates',[2] rather than reporting or non-reporting rates, is continued by Olsen in Chapter 8 of this book.

It might be useful for future research to combine such quantitative observations with additional qualitative research to gain more insight into which alternative responses the respondents used exactly. Particularly interesting in the Australian study is the fact that the reporting results were refined by asking whether the respondents considered the wrongdoing either 'very' or 'extremely' serious (Brown, Mazurski and Olsen 2008: 47). Although this approach is useful to eliminate all those cases that on the respondents' own view might not have been serious enough to warrant reporting, it also implies a risk. The ethnographic study of Loyens (2012a) showed that under particular conditions, police officers or labor inspectors also reported less serious incidents. In highly competitive organizations, respondents reported minor cases of misbehavior to stay on good terms with their supervisor. In organizations with a highly unpredictable manager, respondents reported less serious misbehavior to avoid being considered complicit and thus avoid a potential disproportionately high sanction. By not including less serious cases, these types of whistleblowing are neglected.

In conclusion, the classic whistleblowing/silence dichotomy does not seem to capture all possible responses to the reporting dilemma. Staff members sometimes also use other means to resist organizational misbehavior, such as gossiping, making jokes, using sarcasm or cynicism, reprimanding and openly discussing wrongdoing. Hence, particularly staff members who lack the formal power to impact organizational misbehavior can rely on other sources of (informal) power to show their disagreement. Qualitative studies that use in-depth interviewing and ethnographic methods could provide more insight into why and how staff members use these alternative sources of power, thus broadening the classic whistleblowing/silence dichotomy. The prevalence of these alternative responses could then be studied in quantitative survey research, as was done in the Australian 'Whistling While They Work' project (Brown 2008).

INTRODUCING THE CAUSAL MECHANISM APPROACH IN WHISTLEBLOWING STUDIES

As explained above, various researchers applied theories of power and dependency to the topic of whistleblowing. Particularly interesting is the theory of planned behavior, which states that individuals will refrain from performing certain behaviors if they feel they are not in control of the situation and the likely outcome (Ajzen 1991). This idea is linked to Rotter's theory of locus of control (1966). The latter is considered an individual characteristic that refers to the extent to which individuals believe they are in control of the outcome of their behavior. Individuals with an internal locus of control believe they are largely in control of situations they engage in. Individuals with an external locus of control believe that fate, luck or chance have more impact on the outcomes of their behavior than they themselves do.

Near and Miceli (1985) suggest that locus of control is an important explanatory factor for whistleblowing decisions. Internal locus of control individuals would consider whistleblowing to be an opportunity to influence malpractices they do not normally control, while external locus of control individuals would view the malpractices as being controlled by powerful actors whom they cannot stop. The former are also expected to downplay the likelihood of retaliation, while the latter might exaggerate the risks. This leads to the hypothesis that 'individuals who have internal loci of control might blow the whistle when their external locus of control counterparts would not' (Chiu 2003: 67). The impact of 'locus of control' on reporting organizational misbehavior is suggested by various researchers (e.g., Farrell and Petersen 1982; Dozier and Miceli 1985; Near and Miceli 1985), but only confirmed in a few empirical studies that examine antecedents of whistleblowing intentions (Chiu 2003; Curtis and Taylor 2009). Other studies failed to find a significant relationship between 'locus of control' and whistleblowing decision-making (Miceli *et al.* 1991; Starkey 1998; Oh and Teo 2010), which could be explained by the fact that the decision to report may vary according to the situation or the context (Wise 1995).

In the literature, not so much attention has been given to the combined impact of 'locus of control' and contextual variables. It would be interesting to address the question whether contextual factors might have an impact on the effect a staff member's locus of control has on his behavior. The leadership style that supervisors apply might, for example, strengthen or weaken the impact of locus of control on staff members' behavior. Arguably, staff members with an external locus of control might feel more in control among supervisors who apply a participative leadership style than among supervisors who are perceived to be very dominant and authoritative. Jones and Kavanagh (1996) conducted an experimental study that focused on the combined impact of locus of control and other contextual variables, such as peer influence, managerial influence and quality of work experience. Although they did not find any interaction effects between locus of control and these other variables, it would be interesting to conduct more such research. Particularly significant in this respect is the cross-cultural study of Cherry (2006), comparing ethical judgments (i.e., attitude towards bribes) of American and

Taiwanese business persons. He found that 'locus of control' varies according to national culture, applying Hofstede's theory of culture (1980).

The literature review above indicates that the impact of 'locus of control' on behavior can be influenced by contextual factors. Therefore, more research is needed concerning the combined impact of individual and contextual factors on whistleblowing. Inspiration for this type of research can be drawn from the causal mechanism approach. The fundamental ambition of this approach is to provide insight into the 'black box' between two variables of which the correlation has been determined. What is really at work between those two variables? Which causal mechanisms, if any, explain the impact of the independent on the dependent variable, and under which situational conditions do they occur (Hedström and Swedberg 1998; Mayntz 2004)? By doing so, this approach aims at developing deeper, more fine-grained and more fully integrated theories that can explain how and under which conditions certain factors impact behavior. Applied to the topic of whistleblowing, the causal mechanism approach aims at explaining how organizational and individual variables impact decision-making and how this impact varies according to situational conditions. This concurs with Edwards's argument that research on whistleblowing should aim at gaining 'deeper, more comprehensive understanding of the psychological processes underlying decision-making' (Edwards 2008: 1).

We believe that causal mechanisms, not only from psychology (as Edwards suggests) but also from other disciplines (such as sociology and criminology), could enrich the current whistleblowing literature. Research on reporting dilemmas could either study the impact of causal mechanisms that have already been identified in other disciplines or look for new, more specified causal mechanisms; as for the latter, exploratory and ethnographic research could be conducted to identify specific causal mechanisms to explain whistleblowing. As for existing mechanisms in the literature, the theory of moral disengagement that identifies eight cognitive mechanisms (Bandura 1990) could be applied to the topic of whistleblowing. The basic argument of the moral disengagement theory is that individuals use cognitive mechanisms to reframe their behavior in ways that downplay their ethical content or moral implications. Specifically, this theory states that individuals restructure their behavior by cognitions that make their actions appear worthy, not harmful, or by minimizing personal responsibility. By doing so, individuals release themselves from feelings of guilt that would ensue from violating certain standards, making it easier and more acceptable (at least in one's own perception) to behave in a questionable way (Detert *et al.* 2008: 375).

The theory distinguishes between eight cognitive mechanisms that are classified in three main types (Moore 2008: 130): (1) cognitive restructuring of one's actions so they appear less harmful (i.e., moral justification, euphemistic labeling, advantageous comparison); (2) minimizing one's role in the harm that is caused by one's actions (i.e., displacement of responsibility and diffusion of responsibility); and (3) reframing the effects of one's actions (i.e., distortion of consequences, dehumanization, attribution of blame to the victim). An important assumption of the moral disengagement theory is that, although the mechanisms it proposes operate at the individual level, they are not considered stable personality traits. Rather, moral disengagement is conceptualized as a cognitive orientation to the world that is influenced by social contexts in an interactive relationship between personal and social influences (Bandura 2002). It is considered 'a result of the continued reciprocal influences of the individual on his or her environment and vice versa, rather than a measure of the "bad apple"-ness of an individual' (Moore 2008: 131). Sometimes situational aspects or organizational factors can even 'override' individual values and compel people to engage in actions they would otherwise not take part in (Moore 2008: 131). Furthermore, moral disengagement is considered context dependent, meaning that it is more likely to occur in some situations than others and that different cognitive mechanisms will operate in different situations (Moore 2008: 131). This context dependency makes moral disengagement mechanisms particularly suitable to study the link between individual, organizational and contextual variables in whistleblowing.

Several researchers have applied moral disengagement mechanisms in whistleblowing studies. Berry (2004) refers to the mechanism of 'diffusion of responsibility' when she explains that employees use the argument 'Why should I get involved? After all, I am not the only one aware of what is going on here' (Berry 2004: 6) so as not to have to blow the whistle. In her ethnographic study, Loyens (2012a) uses moral disengagement theory to explain the link between organizational factors and reporting behavior. She found that in organizations with strong hierarchical oversight, respondents more likely reported misbehavior of their colleagues to their supervisor than responding to it themselves. Because they considered themselves, at least partly, responsible for taking some action against the colleague's misbehavior, their conscience troubled them. Therefore, they tried to free themselves from feelings of guilt by actively displacing responsibility for the misbehavior to their supervisor. However, in performance-oriented environments, characterized by colleagues needing each other to get results, the cover up of misbehavior was often justified by minimizing the consequences of the misbehavior

(Loyens 2012a). Such mechanisms of 'moral disengagement' are related to 'locus of control' but also emphasize the interaction effect between psychological factors and contextual variables.

In conclusion, the causal mechanism approach emphasizes that causal mechanisms are context bound, in the sense that they are triggered by a specific set of contextual conditions (Pawson and Tilley 1997). Introducing this approach in whistleblowing studies would thus emphasize the context dependency of whistleblowing behavior, more so than the current state of affairs.

TOWARDS EXPLANATORY COMPLEXITY

Whistleblowing research also seems to suffer from a lack of explanatory complexity. Two examples can illustrate this point. First, whistleblowing studies often provide symmetrical explanations for both the decision to report and the decision to keep silent, while explanations for the occurrence and non-occurrence of behavior are often asymmetrical. Secondly, most whistleblowing studies (particularly when quantitative methods are used) try to identify a single model that can explain decision-making in reporting dilemmas under different circumstances. However, as a result of the empirical complexity of social life, decisions to report can often be explained by different (and incompatible) causal pathways. Arguably, the whistleblowing literature would benefit from studies that capture these kinds of explanatory complexities.

The first problem probably results from the fact that most research on whistleblowing aims at explaining the act of reporting and not the act of keeping silent. By doing so, explanations for the decision to keep silent are largely overlooked. The small number of studies that specifically aim to explain the decision to keep silent (see, for instance, de Graaf 2010; Vermaas *et al.* 2001) mention the risk of retaliation as an important argument not to report misbehavior. Retaliation can be defined as: 'undesirable action taken against a whistleblower – and in direct response to the whistleblowing – who reported wrongdoing' (Rehg *et al.* 2008: 267). Many researchers have documented the occurrence and types of retaliation against whistleblowers (Rehg *et al.* 2008: 267; Brown and Olsen 2008a; Bjørkelo *et al.* 2011). In the literature, a distinction is often made between informal and formal types of reprisals individuals might experience after they have blown the whistle. Informal reprisals include being treated as '*persona non grata*' (Tucker 1995); workplace bullying (Bjørkelo *et al.* 2008); verbal threats (Solano and Kleiner 2003); and even ostracism

(Bjørkelo *et al.* 2011). Formal reprisals include unfavorable job evaluations, denial of promotion, discharge or even blacklisting a person so he can never work in a certain sector again.[3]

Uys (2000) explicitly refers to the power struggle between the whistleblower and the employer in which the choice of battlefield is central. She explains that while the whistleblower wants to draw attention to the reported wrongdoing, the employer prefers to 'fight a separate battle in the labor-relations field' (Uys 2000: 264). The latter refers to means with which the employer can retaliate against the whistleblower by treating him as 'an enemy within' (Davis 1989: 8), questioning his competences, undermining his credibility, isolating him, or paralyzing his career (Devine 1997: 28–29). Retaliation is then an organizational tool 'in balancing the power struggle employees embark upon when reporting wrongdoing' (Bjørkelo *et al.* 2011: 228). Research has indicated that the level of retaliation experienced by the whistleblower is related to the status of both the whistleblower and the wrongdoer. In the Australian 'Whistling While They Work' project, the chance of retaliation increased if the whistle was blown against a senior staff member, illustrating the role of power differential (Brown and Olsen 2008a: 152).

The link between perceived risk of retaliation and whistleblowing has led some researchers and practitioners to conclude that to encourage staff members to report organizational misbehavior, employers should take anti-retaliation measures. They could, for example, implement policies that include sanctions for informal types of retaliation or policies that actively protect whistleblowers, such as anti-dismissal and confidentiality measures. Keil and colleagues (2010) suggest that managers should 'create an organizational culture that is conducive to whistleblowing in which bad news does not "get you killed" … and … a culture in which employees know that being the whistleblower is something that will not get you fired or reprimanded' (Keil *et al.* 2010: 805–6). However, protection measures and sanctions for informal reprisals can lead to undesirable side-effects, such as false disclosures (Martin and Rifkin 2004), over-reporting or the exaggeration of complaints to settle a personal score (Loyens 2012b). Moreover, they might not be effective, because motives for the decision to report are not just the reverse of motives to keep silent. In other words, the decision to blow the whistle can probably be explained by other dynamics and underlying processes than the decision to keep silent (Lamb 2009). Encouraging reporting thus cannot be achieved by just removing or reversing factors that explain keeping silent decisions. Research on whistleblowing should therefore allow for identifying asymmetrical explanations for the decision to report, the decision to keep silent and the decision to act otherwise.

The second problem of explanatory complexity is linked to the fact that most studies on whistleblowing try to find a single causal model to explain decision-making. This is particularly the case in quantitative studies that use surveys or vignettes, but also in experimental studies.[4] Ragin (1999), however, argues that a particular value on the dependent variable can mostly be explained by more than one causal model. He refers to this phenomenon as 'causal complexity' or 'the fact that many of the outcomes that interest social scientists often result from several different, non-overlapping combinations of conditions' (Ragin 1999: 1227). Causal complexity thus implies that no single causal condition is either necessary or sufficient to explain the outcome, which is very common in social sciences (Ragin 1999). Rihoux (2006: 682) refers to this phenomenon as 'multiple conjunctural causation', which implies that:

> (1) most often, it is a combination of conditions (independent variables) that eventually produces a phenomenon – the outcome (dependent variable); (2) several different combinations of conditions may produce the same outcome; and (3) depending on the context, on the conjuncture, a given condition may very well have a different impact on the outcome.

He concludes that 'different causal paths – each path being relevant, in a distinct way – may lead to the same outcome' (Rihoux 2006: 682), which can also be referred to as equifinality. Causality is thus context sensitive and researchers should not look for a single causal model that fits the data best (as in quantitative research), but try to determine the various causal pathways that can explain the outcomes (Ragin 1987; Rihoux 2006). Applied to the topic of whistleblowing, the outcome 'keeping silent' can probably be explained by various causal pathways, each consisting of a combined set of necessary or sufficient conditions. Likewise, and referring to the first problem, the outcome 'reporting' could also be explained by various causal pathways. Research that studies these different pathways to the same outcome (e.g., by using qualitative comparative analysis or process-tracing, see below) would enrich the whistleblowing literature.

RESEARCH ON WHISTLEBLOWING: SOME RECOMMENDATIONS

In the previous parts, we tried to broaden the perspective of the current whistleblowing literature by bringing in three other types of research approaches to study the link between power and whistleblowing. We will now list a number of recommendations on how to conduct empirical studies in each approach.

Going Beyond the Classic Dichotomy

The suggestion was made that future research should go beyond the classic dichotomy of reporting versus silence that is typical in most whistleblowing studies. In practice, researchers could do that by explicitly focusing on other responses than keeping silent or blowing the whistle in exploratory studies, comparable to the study by Teo and Caspersz (2011). Qualitative methods, such as (participant) observation and in-depth interviewing within organizations, seem particularly suitable for this type of research. Such methods imply a holistic perspective in which the researcher aims at providing insight into the complexity of the professional environment in which reporting decisions are made. Combining in-depth interviews with observations will allow for within-methods triangulation (Denzin 1978): a combination of several types of data collection that are used to complement and validate each other. Combining different qualitative methods leads to a more valid and comprehensive view of decision-making of street-level bureaucrats (Denzin 1978; Thurmond 2001).

In the ethnographic study of Loyens (2012a) on ethical decision-making (e.g., peer reporting) in the police and the labor inspection service, the combination of observation, interviewing and informal conversation is said to be beneficial in a threefold way. First, the researcher is convinced that the trust that was built during the months of observation and informal conversations was very beneficial during the in-depth interviews. In particular, street-level bureaucrats mentioned aspects of their work and personal life that they would probably not have told a complete stranger. This can be illustrated by the fact that during in-depth interviews street-level bureaucrats sometimes gave many details about highly sensitive internal affairs (including internal scandals about misconduct by colleagues) that had been very influential for their decision-making processes. Secondly, Loyens (2012a: 119) argues that the street-level bureaucrats opened up on various sensitive issues because they were convinced that the researcher had already heard about them from other street-level bureaucrats and they wanted to tell their version of the story. Thirdly, the street-level bureaucrats probably gave a more reliable account of their work because the researcher had already been there for a while and would therefore be less likely to be fooled by misrepresentations of reality. This can be illustrated by respondents' comments like: 'You know how things are going on around here' and 'I don't have to tell you that it is not perfect here'. Hence, different data collection methods lead to a more comprehensive and a more accurate picture of the research settings.

In sum, qualitative studies could be used to get the overall picture and to develop hypotheses concerning other types of resistance to organizational misbehavior than blowing the whistle or keeping silent. The results of such exploratory, qualitative studies might then be further analyzed or tested in quantitative studies. The latter could be used to gain insight into the prevalence and distribution of such alternative acts, and to test hypotheses about the impact of various independent variables on them. Different survey methods seem suitable, such as Likert-scale questions (to get data on occurrence) and open-ended questions in self-report questionnaires or vignette research (to identify other possible responses). Finally, theoretical work that applies conceptual and theoretical ideas from other disciplines (for instance, 'the glass cage metaphor' by Gabriel 2008, see above) to the topic of whistleblowing could also help to go beyond the dichotomy.

Applying the Causal Mechanism Approach

It was also suggested that applying causal mechanisms in whistleblowing research would enrich the literature and emphasize the context dependency of whistleblowing decision-making. To study causal mechanisms, one would need research methods that allow for in-depth analysis and that take contextual factors into account. Two examples can illustrate this. First, ethnographic methods could be used. Hammersley and Atkinson (1995: 1) state that ethnography involves 'the ethnographer participating ... in people's daily lives for an extended period of time, watching what happens, listening to what is said, asking questions – in fact collecting whatever data are available to throw light on the issues that are the focus of the research'. This approach seems to be particularly suitable for studying causal mechanisms and situational conditions under which they operate, because it is aimed at describing what is going on in groups or institutions in a rich and detailed way, leading to 'thick description' (Geertz 1973). By tracing the various steps in decision-making processes (i.e., process-tracing) the causal mechanisms that explain decisions in reporting dilemmas can be identified (George and Bennett 2005).

Secondly, narrative approaches (e.g., Edwards 2008; Henderson 2008; Peters *et al.* 2011) can also be used for this aim. Respondents are then asked to tell the story of how they responded to a whistleblowing dilemma, either orally or in writing. In these stories, explicit attention should be given to contexts and decision-making processes. Edwards (2008: 1) argues that a fundamental shift is needed in how whistleblowing is studied in empirical research. She argues that whistleblowing should not be viewed as a 'singular event', but 'as a phenomenon shaped by context and sensemaking processes'. In that sense, she considers traditional research methods, such as experiments and surveys, as insufficient to study this behavior. Edwards (2008) suggests the diary method, which is an important data collection method in the tradition of narrative research, as an alternative 'to gain a deeper, more comprehensive understanding of the psychological processes underlying decision-making, and to examine the temporal sequences of events and employees' reactions over time' (Edwards 2008: 1). This narrative approach has been applied recently by various researchers to study different types of whistleblowers (for example, see Henderson 2008; Ohnishi *et al.* 2008; Jackson *et al.* 2010; Peters *et al.* 2011). In her doctoral study, Lamb (2009) used a similar method in the phenomenological tradition by focusing on the lived experiences of 18 individuals when they decided to blow the whistle after witnessing unethical activities.

These ethnographic observations or narratives can then be analyzed by using the method of process-tracing. George and Bennett (2005: 206) define process-tracing as a 'method [that] attempts to identify the intervening causal processes … between an independent variable (or variables) and the outcome of the dependent variable'. Bennett (2010) offers a more specific definition when he refers to process-tracing as: 'the technique of looking for the observable implications of hypothesized causal processes, including alternative explanations to the main theory of interest, within a single case [that] involves looking for as continuous a chain of contiguous and sequential events at as fine a level of detail as the evidence or the patience and resources of the investigator allow'. By tracing the chain of cause–effect relations, several intervening mechanisms can be identified and theories about the interaction of causal processes can be developed or tested (George and Bennett 2005: 209). Steel (2004) argues that process-tracing is particularly suitable to study detailed narratives or stories.

Aiming for More Explanatory Complexity

The previous part suggested two ways to allow for more explanatory complexity in whistleblowing studies. First, researchers should look for asymmetrical explanations, as opposed to symmetrical explanations, because explanations for the occurrence of behavior are often not just the reverse of explanations for the non-occurrence of behavior. In practice, that would at least imply more research on the decision to keep silent, because that seems to have been overlooked in this tradition. Exploratory, qualitative studies can lead to a richer understanding of keeping silent decisions by moving beyond 'fear of retaliation' as an explanatory variable. The impact of these newly identified variables can then be tested in quantitative studies. Researchers could also aim for theory development with an explicit focus on explaining keeping silent decisions. Inspiration can be drawn from grid-group cultural theory, power theories and moral disengagement theory.[5] These insights can then be compared with theories explaining reporting behavior, thus enriching the whistleblowing literature.

Secondly, different causal pathways can be identified to explain the same behavioral outcome (Ragin 1999). This issue of 'causal complexity' can be addressed by using the method of qualitative comparative analysis (QCA).[6] QCA was developed by Charles C. Ragin who refers to it as 'the comparative method' (Ragin 1987) because various cases are systematically compared on the basis of different variables. Specifically, this method analyzes how several combinations of different values on the independent variables lead to a certain outcome of the dependent variable. Hence, it can be used to identify both sufficient and necessary conditions that explain different outcomes. It thus addresses the empirical complexity by identifying the various pathways that lead to a certain outcome (Devillé *et al.* 2007). This analytic method is an application of Boolean algebra, in which each case is reduced to a series of variables (conditions and an outcome). It aims to bridge the gap between qualitative and quantitative approaches by integrating 'the best features of the case-oriented approach with the best features of the variable-oriented approach' (Ragin 1987: 84). It is suitable for application in comparative empirical research with small or medium sample sizes (i.e., five to 50 cases). Applied to the topic of whistleblowing, QCA could be used to indicate which combinations of independent variables are necessary and/or sufficient to explain the decision made (be it silence, reporting or another decision). If QCA is not feasible (e.g., because the number of explanatory variables is too high for the number of cases under study), process-tracing could be used. By tracing the causal pathways and unraveling the various components of the decision-making processes, this technique also helps to address equifinality (Bennett 2010; Loyens 2012a: 123).

CONCLUSION

Much research has already been conducted on the link between whistleblowing and power. This chapter briefly discussed the current research, and then broadened the lens to other types of research opportunities on this topic. It focused on three ways in which the research agenda of whistleblowing studies can be extended. First, the suggestion was made to move beyond the classic 'reporting versus keeping silent' dichotomy by studying alternative reactions to the whistleblowing dilemma. This could be achieved in exploratory, qualitative studies that give a richer and more complete picture of other types of resistance to organizational misbehavior than blowing the whistle or keeping silent. The prevalence of such alternative acts could then be analyzed in quantitative studies.

Secondly, the suggestion was made to conduct whistleblowing studies from a causal mechanism perspective. Applied to the variable 'locus of control', the argument was made that most studies have neglected the impact of context in 'locus of control' explanations for whistleblowing. The causal mechanism approach puts great emphasis on contextual aspects of behavior, because it aims at identifying the causal mechanisms that are triggered by specific situational conditions. The application of the theory of moral disengagement on whistleblowing decision-making seems particularly promising. It would, however, also be interesting to look for other, more whistleblowing-specific causal mechanisms that could provide insight into the underlying decision-making processes of reporting dilemmas in exploratory and ethnographic research.

Thirdly, it was argued that whistleblowing studies should aim for explanatory complexity in at least two ways. First, researchers should beware of formulating over-simplified symmetrical explanations for whistleblowing decision-making. Reporting, for example, cannot be encouraged by simply removing or reversing factors that explain keeping silent, because the empirical world is more complex than that and requires asymmetrical explanations. If the high perceived risk of retaliation is an important factor to explain the decision to keep silent, then the implementation of protection policies and confidentiality measures will not necessarily result in more reporting. Asymmetrical explanations for whistleblowing and keeping silent should thus be looked for. Secondly, researchers should not look for a single model to explain a behavioral outcome in all circumstances. The same behavioral outcome (e.g., the decision to blow the whistle) could be explained by different causal pathways, depending on the specific circumstances. Qualitative comparative analysis and process-tracing could be used to identify the various causal pathways that lead to the decision, respectively, to blow the whistle, keep silent or prefer another alternative.

NOTES

1. See Clegg (1990); Parker (1992); Hassard (1994); Castells (1996); Calas and Smircich (1999); Gabriel (2004).
2. The reporting rate is 'the proportion of respondents who see wrongdoing and then elect to report it' (Brown, Mazurski and Olsen 2008: 47). The inaction rate is the proportion of respondents who do not report misbehavior, who do not deal with it themselves and who do not indicate that anyone else reported it (Brown, Mazurski and Olsen 2008: 48).
3. See Near and Miceli (1986); Lennane (1993); Baucus and Dworkin (1994); de Maria and Jan (1997); Lubalin and Matheson (1999).
4. For quantitative studies see e.g., Brewer and Selden (1998); Sims and Keenan (1999); Miceli *et al.* (1999); Park and Blenkinsopp (2009). For vignettes see Klockars *et al.* (2000); Huberts *et al.* (2003); Rothwell and Baldwin (2007a). For experimental studies see Hopman and van Leeuwen (2009).
5. For grid-group cultural theory see Evans (2008); Loyens (2013). For power theories see French and Raven (1959); Moscovici (1976); Miceli and Near (2002); Hopman and van Leeuwen (2009). For moral disengagement theory see Sumanth *et al.* (2011); Loyens (2012a).
6. For more information on the practical application of QCA and the supporting software package Tosmana, see Ragin (1999); Cronqvist (2003); Rihoux (2006).

PART II

ORGANIZATIONAL CULTURE AND RESPONSIVENESS

8. Reporting versus inaction: How much is there, what explains the differences and what to measure

Jane Olsen

INTRODUCTION

Informed by the important but occasional cases that grab the attention of the media, whistleblowing is often painted as rare – and the employee who does so as extraordinary. This chapter seeks to more fully describe the level of whistleblowing in response to observed wrongdoing in organizations. Drawing on empirical research, it shows the customary notion that whistleblowing is a rare activity to be largely untrue. In doing so, it confirms research demonstrating the importance of whistleblowing and the critical role it has played worldwide in exposing wrongdoing in or by organizations. As explained in Chapter 1, reporting by employees – often in the best position to observe, witness or otherwise know what is occurring in organizations – is often the most common way in which wrongdoing is brought to light (e.g., ACFE 2012; Brown, Mazurski and Olsen 2008; KPMG 2010; Miethe 1999).

This chapter begins by synthesizing what we know from the considerable array of international literature concerning how much whistleblowing occurs. It overviews the research methods used to estimate the level of reporting by employees, as well as their limitations. The chapter seeks to reconcile findings and provide a better context for these estimates, derived from large-scale surveys of employees about the proportion of employees who say they have observed wrongdoing and the proportion of those observers who indicate they went on to blow the whistle. The findings are largely consistent with previous reviews which suggest that across the range of countries and organizations studied to date, on average approximately half of all observers of wrongdoing report it (Near and Miceli 1996, 2008; Miceli and Near 2013).

The chapter then explores the context itself, specifically, how differences across situations, organizations and jurisdictions impact whether or not employees will report wrongdoing, and if and how they are reflected in aggregate reporting rates. The practical implications for research of many of the issues discussed in previous chapters are thus demonstrated here. What is it about particular organizations or industries that impacts upon how often employees report wrongdoing? What is the relative impact of provisions that oblige employees to report, as discussed in Chapter 5 (Leys and Vandekerckhove)? Does legislation appear to encourage employees to blow the whistle, by trying to protect reporters, or provide financial incentives (as discussed in Part III)? Based on these findings, the chapter also suggests some evidence-based lessons for improving practice. Research examining the factors associated with reporting provides managers and policy makers with crucial information to inform their design of successful strategies to encourage employees to speak up when they see something they think is wrong.

As a result, the chapter considers the implications for research. The diversity of methodologies and operational definitions used in research to date have implications for the differences in the estimated level of whistleblowing across studies. As already discussed by Skivenes and Trygstad (Chapter 4), differences exist between individuals, organizations, jurisdictions and cultures in terms of what practices are considered as 'immoral' or 'illegitimate' – and this impacts on estimates from the research about how much whistleblowing occurs. Ways are suggested for how more consistent and effective measurement can be achieved in future research. Finally, the chapter suggests that while research into levels of reporting is crucial, this data on its own only provides part of the answers needed by organizations or policy makers. A simple 'reporting–silence' dichotomy is an inaccurate way of understanding employee responses to wrongdoing (Loyens and Maesschalck, Chapter 7). However, research can and should transcend this dichotomy by giving measures of a spectrum of responses, including whistleblowing but also active intervention and other responses, as well as true 'silence' or inaction. Finally, the chapter proposes that whistleblowing research which not only identifies rates of whistleblowing, but enables organizations and policy makers to accurately identify the rates of 'inaction' in response to perceived wrongdoing, may be the most useful indicator of all.

EXISTING RESEARCH

The incidence of whistleblowing has been estimated by employing a variety of research methodologies.

Experimental studies of college students were one of the first research approaches for estimating the proportion of people who will blow the whistle in certain circumstances (e.g., Brabeck 1984; Dozier 1988; Miceli *et al.* 1991). One such experiment found rates of wrongdoing and reporting that did not significantly vary from those obtained by surveying staff (Burton and Near 1995). While this research design is useful in exploring whether certain factors influence reporting behavior, questions remain about the application of such laboratory findings to real world organizations.

Anecdotal or qualitative case studies, the second category, have the benefit of being able to explore the complexities inherent in whistleblowing incidents and seek detailed explanations from individuals about why they did or did not report. They often profile whistleblowers who have either self-selected, are known publicly for reporting or suffering reprisal, or face other usually extreme situations (e.g., Glazer and Glazer 1989; Richardson and McGlynn 2011).

Content analysis, the third category, was another early approach, used to examine media reports and legal cases. Brewer's (1996) study identified 530 cases of whistleblowing in 30 US newspapers between 1989 and 1995, revealing that 70 per cent of whistleblowing cases occurred in the public sector. While similar studies have gained popularity recently, media reports of whistleblowing are fraught with descriptions of reporting to journalists, which other research has since shown to be atypical (Donkin *et al.* 2008; see also Bosua *et al.*, Chapter 11).

Hypothetical scenarios or questions about what employees think they would do in response to observed wrongdoing in certain situations are the most common form of whistleblowing survey research. This is the fourth category. While providing valuable information on perceptions, there is a tenuous relationship between the propensity of employees to report wrongdoing and their actual behavior (Mesmer-Magnus and Viswesvaran 2005; see also Bjørkelo and Bye, Chapter 6). For example, one study found that while physicians place a high importance on reporting serious medical errors, they were much less likely actually to do so (Campbell *et al.* 2007).

Official data, drawn from administrative and operational information, informs a range of research. It captures how much whistleblowing is formally reported, recorded or registered by government or regulatory agencies. In the United States, for example, the official data collected by agencies has showed a burgeoning of whistleblowing in recent years. Data suggests that around 3,500 whistleblowers are contacting four predominant federal regulatory agencies annually, not accounting for reports made to other federal agencies, state agencies under their own whistleblower protection statutes and internally within organizations.[1] An analysis of the official internal investigation of large public sector agencies in one Australian estimated that a minimum of 1.8 per cent of public servants reported state wrongdoing in any given year (Brown *et al.* 2004), while an examination of reporting via hotlines predominantly in the private sector across a range of industries found that 9.27 incidents were reported per 1,000 employees (The Network 2013).

The problem is that whistleblowing matters splashed across newspaper headlines, heard in courtrooms or assessed by government agencies as meeting certain legislative criteria are not representative of the range of reporting by employees captured by commonly accepted definitions of whistleblowing. While they can shine a light on the 'tip of the iceberg', official data clearly fail to reveal a substantial amount of reporting that is occurring out of sight. In comparison to the number of staff who say they reported wrongdoing, there is a clear under-counting or under-estimate of reporting by employees in official data:

- The 'Whistling While They Work' research, for example, compared the number of internal reports of wrongdoing that had been formally reported by agencies as whistleblowing reports under the legislation relevant to their jurisdiction (5,308) to the estimated incidence of public interest whistleblowing based on a survey of 67,698 employees (Brown, Latimer, McMillan and Wheeler 2008).
- In one Australian state, 39 public interest disclosures (PIDs) were made for every 10,000 public authority employees (0.004 per cent) (NSW Ombudsman 2012). The number of formal PIDs identified (334) was insubstantial when compared to over 4,200 respondents (or 7 per cent) to a survey of state government employees in the same jurisdiction who said they had 'submitted a formal complaint' after witnessing 'improper conduct' at work in the past 12 months.

The differences between such numbers has been attributed to technical legislative definitions that exclude reports from being counted; restrictive procedures for making reports; or the lack of understanding in agencies about how the legislation is intended to apply, as evidenced by a failure to identify and/or assess reports by staff (Brown, Latimer, McMillan and Wheeler 2008). It also depends on whether and how the information is recorded. As a product of an administrative system, official data may be more reflective of known organizational workload and activity than actual levels of reporting. It only provides limited information about a small and discrete group of the population: those who make a formal report. Because of this sensitivity to system changes, the impact of organizational and jurisdictional changes to policies, practices or legislation or an increase in resources is often impossible to quantify relying on official data alone. The quality of the information collected will also vary from one jurisdiction to the next, not to mention fundamental differences in how whistleblowing is defined across statutory regimes. This has implications in terms of policy. By significantly under-estimating how much wrongdoing employees bring to light, the level of resources that are allocated to effectively support these employees and investigate their allegations is also likely to fall short.

In contrast, large-scale studies of random, representative samples of employees can reveal the extent to which reporting wrongdoing occurs in everyday organizational life. Respondents who have observed wrongdoing are then generally asked whether they reported it. The reporting rate is the proportion of respondents who said they knew about wrongdoing then went on to report it. As first noted by Miceli and Near (1984), this questionnaire design allows for the comparison of reporters to non-reporters to non-observers of wrongdoing.

Table 8.1 *Reporting rates across surveys of various samples*

Author	Year of publication	Sample	Reporting rate
Asia			
Davis and Konishi	2007	24 Japanese nurses	0%
Bashir, Khattak, Hanif and Chohan	2011	2,703 Pakistani public sector employees	8%
Australia			
Australian Public Service Commission (APSC)	2004	3,202–10,222 Australian (Commonwealth) public service employees	50%
	2005		50%
	2006		56%
	2007		60%
	2009		59%
	2010		51%
	2011		45%
Commissioner for Public Employment	2007	6,270 South Australian public sector employees	30%
Brown, Mazurski and Olsen	2008	7,663 Australian public sector employees	39%

Author	Year of publication	Sample	Reporting rate
Office of the Public Sector Standards Commissioner	2010	9,992 Western Australian public sector employees	36%
Public Service Commission, NSW	2012	60,779 New South Wales public sector employees	23%
Europe			
Webley and Dryden	2005	759 full-time British employees	48%
Webley and Werner	2008	791 full-time British employees	60%
Waters	2008	752 English nurses	87%
TI Czech Republic in Transparency International	2009	Czech Republic employees	One-third
Moore and McAuliffe	2010	152 Irish nurses	70%
North America			
Merit Systems Protection Board (MSPB)	1981 1984 1993	8,296, 1,944 and 13,342 US federal government employees	30% 40% 50%
Gartrell et al.	1987	1,423 national US psychiatrists	10%
Tangney	1987	245 science professors	10%
Blackburn	1988	1,212 US private sector employees	58%
Keenan	1988	143 first-level managers	46%
Near and Miceli	1988	US and Canadian directors of internal auditing, 892 in private sector and 119 in public sector	90% (public) 91% (private)
Bayer, Strickland and Miethe	1992	326 US (Virginia) employees	48%
Miethe and Rothschild	1995	130 non-profit employees in Nevada (US)	59%

Author	Year of publication	Sample	Reporting rate
Ethics Resource Center (ERC)	1999	US private sector, government sector and non-profit sector employees (National Business Ethics Survey or NBES)	48% (1994)
	2007a	US government sector employees (National Government Ethics Survey)	60% (2000) 62% (2003) 58% (2005) 70% (2007)
	2007b	US private sector employees (NBES)	57% (2000) 65% (2003) 55% (2005) 58% (2007)
	2009		63%
	2012a		65% (2011)
	2008	US non-profit sector employees (National Non-Profit Ethics Survey)	56% (2000) 67% (2003) 58% (2005) 62% (2007)
	2012b	US private sector 'Fortune 500' company employees (NBES)	74%
Rothschild and Miethe	1999a	1,004 US working adults	62%
Near, Rehg, Van Scotter and Miceli	2004	Workers at a large military base (US)	26%
Campbell et al.	2007	1,662 US public and private sector physicians	45%
Miceli, Near, Rehg and Van Scotter	2012	9,906 US military and civilian employees	24%
Ipsos Reid	2013	1,054 Canadian employees	52%
South America			
ERC	2003	62,605 Puerto Rican government employees	36%

Table 8.1 lists a number of identified studies that surveyed employees about their actual behavior in response to observed wrongdoing, along with the rate of reporting among observers of wrongdoing in the particular sample surveyed. Previous reviews on the topic have traditionally focused on academic research published in the United States. In

contrast, the studies listed are not limited by context, geography or time. Most significantly, practitioner studies that were not subject to peer review or secondary analysis by academics are included. The all-inclusive scope has advantages beyond the obvious increase in the amount of relevant information: it draws on a variety of approaches and sources of knowledge, as well as minimizing publication bias (Slavin 1986).

While estimates vary depending on who is asked, how they are asked and where they work, approximately half of all employees who say they observed wrongdoing state that they then reported it. The first MSPB report (MSPB 1981: i) noted that the self-reported experiences of survey respondents may 'reflect a certain degree of misperception of observed events, incomplete understandings of facts, one-sided viewpoints, and self-serving recollections'. Despite this, managers and policy makers should find it concerning that equally as many employees do not report wrongdoing that they observe. Not only this, perceptions on observations of workplace wrongdoing appear relatively common; many employees believe they have encountered wrongdoing in their organization recently.

Even when focusing only on studies that ask about the past experiences of employees (as opposed to their intentions), the estimates of how often staff report wrongdoing vary greatly, not least because studies employ different populations, measures and definitions. As Table 8.1 shows, reporting rates range from 8 per cent of Pakistani public officials considered at high risk of corruption (Bashir *et al.* 2011) to 74 per cent of Fortune 500 company employees (ERC 2012b). While it is tempting to generalize findings to broader populations, this should be resisted given the large variation in reporting levels.

Another reason for treating any comparisons with caution is the wide range in the research and questionnaire designs used. The dramatic variance across studies in the proportion of employees who observe wrongdoing (within Australia alone, ranging from 8 per cent (APSC 2006) to 72 per cent (Brown, Mazurski and Olsen 2008)) is at least partly due to how questionnaires define wrongdoing and reporting. Understanding the different techniques, measures or other methodologies used is essential for drawing appropriate comparisons across studies. In one recent comparison of the incidence of public sector whistleblowing in the United States, Australia and Norway, Miceli and Near (2013) discussed how differences in results may be due to political, cultural, social and legal forces that vary across nations, but are also likely due to the different ways in which variables are measured. For example, definitional issues around whether whistleblowing encompasses reporting internally to the organization, externally to regulatory bodies or publically to the media impact on consistency across reporting rates. This will be discussed further in considering the implications for research.

In an attempt to explain differences in reporting, the majority of research to date has focused predominantly on the individuals involved. Drawing largely on the model of pro-social organizational behavior (POB) described elsewhere in this book (see Bjørkelo and Bye, Chapter 6 and Roberts, Chapter 9), the focus has been on the decision-making process of employees faced with wrongdoing, and the personal and situational variables, and any interactions between them that shape this choice (e.g., Miceli and Near 2010; Miceli *et al.* 2008; Near and Miceli 1996). For example, research suggests that employees are more likely to report if they:

- have more power (Miceli and Near 1984);
- exhibit certain attitudes and beliefs (Brabeck 1984; Donkin *et al.* 2008; Keenan and Sims 1995; Miceli *et al.* 1991; Near and Miceli 1996; Rothschild and Miethe 1999b); or
- have certain personalities (Bjørkelo *et al.* 2010; Miceli *et al.* 2001; Miceli *et al.* 2012).

Despite this, the characteristics of reporters are not inherently different from non-reporters. Reporting is shaped not merely by the attitudes or characteristics of individual employees, but by collective practices and interactions within an organization and the circumstances in which employees find themselves. Most reporters are employees who simply happen to observe wrongdoing, sometimes because of the nature of their job (Near and Miceli 1996). These empirical findings stand in stark contrast to the common stereotypes of whistleblowers as heroes or villains. Research has also consistently shown that environmental factors have a stronger relationship to reporting than the characteristics of the individual employee (Wortley *et al.* 2008; Miceli *et al.* 2008). The next section of this chapter will examine these situational and organizational factors that are associated with reporting.

SITUATIONAL AND ORGANIZATIONAL FACTORS ASSOCIATED WITH REPORTING

Given that individual differences cannot adequately explain the vast differences in reporting rates across organizations (for example, see Roberts *et al.* 2011), what does influence whether or not employees will report observed wrongdoing? Cultural differences in reporting, perhaps shaped by traditionally held values or historical events, were discussed in Vandekerckhove *et al.*, Chapter 2. The relationship between reporting by employees and macroeconomic systems also seems parallel: the Ethics Resource Center (ERC) survey series of US employees show that as the economy worsens, the rate of misconduct rises and the rate of employee reporting drops (e.g., ERC 2012e). However, rather than taking a macro perspective, this chapter goes beyond national and cultural determinants of who is likely to report and instead focuses on who reports under what conditions. In particular, the focus is on situational, organizational and public policy characteristics.

Situational Characteristics

In terms of the immediate context, there are three groups of situational factors: those related to the wrongdoing itself, those concerning social/interpersonal relationships and the role of the employee.

Wrongdoing: Seriousness, frequency, type, evidence

The characteristics of the wrongdoing, particularly its nature and scale, are often associated with whistleblowing empirically. The perceived *seriousness of the wrongdoing* has been positively related to reporting (e.g., Wortley *et al.* 2008; Miceli and Near 1985, 2005; Near and Miceli 1996; Mesmer-Magnus and Viswesvaran 2005; Victor *et al.* 1993; Singer *et al.* 1998; Rothschild and Miethe 1999a, 1999b; MSPB 2011), as has the perceived *frequency of the wrongdoing* (e.g., Wortley *et al.* 2008). This has been explained using a pro-social model of behavior because it is indicative of a need for corrective action. It is also consistent with the dominant view in many Western countries that whistleblowing is warranted if it is in the public interest (Near and Miceli 1996).

Significantly related to an indicator of seriousness (cost), the *type of wrongdoing* perceived also makes a difference in reporting behavior. For example, employees of a large military base who observed mismanagement and sexual harassment were significantly more likely to report the wrongdoing than were employees who observed stealing, waste, safety problems or discrimination (Near *et al.* 2004). However, the higher rate for reporting mismanagement is inconsistent with the theory that *intentionality* (as opposed to inadvertent wrongdoing) may affect an employee's emotional response to the wrongdoing and, in turn, triggers reporting behavior (Gundlach *et al.* 2003). The type of wrongdoing is also significantly related to the *quality of evidence* about the wrongdoing that the observer has (MSPB 2011), perhaps because it provides some indication of the accuracy of the employee's observation of the facts surrounding the wrongdoing (Near and Miceli 1996).

This touches on an important issue: that wrongdoing is in the 'eye of the beholder'. Reasonable people will sometimes differ on what they think constitutes wrongdoing – what some consider serious, may be trivial to others. Statutory definitions of wrongdoing are inconsistent (although generally include corruption), and what the culture of the organization will accept or tolerate often provides the observer with different cues about seriousness. In accordance with the POB model, an employees' knowledge about what is considered wrongdoing is a prerequisite to even considering reporting as a course of action (Near and Miceli 1996). Employee education and awareness is important to a common understanding of wrongdoing and why reporting is important.

Key actors and their existing relationships

Taking an ecological perspective, whistleblowing can be seen as a dynamic phenomenon that occurs in a complex web of existing relationships between many social actors: the observer, the perceived wrongdoer, the potential recipient of the report, co-workers (also referred to as peers), supervisors, senior management, and other potential sources of support, threat or reprisal. For example:

- Although contradictory to theories of power dynamics, research proposes that reporting peers is more difficult than reporting a supervisor and attributes this to group norms against reporting on peers and stronger identification and empathy with them. It may also be because employees are less likely to report wrongdoing by people with whom they have a *close interpersonal relationship* (King 1997).
- While most research only considers relationships with other organizational members, *support from family and friends* has also been associated with the likelihood of reporting (ERC 2012c).

Conversely, research has also shown that employees who reported wrongdoing had a *history of conflict* in the workplace, with colleagues, managers or even the organization itself (Wortley *et al.* 2008). The same research found that motivation to report increases when the wrongdoing is *directed at the observer*. This highlights that bullying, disagreement about performance management or other dissatisfaction with the immediate workplace environment are common triggers for employees to come forward with information they may have otherwise kept quiet.

Employee role

An employee's belief that their role requires them to address wrongdoing often leads them to do so (e.g., Mesmer-Magnus and Viswesvaran 2005; Miceli *et al.* 1991; Miceli and Near 2005; Near and Miceli 1996; Victor *et al.* 1993). When employees generally are asked why they reported, perceptions that it was their duty or that they had a legal responsibility to do so were important considerations (Miceli *et al.* 1991; Wortley *et al.* 2008). Supervisors, whose duties are likely to explicitly or implicitly prescribe taking action in response to wrongdoing, are more likely to report than other staff.

Employees in particular occupations or industries also differ in their tendency to report wrongdoing that they observe because of certain *responsibilities or obligations*. For example, one sample of internal auditors reported wrongdoing at a much higher rate than other samples (90 per cent in Near and Miceli 1988). This is unsurprising, considering their day-to-day responsibilities include examining activity within organizations, assessing possible risks and opportunities, and deciding on a particular course of action – a very similar decision-making process to whether or not to blow the whistle. Discovering wrongdoing is also directly part of their role and they often have better access to information than typical employees (Miceli and Near 1994).

Organizational Factors

Organizations show great differences in the degree of success that different agencies appear to be having in encouraging employees to speak up, which suggests that differences in context, approach and management culture have strong, measurable effects at the organizational level.

Sector/Industry

The type of wrongdoing observed and the acceptance of reporting also appears to differ across sectors and industries. Highly regulated industries such as financial services and insurance may experience a high rate of external reporting because of the existence of regulatory bodies which offer observers of wrongdoing alternative pathways to which they may logically and easily report (Miceli *et al.* 1991).

Reporting rates also appear to differ between the private, public and non-profit sectors. Government employees have been shown most likely to both observe and report wrongdoing, while the non-profit sector was least likely to observe wrongdoing and the business sector least likely to report wrongdoing that they observed (ERC 2007a, 2007b, 2008). Other research of external disclosures found a considerably higher rate of external disclosure among public sector employees (70 per cent), compared to their non-profit (18 per cent) and private (13 per cent) sector counterparts, even after controlling for differences such as the level of wrongdoing and the perceived ethical standards of the organization (Rothschild and Miethe 1999b). This may be because of the availability of external bodies to which such reports can be made by public sector employees. A content analysis of media articles that found 70 per cent of whistleblowing reports were from the public sector. Brewer (1996) described some of the other key differences between sectors:

(1) Public sector employees have greater legal protection from retaliation and 'at will firing' than private sector employees.
(2) Many government agencies have established special hotlines to encourage the reporting of wrongdoing by employees.
(3) Public sector employees are more likely to have 'public service motivation', leading them to take action when it is in the public interest.
(4) Alternatively, government agencies tend to be larger, more bureaucratic and are perceived as less responsive to workers' comments and suggestions.[2]

Climate

An organization's positive climate has been described as influencing perceptions about the appropriateness of reporting by discouraging wrongdoing and encouraging reporting (Near and Miceli 1995). Studies show that organizations which constantly pressure their employees have higher rates of wrongdoing and lower rates of reporting (ERC 2012e; Vaughn 1999) – misconduct may be seen as the only way to achieve goals and meet unreasonable expectations. Climate can encourage reporting by shaping three key expectations:

(1) *That responsive action will be taken*: employees in organizations that are responsive to complaints (e.g., Miceli and Near 1988) and have a 'low defensive organization climate' (Keenan 1988: 250) or that are perceived as just (Near and Miceli 1996) are more likely to report than other employees. When Western respondents are directly asked why they did or did not report, their belief that something will or could be done in response is often the most frequent answer (ERC 2003; Keenan and McLain 1992; MSPB 1981, 1984; 1993, 2011; Near and Miceli 1996; Near *et al.* 2004; Wortley *et al.* 2008). While this initially seems to indicate that

reporting is altruistic in nature, an alternative explanation is that responsive action increases the likelihood of a reward or minimizes the risk of reprisal, for example. From this perspective, even reporters with improper motives are likely to place importance on their desired action being taken.

(2) *That they will be supported*: supportive ethical climates have been associated with intentions to report (Near and Miceli 1995; Keenan 1988), although their relationship to reporting behavior has not been examined (Mesmer-Magnus and Viswesvaran 2005). Reporting is also more likely when there is greater value congruence between employees and senior management (Near and Miceli 1996).

(3) *That they will not suffer reprisal*: observers that perceive a threat of retaliation (by the organization, immediate supervisors or co-workers) are much less likely to blow the whistle than those who do not perceive a retaliatory climate (Keenan 1995; King 1999; Mesmer-Magnus and Viswesvaran 2005; Near and Miceli 1996). Early research showed this was not always the case (e.g., Miceli and Near 1984) and suggested a more complex relationship: that the expectation of reprisals may actually encourage some observers to report wrongdoing to the media or others external to their organization (Jos *et al.* 1989; Miceli and Near 1985; Miceli and Near 1989; Near and Miceli 1986). While non-reporters draw on fear of reprisal to explain their decision, those that did report did not consider it to be important (Wortley *et al.* 2008).

PUBLIC POLICY AND ITS IMPLICATIONS

Public Policy as a Situational Variable

Legislative instruments dedicated to whistleblowing are also an important variable for research, as they combine a range of elements that may encourage reporting, including by trying to influence the climate, as discussed above. Beginning in the United States, legislation has traditionally focused on *protecting whistleblowers* by discouraging reprisal, with this also intended to indirectly encourage whistleblowing (see Fasterling, Chapter 14, and Lewis, Devine and Harpur, Chapter 15). The significant increase in the MSPB reporting rates over time has been attributed to the successful implementation and awareness of legislation (Miceli and Near 1989; Miceli *et al.* 1999), while recent increases in reporting have followed the introduction or improvement of whistleblowing legislation

(Miceli *et al.* 2012; Miceli and Near 2013). In contrast, the passage of state laws providing protection appeared not to increase the incidence of reporting in those states (Dworkin and Near 1987). Australian respondents also indicated that legal protection plays a role in their intentions to report (Zipparo 1999a) and it also seems to play a role in their behavior (Roberts 2008).

More recently, the focus in the United States has shifted to encouraging whistleblowers by improving *incentives* and providing *multiple reporting pathways* (Moberly 2006). While US federal government employees indicate that they would not be more willing to report if they received financial rewards (MSPB 1981), in reality, the adoption or strengthening of financial incentive schemes in the United States has seen the number of whistleblowing matters rise. Following changes to the False Claims Act for example, the number of claims increased steadily; a continuing trend that has seen an upsurge in recent years (DOJ 2011; see Faunce *et al.*, Chapter 16). This growth has led to support for the effectiveness of rewards in encouraging reporting compared to the relatively modest number of formal whistleblowers under legislation providing protection against reprisal (Dworkin and Near 1997; Moberly 2006).

The authors of one experimental study concluded that external incentives to report (such as rewards and punishments) may undermine internal moral motivations (Feldman and Lobel 2011). When faced with hypothetical wrongdoing, college students were less likely to indicate that they would report where fines for liability failures and protections from retaliation were present; intentions to report were highest when there was a duty to, and a reward of a high magnitude was available. Participants downplayed the influence of incentives on themselves personally (although not on others) and rated incentives as the least effective in practice. The effectiveness of incentives also depended on context: reporting rates were consistently high when the misconduct was perceived as serious, and when perceived not to be serious, the presence of an incentive lowered reporting.

However, relatively little attention has been given to the effectiveness of statutory *requirements on organizations*. Given the importance placed by reporters and non-reporters of wrongdoing alike on what action will be taken in response to a report, obliging organizations to take action in response to a report and providing penalties for non-compliance may prove effective (Miceli and Near 2006). This highlights an important point. While law may have some expressive value, its success in normalizing employee reporting largely depends on how well it is implemented (Moberly 2006). This is a crucial issue which is also taken up elsewhere (see Brown *et al.*, Chapter 19).

Statutory encouragement and protection of whistleblowers also depends on fundamental issues such as employees' confidence in the *legal system* and its accessibility. The existence of other legislation or common law rules acts to increase the cost of reporting (e.g., official secrecy laws, defamation or denunciation laws) or reduce their likelihood, primarily by providing employment or industrial relations standards. Skivenes and Trygstad (2010a) attribute the relatively high rate of reporting in their study to the Norwegian culture and a legal system that is supportive of whistleblowers. For example, the United States is one of many countries with a dominant 'employment-at-will' doctrine that allows employers to fire an employee for any reason, including reporting (see Miceli and Near 2013; see also Lewis, Devine and Harpur, Chapter 15). This stands in contrast to the United Kingdom, where the dismissal of employees requires a justified reason, and the supportive employment rights existing in Norway facilitated by strong unionism. For example, the lower incidence of external whistleblowing in Western Europe compared to East Asia was seen to reflect the preference for other channels, such as work councils, labor unions or executives (Arvis and Berenbeim 2003).

Policy Implications

From all of the above, the implications of high quality research into levels of whistleblowing become clear. Despite the differences in reporting across contexts and studies, many employees plainly not only observe wrongdoing, but also report it either within their organization or to external recipients they believe will take action to deal with it. Information about the level of reporting is necessary to determine appropriate reporting structures and to allocate resources accordingly (Roberts *et al.* 2011). Research also allows for links to be drawn between what empirical findings suggest leads to a greater likelihood of reporting and the practical action that managers and policy makers can take to encourage employees to report wrongdoing. Table 8.2 lists these actions according to the element of the POB model where they seek to intervene and the key messages organizations and governments need to send to employees.

An internal reporting policy is one key mechanism for organizations to demonstrate that they will take appropriate action when wrongdoing is reported and support and protect employees who report. Increased internal reporting has been associated with having specific, identified whistleblowing pathways, a particular person identified to receive and follow up the information, and a strong, supportive policy encouraging whistleblowing (Keenan and Sims 1995; Miceli and Near 1992). In one study, US company human resource executives reported a significant increase in the number of internal disclosures by employees after implementation of internal disclosure policies and a corresponding significant decrease in external disclosures (Barnett *et al.* 1993).

Yet policies alone will be ineffective in encouraging reporting unless employees are aware of them (Near and Miceli 1996). The rate of employee inaction after observing serious wrongdoing was lower in agencies in which more staff were aware of and confident in whistleblowing legislation (Roberts 2008). Drawing on official data, organizations that had not established an internal reporting policy or had not undertaken relevant staff awareness training reported receiving no public interest disclosures over a six-month period (NSW Ombudsman 2012).

Centralized oversight or regulatory agencies are a critical link between policy and organizations. They can build employee confidence to report by monitoring, auditing and enforcing any non-compliance by organizations with their obligations when a report is received, and to establish systems, including internal policies. They can encourage reporting by promoting public awareness of whistleblowing or support good practice in organizations through the provision of information, advice, training and guidance. How well oversight agencies perform their functions is likely to depend on the resources invested in them and their ability to build relationships with organizations. They also need the information on how these systems are working, provided by research (see further Brown *et al.*, Chapter 19).

By and large the effectiveness of the organizational strategies suggested in Table 8.2 and their applicability across contexts has not been evaluated, however (or at least not reported publicly). While recent years have seen a flurry of whistleblowing research (and not minimizing its value), much of this effort replicates previous studies, albeit in different contexts. Assessing the effectiveness of commonly suggested strategies in use by organizations and legislation is vital to ensuring policy is evidence-based. Such collaboration between researchers and practitioners may also provide opportunities to conduct stronger research designs, for example, cause-effect relationships that can be tested directly by measuring differences over time.

The unintended consequences of efforts to encourage staff to report also need to be considered. A recent Ethics Research Center study (2012e) showed not only an increased reporting rate, but also an increase in retaliation for reporting. While most strategies, such as those aimed at building a supportive culture discouraging of wrongdoing, will improve both outcomes, others may not. One experiment of college students found reporting increased when people had a duty to do so, while the introduction of a reward had the opposite effect (Feldman and Lobel 2011). Following legislation requiring the reporting of child sexual abuse, for example, the number of reports made increased but the proportion of reports that were investigated or that were substantiated decreased (Levanthal 2001 cited in Johnson 2003). This may also lead to an increase in the number of people that have reports made about them, typically a stressful situation, regardless of whether the allegations are true. Organizations and governments requiring employees to report, as well as those that adopt an 'if in doubt, report' approach and encourage employees to raise all concerns (Brown and Donkin 2008: 14), should therefore ensure that:

- sufficient resources are available to appropriately assess and respond to reports; if they are not, reporting rates will again decline as employees come to realize reporting is ineffectual;
- there is a corresponding focus on improving the identification and assessment of wrongdoing by employees;
- systems are integrated so reports can be appropriately streamed depending on the issues that they raise (e.g., grievance resolution versus investigations of corruption), and employees know that their report may be dealt with in a number of ways depending on the content;
- when a decision is made to take no further action in response to a report, a thorough explanation is provided to the reporter so they understand the reasons why;
- support is provided to subjects of reports throughout the process, particularly if the allegations against them are proven incorrect.

In an ideal environment, where reporting is truly viewed as an everyday part of organizational life, the emotion and stress that often surrounds those involved are minimized. The result is managers who are responsive rather than defensive, reporters without a need for vindication and subjects of reports who trust in an impartial, and necessary, process.

Table 8.2 Practical action to encourage reporting based on the POB model

Element of POB model	Message for employees	Organizations / managers	Governments / policy makers
Wrongdoing identified	'Report all concerns – we think any wrongdoing is serious'	• Emphasize the importance the values of integrity and fairness, and reframe reporting as an act of loyalty to the organization (Waytz *et al.* 2013) • Provide advice to employees about what constitutes wrongdoing, that they should report any concerns they may have and do not need to provide evidence • Advice can be provided through general communications, codes of conduct and other policies and procedures, dedicated or other ethics-related education and training, induction programs, an advice line/hotline, managers or ad hoc 'risk alerts'	• Ensure whistleblowing legislation applies to reports about a wide range of behavior rather than limiting its scope to particular types, levels of seriousness or public interest wrongdoing (Miceli *et al.* 2008) • Criminalize organizational wrongdoing with strong penalties that deter
Social norms	'We value reports and will take responsive action'	• Establish an internal reporting policy endorsed by head of the organization • Ensure appropriate systems are in place for timely assessment, investigation and or other responsive action • Share/publish examples of reports, the action taken in response and any changes or improvements that resulted, particularly to those proximal to the reporter (region, work unit, profession)	• Enact whistleblowing legislation – this alone can legitimatize and normalize reporting by making it seem significant and valued (Feldman and Lobel 2011) – although depends on awareness and confidence • Raise public awareness of the statutory regime • Motivate organizations by sharing examples of good practice

Element of POB model	Message for employees	Organizations / managers	Governments / policy makers
Responsibility	'You have a duty to report wrongdoing'	● Oblige employees to report wrongdoing in code of conduct or other policies ● Monitor compliance (e.g., managers directly ask employees at least annually through performance management program) ● Send employees the message that reporting is part of their job and a valuable public service (MSPB 2011)	● Oblige employees to report wrongdoing in statutory codes of conduct ● Oblige organizations to receive, assess and take action on a report (Miceli and Near 2006) – and make this information available publicly or provide to an oversight body ● Oblige head of the organization personally to take or attest to certain actions ● Provide penalties for non-compliance and ability to reduce penalties if have robust system
Option available	'You have multiple options for reporting easily and safely'	● Provide multiple safe and easily accessible reporting pathways ● Employees who receive reports have knowledge, skills and experience ● Communicate when policy first established and regular reminders	● Allow for multiple safe and easily accessible reporting pathways – internal to the organization, external to other organizations that can take action, or to a media or journalist (public reporting). ● Remove or minimize 'procedural hurdles' such as circumstances for reporting to external/media, excluding anonymous reports, 'good faith' requirement or time limits on reporting (Miceli and Near 2006)
Risks	'We will take action to protect you from reprisal'	● Reassure employees that reasonable action will be taken to protect them – in consultation with themselves ● Take effective and timely action when allegations of reprisal are made, including independently investigating and taking disciplinary action if substantiated	● Criminalize reprisal and provide strong penalties ● Require that the identity of the reporter is kept confidential ● Provide ability for reporters to seek injunctive relief or compensation

Element of POB model	Message for employees	Organizations / managers	Governments / policy makers
Opportunities	'You will be supported for reporting'	• Establish support networks for reporters and subjects of reports • Provide incentives for exemplary ethical conduct such as reporting: – Evaluate as part of performance management – Regular ethical decision-making award or other recognition schemes – Rewards (financial or otherwise)	• Provide financial rewards or 'tokens of appreciation' for employees if report is substantiated • Establish a recognition/award system

RESEARCH IMPLICATIONS

There are many lessons from research to date for future researchers seeking to examine the incidence of reporting by surveying employees. It is important to take stock of the questionnaires used previously in studies, and any associated biases that may limit the relevance of the findings to policy makers. The crucial objective is ensuring the validity of the research: the extent to which a study's findings are warranted, taking into account its research methods and the characteristics of participants. Collaboration with policy makers is one way in which to build validity into research:

- investing in stronger research designs and triangulating data sources improves *internal validity*, the ability to make accurate assessments without bias or error;
- selecting appropriate sampling strategies to minimize potential bias improves *external validity*, the extent to which a study's results can be generalized to a larger or different population beyond the participants in the study;
- striking the balance between operationalizing key concepts consistently to facilitate comparison and maintaining their relevance to their corresponding population improves *measurement validity*, the degree to which a measurement measures what it purports to measure.

Strong Research Designs More Likely to Provide Conclusive Answers

Most survey findings are taken from cross-sectional studies where a proportion of the relevant population is surveyed at a particular point in time. Even though the Ethics Resource Center describes its series of surveys as 'longitudinal', a different sample is selected to participate each time, as is the case for the series of government surveys which sometimes select different organizations to participate (e.g., MPSB 1981, 1984, 1993; APSC 2004–2011). The problem, as noted by Miceli and Near (1984: 691), is that any relationship between variables found in the research cannot be conclusively determined as one having caused the other. The 'gold standard' in research designs are randomized controlled trials because they are able to attribute a cause and effect relationship. Although such research would be particularly valuable to figuring out 'what works' in encouraging staff to report wrongdoing for governments and organizations, their use is necessarily limited in the whistleblowing sphere. A strong research design is important to policy makers because it helps to more conclusively answer two important questions:

(1) Why don't employees report wrongdoing that they know about?
(2) What strategies are effective in increasing the proportion of employees who report wrongdoing that they know about?

Large-scale, longitudinal research has been called for because of its greater applicability to the general population and ability to track critical indicators such as reporting and inaction over time, as well identify cause-and-effect relationships and the impact of events, such as legislative change or policy implementation. Of course, as noted by Rothschild and Miethe (1999b), gaining accessing to employees and surveying a large group of them is difficult, time-consuming and expensive. Collaborative, complementary and coordinated research involving policy makers may be one way to facilitate research, integrate datasets and minimize these costs. The model taken with the early MSPB surveys could be used, providing researchers with a large and rich data source for in-depth secondary analyses; which in turn ensures findings are fed back to practitioners to adopt better practice and turns evidence into action. There is also the opportunity to develop alternate methodologies such as action research, time-series designs (which allow for changes over time to be properly assessed by plotting reporting rates while controlling for any confounding variables) and less stringent but still rigorous research designs such as matched groups or quasi-experimental designs.

Generalizability Depends on Appropriate Sampling

The extent to which a study's results can be generalized depends on its sampling strategy, including the level of diversity in the organizations and industries that are the focus of the research. Even with a powerful research design and well conceptualized survey instrument, a biased sample leads to information that is of little value to policy makers. Policy makers are limited in their ability to draw conclusions across studies because:

- Reporting rates will vary depending on the *scope of the possible sample*, for example, their profession, organization or industry. Studies that do not restrict their sample typically find greater variability in the responses of employees. There is even likely to be significant diversity within some organizations, and this is taken into account in any sampling frame.

- Other studies have not employed a *random recruitment strategy* when seeking participants, one method of limiting bias in a sample, and many others do not indicate whether their sample was chosen at random or not. This is particularly important when research is seeking to estimate the incidence of reporting or inaction.
- The larger the *sample size*, the greater the certainty that their responses reflect the views of the whole population. In whistleblowing research this is particularly important because only a proportion of respondents will observe wrongdoing and only a proportion of these will report it. This subset of reporters needs to be of sufficient size to ensure the information they provide about their situation is as representative as possible (Near and Miceli 2008).

Despite the increasing interest in whistleblowing research, there have been calls for more large-scale, multi-organizational and cross-jurisdictional projects. By bridging the divide across jurisdictional boundaries and countries, research of this nature is more amenable to generalization to other groups, has greater relevance and, as such, would represent a significant contribution to the evidence base for policy makers. Comparative research across multiple contexts also allows for the impact of place and setting (at a national, jurisdictional and organizational level) to be shown empirically and can lead to new hypotheses about why employees do not report and the strategies that are effective in tackling these barriers.

Appropriate Survey Administration can Minimize Bias

All modes of administering surveys (face-to-face, telephone, self-administered on paper or electronically) have advantages and disadvantages that are not relevant for discussion here. However, it is worth noting that two particularly salient respondent characteristics, their *willingness to disclose* sensitive information and *desire to present themselves in the best possible light*, are minimized if surveys are self-administered (Bradburn 1983). Employees are more likely to respond to items and respond more accurately to sensitive questions if there is a weak social presence and they can remain anonymous (Tourangeau *et al.* 2000). Traditionally, postal surveys have been suggested to improve the willingness of respondents to disclose information, although research assessing computer-based surveys has suggested an even greater willingness. Similarly, *social desirability bias* results in the over-disclosure of desirable behaviors and under-disclosure of undesirable behavior. Assurances of confidentiality and anonymity lead to more honest answers.

At the same time, participants may be less likely to respond to self-administered surveys. The lower the *response rate*, the greater the chance that those who choose not to participate in the research differ from respondents in a way that is important. For example, it could be assumed that employees without experiences or concerns of wrongdoing and reporting are less likely to respond, thereby inflating estimates of the prevalence of whistleblowing. Organizations with a poor ethical culture might be less likely to participate in such research. Irrespective of the particular direction, *non-response bias* can weaken the precision of estimates of the population, as well as the generalizability of any findings.

Consistent Operationalization Facilitates Comparison

As already noted, the way in which employees are asked about witnessing wrongdoing and what action they took in response impacts dramatically on reporting rates. Psychological or legal styles of questioning, for example, directly ask respondents whether they have blown the whistle (e.g., Bjørkelo *et al.* 2011). However, this style of questionnaire does not allow for comparison across countries as it relies on cultural-specific interpretations of what is considered to be whistleblowing and means that respondents must personally identify themselves as whistleblowers, which many may be reluctant to do.

A behavioral approach, however, typically provides respondents with a list of activities or wrongdoing types and asks them to select which they have 'observed', 'witnessed' or which they are 'aware of'. As discussed elsewhere in this book, one major operational difference in the existing research is how broadly wrongdoing is defined, including its level of seriousness, how many examples of wrongdoing are presented to respondents and the period of time in which the wrongdoing has been observed. Relevant here is that, as the rate of observation increased, the rate of reporting decreased (with the notable exceptions of ERC 2011, which had the highest rates of both observation and reporting, and Webley and Werner 2008). This could reflect the culture of organizations, whereby if wrongdoing is perceived to be tolerated, it is less likely to be reported. However, this finding could also be a product of questionnaire items about wrongdoing: if limited to wrongdoing seen as more serious, staff are naturally more likely to indicate that they reported.

Inaction Versus Reporting

Finally, according to the POB model, it is only when the perceived wrongdoing has not been reported or otherwise resolved that the reporter moves on from the second to third phase of the decision-making process: whether they consider it is their responsibility to act, whether they have opportunity to act, and whether the benefits of acting outweigh the costs. Whistleblowing research has often, perhaps intuitively, been specifically focused on the action of *reporting* the wrongdoing and the use of the 'reporting rate' as an indicator of an ethical organizational culture.

Miceli and Near (1992: 9) have noted that 'alternative actions' are not the primary focus, and 'quite varied in their form and likely consequences'. However, employees who do not report observed wrongdoing may have many valid reasons for not doing so: the wrongdoing may have been reported by someone else or otherwise resolved, or they have taken some other action, such as speaking directly to the person. When employees are asked why they did not report, consistently a substantial proportion says it is because they had resolved or taken care of the problem themselves (e.g., one-third in ERC 2007a, 2007b; one-quarter of sexual harassment victims in Human Rights and Equal Opportunity Commission 2004). Respondents drawn from samples of police (CMC 2010) and scientists (Wenger *et al.* 1999) also indicate a preference for directly raising the matter with the person involved rather than via official channels when presented with hypothetical scenarios of wrongdoing. Many employees may also observe the same wrongdoing, but it might only take one person to alert management before it is resolved.

In some cases the action taken by the observer can be quite severe. While only 30 per cent of academic biochemists with personal experience of severe incidents of misconduct reported it, 3 per cent took personal action that resulted in the termination of the person's employment and a further 14 per cent confronted the person directly (Braxton and Bayer 1996). Conversely, if issues are minor or the result of misperceptions, employee reporting of these matters rather than attempting to resolve them personally may actually create a burden for an organization. In a study of the US Naval Academy, Pershing (2003) describes how reporting may violate informal norms about peer loyalty, while inaction may be seen as betraying loyalty to the institution – so counselling peers about their misconduct enables the observer to appeal to both loyalties.

To address this issue, Brown, Mazurski and Olsen (2008) developed the concept of the *inaction rate* as a more robust measure of the performance of organizations. When analysing the employee survey data as part of the Australian WWTW research, an inaction rate was calculated based on the proportion of respondents who had observed very or extremely serious wrongdoing and either not reported it, or not provided a reason for not reporting it which indicated alternative action by themselves or others. This requires asking staff who do not report for their reasons, and including options that cover situations where the wrongdoing has already been reported by someone else, the wrongdoing has already been resolved, they spoke directly to the wrongdoer and resolved the situation, or they took some other action to resolve the matter. The inaction rate was also limited to wrongdoing considered by the respondent to be very or extremely serious to avoid capturing situations where the wrongdoing was not serious enough to warrant reporting. Figure 8.1 shows the difference between the reporting and inaction rates of employees from 11 case study agencies.

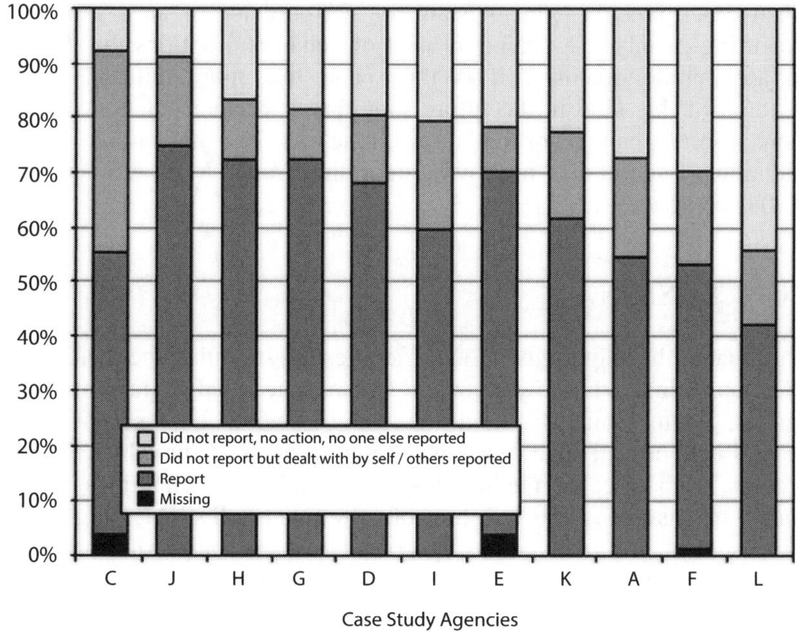

Source: Brown, Mazurski and Olsen 2008: 49

Figure 8.1 'Reporting' and 'inaction' rates

While across all employees surveyed there was an 'average' inaction rate of 29 per cent, Figure 8.1 shows that the rate across only these agencies varies from less than 10 per cent to almost 50 per cent. When all 120 agencies that participated in the research are included, the range of inaction rates was considerably wider: in some, the inaction rate was less than 10 per cent of employees, but in at least one agency in each of the four jurisdictions studied, the inaction rate was more than 55 per cent (Roberts *et al.* 2011). Rates of inaction at a jurisdictional level were similar, despite statutory regimes providing differing levels of protection. Despite this, the inaction rate was significantly lower in agencies in which more employees were aware of and confident in whistleblowing legislation (Roberts 2008). The differences are very clearly at an organizational level.

From a policy perspective, it is important to measure what matters. Is the real problem for organizations that employees don't report or that the wrongdoing does not get resolved? By addressing this question, future research can draw on the potentially more useful measure of inaction when describing the ethical health or performance of an organization. Reporting is only one choice in a set of behavioral options that leads to an appropriate outcome. It is thus clear that more holistic, applied research of this kind in the future should test whether inaction rates are more useful than reporting rates alone, as key indicators, perhaps beginning with but also improving upon the Brown, Mazurski and Olsen (2008) approach.

CONCLUSION

This chapter has highlighted the difficulties in estimating the incidence of whistleblowing. While experimental studies, anecdotal or qualitative case studies, content analysis, and the use of hypothetical scenarios and official data can all shed light on different aspects of the whistleblowing process, such research methodologies also all have limitations when it comes to answering the question of how much whistleblowing occurs. This is most accurately done by considering the range of studies that surveyed random, representative samples of employees about their past experiences. This body of research tends to confirm that whistleblowing is a relatively routine activity in the organizational life of employees (Brown and Donkin 2008). While estimates vary considerably depending on the profession and location of the employees and, most significantly, how they are asked, approximately half of all employees who say they observed wrongdoing go to report it.

In contrast to a large body of whistleblowing research that focuses on the differences between individuals in an attempt to understand why some individuals report wrongdoing when others do not, this chapter has explored the situational, organizational and public policy factors that are most likely to play a role. Any employee can be a whistleblower if they come across serious and frequent wrongdoing, sometimes as part of their day-to-day responsibilities, although the trigger to come forward may be conflict in their working environment. Public sector employees tend to report more often, perhaps because of the range of bodies external to their own organization to which they can disclose. While whistleblowing legislation is also likely to shape reporting rates by protecting whistle-blowers, providing incentives, offering multiple reporting pathways and placing requirements on organizations, further research is warranted into the effectiveness of these different elements in encouraging employees to report.

Despite this, organizations can dramatically increase the likelihood of their staff reporting by creating a culture where employees are encouraged to report their concerns and believe that responsive action will be taken, they will be supported for doing so and will not face reprisal. An organization's internal reporting policy should emphasize these messages and provide employees with multiple reporting options. Building awareness is also critical. Oversight and regulatory bodies can play an important role by ensuring that organizations have internal reporting systems in place and by monitoring their effectiveness. The implementation of systems also provides researchers with a valuable opportunity to examine 'what works' in encouraging reporting behavior.

To increase relevancy to policy makers, research is needed that is well designed; draws on multiple sources of data; uses appropriate sampling techniques and survey administration; can be generalized to a broader population; and facilitates comparison with other studies. While often seeming difficult to achieve, collaborative research involving policy makers can assist in achieving these objectives. There are clearly many different conceptual variations when defining whistleblowing: at an organizational or legal level, in how it is understood across cultures, and in its operationalization in questionnaire items. It is essential, however, that any research consistently defines and measures wrongdoing, reporting and – as shown in this chapter as most important – inaction. It is only then that the influence of context can be fully explored and firm conclusions drawn about the factors that shape an employee's decision to respond to wrongdoing.

The lack of standardized definitions of reporting by employees is a challenge for research in this area, as it means valid and reliable comparisons often cannot be made across studies, time, countries, organizations and sectors, and therefore generalizability is limited. The use of different instruments leads to quite different rates of reporting, even within the same population. This makes it difficult to discern the impact of context on whether or not employees will report and to identify what works in encouraging them to do so. Limiting the evidence base available for managers and policy makers means that their ability to implement and evaluate effective organizational strategies and statutory regimes is also limited. While every measure is inevitably flawed to some extent, crucial to an international focus in whistleblowing research is the development of a common data measurement, collection and analytical framework on the incidence of wrongdoing, reporting and inaction.

The overall aim, and one serving the public interest, is to strengthen strategies seeking to engender confidence in employees to take appropriate action, which may or may not include reporting it to someone else, when they see something they believe is wrong. The message to organizations striving to create a positive reporting environment and to policy makers considering enacting legislation is largely positive: even where cultural or social barriers to reporting exist, it is possible to take action that improves the likelihood of known wrongdoing being reported.

NOTES

1. Based on the following: (i) The Department of Justice (DOJ 2011b indicated that 638 new *qui tam* matters were filed under the False Claims Act in the financial year ending 30 September 2011, demonstrating a steady increase in *qui tam* matters over the past five years. (ii) Since establishing its whistleblower program in August 2011 under the Dodd-Frank Act 2010, the SEC (2012) has reported receiving about eight tips per day; this is a number that would equate to close to 3,000 per year. (iii) The Commodity Futures Trading Commission is also required to establish a whistleblower program as part of the financial reports; it received only a fraction (46) in the eight-month period ending in August 2012 (Alper 2012). (iv) The IRS received close to 1,000 submissions to its whistleblower officer over the four fiscal years ending September 2010 (Rettig 2012).
2. The relevant research examining differences across sectors was conducted in the United States and may not be applicable in other contexts. It also may no longer be relevant given the subsequent increased focus on whistleblowing in the corporate world triggered by the introduction of legislation such as the Dodd-Frank Act (2010) and the Sarbanes-Oxley Act (2002).

9. Motivations for whistleblowing: Personal, private and public interests

Peter Roberts[*]

INTRODUCTION

In the popular understanding of whistleblowing, motivation is a key component of the narrative. The stereotypical whistleblower is a person who is motivated by a strong belief that wrongdoing has occurred and that it needs to be corrected. However, the precise role that motivation plays in the whistleblowing process is more complex.

Motivation, for the purposes of this chapter, is dealt with as the driving force which causes employees to come forward and report wrongdoing. The definition of whistleblowing is one that has been commonly used in the research literature: 'the disclosure by organization members (former or current) of illegal, immoral, or illegitimate practices under the control of their employers, to persons or organizations that may be able to effect action' (Near and Miceli 1985: 4).

This chapter investigates where motivation is located within the whistleblowing research landscape and attempts a typology of motivation as it relates to whistleblowing. The broad categorization of motivation for whistleblowing into altruistic and self-interest reasons is proposed as a mechanism for describing and analyzing these motivations, notwithstanding that there is overlap between these categories and whistleblowers can simultaneously express motivations in both categories. Altruistic motivations for whistleblowing are further analyzed and described, with the observation that whistleblowers motivated for altruistic reasons frequently use the nature of the issue being reported as a proxy for their motivation. Bullying and harassment, including sexual harassment, are commonly reported in the category of whistleblowers motivated by self-interest.

Whistleblowing action can be an explicit mechanism for protecting whistleblower interests in a conflict with management. The limitations of using survey descriptions of types of wrongdoing are also explored and the implications for research and the management of whistleblowers are discussed. The analyses in this chapter are based upon a sample of self-selected Australian public sector whistleblowers (n = 253) who completed a survey, with a subset of that sample (n = 58) who went on to participate in semi-structured interviews about their whistleblowing experience. The focus of the study was on the motivations to blow the whistle and the delineation between those whistleblowers motivated by self-interest and those indicating altruistic motives.

MOTIVATION AND WHISTLEBLOWING RESEARCH

Many researchers investigating the phenomenon of whistleblowing focus upon the moral and ethical dimension, while others focus upon the phenomenon even more closely in terms of financial crime.[1] This is not to suggest that those researchers would dispute that there are other motivations, only to observe that other dimensions can be overlooked. Vandekerckhove (2006) notes that in the many definitions of whistleblowing, motivation is more often an implicit than an explicit factor. He goes on to make the important distinction between altruistic motives, which accord with the more commonly identified public interest notion of whistleblowing, and egotistical motivations for whistleblowing, where the whistleblower is motivated by personal interest. This chapter analyzes the relationship between altruistic motives of whistleblowing and egotistical motives, referred to as self-interest motives.

Arguably the most influential theoretical framework in the analysis of the whistleblowing experience is the pro-social behavior model. Brief and Motowidlo (1986: 711) define 'prosocial organizational behavior' as behavior that is (a) performed by a member of an organization; (b) directed towards an individual, group, organization with whom he or she interacts while carrying out his or her organizational role; and (c) performed with the intention of promoting the welfare of the individual, group or organization towards which it is directed. The pro-social behavior model focuses upon the impact of the whistleblowing action rather than motivation, but motivation plays an important role. Miceli *et al.* (2008) make the point that behavior does not have to be altruistic to be considered pro-social and that while whistleblowers may feel morally compelled to act, they may contemporaneously hold the view that the disclosure will result in some personal gain for themselves. The authors provide as an example disclosures about unsafe working conditions which potentially may directly benefit the whistleblower as well as the organization as a whole.

While limiting the definition of whistleblowing to require altruistic motives certainly sets an unrealistically high barrier, it does need to be recognized that at the other end of the altruistic/personal interest spectrum will be disclosures which are overwhelmingly in the interest of the whistleblower, with often limited identifiable relevance or any broader group or organization. An example of this would be disclosures about perceived unfairness in promotion or selection decisions where the motivation is primarily self-interest. In legal and procedural terms this spectrum is defined by notions of public interest and personnel grievances. It has been frequently observed that while these two constructs may appear to be distinct, research indicates that there is, at the very least, a blurring of the boundaries between them (Brown, Mazurski and Olsen 2008: 36). Roberts (2012) found that whistleblowers frequently report simultaneously on both public interest issues and personnel grievances.

In their influential meta-analysis of whistleblowing studies, Mesmer-Magnus and Viswesvaran (2005) observe that ethical considerations and perceptions about self-interest are related to whistleblowing intention but not to the actual whistleblowing. In line with the pro-social behavior model, there have been a number of studies which have discussed the contextual factors that, along with motivation, factor into the process of deciding to report. Those contextual factors can be seen, with the exceptions set out below, in terms of the presence or absence of impediments to the whistleblowing action. One contextual factor which has received considerable attention is the degree to which the belief that the whistleblower will suffer retaliation is an impediment to reporting. Considerable evidence supports this proposition (King 1999; Miceli *et al.* 2008; Near *et al.* 2004; Parmerlee *et al.* 1982; Wortley *et al.* 2008). Another potent impediment to reporting is the belief that nothing will be done as a result of the report, in certain circumstances even more influential than fear of retaliation as observed by Near *et al.* (2004) and reported by Wortley *et al.* (2008).

Another cluster of contextual variables centers on the organizational environment in which the whistleblowing takes place. Confidence in the efficacy of legislative protection and the comprehensiveness of organizational procedures is likely to enhance whistleblowing (Roberts 2008). Perceptions of the preparedness of managers and supervisors to support whistleblowers is another incentive to act upon the motivation to report (Donkin *et al.* 2008; Keenan 2000; Sims and Keenan 1998). At the broader level of organizational climate and values, trust in management has been found to enhance whistleblowing (Berry 2004; Near and Miceli 1996; Wortley *et al.* 2008).

A contextual issue that does bear more directly upon the motivation to report is that of seriousness of the wrongdoing. A number of studies have found that there is a positive link between seriousness and the propensity to report (Near and Miceli 1996; Near *et al.* 2004; Wortley *et al.* 2008). Associated with the issue of seriousness is whether the activity was directed towards the whistleblower, something that occurs frequently in cases like bullying and sexual harassment. That factor has also been found to be positively associated with the whistleblowing (Wortley *et al.* 2008).

As mentioned, there has been a tendency in the research to focus upon altruistic motives for whistleblowing. Nevertheless, self-interest motivations do play an important part in whistleblowing, as will be explored further below. A corollary of the emphasis given to altruistic whistleblowing is that self-interest whistleblowing can be regarded by administrators as a less justifiable form of the activity. Consequently, there can be a destructive tendency to explore the motivation of whistleblowers to determine whether or not the driving force behind their reporting is altruism or self-interest. Taking whistleblowers' motivations into account when assessing the validity of their claim can lead to whistleblowers being interrogated about how they formed the view that wrongdoing had occurred, thus making an already stressful situation even more problematic. In designing procedures and legislation, as observed by Brown, Latimer, McMillan and Wheeler (2008: 261), organizations and legislators should resist the temptation to encourage the exploration of the motivation for reporting and base their actions purely upon the objective tests as to whether the person holds a reasonable and honest belief that wrongdoing has occurred or the disclosure demonstrates that the wrongdoing has occurred.

METHODOLOGY

A valuable resource for examining a range of motivations for whistleblowing are the interview transcripts recorded as part of the 'Whistling While They Work' research project in Australian public sector organizations (Brown 2008; Roberts, Brown and Olsen 2011). Among the data collected in this wide-ranging study were interviews and survey material from 15 case study agencies. These case study agencies included large departments of state dealing with public administration, education and health, including respondents from administrators to frontline teachers and nursing staff. Also included are police organizations and local government entities. While not in any way purporting to present an exhaustive list of whistleblowing contexts, the material from these 15 agencies represents a wide range of organizational and professional situations. Consequently, these data enable the analysis and grouping of whistleblowing contexts from which conclusions can be drawn about motivation.

Of the 253 survey participants, 58 agreed to be interviewed.[2] The interviews were semi-structured and narrative in style; a schedule of key themes was utilized, focused upon getting the interviewee to relate the reason why wrongdoing was reported, the sequence of events and their experience after reporting. Interviewees were not specifically asked about their motives for reporting. Rather, they were given an open-ended invitation to relate to the interviewer what had occurred to them in their whistleblowing experience. Consequently, the interviews contained a variety of information about motivation.[3]

Some interviewees were quite explicit in what motivated them to report, while for others motivations could only be surmised by reading the context of their experience. Care was taken in analyzing the transcripts to identify the primary motivation for reporting. Many interviewees expressed attitudes about their organization which could be construed as motivations for reporting, but on close analysis of the narratives, those attitudes were formed consequent to the interviewee making the decision to report.

ALTRUISTIC MOTIVATIONS FOR WHISTLEBLOWING

In this analysis, the motivations of the reporters were transposed on the spectrum of altruism through to self-interest. The starting point for this analysis is a group of interviewees broadly critical of the actions of their organizations.

Policy Disagreements

Given that the individuals in the interview sample were all public sector employees, it was not surprising to find a significant proportion (10) whose motivation was a disagreement with the policies of the organization and frequently these were expressed in specifically ethical terms. Nick,[4] a middle-level manager in a regional office of a large organization was sidelined because management did not wish to proceed with the project that he was working on. Nick expressed the view that his marginalization had occurred because of his team's location and specifically questioned what he saw as a departure from the organizational code of ethics:

> I guess it's the total disregard for the values. We often see in our organization values being put up there and saying yes, we live for values ... it's tokenism in its form and its content. So that when we actually were in a situation and we had the evidence and we put it forward, nothing was done. So the values weren't upheld.

Gary was a junior employee and a union delegate in a large organization. As union delegate he became involved with industrial relations negotiations and acted upon what he saw as the organization being the ideological frontline for the government's industrial relations policies:

> but they [the departments] were influencing [industrial relations] policy within the [organization]. They were actually acting in a way not just to implement government policy but actually to push for government policy. So they were acting in a way that was sort of ideological rather than just, you know, as they should as departments.

Disagreements with organizational policies can be at a much more local level and involve issues of self-interest. John, a high school music teacher whose music program was suspended for budgetary reasons, mobilized community support for the program's retention, resulting in a conflict situation with his principal. John was formally disciplined, appealed and lost. The motive in this case appears to be a mix of policy disagreement and personality conflict.

Going back to the definition of whistleblowing being used in this chapter, it could be argued that reporters who are motivated by a disagreement with the organizational policy fall outside the definition of whistleblowing. As Near and Miceli observe (1985: 3), 'When organization members attempted to change the organization's actions which are legitimate, this is not whistleblowing'. However, this observation depends on whose perception of illegal or immoral behavior is going to be dominant. In the cases mentioned above, it would be most unlikely that management would agree that the actions that were taken were illegal or immoral. But as demonstrated by the selection of quotations from the transcripts, it is clearly a perception of the reporters that the action is ethically wrong and that this is what motivated them to continue with their whistleblowing activity, even to the point of suffering retaliation.

Ethical Breaches

The next category of interviewees was a group who indicated motivations with an ethical dimension set within an organizational context. Here, 13 respondents could be identified as having motivations related to activities identified as breaches of some law or code of conduct. The largest subset of this contextual category appeared to take the view that the naming category of the wrongdoing that they had observed, and reported upon, did not require any further clarification as to motivation. The sorts of nominated wrongdoings were:

- fraud;
- theft;
- breaches of code of conduct;
- misuse of allowances;
- falsification of records.

Analyzing the transcripts in terms of a narrative, the interviewees in this grouping appear to have made the assumption that the sorts of wrongdoing that they had witnessed were commonly accepted as being motivation enough for reporting and thus naming the wrongdoing implied an explanation of motivation. The issues in the list above include activities that are illegal or at the very least commonly regarded as fraudulent. Only one interviewee, who reported on a supervisor misrepresenting their hours of work, felt the need for further explanation about motivation, saying 'We felt it was not quite right'.

Within this context of ethical considerations in an organizational setting, the following situations occurred.

David, a junior officer in a large organization and a union delegate, made a number of internal reports about policies and procedures in the organization which he considered to be incorrect. He was eventually dismissed for misuse of organizational internal communication networks. He explained his motivations in the following terms:

> Why did I report them? Because they were a major concern. I suppose I believe when I see something which is wrong I hope somebody has got enough willpower to acknowledge there's something wrong and try and correct it. Unfortunately it seems [the organization]'s attitude is to just sweep it under the carpet and ignore what's going on.

Alice is a paramedical professional contracted to a government-funded organization. She witnessed that organization misrepresenting information so that it would gain more government funding. She explained her motivations for reporting in the following terms:

> I thought that [the activity] was unethical and basically trying to rewrite history for their funding purposes.

Jim witnessed a work colleague bullying an airline steward and was given a specific instruction to formally report that activity. His motivation was obeying a direction from a superior and in the interview he expressed the view that had he not received the instruction, he would not have reported the wrongdoing.

A number of interviewees reported because of what they perceived to be their management responsibilities. Liz, a health professional supervisor, reported another health professional for engaging in private practice contrary to the policies of the organization. She explained her motives in the following terms:

> I reported it, and I was assured I'd be given all consideration and respect – in fact, what else could one do?.

There were a number of interviewees who were reporting upon issues involving individuals at a lower level than themselves. While there is some logic in excluding such incidents from an analysis of whistleblowing on the basis that their reporting was part of their managerial function, it is clear from the transcripts that, in a complex organizational structure, the fact that the report may be about a subordinate officer does not mean that the reporter is immune from retaliatory action.

Finally, there were interviewees in this motivation category who, while being primarily altruistic, also carried elements of self-interest. One interviewee reported on a theft within the workplace, noting that had she not reported it, she may have been suspected herself. Beth reported a supervisor in an educational setting, saying:

> Oh well, I guess it came to the end of being used and abused. Eventually I'd been witnessing for a long time the misuse. But it's sort of resulted in the putting down of other people that made me do something about it basically or put it in somebody's hands that could do something about it.

Between these two groups, motivations with an ethical dimension set within an organizational context and disagreement on policy direction of the organization, five respondents were recorded as having a secondary motivation from the other group, indicating that there is not a clear delineation between these two categories of altruistic motivation.

Legal Obligation to Report Wrongdoing

Another category of altruistic motivation is where respondents report because of a specific legal obligation. This occurs in the public sector, for example, with law-enforcement officers and persons working with children where there are active obligations to report any suspicion of illegal behavior. In the group examined, there were only a small number (3) whose motivation could be categorized as arising from a legal obligation. Police officer Anna witnessed a subordinate seriously assaulting a member of the public resulting in this person being hospitalized. She was aware of her legal obligations to report, did so, but suffered retaliatory consequences. Sarah witnessed inappropriate behavior from a colleague towards a teenage student in an educational setting. A motivation to report where there is an active legal obligation, contravention of which could result in disciplinary action, transcends into self-interest reporting. Sarah acknowledged that she risked being disciplined if she did not report what had been observed:

> They [my colleagues] said you have no option; you must report her. If it comes out that she had a kid in the bed and you knew about it and you did nothing you can lose your job. I'm thinking, well, I don't want to lose my job and they said and your super [superannuation entitlements]. I definitely don't want to lose my super.

A category of altruistic motivation which was expected to figure prominently was whistleblowing because of a violation of professional ethics. Only one of the interviewees appeared primarily motivated by considerations of professional ethics. This was Tammy, a senior nurse reporting externally on the clinical competence of a surgeon. That case resulted in criminal charges being laid and the surgeon being prosecuted. The nurse in her interview did not specifically mention professional ethics; however, the context of the transcript makes it clear that this was her motivation for reporting.

Personal Morality

The final category identified in altruistic motivation is personal morality. Two interviewees expressed the view that their reason for reporting was an incident which they considered violated their personal morality or ethical standards. Police officer Phil acted to have a recruit removed because he had come into knowledge about that person's corrupt behavior. He said:

> and as far as I was concerned, you know, I had zero tolerance for any form of dishonesty.

SELF-INTEREST MOTIVATIONS FOR WHISTLEBLOWING

Bullying and Harassment

Turning to the group of motivations defined as self-interest, the first and most obvious one is reporting about bullying and harassment. For the purposes of this analysis, bullying and sexual harassment were bracketed together in terms of identifying motivation. Of the interviews examined, nine respondents identified bullying or harassment as the motivating factor for their reporting. While most interviewees identified bullying, there were two cases involving harassment. One of those, Jill, was an experienced teacher who had a mild disability and was sexually harassed, including inappropriate physical contact, by a fellow colleague. She went on to report the matter which was successfully dealt with.

Not all the bullying cases were straightforward one-on-one bullying. Lorraine and her colleagues in a work unit were concerned about bullying from a supervisor and the group reported through the union (even though not all of the group were union members) to have the case dealt with.

As noted when discussing ethical issues in an organizational setting, interviewees made the assumption that the sorts of wrongdoing that they had witnessed were commonly accepted as being motivating enough for reporting. A similar factor appears to be at work when discussing bullying and harassment. In other words, when an interviewee mentions such an activity, there appears to be an implicit assumption that there is a common agreement of the seriousness of such wrongdoing which requires no further explanation of motivation. On occasions, interviewees explained their ethical perceptions of the action. This is what Jane, a health administrator, said about her motivation for whistleblowing about bullying:

> It was about the inconsistency of the manager, the culture in the work place, the fact that there was lack of values for staff members. A lot of staff members had left because they were distressed about being in that work place.

The context of these interviews was a selection of public sector agencies in Australia. It is common practice in these environments to have one process for the handling of grievances and another separate one for the handling of whistleblowing. In most Australian organizational contexts, bullying and harassment are considered as falling within grievance mechanisms. This may have the effect of under-estimating the proportion of bullying cases that came within the parameters of the study. Going back to the Near and Miceli (1985) definition quoted above, it appears that bullying and harassment fall within the research definition of whistleblowing. Indeed, Miceli *et al.* (2008a) explicitly include sexual harassment in their analysis of organizational whistleblowing. This reflects changes in public attitude towards bullying and sexual harassment, both of which are prohibited in legislation and codes of conduct. By virtue of this elevation of the activity into a generally accepted category of misconduct, the motivation driving reporting would appear to meet both the definition of altruism, in the sense that it is in the public good that these matters be brought to light and dealt with, and the definition of self-interest, in that the whistleblowers are seeking to have the wrongdoing stopped and dealt with for their own wellbeing.

Self-Protection

The final motivation category to be examined in this analysis is one in which respondents appeared to be motivated by self-protection. The interview sample was drawn from the larger survey group (n = 253) who had either volunteered or identified as having reported wrongdoing. One of the survey questions related to whether there had been conflict or serious disagreement with the participants' manager(s) or supervisor(s). Overall, 37.1 per cent of respondents circled that option (Roberts *et al.* 2011: 58), indicating that the circumstance of pre-existing or contemporaneous conflict appears to be a key issue in some whistleblowers' experiences. Consequently, it was expected that the analysis of the interviewees would indicate the existence of that pre-existing conflict. Examination of the interview transcripts revealed a group of respondents (10) where the reporting had elements of self-protection. Every one of the respondents in that group discussed a conflict situation that existed prior to the report being made. Illustrative of these cases were the following.

- Peter, a manager in a medical institution, refused a direct instruction to dismiss a subordinate on the basis that he considered the directive was unlawful. A number of bullying complaints were made against him. Peter maintained that these complaints were management initiated, and so Peter submitted a public interest disclosure claiming retaliation for his original decision for the specific reason of protecting his own interests.
- Margaret, a nurse, was the subject of complaints about bullying. She reached the conclusion that the investigation was biased and

complained to the head of the organization. Her complaint was upheld on the basis of a lack of procedural fairness and the original complaints were overturned.
- Julie, a high school teacher, raised the issue of discipline in the playground with the principal motivated by professional considerations. Examination of the transcript indicates that there was a contemporaneous issue of her being accused of bullying children and having to defend herself against disciplinary action.

Even though the transcripts in this final group were quite diverse, there were some common elements:

- Many of the narratives in this final category of self-protection involved tortuous and complicated tales of tit-for-tat action, with the organization reportedly acting against the interests of the reporter and the whistleblower taking action to protect his or her own interests. In all these cases, that action included making some sort of complaint or report.
- All of the respondents in this group, at some stage in the process, were the subject of complaint from other parts of the organization.
- While in a number of cases the respondents made critical observations about the ethical standards in the organization, they are open to interpretation as constituting a rationalization for the use of the reporting process as a self-protection mechanism.

Interviewees in all of the categories that were identified as being motivated by self-interest were more likely to have mentioned pre-existing conflict than the interviewees in the categories identified as altruistic.[5]

Consideration of the cases in this final category against the definition of whistleblowing raises issues about whether these cases can be considered whistleblowing at all. As noted above, the substance of Julie's whistleblowing report was far less serious than the issue for which she was facing disciplinary action, indicating that her motivation was primarily driven by self-interest rather than the interests of discipline in the school. On the other hand, Margaret's case appears to have had an altruistic outcome, even though that may have been inadvertent.

COMPARISON OF INTERVIEW AND SURVEY DATA

In a number of instances during the analysis of interview transcripts, it appeared that the interviewee believed that naming the particular wrongdoing was enough to indicate motivation. This raises the issue of whether the identification of wrongdoing in a survey instrument can be used as a proxy for motivation. Some insight into this issue can be gained because the responses in the 54 interviews analyzed can be compared with the participants' responses to the Internal Witness Survey (n = 253). That survey instrument contained a list of 38 nominated categories of wrongdoing that were assembled using previous research studies.[6] Respondents were able to identify more than one category of wrongdoing that they had reported on and had the opportunity to provide a free text response if the wrongdoing had not been nominated in the list. The 38 nominated categories were items of a list of matters commonly perceived as public interest wrongdoing where the reporting would be based upon altruistic motivation. However, there were nine items in that list which could also be characterized as reporting based upon self-interest.

Using the distinction between self-interest and altruism, the respondents were divided into three groups:

- those who had reported on self-interest matters only;
- those who had reported on altruistic matters items; and
- those who had reported items out of both categories; this category is described as 'Cross-over'.

Table 9.1 Number of reports by reporting category

Number of reports	Altruism	Self-interest	Cross-over
1	24	22	Not valid
2	15	6	12
3	8	2	11
4	8		11
5	8		13
6	2		17
7	2		10
8	1		9
More than 8	2		32
TOTAL	70	30	115

Source: 'Whistling While They Work' research project, Internal Witness Survey, Q2

In designing the survey instrument, there was an assumption that respondents had acted upon one, or possibly two, issues of wrongdoing. On its face, the result outlined in Table 9.1 is counter-intuitive. Respondents had been asked to identify the nature of the wrongdoing that they had reported and a majority nominated multiple issues. One respondent in the survey group circled 22 out of the 38 categories of wrongdoing. Also counter-intuitive is the majority of respondents nominating wrongdoing that could be characterized as crossing over the boundary between altruistic and self-interest reporting. It was expected that where respondents nominated more than one type of wrongdoing, those types of wrongdoing would be cognate.

To further explore this unexpected result, the individual items nominated by those survey respondents who were also interviewed were listed and examined. To illustrate the pattern of responses found, those interviewees mentioned by name above have been detailed.

Table 9.2 Interviewees identified as acting from primarily altruistic motivations

Name	Description of wrongdoing witnessed from interview transcript	Wrongdoing identified in survey (self-interest items italicized)
David	Disagreement with organizational policies and procedures	Incompetent or negligent decision-making, waste of work funds, *bullying*
Alice	Organization misrepresented activities to gain more funding	Improper use of agency facilities or resources for private purposes, unlawfully altering or destroying records
Jim	Employee colleague harassed an airline staff member	Bullying, reprisal against whistleblowers
Liz	Health professional colleague engaged in unauthorized external employment	Improper use of agency facilities or resources for private purposes, misuse of overtime or leave provisions, acting against organizational policy, regulations or laws, unlawfully altering or destroying records, *reprisal against whistleblowers, bullying*

Name	Description of wrongdoing witnessed from interview transcript	Wrongdoing identified in survey (self-interest items italicized)
Beth	Work colleague incompetent and not fulfilling duties	Improper use of agency facilities or resources for private purposes, incompetent or negligent decision-making, failure to correct, inadequate record-keeping, failure to follow correct staff selection procedures
Nick	Organization abandoned a major project and sidelined team members	Free text description of wrongdoing provided as well as identifying incompetent or negligent decision-making, *bullying*
Gary	Disagreement with organizational policies and procedures	Free text description of wrongdoing provided
John	High school music program discontinued	Misuse of confidential information, incompetent decision-making, failure to correct serious mistakes, inadequate record-keeping, negligent purchases or leases, acting against organizational policy, regulations or laws, misleading or false reporting of agency activity, covering up corruption, hindering an official investigation, unlawfully altering or destroying official records, *failure to follow correct staff selection procedures, favoritism in selection or promotion, reprisal against whistleblowers, bullying*
Anna	Police subordinate assaulted a suspect	Free text description of wrongdoing provided
Sarah	Inappropriate behavior from teacher colleague towards a student	Acting against organizational policy, regulations or laws
Tammy	Clinical incompetence by a surgeon	Incompetent decision-making, failure to correct, endangering public health, allowing dangerous working conditions, inadequate record-keeping, covering a poor performance, unlawfully altering or destroying records, *bullying*
Phil	Police recruit identified as cheating	Misleading or false reporting, reprisal against whistleblowers, *bullying*

Source: 'Whistling While They Work' research project, interview transcripts and Internal Witness Survey.

Table 9.3 Interviewees identified as acting from primarily self-interest motivations

Name	Description of wrongdoing witnessed from interview transcript	Wrongdoing identified in survey (altruistic items italicized)
Jill	Teacher sexually harassed by colleague	Theft of money, improper use of agency facilities or resources for private purposes, misuse of overtime or leave provisions, intervening in a decision, incompetent decision-making, covering up poor performance, *sexual harassment, bullying*
Lorraine	Bullying of a work group	Free text description of wrongdoing provided as well as identifying allowing dangerous working conditions, inadequate record keeping, *bullying*
Jane	Bullied at a workplace meeting	Free text description of wrongdoing provided as well as *bullying*
Peter	Asked to dismiss an employee without due process	Incompetent decision-making, acting against organizational policy, regulations or laws, *sexual assault, sexual harassment, unfair dismissal, reprisal, bullying*
Margaret	Challenged procedures for investigating a complaint about her	Covering up poor performance, favoritism in selection or promotion, bullying
Julie	Complained about schoolyard discipline	Intervening in a decision on behalf of a friend or relative, misuse of confidential information, failure to correct serious mistakes, endangering public health or safety, allowing dangerous working conditions, inadequate record-keeping, acting against organizational policy, regulations or laws, misleading or false reporting of agency activity, covering up corruption, hindering official investigation, unlawfully altering or destroying records

Source: 'Whistling While They Work' research project

Looking at Tables 9.2 and 9.3, there is little consistency in terms of matching the survey items to the action that took place. With Tammy and Sarah in Table 9.2, relying upon the survey data would give little idea of the nature of the wrongdoing or, more importantly, its seriousness. In John's case in the same table, a routine management action within his school provoked an extraordinarily long list of perceived wrongdoings, quite out of proportion with the nature of the action and not at all informative to the researcher. In some of the transcripts examined, there was a stark disjunction between what was reported in the survey and what those same respondents said in the interview. In Jill's case, she nominated theft of money as a wrongdoing that she had observed. That was not mentioned at all in the transcript. Similarly, Peter nominated issues about sexual assault and sexual harassment, yet the transcript of his case was restricted to issues about his management of a dismissal case.

Comparing the transcripts with the survey items, there is a good case for arguing that a significant number of respondents used the request to nominate wrongdoing as an opportunity to express their overall frustration and attitude towards the organization. Almost certainly this is a function of a survey instrument (and indeed the interview) being based upon the recollection of the participant well after the events had concluded. One plausible explanation for the high number of self-interest items nominated by the survey respondents and the high number of respondents who nominated both altruistic and self-interest type issues would be that they are reporting upon their perceptions of the totality of the wrongdoing that they had experienced in reporting, rather than the trigger issue that was being sought by the survey instrument. In other words, what appears to be being nominated is an affective reaction to the totality of the whistleblowing experience. This would certainly explain the very high incidence of bullying being nominated (of the 253 survey respondents, 115 nominated bullying) which would indicate that many respondents are reporting upon the retaliation that they suffered. Also, the high incidence of items like acting against organizational policy, incompetent decision-making, covering a poor performance, failure to correct serious mistakes and inadequate record-keeping can be best explained by the respondents reporting upon what they see as the shortcomings in the way in which the organization dealt with their seminal whistleblowing report.

DISCUSSION

In summary, a number of issues were explored in the study:

(1) the distinction between whistleblowing reports being motivated by self-interest or public interest;
(2) what motivations indicate about the parameters of the whistleblowing experience; and
(3) collecting and analyzing data on motivation in whistleblowing.

For each of these issues, the research and practice implications are differentiated and discussed.

Distinction Between Whistleblowing Reports being Motivated by Self-Interest or Public Interest

One of the key conclusions that can be reached from this analysis is the important distinction between altruistic reporting and reporting for self-interest reasons. This distinction goes to the heart of the issue of differentiating between public interest matters and those where motivation arises from the individual's perspective of wrongdoing that affects them directly. Wrongdoings like bullying and sexual harassment, while having a strong self-interest dimension, are simultaneously matters where there are altruistic elements in the outcomes of reporting. While the immediate motivation may well be personal outrage due to the bullying or to the sexual harassment, community standards and attitudes ensure that those issues also have a strong public interest dimension.

Implications for managers and legislators

The blurred distinction between public interest matters (where the motivation for reporting is altruistic) and grievance matters (where the primary motivation is self-interest) creates a problem for organizations developing policies or procedures for whistleblowing. From the perspective of supporting whistleblowers, the adage 'when in doubt report' is a noble objective. However, as any manager experienced in these matters will attest, many of these issues are better handled through grievance mechanisms with the objective of mediating the conflict between the individual reporter and the person responsible for the wrongdoing. If some of those cases have a strong public altruistic or interest element, the person should be identified as a whistleblower and therefore attract the support and protection of the organization. This places an added onus on organizations to carefully monitor grievance processes to ensure that, at line-management level, serious public interest issues are not being ignored. In practice, this may be difficult to achieve because some line managers have a tendency to be dismissive about grievance issues and hostile to allegations of wrongdoing that may impact upon themselves or their managerial colleagues (Roberts *et al.* 2011: 23–4).

Implications for researchers

As noted earlier, this study used the definition of whistleblowing which considers the activity as the disclosure of practices which are 'illegal, immoral, or illegitimate' (Near and Miceli 1985: 4). The terms 'illegal' and 'illegitimate' have a specific meaning, particularly when it comes to organizational practices. However, the term 'immoral' is a lot broader and is not one which is commonly reflected in whistleblowing legislation and procedures. Administrators prefer more precision when they are designing procedures and they will commonly use specific terms like 'maladministration', 'breaches of ethical conduct', 'waste of public monies', and so forth. Not only does the term 'immoral' not easily equate to such definitional terms, it is also subjective. What an employee may consider immoral may be fundamentally different to the approach of organizational management. Some practices, like bullying and sexual harassment, are both immoral and, if not illegal, specifically contrary to organizational codes of conduct. The whistleblowers' interview transcripts in this study gave little indication that whistleblowers put their mind to the difference between the public interest and what they considered to be wrong in their own terms. The effect of this in whistleblowing research is that many of the activities being investigated will fall outside the organizational parameters of whistleblowing. This has the advantage of alerting researchers to issues that may be concerning employees which are being overlooked by management, but careful definition of study outcomes is required so as to align the two perspectives.

Motivations and the Parameters of the Whistleblowing Experience

Participants in both the survey and the interviews volunteered to participate after being approached by the organizations on the basis of their experience in reporting wrongdoing. Consequently, a number of participants fell outside what is considered to be the normal whistleblowing process. The study included managers (for example, from this study, Anna) who reported on wrongdoing by their subordinates. Potentially there are employees whose organizational roles expose them to wrongdoing in the workplace, in particular, investigators and auditors. For those employees, the motivation to disclose will stem from their organizational responsibilities often overlaid by their perception of their professional duties. Another category was employees who considered that a policy direction of the organization was wrong (for example, from this study, Nick, Gary and John) and raised that issue. While falling within the definition of whistleblowing used in this study, such actions are rarely considered as whistleblowing by organizations; indeed, most legislative and procedural structures specifically preclude raising policy issues from whistleblowing schemes. As indicated earlier, many respondents who had reported on policy issues or wrongdoing by subordinates as part of their management role suffered retaliation.

Implications for managers and legislators

Both of the issues raised above have significant practical implications. Looking at the issue of organizational members reporting on wrongdoing on the basis of their responsibilities, the fact that such persons may suffer retaliation as a result of undertaking what they considered to be their professional duty, is indicative of a significant breakdown in governance processes and organizational culture. Certainly, the whistleblowing procedures should be able to protect such persons, but retaliation against employees in this situation is surely a red flag to senior management that there is something fundamentally amiss in the organizational culture. The issue of protecting employees who criticize organizational policy is more vexed. Inevitably, organizations are going to take decisions that some employees are going to disagree with. Again, while ideally these persons should be given the same level of protection as other whistleblowers, the fact that such persons are using whistleblowing processes to air these disagreements is indicative of a breakdown in organizational communication. At a practical level, organizations would be well advised to closely monitor their whistleblowing processes to identify whether the motivations discussed above are triggering disclosures, and if so, recognize that this may be symptomatic of more fundamental governance issues.

Implications for researchers

In the discussion of the differentiation between reports motivated by self-interest and reports motivated by public interest, a number of observations were made above about the utility of researchers looking at the parameters of the whistleblowing experience. Those observations have relevance to the two issues raised above.

Collecting and Analyzing Data on Motivation in Whistleblowing

The examination of the motivation of whistleblowers in this study indicates that many whistleblowers, when participating in whistleblower research, fall back upon assumptions about community values in their thinking about motivation for reporting. For researchers, this has particular implications in that identifying the wrongdoing may be conflated with motivation for reporting. This would lead to the conclusion that in the design of survey instruments, participants, when being asked about their whistleblowing activities, should be separately asked about what wrongdoing they observed and why they felt that it deserved being reported.

Associated with that matter are issues about the utility of asking respondents to identify wrongdoing from what a researcher thinks is an exhaustive list of possible wrongdoing. As discussed, respondents appear to use that opportunity to express a wider range of feelings about the organization. Of more concern is how realistic to an outcome it is to assume that it is possible to generically list wrongdoing that could potentially occur. In the data analyzed in this chapter, only a minority of respondents took the trouble of entering a free text description of the wrongdoing, most preferring to circle items that approximated the wrongdoing that occurred. The end result is a false sense of precision in categorizing wrongdoing and from that could flow some logical flaws in the conclusions drawn about other elements of whistleblowing research. This is a particular issue with bullying, where survey respondents may be nominating bullying for a variety of reasons:

- a wrongdoing directed at the reporter;
- a wrongdoing witnessed by the reporter then directed to another person;
- in retaliation to an earlier report of wrongdoing; or
- part of an ongoing conflict situation within the organization.

This study has focused upon the attitudes and the views of the whistleblowers themselves. It was outside the scope of the research project to align the account of the whistleblowers with the views of management, or indeed to verify the accuracy of the statements that they were making. Consequently, an external observer like a researcher is not in a position to make any judgment about the facts of the issue and has to take the narrative of the whistleblower at face value.

Implications for researchers

Unless steps are taken to precisely identify who should be considered a whistleblower and who should be treated as a person using the whistle-blowing mechanism for self-protection, there is a danger that persons who are primarily motivated by attempts to protect their own interests in an ongoing conflict with the organization can be wrongly assumed to be whistleblowers. If that occurs, then it is likely that the information provided on issues like retaliation, lack of trust in management and ineffectiveness of whistleblowing procedures, is likely to be influenced by prior to and post-disclosure events, thus skewing the results of whistleblowing research in a direction that over-estimates the degree of retaliation that is occurring.

To draw conclusions from that nomination requires the construction of a sophisticated survey instrument that avoids the time-consuming analysis of interview transcripts as has occurred in the analysis for this chapter.

CONCLUSION

There is a stark divide between the popular view of whistleblowers being motivated by an altruistic desire to right serious wrongs at the expense of their own career and health, and a view, often expressed by managers, that whistleblowers are self-interested trouble-makers who use the protection offered by whistleblowing procedures to further their own interests. The analysis in this chapter indicates a much more complex reality. While some whistleblowers are motivated by purely altruistic reasons, others are motivated by self-interest, and the two concepts overlap with some ambiguity. This analysis does not result in any easy solution to the difficulties faced both by managers and researchers when dealing with whistleblowers. For researchers, it is a daunting task to separate out the messy contextual issues that bear upon identifying the motivations for whistleblowing. For managers, they have the equally difficult task of not letting the presence of self-interested motivations divert them from their responsibility for providing protection for whistleblowers and dealing effectively with the issues that they raise.

NOTES

* A complete description of this study is provided in the final report of the 'Whistling While They Work' research project (Roberts *et al.* 2011). This project was made possible by funding from the Australian Research Council (ARC Linkage Project LP0560303) and the various industry partners to this project, as listed on the project website: www.griffith.edu.au/whistleblowing. The author thanks his colleagues on the 'Whistling While They Work' Project team as well as these industry partners and the participants for their assistance with this research. The findings and views expressed in this chapter are those of the author and do not necessarily represent the views of the Australian Research Council or the project industry partners.

1. For the first category see Alford 2001, 2007; Bouville 2008; Brody *et al.* 1998; Chiu 2003; Henik 2008; Jensen 1987; Lindblom 2007; Teo and Caspersz 2011. For the second category see Dyck *et al.* 2010; Fredin 2011; Moberly 2006.
2. Interviews were conducted either by telephone or face-to-face. The interviewers were research staff associated with the project. All interviews were recorded and transcribed, with each participant given the opportunity to examine the interview's transcript and make clarifications or amendments. The transcripts were analyzed both to record specific factual issues as well as examining the narrative reporters were relating in presenting their version of the issue. The interview transcripts were all coded using NVivo9 software using a coding tree of some 150 items.
3. Five transcripts were omitted from the analysis because it was not possible to make any judgment about motivation.
4. The names used are not the real names of the interviewees.
5. This difference was found to be statistically significant: Pearson Chi Square $\chi2$ = 24.79, p = ≤.001 – n = 54.
6. A more complete discussion of the methodology used in the design of the survey instrument can be found in Brown and Donkin 2008. As noted by Miceli *et al.* 2008 in their discussion on methodological issues on whistleblowing research, asking respondents to identify wrongdoing from the list of definitions is a common method for exploring the nature of the wrongdoing disclosed.

10. Whistleblowers and suffering

Rodney Smith

INTRODUCTION: THE SUFFERING WHISTLEBLOWER STEREOTYPE

Suffering has long preoccupied practitioners, commentators and academics concerned with whistleblowing. Advocacy groups and professional associations have pressed for whistleblower suffering to be recognized and addressed (Borrie 1996; Vandekerckhove and Lewis 2012). Whistleblowing laws typically include provisions that outlaw mistreatment of whistleblowers and offer redress for those whistleblowers who do suffer (Miceli and Near 1992: ch. 6; Brown, Latimer, McMillan and Wheeler 2008). These provisions are elaborated throughout numerous organizational policies, procedures and codes of ethics in both the public and private sectors (see Lewis 2006; Hassink *et al.* 2007; Brown and Olsen 2008b; Moberly and Wylie 2011).

Despite these efforts to prevent whistleblower suffering, a very common view among academics and other public commentators is that whistleblowers will typically lose much in their commitment to reporting wrongdoing. Their careers, incomes, health, homes and relationships are all likely to be negatively affected.[1] One scholar summarizes their fate as follows: 'Reviled by management and shunned by co-workers, whistleblowers face a lonely existence' (Culp 1995: 112–13). For another, whistleblowers 'risk obliteration' (Alford 2001: 4).

The association between whistleblowers and suffering is so strong among some commentators that they see them as inseparable. William De Maria (1994: 12), for example, has argued that 'one must actually suffer reprisal to earn the title whistleblower'. The 'non-suffering' whistleblower is 'a contradiction in terms' (De Maria 1999: 25). In other cases, researchers acknowledge that some whistleblowers do not suffer, but they focus exclusively on those that do (see, for example, Martin and Rifkin 2004: 227; Mansbach 2011: 14–15). Survey research suggests that the common scholarly expectation that whistleblowers must suffer is also widespread in workplaces and among the general public (Gorta and Forell 1995: 331; Zipparo 1999a: 83, 86).

The ubiquity of the idea of the suffering whistleblower has had important theoretical and practical consequences. One theoretical consequence has been the conceptualization of whistleblowers as rare, exceptional people who are prepared to pay the heavy price of their revelations. Religious metaphors – the whistleblower as 'scapegoat', 'sacrifice', or 'saint of secular culture' – are invoked to capture this special character (Alford 2001: 31, 125; Grant 2002: 391; see also O'Day 1974: 381). In more secular terms, suffering whistleblowers are 'ethical resisters' (Glazer and Glazer 1989), unusually committed to 'universal moral standards', regardless of the consequences (Jos *et al.* 1989: 557). One practical consequence of the suffering whistleblower stereotype is that employees may refrain from reporting observed wrongdoing, since they are not prepared for the martyrdom that they are warned will inevitably follow their action. Such an outcome would be unfortunate in cases where employees would not, in fact, have suffered retaliation for blowing the whistle and doing so would have led to effective organizational responses to wrongdoing. Rather than promoting integrity in organizations, constant warnings about the inevitability of whistleblower suffering may unnecessarily reduce organizational integrity (Smith 2010).

As Miceli and Near (1992: 81) point out, the suggestion that not all whistleblowers suffer 'is not to deny that retaliation occurs or to minimize its devastating impact where it does occur … any retaliation against a whistleblower who is acting in good faith is too much retaliation'. At the same time, understandings of the extent, nature and causes of whistleblower suffering are so central to the ways in which scholars, practitioners and employees view whistleblowing itself that it is critical to get those understandings right. In an attempt to achieve this goal, the rest of this chapter reviews the current state of research on whistleblower suffering. The chapter covers the following issues:

- 'suffering' defined in the whistleblowing literature;
- rates of retaliation and suffering;
- types of whistleblower suffering;
- differential rates of suffering and their causes;
- effects of suffering on individuals and organizations;
- research limitations and future research questions.

'SUFFERING' DEFINED IN THE WHISTLEBLOWING LITERATURE

The concept of suffering is ambiguous. It often refers to subjective experiences – feelings of pain and distress. On the other hand, it is also commonly used to describe objective experiences involving penalty, injury or loss. The two senses of suffering can be distinguished, as when someone experiences a financial loss without being concerned by it ('easy come, easy go'); however, the two senses are often run together, so that objective loss or injury is taken as a sign of subjective distress ('she suffered financial loss'). This ambiguity, commonly found in ordinary speech, is also evident throughout the whistleblowing literature. Whistleblowing researchers rarely distinguish between objective losses experienced by whistleblowers and those whistleblowers' subjective states. The interconnectedness of the two is generally assumed. In biographies and case studies of whistleblowers, accounts of the objective penalties and punishments meted out to whistleblowers are interwoven with the feelings and responses of the whistleblowers themselves (see, for example, De Maria 1999). The survey research generally avoids attempts to measure subjective feelings of harm among whistleblowers in favor of measuring different types of negative action (ostracism, demotion, sacking, and so on) that whistleblowers experience. The whistleblowing literature commonly describes these negative actions as 'retaliation' (see, for example, Miceli *et al.* 2008), although other terms such as 'reprisals' are also used (see, for example, Smith and Brown 2008). The rest of this chapter follows the whistleblowing literature in assuming that the objective and subjective suffering of whistleblowers are tightly linked.

RATES OF RETALIATION AND SUFFERING

Estimates of how many whistleblowers suffer 'vary dramatically' (Miceli *et al.* 2008: 23). In some studies, the rates are at or near 100 per cent: all 18 whistleblowers in a South African study (Uys 2008: 908–9); 34 of 35 respondents in Australian research (Lennane 1993: 668); 95 per cent of whistleblowers surveyed in the United States (Jos *et al.* 1989: 554); 24 of 28 public sector whistleblowers in Sweden (Hedin and Månsson 2012: 160), and so on.

In other research, rates of retaliation and suffering are much lower (Miceli and Near 2013). Reviews of various US surveys of public sector employees over several decades indicate that between 16 and 38 per cent of whistleblowers experience retaliation (Miceli and Near 1989: 101;

Near *et al.* 1993; Miceli *et al.* 2008: 24). Results from the large surveys of US private sector employees conducted by the Ethics Resource Center also fall within this range. In 2011, for example, 22 per cent of private sector whistleblowers reported that they had experienced retaliation (ERC 2012d: 1). The same percentage of Australian public sector whistleblowers reported mistreatment in 2006 (Smith and Brown 2008: 123). In the United Kingdom, 35 per cent of whistleblowers who called the Public Concern at Work helpline reported retaliation (PCaW 2010: 12). The lowest reported retaliation rates (only 8 per cent) were found among whistleblowers in a 2005 Norwegian workforce survey (Bjørkelo *et al.* 2011: 219). In another study, just 6 per cent of US private sector auditors who reported wrongdoing experienced retaliation; however, their reporting occurred as part of their formal roles, rather than as whistleblowing per se (Miceli *et al.* 2008: 24).

The main reasons for the large differences in estimates of retaliation and suffering between the first and second groups of studies reported above have to do with their sampling methodologies. The studies in the first group, which find near universal suffering, rely on relatively small and unrepresentative samples, often explicitly drawn from contexts in which whistleblowing events are already known to have gone wrong (Whitton 1995: 459–60). Such research is closely related to the whistleblowing literature based on biographical case studies, in which the focus is on a few prominent whistleblowers whose negative experiences have gained media attention and public controversy (see Peters and Branch 1972; Glazer and Glazer 1989; Dempster 1997; De Maria 1999; Alford 2001).

The studies in the second group are based on broader systematic samples of workforces, in which only some respondents in the total samples will have observed wrongdoing, smaller subsamples will have reported it, and smaller subsamples again will have suffered for doing so. Their design means that these studies are likely to pick up a wider range of whistleblower experiences, including suffering, than the studies in the first group. Workforce surveys present their own methodological problems in estimating rates of whistleblower suffering. In particular, former employees who have lost their jobs for reporting wrongdoing are missing from workforce samples, artificially depressing the rates of whistleblower suffering (Cortina and Magley 2003: 260; Miceli *et al.* 2008: 11). On the other hand, the effect of including these former workers on the overall estimated whistleblower suffering rates appears to be relatively small (Smith and Brown 2008: 124).

In summary, while the exact rates of suffering vary from study to study, they rarely appear to exceed two-fifths of all whistleblowers and most of them appear to be considerably lower. Contrary to the popular wisdom, most whistleblowers do not suffer.

CONCEPTUALIZING TYPES OF WHISTLEBLOWER SUFFERING

While not all whistleblowers suffer, when they do, they tend to suffer in multiple ways (Cortina and Magley 2003: 255; Smith and Brown 2008: 129; Miceli *et al.* 2008: 16). This point is repeatedly brought out in biographical accounts of whistleblowers and in survey studies. The types of suffering range in severity from relatively minor ostracism through to changed job conditions, demotion, job loss, loss of income, medical and psychological problems, destruction of property, assault and even murder.[2] Harms suffered by whistleblowers may be strictly 'work related' or 'formal' (for example, demotion, transfer or reduction in work hours) but they may also be 'social' or 'informal' (for example, being shunned by former friends) (Cortina and Magley 2003: 248; Miceli *et al.* 2008: 14–16; Bjørkelo and Matthiesen 2011: 131–2). Suffering can extend beyond whistleblowers themselves to affect their families and friends. In one study, for example, Lennane (1993: 668) found that of 77 children who had a whistleblower parent, 60 had been affected by parental divorces.

Researchers have not developed a consensual approach to categorizing and measuring specific types of whistleblower suffering. Their various questionnaires include quite different batteries of suffering items. Items relating to the same type of suffering are often worded differently. The same harms (for example, physical or property damage) may be presented as a single item or separated into multiple items. This makes it difficult, if not impossible, to assess whether some types of suffering are consistently more common than others over time and across different contexts. The most comprehensive list of harms is found in the Australian 'Whistling While They Work' (WWTW) questionnaire, which included 27 possible types of bad treatment. According to WWTW respondents from public sector organizations, the most common types of harm experienced by whistleblowers who had suffered any harm at all were threats, intimidation, harassment or torment (64 per cent), undermined authority (44 per cent), heavily scrutinized work (43 per cent) and ostracism by colleagues (42 per cent). The least common harms were sacking, suspension, demotion, being put on probation, assault or physical harm, which were all experienced by less than 10 per cent of whistleblowers who suffered harm. Smith and Brown (2008: 128–9) concluded from these patterns that what characterized the most common types of suffering was that they could 'all be achieved more or less surreptitiously and without formal change to the status of the whistleblower', while the least common types all involved 'more drastic and tangible action against the whistleblower' that would leave either physical evidence (assault) or a paper trail (sacking etc.).

This explanation as to why some types of harm are more common than others is plausible; however, it is hard to transfer to other surveys, which use different suffering items. For example, the well-known series of US Merit Systems Protection Board (MSPB) surveys, conducted in the 1980s, included items covering eight types of formal workplace retaliation but no items dealing with the informal or social harms potentially experienced by whistleblowers (Near and Miceli 1986: 139; Miceli and Near 1989: 96). Later research by Miceli, Near and others expanded the battery of retaliation types to 24 items, including items on two informal harms (see Near *et al.* 2004; Rehg *et al.* 2008). Only around half the items in the Australian WWTW survey are even roughly comparable to the US items and none use the same wording. These problems multiply when other whistleblower surveys are compared. The United States Resource Research Center private sector surveys now collect data on whistleblower suffering using a battery of 12 items (ERC 2011: 16), which mostly differ from the items in both the Miceli and Near and the WWTW batteries. Development of a standard set of measures for types of whistleblowing suffering is necessary before our comparative knowledge in this area can progress far.

Similarly limited progress can be discerned in efforts to identify patterns in the types of suffering experienced by whistleblowers. One such effort was set out by O'Day (1974), who suggested that whistleblowers face a 'first phase' of 'indirect intimidation', followed by a 'second phase' of 'direct intimidation'. The 'rituals' of the first phase are 'nullification' (denial that the whistleblower has identified a genuine problem), followed by 'isolation' of the whistleblower from his or her colleagues. Second-phase rituals are 'defamation' of the whistleblower and, finally, 'expulsion' of the whistleblower from the organization. The aim of the first three rituals is to cause a 'voluntary withdrawal' by the whistleblower in the face of growing suffering. The final expulsion ritual forces 'involuntary withdrawal' on any whistleblowers who remain unrepentant.

Although some research studies appear to support the idea of whistleblower suffering progressing through phases (see, for example, Hedin and Månsson 2012: 154), others do not. A study of US legal cases by Dworkin and Baucus (1998), for example, found that whistleblowers were almost never subjected to all four of O'Day's phases. Moreover, in a number of cases, managers resorted to expulsion as their first and only retaliatory response, rather than trying the other phases first. Whistleblowers who anticipate retaliation seem best advised to prepare for any and all of the possible management responses identified by O'Day from the very outset. These responses may increase over time, so as 'to overwhelm the whistleblower in a struggle for self-preservation – of career, family, bank account, even sanity – until the point of the dissent is forgotten or put behind weightier survival priorities' (Devine and Alpin 1988: 227). However, retaliation seems unlikely to follow a specific pattern of escalation.[3]

In any case, we do not know which types of retaliation and suffering will prove more or less important for whistleblowers in different circumstances: 'For example, a geographic transfer might represent a more severe penalty to one individual, whereas a denial of promotion would be of more consequence to another' (Near and Miceli 1986: 139; see also Miceli and Near 1989: 96–7). Miceli and Near's solution to this problem has been to give the same weight to all types of retaliation and associated suffering and summing them, along with the number of types of threatened retaliation and the number of types of organization members who retaliated against them, into a single 'comprehensiveness of retaliation' index. This solution has proved an enduring one (see Miceli *et al.* 2008: 15–16, 105); however, one of its effects has been to help direct attention away from analysis of specific types of whistleblower suffering.

DIFFERENTIAL RISKS OF SUFFERING

The question of whether some whistleblowers are more likely to suffer than others has preoccupied much of the research in the field. Four factors that are repeatedly addressed in the research are: the characteristics of the whistleblower; the characteristics of the organization; the characteristics of the reported wrongdoing; and the reporting path taken by the whistleblower. Another factor that has received more limited attention is the impact of national culture on whistleblower suffering (for whistleblowing and cultural context see Vandekerckhove *et al.* Chapter 2). These five factors are considered in turn.

Whistleblower Characteristics

Relevant whistleblower characteristics include their psychological dispositions, socio-economic characteristics and positions within their organizations. The impact of psychological dispositions on whistleblowing suffering has received relatively little attention, perhaps because psychological correlates of whistleblowing itself have been difficult to establish (see, for example, Rothschild and Miethe 1999a: 116; Mesmer-Magnus and Viswesvaran 2005: 285–6; Wortley *et al.* 2008: 59–62). Miceli and Near (1997: 144–5) speculate that 'anti-social' whistleblowers – those motivated by negative emotions such as anger and vengefulness to harm their organizations – will be more likely to experience retaliation from co-workers and managers because they lack credibility and threaten jobs and the organization's future. The Australian WWTW public sector study found no support for this idea: 'Overall, the data do not show that those whistleblowers who said they were mistreated were any more likely to be troublemakers, disgruntled employees or individuals predisposed to fall into conflict with management' (Brown and Olsen 2008a: 141). Instead, the public sector workers who were most likely to suffer appeared to be those with naive levels of trust in the capacity and willingness of managers, co-workers and legal processes to protect them (Brown and Olsen 2008a: 141–2).

More effort has been devoted to identifying possible socio-economic correlates of whistleblower suffering, although the research remains patchy and the results have been inconsistent.[4] On gender, for example, some studies have found that female whistleblowers are more likely to be mistreated than male whistleblowers (Rehg *et al.* 2008: 235), while others have found no consistent differences (Rothschild and Miethe 1999a: 123; Mesmer-Magnus and Viswesvaran 2005; ERC 2010b: 7–9) and in one study men were more likely than women to be sacked for reporting wrongdoing (Baucus and Dworkin 1994: 197).

The individual whistleblower characteristics that seem most consistently to predict retaliation have to do with position and power in the workplace. Higher rates of retaliation are generally associated with individuals in more precarious employment, including part-time, casual or contract workers, newer employees, lower-level workers and employees under financial pressure. Employees at more senior occupational levels who enjoy stronger tenure and better pay are less likely to face retaliation for exposing wrongdoing.[5]

There have been some exceptions to these patterns (see Mesmer-Magnus and Viswesvaran 2005: 293; Miceli *et al.* 2008: 106–7); however, the patterns occur regularly enough to suggest that occupational class is an important element in explaining whistleblower suffering. Miceli *et al.* (2008: 103–4) hypothesize that employees who are 'credible, confident, competent and objective', who have expertise, and who are essential to their organizations will be less likely to suffer retaliation than those who lack these attributes. A strong connection can be drawn here with the ways in which neo-Marxist and neo-Weberian class theories use authority and expertise, along with lack of capital ownership, to help define the different class positions of workers (see, for example, Wright 2005). Professional and managerial employees who are able to use their expertise and authority to reduce their level of economic exploitation also often seem to be able to use these same resources to blow the whistle without suffering.

The potential importance of class for understanding whistleblower suffering is further suggested by the repeated finding that the relative power of wrongdoers and whistleblowers predicts retaliation. Where wrongdoers hold more senior and powerful positions within organizations than whistleblowers, the likelihood and extent of retaliation increase, compared with situations in which wrongdoers and whistleblowers are in similar positions, or wrongdoers are in less powerful positions than whistleblowers (see Keenan 2000: 204, 213; Cortina and Magley 2003: 260; Miceli *et al.* 2008: 109–12; Brown and Olsen 2008a: 150).

Organizational Characteristics

One corollary of the common view that all whistleblowers suffer is that all organizations within which whistleblowers work are essentially the same and respond in the same way to whistleblowing. The literature often adopts a simple assumption of opposition between the whistle-blowers as 'ethical resister' and the organization as 'bureaucratic hierarchy' (Glazer and Glazer 1989). This oppositional logic became prominent in the 1970s and has persisted since.[6] In a recent example, Uys (2008: 905) writes:

> Organizations typically regard whistleblowing as a form of betrayal. They believe that whistleblowing is a deviant act, which threatens the profitability of the organization and tarnishes its reputation. They therefore tend to deal with whistleblowers as traitors by punishing those who engage in this kind of activity.

This common view is challenged by research that shows that not all organizations react in the same way to whistleblowers (Smith 2010). Miceli and Near (1992: 82–8) suggest that organizations can respond to reports of wrongdoing in three ways: by resisting whistleblowers, by accommodating their concerns, or by a combination of the first two responses. Potential factors that might lead organizations to follow these different paths are: organizational sector; organizational or workgroup size; the external pressures faced by an organization; the intensity of group loyalty within an organization; the ethical culture of the organization and its leadership.

No research has systematically compared the suffering of whistleblowers in the public, private and not-for-profit community sectors. Almost all whistleblower research to date has focused either on public sector organizations or private sector organizations. Even where employees from both sectors are sampled (e.g., Bjørkelo *et al.* 2011), the experiences of whistleblowers in the two sectors have not been compared. Virtually no research exists on the not-for-profit community sector, although there is evidence that whistleblowing is not uncommon within not-for-profit organizations (see, for example, PCaW 2010: 11).

The very rough comparisons possible between the separate studies of public sector and private sector whistleblowing suggest that forms of formal retaliation (sacking, suspension, demotion, etc.) may be more common in the private sector than in the public sector. The reasons for expecting public and private sector treatment of whistleblowers to vary might include differences in public and private sector organizational values (van der Wal 2008) and differences in the legal and regulatory regimes governing the two sectors (Bowden and Smythe 2010). These differences need not specifically relate to whistleblowing; for example, employment laws and regulations may make it harder in general to dismiss public sector employees than their private sector counterparts, offering greater indirect protection to public sector whistleblowers.

A second organizational factor which may affect the likelihood of retaliation is the size of the organization and its workgroups. Reporting the finding that Australian public sector whistleblowers in smaller workgroups were more likely to face retaliation than those in larger workgroups, Brown and Olsen (2008a: 147–8) argue that 'when the size of a reporter's immediate workgroup is smaller, there is greater opportunity for … reprisals (given the likely higher level of workplace interaction with the wrongdoer[s]) and there is more likely to be an environment conducive to them'. This finding is supported by recent research on the US private sector (ERC 2010b: 3), although not by earlier US research, which found higher rates of retaliation in larger companies (Miceli and Near 1992: 215).

Whistleblowers in organizations that operate in high-pressure environments seem more prone to suffer retaliation than those working in low-pressure contexts (Miceli and Near 1992: 217; ERC 2010b: 4). A 2011 study comparing Fortune 500 companies with other US companies found that whistleblowers in the Fortune 500 companies were four times more likely to experience retaliation (53 per cent versus 12 per cent)

(ERC 2012b: 9–10; 2012d: 7–8). Similarly, whistleblowers in US companies going through mergers and acquisitions were twice as likely to suffer retaliation as those working in stable companies (34 per cent versus 16 per cent) (ERC 2012d: 7–8). The recent US recession also appears to have produced a doubling in whistleblower suffering from 2007 to 2011 (ERC 2011: 15).

One reason high-pressure environments increase risks of retaliation is that they produce strong cultures of group loyalty in the face of external threats. This phenomenon is well-known in policing. Police cultures excuse 'noble cause' corruption by officers on the basis that it is essential to the work of protecting society from criminals (Goldschmidt and Anonymous 2008; Cooper 2012). Officers who break the 'blue code of silence' by reporting such corruption face heightened risks of retaliation (Westmarland 2006; Alain and Grégoire 2008: 182–6; Gottschalk and Holgersson 2011: 397–8). Interestingly, the only published study directly comparing police and civilian officials, conducted in Georgia (US), found police had a weaker code of silence than their non-uniformed counterparts and were more likely to report wrongdoing (Rothwell and Baldwin 2007a). Previously unreported results from the 2006–2007 WWTW Employee Survey and WWTW Internal Witness Survey offer some support for the 'blue code' thesis. They show that Australian police and civilian officials were equally likely to report wrongdoing, but that the police who did so were more likely to be treated 'quite badly' or 'extremely badly' by both co-workers and managers. The differences were small but statistically significant ($p < .05$).

Organizational cultures can have positive as well as negative effects on whistleblowers. The Ethics Resource Center surveys consistently show that companies that develop strong ethical cultures and more comprehensive integrity programs reduce retaliation against whistleblowers by almost half.[7] These findings are consistent with public sector research (Zipparo 1999b: 284; PCaW 2010: 16). The role of leaders in setting ethical cultures within organizations and influencing the treatment of whistleblowers is widely recognized.[8] In this context, leadership is not limited to the top levels of an organization. Where CEOs, managers and supervisors promote strong ethical values, policies and programs within their organizations and actively support specific instances of whistleblowing, suffering among whistleblowers is considerably lower than it is in organizations where leaders either do not play these roles or are instigators of retaliation themselves.[9]

This research indicates that the way in which individual leaders exercise their *agency* within organizations is more important to the fate of whistleblowers than the bureaucratic *structures* within which leaders and whistleblowers operate. The impact of leaders on the treatment of whistleblowers points to the value of a move away from research that focuses on the characteristics of organizations as a whole, towards research that examines the micro-level 'dyadic interactions or relationships' between individuals within those organizations (Mesmer-Magnus and Viswesvaran 2005: 293) – a theme taken up in detail by Vandekerckhove, Brown and Tsahuridu (Chapter 13).

Wrongdoing Characteristics

Characteristics of wrongdoing that potentially affect the likelihood of whistleblower suffering include: the type of wrongdoing involved; the seriousness of the wrongdoing; the frequency of the wrongdoing; and its level of organization. These characteristics will often overlap. Frequent bribery to bypass regulations, for example, is likely to be more serious (due to its cumulative effects) and requires a greater level of organization than the one-off opportunistic misuse of company equipment.

Only one study appears to have explored the impact of general wrongdoing types on the whistleblowers who report them. Near *et al.* (2004) found that US Department of Defense employees who reported financial, program or resource waste were less likely to suffer retaliation than those who reported other violations, such as mismanagement, stealing, safety breaches, sexual harassment and discrimination. Miceli *et al.* (2008: 113–14) later speculated that the reason for the difference is that, since waste 'does not benefit anyone', those reporting the waste would be seen as doing the organization a service. It is worth noting, however, that at least one of the types of waste included in Near *et al.*'s survey ('ineligible people receiving benefits' (2004: 227)) does have a clear beneficiary, so the explanation is not entirely convincing.

More serious wrongdoing appears to be more likely to end in reprisals for whistleblowers than less serious wrongdoing. Different studies have used varied measures of seriousness, including estimates of monetary value, frequency, whistleblowers' own perceptions, and scales using combinations of these measures. Studies since the 1980s have mostly found positive correlations between wrongdoing seriousness and retaliation, with the small remainder of studies finding no relationship.[10] In their meta-analysis, Mesmer-Magnus and Viswesvaran (2005: 288) separated the effects of seriousness and frequency on retaliation. Both variables had effects, with frequency of wrongdoing the more powerful predictor of retaliation.

A related element of wrongdoing that affects whistleblowers is the extent to which it is organized. Bjørkelo and Matthiesen (2011: 133) argue that whistleblowers face lower risks of retaliation when wrongdoing is ad hoc and opportunistic than they do when their organizations are 'enmeshed in fraud'. At the extreme, systematic corruption presents significant challenges and costs for its perpetrators, since it relies on relatively large and complex exchange networks that must remain hidden. The 'governance structures' of corrupt networks are therefore highly vulnerable to whistleblowing, which in turn makes the effective punishment of actual or potential whistleblowers a vital part of continued organized corruption (Della Porta and Vannucci 2012: 30 especially). If the numbers involved in wrongdoing can be taken as a reasonable proxy for this dimension of organization, the available survey data have produced mixed results. Near and Miceli (1986: 141–2) discovered no relationship between the number of different groups involved in wrongdoing and the extent of retaliation against whistleblowers. Brown and Olson (2008a: 147–8), by contrast, found that the risk of retaliation increased with the number of wrongdoers.

Reporting Paths

Where and how whistleblowers report also appears to affect their risk of suffering. Whistleblowers whose first move is to take their concerns outside their organization to a watchdog agency, politician, journalist, or the like are more likely to experience retaliation than those who initially try to have their concerns dealt with internally by supervisors, managers or specialist officers.[11] A possible explanation is that initial reporting through external avenues breaks with the 'proper channels' set out in the law (Miceli and Near 1997: 145–6; Dworkin and Baucus 1998: 1281–2), or less formally in the norms of workplace culture (Callahan and Collins 1992). External reporting in the first instance could be viewed as an expression of disloyalty to the organization and its members.

By the same token, Dworkin and Baucus (1998: 1295–6) found that the differences in the suffering of internal and external reporters had to do with the *type* of suffering they faced. Whistleblowers who reported internally were more likely to be sacked quickly, while external whistleblowers faced a longer process of discrediting before they were sacked. Moreover, other research suggests that external reporting *at any stage* results in greater chances of whistleblower suffering.[12]

The greater likelihood of retaliation following external reporting may reflect the fact that by the time whistleblowers report externally, internal processes for handling their reports have already gone badly wrong, so that further action *from any source* is unlikely to improve the situation. The finding that the more authorities who handle a whistleblowing report before it is finalized, the more whistleblowers are likely to suffer, is consistent with this interpretation (Miceli and Near 1988; Brown and Olsen 2008a: 157; ERC 2012d: 7). In part, this may be because whistleblowers lose control over who is investigating their concerns. One Australian study examined the practice of external watchdog agencies returning most wrongdoing reports to the whistleblowers' own organizations for investigation, even where those organizations had earlier failed to investigate wrongdoing properly or to protect the whistleblowers. In most cases, whisteblowers were not warned of this practice, with predictably damaging consequences (Annakin 2011).

A different form of loss of control over the reporting and investigation process occurs when whistleblowers who have reported anonymously become identified. While at least one study suggests that open reporting may not expose whistleblowers to greater risk of harm than anonymous reporting (Brown and Olsen 2008a: 149), another study indicates that whistleblowers whose attempts to report anonymously become known are at a heightened risk of retaliation (Miceli and Near 1992: 221–2).

The overall conclusion to draw from these different aspects of the reporting and investigation process is that whenever whistleblowing is not handled effectively in the first instance by supervisors, managers and/or specialist officers within organizations, it is likely to spiral out of control, with detrimental effects on the whistleblower (for a discussion of the variety of consequences resulting from the decision to report internally or externally, see Moberly, Chapter 12).

National Culture

The possible role of national cultures in the mistreatment of whistleblowers has been a source of speculation but not of systematic research. Musings about the impact on whistleblowers of historically ingrained national assumptions about authority – negative Western European memories of collaboration during the Second World War, ingrained Eastern European suspicion of authoritarian states, the Australian 'anti-dobber' mentality dating from the convict era, and so on – recur during informal discussions of whistleblowing at academic conferences and elsewhere.

This type of conjecture seems reasonable for at least two reasons. The first is the power of cultural forces to shape individual attitudes well before those individuals enter the workforce. McLain and Keenan, for example, argue that '[n]egative societal attitudes toward "ratting on" wrongdoers are formed early in childhood' (1999: 266). Secondly, cross-national quantitative research based on theories of national culture, such as the widely used typologies advanced by Geert Hofstede and his colleagues, has demonstrated the impact of national culture on a range of aspects of organizational behavior (Hofstede 1980; Hofstede *et al.* 2010). Hosfstede's 'power distance' dimension of national culture has been of interest to some whistleblower researchers. Put simply, 'power distance' refers to distribution of power that members of a society see as normal.

Unfortunately, as discussed in more detail in Chapter 2, the systematic cross-national research required to test this sort of hypothesis has not been conducted. For example, the case of China suggests that the impact of culture on whistleblower suffering needs careful research. China is often depicted as a high 'power distance' culture (Hofstede *et al.* 2010). Other cultural factors that might be expected to count against Chinese whistleblowers are 'pressure to keep unity within the in-group' (Zhang *et al.* 2009b: 36) and the 'code of silence' within the intertwined Communist Party and state hierarchies (Ma 2008: 157). Nonetheless, although many Chinese whistleblowers suffer (Gong 2000: 1903), not all do (see Van Den Hende 2004). Whether a higher proportion of whistleblowers suffer in China than in, say, the United States, is unknown. One comparative study did find that, despite other differences in their attitudes toward whistleblowing, Chinese and US managers were equally likely to fear retaliation for blowing the whistle (Keenan 2007: 91–2). Finally, the focus on national culture might conceal important regional cultural differences, which make whistleblowing more acceptable in some parts of China than in other areas (Zhang *et al.* 2009b: 36). Whistleblowing research remains a long way from being able to provide confident answers to questions about the impact of culture on whistleblower suffering.

EFFECTS OF RETALIATION

For many whistleblowers who experience retaliation, the personal impact is dramatic. They are left, in Alford's (2001) words, with 'broken lives'. Within the workplace, whistleblowers who suffer mistreatment are likely to become disengaged, dissatisfied, distrusting of managers and workmates, and likely to seek other jobs.[13] The effects extend beyond the workplace. A recent account of retaliation against Swedish public sector whistleblowers provides a good summary of the effects found in other studies:

> [T]he consequences were conspicuous. Many were forced to leave their work assignments, transferred or terminated. Some described the retaliation they experienced up until their departure as a kind of psychic trauma. They were enveloped in chaos, felt confused and found it difficult to understand and deal with what had happened. In the group of respondents there were many who described various emotional reactions. They had been plagued with anxiety, depression, irritability or dread, even suicidal thoughts. The respondents found different ways of dealing with these reactions. About one-third of them described long periods of sick leave as a result of crisis-like symptoms. Others made up their mind to continue working at the workplace and not reveal anything outwardly. Still others changed jobs during the retaliation phase to distance themselves from the conflict-filled workplace. (Hedin and Månsson 2012: 162)

Even where whistleblowers who have suffered in these ways have been able to remake their professional and personal lives, this has often been a long and difficult process (see, for example, Glazer and Glazer 1989: ch. 7).

Given the widespread, if mistaken, view that all whistleblowers suffer such consequences, we would expect anticipated suffering to deter potential whistleblowers. The experiences of prominent whistleblowers often seem to reinforce this point. 'My advice to potential whistleblowers ... Forget it!', said one of Glazer and Glazer's US whistleblowers (1989: 206). 'Tell them to fuck off', was the pithy recommendation of a well-known Australian police whistleblower (Padraic 2005: 233). A number of survey studies since the 1980s have shown that employees who fear retaliation are less willing to report wrongdoing than those who have no such fears.[14] Other studies have suggested that, although fear of retaliation is one reason for employees remaining silent about wrongdoing, it may not be the most important or widespread reason. Beliefs that nothing will be done about the reported wrongdoing, perceptions of the seriousness of the wrongdoing and lack of an anonymous reporting option have been more telling considerations in one or more studies (Gorta and Forell 1995: 331–5; ERC 2012b: 15; 2012c: 5).

In addition, expectations of suffering may have greater effects on employees' abstract claims about their willingness to report wrongdoing in general than they do on their actual reporting when they see wrongdoing in their organizations. In their meta-analysis of whistleblowing studies, Mesmer-Magnus and Viswesvaran (2005: 287) report that the 'threat of retaliation is negatively related to the intent to blow the whistle, but appears to be unrelated to actual whistleblowing behaviors (r = –0.27 and 0.04, respectively)'. Whistleblowers are equally likely to have acted whether the risk of retaliation is high or low. This finding throws into doubt the extent to which potential whistleblowers follow the sort of rational calculating decision-making process assumed by some scholars, including Mesmer-Magnus and Viswesvaran themselves (2005: 291; see also, for example, Miceli *et al.* 1991). If employees do calculate risks and other factors before acting, they often seem to ignore the results, reporting wrongdoing despite their anticipation of mistreatment, or they get the calculations wrong, over-confidently assuming they won't be mistreated. A more plausible suggestion for the lack of relationship between perceptions of retaliation risk and reporting, also made by Mesmer-Magnus and Viswesvaran (2005: 291), reverses the assumed causality: once whistleblowers have actually reported wrongdoing, 'they may be so committed to taking action that they are no longer able to back out', whether or not they encounter retaliation as a result. This suggestion fits many of the narratives in the biographical and other qualitative research (see, for example, De Maria 1999; see also Bjørkelo and Bye, Chapter 6, for another theory on the noted distinction between intentional and actual whistleblowing).

If retaliation is designed specifically to silence those who have begun to report wrongdoing, the suggestion in the research is that it does not do so in practice. Instead, it seems to redirect the whistleblowers' efforts externally. Glazer and Glazer (1989: 136) report that '[t]he more abuse the resisters faced, the more confirmed they became that active opposition was the only path to ending the chain of lawless acts. Propelled by various forms of retaliation, resisters sought out new allies and alternative authority structures'. Survey studies also show that where whistleblowers face internal retaliation, they are more likely to pursue their concerns externally.[15] In line with the warnings of seasoned veterans quoted above, some whistleblowers who have experienced suffering are unwilling to report wrongdoing again (Lennane 1993: 669; ERC 2012b: 15). It is unclear whether whistleblowers who suffered past retaliation are *less* likely to report again than those who experienced no retaliation. US research on public sector whistleblowers suggests not, especially where those whistleblowers believe that their first report was effective: 'Whistle-blowers appear to be strongly motivated by the opportunity to bring about change, and retaliation is of lesser concern to them' (Near and Miceli 1986: 143; see also Miceli and Near 1989: 92). Research on the Australian public sector, by contrast, indicates that 'as bad treatment increases, preparedness to report again falls away'. At the extremes, 82 per cent of whistleblowers who were treated well by both managers and co-workers said they would report again, compared with just 35 per cent of those treated badly by both (Smith and Brown 2008: 127).

A final possible effect of retaliation worth considering is the conversion of the suffering whistleblower into a campaigner for broad socio-political change. Rothschild and Miethe (1994: 271) identify this possibility:

> The ordeal of the whistleblowing experience affects people in different ways. In some cases, people may be so ruined ... that they become permanently embittered ... In other cases, however, the retaliation transforms former whistleblowers into persistent political resisters. Their critique evolves from the organizational level to the societal level.

Mansbach (2011:16) makes a similar argument for the politicizing effects of whistleblower suffering. Although these studies present some anecdotal examples of such politicization (Rothschild and Miethe 1994: 268; Rothschild 2008: 899; Mansbach 2011: 16), it seems to occur only in a tiny minority of cases.

CONCLUSION: THE STATE OF RESEARCH ON WHISTLEBLOWER SUFFERING

The core finding of the research reviewed in this chapter is that while some whistleblowers suffer, most do not. This finding might seem straightforward enough; however, the variability of whistleblower experience to which it points provides the key to all the other research topics discussed in this chapter. If not all whistleblowers suffer, what distinguishes those that do from those that do not? Are some types of suffering more widespread than others? Where suffering occurs, what difference does it make, compared with whistleblowing without suffering, for individuals and organizations? And so on. The finding that not all whistleblowers suffer also presents serious challenges to common ways of theorizing whistleblowers and their organizations, pointing to the need for a move away from thinking in terms of broad-brush antinomies of 'bureaucracy' and 'resisters'.

If we can be sure that not all whistleblowers suffer, we know considerably less about the answers to the questions that follow from this point, such as why rates of whistleblower suffering vary across samples in different research studies and among whistleblowers in particular studies. In part, this is because we still lack a critical mass of research studies to compare. It has been a repeated occurrence in this chapter to find that only a few studies have addressed particular aspects of whistleblower suffering and these few studies have sometimes presented fairly meagre and contradictory findings. This situation can be improved with more research studies; however, it will be improved most effectively if attention is turned to systematic and disciplined comparative research. The dominance of US studies, as Bjørkelo *et al.* (2011: 207) note, means that most of what we know about whistleblower suffering is drawn from the United States. Only one genuinely cross-national comparative study (Keenan 2007) was identified in the research for this chapter. Research on whistleblower suffering has been conducted across a relatively small number of countries other than the United States (notably the United Kingdom, Australia, Norway, Sweden, China and South Africa); however, it has used a range of methodologies. The development of standard questionnaire items on suffering, whistleblower characteristics, organizational characteristics, reporting paths, and the like is essential if we want to know whether, for example, national cultures really do affect the rates, types and causes of whistleblower suffering. The same points hold true if we are to make comparisons of whistleblower suffering across the public, private and not-for-profit community sectors, or within different organizational cultures (police versus civilian, for example), or in the same sorts of organizations over time (the Ethics Resource Center surveys of US companies are a start in this last area).

Other problems with research on whistleblower suffering have been noted in the past. No method of researching whistleblowing will be perfect (Miceli *et al.* 2008: 26–32). The particular flaws that can be found in any one of the existing whistleblower research studies, however, seem less important to future progress in understanding whistleblower suffering than the incompatibilities and gaps that appear when those existing studies are viewed as a whole. Summing up the research on retaliation against whistleblowers 20 years ago, Miceli and Near concluded that 'the picture is less than clear' (1992: 231). Parts of the picture are clearer now, but much of the canvas remains to be filled in.

NOTES

1. See e.g., O'Day 1974; Jos *et al.* 1989; De Maria 1994; Culp 1995; Martin 1997; 1999; De Maria 1999; Alford 2001; Grant 2002; Cooper 2006: 222–6.
2. See e.g., Lennane 1993: 668; Gong 2000: 1910–11; Smith and Brown 2008: 129; ERC 2011: 16; Bjørkelo and Matthiesen 2011: 134; ERC 2012b: 28.
3. See Glazer and Glazer 1989: ch. 5; Devine 1997: 14–29; Martin and Rifkin 2004; Devine and Maassarani 2011: 19–40.

4. For summaries see Miceli and Near 1992: 204; Mesmer-Magnus and Viswesvaran 2005; Near and Miceli 2008: 273; Miceli *et al.* 2008: 106.
5. See Near and Jensen 1983: 7–8; Baucus and Dworkin 1994: 198; Rothschild and Miethe 1999a: 122–3; Brown and Olsen 2008a: 157; ERC 2010b: 3–4; 2010c: 9.
6. See e.g., O'Day 1974; Dempster 1997; De Maria 1999; Alford 2001; Ben-Yehuda 2001; Martin and Rifkin 2004.
7. ERC 2010b: 10; 2011: 35; 2012b: 19–20; 2012d: 13–14.
8. See e.g., Cooper and Wright 1992; Brown and Trevino 2006; Manz *et al.* 2008; Pelletier 2012; Thoroughgood *et al.* 2012.
9. See Near and Jensen 1983: 19, 21; Near and Miceli 1986: 141–2; Miceli and Near 1989: 105; Mesmer-Magnus and Viswesvaran 2005: 288; Near and Miceli 2008: 273; Miceli *et al.* 2008: 109–10; Smith and Brown 2008: 121–5, 130–1; ERC 2010b: 11; 2012d: 15; Pelletier 2012: 414; Thoroughgood *et al.* 2012: 902, 911.
10. See e.g., Near and Miceli 1986: 141–2; Miceli and Near 1992: 104; Rothschild and Miethe 1999a: 122–3; Miceli *et al.* 2008: 122–3; Brown and Olsen 2008a: 147, 150.
11. See Miceli and Near 1992: 204; Dworkin and Baucus 1998; McLain and Keenan 1999: 258, 263–4; Near and Miceli 2008: 273; Miceli *et al.* 2008: 109, 114–16; Annakin 2011.
12. See Near and Miceli 1986: 141–2; Rothschild and Miethe 1999a: 122–3; Mesmer-Magnus and Viswesvaran 2005: 288; Brown and Olsen 2008a: 150.
13. See Cortina and Magley 2003: 258, 262; ERC 2010b: 12, 15, 17; 2011: 17; 2012d: 3–4.
14. See Devine and Aplin 1988; Callahan and Collins 1992: 944–5; McLain and Keenan 1999: 257–8, 265; Keenan 2000: 210–11; Brown and Olsen 2008a: 140–2; Rothschild 2008: 891.
15. See Miceli and Near 1985: 537–8; ERC 2011: 37; 2012b: 2, 14, 16; 2012d: 4.

11. Going public: Researching external whistleblowing in a new media age

*Rachelle Bosua, Simon Milton, Suelette Dreyfus and Reeva Lederman**

INTRODUCTION

The information revolution in all its facets presents challenges and opportunities for the media. One of the biggest opportunities of this revolution is the proliferation of information and communication technology (ICT) that allow individuals, groups and teams to socialize, collaborate and connect to online content across time and space. This ability, particularly the use of social media, is extremely significant in terms of its impact on whistleblowing. External whistleblowing, including whistleblowing to the media, is clearly affected by the information revolution. Evidence of this includes the emergence of a new media organization, WikiLeaks. To date little research has been undertaken to study the impact of the information revolution on external whistleblowing.

In Chapter 12 of this volume, Moberly addresses the bulk of whistleblowing which goes to non-media recipients. In this chapter we investigate the implications of the information age for whistleblowers and for whistleblowers interacting with journalists. We present our findings into the impact of new media and the information age on whistleblowing. Our findings present the dual perspectives of journalists and whistleblowers. We interviewed 17 investigative journalists and four high-profile whistleblowers seeking to understand how the information age has impacted on the interaction between journalists and whistleblowers. We have found that there is a false sense of security in information technology amongst journalists and whistleblowers. Additionally, both journalists and whistleblowers prefer the personal touch in blowing the whistle. On the face of it, new technology presents barriers for communicating with whistleblowers. On the other hand, interaction could be facilitated by technology in ways that protect the whistleblower. Furthermore, there are some doubts about whether journalists, generally, are still relevant, given 'old media' is reducing its employment of journalists. Finally, we have found evidence that social media plays a very positive role in garnering more information from communities once the journalist is 'set on the path' by information from a whistleblower.

BACKGROUND: EXTERNAL WHISTLEBLOWING AND THE INFORMATION AGE

Whistleblowing is 'the disclosure by organization members (former or current) of illegal, immoral or illegitimate practices under the control of their employers, to persons or organizations that may be able to effect action' (Near and Miceli 1985: 4; Tavakoli *et al.* 2003). Using this definition, 'the person or agency who received the complaint' (Near and Miceli 1985: 3) sometimes include the media who, in the eyes of the whistleblower, may be able to help address what the whistleblower perceives as a wrongdoing. Indeed, the latter can be seen as part of 'public interest' whistleblowing and concerns wrongdoing that affects more than the private interests of the whistleblower (Brown and Donkin 2008).

External Whistleblowing

External whistleblowing is described as reporting wrongdoing to any party outside the organization who may be able to correct or stop the wrongdoing. External whistleblowing, including that to the media, remains highly debated as it could not only expose wrongdoing but a failing organization (see Moberly, Chapter 12; Dworkin and Baucus 1998; Kaptein 2011). Some argue that external disclosure is the only 'true' form of whistleblowing, since internal disclosure is often insufficient to deal with serious wrongdoing, and cannot provide adequate protection to the whistleblower (Grace and Cohen 1998; Dawson 2000; Truelson 2001). In the United Kingdom, Japan, South Africa and some Australian jurisdictions, legal protections apply to external whistleblowing. However, many other countries do not accord such protections (Vandekerckhove 2010; Brown 2011a; Dworkin and Brown 2013; see Fasterling, Chapter 14 and Lewis, Devine and Harpur, Chapter 15).

As also described by Moberly in Chapter 12, the list of external whistleblowing avenues is extensive, including 'government watchdog and investigation agencies, external anti-corruption hotlines, external counselling services, relevant trade unions, members of parliament and journalists' (Donkin *et al.* 2008). Traditionally, journalists have been employed in media organizations. However, there is an increasing trend for investigative journalists to operate as freelancers, driven by the down-sizing necessitated by the breakdown of the 'business model' of traditional media and the fact that these journalists are relatively expensive to employ. Our focus is on the impact of online technologies on the relationship between journalists and whistleblowers.

Most observers of wrongdoing report internally while most external whistleblowers also first blow the whistle internally (Donkin *et al.* 2008; Miceli *et al.* 2008). The choice about whether to proceed externally is influenced by many different things. For example, an observer of wrongdoing may perceive, rightly or wrongly, that there is little support for those who report internally. Further, they may perceive that observers of similar past wrongdoings were not taken seriously enough and no action was taken, or the observers may have been punished for speaking out (Miceli *et al.* 1991; Dworkin and Baucus 1998). However, in other cases there may be a healthy attitude to reporting wrongdoing internally, rendering the need to go externally redundant. Often it depends on whether the whistleblower views the wrongdoing, such as corruption, as going all the way to the top of an organization.

The Media and Journalists

Journalists and the media broadly play a role in realizing the duties of the society with respect to whistleblowing articulated by Vandekerckhove and Tsahuridu (2010) as a series of 'demands' to society regarding whistleblowing. Specifically, the media can warn the society at large about wrongdoing by airing whistleblower grievances (Demand 10). However, this is tempered by the need to protect against malicious whistleblowing (Demand 7), which most seasoned journalists are well aware of as an issue. It was certainly expressed by a number of them to us in our qualitative data gathering. Demand 2, to protect whistleblowers against retaliating organizations, is helped by media organizations supporting journalists' protection of sources, or by more formal nation-wide freedom for journalists to protect sources. In many cases sources are whistleblowers. However, protections for whistleblowers going to the media have historically been patchy (Callahan and Dworkin 1994), despite the aforementioned powerful role in delivering societal duties (Vandekerckhove and Tsahuridu 2010) and the increasing, but slow recognition of the role of the media in whistleblower protection laws.

Impact of the Information Age

The information age has impacted on every aspect of society; providing information externally through whistleblowing is just one of the ways. What has changed in the information age includes: connectivity, including social networks, virtual collaboration through networking, instant access to information and evidence, automatic searching and the ease of generating information from many different sources.

All employees are nowadays connected to intra-organizational networks and most organizations also provide access to the Internet. This means transmission of information is easy. Further, technology can also provide a way to cloak the sites being visited and to encrypt the information provided. All of this makes organizations much more porous and perhaps more vulnerable than previously. Beyond electronic connectivity, connectivity through social networks is made much easier through ICT (e.g., Facebook). This means that in the information age it is possible to connect with more people more easily.

Digital information is now the primary form of information for organizations. Further, non-digital information can easily be transformed into a digital form (e.g., using scanning photocopiers). This makes documentary evidence about wrongdoing much more accessible for observers of wrongdoing. Together with connectivity, digitized information about wrongdoing can now be more easily accessed and transmitted.

The information age has also made it possible to link information much more easily. Specifically, information can be searched intelligently using IT systems enabling people to gather related documents very easily. This can be used by whistleblowers to gather required evidence prior to going external.

Finally, IT allows for documents to be written and transmitted very easily. Further, wide publication of information is similarly much easier, evidenced by the challenge to the business model of 'old media' publishers in television and newspapers. In these ways, a whistleblower can put in writing a summary of the evidence gathered and transmit it easily to others. The summary can be complex and large in its own right. The author, however, needs to take steps to protect their identity and the origin of the document. Once received, journalists and the media can make documents public directly to readers in a raw form.

Whistleblowing in the Information Age

Considering the power of technology and changing nature of external whistleblowing, the implications for whistleblowing in the information age are profound. Whistleblowers can gather and disseminate information very easily. Whistleblowers no longer need a third party to transmit (e.g., a journalist) by using new media organizations (e.g., WikiLeaks) as a way to reveal inside information. However, information technology also enables greater connectivity and discussion of information either in closed forums (e.g., a private chat) or publicly (e.g., a blog or Internet forum). The information age also helps whistleblowers connect over long distances with trusted recipients such as well-known investigative journalists.

Summarizing, the information age lowers the barrier for whistleblowers in finding and transmitting information about serious wrongdoing externally. Moreover, the information age also opens up new ways journalists and whistleblowers can communicate.

WikiLeaks: A New Media Organization

WikiLeaks initiated its website in 2006 and provides a unique approach for whistleblowers to provide documentary evidence of wrongdoing. Aimed at providing newsworthy information to the public, it has been publishing original source material alongside stories as evidence of the truth associated with wrongdoing. Within a year of its launch, it claimed a database of more than 1.2 million documents which has since grown exponentially (Benkler 2011). Using various technical approaches, WikiLeaks can provide anonymity and security of sensitive and confidential information submitted to the website. Anonymity is achieved by ensuring the computer used to transmit information is very difficult if not impossible to trace back to the information source. This process uses an approach called TOR (www.torproject.org) or TCPIP Onion Routing. Security of information is achieved by guiding whistleblowers through the process of information encryption. Encryption processes the files being transmitted so that only people with access to a key generated during encryption can read the contents.

Together, these approaches followed by WikiLeaks provide important safeguards for whistleblowers to protect their identity. However, little is known about:

- how whistleblowers and journalists use ICT;
- the awareness of risks in using technology other than that provided by WikiLeaks;
- the various advantages and drawbacks of using ICT during external whistleblowing activities.

To explore these aspects further, we are interested in the following questions:

(1) What is the impact of technology on whistleblower-journalist interaction?
(2) What awareness is there from both whistleblowers and journalists about the risks of ICT?

In the next section we discuss the research design for the study. Following this, we present the findings in two sections. The first discusses the question of how whistleblowing has been changed by ICT. We then examine the level of awareness of the risks of providing information electronically. This is followed by our conclusion.

RESEARCH DESIGN

We interviewed 17 investigative journalists and four high-profile whistleblowers to pursue our objectives of this study (see also previously, Dreyfus *et al.* 2013). We interviewed both groups because we were interested in both sides of the story. It should be noted that due to confidentiality issues and the sensitivity of whistleblowing, whistleblowers are difficult to recruit. Specifically, we asked open-ended questions exploring interviewees' attitudes to technology and its role in the light of organizations such as WikiLeaks. Table 11.1 shows the breakdown of our interviewees by location, role (whistleblower or investigative journalist), gender and, in the case of journalists, the journalist's preferred media or media involvement. We chose not to disclose the avenue preferred by our whistleblowers. For the purpose of this chapter, we have assigned numbers to the interviewees that do not necessarily correspond to the identifiers we used in the study and to further protect interviewees' privacy, we use the term 'he' to describe participants regardless of their gender.

The interviewees, in the case of journalists, were selected based on their status in the industry and the fact that they had interacted (sometimes very routinely) with whistleblowers. Specifically, journalists needed to have a history of at least five major stories involving revelation of serious wrongdoing in organizations involving one or more sources with inside information about the wrongdoings discussed. In the case of whistleblowers, it had to do with the significance of the matter disclosed. Further, whistleblowers needed to have provided at least one major example of serious wrongdoing in their organization by revealing inside information to a journalist and having the story published. Not surprisingly, there are comparatively fewer whistleblowers than journalists. All whistleblowers have had their names exposed via media reports in their respective country or region, or in a specific industry or line of work.

We then analyzed the data we gathered by coding the interviews according to the meaning of the text. Specifically, we examined fragments of text and then ascribed a reasonable interpretation of what the interviewee meant. The fragments of text ranged in size including words, word phrases, sentences and multiple sentences. We then assigned codes against the fragments of text that reflected a balanced interpretation of the meaning of the text. We also considered all possible interpretations of the text when determining codes assigned. Two of us independently coded this way and after coding six interviews we met and consolidated our codes. Very few discrepancies came to light and so we coded the remaining interviews in a similar way. As we proceeded, we created more abstract groupings of codes that reflected the general meaning of the text, and the emerging consolidated view answering the research questions. We also refined the codes as we proceeded.

Our objective was to report our interviewees' attitudes to technology in the information age and its role in whistleblowing to the media about serious wrongdoing and not to develop a theory, grounded in the data, to explain why our subjects responded in the way they did. Consequently, we present our findings in a descriptive manner. By this we mean that we present our consolidated summary of all interviewees' responses we found in the text substantiated by quotes as appropriate.

IMPACT OF TECHNOLOGY ON EXTERNAL WHISTLEBLOWING

In this section we examine the impact of technology on whistleblowing to the media. We found new media and the information age, both enabled by ICT, impacted on trust, on communication with journalists, on documents provided, and on broader social engagement via social media.

Building Trust in Whistleblower-Journalist Interactions

Both journalists and whistleblowers seek a degree of trust when interacting. Interviewee 101 was typical in saying that they 'build up relationships based on, if not trust, then mutual understanding'. In this way a relationship is established with the whistleblower that then leads to them revealing inside information about serious wrongdoing. This is important

Table 11.1 Participant details: Location, type of participants, gender and media involvement

Interviewee number	Location	Investigative journalist or whistleblower	Gender	Media involvement
101	UK	Investigative journalist	Male	Print
102	Germany	Investigative journalist	Male	Print
103	Bulgaria	Investigative journalist	Male	Online
104	Central Asia*	Investigative journalist	Male	Online
105, 106	UK	Investigative journalist	Male	Print
107	Russia	Investigative journalist	Male	Print
108	Iceland	Investigative journalist	Male	Television
109	Germany	Investigative journalist	Male	Print
110	UK	Investigative journalist	Male	Television
111	UK	Investigative journalist	Female	Radio
112, 113	Iceland	Investigative journalist	Male	Television
114, 115	Australia	Investigative journalist	Male	Print
116	Australia	Investigative journalist	Female	Print
117, 118	Australia	Whistleblower	Male	None
119	Australia	Investigative journalist	Male	Television
120	Australia	Whistleblower	Male	None
121	Australia	Whistleblower	Female	None
	TOTAL: 21 interviewees across 7 countries	17 journalists and 4 whistleblowers	19 males and 2 females	9 print, 5 television, 2 online, 1 radio

* Central Asia includes Kazakhstan, Uzbekistan, Turkmenistan, Tajikstan and Krygyzstan

because whistleblowers are, by the nature of the business, wary, as recounted by Interviewee 104: 'they're all risk avoidant by nature, right, because of the type of scenario they are in … none of them are walking into this willy-nilly'.

Experienced investigative journalists, such as Interviewee 110, go to great lengths to build trust in the light of this:

> My preference is to meet with them first of all in person … even if it means a research trip to the far corners of the earth because there is so much more you're going to get out of them face-to-face, so much more trust you're going to establish with them – all that sort of basic stuff.

Interviewee 119 described the importance of personal connection as well by saying 'for the genuine high impact people, personal connection is necessary to them to feel safe enough to spill the beans. You're never going to get rid of the personal connection'. This clearly has implications for using ICT alone in whistleblowing, particularly to the media. Willingness to trust in this way can lead to a long-term relationship between the giver of information and the journalist where the whistleblower will 'go out of their way to help you further' (Interviewee 116).

Whilst journalists value trust built face-to-face, whistleblowers sometimes use technology to test journalists before they can trust them. For example, Interviewee 111 related cases where fake e-mail addresses were used by whistleblowers:

> usually to test me or I mean to sort of see if I can be trusted. You know, they are afraid to get in touch because they're afraid to convey information about themselves. You know, not quite knowing how I will handle it.

Journalists as trusted advisors

However, often journalists become trusted advisors for whistleblowers (Hollings 2011). One whistleblower, Interviewee 117, described advice that he sought from a trusted journalist that motivated the whistleblower to discuss the matter with a politician under whistleblower protection:

> Yes, on a Saturday I was … I done [*sic*] it over the phone. I told [the person in authority] what we'd done and [the person in authority] said [they] would contact the relevant authorities and take advice, and for me … and I think it was for me [the person in authority] would ring me back on the Tuesday and we'd go from there.

This allowed the whistleblower to seek redress formally through anti-corruption avenues. Without having trusted the journalist, the whistleblower would not have known about the provisions that the whistleblower then used to bring the serious wrongdoing to the attention of relevant authorities. The journalist had told the whistleblower about the provisions. However, the whistleblower was unhappy with the level of support from the relevant authorities (rather than the investigative journalist): 'I wouldn't do it again unless the circumstances changed. Unless there was better support from the authorities'. Indeed, in one case the poor support perceived by the whistleblower was in stark contrast to the superior support given by the journalist. The whistleblower and others involved in this first-mentioned case suffered serious repercussions as a result of the information they provided. This is common for whistleblowers; the interviewee indicated that whistleblowers 'have to be strong'.

Trust and ICT

Trust and ICT present a tension for whistleblowing. Technology affords many things, but without trust both parties are loath to fully engage. For example, all empathy and subtlety about the story around a wrongdoing disappear because there is a much poorer quality of interaction between the journalist and whistleblower. Specifically, Interviewee 106 said of online interaction that there is 'a lack of [emotional] bandwidth … that so much just isn't there in the interaction. And then empathy disappears and subtlety disappears'. Others found that the medium was 'more distant and therefore less intimate but … encourages disclosure … and people will say and do the most appalling things online' (Interviewee 105). To overcome this, journalists frequently seek face-to-face contact with the information provider.

Online avenues removed from reality

Whistleblowers may also find that online avenues potentially remove or disconnect them from the reality of providing potentially significant material, when compared with traditional means. Interviewee 110 put it best by saying: 'there is a detachment, it is less real, you know, because you don't meet someone, because you don't hand over a manila folder'. Specifically, documents disappear into the void of the Internet and don't have the 'cloak and dagger' of mail drop or a clandestine meeting. There is also a sense that the ease of providing information via online whistleblowing attracts outraged hearts commonly found on the Internet. In a sense, this is a spillover effect, but nonetheless one that heightens the risk of fallacious information. Specifically, journalists are uncertain 'under what circumstances were the documents obtained' (Interviewee 116) and whether 'they are authentic' (Interviewee 116). This brings into sharp relief that journalists need further information to judge the veracity of documents. Often this may only be obtained by interacting with the whistleblower (either face-to-face or technology-mediated).

Communication with Whistleblowers

While technology can facilitate whistleblower to journalist communication about wrongdoing, it can also be a source of risk for the whistleblower. This is increasingly so as the traceability of contact increases with ever-improving audit and spying software. Indeed, whistleblowers are often given a false sense of security by using ICT. For example, Interviewee 116 cites a case where a whistleblower 'made the mistake of sending an e-mail to me from his work computer and got called in' by his managers. Clearly, in this case the whistleblower misjudged the security provided by e-mail.

ICT facilitates communication

Indeed, some journalists use a technique common in intelligence gathering where multiple channels are used to communicate with potential whistleblowers:

> I might use a combination of e-mail, Skype, chat and phone … and if it's sensitive I might start to spread the information across those sort of four sources so there's not one place where I've got one bit of information. (Interviewee 110)

Journalists' use of Skype

In contacting whistleblowers, some journalists use Skype. Interviewee 106 said 'People [are] preferring to use Skype at the moment where you communicate voice, not text, in certain situations'. He cautioned about the danger of using trigger words in conversations (e.g., 'Osama bin Laden') that might alert others to the content conveyed.

However, more recently Skype has attracted criticism in the ICT media for its lack of security. Notably, the well-respected non-government organization Privacy International (PI) felt compelled to ask Skype to improve voice services security in order to protect users' privacy (King 2012). In particular, PI identified the risk to those in oppressive regimes who could face a loss of life (Smith 2011). The criticisms included ease of impersonating users, 'poor audio encoding … allow[ing] eavesdropping, and the lack of HTTPS for Skype download … which could be spoofed so users download' a fake version of the software that might have a backdoor (Smith 2011). Microsoft's acquisition of Skype in 2012 only heightened concerns among privacy activists about who had access to people's private Voice over Internet Protocol (VoIP) conversations (Gallagher 2012).

In many ways, this Skype example provides a good illustration of the contrast between what ICT security experts highlight as a security risk and what whistleblowers believe is safe for communicating with reporters. This gap, based on lack of technological knowledge and expertise, will continue to be a risk for whistleblowers, and therefore a problem to be managed by journalists.

First journalist-whistleblower contact

It is interesting to note that the research team's qualitative data showed that many journalists want to meet in person, and particularly that they prefer that the first contact be face-to-face. This meeting is then followed by documents detailing the serious wrongdoing. While this face-to-face engagement is more about 'reading' the whistleblower and their motives, it also circumvents the problem of not knowing which technologies are safe or risky for anonymous contact.

When it becomes clearer that the informant, who hitherto has communicated through open e-mail, has valuable and sensitive documents to divulge, experienced journalists warn the informant 'to switch to a more secure mode of communication ... we did that on several occasions' (Interviewee 109). Where possible, journalists would meet with the whistleblower as soon as possible.

WikiLeaks as a secure technology

WikiLeaks uses technology that goes a long way to protecting whistleblowers. Most whistleblowers want to remain anonymous and are often aware of the risk of technology and in some cases shun its use in providing information to journalists. Awareness of new media such as WikiLeaks is growing. Interviewee 102 said: 'I think people are getting more and more aware about it [new secure anonymous online digital technologies]' compared with several years ago. The same interviewee further commented: 'Like a couple of years ago it wasn't an issue, I would even get e-mails via Facebook. That doesn't happen anymore at all'. This was echoed elsewhere in the qualitative data: 'people [are getting] more and more aware of the possibility of passing information and who use [the channel] more often' (Interviewee 112).

Providing Documents Using Technology

Another important way in which ICT has changed whistleblowing is the way in which documents are provided by whistleblowers (Caryl 2011). Specifically, more documents can be given and distributed easily. They can be deposited without any context but in volumes not seen before. This ability to provide such volume of documents instantly is quite different from earlier times, as Interviewee 111 remarked:

> comparing Daniel Elsberg in the 70s and earlier whistleblowers who had to photocopy hundreds of thousands of pages, and as I say just the sheer operation is staggering. So to my mind, there's no doubt that [the new technologies] encourage whistleblowing.

Documentary evidence alone is not useful

Documents are often written in jargon and lack context. This means that contact with whistleblowers is important in understanding the information contained in the documents. Further, journalists don't know what documents signify and therefore need further contact with whistleblowers. The documents may contain little information about the context, thus making writing a story about the wrongdoing evidenced by the document more difficult. This is accentuated because documents, without any contextual information, provide little understanding about the story. The volume of documents also makes this doubly challenging. Interviewee 106 put this well by stating:

> [The] documents by themselves are pretty sterile ... you don't really know what they mean, you don't really know what the context is, you don't really know what the authenticity is ... I don't want somebody to say 'here is a document'.

If documents are provided electronically, without any contact with whistleblowers, then the journalists do not know the authenticity of the documents. Interviewee 110 often used face-to-face meetings to 'figure out the strength of what they've got [documents]'. Further, journalists find it difficult to check or to verify the information contained in the documents without being more aware of the whistleblower providing the documents, or as Interviewee 110 puts it, 'you can actually at least crosscheck with a source'. In this way, the journalists are ascertaining whether or not the information and the whistleblower are genuine. All of this is critical in building a story about the wrongdoing based on evidence.

Establishing a whistleblower relationship prior to sharing documents

Sometimes, whistleblowers will not release documents to journalists until a relationship is firmly established. Interviewee 116 gave a specific example in saying:

> Because that person, that doctor I was telling you about, originally contacted us anonymously by phone and then by e-mail and then we convinced her to talk to us and then after she talked to us she then gave us all the documents. She was just fantastic.

Organizations relying on ICT for conveying documents, without contact with the sender, face a common problem. Specifically, the organization needs to vet documents and do so by checking that 'files, documents are real documents and not fake. Then if they are not fake, [whether] they are in the public interest' (Interviewee 103) and warrant publication. Then, sites have the challenge of making the world aware of the documents. This is often done via social media: 'we have RSS and we use Twitter to announce new documents published on the website' (Interviewee 103).

Providing a way for potential whistleblowers to discuss with people inside the media organization to which they have provided documents is therefore important. Specifically, whistleblowers seek a 'backchannel' (Interviewee 109) to discuss the documents provided. Invariably, the whistleblower also wants to know 'when will it be published'. Indeed, providing a way to interact will be critical for the future of organizations like WikiLeaks: 'you need somebody like 24/7 ready to answer questions. And the other thing is the trust issue' that personal contact will help establish (Interviewee 109). Verification and context setting can also be achieved this way. The future, therefore, for media organizations like WikiLeaks and the more than dozen online publishing sites of that type that have popped up since, is in establishing trust with whistleblowers through interaction with their journalists.

Destroying or hiding documentary evidence

Journalists are requested by courts, from time to time, through subpoenas, to provide documents they possess. Our interviewees were conscious of this. In the 'old-school' (Interviewee 114) where actual printed documents were provided they 'might just burn [the documents]' or put 'it somewhere else' to protect the identity of the whistleblower. Today, 'you can get a lot more material in a manner that protects the journalist and the source' but 'It's also causing more and more "security control" prosecution of whistleblowers in government because of that [and] it's got everyone very much scared. It's fundamentally changed the way [journalists] receive information' (Interviewee 114). In response 'there's a lot of information that's kept in a far more secret manner than it used to be' in organizations (Interviewee 114).

Destroying data by erasing it can prove challenging, as it is prone to recovery using digital forensics unless the data storage device is well and truly destroyed (for example, with a hammer). This is clearly more difficult than simply burning a piece of paper. Further, some digital barriers come from data logs tracking who in an organization had accessed which material, and when. These logs cannot just be destroyed with a hammer. Long-term electronic tracking undermines anonymity, thus making the job of the whistleblower and journalist working together much more difficult.

Use of dropboxes for documentary evidence

A number of newspapers and other media provide a dropbox to provide documents and information about stories, particularly those that might need confidentiality, including reports of wrongdoing. Journalists were divided about whether dropboxes are good. Some thought it was a bad idea because it provided no backchannel for whistleblowers. Specifically, those providing information:

> don't really know where the information is going to end up … It partly makes sure they are anonymous but then again they don't know that it reaches the right person that can deal with it. (Interviewee 102)

Getting the documents into the hands of the right person is critical to get a story up, and this is, and remains, a problem with dropboxes in news organizations. Further, journalists like to maintain some contact with the providers of information so that the veracity of the information can be tested and so that trust can be developed with the whistleblower.

It was unclear for many journalists whether or not the claims of security and anonymity provided by boxes could be trusted. Some were 'very, very cautious about' the security of them and other Internet technologies (Interviewee 118). However, in some countries, for instance Germany, there is infrastructure set up to enable private interaction between journalists. Interviewee 109 described it: 'We have another thing in Germany like a "private box" which is a more secure way of getting in touch and the journalist can open one. It is a service from journalists for other journalists called privacy box'. Nevertheless, risks in using this sort of technology remain.

Despite the risks of dropboxes, other journalists thought that dropboxes provided a tipping point for some whistleblowers. Having used the dropbox, a whistleblower may then make contact with the journalist directly after seeing the story coming from information they provided through the dropbox. Journalists certainly see a future for electronic dropboxes. Interviewee 119, a whistleblower, said: 'I think the dropbox thing is going to be more and more prevalent and I think that's a good thing. Because it will keep people on their toes'. Whistleblowers, like Interviewee 117, expressed a lack of certainty about the security of dropboxes by saying 'I don't think it's secure. Is it?'. Such lack of confidence in the dropbox owner's ability to protect a whistleblower in a digital setting may slow the use of the technology by whistleblowers.

Using Social Media to Engage Informants

Journalists now actively use social media to encourage whistleblowers. Specifically, they use Twitter to announce new publications on sites and to inform followers of a topic or story related to a leak they have received. In this way, they encourage further contact from people, other than the whistleblower, who may be knowledgeable or familiar with the story. Journalists often use Twitter to hint to followers about a story they are writing and to ask for help. In this way, journalists gather information from people who may be in a position of power in the organization about which they are writing. These people may then whistleblow in response. Others use Facebook and other social media. Interviewee 109 says: 'We have all kinds of approaches, even on social media. I'm using Twitter and Facebook. Which is not advisable, of course, but we even have those approaches'.

Twitter and crowdsourcing

The use of social media can be quite sophisticated. For example, one interviewee uses Twitter in a way that brings further information about a story. The information is a little like a snowball gathering more snow. Interviewee 119 relates a recent experience where:

> I got a tipoff from someone saying that a particular psychiatric facility in [province] was using ropes and illegal means to restrain patients. So I sent out [tweeted] things saying 'does anyone know of an instance of this in [province]?' And within 30 minutes I had everything.

This journalist had several examples. The common theme was that early stories helped gather momentum about the topic. In this sense, a tipping point was reached, where the journalist would get 'e-mail after e-mail after e-mail' (Interviewee 119) from informants. The power of these new avenues to communicate means that others can 'point you to stories where people are disempowered but this feeling that there is this great injustice going on and that's where you get a high impact' (Interviewee 119). Other journalists 'refer to [this] as crowdsourcing' (Interviewee 105).

Blogs

Journalists see blogging as an extension of Twitter. Specifically, they use blogs as an extended way to explore a story. This also allows a conversation to be opened with potential whistleblowers and the public more broadly. It also helps to smoke out whistleblowers because the journalist can indicate in more depth the sort of story they are writing. However, journalists are mindful that training and education about blogging is required for this medium to be effective.

Chat rooms

Chat rooms enable journalists to reach the level of trust with a potential source so that the provider of information is comfortable to divulge the information they have. Chat rooms, however, have their own risks that some of the journalists pointed out: 'Yeah I'd be said to be suspicious of chat rooms because, I mean around the world they're used by pedophiles to pick up kids. You know, philanderers to pick up women … The whole thing … You don't really know who you're talking to' (Interviewee 118). Nevertheless, chat rooms that are attached to trusted sites, such as those that have been used in the past by websites like WikiLeaks, may be different. Thus brand is very important for trust, and this may help either more established media organizations (or those that are less established but with a clear brand like WikiLeaks) to the disadvantage of lesser known digital-only journalism sites, regardless of their quality or adherence to journalistic ethics.

Snowballing of stories through social media

The use of social media is also influenced by the fact that 'someone could be anywhere with a mobile phone taking a photo or a video of [wrongdoing]' (Interviewee 120). There is potential for photos or video gathered in this way to give impetus to those in authority to pursue those people implicated.

Using social media, journalists can gain confidence that can lead to an outpouring by the community. Interviewee 107 recalls an experience of using social media:

> The public outrage was enormous … There is an injustice, the police, the prosecutor's office, the investigation people, they don't do anything because someone highly placed is involved but then there's this sort of popular outrage which finds expression in blogs and in the Internet and in chat forums, it starts out and needs new Internet and it spills out into newspapers as well … The first 48 hours or so [before the use of the Internet] there weren't [*sic*] a lot of traction on the story.

The interviewee then went on to describe how the use of social media gave the story 'legs' – that is, interesting twists and angles that kept it alive over a period of time. This is interesting in itself because digital media (particularly interactive social media) can thus flesh out a whistleblower's initial story with new leads in a short time frame. This may not only provide supporting stories (verification) that might not otherwise have come forward, but also very importantly gives the whistleblowers fast turnaround, and a highly transparent feedback loop on their leak. In the past they may have shown up at the reporter's office day after day to learn what new spin-off stories might be published the next day or week. Now they can sit at their home computer and watch it unfold, sometimes with lightning speed. Interviewees spoke frequently about how important it was to whistleblowers to know when the story was breaking and what would happen next, thus digital technologies are a perfect fit to meet this need.

Nevertheless, for journalists, one story involving whistleblower information frequently leads to another story and social media facilitates this and makes it possible for more leads to contribute easily and anonymously. Further, in order to encourage contact, journalists increasingly leave an e-mail address at the end of high profile stories to invite leaks. This is seen as particularly effective in generating further detail from those 'in the know' about the story. It also encourages new whistleblowers to provide further information about the serious wrongdoing to trusted investigative reporters.

Interviewee 106 gave a typical instance where writing a story about corruption resulted in more leads:

> Yeah, because we kept writing about the subject and people kept coming forward and it was sort of interesting because each one of them that came forward said you only just scratched the surface there is much more going on than you realize.

JOURNALIST AND WHISTLEBLOWER AWARENESS OF RISKS IN INFORMATION TECHNOLOGY

Our research shows a variety of attitudes to technology that journalists and whistleblowers hold about providing inside information of serious wrongdoing using ICT. Uppermost in the minds of journalists about using technology to provide inside information about serious wrongdoing is the need to simultaneously build trust with the whistleblower and also to protect their identity. Therefore, journalists are wary about setting up a trace back to whistleblowers through technology. We also found a degree of naivety about the safety of using many forms of ICT. We have covered some of these risks in the previous section.

Caution of Technology and Security of ICT

Journalists are cautious about the use of some technology for providing inside information. Many journalists do not use electronic means to pass confidential documents:

> My preference is that if it is something very sensitive and we do sensitive stuff a lot, we keep communications, electronic communications, to a minimum and we do it face-to-face, and reorganize the filming on the ground. (Interviewee 110)

Journalists encourage whistleblowers to provide documents in a safe way. Some journalists do not trust the security of online and information technology: 'You can't really trust online I don't think at the moment' (Interviewee 110). Further, they are conscious of ICT and regularly check for viruses and other security tampering techniques. However, the degree to which the journalist protects a whistleblower 'depends on the level of the person's [whistleblower's] ability' (Interviewee 103) to understand the technology. This interviewee prefers to use 'secure communication by "Jabber" or "OTR" if not Skype and [as a last resort] by e-mail' and takes steps that are more sophisticated than most journalists do.

Others are not concerned about security or are ignorant of the risks involved. Indeed, some journalists believe that both whistleblowers and their fellow journalists are naive about the risks and capabilities of ICT to support whistleblowing. Interviewee 110 put it as follows when discussing how to protect whistleblowers from the risk of using the Internet:

> We use various methods to try and increase the security as much as we can even though I don't know anywhere near as much as I need to know about it

> and I don't think a lot of journalists do when it comes to online security when it comes to those sorts of contacts.

Some journalists prefer 'old fashioned' phone calls followed by meeting in person. However, there is often caution about this, as Interviewee 117, a whistleblower, put it because 'They can trace everything' when discussing phoning someone about wrongdoing, 'My [work colleague] made an anonymous phone call [to a journalist] and they were able to trace the phone line'. Others are cautious to judge veracity and reputation and therefore the significance of the information given by whistleblowers without meeting. Nevertheless, meeting in person helps with further online contact with whistleblowers.

Importance of Anonymity

Despite security being important for both whistleblowers and journalists, anonymity is most important. Both whistleblowers and journalists seek circumstances where the whistleblower's identity cannot be traced by a third party. Sometimes, whistleblowers seek complete anonymity and this is nowadays provided online through media organizations such as WikiLeaks. However, traditional media such as newspapers also allowed completely anonymous communications with their reporters in some cases, as revealed to us in interview data.

While anonymity is important to whistleblowers, it also gives journalists increased freedom to use the information provided. Interviewee 103 gave an example where anonymity gave him more freedom:

> I think the anonymous sources give you more freedom … like an editorial, because we don't … have guidelines by the author which are given in a conversation with the source.

When comparing security of information (keeping the carriage of information opaque) and anonymity (keeping the identity of the source secret), anonymity is the more critical:

> Anonymity comes before security … imagine someone leaks the document and the document is not kept securely and it leaks to some intelligence agency … and the damages are not enormous … but if the system is set in such a way that they can trace back the leaker the damages will be serious. So, anonymity first, and security second. (Interviewee 103)

Nevertheless, in an ideal world 'we want to have both' (Interviewee 103). Further, failure to keep anonymity has a fallout for the journalist in that it 'can change [whistleblowers'] attitude[s] to continuing to work with you' (Interviewee 103). Interviewee 108 also said that both anonymity and security are important, but anonymity is 'the first one – [the whistleblowers] are afraid for themselves'.

CONCLUSIONS AND FUTURE DIRECTIONS

Recall that this chapter explored two specific questions:

(1) What is the impact of technology on whistleblower-journalist interaction?
(2) What awareness is there from both whistleblowers and journalists about the risks of ICT?

Social media has changed the way journalists interact with potential providers of information about serious wrongdoing, including whistleblowers. By crowdsourcing, journalists can broaden the number of informants and provide a degree of cover for whistleblowers. It is likely the use of social media by journalists is also encouraging potential whistleblowers to contact journalists by lowering barriers.

Thanks to pervasive ICT and networks, huge quantities of documents can now be provided with whistleblower-generated contextualizing information, thus allowing whistleblowers to fully inform journalists. Further, tools allow for searching of publicly available information, thus making the task of journalists piecing together other parts of the bigger picture related to the specific documents much easier. However, the sheer volume and ease with which documents can be provided leaves journalists with a challenge of sifting and sorting the information provided. It also adds a block between the 'input' side of media sites with journalists and others seeking to understand the importance of the information. Those seeking to understand the documents are often reached using 'backchannels'.

By far, the biggest impact of ICT is in trust and communication between journalist and whistleblower. ICT can provide an easy avenue for the first contact and in general facilitation of new contacts. However, the technology does not help to build trust between the two. We have found journalists and whistleblowers seek to establish trust in many cases. Further, there are clear risks in using ICT to give inside information about serious wrongdoing. Whistleblowers need reassurance about the use of technology in the carriage of documents about serious wrongdoing. WikiLeaks provides such an assured path. The technology underpinning WikiLeaks can be used by any organization seeking information about serious wrongdoing. Therefore, it is likely a proliferation of similar websites will occur with a much more targeted purpose. These may be regulatory (e.g., by a securities commission); within a specific organization (e.g., a specific bank) or industry (e.g., the banking industry); or concerned with systemic corruption (e.g., for a crime commission or ombudsman). Supporting personal contact at these sites in a safe way will increase whistleblower trust of the avenue to provide information, by enabling them contact with someone 'behind the scenes'. However, awareness of the technology underpinning the WikiLeaks model remains poor.

Awareness of the risks of technology was mixed. Indeed, there is a degree of naivety about the risks of technology when conveying documents about serious wrongdoing to someone outside the organization. This brings a false sense of security when using some avenues. For example, some try to use e-mail or unsecured dropboxes to give sensitive information. This risks the information being read in transit, and the identity of the sender being uncovered by tracing the sending back to a specific computer. Others are more cautious and understand the risks taken.

The WikiLeaks model has provided a secure and anonymous way of document provision, thereby keeping the whistleblower safe. Nevertheless, allowing for one-on-one contact between members of the publishing organization and the prospective whistleblower is crucial to the ongoing success of this model. As whistleblower Interviewee 117 put it, he 'wouldn't use the Internet to leak something because you don't have that trust relationship with a computer as opposed to [a journalist]' with whom he has a relationship. Further, even if WikiLeaks is not completely secure or anonymous, it is head-and-shoulders better than other forms of digital communication (e.g., Skype or e-mail). Our results show that some journalists realize this risk, but in general there is also a degree of naivety in both the whistleblowing and journalist communities about the use of technology for providing details of serious wrongdoing. Specifically, we found that some journalists and whistleblowers overly trust technology, and apply to it in their own minds a degree of anonymity that it often does not truly offer. However, we also found a degree of maturity with whistleblowers and the most experienced journalists in our sample.

We now see the first purely technical avenues for whistleblowers to provide inside information to media organizations and to journalists. Specifically, whistleblowers can now provide the information easily, untraced, without any human contact to the media via truly anonymizing electronic means. The technology is lowering the barriers for whistle-blowers. Therefore, one avenue for future research would be to analyze whistleblowing via ICT through the lens of 'the theory of planned behavior' (Taylor and Todd 1995). This theory is often applied in information systems to explain how human actors decide to use specific technology and is particularly useful in situations where the use of technology is entirely volitional. The use of WikiLeaks is such an example. Further, the theory of planned behavior is superior to other technology adoption theories applied in information systems because the unit of analysis is the individual user, the use context of the technology is not assumed to be an organization, and there are clear social norms and individual attitudes that apply in this context. Also, many studies in information systems that examine the adoption of technology often do so where the individual user has no power to reject the technology, which does not apply in this setting.

Despite the devastating impact of the Web on media companies, new media sites following the WikiLeaks technical model will play an important role in ensuring the remaining investigative journalists, many in freelance roles, will have access to whistleblowers and their documents. In turn, this will help the new media to continue to be the fourth estate critical to contemporary democracy. One important part of this is enabling journalists to fulfil the demands Vandekerckhove and Tsahuridu (2010) identify. Provision of large numbers of documents *directly* from whistleblowers to the public may not be as easy to facilitate in the future.

Online technology, such as the technology underpinning WikiLeaks, will be important for regulatory authorities, industries, journalists, media outlets and others playing the role of 'the person or agency who received the complaint' (Near and Miceli 1985) to help the whistleblower redress the wrong she/he has seen. Policy responses will have to be formulated to help achieve this objective.

NOTE

* We thank our project team colleague A.J. Brown of Griffith University for his inputs into this research, and the Australian Research Council for funding support under DP1095696.

12. 'To persons or organizations that may be able to effect action': Whistleblowing recipients

Richard Moberly

INTRODUCTION

As this book demonstrates, scholars have conducted substantial research on whistleblowers. However, the *recipients* of whistleblower disclosures receive much less academic attention, which is surprising because they play a crucial and difficult role in the whistleblowing process (Near and Miceli 1995: 693).

Indeed, Miceli *et al.* (2008: 140) call the recipient 'the most important ... member' in the whistleblowing process other than the whistleblower, 'because he or she will decide what action will be taken'. Classically defined as 'persons or organizations that may be able to effect action' after they receive a report of misconduct (Near and Miceli 1985: 4), recipients can respond to the allegation in numerous ways that will help determine the impact of the whistleblower's complaint.

Recipients can work to alleviate the underlying misconduct or they can ignore the complaint and/or retaliate against the whistleblower (see Miceli and Near 1992: 179; Mesmer-Magnus and Viswesvaran 2005: 281; Near and Miceli 1986: 138–41). Whistleblowers will assess the recipient's response and act accordingly: if they are ignored, they may continue to blow the whistle to a different recipient, or they may give up. They may exit the company. If they are retaliated against, they may file an additional complaint, either internally or to an administrative or judicial body if they are protected by anti-retaliation protections (Miceli and Near 1992: 56–8). Recipients affect not only the specific whistle-blower in a specific instance, but also 'the propensity of other observers of wrongdoing to report concerns internally' (Miceli and Near 1992: 77). Even the whistleblower's perceptions about the recipient's potential responsiveness or likelihood to retaliate could matter to an individual's decision to report misconduct, as well as whether to remain anonymous when reporting (Miceli and Near 1992: 151).

The recipient's job is challenging and potentially problematic (Miceli and Near 1992: 183). As put by Roberts *et al.* (2011: 45), 'recipients of reports face a difficult task, needing to stand above personal interest and look to the long-term benefit for the organization while at the same time dealing responsibly and professionally with a reporter who is likely to be under considerable stress … A major issue for organizations is that so many of their staff, sometimes at relatively junior levels, might not have the skills to conduct careful assessment of reports'. Other problems may arise because a recipient often is also the whistleblower's supervisor. Miceli and Near (1992: 184) note that 'these may be conflicting roles, because the supervisor, when acting in the company recipient mode, may agree that the wrongdoing has occurred and feel compelled to act to terminate it, yet feel defensive that the subordinate has implicitly criticized her or his behavior in somehow allowing the wrongdoing to occur, even if she or he is not directly responsible for committing the wrongdoing'.

Because of their important and complicated role, this chapter takes an in-depth look at disclosure recipients. First, the chapter presents a taxonomy for considering types of recipients and also summarizes the sometimes problematic and inconsistent approach taken by policy makers and the law towards these players. Secondly, the chapter identifies predictions about recipients made by whistleblowing theory and highlights studies focusing on various recipients. Finally, the chapter offers some insight into future research that could be conducted in order to better understand how recipients can more effectively correct wrongdoing and protect whistleblowers.

A TAXONOMY OF RECIPIENTS

Scholars typically identify two types of recipients: those who are in the same organization as the whistleblower (an 'internal' recipient) and those who are outside of the organization ('external') (Miceli and Near 1992: 25). Given the accepted definition of a recipient as one who can 'effect action', there is general agreement that co-workers, friends and family are not proper whistleblowing recipients because they cannot correct the problem disclosed by the whistleblower (Miceli and Near 1992: 16). Recently, Vandekerckhove modified this approach by splitting the 'external' category into two types of recipients: regulatory and the general public, typically thought of as the media (Vandekerckhove 2010: 17). While Bosua *et al.* (Chapter 11) examine whistleblowing to the media, this chapter will discuss internal recipients and external recipients such as administrative, regulatory or law enforcement bodies.

The simplicity of these labels belies the many different roles recipients can take. In Australia, for example, 'external recipients of disclosures potentially include government watchdog and investigation agencies, auditors general, ombudspersons, external anti-corruption hotlines, corruption commissioners, external counseling services, public service commissions, relevant trade unions, and members of parliament' (Donkin *et al.* 2008: 86; Annakin 2011: 33–6).

Internal recipients run the gamut too. A whistleblower's direct supervisor presents the most obvious internal choice to receive a disclosure. But numerous other internal recipients exist as well, such as human resources personnel, department heads, legal counsel, ombudspersons, the board of directors and internal hotlines (Miceli and Near 1992: 57, 78; Moberly 2006: 1138). Some organizations have entire 'ethical standard units' or 'fraud investigation units' that receive and investigate whistleblower reports (Donkin *et al.* 2008: 86).

To complicate matters more, some recipients blend the categories. Jonathan Brock has written about a unique effort at the Hanford Nuclear Site in Washington state, called the Hanford Joint Council for Resolving Employee Concerns. The Council consists of employee and management representatives, as well as outside public interest and advocacy groups, and neutrals. Employees at the plant who feel that a safety problem has not been resolved sufficiently can report to the independent Council, which will investigate the problem and make provisions to protect the employee from retaliation (Brock 1999: 511–12). According to Brock, the Council works because of the combination of numerous factors:

> the membership composition and the tools it brings, including the capacity to immediately bring the right level of authority and perspective to the case; independence and neutrality; the fact that the system's existence, features, and its operating authority are the product of agreement by all relevant direct and indirect parties; the rule of working and recommending by consensus; the agreement to presumptively implement consensus decisions; the stable and rapid availability of a multi-tool mechanism; and mutual risk-taking to let the process work. (Brock 1999: 517)

From a definitional perspective, the choice among these recipients matters little to whether an act of disclosure should be considered 'whistleblowing'. Miceli and Near argue that because almost all whistleblowers who report externally initially report internally; the external report is a continuation of a process that began with an internal report, 'rather than doing something radically different' (Miceli *et al.* 2008: 8;

Miceli and Near 1992: 25). It is certainly clear from existing research that contrary to some stereotypes, whistleblowers overwhelmingly report misconduct to an internal recipient first and often stop before reporting externally (see Miceli and Near 1992: 13, 26, 194; Donkin *et al.* 2008: 106; Rothschild and Miethe 1999a: 112). They make external disclosures only after they have met with opposition or retaliation from inside their organization (see Skivenes and Trygstad 2010a: 1083; Annakin 2011: 166; Rothschild and Miethe 1999a: 119). This picture is borne out by recent research in Australia (Donkin *et al.* 2008: 83–91), the United States (ERC 2010a: 15; MSPB 2011: 2, 8–9), and Norway (Skivenes and Trygstad 2010a: 1083). In all these studies, less than 10 per cent of whistleblowers ever went outside their own organization, and overwhelmingly, those who did only acted after receiving an adverse internal response.

The recipient's status as an organizational member or an outsider does not alter the essential component of whistleblowing, that an insider wants to report wrongdoing and to use voice to change the organization (Miceli and Near 1992: 25).[1] However, this choice between an internal and an external recipient can matter significantly beyond mere definitions. As Miceli and Near (1992: 27) also noted, the choice of the complaint recipient may not define the act of whistleblowing, but it certainly affects 'how the whistle-blowing process is played out'. The distinction between internal and external (regulatory) recipients provides a categorical schemata to assess the trade-offs reporting to each type of recipient creates, while trying to advance the dual goals of reducing wrongdoing and protecting whistleblowers. Society, organizations, the law, whistleblowers, and even the recipients themselves each have a perspective on who the 'best' recipient may be. Indeed, Dworkin and Callahan noted in 1991 that whistleblowing involves the balancing of several interests: the individual whistleblower desires to report misconduct without suffering a reprisal; the organization has an interest in 'control and efficiency'; and society wants to encourage 'lawful behavior and public accountability'. The recipient's identity plays an essential role in this balancing. Thus, '[d]ecisions regarding the appropriateness of outlets [i.e., recipients] are crucial to the interests of the parties involved, because they determine who can act upon the information, when and how a remedial or punitive response may be made, and whose interests are furthered or impaired' (Dworkin and Callahan 1991: 268).

Yet, as discussed in more detail below, despite attempts by society, organizations and the law to influence a recipient's response to a whistleblower, how these important players react to whistleblower disclosures remains under-studied and relatively indeterminate.

External Recipients: Promoting Law Enforcement and the Public Good

Some have argued that external reporting should be required, or at least prioritized, because external recipients will correct the underlying wrongdoing more readily than an internal, organizational recipient who may be tempted to ignore or cover up the problem (Mesmer-Magnus and Viswesvaran 2005: 278; Dworkin and Baucus 1998: 1286). As Sinzdak noted (2008: 1651), '[p]roponents of an external reporting requirement emphasize the whistleblower's role in protecting the public's welfare and in promoting enforcement of particular statutes'.

The ability of an external recipient to respond to wrongdoing could be crucial, because some studies have indicated that whistleblowers report externally when the misconduct involves severe or physically harmful wrongdoing as opposed to economic or psychological harms (see Dworkin and Baucus 1998: 1285, 1294; Callahan and Dworkin 1994; Near and Miceli 1985). Indeed, particularly in situations when an organization depends on the wrongdoing, organizational power theory predicts that external whistleblowing will be more effective than internal disclosures (Near and Miceli 1995: 697). This may also be true because internal whistleblowers most frequently report to their supervisor, which according to at least one study leads to reduced effectiveness at getting the wrongdoing to end compared to external whistleblowers (Dworkin and Baucus 1998: 1295).[2]

One problem with external whistleblowing, of course, may be that it can be disruptive to the organization, even while benefiting society generally (Donkin *et al.* 2008: 94). Donkin *et al.* note another problem with external whistleblowing: it may be anti-social, rather than pro-social, if a whistleblower reports externally to gain some sort of individual benefit without reporting internally first (2008: 94).

Internal Recipients: Promoting Efficiency and Organizational Control

From the organization's perspective, the opposite is true: organizations likely prefer internal whistleblowing because the wrongdoing can be addressed without tremendous upheaval. As Callahan *et al.* argue (2004: 905), '[i]nternal disclosures … minimize the organizational costs of whistleblowing by permitting employers to rectify misconduct confidentially and with little disruption to employer-employee relationships. Internal reports also enable the correction of misunderstandings, reducing the likelihood that the organization will unfairly suffer harm due to external exposure'. Organizations can 'take corrective action and thereby reduce the likelihood of lost business, adverse publicity, litigation, fines or other criminal sanctions, and other adverse consequences' (Dworkin and Callahan 1991: 300). Moreover, organizations that fix problems reported to them may find an increase in employee loyalty, which enhances organizational culture (Miceli *et al.* 2009: 380).

The downside of internal whistleblowing appears when it does not work and the organization either ignores the misconduct, retaliates against the whistleblower, or both. Other downsides often mentioned about internal whistleblowing, such as that it disrupts employee productivity and serves a private, rather than a public interest, lack empirical support according to Dworkin and Callahan (1991: 303), because whistleblowers rarely act out of spite or malice.

The Law: Betwixt and Between

The balancing between the benefits and drawbacks of internal and external whistleblowing does not occur in a vacuum. At times, the law distinguishes between internal and external recipients by protecting whistleblowers from retaliation only if they choose the law's preferred recipient. As put by Dworkin and Near (1997: 3), our typical social science definition of whistleblowing as reporting 'to any party who can effect action' differs from the legal definition, which often is 'more restrictive'. Moreover, some laws attempt to influence a whistleblower's choice of recipient, either by requiring organizations to create disclosure channels or by rewarding whistleblowers who report to a particular recipient.

With regard to retaliation protection, Callahan and Dehn (2004a: 904–5) noted that '[i]nternal reports are strongly favored in the United Kingdom, while US and Australian laws tend to emphasize external whistleblowing'. However, such generalizations overlook the great diversity of reporting options embraced even within a single jurisdiction. For example, the United Kingdom's Public Interest Disclosure Act (PIDA) 1998 utilizes a tiered reporting system (Vandekerckhove 2010: 17). PIDA 1998 readily protects internal disclosures to a whistleblower's employer, but also permits reports to a prescribed external regulator and, potentially, to an even wider group of recipients, including the media. Employers can designate internal recipients, and the government can designate certain regulatory recipients. With each tier, the whistleblower must satisfy increasingly stringent requirements, such as proving that the allegations are substantially true or showing that the whistleblower will not personally gain from the disclosure. Thus, while the easiest route is internal,

PIDA recognizes that whistleblowers may also need to report externally in certain situations, such as when the internal recipient is not responsive or when reporting about misconduct of an 'exceptionally serious nature' (Lewis 2008: 500–2). Other jurisdictions, such as Romania, embrace a variety of recipients at once by permitting a whistleblower to report internally to the employer or externally to parliamentary commissions, trade unions, professional bodies or the press, without requiring progression through the various tiers (Vandekerckhove 2010: 21–2).

Moreover, the law in Australia and the United States has shifted to further encourage internal whistleblowing more directly in the decade since the report by Callahan *et al.* In Australia, from 1994, Queensland whistleblowing law always identified the entire management chain as possible recipients of whistleblower disclosures (including anyone in the organization 'who, directly or indirectly, supervises or manages' the whistleblower, or 'who has the function of receiving or taking action on the type of information being disclosed', such as internal auditors). This approach, indirectly reflected in many Australian laws, has also been more explicitly recognized in recent ACT and federal legislation.[3] Similarly, in the United States many newer statutes, such as the Sarbanes-Oxley Act of 2002, protect whistleblowers who report to either internal or designated external recipients in the government. The primary US law covering federal government workers, the Whistleblower Protection Act, protects internal whistleblowers as well as those who report to the media. State law in the United States can be more inconsistent, as '[s]ome [state] jurisdictions protect whistleblowers who report misconduct to a supervisor or another person inside the company, while other states' common law protects only external whistleblowers, under the rationale that reporting misconduct internally does not sufficiently advance the public interest' (Moberly 2008: 984–5).

The law also can incentivize reporting by requiring organizations to implement disclosure channels to certain recipients. The Sarbanes-Oxley Act in the United States requires that each publicly traded company offer a whistleblower hotline for employees to report misconduct directly to the company's board of directors (Moberly 2006: 1138). After Sarbanes-Oxley and PIDA 1998 were passed in the United States and the United Kingdom, respectively, employers institutionalized reporting channels in order to encourage employees to report misconduct internally rather than externally (see Moberly and Wylie 2011; Vandekerckhove and Lewis 2012; Lewis and Kender 2010). Similarly, laws in the United States and Australia, among other places, have created specific departments charged with receiving and investigating disclosures from government employees, thereby providing a recipient external to the whistleblower's own department. In the United States, federal government employees can report to the Office of Special Counsel or to an Inspector General designated for each agency. In Australia, legislation in the various states permits disclosures to an external oversight agency. As Roberts and Brown note (2010: 64–5), 'these agencies differed quite considerably between the jurisdictions, the most common oversight bodies being Ombudsman Offices, anti-corruption agencies, Auditor General's Offices and public sector employment agencies'.

Some laws direct private sector whistleblowers to certain government agencies as well. For example, in the United Kingdom, the PIDA 1998 protects whistleblowers who report to 'prescribed persons' that oversee certain regulatory areas, such as the Health and Safety Executive and the Financial Services Authority.

Finally, some US laws provide rewards, or bounties, to whistleblowers. This phenomenon is limited to the United States, for now, and includes the recently passed Dodd-Frank Wall Street Reform and Consumer Protection Act, which provides rewards of 10 to 30 per cent of any fines or penalties collected from whistleblowers who provide the Securities and Exchange Commission information about securities fraud. The United States also provides rewards to whistleblowers who report tax fraud and other fraud against the federal government. Each of these laws designates an external recipient, such as the SEC or the Department of Justice, to receive whistleblower complaints. In fact, Dodd-Frank created from scratch an entire Office of the Whistleblower in the SEC specifically designed for this purpose (Moberly 2012a: 52) The potential for financial reward encourages whistleblowers to report externally to the government rather than reporting internally (Dworkin and Callahan 1991: 273; see also Faunce *et al.*, Chapter 16).

These various legal models – anti-retaliation, structural and bounty – emphasize the role of the recipient in different ways. The anti-retaliation model incentivizes reports to specific recipients by only protecting whistleblowers from retaliation if they report to the approved recipient. However, Near *et al.* (1993: 409) criticize this model for not being effective because it ignores the recipient's behavior once he or she receives the disclosure in addressing the underlying wrongdoing:

> the legal mechanisms used to date have been less effective than legalistic organizational mechanisms to encourage whistle-blowing, probably because the legal mechanisms have focused on the behavior of only one party to the interaction, namely, the organization that retaliates against the whistle-blower.

> In contrast, research findings suggest that legalistic organizational mechanisms used to encourage whistle-blowing, especially the use of role prescription as such a mechanism, seems to have the desired effect of changing both the organization's behavior and that of the potential whistle-blower.

'Legalistic organizational mechanisms', also called the 'structural model' by Moberly, and bounty laws might better address Near *et al.*'s concern about effectiveness. These laws specifically designate a recipient that not only should protect a whistleblower from retaliation, but also should investigate the merits of the underlying disclosure. For example, a company's board of directors receiving disclosures from a legally mandated hotline is under an affirmative obligation to examine credible reports of misconduct in the company (Moberly 2006: 1143–5, 1151). Similarly, the government agencies that bounty laws designate as recipients of disclosures must evaluate the claims of misconduct; indeed, the whistleblower only receives a reward if the agency prosecutes or settles a claim against the wrongdoer. Moberly has argued that this reward system could better address the underlying misconduct because it forces the wrongdoer to pay damages for its misconduct rather than just damages from retaliation (Moberly 2012a: 49).

Balance: the Normative View

Perhaps as a result of the complex interrelationship of variables that might lead a whistleblower to report internal or externally, or both, the consensus among whistleblowing scholars and legal policy makers seems to be that the law should permit whistleblowers to report either internally or externally to a regulatory body and it should protect whistleblowers from retaliation when they do (Dworkin and Near 1997: 3). As put by one commentator, '[a] rigid report recipient requirement – whether external or internal – cannot match the diversity of situations in which employees find themselves' (Sinzdak 2008: 1634).

Some commentators feel strongly that internal reporting should always be the first priority, but that external reporting channels should be available if the internal channel does not work. For example, Calland and Dehn (2004a) argued that making internal recipients available for employees is in the organizations' self-interest and furthers self-regulation, particularly if internal mechanisms have an alternative reporting channel outside of the normal supervisor reporting regime. This alternative channel 'reminds everyone in an organization that they owe a loyalty to the organization and not just to their manager' and can also be effective in deterring and discouraging supervisory abuse of authority

(Calland and Dehn 2004b: 5–8). But these authors also recognize the value of external recipients, in large part because an external option gives incentives to organizations to have strong internal channels. Others have argued that the law should prefer an internal recipient, but protect external whistleblowing when 'internal channels are blocked, provoke retaliation, or would prove futile' (Dworkin and Callahan 1991: 268).

Vandekerckhove's three-tiered system calls for a strong normative preference for an internal recipient with the option for subsequent reports to an external recipient. If an internal disclosure fails, the whistleblower should be permitted to report to an external regulator placed outside of the initial organization. Ideally, this regulator has a mandate as a political representative of society. Finally, a third tier recipient exists as another watchdog, permitting disclosure to the wider society, often through the media (Vandekerckhove 2010: 17–18). PIDA 1998 in the United Kingdom reflects this tiered disclosure system that promotes internal disclosures but that also has external reporting options to key regulators of various industries. To go outside of these internal and regulatory recipients is more difficult and less protected: it has to be reasonable in all the circumstances to go more public, such as to the media (Myers 2004: 107–8).

Despite this normative preference, other factors may outweigh allowing an expansive group of recipients. For example, the United States' Sarbanes-Oxley Act of 2002 permits corporate lawyers to report misconduct up the chain of command to the company's board of directors, but it does not permit reports to external recipients because of the high value the law places on attorney-client confidentiality.[4] National security whistleblowers in the United States may be permitted to report misconduct to Congress under certain circumstances, but the law does not allow them to disclose to the media if doing so would disclose classified information (Moberly 2012b: 96–111). Thus, the normative choice for the 'ideal' recipient can become even more complex when other considerations are present.

RESEARCHING RECIPIENTS

In 1992, Miceli and Near concluded that 'no research has yet addressed the role of the complaint recipient in the whistle-blowing process' (Miceli and Near 1992: 73). Twenty years later, that conclusion would no longer be accurate. Although the recipient's role is still under-studied, some scholars have begun to pay more attention to the recipients themselves as opposed to the whistleblower's choice of recipient.[5] To discuss this research, this section proceeds as follows. First, it examines two prominent theories that provide hypotheses about the effect of recipients on whistleblowing. Secondly, it discusses the few studies that have examined internal recipients, specifically reports made to supervisors and internal disclosure channels. Finally, it concludes by describing the only study focusing primarily on an external recipient.

Theories about the Recipient's Role

Whistleblowing is a process, not a one-time event (Near and Miceli 1995: 686). Many different theories attempt to explain various aspects of that process, from predicting when individuals might blow the whistle to describing the likelihood of retaliation occurring. Two of the most prominent theories account for the recipient's role in that process.[6]

First, Miceli and Near (1985: 540) propose that power theory plays an important role in explaining whistleblowing – not just whether to blow the whistle, but also '*to whom* one would blow the whistle'. Specifically, they argue that 'the power plays among the individuals involved,' including the recipient of the disclosure, might predict (1) whether whistleblowing would be effective and (2) whether retaliation would occur (Miceli and Near 1992: 196; for more on whistleblowing and power see Loyens and Maesschalck, Chapter 7).[7] With regard to the power of the recipient, Miceli and Near predicted that the more power the recipient has within an organization, the more effective a whistleblower would be at stopping the misconduct (assuming the recipient agrees that misconduct occurred), because the recipient's power enhances the whistleblower's credibility (Near and Miceli 1995: 693; Miceli and Near 1992: 197, 221). If a whistleblower reports externally to the company, the power theory would predict that the whistleblower initially reported internally to a weaker recipient and was not satisfied with the outcome (Miceli and Near 2002: 460). Alternatively, Callahan and Dworkin (1994: 165) theorized that a whistleblower would be more likely to report externally when the wrongdoer is influential in the organization. 'The wrongdoer's success in resisting change, suppressing information, and retaliating depends on his or her organizational influence'. The more powerful the wrongdoer, the more likely the whistleblower will be to report externally in order to affect organizational change.

Surprisingly little research has been conducted to test hypotheses related to effectiveness, perhaps because of the difficulty of determining when whistleblowing has been effective at stopping misconduct. However, Miceli and Near have begun to test their theory. In 2002, they conducted a pair of studies that preliminarily examined a hypothesis related to the power theory: that whistleblowing will be more effective when a disclosure is made internally to a recipient of high status (Miceli and Near 2002: 460). In the first study they examined data from the well-known 1980 Merit System Protection Board study of federal employees in the United States, focusing on whether a whistleblower reported to a manager, someone higher up in the organization, the Office of Inspector General (OIG), and/or someone external to the organization. They found that their hypothesis was partially supported in that reports to the OIG were significantly more effective than reporting to a supervisor. However, they also found that reporting to higher level management was not more effective (Miceli and Near 2002: 466). In the second study, they surveyed internal auditors and found support for their hypothesis: auditors who reported to top management or the audit committee of their company were more effective than auditors who reported to less powerful recipients (Miceli and Near 2002: 469).

With regard to retaliation, Miceli and Near (1992: 221) predicted that a powerful recipient would be able to protect a whistleblower from retaliation. To test this prediction, the authors surveyed auditors and found 'some support for a theoretical framework that includes power relationships as the source of some retaliation'. But they also indicated that the concept of retaliation might need to be reconsidered: sometimes it appeared to be an organizational response, while at other times it was an individual wrongdoer who directed the retaliation (Miceli and Near 1994: 790–1).

Although power theory predicts that whistleblowers will simply choose a powerful recipient in order to be more effective and avoid retaliation, it becomes more complicated. Miceli and Near (2002: 460) also noted that, 'an influence target who is powerful enough to stop wrongdoing is also likely powerful enough to harm the influence agent, so some whistleblowers may select less powerful complaint recipients in order to reduce retaliation risk, thereby reducing whistle-blowing effectiveness'.

A second theory involves justice, both procedural justice affecting individual satisfaction with an organization's disclosure system and distributive justice related to the actual outcome of a whistleblower's report (Near *et al.* 1993: 395). While this has applications for whistleblowers, the authors also applied justice theory to recipients of a whistleblowing disclosure. As they hypothesized:

> from the organization members' point of view, distributive justice occurs when the organization is not harmed by the wrongdoing (i.e., a satisfactory outcome for them as organization members) and procedural justice when the whistle-blower follows "fair" reporting procedures, probably reporting the

> wrongdoing through internal channels rather than making it public knowledge by reporting it to some outside agency or the media. (Near *et al.* 1993: 395–6)

They then argued that if procedural and distributive justice of disclosure channels are improved, the *recipients* will feel higher satisfaction with the whistleblowing process, which will subsequently help whistleblowers (Near *et al.* 1993: 397). Legalistic procedures in organizations to receive complaints and respond to them will reduce retaliation, in part because they will affect the recipient's perspective on procedural justice, not just the whistleblower's:

> That is, if whistle-blowing is seen as a normatively correct thing to do and if organizational mechanisms are provided that permit individuals to do it in a way perceived to be fair by others, satisfaction with the system should be greater for organization members other than the whistle-blower. Our prediction is that such individuals will be less likely to retaliate against the whistle-blower and more likely to consider his charges objectively, with the express intention of terminating wrongdoing if it has occurred. (Near *et al.* 1993: 399)

The authors admitted that, at the time, their prediction had not been tested empirically.

Internal Recipients

The recipient's possible reactions to receiving a whistleblower disclosure can vary dramatically depending upon the role the recipient plays. And, particularly for internal recipients, those roles often are complex. Moreover, it can be difficult to distinguish between an organization's reaction compared to the initial individual recipient's reaction. For example, Near and Miceli discussed the variety of responses a whistleblower might receive from the 'organization', and noted that the responses will not always be the same: whistleblowers might get responses from co-workers, supervisors, the recipient of the disclosure and the 'dominant coalition' (which is often called the management team in studies, see Near and Miceli 1995: 685). Moreover, disentangling the reaction towards the whistleblower and the response to the underlying wrongdoing can be hard (Miceli and Near 1992: 179–80). This complexity explains why a more focused research effort should be directed towards understanding the internal recipient's vital role in the whistleblowing process.

Supervisors

That said, three important issues become clear from the studies of internal recipients. First, when studying recipients, the front-line managers are the key players to understand because so many whistleblowers report to them first (Donkin *et al.* 2008: 91–3; Mazerolle and Brown 2008: 165–6). Keenan (2002b: 25) studied different levels of management to examine their perception of various aspects of whistleblowing behavior. He found that upper level managers are more likely to blow the whistle themselves, and less likely to be concerned with retaliation. To the extent that first level managers receive complaints but then have to decide to go up the chain with bad news, this might make it more difficult for whistleblowing to work when the news is first delivered to first level managers. 'First level managers… are at the bottom of the organizational hierarchy, perceiving themselves as caught in the middle between higher levels of management and workers, having little allegiance to either group' (Keenan 2002b: 29). In fact, when deciding what to do about a whistleblower report, low level recipients of disclosures often go through the same decision process as whistleblowers before they report (Miceli and Near 1992: 73).

Additionally, the Australian 'Whistling While They Work' (WWTW) study found that mistreatment of whistleblowers occurred more frequently when a whistleblower had to report through several levels of management, as opposed to when a whistleblower disclosure was resolved after the first internal report (Brown and Olsen 2008a: 156–7). Brown and Olsen concluded that '[t]hese findings further reinforce the importance of a competent initial response to a disclosure, preventing the need for a second or further report, if the chances of protecting even lower-risk whistleblowers are to be maximized' (Brown and Olsen 2008a: 157). The authors of the WWTW study put it this way:

> It is up to those line managers, as the immediate recipient of most reports:
>
> - how they react to the report from their subordinate;
> - how they make initial judgments about the validity of the claims that are being presented to them;
> - how supportive (or non-supportive) they are of the reporter;
> - how knowledgeable they are about the organizational policies and processes;
> - how knowledgeable they are about the general principles of investigation and the need to determine the truth of the matter in a disinterested manner;
> - how committed they are to remedying any wrongdoing that is proven. (Roberts *et al.* 2011: 23)

Secondly, the perceptions of the initial recipients matter greatly to the outcome of the whistleblowing process. For example, although the focus of the recipient should not be on the whistleblower, sometimes the recipient's perception of the whistleblower matters, such as when there is little evidence of misconduct other than the whistleblower's claims (Miceli *et al.* 2008: 140). It might be hard for the recipient to look past her or his views of the credibility of the whistleblower, even though ideally that is not what matters. As Miceli *et al.* (2008: 141) noted: 'One implication is that, if perceived validity is low, the whistle-blower will be ineffective, because there is no felt need to take action if the complaint recipient does not believe wrongdoing has taken place'. Another perception that matters is whether wrongdoing has occurred. A positive agent acting in the organization's best interest will act to end the wrongdoing as quickly as possible, because the costs of wrongdoing can escalate quickly (Miceli *et al.* 2008: 141). Other factors may matter to the complaint recipient: 'corroboration by others, the views of others of the whistle-blower's motives, and the process used' (Miceli *et al.* 2008: 142).

Problematically, front-line managers may have misperceptions about whistleblowers and their disclosures that impede ideal responses. One difficulty with investigating and dealing with reported misconduct is the recipients' belief that only a few complaints actually have any validity.[8] As Miceli *et al.* assert (2009: 388–9):

> Obviously, employers who perceive that complaints are frivolous are unlikely to take corrective action, and if they refuse to act on a large proportion that are valid, then even employees with valid concerns will quickly conclude that nothing will happen if they complain. This creates a vicious circle in which employees rarely report real wrongdoing, so officials take few corrective actions, to which employees react by believing nothing would be done to correct wrongdoing if it were reported, and reports drop further.

Also, recipients can have a difficult time distinguishing between personnel grievances and public interest disclosures. In reality, those two problems are intertwined and tangled (Roberts *et al.* 2011: 57–60).

Miceli and Near pointed to literature on attribution theory to note the danger of these misperceptions: recipients will be influenced by the recipient's evaluation of the whistleblower's motivations (is he or she a complainer?), and the type of channel the whistleblower used to report (was it an official channel?). Attribution theory suggests 'that characteristics of the complainant, such as her or his credibility, and characteristics of the complaint, such as the seriousness of the wrongdoing reported, may affect' the recipient's response (Miceli and Near 1992: 78–9). In other words, as these same scholars argued ten years later:

> complaint recipients, top management, and other parties are *not* unbiased observers. They may: (i) not recognize wrongdoing as others define it, (ii) not be willing to take responsibility for wrongdoing under their control, or (iii) have vested interests in the continuation of wrongdoing. (Miceli and Near 2002: 474)

Moreover, the perceptions of recipients and whistleblowers differ dramatically, which can lead to problems in the whistleblowing process. Using the WWTW data, Annakin concluded that few recipients understood the importance of trust and loyalty to whistleblowers and 'the complex process that underlies a whistleblower's decision to make their disclosure externally' (Annakin 2011: 166). The WWTW data also demonstrated that whistleblowers often focused on the outcome of a particular report, while supervisors tended to focus on following the proper process for managing the disclosure. As put by Smith (2010: 716), '[w]hat develops among managers is a case of cognitive dissonance, in that they see whistle-blowers as dispassionate Weberian public servants like themselves, concerned with procedure and not determined to achieve particular outcomes'. Case managers (those who received the reports) systematically under-estimated the importance to whistleblowers of being vindicated substantively; the recipients had little idea that being proven right mattered so much to the whistleblowers (Smith and Brown 2008: 120). Fewer than half of recipients in the WWTW study thought that confirmation of their complaints would be important to whistleblowers, while whistleblowers would almost never be satisfied without that substantiation.. This 'mutual misunderstanding between whistle-blowers and managers' impedes the whistleblowing process (Smith 2010: 716).

Similarly, after surveying internal auditors, Miceli and Near (1994: 789–90) expected to find that managers who received whistleblower reports would retaliate less when the wrongdoing harmed the organization, because they 'would appreciate the information from whistleblowers when the organization is being harmed by the wrong-doing'. The opposite happened though: whistleblowers were *more* likely to be retaliated against when the wrongdoing reported was harmful to the organization's climate or culture. According to Miceli and Near (1994: 790), this could be because whistleblowers and managers have different views of what is harmful to the organization's culture and climate; or it could be that the same managers who retaliate also are responsible for the wrongdoing.

A third issue arising from studies of internal recipients is that front-line supervisors are often unequipped to adequately handle the whistleblower or the report about misconduct (Donkin *et al.* 2008: 91–3; Smith 2010:

714). Training supervisors could provide a solution to the problem of managers misperceiving a whistleblower's motivations or not responding appropriately to whistleblowers (Miceli and Near 1992: 293). Because whistleblowers so often report initially to their supervisor, Brown and Olsen (2008a: 157) advocated for better training of front-line managers as a way to increase whistleblower effectiveness and reduce retaliation. The WWTW study also found that few agencies had risk assessment systems in place for recipients of disclosures to evaluate the potential for retaliation against the whistleblower (Roberts *et al.* 2011: 60–1). This underscores the dual obligations of recipients: not only to deal with the substantive problems disclosed by the whistleblower, but also to protect the whistleblower from retaliation.

In addition to better training, better procedures could be helpful. Smith argued that Australian public agencies often had 'underdeveloped' procedures for dealing with whistleblower reports (Smith 2010: 713). Even agencies with policies do not discuss how recipients should support whistleblowers or manage complaints – they just deal with how to make reports (Smith 2010: 714). Specifically, Roberts *et al.* (2011: 53) concluded that organizations should plan for the fact that most disclosures are made internally to line managers by clearly explaining when managers should handle disclosures themselves, how they should document their report and investigations, and when managers should refer a disclosure up the chain of command.

In other words, organizations not only should support whistleblowers, but also need to support the initial recipients of whistleblower disclosures. As put by some of the WWTW scholars:

> Line managers also have the capacity to be passive in the reporting process in order to 'stay out of the firing line'. In larger, complex hierarchies, the line manager who fulfills organisational responsibilities is also placed in a difficult situation. This might not make the line manager as vulnerable as a reporter, but it is vulnerability nevertheless. Consequently, when organisations express commitment to supporting the reporters of wrongdoing, that support should extend to the direct recipient of the report. It is not an easy task for organisations to ensure their line managers take risks in supporting reporters of wrongdoing. That is, however, what is being suggested here. Line managers should be encouraged to take on reports of wrongdoing as if they were their own, up to the point that it is clear, on the balance of probabilities, that the report has no substance and no further action is warranted. (Roberts *et al.* 2011: 25)

Internal disclosure channels

Organizations can influence whistleblowing in a variety of ways, such as creating a culture that encourages employees to report misconduct. With regard to the topic of this chapter, organizations can also institutionalize the receipt of whistleblowers' disclosures. Whistleblower researchers have examined how an organization (as opposed to an individual line manager) acts as a recipient of disclosures. The most common practice is for the organization to implement an internal disclosure channel for whistleblowers to circumvent a direct supervisor and report immediately to high level company officials (Moberly 2006: 1131–2). This channel permits whistleblowers to avoid the 'blocking and filtering' that can result if a supervisor is involved in the wrongdoing or hostile to the whistleblower (Miceli and Near 1992: 291; Moberly 2006: 1149). Additionally, disclosure channels provide whistleblowers a powerful, credible recipient to disclose to: someone the organizational leaders will listen to. They may also reduce the threat to the bureaucratic organizational structure that whistleblowing can otherwise cause, making the disclosures more effective as well (Near and Miceli 1995: 702).

Such channels rely upon the view of whistleblowers as pro-social actors who can be influenced by an environment where they feel that upper management will correct misconduct if they are informed of it. Miceli and Near hypothesized that when inactive observers of misconduct believe their organization will correct misconduct, they are more likely to report wrongdoing than in other organizations where people do not have that perceptions (Miceli and Near 1988: 270). Their study was based on MSPB surveys from 1983, and the data supported their hypothesis (Miceli and Near 1988: 274). Publicized disclosure channels can help convince potential whistleblowers that the organization will correct the misconduct.

Among the vast variety of options for implementing a whistleblowing channel, organizations can utilize a hotline, designate an ombudsperson, or install a separate unit. Organizations can task these recipients with simply receiving and reporting disclosures to management, or mandate that they investigate the disclosure and protect the whistleblower from retaliation.

Some studies have focused on the impact on whistleblowing when organizations implement internal disclosure channels. In general, internal whistleblowing increases when an organization provides a channel for whistleblowers to use, identifies a specific recipient to follow-up on the information, and implements a strong anti-retaliation policy (see Miceli *et al.* 2008: 194; Barnett *et al.* 1993: 133; Barnett 1992: 949–50; Miceli and Near 1992: 290). For example, Barnett *et al.* surveyed 300 human resources executives and found that companies had a significant increase in internal disclosures after implementing internal disclosures policies and procedures (Barnett *et al.* 1993: 127, 133). The authors concluded that these channels helped increase disclosures, but only if the employees thought the channels would be effective (Barnett *et al.* 1993: 129).

Not surprisingly, the form and function of these recipient structures can matter. After studying US accountants, Seifert *et al.* concluded that:

> when organizational policies and procedures for whistleblowing are designed to incorporate the dimensions of fairness or justice, organizational accountants perceive a higher likelihood that financial statement fraud will be disclosed by a whistleblower … [suggesting] that management can take actions that may positively impact the likelihood that organizational accountants will report financial statement fraud. (Seifert *et al.* 2010: 714)

Thus, studies have provided a laundry list of advice for organizations intent on establishing a way to receive whistleblower complaints formally. Most focus on demonstrating procedural fairness, because if individuals perceive that whistleblowing channels are unjust, a whistleblower might report externally rather than internally (Miceli *et al.* 2008: 85). For example, Wortley *et al.* (2008: 81) assert that organizations can encourage whistleblowing 'by checking the accuracy of information, taking all reports seriously, referring all reports to an unbiased, well-respected arbiter, giving all involved the opportunity to provide input and the other features of good investigation'. Others emphasize that the designated recipient should be 'trusted, independent, [and] powerful' (Miceli and Near 1992: 292). The organization should name several different recipients and train employees in the availability of the various channels to report (Donkin *et al.* 2008: 107; Miceli *et al.* 2009: 389–90). Some commentators suggested that reporting channels should even include external pathways and instructions on when to report to the media (Roberts *et al.* 2011: 13–14).

Documenting and explaining comprehensive procedures for reporters and receivers has been shown to be effective. The WWTW project found that 'the agencies with more comprehensive procedures were also those whose staff had more professed knowledge of whistle-blowing procedures and a greater confidence in whistle-blowing. The same agencies also tended to treat whistle-blowers better than agencies with less developed formal procedures' (cited in Smith 2010: 717).

After receiving reports, management should investigate, and those investigations should be efficient and impartial, with a fair hearing procedure (Miceli and Near 1992: 293; Roberts *et al.* 2011: 22).

Recipients should respect a whistleblower's desire to remain anonymous. Indeed, the WWTW group emphasized the importance that internal disclosure channels create trust with whistleblowers. Organizations must 'respond well in their investigation and remediation of alleged wrongdoing and … ensure unnecessary adverse consequences do not befall those who report' (Donkin *et al.* 2008: 106). This trust, in turn, encourages the use of internal, as opposed to external, reporting (Donkin *et al.* 2008: 103). As put by Roberts *et al.* (2011: 19), '[a]t an individual level, trust in the recipient of the report is an important factor in the decision about reporting pathways, in particular the selection of internal reporting pathways over external reporting pathways'.

Thus, disclosure channels that provide feedback to whistleblowers on an investigation's progress may be more effective (Smith and Brown 2008: 120–1). Miceli *et al.* (2009: 389) note that:

> implementing this recommendation would likely help counteract employees' tendency – demonstrated in controlled research – to believe nothing could or would be done if wrongdoing were reported. Consistent with this advice, research suggests that encouraging reporting and immediate correction about which employees are informed may also have desirable effects almost as good as those resulting from preventing wrongdoing in the first place.

After a massive 2010 study of federal employees by the Merit Systems Protection Board, the Board recommended that, regardless of the substantive merits of the whistleblower's claim, management inform the whistleblower about the outcome of any investigation in order to let whistleblowers know it was taken seriously and to inform them that they acted correctly in reporting their suspicions (MSPB 2011: 18).

Importantly, despite being the source for much of this advice, Miceli *et al.* (2009: 389) also noted the 'dearth of controlled empirical research' that examines the effect of such recommendations, even though the recommendations 'seem reasonable'. Moreover, procedures without management support and financial backing will likely be worthless. As one of the WWTW investigators put it, 'procedures themselves do not guarantee a good outcome; this is likely to hinge on management commitment, promulgation of the procedures and effective resources devoted to investigation and to supporting staff' (Roberts 2008: 259).

External Recipients

In contrast to the existing literature regarding how organizations can and should set up internal disclosure channels, little attention has been given to how external recipients impact whistleblowing. One prominent exception to this conclusion arises out of the WWTW project. Annakin examined the role public accountability agencies play in Australian public sector whistleblowing. Australia has a complex set of external accountability agencies to which a whistleblower could report, including auditors general, ombudsmen, corruption commissioners and public service commissions (Annakin 2011: 33–6). Annakin (2011: 39) found, however, that rather than take an independent approach to investigating whistleblower disclosures and protecting them from retaliation, these external agencies rely upon a concept of 'distributed integrity', in which the agency trusts the whistleblower's own government department to investigate and resolve whistleblower allegations. These agencies refer disclosures back to the departments to investigate, which is how the integrity agencies deal with complaints from the public. But, according to Annakin (2011: 6), this process ignores the special nature of whistleblower complaints, which have often already been made within the department. The agencies compound this by also referring claims of retaliation back to the departments. The external agencies' failure 'to develop and use additional procedures for dealing with whistleblowers and their disclosures has severely limited the effectiveness of their role in institutionalising the legislative objectives' (Annakin 2011: 10).

Annakin examined three different Australian jurisdictions to see how external agency reporting was set up through legislation. She found that:

> [d]espite the importance attributed to the roles and responsibilities of accountability agencies, none of the Acts describe in much detail the actions to be taken when disclosures are received. No new powers to deal with disclosures were given to any agency, with the exception of increasing the jurisdiction of nominated agencies to investigate allegations of reprisal action against whistleblowers. (Annakin 2011: 102)

Also, the legislation did not really address specific issues related to whistleblowing, other than retaliation protection. 'The legislation prescribes no additional requirements to ensure investigation or rectification of wrongdoing revealed by whistleblowers, relying solely on the existing capacity of accountability structures and institutions' (Annakin 2011: 103).

Annakin relied on survey results from whistleblowers, department heads and case managers involved in the WWTW. Based on these results, Annakin made three conclusions regarding the external agencies' responses to whistleblowers. First, because of resource limitations and insufficient skill in its professional staff, the external agencies had difficulties sufficiently assessing and reacting to whistleblower complaints. Increases in responsibilities to include whistleblower assessment did not necessarily include increased funding, which led to whistleblowers' overwhelming feeling that their complaints were not being taken seriously (Annakin 2011: 191). Interestingly, the same thing happened in the United States when the Sarbanes-Oxley Act of 2002 mandated that the Department of Labor begin investigating retaliation claims under the Act, but Congress did not allocate the Department any new resources despite hundreds of new claims (see Moberly 2007: 124–5).

Secondly, the agencies simply did not investigate the claims well. For example, they took too long in their investigations. More important, perhaps, they referred too many whistleblower complaints back to the whistleblower's department for investigation, which can be problematic because the whistleblower likely reported to the external agency precisely because the departmental investigation was unsatisfactory. Finally, despite the universally recognized importance of maintaining confidentiality, external agencies often revealed a whistleblower's identity to the whistleblower's employing department (Annakin 2011: 203–15).

Thirdly, Annakin (2011: 215–17) uncovered a lack of coordinated oversight among the various external agencies and the departments. Some whistleblowers were caught in the gaps between different agencies' jurisdictions, resulting in being referred from agency to agency, with no group taking responsibility.

As a result, whistleblowers in the WWTW study had a remarkably low level of satisfaction when reporting to an external agency: only 5 per cent had any level of satisfaction (Annakin 2011: 185). Annakin (2011: 186) summarizes the reasons why the satisfaction is so abysmal:

> whistleblowers having very high expectations of accountability agencies, being disappointed by accountability agencies' decisions to take no action, viewing investigative action as insufficiently independent or thorough and falling through the gaps in coordination between accountability agencies.

Of course, Annakin's work deals with the specific arrangements in Australia between government departments and external integrity agencies, set up by various Australian laws. However, researchers in other jurisdictions could take a similar approach when studying external reporting agencies because many countries have similar arrangements by which a whistleblower could report internally and then externally to an outside regulatory group. Examining the interaction between internal and external reporting, as well as the processes set up by external recipients, would be an important step to better understand the role external recipients can play in the whistleblowing process.

FUTURE RESEARCH AND CONCLUSIONS

Progress has been made since Miceli and Near concluded 20 years ago that no research had been conducted about the recipients of whistleblower disclosures. However, compared to other aspects of the whistleblowing process, this key player is still under-studied. Several areas could be examined in future research.

First, future research could examine the role recipients play in whether a whistleblower disclosure is effectively resolved. For example, Miceli *et al.* (2008) use power theory to make predictions about effectiveness. They assert that the more agreement recipients and whistleblowers have about the existence of misconduct, the more likely the wrongdoing will stop. As a result, they predicted that 'in well-managed organizations that are behaviorally committed to high ethical standards, whistle-blowers will probably be more effective when the internal party to whom the wrongdoing is reported agrees that the complaint's content is meritorious or valid' (Miceli *et al.* 2008: 141). Also, the authors expected 'that this effect would be stronger when there is independent evidence that good management and maintenance of high ethical standards is part of the organizational operations' (Miceli *et al.* 2008: 141). However, they acknowledged that this proposition has not been tested (Miceli *et al.* 2008: 141).

Secondly, as noted above, numerous commentators suggested the importance of training managers and hotline operators regarding the best practices for receiving whistleblower disclosures. However, no research has examined the effectiveness of such training, which Miceli *et al.* noted is 'sorely needed' (Miceli *et al.* 2009: 385).

Thirdly, organizations have incorporated a wide variety of internal procedures to receive whistleblower complaints and encourage whistleblowing, including ombudsmen, internal review boards, hotlines and suggestions boxes. However, research on the comparative advantages and disadvantages of each does not exist (King 1999: 324–5). Miceli *et al.* (2008: 122) concluded that, for organizations that want to encourage internal whistleblowing:

> there is little guidance to offer as to which concrete steps will 'work' when employees are fearful or reluctant to come forward. For example, what types of training have proven useful, or not useful, in reducing the perceived threat

> of retaliation and improving managerial responses to wrongdoing and whistleblowing? Which complaint channels are more trusted, and why? Should employees always be encouraged first to report problems to a supervisor, or does some form of ombudsperson approach work more effectively? Can a 360-degree appraisal system generate suggestions for operation improvement, including responses to wrongdoing, in a nonthreatening way? And do the answers to any of these questions depend on situational conditions, such as the demographics of the workforce?

While scholars have provided reasonable, thoughtful advice about the components of a successful whistleblowing system, rigorous empirical evidence of what works and what does not would be extremely helpful.

Fourthly, more research could be conducted on the response of various external agencies to whistleblower disclosures. The Dodd-Frank Act will not be the last whistleblower law to identify a specific agency charged with receiving whistleblower disclosures, and studies could attempt to provide a list of best practices based on an examination of what has worked in the past. For example, Lewis has made reasonable suggestions for amending the United Kingdom's PIDA 1998 to add external recipients, such as unions or a new Public Interest Disclosure Agency (Lewis 2008: 504). Future research could follow Annakin's lead and examine both the effectiveness of external agency recipients at addressing wrongdoing reported by whistleblowers, as well as their ability to protect whistleblowers from retaliation.

Finally, research that surveyed supervisory recipients to examine their beliefs and actions would be very helpful. Supervisors are the most common recipients of disclosures, yet they are the least studied. Are they 'pro-social' in their outlook when they act on whistleblower disclosures? Do they exhibit organizational citizenship behavior so that they pass along reports? In other words, do effective supervisor recipients act the same as whistleblowers? This area is complicated by the fact that whistleblower reports are often mixed with personnel grievances and made informally with difficult-to-grant requests for confidentiality (Roberts *et al.* 2011: 50–77). Also, Roberts *et al.* (2011: 54–6) noted that the WWTW study revealed the importance of *informal* reports to line managers and the managers dealing with problems informally. Disentangling the formal whistleblower report from the informal complaint complicates the recipient's job dramatically. Managers then must investigate disclosures and protect whistleblowers from reprisal – all while themselves being put in a similar position as the whistleblower in deciding whether to send the report up the company ladder. These supervisor recipients play a crucial role in protecting the whistleblower from retaliation, addressing the wrongdoing effectively and ultimately creating a climate in which employees are willing to report. They should be studied more directly.

NOTES

1. By contrast, it should be noted that some have argued that a whistleblower must 'go public', i.e., blow the whistle to someone outside of their organization, in order to be considered a true whistleblower (Miceli *et al.* 2008: 8; Annakin 2011: 45 citing papers taking this position). For example, when Sherron Watkins, the Enron whistleblower, testified before a Congressional committee in 2002 about the company's accounting fraud, one Congressperson noted that she was not a 'whistleblower in the conventional sense' because she acted out of loyalty and only reported her concerns internally to Enron's CEO Ken Lay (Anon 2002: 4).
2. This conclusion regarding effectiveness is tempered by a different study from Miceli and Near which found that the recipient of a disclosure did not correlate to whether the disclosure was effective or not. However, this result may be peculiar to the group of whistleblowers they studied: auditors who are expected to use internal channels before reporting externally (Miceli and Near 1992: 194–5).
3. See Whistleblower Protection Act 1994 (Qld, Australia), s. 27(3)(c) and (d); now Public Interest Disclosure Act 2010 (Qld, Australia), s. 17(3)(d) and (e); Public Interest Disclosure Act 2012 (ACT, Australia), s. 15(1)(c); Public Interest Disclosure Act 2013 (Cth, Australia), ss. 26 and 34.
4. Sarbanes-Oxley Act 2002; 17 C.F.R. s. 205.3.
5. In other words, numerous studies have examined whether whistleblowers report internally or externally, and the consequences of that choice (Miceli and Near 1992: 13, 26, 194; Donkin *et al.* 2008: 106; Rothschild and Miethe 1999a: 112; Skivenes and Trygstad 2010a: 1083; ERC 2010a: 15; MSPB 2011: 2, 8–9; Miceli and Near 1985: 537; Rehg *et al.* 2004: E6; Miceli *et al.* 1991: 127; Dworkin and Baucus 1998: 1281, 1295; Brown and Olsen 2008a: 138; Mesmer-Magnus and Viswesvaran 2005: 282; Miceli *et al.* 1999: 147). However, these studies focused on the *whistleblower's* actions, not on the *recipient's* actions in response to a whistleblower's disclosure.
6. A third theory, pro-social theory, helps explain why individuals become whistle-blowers. This theory might be applied to recipients similarly to its application to the whistleblower: the recipient must decide whether misconduct actually happened, whether the recipient must do anything about it, and whether the recipient has the power to change the conduct (Near and Miceli 1995: 693). In this way, recipients often have the same considerations and concerns as whistleblowers, particularly when recipients must determine how to handle a whistleblower complaint.
7. Of course, the power of the various actors does not tell the whole story. Other variables matter, such as the level of dependence on the wrongdoing by the recipient or the organization. The more dependent they are, the more resistant to change the organization will be (Miceli *et al.* 1999: 133).
8. Even though other studies belie this belief, see Miceli *et al.* (2009: 388); Miceli *et al.* (2008: 22, 195). It should be noted that this problem can occur with recipients other than front-line supervisors. For example, Curtis surveyed those responsible for 'screening, researching, and evaluating' disclosures received by a whistleblower hotline and found that they had a 'troubling low' view about whether reports were valid, averaging 3.04 on a 10-point scale, with 10 meaning completely valid (Curtis 2006: 4, 19, 26).

13. Managerial responsiveness to whistleblowing: Expanding the research horizon

*Wim Vandekerckhove, A.J. Brown and Eva Tsahuridu**

INTRODUCTION

Over the past 40 years, most whistleblowing research has focused on the whistleblower. Given the historical, political and organizational context in which the notion of 'whistleblowing' appeared in Western public affairs from the early 1970s (Vandekerckhove 2006), this focus on the whistleblower is not surprising. When systematic empirical research began in the 1980s, the researchers faced an agenda determined largely by an antagonism between managers in organizations, on the one hand, and activists, including whistleblowers, who were trying to change corporate and governmental behavior, on the other. The result was a crude antagonism between whistleblowers as 'ethical resisters' and organizations as 'bureaucratic hierarchies' (Glazer and Glazer 1989). This dichotomy has proved enduring (e.g. O'Day 1974; De Maria 1999; Alford 2001; Uys 2008). It has naturally flowed through to research questions based on attempts to identify: Who is the whistleblower? Are they heroes or villains? Do they harm organizations? Should we protect these individuals?

Forty years later, the political and organizational context seems to be a different one. As set out in Chapter 1, and in more detail in later chapters, legislation protecting or rewarding external whistleblowers is no longer a rarity. Whistleblowing policies and procedures are widely advocated as elements for strengthening public integrity, corporate governance, and efforts to combat corruption and fraud. In this sense, whistleblowing is now seen by many managers and regulators alike, not as a threat to organizations, but as a necessary part of the regulatory and self-regulatory environment which sustains their ability to operate, and even as directly enhancing organizational efficiency (Vandekerckhove 2006).

In addition, the strong competing relationship between whistleblowers and organizational managers has often been dominated by those whistleblowing cases which reach the media, in situations which entrench a sense of conflict because they involve maximum reputational risk and damage. However, research has now consistently shown (at least in developed world settings) that before people blow the whistle outside their organization, they almost always try to raise their concern internally (Miceli and Near 1992; Donkin *et al.* 2008). Public policy has increasingly followed this reality, with a growing trend towards 'three-tiered' whistleblowing regimes: first, measures to encourage and protect whistleblowing inside the organization; secondly, measures to encourage and protect whistleblowing to independent, publicly accountable agencies (e.g., a regulator or a parliamentary ombudsperson) if internal whistleblowing is not effective or appropriate; and only thirdly, protection of public whistleblowing (e.g., to the media) where neither of the first two tiers are effective to resolve the matter (Vandekerckhove 2010).

These developments have opened a whole new dimension within whistleblowing research and practice, namely, that of internal whistleblowing. The policy debate is no longer simply about protecting whistleblowers from organizations. Rather, it is shifting towards the protection of *society* from organizations that are unable or unwilling to heed whistleblowing disclosures, correct any wrongdoing occurring under their responsibility, or grant justice to individuals who play this role. Whistleblowers expose wrongdoing, but not necessarily to the public. More precisely, they are usually likely to expose it to the public only as a last resort. An internal organizational whistleblowing policy thus becomes a risk management tool at multiple levels (Tsahuridu 2011). The implication is that it is not necessarily in the public interest to know about what goes wrong in organizations, unless the circumstances are such that the organization cannot, or will not self-rectify – but it is generally in the public interest to know when organizations fail to correct their own malpractices. Hence organizations can be held accountable for responding inadequately to concerns raised internally. The fact that external whistleblowing is almost always preceded by people raising concerns internally suggests that most news stories about organizational wrongdoing are indicators of management missing an opportunity to correct malpractice themselves. Among regulators and managers, awareness of the benefits of responding appropriately to the early warning signs is slowly growing.

This chapter explores the implications of this major shift. It addresses how research into whistleblowing may need to evolve if it is to inform new priorities in management, regulation and public policy. It becomes crucial that more insight is gained into how the management processes of organizations and whistleblowing interact and interrelate – not simply in bad ways or with bad outcomes for whistleblowers, but across the spectrum. After all, research in different advanced democracies suggests that in these contexts, 50 per cent or more of internally voiced concerns are successful in having wrongdoing addressed or corporate practices changed; and that retaliation against whistleblowers is not as ubiquitous as generally assumed (see Smith, Chapter 10; also Smith and Brown 2008; Skivenes and Trygstad 2010b; Bjorkelo *et al.* 2010). Different success rates between organizations, industry sectors and legal regimes make it possible to begin cracking the code of what makes internal and regulatory whistleblowing successful in some cases, but not others.

The first section follows many of the preceding chapters, by reviewing what is currently known about whistleblowing from existing research, and in particular, the limits to existing knowledge given that most of this research has been focused on whistleblowers, more than on organizational responses. Evidently, the characteristics of whistleblowers represent only one set of factors in this code, among many. We thus identify the gaps in knowledge about managers' responses to whistleblowing and relevant managerial practices, and the importance of filling these. We identify managerial responses to whistleblowing as falling into two broad, interrelated categories: managerial responsiveness to primary concerns about wrongdoing (which we call 'hearer action'), and, secondarily, managerial ability or willingness to refrain from, or protect the whistleblower against, retaliation or reprisals for airing those concerns (which we call 'protector action'). Both clearly need to be studied.

In the second section we explore some of the rare available data on at least one of these dimensions, collected in surveys of 532 managers in 15 Australian organizations in 2007–2008, in order to begin establishing the feasibility of more systematic study of the nature and influences of both 'hearer action' and 'protector action'. The results support this feasibility. The third section of the chapter then develops a research model into the nature and effectiveness of managerial 'hearer action' and 'protector action', as an extension of existing research into whistleblowing. We see this model as providing a new departure point for the development of more efficient and effective measures of organizational responsiveness to whistleblowing. The fourth section of the chapter discusses implications for further research, and overall conclusions.

FOCUSING ON THE WHISTLEBLOWER: WHAT WE KNOW FROM EXISTING RESEARCH

On Whistleblowing

As elsewhere in this book, we understand whistleblowing as 'the disclosure by organization members (former or current) of illegal, immoral or illegitimate practices under the control of their employers, to persons or organizations that may be able to effect action' (Near and Miceli 1985: 4). This definition involves at least four parties in the whistleblowing process: those responsible for wrongdoing, the whistleblower(s), the complaint recipient, and the organization that it is hoped will act.

To date, research has focused primarily on the second of these parties; to a lesser extent on the first; and only to a very limited extent, in a generalized way, on the third (the complaint recipient) or fourth party (the organization). Near and Miceli (2008) explain that most research has been concerned with (1) assessing levels or incidences of wrongdoing, whistleblowing and retaliation against whistleblowers; (2) identifying the differences between whistleblowers and inactive observers of wrongdoing; (3) predicting retaliation; and (4) exploring conditions that would lead to effective whistleblowing (Near and Miceli 2008: 270). There has been little direct focus on the complaint recipient, and even where it is addressed, it tends to suffer from similar limitations to those that affect our understanding of whistleblowers. For example, Knapp *et al.* (1997) comment that whistleblowing research literature tends not to provide for a continuum of reactions to wrongdoing, instead crudely categorizing the actions of observers as 'report' or 'not report' (see also Loyens and Maesschalck, Chapter 7). Similarly, research has tended to categorize the response from the complaint recipient as either 'address' or 'retaliate'. In fact, this dichotomy itself collapses two quite distinct dimensions – response to the wrongdoing and response to the whistleblower – when these are two potentially independent variables.

Even Near and Miceli's (1985) standard definition of whistleblowing tends to limit the focus, by suggesting that there is one recipient. In fact, whistleblowers do not normally encounter a single, consistent and explicit organizational response, but rather a range of responses from different individuals in the organization (Near and Miceli 1995: 685). Original recipients may be inside or outside the organization, the supervisor, or the dominant coalition (which is operationalized in many studies as the top management team), as may be additional or subsequent recipients. In addition to the response to the disclosure itself, there is the question of support for having made it, which may be provided by some managers, or some colleagues, but not others.

Typically, managerial responsiveness to whistleblowing has received, at best, indirect treatment in research. Near and Miceli's (1995) model of individual and situational variables that affect whistleblowing, after the whistle has been blown, includes the credibility and power of the complaint recipient as variables influencing the organization's willingness to change. In this model, the recipient's characteristics interact with support for the whistleblower or the wrongdoer. However, while many studies distinguish the whistleblower's characteristics, contextual characteristics, and those of the wrongdoing and the wrongdoer, fewer distinguish the recipient's characteristics (Mesmer-Magnus and Viswesvaran 2005).

As noted earlier, quantitative measures of 'organizational courage' have been suggested which investigate the collective willingness of organization members to speak up (Kilmann et al. 2013), but even more central to the organization's performance is the courage of the managers who control that organization, in terms of whether and how they discharge these quite specific responsibilities.

On Effectiveness

While little research has been undertaken directly into different managerial responses, the overall issue of whistleblowing effectiveness has attracted slightly more attention. Near and Miceli (1995: 681) define effective whistleblowing as 'the extent to which the questionable or wrongful practice (or omission) is terminated at least partly because of whistle-blowing and within a reasonable time frame'. However, there has continued to be little theory or research about the conditions associated with such effectiveness. Miceli and Near (2002) have tested several propositions of their Near and Miceli (1995) model, then the only published model of effectiveness, using resource dependence, minority influence and social power theories. In the three studies reported, similar results were found (Miceli and Near 2002). The position and power of the whistleblower and the organization's dependence on the wrongdoing influenced whistleblowing effectiveness. Managerial responsiveness played only an indirect role, with high status complaint recipients associated with more effective internal whistleblowing (but sometimes with less effective external whistleblowing). Whistleblowing that was role prescribed, that is, undertaken by auditors or others who were involved in identifying and reporting wrongdoing, was consistently associated with whistleblowing effectiveness. More effective whistleblowers experienced significantly less retaliation, but as noted earlier, retaliation and effectiveness are distinct constructs. Demographic and other control variables of the whistleblower generally did not predict effectiveness.

The gaps in knowledge left by research to date are significant. For example, when discussing the likely impact of a recipient's assessment of the validity of whistleblowing upon effectiveness, Miceli and Near comment that 'complaint recipients think that few whistleblowing reports are well founded' (2002: 474). Similar conclusions were reached by Hunton and Rose (2011) after studying how members of audit committees assess the credibility of anonymous versus eponymous reports of wrongdoing. However, such conclusions suggest that managers are generally unable to make any positive difference to the organization's response, and instead are always destined to be more or less willing accomplices in cover-ups and whistleblower mistreatment, when there is good reason to suspect that this cannot be accurate (Smith 2010).

By contrast, other evidence suggests that many complaint recipients do recognize the legitimacy and potential value of employee reports. As part of the research which will be further explored below, the majority of a sample of over 750 managers and integrity officers from 14 Australian public sector agencies, surveyed in 2007, rated employee reporting as a more important means by which wrongdoing was brought to light in their organizations, than direct observation, routine controls, internal audits, external investigations or external complaints (Brown, Mazurski and Olsen 2008). Only a minority saw employee reports as 'wholly trivial', or likely to be false or vexatious, even when accepting that whistleblowing may sometimes be mistaken, or mixed with personal or employment grievances. We draw further on this evidence below, in order to identify some of the directions in which research needs to be developed.

In addition, Miceli and Near (2002) point to evidence that whistleblowing about less serious or less entrenched wrongdoing is more likely to be effective, as is the use of internal designated channels. This evidence suggests that the quality of the relationship between the observer of wrongdoing and potential complaint recipient should be explored further (for more on whistleblowing recipients see Moberly, Chapter 12). Similarly, while whistleblowing is often and correctly investigated as a form of 'pro-social behavior', there is no research on how pro-social behavior affects reactions to whistleblowers (Near and Miceli 1995). Complaint recipients may be confronted with decisions similar to those facing whistleblowers, that is, by determining '(a) whether wrongdoing has occurred, (b) if so, whether they are responsible for acting, and (c) if so, whether they have the power to change the wrongdoing' (Near and Miceli 1995: 693). If the complaint recipients lack power, they must consider if they have any potentially effective actions available to them.

However, if a powerful, high status complaint recipient supports a whistleblower, it may enhance the whistleblower's credibility and status, or raise the status of the complaint. Further, the ethical climate of the organization may also be a more important influence on the responses of complaint recipients, than the particular personalities or merits of whistleblowers. While preliminary evidence (Near and Miceli 1991, cited in Near and Miceli 1995) did not suggest that the complaint recipient's status is important, the degree of support for the whistleblower was not measured. As we will explore below, more recent evidence from whistleblowers and managers alike provides evidence that support from within the management hierarchy is important to the relative success of the outcome, especially support from front-line supervisors, problematic as this may be (Brown and Olsen 2008a).

On Power

Miceli and Near (1995) postulate that the power of the whistleblower will affect the effectiveness of whistleblowing. Generally, the individual is more dependent on the organization than vice versa. If the whistleblower possesses powerful resources then the organization would be more likely to address wrongdoing. But in cases where both the wrongdoer and the whistleblower are powerful, or the organization depends on the wrongdoing to survive, then a more powerful whistleblower may be more likely to face retaliation than a less powerful whistleblower. This is because he or she is perceived to be a bigger threat.

If the whistleblower is powerless and depends on the organization, then whistleblowing may be ignored. The value congruence between the whistleblower and the dominant coalition makes the whistleblower more powerful and thus more likely to influence top management to terminate wrongdoing. Finally, Miceli and Near (2002) found that ineffective whistleblowing is more likely when top management perceives whistleblowing as a threat to the organization's authority structure.

On Retaliation

Finally, existing research does often deal with retaliation as one of the key foci for study. Mesmer-Magnus and Viswesvaran's (2005: 282) meta-analysis of the personal and contextual correlates of whistleblowing intention and behavior identified four predictors or correlates of retaliation against whistleblowers: '(1) characteristics of the whistleblower, (2) actions taken by the whistleblower in reporting organizational wrongdoing, (3) situational or environmental variables related to the organization, and (4) characteristics of the wrongdoing or wrongdoer'. In their view, situational or environmental variables include top management, supervisor and co-worker support, even if the characteristics of the complaint recipient are not included as a factor.

From this, it can be seen that both the characteristics and the behavior of top management, supervisors and co-workers provide important elements for study in relation to retaliation. Research has also examined how the characteristics of the wrongdoing may influence retaliation (see Brown and Olsen 2008b), with positive correlations found between retaliation and severity and frequency of wrongdoing. Possession of convincing evidence or the whistleblower's ability to stop the wrongdoing is associated with lower likelihood of retaliation. The use of an external channel to report wrongdoing is associated with more retaliation, although, as also noted elsewhere, the retaliation may also precede or indeed trigger the use of the external channel (e.g., Smith and Brown 2008; Moberly, Chapter 12). A small negative relationship between job level and retaliation was found.

However, little research has been undertaken to examine how the characteristics or the specific actions of management may influence retaliation, whether by causing it, limiting it or preventing it. For example, in line with most research to date, Near and Miceli (2008) explored retaliation in terms of whistleblower characteristics rather than complaint recipient characteristics. It remains axiomatic that retaliation may be used by managers so that the organization's authority structure is not violated, and that this is more likely in bureaucratic organizations (Weinstein 1979). Near and Miceli (2008) comment that whistleblowers may be ignored, retaliated against or silenced, but they may also face a variety of these responses, as they are not mutually exclusive. They also argue that increasing sensitivity to and penalties for wrongdoing may affect the incidence of whistleblowing, by fostering a more positive management response to it, more than laws that aim to reduce retaliation against whistleblowers. The timely termination of the wrongdoing would encourage other observers of wrongdoing to report. This argument draws on continuing evidence that for employees, the question of whether they perceive anyone to be interested in listening is a more important predictor of their likelihood to speak up than considerations of the likelihood of retaliation (e.g., Wortley *et al.* 2008: 74–7).

Overall, Mesmer-Magnus and Viswesvaran call for more research to explore whether retaliation is better predicted, or prevented, by examining dyadic interactions or relationships (between whistleblower and complaint recipient), than by examining the position of individual whistleblowers through proxies such as their job level or perceived value to the organization. This aligns with the view of Near and Miceli that responses to whistleblowing may be more strongly influenced by other factors, including managerial attitudes to the wrongdoing involved, than anything to do with the whistleblower at all:

> executives may be more likely to listen to whistleblowers and terminate the wrongdoing if they clearly understand what constitutes wrongdoing and the penalties they would suffer if they were to allow the wrongdoing to continue. Clearly, we need more research on this question, but the initial evidence suggests that policy would be better served to focus on penalties for wrongdoing, as a way to increase reporting of organizational wrongdoing. (Near and Miceli 2008: 278)

Finally, research into the relationship between whistleblowing and employee voice has also confirmed the need to focus on actual management of the whistleblowing process. In this field, all the indications are that organizations who want to derive more benefit from employee voice, in general, need to 'help supervisors understand that they most likely are part of the problem'; but significantly, the same authors note that as yet, 'prior research has not unpacked the psychological processes that explain different supervisor reactions to subordinate voice' (Chiaburu *et al.* 2013: 246, 248).

EXPLORATORY FINDINGS ON MANAGERIAL RESPONSES TO WHISTLEBLOWING

How feasible is it to collect the type of data that would fill out the rest of this picture? From the roles played by managerial and organizational responses in research to date, described above, it is first clear that two quite different, intertwined dimensions need to be studied. Each of these dimensions is necessary for whistleblowing to be regarded as successful: managerial responsiveness to the primary concerns aired by the whistleblower about wrongdoing; and ability or willingness to refrain from, or protect the whistleblower against retaliation or reprisals for having aired those concerns. We call these, respectively, 'hearer action' and 'protector action'.

As noted above, fewer studies have tended to collect data on the characteristics of 'hearers', or disclosure recipients, than on whistleblowers' characteristics and other contextual factors. More recently, however, empirical surveys have begun to ask participants to whom they did, or would blow the whistle if they observed wrongdoing; and to allow them to identify multiple recipients, and the order or sequence in which they would make their disclosure to different recipients (e.g., Donkin *et al.* 2008; Dreyfus and Brown 2013; PCaW 2013). Such research thus demonstrates the feasibility of identifying the types of recipients and potential recipients whose individual characteristics, responses and responsiveness could be studied in further detail. The full spectrum of potential recipients, inside and outside organizations, is discussed in Chapter 12 by Moberly and in Chapter 11 by Bosua *et al.* What is clear is that provided organizations can be persuaded to participate in research, or sufficient samples of recipients can otherwise be accessed, there is no particular barrier to studying the different ways that different managers respond to a primary disclosure, at different stages of its handling within a given organization.

Studying 'protector action' may seem more challenging. After all, managers are not likely to concede that they have, or would be likely to, undertake retaliation, or fail to offer support and protection to whistleblowers when arguably needed. However, some previously unreported data from the Australian study mentioned earlier helps demonstrate that this too, is not only feasible, but likely to be rewarding. Full details of the 'Whistling While They Work' research project where this data was collected are found elsewhere (Brown 2008; Roberts *et al.* 2011). As part of this research, survey responses were collected from 532 randomly selected managers in 15 Australian public sector organizations in 2007–2008. Among other issues, managers were asked what they would consider to be 'the best way for you to respond to the following events, if they happened to an employee you are dealing with who has reported wrongdoing?'. The four events were drawn from a range of known research and case results, indicating early warning signs of adverse outcomes or reprisals against whistleblowers, of ascending order of seriousness or complexity:

(1) Co-workers cease to associate with the employee at work.
(2) Co-workers begin spreading rumours about the employee.
(3) A manager makes negative comments about the employee's personality.
(4) A manager plans to refer the employee for psychiatric assessment.

In relation to each, respondents were offered the following five choices, which for the purposes of analysis have been grouped to permit construction of a scale, as a measure of preparedness to intervene in order to prevent or limit adverse action against the whistleblower. Low preparedness (0) is indicated by the responses 'Take no action (not my role)' or 'Wait and see if a problem emerges'; moderate preparedness (1) is indicated by the responses 'Advise/consult senior managers' or 'Advise/consult an external agency'; and high preparedness (2) is indicated by the response 'Counsel the staff or manager involved' being the only response involving direct intervention or action.

Table 13.1 contains the responses to the four events; while Tables 13.2–13.6 show response means in relation to a number of variables involving the perceptions and attitudes of these managers towards whistleblowing:

(1) Their perceived importance of employee reporting as a means of bringing wrongdoing to light in the organization (Table 13.2).
(2) Their view of the proportion of employee reports that are generally vexatious or unfounded, mentioned earlier (Table 13.3).
(3) Their level of training (Table 13.4).
(4) Their experience with whistleblowing, measured by the number of cases they reported having dealt with during the five years preceding the survey (Table 13.5).
(5) Their perception of the quality of risk management within the organization (Table 13.6).

Overall, these results suggest that on their own account, both lower and more senior managers are more inclined to intervene than not. However, intervention was most likely for rumors and negative comments about the employee's personality, and not when there was a planned psychiatric assessment (which we see as the worst scenario). There is an increase, however, in preparedness to take the matter further or elsewhere (advise/consult senior managers or external agency) as behaviors worsen. This tendency is slightly less pronounced for more senior managers compared to lower managers, which could be explained by more relative power of the senior managers.

Further differences in their stated preparedness to take action emerge, moreover, depending on the range of the perceptions and experiences of different managers, within and across each of these two broad groups, as shown by the remaining tables.

Table 13.2 shows that almost across the board, the greater the importance that managers attach to employee reporting as a means of

Table 13.1 Manager preparedness to intervene (%)

What do you think would be the best way for you to respond to the following events, if they happened to an employee you are dealing with who has reported wrongdoing?	Manager level	(n)	0 Take no action/ Wait and see if problem	1 Advise/ Consult senior mgrs or external agency	2 Counsel the staff or mgr involved	
(a) Co-workers cease to associate with the employee at work	1st and 2nd	(279)	14.0	22.6	63.4	100
	More senior	(248)	8.5	18.9	72.6	100
	Total	**(532)**	**11.3**	**20.4**	**67.3**	**100**
(b) Co-workers begin spreading rumors about the employee	1st and 2nd	(279)	1.5	25.1	73.5	100
	More senior	(248)	0.0	25.8	74.2	100
	Total	**(532)**	**0.8**	**25.5**	**60.0**	**100**
(c) A manager makes negative comments about the employee's personality	1st and 2nd	(279)	3.2	49.8	47.0	100
	More senior	(248)	1.6	35.1	63.3	100
	Total	**(532)**	**2.5**	**42.9**	**54.7**	**100**
(d) A manager plans to refer the employee for psychiatric assessment	1st and 2nd	(278)	5.4	76.3	18.3	100
	More senior	(245)	9.8	61.8	27.3	100
	Total	**(528)**	**7.6**	**69.8**	**22.5**	**100**

Source: 'Whistling While They Work' project, Manager Survey ('Managing the Internal Reporting of Wrongdoing', 2007), Q44

bringing wrongdoing to light in their organizations, relative to other means, the stronger their stated preparedness to take action in response to signs of reprisal risk. The only possible exception is on the part of some senior managers (n = 11). Consistently with Miceli and Near's (2002) suggestions, just as not all managers see whistleblowing as equally valuable or otherwise, they vary in their preparedness to intervene, with a clear relation between the two.

Table 13.2 Perceived value of whistleblowing

Importance of employee reporting for bringing wrongdoing to light in my organization		1st and 2nd level managers	More senior managers
		Four item scale (a–d) (0–8)	
Not /somewhat important /missing	Mean	5.63	5.76
	N	27	29
Important but at least one other thing more important	Mean	5.67	6.01
	N	83	67
Very important and as important as anything else	Mean	5.77	6.30
	N	48	54
Extremely important and as important as anything else	Mean	5.86	6.34
	N	108	87
Very/extremely important and more important than anything else	Mean	6.08	6.00
	N	13	11
Total	Mean	5.78	6.16
	N	279	248

Source: 'Whistling While They Work' project, Manager Survey ('Managing the Internal Reporting of Wrongdoing', 2007), Q14

When asked whether they agreed that 'most employee reports [of wrongdoing] are wholly trivial (no information merits investigation)' or that 'reports are often vexatious (an abuse of process)', relatively few managers did so, and many managers disagreed strongly. In general, Table 13.3 shows, again, that those managers who tended to agree with these statements tended to show lower preparedness to take 'protector' action (with one outlier among the senior managers, n = 1).

The findings in Table 13.4 suggest that receiving training on how to deal with whistleblowers is more important than the kind of training managers received. Managers who had received training showed more preparedness to intervene (they had a higher mean on how they answered the four scenarios). Professional training seemed to have more impact for senior managers, whereas informal or on the job training seems to have more impact for lower level managers.

Table 13.3 Perceived problems with whistleblowing

When public employees report wrongdoing, what type of information do they provide? – Most employee reports are wholly trivial (no information merits investigation) – Reports are often vexatious (an abuse of process)		1st and 2nd level managers	More senior managers
		Four item scale (a–d) (0–8)	
Strongly disagree both statements/one, disagree other	Mean	5.64	6.25
	N	47	36
Disagree both statements	Mean	5.83	6.16
	N	76	68
Disagree one, neither dis/agree other	Mean	5.84	6.04
	N	74	74
Disagree one, agree other	Mean	5.85	6.32
	N	27	22
Neither dis/agree both	Mean	5.79	6.25
	N	29	28
Agree one, neither dis/agree other	Mean	5.20	5.80
	N	10	15
Agree both	Mean	5.56	8.00
	N	9	1
Total	Mean	5.76	6.15
	N	272	244

Source: 'Whistling While They Work' project, Manager Survey ('Managing the Internal Reporting of Wrongdoing', 2007), Q27

Table 13.5 also suggests there might be some association between managerial intention to intervene on behalf of a whistleblower and their direct experience of dealing with whistleblowers. Those managers who had no experience showed the weakest intention to intervene, whilst managers who had experience of more than ten cases also tended to show the strongest intention to intervene. Although our findings do not indicate this relation to be linear, they do suggest that preparedness to act may relate to direct knowledge of either the need or the feasibility of acting, in practice.

Table 13.4 Level of relevant training

What training have you had about how to deal with cases where employees have reported wrongdoing?		1st and 2nd level managers	More senior managers
		Four item scale (a–d) (0–8)	
No particular training/ missing	Mean	5.64	5.98
	N	84	44
Informal/on the job training	Mean	5.87	6.18
	N	134	119
Professional training	Mean	5.77	6.24
	N	61	85
Total	Mean	5.78	6.16
	N	279	248

Source: 'Whistling While They Work' project, Manager Survey ('Managing the Internal Reporting of Wrongdoing', 2007), Q22

Table 13.5 Experience with cases

Since the middle of 2002, approximately how many different cases have you dealt with involving employees who have reported wrongdoing in your organization?		1st and 2nd level managers	More senior managers
		Four item scale (a–d) (0–8)	
None	Mean	5.80	5.79
	N	79	19
One or two	Mean	5.63	6.24
	N	83	59
3–10	Mean	5.83	5.99
	N	70	109
11–20	Mean	5.70	6.78
	N	20	27
More than 20	Mean	6.18	6.36
	N	22	33
Total	Mean	5.78	6.17
	N	274	247

Source: 'Whistling While They Work' project, Manager Survey ('Managing the Internal Reporting of Wrongdoing', 2007), Q9

Table 13.6 Quality of risk management in the organization

In your view, how well are the risks of wrongdoing managed in your organization?		1st and 2nd level managers	More senior managers
		Four item scale (a–d) (0–8)	
Not at all	Mean	5.50	6.00
	N	6	1
Not very well	Mean	5.70	6.30
	N	43	30
Somewhat	Mean	5.84	6.11
	N	105	90
Very well	Mean	5.81	6.24
	N	116	116
Extremely well	Mean	5.63	5.38
	N	8	8
Total	Mean	5.79	6.17
	N	278	245

Source: 'Whistling While They Work' project, Manager Survey ('Managing the Internal Reporting of Wrongdoing', 2007), Q13

Finally, Table 13.6 shows a potentially complex relationship between managers' intention to intervene and their organizational context, as measured by their perception of the overall quality of risk management in their organization. Both low level and senior managers are least prepared to take protector action if they perceive risks to be managed either extremely well or not at all. A possible explanation is that if people perceive risks to be managed extremely well anyway, there is less need for them to take action. This is in line with findings from Kaptein (2011), who found that in organizations that scored high on the Corporate Ethical Values model, people see less need to take responsible action (i.e., blow the whistle) if things go wrong. However, the low means for intention to intervene when perception of risk management quality was lowest could also be explained by seeing this as an indicator that the organization is not interested in addressing concerns about organizational risks, and thus that managers' perceptions of the leadership culture around them may be just as important as their own individual attitudes or values.

Low level managers show a strong intention to intervene if they perceive risk to be 'somewhat' managed well. A possible explanation is that, in that case, there is some indication within the organizations that *risks* are important to pay attention to, but that whistleblowing is important because other risk management systems are not adequate. More senior managers show a small decrease in intention when the quality of organizational risk management is perceived 'somewhat well'. In contrast to lower managers, more senior managers might have a stronger intention when they perceive risk management quality as low, because they rely more on whistleblowers and have the power to intervene. Similarly, more senior managers might be showing a stronger intention to intervene when they perceive risk management quality as high, because there are whistleblowing procedures within the organization and they know how to work with them.

None of these findings are straightforward – rather, they all call for further research. Nevertheless, these data, from a considerable sample of managers, indicate that it is indeed possible to measure managers' intentions and preparedness to take action with respect to their own whistleblowers, and to identify personal and situational variables which help explain which managers are more likely to show such preparedness to act on behalf of whistleblowers, and which are less likely. Further analysis would show the relative significance and interaction between these and other factors as predictors of managerial preparedness to take action on behalf of whistleblowers. These results, therefore, have many implications for further research into managerial responsiveness.

Above all, these exploratory data confirm that relations between variables are not straightforward or linear. The question becomes how managerial responsiveness should be theorized for the purposes of empirical research, and how those theories can then be tested, through methods and incorporating variables such as those demonstrated above.

TOWARDS A MODEL FOR TESTING 'HEARER COURAGE'

As already outlined, the first of two major dimensions on which managerial responsiveness needed to be studied is that of 'hearer action', or responsiveness to the primary concerns about wrongdoing. If a better understanding of the different responses of organizations to different instances of whistleblowing is to be achieved, a stronger focus becomes necessary on how disclosures are received, by whom, and who makes decisions affecting the multiple dimensions of the response. As an extension of studies into the nature and characteristics of whistleblowing, it becomes necessary to research the nature and characteristics of the individuals who must respond, within their organizational context.

Recently, Mansbach (2011) and Vandekerckhove and Langenberg (2012) have developed Foucault's concept of *parrhesia* as a new perspective in whistleblowing research. The ancient Greek term 'parrhesia' means 'frankly speaking truth'. It denotes an act of denouncing a perceived practice, without having an alternative 'better way'. As such, parrhesia may appropriately describe the initial step of the whistleblowing process, when members of an organization (in Near and Miceli's definition) denounce something as unacceptable, a mistake, or simply wrong, even before identifying themselves as a whistleblower.

While Mansbach (2011) points to the democratic value of parrhesia along with the inherent risks for the parrhesiastes, or the person performing parrhesia, Vandekerckhove and Langenberg (2012) link it to courage and discuss this in an organizational context. They argue that the social meaning of parrhesia stems from perceiving it as an interactional event rather than as a solitary act of the parrhesiastes. Likewise, to understand the social meaning of internal whistleblowing we must perceive whistleblowing not just as an act of the whistleblower, but rather as an interaction between whistleblower and recipient. This leads Vandekerckhove and Langenberg (2012) to theorize that it is not only the speaker who requires courage to speak up. Just as importantly, the recipient or hearer needs courage to hear what is being said, take appropriate action, and refrain from inappropriate action. Obviously, if the speaker lacks courage, he or she may be unlikely to speak up (or will revert to gossip: see Leys and Vandekerckhove, Chapter 5). In this sense, to the extent that whistleblowing research has so far focused on the whistleblower, as discussed above, this can be understood as a search for those variables that determine who has courage to speak, under what circumstances, and with regard to which perceived wrongs. One way this has impacted practice is through socio-technical interventions aimed at lowering the speaker-courage threshold: for example, through rewards for whistleblowers, anonymous hotlines, computer mediated reporting channels and protection strategies.

The gaps in whistleblowing research highlighted earlier point to a new search: for those variables which determine courage on the part of disclosure recipients. This is significant, because whereas it is often unclear as to whether or when an employee is subject to any positive duty to blow the whistle (see Leys and Vandekerckhove, Chapter 5), managers in organizations are frequently subject to much clearer responsibilities, either ethical or formal, to respond in various ways to employees who blow the whistle. As noted earlier, however, even in the field of employee voice, research is yet to unpack the processes that explain 'different supervisor reactions to subordinate voice' (Chiaburu *et al* 2013: 248). Similarly, while quantitative measures of 'organizational courage' have been suggested to investigate the collective willingness of organization members to speak up (Kilmann *et al* 2013), it is the courage and other variables that influence the performance of the managers in control of the organization, in terms of whether or how they discharge these quite specific responsibilities, which would seem to be the most central and important focus. As discussed in the next Part of this book (see Fasterling, Chapter 14, and chapters following), such responsibilities might stem from their general duties towards employee well-being, or to public safety, or specific duties to their organization, or they may be even more specifically imposed by whistleblowing laws or other regulations. This reinforces a crucial question: why is it that some managers step up, recognize and discharge these responsibilities in an effective manner, when others do not?

If critical aspects of whistleblowing action can be usefully understood through the prism of courage, so too can 'hearer action'. Hearer courage is a way of understanding which managers have the courage to hear, under which circumstances, and with regard to which wrongs.

In relation to 'hearer action' and courage, if we perceive whistleblowing as an interactional event between speaker and hearer, then what does hearing mean? What must the recipient do to hear? Based on the definition of Near and Miceli (1985: 4), internal whistleblowing is done to persons who 'may be able to effect action'. Recipients must therefore effect action in response to what has been said to them. Arguably, neglecting a concern raised is also an action. However, like Miceli and Near (1995), we will focus on the first dimension of effective whistleblowing, i.e., whether investigative and remedial action is taken, so that any malpractice is corrected. Thus, we will not include retaliation or neglect in what we call 'hearer action' – these will be pursued in the next section.

'Hearer action' is what makes a recipient a hearer. What does 'hearer action' involve? From what we know about the whistleblowing process, whistleblowers often initially raise their concerns with their line manager or with someone above that, or with a specific policy-designated person. The implication is that quite often, the initial recipient will not be mandated to investigate the concern, correct the malpractice or sanction wrongdoers. Instead, the initial recipient might have to pass the concern to an appropriate function within the organization, i.e., internal audit, HR, CFO, CEO, or even the board. Thus 'hearer action' for the initial recipients can mean correcting malpractice or becoming a speaker themselves. It is in this sense that Vandekerckhove and Langenberg (2012) theorize that internal whistleblowing often requires a 'parrhesiastic chain' of courageous speakers-hearers-speakers.

If research on the whistleblower has improved practice by finding out how to lower the speaker-courage threshold, research into managerial responses could improve practice by finding out how to lower the hearer-courage threshold. For example, it seems obvious that role-prescribed and specialized hearer-speakers, such as internal auditors or outsourced hotline providers, should require less courage to pass on concerns or information about malpractices to those who can correct them, than an HR manager or a sales team leader. This does not imply that internal auditors or outsourced hotline providers are the panacea for effective whistleblowing. A chain is as strong as its weakest link, and if the weakest link in a parrhesiastic chain is an unwilling frontline manager, corrupt CEO or incompetent board, then any kind of low-courage whistleblowing channel will remain ineffective.

The implication is that research on recipients of whistleblowing should include all hearer-speakers, including recipients within the wider society such as regulators, law enforcement agencies, professional bodies and media. When it comes to a model which can be used to research managerial responses to whistleblowing, this clearly must include managers at any level in an organization.

'Hearer action' may form part of a person's role description, depending on the internal whistleblowing policy. However, we distinguish between those functions designated specifically as whistleblowing recipients (e.g., compliance and ethics officers, auditors, hotline operators) and managers for whom these functions are at best collateral or secondary roles.

Since we do not yet know to what extent context and personality determine, moderate or mediate manager responses to whistleblowing, we propose the theory of planned behavior (Ajzen 1991) as a useful initial entry into this field of research, and a way of operationalizing the elements developed above. The usefulness of this approach for linking intention and actual behavior is also discussed by Bjørkelo and Bye (Chapter 6). We will briefly outline the main elements of the theory and develop some propositions from it.

The theory of planned behavior can be used to predict behavior. It takes a dispositional approach assuming individuals' ability for cognitive self-regulation. This means that intentions lead to behavior, if we understand intention to be comprised of both motivational and non-motivational factors. Motivational factors include someone's attitude towards the behavior and the subjective norm. Non-motivational factors include the perceived availability of opportunities and resources to perform the behavior, like time, money, skills, and the cooperation of others. Hence, from Ajzen's theory of planned behavior, intention can be formulated as:

$$I = f(A,N,PBC)$$

Intention (I) is a function of attitude (A), subjective norm (N), and perceived behavioral control (PBC).

Ajzen (1991: 183) points out that perceived behavioral control is not the same as perceived locus of control. The latter is a generalized expectancy which tends to be stable across situations and forms of action. Perceived behavioral control, however, refers to 'people's perception of the ease or difficulty of performing the behavior of interest'.

Our emphasis is on the development of propositions on behavioral performance, not behavioral achievement. In other words, using the theory of planned behavior we will develop propositions on when managers will take 'hearer action' but not on whether or not that 'hearer action' will eventually lead to effective whistleblowing. As mentioned above, a chain is only as strong as its weakest link. Our propositions could be used to test the strength of each link of a parrhesiastic chain within an organization, or where the weakest links tend to be across organizations.

According to Ajzen, there are three antecedents to planned behavior, which we see as relevant to the context of a manager's response to whistleblowing, and suggest can be formulated into testable propositions on 'hearer action'.

Attitude Towards the Behavior

This first antecedent refers to the 'degree to which a person has a favorable or unfavorable evaluation or appraisal of the behavior in question' (Ajzen 1991: 188). Ajzen's model was initially tested for ethically neutral behavior like going to the beach, mountain biking and jogging. Ajzen suggests that because ethical issues tend to take on added belief salience, some measure of perceived ethical obligation could add predictive power to the model. The behavior in question here is 'hearer action', which is one or a combination of the following: investigate the concern, pass on the information or concern, correct the malpractice, and take sanctions against the wrongdoer.

A person's attitude towards 'hearer action' and a person's perceived ethical obligation towards such action are not easily distinguishable.

However, Ajzen suggested that a notion of ethical obligation a person might have with regard to 'hearer action' would be relevant for that person's attitude towards responding to whistleblowing. Hence we suggest that a recipient or manager's personal attitude to whistleblowing, including their own whistleblowing propensity (see Loyens and Maesschalck, Chapter 7 and also Moberly, Chapter 12), could be used as a measurement of that attitude. Previous research has shown positive attitudes to whistleblowing, including propensity, to be just as high or higher among samples of managers than in general employee samples (e.g., Keenan 2007; Mazerolle and Brown 2008). Higher whistleblowing propensity would, therefore, be more likely to lead to a more favorable evaluation of 'hearer action', and hence towards a higher intention towards 'hearer action'.

Subjective Norm

The second antecedent refers to 'perceived social pressure to perform or not perform the behavior' (Ajzen 1991: 188). A number of items could be used to measure this, and it might be useful to include both internal, as well as external, perceived social pressures. Internally these might be: whether whistleblowing recipients have seen others take 'hearer action' in the past and whether they were positively sanctioned for it within the organization; whether whistleblowing is included in managers' performance indicators; whether wrongdoing is clearly defined within the organization; and whether it is espoused as a desirable action to take. External indicators might be: whether one's family or social network would expect it; and whether legislation requires such 'hearer action'.

Perceived Behavioral Control

The third antecedent refers to the 'perceived ease or difficulty of performing the behavior and reflects past experience as well as anticipated impediments and obstacles' (Ajzen 1991: 188). Indicators which could be used to measure this include perceptions and knowledge of: internal whistleblowing procedures and whether recipients have a defined role in these; one's skill in performing 'hearer action' (including investigating, avoiding conflict and protecting the whistleblower); and whether there is a helpline available for managers. Some research has already probed this territory, with Mazerolle and Brown (2008) having highlighted the fact that managers may have strongly positive attitudes to whistleblowing as a general notion, but be left severely under-informed or under-equipped as to how to manage it in practice. These tensions were found to correlate with problems of poorer organizational outcomes in relation to whistleblowing cases (Roberts 2008).

Propositions

Ajzen's model of planned behavior focuses on intention, and given that intention can influence behavior, even if it does not dictate it, we propose the following:

> *Proposition 1*: managers with a more positive attitude towards whistleblowing will report a higher intention to take 'hearer action'.

> *Proposition 2*: managers who perceive more social or professional pressure to take 'hearer action' will report a higher intention to take 'hearer action'.

> *Proposition 3*: managers who have a higher perceived behavioral control will report a higher intention to take 'hearer action'.

Ajzen states that the relative importance of attitude, subjective norm and perceived behavioral control in predicting intention as planned behavior will vary across behaviors and situations. Hence, one research aim could be to find out which of these variables are causal, mediating or moderating. In that sense, we might expect intention to be a function of motivating and non-motivating factors in the following way: $I = (A,N) \times (PBC)$. On the one hand, managers' whistleblowing propensity and perceived social pressure for 'hearer action' might make them motivated to take such action, but still not have the intention to do so because of lack of knowledge or skill. On the other hand, managers might receive training and have an explicit role within the whistleblowing procedure, yet would not report an intention to take 'hearer action' because they are not motivated to do so (for a variety of reasons, such as experience of how others who took hearer action were treated, or signals from top management that cutting a corner is OK as long as one meets the target). Hence our two final propositions:

> *Proposition 4*: managers with a positive attitude to whistleblowing or who perceive high social pressure to take 'hearer action', but who report a low perceived behavioral control, will also report a lower intention to take 'hearer action'.

> *Proposition 5*: managers with a negative attitude to whistleblowing or who perceive low social pressure to take 'hearer action', yet report a high perceived behavioral control, will also report a lower intention to take 'hearer action'.

PROPOSITIONS FOR 'PROTECTOR' COURAGE: PROACTIVE MANAGEMENT OF RETALIATION RISKS

If effective internal whistleblowing requires a 'parrhesiastic chain' of courageous speakers-hearers-speakers, it also requires a similar chain of decision-making in which individual managers make an effort to protect those who have spoken up from adverse reactions that might befall them. Just as critical aspects of whistleblowing action and 'hearer action' can be usefully understood through the prism of courage, so too can 'protector action'. Protector courage is thus a way of understanding which managers have the courage to stand up for, or organize interventions around, those who blow the whistle within areas under their influence or control, in order to reduce or combat the familiar risks of retaliation, conflict or suspicion of the reporting action.

As shown by the exploratory data earlier, these risks range from simple workplace stress to a wide range of adverse consequences, and from low level informal reprisals to high level formal reprisals (see Smith, Chapter 10). Research also indicates that whistleblowers look to, and find, a multiplicity of different sources of support and protection in response to the risks and problems they face, but that successful delivery of that support can be highly variable (Brown and Olsen 2008b). A manager in a position to take 'protector' action may also be taking 'hearer' action. Alternatively, circumstances, roles or seniority may dictate that those in a position to take 'protector' action are different to the 'hearing' actors. Defining 'protector action' remains challenging given the lack of research to date on the different strategies or choices that exist for managers, who might seek to support or protect staff who report: much is known about the nature of the reprisals that managers are capable of undertaking, or of allowing to occur, but less is known about what they can do to prevent this from happening. Yet, this understanding is crucial, given that statutes increasingly impose obligations on organizations to support and protect whistleblowers. As will be discussed in the next Part of the book, duties to refrain from deliberate reprisals have been in place in several countries for up to three decades. These anti-retaliation measures under general law, and whistleblowing laws, are predicated on an assumption that individuals and organizations have an enforceable duty not to undertake retaliation, the breach of which will trigger rights to remedies including compensation. More recently this has extended into legislation and corporate governance standards which require an active management approach to the provision of support and reprisal prevention, including assessing and managing the risks that are consistent with, or might lead to, breakdowns in trust and retaliation in general.

On this second major dimension of managerial responsiveness, therefore, an equivalent model is also needed for evaluating how managers assess and respond to the risks of retaliation, irrespective of whether they have any responsibility to take 'hearer action'. Different managers are likely to perceive risks differently, for example, the risk of embarrassment if they get a decision wrong; or the greater risk to themselves or the organization if they spend too much time worrying about how a whistleblower is faring, as opposed to getting on with core business; or the longer term risks to both the reputation and the bottom line of the organization if retaliation eventuates and conflict escalates.

Propositions

We posit that Ajzen's three antecedents to intention as planned behavior can also be used to research manager responses to whistleblowing, in terms of preparedness to take 'protector action'. Indeed, the exploratory data earlier shows not only that it is feasible to measure intention to take such action, but to identify a range of variables that would either directly satisfy, or serve as close proxies for these antecedents (Tables 13.2–13.6). Equivalent propositions to those related to 'hearer courage' can therefore be proposed:

> *Proposition 6*: managers with a more positive attitude towards whistleblowing will report a higher intention to take 'protector action'.

> *Proposition 7*: managers who perceive more social or professional pressure to take 'protector action' will report a higher intention to take 'protector action'.

> *Proposition 8*: managers who have a higher perceived behavioral control will report a higher intention to take 'protector action'.

> *Proposition 9*: managers with a positive attitude to whistleblowing or who perceive high social pressure to take 'protector action', but who report a low perceived behavioral control, will also report a lower intention to take 'protector action'.

> *Proposition 10*: managers with a negative attitude to whistleblowing or who perceive low social pressure to take 'protector action', yet report a high perceived behavioral control, will also report a lower intention to take 'protector action'.

Our adaptation of Ajzen's model to recipients of internal whistleblowing, and our development of ten propositions on 'hearer action' and 'protector action' can be used for the kind of research called for by Mesmer-Magnus and Viswesvaran (2005) and Near and Miceli (2008), along with that needed in the field of employee voice. As noted earlier, because responses to whistleblowing may be more strongly influenced by managerial attitudes than by anything to do with the whistleblower, successful whistleblowing might be more predictable by researching these attitudes and behaviors of recipients towards wrongdoing and the whistleblower, rather than characteristics of the individual whistleblower.

IMPLICATIONS FOR FURTHER RESEARCH

As discussed at the outset, whistleblowing research has tended to suffer from a range of limitations, stereotypes and dichotomies. So far, we believe we have demonstrated both the need to move beyond these, and the feasibility of doing so. It is apparent that not all organizations are the same in the manner in which they respond to their own whistleblowers. While many may experience problems, and all may be capable of undertaking reprisals, it is clear that some do so less than others, or in differing circumstances, and to differing degrees.

Similarly, within organizations, not all managers are the same. Some are likely to be more willing and/or able to take effective 'hearer action' than others, depending on personal attitude, organizational norms, and their power or ability to do so. Some managers are shown to be more willing and/or able to take effective 'protector action' than others, depending on all these and perhaps other circumstances. It is therefore apparent that further research into managerial responsiveness, individually and collectively, is both feasible and stands to provide a whole new level of insight into how whistleblowing is being managed in practice; how it could be managed; and how it should be managed, in the interest of effectiveness.

In this process, it is apparent that research into managerial responses needs to learn from and leapfrog some of the limitations of the early research into whistleblowers. For example, just as early research into whistleblowers tended to presuppose that observers of wrongdoing had only two options (report or stay silent), research into managerial responses tended to categorize the response of complaint recipients as a dichotomy of either 'address' or 'retaliate'. This basic dichotomy is inappropriate, as it conflates two quite distinct dimensions – response to the wrongdoing, and response to the whistleblower – when these are potentially two independent variables. In addition, there is also likely to be a range of possible responses, not a simple dichotomy. The analyses provided earlier show both the feasibility and utility of research into a spectrum of possible responses, in order to establish the variables which contribute to, or derogate from, greater managerial capacity to respond effectively to whistleblowing incidents.

The potential benefits of this research are profound. By understanding the factors that influence managerial responsiveness in this way, it will be possible for organizations and regulators alike to identify what is going wrong and right with institutions' efforts to manage whistleblowing more effectively, and use it for the advantages that most managers (contrary to some assumptions) appear to recognize. From this knowledge, more appropriate policies and practices, clearer understanding of where and how responsibility needs to be attributed for the management of whistleblowing and reprisal risks, and more effective training and awareness interventions, can emerge.

From the above discussion, it can also be seen that research into managerial responsiveness should proceed with the benefit of a more detailed theoretical model, derived from existing models of organizational and managerial behavior, but informed by the unique complexities of whistleblowing dynamics and processes. Attitude, subjective norms and perceived behavioral control, as suggested by Ajzen (1991), are likely to remain fundamentally relevant. However, each of these has already been shown to involve a wide range of potential influences and parameters; and the interactions between them are likely to be decisive.

Taking into account the insights above, and the existing research into whistleblowing and its outcomes, we can suggest a more detailed framework for seeking answers to the fundamental question: why do managers and organizations not respond more effectively to whistleblowing? In our view, both 'hearer courage' and 'protector courage' should be researched, but in seeking to explain what supports or leads to these, research might usefully apply Ajzen's model by looking to measure quite specific aspects of the knowledge, attitudes and experience of individual managers, as follows.

Attitudes

(1) Relative *awareness* of the incidence, nature and benefits of whistleblowing as an organizational phenomenon.
(2) Relative exposure to, and/or tolerance for, the *risks of wrongdoing* that give rise to the need for whistleblowing.

(3) Particular *perceptions* about particular disclosures, including (3a) validity/accuracy, etc. of the information in disclosures; (3b) perceived motive of the reporter (e.g., disaffected employee = perceived malice = low validity); (3c) rationalization processes (e.g., that in the circumstances conduct is not so serious as to warrant a formal process); (3d) cost/benefit, that the time and effort spent trying to support and protect whistleblowers is just not worth it.

(4) Other individual attitudes or beliefs about *how to respond to conflicts/challenges*, including personality, unwillingness to rock the boat/make waves/take risks, etc.

Subjective Norms

(5) Individual attitudes or beliefs about *appropriate organizational responses*; e.g., (5a) *loyalty*, taking action on a disclosure seen as being disloyal to colleagues generally or friends in particular, or to the organization; (5b) *fear*, that action will not be supported by management and career will suffer as a consequence; (5c) *organizational culture*, including trust in own management generally; (5d) *futility,* that no good purpose is served by taking action because nothing will come of it due to reluctance of management to take appropriate action.

(6) *Self-interest/complicity*, e.g., the presence of risks that the recipient of the report, or persons above them, are either involved in the wrongdoing, have turned a blind eye to it in the past, or are otherwise responsible.

Perceived Behavioral Control

(7) *Knowledge* about *how* to manage whistleblowing, including how to receive and respond to disclosures, and options for whistleblower support (including training).

(8) *Rank, seniority, position description, roles.*

(9) *Career stage, career progression and outlook, job satisfaction.*

(10) Attitudes, beliefs and fears regarding *external impacts*, e.g., (10a) *reputational consequences* for self, the unit or the organization (or government); (10b) *regulatory consequences* for self, others, organization, profession or industry, of acting in response to reported wrongdoing and/or taking protective action.

Research indicates that almost any organization member may be capable of becoming a whistleblower, depending on the circumstances and triggers. What is less clear, but could be more effectively researched, is whether any and every manager is equally capable of responding effectively or poorly to the circumstances in which employees report wrongdoing; and more particularly, which factors and combinations of factors in organizations influence the ability of their managers to do so. We suggest the above as a framework for answering these questions.

CONCLUSIONS

This chapter discussed gaps in existing whistleblowing research, in relation to understanding the nature and causes of different management responses to employee-reported wrongdoing. It has also identified the importance of filling these gaps, if the crucial issue of how to ensure more effective outcomes from whistleblowing is to be adequately addressed by organizations and regulators.

Fortunately, the transition is now underway, away from previous stereotypes of organizations as generally uninterested or incapable of either hearing or protecting their whistleblowers. It is naive to believe that organizations can be taught to want to hear and protect whistleblowers in every case. Instead, it is reasonable to expect that there may always be some circumstances in which the challenges posed by whistleblowing, in terms of the wrongdoing exposed or reprisal risks, are beyond the capacity of any organization to manage alone, or at all. The next Part of this book deals with the regulatory and legal frameworks around whistleblowing that have been developed in response to this reality. They include the need for regulatory oversight, so that whistleblowers can still be heard at an industry or societal level, in circumstances where no individual manager or managers could be expected to show the type of 'hearer courage' needed for an effective internal response to concerns. They also include the need for legal redress, such as regulator intervention and compensation rights and mechanisms, to cover circumstances where no individual manager or managers can be expected to show effective 'protector courage' towards the whistleblower, or where the efforts to take protector action break down.

At the same time, the growing recognition of whistleblowing as a crucial source of management information, and risk management tool, is now providing organizations with a large range of incentives to foster and institutionalize 'hearer courage' and 'protector courage' in their own management styles and cultures. Following Ajzen (1991), we suggested a model for research to better understand the factors that support and promote hearer action, incorporating managers' individual attitudes, subjective norms and perceived behavioral control. We presented some exploratory data from surveys with 532 managers in 15 public sector organizations in 2007–2008, as part of exploratory Australian research. These suggest that managers' attitudes towards employee reporting of wrongdoing, their level of training in the handling of such cases, and their degree of experience, position and seniority might all relate positively to their stated preparedness to take 'protector action' in relation to a whistleblower facing retaliation risks, albeit with some interesting variations. The managers who showed lowest preparedness to take 'protector action' were those who saw employee reporting as relatively unimportant and/or more likely to be unfounded, had received the least or less adequate training in respect of the handling of such cases, and were at mid-stages rather than early or late stages of their management career.

These results are significant in themselves, in pointing towards actions that organizations can take to increase their own capacity to provide effective whistleblower support. They show that practical decisions do matter, regarding how whistleblower management obligations are distributed, what training is provided to managers, and what criteria might be included in managerial selection or promotion procedures, by organizations who seek to more seriously embed their commitment to the effective handling of employee concerns. However, these discussions and results also point the way to further and better research, by enabling us to suggest a more detailed model of those factors that might be usefully investigated to provide a more comprehensive picture of what is influencing these different managerial outcomes. Organizations that recognize the role of whistleblowing as a risk management tool, and seek to utilize it, stand to benefit greatly from the self-diagnoses of their own capacities, strengths and weaknesses that this form of research can provide.

NOTE

* The views and opinions expressed in this chapter are those of the authors and do not necessarily represent the views of, and should not be attributed to, CPA Australia.

PART III

RESEARCH IN ACTION

14. Whistleblower protection: A comparative law perspective

Björn Fasterling

INTRODUCTION

In this chapter, a programme for comparative legislative research in the field of whistleblowing is proposed, identifying research questions along two basic public policy objectives that laws typically pursue in the context of whistleblowing. One is centered on guaranteeing the individual rights of the discloser, with particular regard to the whistleblower's freedom of expression, and the other towards a more effective prevention and detection of violations of the law and dangers to health and security. The following two prominent whistleblower cases may provide an illustration of how the law operates with regard to these two objectives.

Robert Ferro was a scientific researcher employed at Aerospace Corp., a private research company that had a contract with TRW Inc. Ferro discovered in 1995 that electrical components for use in defense satellites were likely to fail. TRW Inc. sold the components to the US government. In 2001 the government experienced critical failures of satellites in orbit as a result of the faulty electrical components, but TRW did not disclose the research Ferro had conducted. TRW, meanwhile acquired by Northrop Grumman Corp., insisted on a non-disclosure agreement and refused to allow Ferro and his employer to disclose the negative results of the research to anyone. Ferro filed a *qui tam* suit under the US False Claims Act 1986 against Northrop Grumman (Faunce *et al.* examine *qui tam* statutes in greater detail in Chapter 16). The US government joined the lawsuit. In 2009 the case resulted in a settlement that obliged Northrop Grumman to pay US$325 million to the government for the fraud. Ferro was entitled to receive US$48.7 million.

Brigitte Heinisch was employed as a geriatric nurse in a nursing home for the elderly operated by Vivantes Netzwerk für Gesundheit GmbH, a state-controlled company specializing in health care and assistance to the elderly. On several occasions Heinisch made the company's management aware of staff shortages. When the company refused to take measures, Heinisch brought a criminal complaint against the company for severe fraud. The prosecutor decided not to take further action upon the complaint. In the meantime, Heinisch was dismissed with due notice on account of her repeated illness. She then distributed leaflets, in which she denounced the dismissal as a 'political disciplinary measure taken in order to gag those employed'. When the employer obtained knowledge about the (fruitless) criminal complaint that Heinisch had brought against the company, she was dismissed again, but this time for fault. Heinisch unsuccessfully challenged this dismissal in German courts. When the applicant turned to the European Court of Human Rights (ECtHR), the court ruled that the employer's interests did not outweigh the public interest in exposing possible abuses by nursing homes. Heinisch was awarded a compensation of €15,000 by the ECtHR.

In both cases the law eventually helped the whistleblower. However, the way the law operated was quite different from one case to the other. In the Ferro case, specific provisions in the law enabled the participation of the whistleblower in a lawsuit against the suspected wrongdoer. In the Heinisch case, the whistleblower successfully fought against her employer's retaliation for having blown the whistle by invoking her right to freedom of expression. The reported staff shortages were not the subject matter of the case (although the case did spark a public debate about problems related to the privatization of health care for the elderly). In Heinisch, the law did not help the whistleblower for the sake of law enforcement, but in order to safeguard the exercise of her fundamental rights. The law may have also facilitated the freedom of expression in the Ferro case, but in this case the law's primary objective was to enforce the state's interests by 'deputizing' a private individual with inside knowledge about an alleged fraud.

While many countries agree to promote both policy objectives through the law, each legal system will need to draw up limits in order to protect the legitimate interests of other persons that may be affected by a whistleblower's disclosure, for example, those of employers, employees, employee representatives within organizations, suspected wrongdoers or the state. Comparative legislative research can reveal differences and convergence in public policy.

To the author's knowledge there is no comprehensive comparative law study on whistleblowing that covers several nations spanning over different legal families.[1] Vaughn (2012), however, provides a historical account of whistleblowing laws, drawing on personal, US and wider experience, and on this basis compares the effectiveness of whistleblower laws in different countries. There are also various country reports. For example, the Council of Europe gives a brief overview over existing and proposed legislation (PACE 2009). Transparency International offers a synopsis over ten European countries with an emphasis on Eastern Europe (Osterhaus and Fagan 2009; see also more recently Worth 2013). Banisar (2011) discusses whistleblower provisions in international treaties and in various national laws, focusing essentially on general and sectoral laws that specifically address whistleblowing. Furthermore, there are several two or three country comparisons that allow for a deeper comparative analysis. For example, Callahan *et al.* (2004) compare whistleblowing statutes in the United Kingdom, the United States and Australia. Lewis and Trygstad (2009) review the situation in Norwegian and UK law, also taking into account the different levels of power of employees and their representative organizations. Fasterling and Lewis (2014) discuss leaking, whistleblowing and freedom of speech under a comparative analysis that takes UK, US, French and German laws into account.

Dworkin and Brown (2013) compare US and Australian laws applying an analytical framework that distinguishes four legislative models for whistleblowing: (1) anti-retaliation or organizational justice; (2) reward or bounty; (3) structural or institutional; and (4) public or media. Dworkin and Brown's 'four-model' approach is helpful for comparative research that examines legal systems in which there have been targeted efforts to enact laws that protect or encourage whistleblowing. It becomes less obvious, however, how to apply their approach to legal systems that have no or hardly any legislation on whistleblowing. Even if legal systems lack any legislative strategy on whistleblowing, they do not necessarily leave the whistleblower unprotected. Morvan (2009), for example, compares French law (which has only a few whistleblower provisions) and US law (which has many), coming to the conclusion that general freedom of expression protection at the workplace and a high level of protection against wrongful termination in France may make whistleblower statutes less necessary than in the United States, where such protections are weak. Morvan's analysis shows that comparative legislative research, if it is to reveal policy convergence and differences – not only in form but also in substance – needs to provide the general context in which laws pertaining to disclosures made by organization insiders operate, for example, general employment law (termination protection versus employment at will); human rights law (the scope and limits of freedom of expression at the workplace); disclosure and secrecy laws in general; or procedural law (burden of evidence rules).

In the subsequent sections the missing comparative law analysis cannot be undertaken (a book chapter would be overwhelmed by such a task). However, the following sections will prepare the essential questions that a comparative law analysis must address. They will refer to Dworkin and

Brown's four models (2013), but will integrate them in an analytical structure which, in the author's opinion, deals more easily with legal systems that have no targeted legislative approach to whistleblowing (see above). The 'programme' suggested here separates the two above-mentioned basic policy objectives of whistleblowing. Consequently, the next section deals with the whistleblower's right to report and limits to such right, followed by a section that discusses the instrumentalization of the whistleblower as a monitor in the public interest.

RIGHT TO REPORT AND ITS LIMITS

The first element of comparative law research would consider by which means and to what extent a legal system offers rights to individuals to report about perceived wrongdoings within an organization.

Right to Report

The often cited definition of the term 'whistleblowing' by Near and Miceli (1985: 4) is 'the disclosure by organization members (former or current) of illegal, immoral or illegitimate practices under the control of their employers, to persons or organizations that may be able to effect action'. This definition is problematic because rather than disclosing illegal, immoral or illegitimate practices, the whistleblower discloses information that he or she believes will provide evidence or at least a substantiated indication of illegal, immoral or illegitimate practice.[2] The disclosure can under no circumstances be independent of the whistle-blower's own subjective judgment. The subjective interpretation of the circumstances and a personalized syllogistic application to a norm is implicit when a whistleblower reports facts as illegal, immoral or illegitimate. With this subjective element, whistleblowing easily qualifies as speech and therefore could benefit from the right to the freedom of expression. If a legal system guarantees freedom of expression to an organization insider, the right to report is the default legal setting and does not require any other basis in the law. For example, in article L1121–11 of the French Labor Code there is an explicit guarantee of fundamental rights at the workplace that applies to any employment, whether it is public or private: 'No restrictions to individual and collective human rights and civil liberties could be undertaken if they are not justified by the nature of the task and are proportional to the aim of such task.'

In other jurisdictions such guarantees may be less obvious. In Germany, freedom of expression is directly applicable in the public sector, but applies to horizontal, i.e., non-state to non-state relationships only indirectly. According to the principle of 'indirect third party effect' (*mittelbare Drittwirkung der Grundrechte*), courts are obliged to take into account the importance of human rights when they interpret general clauses of the Civil Code, for example, good faith. Whistleblowers' rights to report have been based on the freedom of expression and civic rights in German court decisions.[3]

The situation becomes more difficult for the whistleblower in the United States. Here, the First Amendment protection in private employment relationships is restricted by the fact that the potential violation of the constitution requires a state action. In essence, this excludes any horizontal application of constitutional protections. However, US courts have exceptionally applied the First Amendment in certain 'private' cases, where a public function or public forum was involved or if there was a close nexus between the state and the private party concerned. Outside these narrow confines private sector employees are not able to invoke freedom of expression as a basis for a right to report.[4] Thus, where freedom of expression is an insufficient basis, whistleblowers, as in the case of the United States, are dependent on statutes that explicitly authorize or encourage certain types of disclosures. For example, section 806 of the US Sarbanes-Oxley Act 2002 only protects disclosures pertaining to infringements of that statute and other US federal securities laws.

The piecemeal protection through such 'sectoral' approaches could be overcome through broader legislation, such as the UK Public Interest Disclosure Act (PIDA) 1998 (which inserted a new Part IVA into the Employment Rights Act (ERA) 1996). However, any whistleblower statute, no matter how general its scope, will delimit the range of protected disclosures and not cover reports that fall short of the statutory definition. For example, criticism of work conditions that do not amount to a breach of legal obligations would probably not fall within the ambit of many whistleblower statutes but could still be treated as an exercise of freedom of expression. The French *Clavaud* ruling[5] that an employee of the Dunlop Company acted within the limits of freedom of expression when he gave an interview in a newspaper criticizing work conditions, would not have been possible under much whistleblowing legislation.

This being said, nothing (except for lacking political will) prevents a legal system from doing both: offering basic freedom of expression guarantees as well as providing one or several statutory bases for rights to report perceived wrongdoing within organizations.

Remedies and Burden of Evidence

When a whistleblower has the right to report, the next issue concerns the availability of remedies. In other words, how does the right to report serve the whistleblower in a situation of conflict? Rights could become helpful in order to defend against retaliation, damages claims or at least to alleviate the negative consequences of having blown the whistle. In the case of an employment relationship, retaliation by the employer often takes the form of a dismissal (as in Heinisch). Laws could make such dismissals void where employees exercise the right to report perceived wrongdoings. In a comparative analysis, it is important in this context, however, not to evaluate and compare solely anti-retaliation provisions, but also to take into account the general level of termination protection in the analyzed jurisdictions. For example, the at will employee in the United States relies more on specific whistleblower protections (Cavico 2004; Dworkin and Brown 2013), than the French or German employee who benefits from a comparatively high level of termination protection.

Further, research should take burden of evidence rules into account when evaluating remedies. Evidence rules can have a significant effect on how rights can be asserted, for example, in challenging dismissals. Above we have seen that French employment law is comparatively protective of whistleblowers. Nevertheless, in order to claim wrongful dismissal the employee must not only prove that a disclosure of alleged wrongdoing was made, but also that the employer terminated the employment relationship because of this – something that may be difficult to establish in practice (see Adam 2010).[6] The problem worsens in legal systems that have similar evidence rules but additionally provide for a low termination protection in general. If the employer can terminate employment contracts for any reason, absent any legal presumption that would shift the burden of evidence to the employer, it will become even more complicated for the whistleblower to prove that the termination of the employment was predominantly motivated by his or her disclosure.

Comparative law analysis will further deal with remedies that help overcome detriments short of dismissal.[7] Outside of employment contracts, rights to report wrongdoing could protect against damages claims or offer a defense in criminal or administrative proceedings against secrecy violations.

Limits to the Right to Report

Once a comparative study has identified the whistleblowers' rights to report, it will analyze the limits to such rights. The exercise of the whistleblowers' right to report could either be limited by the law or by contract. Typical limits are duties of confidentiality and, in the case of employment, duties of loyalty or similarly named implicit duties that employees owe to employers.

Duties of confidentiality

The law or a contract may impose confidentiality or non-disclosure duties on civil servants, individuals or on organizations including their employees. The question arises as to which extent those who have confidentiality duties are precluded from acting as whistleblowers. With regard to statutory duties of confidentiality, comparative law research would examine and compare justifications for such duties and their public policy exemptions. For example, section 37(1) of the German Law on the Status of Civil Servants imposes in a quite general manner secrecy obligations on civil servants with regard to their service. An exception to this obligation is the right to report a substantiated suspicion of corruption directly to the public prosecutor.[8]

With regard to contractual confidentiality duties, a comparative analysis would examine the extent to which the law can override the contractual confidentiality norm. As examples we could consider section 43J of Part IVA of the UK ERA 1996 (pertaining to confidentiality agreements) or the Securities and Exchange Commission (SEC) rule 240.21F–117(a), which implements the US Dodd-Frank Act's whistleblower provisions and prohibits target entities from enforcing confidentiality agreements to prevent whistleblowers from communicating with the staff of the SEC.[9]

Duties of loyalty or similar duties towards the employer

In employment relationships duties of loyalty or similarly labelled implicit duties could also limit the right of employees to report wrongdoing (cf. Lewis 2011a). To determine these limits any legal system will, in some form, undertake a balance between the rights of the whistleblower, the public interest in the disclosure, and the employer's interests. Striking the balance will depend on certain characteristics of the disclosure, among which typically figure the following factors:

(a) the severity of the alleged misconduct or the seriousness and imminence of the reported danger;
(b) the degree of substantiation of the whistleblower's allegations;
(c) the communication channel used by the whistleblower; and possibly
(d) the whistleblower's subjective perceptions and motivations.

There are different techniques by which the law takes the above factors into account when balancing the whistleblower's right to report against conflicting interests. We could crudely distinguish between two approaches. First, a law could spell out in detail the types of disclosure that may be made and to whom, and the extent to which allegations must be substantiated and so forth. An example of such a law is Part IVA of the UK ERA 1996 that defines the term 'protected disclosure' and determines under what circumstances a report can be made internally and when a whistleblower may use other communication channels. This approach has the advantage of providing a good degree of legal certainty to the employee.[10] The downside of a detailed statutory solution lies in its rigidity. For example, if an employee in the United Kingdom reports unethical behavior or criticizes workplace conditions, but the employee's motivation does not pass the public interest requirement[11] or the disclosure does not tend to show a case explicitly mentioned in section 43B(1) of the ERA 1996, the whistleblower remains unprotected. The alternative approach to clear and detailed but rigid legislation would be that the law balances interests through a flexible principle of judgment, such as proportionality. For example, referring to article L1121–1 of the French Labor Code, French courts have ruled that, save for cases of abuse, employees do not breach their duty of loyalty towards the employer if they exercise their fundamental rights, including freedom of expression at the workplace.[12]

Proportionality analysis may suggest that internal reporting channels must be used by the employee under certain circumstances (see, for example, in Germany Rieble and Wiebauer 2010: 91). Proportionality facilitates judgments that can take all circumstances of the individual case into account.[13] The flexibility advantage of the proportionality principle for whistleblowing cases comes at the cost of its lack of clarity for the whistleblower. The Heinisch case mentioned above illustrates this predicament: similar to French law, German employment law undertakes a balance of interests under application of the proportionality principle. Heinisch had brought a criminal complaint against her employer without having thoroughly substantiated her allegations. Suspected serious wrongdoing could justify an immediate external report even if the allegation turns out to be untrue and reporting relatively minor concerns may be regarded as disproportionate even where wrongdoing is subsequently established.[14] The uncertainty for Heinisch existed because it was unclear whether the seriousness of the alleged wrongdoing justified her actions and to what extent it should be taken into account that she had initially tried to raise the issue with the employer internally. The lack of legal clarity is reflected in the different positions taken by the various courts that have dealt with the case. The ECtHR in *Heinisch v Germany*[15] tilted the balance in favor of the freedom of expression and concluded that 'the public interest in having information about shortcomings in the provision of institutional care for the elderly by a state-owned company is so important in a democratic society that it outweighs the interest in protecting the latter's business reputation and interests'.

'Structural Approach': The Institutionalization of Communication Channels to Facilitate Whistleblowing

Despite legal protections against retaliation at the workplace and the provision of defences against legal sanctions or damages claims, organization insiders may still be restrained from 'speaking up'. Laws, under a 'structural approach' (Moberly 2006; Dworkin and Brown 2013), can encourage organization insiders to report misconduct by obliging or incentivizing organizations to institutionalize communication channels designed to receive such reports and follow up on them. For example, section 406 of the US Sarbanes-Oxley Act 2002 requires companies to state that they have adopted a code of ethics for senior financial officers or explain the reasons why not. In implementing section 406, the SEC states in its rule 229.406(a)(4)[16] that such 'codes of ethics' must promote the 'prompt internal reporting of violations of the code to an appropriate person or persons identified in the code'. Similarly, section 7(2) of the UK Bribery Act 2010 provides a complete defense to the crime of failing to prevent bribery if the organization can prove that it had 'adequate procedures'. In the United States, we find judicial incentives for the adoption of internal whistleblowing schemes: the US Federal Sentencing Guidelines give judges the discretion to mitigate sanctions for companies that have an effective compliance and ethics programme in place. For these purposes, internal whistleblower arrangements can be treated as relevant (Hess 2007).

The above examples deal with the introduction of communication channels within an organization. We can also imagine the establishment of communication channels outside of an organization. Laws could institutionalize public ombudsman offices, or give powers to independent organizations to receive whistleblower complaints.[17] Such structural measures may indeed facilitate the exercise of rights to express freely, possibly leading to more openness in organizations. On the one hand, internal whistleblowing schemes may ease the burden of employees to 'speak out' by providing them with information on whom to contact and what steps to take, if an employee sees a cause for disclosure. On the other hand, the existence of formal internal reporting procedures can raise an employer's expectation that employees will actually report wrongdoings when they have the possibility to do so.[18] The increased incidence of internal whistleblowing procedures may also produce a legal effect. Irrespective of whether such procedures directly create legal rights and obligations, they can generate expectations which affect the interpretation of legal terms. For example, it might be argued that an implied duty to cooperate obliges employees to make use of a disclosure procedure if it is readily available. Comparative legislative research could compare structural models in the light of promoting freedom of expression for the organization insider. Structural approaches may not only facilitate expression, but also aim at deputizing organization insiders as monitors in the public interest. This is the topic of the next section.

THE WHISTLEBLOWER AS MONITOR

The previous section dealt with how to compare the individual rights of the whistleblower, with particular emphasis on freedom of expression. This section will focus on the second policy thrust of whistleblowing legislation, namely, effective law enforcement and the prevention and detection of dangers.

Instrumentalization of the Whistleblower

Laws that deputize organization insiders as monitors must be analyzed and compared in the light of the rule of law and respect of human rights guaranteed in a given jurisdiction. In the absence of a satisfactory rule of law and adequate human rights protection, whistleblowing legislation will most likely result in excessive policing. In jurisdictions with laws that effectively guarantee fundamental freedoms, the instrumentalization of the whistleblower through legal measures is justified if it promotes the public interest without disproportionately impinging on the legitimate interests of individuals. For example, the encouragement to establish internal reporting schemes has produced conflicts with fundamental rights of individuals, in particular with regard to privacy and data protection. In order to reconcile reporting procedures (including anonymous hotlines) with data protection provisions, laws must pay detailed attention to the protection of the identity of both whistleblowers and those who are the subject of allegations (Lewis 2011b; Pagnattaro and Peirce 2008).

With regard to corporate reporting schemes, a further, fundamental reservation should be mentioned. The prime objective of any corporate whistleblowing system is to secure and control potentially sensitive information that, if disclosed to legal authorities or to third parties, could endanger the company's interests. Controlling such information improves a company's capacity to manage liability risks, or prevent and detect criminal or other conduct for which the organization would be vicariously liable. In other words, the internal whistleblower becomes an instrument of a company's risk management and does not necessarily act in the public interest.[19] When legislation attempts to protect whistleblowers or offers incentives to those who report suspected wrongdoing directly to competent authorities, it could be argued that the legal authorities compete with companies for the control of information. This is the case even where the relevant law encourages or prioritizes whistleblowing within an organization. The competition exists because it is not guaranteed that corporate compliance systems always operate in the public interest. An internal system will only serve the public interest in the reporting and sanctioning of wrongdoing to the extent that this is consistent with the organization's risk management interests. If these interests do not converge, there may be situations where companies do not want to reveal wrongdoing that they become aware of through their internal whistleblowing procedures. Therefore, it is questionable whether whistleblower protection or structural whistleblowing laws should make internal reporting an absolute prerequisite, because this would amount to a prioritization of the company's risk management interests over the public interest in learning about wrongdoing.

Reporting Obligations

One deputization strategy would be to impose duties on organization insiders to report suspected wrongdoings. Such duties are also discussed elsewhere in this book (Leys and Vandekerckhove, Chapter 5). Most legal systems will have minimal reporting obligations for anyone. However, such obligations will be confined to reporting suspected serious crime. In some situations an individual's professional position or function within an organization may give rise to additional reporting duties.[20] In specific areas, such as anti-money laundering or anti-bribery legislation we find laws that oblige companies to implement compliance functions, with public reporting requirements for compliance managers. A general obligation for all organization insiders to report suspected wrongdoing, however, would probably violate the freedom of expression in so far as it includes the freedom not to speak. In addition, an organization insider would face heavy uncertainties when confronted with whistleblowing duties, in particular when it is not clear at which level of substantiation the duty to disclose is triggered or whether the duty implies that a person must investigate suspicious activity (see also Lewis 2011a). Often the organization insider will not have full knowledge of illegal activity but merely clues. Imposing a general whistleblowing duty on organization insiders would combine the risk of being a potential victim of inadequate whistleblower protection with the risk of being sanctioned for not blowing the whistle.[21]

Deputizing through Rewards: Financial Incentives to Report

While disclosure obligations pressurize organization insiders to report wrongdoings, financial rewards could incentivize them to do so. US laws have most experience with such 'reward' or 'bounty' models (Dworkin and Brown 2013; Faunce *et al.*, Chapter 16). The above-mentioned Ferro case dealt with a financial reward for a person who disclosed inside information that provided evidence of a fraud committed against the state. Ferro brought his case on the basis of the US False Claims Act (FCA). This law was introduced in 1863, revised in 1986, and contains the oldest private enforcement mechanism still in force today: an individual, often a former employee of a company (or as in Ferro the employee of a sub-contractor bound by confidentiality), who is called the 'relator', may file a *qui tam* action against federal contractors claiming that they committed fraud against the government. The government may join the action or the relator pursues the action alone. Depending on the case, the relator may collect between 15–30 per cent of the awarded damages in case of the action's success.

Carson *et al.* (2008) and Callahan *et al.* (2004) relate figures displaying a certain effectiveness of *qui tam* under the reformed FCA with regard to combating government fraud committed by private contractors. Given the apparent success of the FCA it comes as no surprise that the *qui tam* motivation and reasoning has been expanded in recent US whistleblower legislation. The US SEC (see SEC 2011) adopted a final rule implementing the Dodd-Frank Wall Street Reform and Consumer Protection Act's 'Securities Whistleblower Incentives and Protection' measures that offer rewards of 10–30 per cent of the monetary sanctions that the SEC and the other authorities are able to collect, for whistleblowers who report potential violations of US federal securities laws directly to the authorities. Accordingly, the program is often labelled 'the bounty program'.[22] The difference between the SEC's 'bounty program' and *qui tam* is that the whistleblower does not become a party to the action initiated against the company. However, both mechanisms are (from a law enforcement perspective) functionally equivalent. In both the state enlists private citizens to acquire information for the benefit of public law enforcement and the private individual may collect part of the monetary sanction or damages imposed upon the defendant. It is no wonder that *qui tam* is sometimes referred to as a 'whistleblower law' (see, for example, Carson *et al.* 2008).

From a historical perspective, the idea that governments deputize individuals for enforcing law under promise of reward goes back to medieval times. Such private law enforcement schemes were used when the state's own law enforcement institutions were deemed insufficient or when the state held that certain violations of the law could be prosecuted more efficiently with the help of private citizens (Pitzer 1972). The parallels to the historic *qui tam* justification become apparent when states introduce whistleblower laws, invoking the state's difficulties with law enforcement, in particular with regard to certain forms of economic crime committed within large complex and powerful organizations (cf. Callahan *et al.* 2004: 881). In this context, it may be more than a coincidence that jurisdictions where private law enforcement has no long-standing tradition (Germany and France have only recently introduced limited private enforcement schemes), and where the concept that private citizens are financially incentivized to pursue the law enforcement interests of the state may be viewed as incompatible with the rule of law and division of powers principle, are also reluctant to adopt whistleblowing statutes (for Germany see Kölbel 2008). Financial incentives to blow the whistle may, however, become more common in Europe to the extent that Member States of the EU implement procedures similar to the above mentioned 'bounty program' under Article 29(2) of the proposed Regulation on Market Abuse (see EC 2011; for a discussion see Fleischer and Schmolke 2012).

Deputization through Whistleblower Protection and Structural Approaches

To the extent that legislation views whistleblowing as an instrument to regain societal control over powerful private organizations (Callahan *et al.* 2004), it is appropriate to situate anti-retaliation and structural measures (see above) which do not provide financial rewards in the same law enforcement context as *qui tam* or similar 'reward' schemes. Whistleblowing laws that protect against retaliation and offer readily available communication channels rather than financial incentives rely on the various other motivations that may induce individuals to disclose suspected wrongdoing in the public interest (on the various motivations, see Miceli *et al.* 2008). Some countries have been reluctant to offer financial rewards to whistleblowers on the grounds that this would undermine the moral quality of disclosing in the public interest. However, empirical evidence demonstrates that rewards improve the success of whistleblowing, if success is measured in terms of willingness to report wrongdoing (see, for example, figures reported by Carson *et al.* 2008; Callahan *et al.* 2004; Dyck *et al.* 2010). Rewards offset the substantial personal risks that disclosers incur despite the existence of whistleblowing legislation. Between October 1987 and October 2010 the sum paid to whistleblowers under the US False Claims Act was US$2.877 billion. It is also necessary to mention the disappointing level of protection for whistleblowers under section 806 of the Sarbanes-Oxley Act 2002 (see Dworkin 2007; for an empirical study see Moberly 2007). It would seem that protection without financial reward may promote the moral reputation of whistleblowing. However, from a pure law enforcement perspective, protection without reward is low cost recruitment of the private citizen which does not appear to be particularly effective.

Analysis of the Effectiveness of Monitoring Systems

The effectiveness and costs of deputizing organization insiders through pressure, incentives or encouragement should be compared with their functional equivalents, meaning other monitoring or disclosure systems that have the objective to detect and prevent crime and dangers to human health and safety.

Whistleblower deputization has the advantage that it increases the possibility of competent authorities getting hold of information that only few people have and that general disclosure laws cannot produce. However, deputization's downside lies in the risk of abusive and frivolous complaints (well designed laws could offer effective disincentives to such practice) or simply badly substantiated allegations or judgment that results in unnecessary suspicion and disruption of work processes (for example, when a corporate internal investigation is conducted following a whistleblower complaint). The effectiveness of whistleblower deputization is likely to vary in different legal contexts. For example, corporate crime that is notoriously difficult to investigate (because its detection is largely dependent on the cooperation of organization insiders) might justify sophisticated legal deputization strategies. This may explain the widespread recourse to whistleblower systems in the fight against corruption or insider trading. In other areas, where irregularities are more effectively uncovered by trained specialists who conduct regular audits, for example, in the field of occupational safety, deputization of whistleblowers may still be helpful but is probably less essential.

Comparative legislative research should therefore consider how deputization systems harmonize with other monitoring systems in a given legal context. As a matter of principle, to the extent that legal systems succeed in obliging or incentivizing organizations to disclose information in the public interest through appropriate channels, reliance on disclosures made by individual organization insiders becomes less crucial. Therefore, a full appreciation of the effectiveness of deputizing of whistleblowers can only be made against the backdrop of the scope of duties for organizations to disclose information, either to competent authorities or to the public (see Vandekerckhove and Tsahuridu 2010 for an overview over disclosure and confidentiality obligations of individuals and organizations).

We could well imagine that monitoring through whistleblowing may be a complementary measure in support of existing monitoring and disclosure devices, or that it may be a residual measure that becomes of vital importance only to the extent that other monitoring and disclosure systems are non-existent, fail or underperform.

CONCLUSIONS AND SUGGESTIONS FOR COMPARATIVE RESEARCH

In some jurisdictions whistleblowers are portrayed as the 'eyes and ears of the law'. In corporate compliance programs they become the 'eyes and ears of the company'. The metaphors overlay the obvious that the 'eyes and ears' of the whistleblowers are their own. For this reason this chapter proposed that the first issue for comparative legislative research on whistleblowing would be to analyze how legal systems protect and enable the freedom of expression of the individual who has access to sensitive information about possible wrongdoings or dangers to health and security. If we accept that freedom of expression is a human right, an intrinsic good, and in this respect a cornerstone of democracy, it is recommended that we treat the question of instrumentalizing the whistleblower's disclosures for public interest purposes separately. Distinguishing the two issues, promoting individual freedom on the one side and the public interest on the other, may seem artificial because whistleblowers use their freedom of expression at the same time as they promote the public interest. Nevertheless, conclusions can differ with regard to the realization of these two policy concerns in different legal systems and contexts. It could be, for example, that the whistleblower's freedom of expression is best promoted through far-reaching guarantees of fundamental rights or stand-alone whistleblowing statutes with a wide and general scope. By way of contrast, sectoral solutions could be more effective with regard to deputizing whistleblowers for law enforcement purposes.

A second concern expressed in this chapter is to avoid drawing premature conclusions from comparative legislative research that remains on the surface. We have seen, for example, that the absence of whistleblowing statutes does not mean that whistleblowers are less protected than in jurisdictions that have adopted whistleblowing statutes. Comparative legislative research must be able discern the general legal context relevant for whistleblowing situations and identify and evaluate functional equivalents to whistleblowing in each legal system before supposing that one legislative model is *per se* superior to the other and could be exported to any kind of legal system without friction.

Finally, by proposing a 'programme for comparative research', this chapter does not seek to compete with other comparative analytical frameworks. It has been argued above that the 'double-thrust' approach proposed here has the advantage that it can adequately compare the treatment of whistleblowers in all legal systems, including legal systems that do not have whistleblowing legislation. With this advantage, this approach can complement or be complemented by other analytical frameworks for comparative analysis, in particular the four model approach by Dworkin and Brown mentioned above. However, with regard to the latter, at least two conditions must be met if it is to be combined with the programme proposed in this chapter: (1) the four model approach must not focus on whistleblowing legislation only but also take its functional equivalents into account (see Zweigert and Kötz 1998: 36–40 for the research of 'functionally equivalent' rules in comparative law); (2) while each of the four models can be analyzed in the light of the instrumentalization of the whistleblower as monitor, they are more difficult to apply in the context of protecting freedom of expression. In particular, freedom of expression needs to be enabled and facilitated but not specifically encouraged (for example, through rewards), so that certain 'structural' or 'reward' approaches are not necessary or even misplaced, for the protection of freedom of expression as a human right.

NOTES

1. Cf. Zweigert and Kötz 1998: 63 on the notion of 'legal family'.
2. Near and Miceli 1985, explaining the single elements of their definition, clarify that employees disclose information that they believe to be illegal, immoral or illegitimate.

3. See Rieble and Wiebauer 2010: 72, 88 and Berthold 2010 for a collection and commentary of German jurisprudence.
4. Cf. Morvan 2009: 1023; Mendelsohn 2009: 726; Barry 2007: 268. By way of contrast, US government employees can comment on their employer's activities and have free speech guaranteed. The First Amendment has been applied to public employees and interpreted to protect both state and local government whistleblowers. Remedies are available through the federal courts and include damages and costs as well reinstatement and back pay. Nevertheless, public sector employees may also face considerable difficulties (Barry 2007; Morvan 2009; Mendelsohn 2009). For example, in *Garcetti v Ceballos* a deputy district attorney filed a civil rights complaint alleging that he had suffered reprisals at work because he wrote a memorandum recommending the dismissal of a case involving governmental misconduct. In denying his claims, the Supreme Court rejected 'the notion that the First Amendment shields from discipline the expressions employees make pursuant to their professional duties'. Thus it is argued that a US government employee has more legal protection speaking on a public platform or taking allegations to the media than reporting to a supervisor.
5. Cour de Cassation, Chambre Sociale, 28 April 1988, Bull. civ. V., No. 257.
6. A specific French whistleblower statute confined to allegations of corruption reverses the evidence rule that is disadvantageous to the whistleblower: if an employee shows that a concern was raised, the employer must prove that the dismissal was for reasons other than this (see Adam 2010).
7. For an example of a legal provision that does not go beyond protection against dismissal see art. 5(c) of the International Labor Organization Convention No. 158 on Termination of Employment (68th Session, 1982).
8. Thus bypassing any chain of command within the public service, see s. 37(2) No. 3 of the said law.
9. Public policy exemptions to contractual confidentiality can be difficult to establish. For example, in *qui tam* proceedings under the US False Claims Act, a US federal court held that the *qui tam* relator may not breach confidentiality duties in order to collect evidence for the alleged fraud: 'statutory incentives encouraging investigation of possible fraud under the FCA do not establish a public policy in favor of violating an employer's contractual confidentiality and non-disclosure rights'. See *United States ex rel. Cafasso v Gen. Dynamics C4 Sys., Inc.*, 637 F.3d 1047, 1061–2 (9th Cir. 2011).
10. Legal certainty and clarity are the reasons that Transparency International expresses a preference for such a stand-alone legislative approach. See point 23 of the 'Recommended Principles for Whistleblowing Legislation' (Osterhaus and Fagan 2009).
11. See Enterprise and Regulatory Reform Act 2013 (UK) and ERA 1996, s. 43B (UK). The public interest requirement replaces the good faith requirement in Part IVA of ERA 1996. The good faith requirement may well have inhibited the disclosure of serious wrongdoing if a worker feared that his or her motive might become an issue (see Lewis 2008). This requirement was recently removed from the key stages of whistleblowing liability hearings, but remains a factor that can result in compensation being reduced by up to 25 per cent. The new public interest requirement is less onerous for whistleblowing claimants.
12. Morvan 2009; Adam 2010; Leborgne-Ingelaere 2011. A legal provision such as art. L1121–1 of the French Labor Code contains a principle that employees may exercise their freedom of expression using any communication channel they wish, but that this exercise may be limited in cases of abuse or in order to protect conflicting legitimate interests. By contrast, some legal systems without stringent freedom of expression guarantees may positively regulate available communication channels for

organization insiders. Yet, such legal systems start from the reverse principle that organization insiders require an express right to use certain communication channels, for example, the press. See Dworkin and Brown 2013 for the 'public or media' legislative model under Australian law.

13. For a discussion on French law, see Adam 2010. For relatively recent French jurisprudence see Cour de Cassation that has dealt with art. L1121–1 of the Labor Code in two whistleblowing cases decided on the same day; they confirmed that French jurisprudence is comparatively permissive with regard to freedom of expression at the workplace. In one, the employee claimed damages for wrongful termination despite the fact that her allegations of sexual harassment by her superior were unproven. The court upheld the claim because the employee's right to freedom of speech had not been abused; the fact that the allegations could not be proven was insufficient to establish that the report was made abusively. The second decision involved a woman employed by a Member of Parliament. She was dismissed after she had reported to the public prosecutor and the press that her employer had created a fictitious post for his daughter. The termination of employment was considered wrongful whether or not the Member of Parliament had actually broken the law and independently of the fact that the prosecutor discontinued the investigation. See *F–D, Mme M v SA Spring Technologies*, Cour de Cassation, Chambre Sociale, 29 September 2010, no. 09–42.057; *F–D, MJ v Mme K*, Cour de Cassation, Chambre Sociale, 29 September 2010, no. 09–41.544. See also the commentary of the judgments in Leborgne-Ingelaere 2011.
14. Cf. Federal Labor Court (Bundesarbeitsgericht), 7 December 2006, 2 AZR 400/05, *Neue Zeitschrift für Arbeitsrecht* 2007, 502.
15. App. no. 28274/08 [2011] IRLR 922 (21 July).
16. See 17 CFR Ch. II (4–1–10 Edition), 430, available at http://edocket.access.gpo.gov/cfr_2010/aprqtr/pdf/17cfr229.406.pdf.
17. Some companies, too, have outsourced reporting channels by creating external ombudsman systems. Even if they appear to be independent external communication channels, a closer look may reveal that they are not. For example, in Germany, the external ombudsmen are often law firms that are retained by the company. This has the effect that only communications between ombudsman and company are privileged, whereas the whistleblower's disclosure is unprotected, unless a contractual agreement between company and ombudsman provides certain rights for the benefit of the whistleblower. By using external ombudsmen, the company contracts out the collection of information from whistleblowers but fully retains control over it. If the company wished to offer help solely in the interest of the employee, it could set up a fund, from which employees would draw in order to consult a lawyer, who would advise the employee on the legal risks connected to the employee's desire to disclose information and on the most appropriate steps to take. An anonymous reporting facility would not be necessary in such a case, since the employee would be the client and the employee's communication with the lawyer would be privileged. However, obviously no companies provide this kind of help, since it does not forward the company's interests in retaining control over sensitive information, which is generally the purpose of any corporate reporting system.
18. Such expectation could be reflected by the loss of moral autonomy on the side of the employee. If an employee is threatened by legal or informal sanction to report facts that could constitute violations of the law or unethical behavior, the employee's autonomous motivation to speak up against such illegal or unethical behavior is at stake, which could frustrate his or her moral responsibility (Vandekerckhove and Tsahuridu 2010). This is, in principle, also the case when policies merely encourage informing. Tsahuridu and Vandekerckhove 2008 observe a 'slippery slope' problem that by encouraging employees to raise concerns internally through the introduction

of formal communication channels, these policies could transform into implicit moral duties, as employees may feel morally compelled to blow the whistle.

19. Some would question whether the term 'whistleblowing' is still appropriate when applied to corporate reporting policies. Those who view 'whistleblowing' as a form of organizational dissent would refrain from using the term to the extent that an employee, when reporting wrongdoings, simply complies with readily available internal communication procedures (cf. Chambers 1995: 192–3; Jubb 1999). The dissent reappears when the employee bypasses such policies by reporting externally, for example, to the press or leaks information via Internet platforms.
20. Whistleblowing duties of employees should therefore not be confused with gatekeeper duties of lawyers, auditors, etc. that in some legal contexts could resemble forms of compulsory whistleblowing. It could also be that individuals entrusted with compliance management tasks within an organization have further-reaching duties to report irregularities than other employees. For German jurisprudence, see Bundesgerichtshof, 5 StR 394/08, 17 July 2009, available at http://juris.bundesgerichtshof.de/cgi-bin/rechtsprechung/document.py?Gericht=bgh&Art=pm&sid=2943943bfa221c46770949da621b0d02&nr=48874&linked=urt&Blank=1&file=dokument.pdf. Tippett 2006 suggests that whistleblowing duties should be more amply imposed on top management, arguing that this could have the effect of lightening the burden for lower rank employees to speak up.
21. Vandekerckhove and Tsahuridu 2010. In the case of employees, some of these risks could be mitigated, if the employee only had to report obvious illegal activity and there are legal presumptions in place that shift the burden of evidence to the employer with regard to the employees' positive knowledge or gross negligent ignorance.
22. When the rules were initially proposed, companies raised concerns that whistleblowers would bypass internal whistleblowing procedures, thereby weakening them, or would delay reports in order to increase sanctions (and therewith the 'bounty'). The final rules alleviate these problems to some extent by providing incentives for employees to report internally first and without delay (SEC 2011: 5–6). However, the SEC discarded an unsuccessful internal reporting process as prerequisite for a reward (SEC 2011), since this would have prioritized corporate risk management interests over the public interest (see above).

15. The key to protection: Civil and employment law remedies

David Lewis, Tom Devine and Paul Harpur

INTRODUCTION

In this chapter we focus on lessons that can be learned from the civil and employment remedies for whistleblowing that exist in the United States, United Kingdom, Australia, New Zealand and Canada. These five English speaking common law countries have been selected as they have the most extensive experience with stand-alone or special purpose legislation aiming to provide remedies for whistleblowers; and there have been recent developments in the first three.[1] As discussed in the previous chapter (Fasterling, Chapter 14), they provide only one snapshot – or range of snapshots – of the legal provisions and approaches that govern whistleblowing. Moreover, the two following chapters (Faunce *et al.*, Chapter 16 and Spencer and Spencer, Chapter 17) deal in turn, and in more detail, with how the law can provide bounty incentives and remedies and with criminal remedies. Civil remedies as reviewed here, however, are plainly crucial to the types of different measures that need to be considered by researchers (see generally Vaughn 2012).

It will be seen that there are a range of civil and employment remedies available in these countries: statutory, common law, administrative and contractual. Generally, these remedies flow from the anti-retaliation model discussed by Dworkin and Brown (2013), and by Fasterling above, which may or may not adopt an employment rights approach. However, some reference will also be made to the bounty model, which uses different strategies for encouraging and compensating whistleblowers. We ask to what extent financial incentives and rewards are a credible alternative to anti-retaliation statutes, or whether countries ought to adopt a combination of the two approaches. In all cases, the remedies afforded must be seen in the light of the rights to which they relate and, inevitably, some explanation of the context in which they apply. For example, in some countries whistleblowing policies and procedures are common in both the public and private sectors, and internal disciplinary sanctions can be imposed where appropriate. Even small legal differences can be of enormous importance to the practical strategies used to pursue whistleblower support, as highlighted later (Brown *et al.*, Chapter 19). However, we do not repeat the political history or background to these laws.

Some of the main questions we address include whether, in principle, general civil remedies are more advantageous to whistleblowers than employment ones. For example, are alternative dispute resolution mechanisms more likely to meet the objective of rectifying wrongdoing? If legal remedies are desirable, is it sufficient to rely on any constitutional, administrative and common law measures or do whistleblowers benefit more from statutory employment protection? As regards legislation, should whistleblowing come under the umbrella of discrimination law, or is it preferable to have a specific whistleblowing statute? Related to this is the question of whether remedies should be made available through the ordinary civil court system or through specialist tribunals. Whatever route is chosen, a range of issues arises about the nature of the remedies offered. For example, should interim relief, re-employment and relocation all be available or merely compensation/damages? Other residual matters that need to be considered include: the imposition of vicarious as well as personal liability; restrictions on gagging clauses; the imposition of time limits for bringing claims; and the availability of legal aid and advice. Finally, we consider some of the main implications for further research.

In looking at these provisions, as Fasterling (Chapter 14) has also already explained, it is important to acknowledge the impact of constitutional rights to freedom of expression, and especially free speech on issues of politics, governance, legal compliance and corporate responsibility. These rights may be provided explicitly by national constitutions, as in the United States, France, Germany and Norway; even article 41 of the Chinese Constitution gives citizens a specific right to report unlawful conduct and forbids retaliation. They may be implicit in constitutions, as in Australia. They may be provided indirectly through human rights conventions, such as the UN Universal Declaration of Human Rights (Article 19) and the European Convention on Human Rights (Article 10). Compensation flowing from breach of such rights is particularly important in light of the changing and increasing role of the media as a whistleblowing avenue (see Bosua *et al.*, Chapter 11).

However, even if such a constitutional right applies to both the private and public sectors, it could be argued this is not an adequate substitute for providing specific incentives or protection for the bulk of whistleblowing. While the interpretation of constitutional rights gives the judiciary considerable flexibility, it is vital that potential whistleblowers know in advance whether or not their actions will be supported and what remedies are likely to be available. Like the common law public interest defense in the United Kingdom or Australia, and the public policy exception to the doctrine of employment at will in the United States, the proportionality test used by conventions and constitutional provisions generates much uncertainty. It means that the courts weigh the employee's freedom to report suspected wrongdoing against the business and property interests of the employer.[2] More significantly, the remedies take a long time to achieve and normally do not reflect the suffering incurred by a successful litigant (on suffering see Smith, Chapter 10). Accordingly, we conclude that civil and employment remedies will remain the backbone of achieving more effective whistleblowing regimes. We begin our tour with the United States.

UNITED STATES

Statutory rights are the primary source of protection for employees in the United States. These are highly fragmented, with at least 57 federal pieces of legislation (47 for corporate workers and ten for federal government employees), as well as 18 for state government employees (Devine and Maassarani 2011: 151).

Federal Civil Service System

Statutory whistleblower rights largely began with post-Watergate reforms in the Civil Service Reform Act 1978, which also substitutes for constitutional remedies.[3] They were refined and expanded for federal civilian employees in the Whistleblower Protection Act (WPA) of 1989.[4] On paper the law covers nearly all public policy misconduct by the federal government. It protects disclosures of illegality, gross waste, gross mismanagement, abuse of authority and substantial and specific danger to public health or safety, as well as assisting in or exercising rights, all testimony to internal federal law enforcement watchdogs, and refusal to violate the law. It provides informal remedies through investigations and pursuit of corrective action from negotiations and, if necessary, litigation by an Office of Special Counsel (OSC). Formal remedies are provided through administrative hearings at the US Merit Systems Protection Board (MSPB) and there is appellate review by the Federal Circuit Court of Appeals.[5] The Whistleblower Protection Enhancement Act (WPEA), which came into effect in December 2012, includes a two-year pilot program giving employees the option to choose their regional courts of appeal.[6]

Under the WPA, federal employees who are covered can choose among three options to enforce their rights. First, they can seek OSC advocacy without incurring the financial burden of bringing their own lawsuit. Alternatively, they can file MSPB appeals for administrative due process hearings (directly if the alleged violation is a suspension of two weeks or greater) and challenge any harassment through an 'individual right of action' if the employee is not satisfied 120 days after filing an OSC complaint. Potential Supreme Court review has never occurred, largely due to the Federal Circuit's recently interrupted monopoly, which prevented contradictory regional circuit decisions. If the employee wins at the MSPB, the government cannot appeal unless its Office of Personnel Management convinces the Federal Circuit that the Board's ruling was not only erroneous, but would have a 'substantial impact' on the merit system.[7]

Other scattered rights exist for federal employees, but they are incomplete or under-utilized. For example, the Lloyd-La Follette Act outlaws harassment for communicating with Congress but it does not include a remedy for enforcement. Nuclear Regulatory Commission and Department of Energy employees have access to jury trials through the Energy Policy Act for nuclear industry employees. Any government employee can go to court complaining about retaliation for making a disclosure to the Securities and Exchange Commission. From a related perspective, anti-discrimination laws also have witness protection clauses against retaliation for assisting in, testifying or exercising anti-discrimination rights, such as those against race, sex or religious discrimination.[8]

Private Sector Employees

Since 2000 there has been a legal revolution in corporate free speech rights with 12 new statutes covering the vast majority of the domestic labor force. Corporate rights have been consistently included as enforcement provisions of environmental, financial regulation or consumer protection statutes. Protection is based on challenges to relevant illegality and, with more recent additions, refusal to violate the law (Devine and Maassarani 2011: 150–1). While the first corporate rights were primitive, those since 2002 have consistently offered the following: strong WPA legal burdens of proof (Devine and Maassarani 2011: 6); informal investigations and formal administrative hearings at the Department of Labor (DOL); access to court for jury trials if there is not a speedy administrative ruling; and at least a 'make whole' remedy with compensatory damages. A few statutes also provide for punitive damages. For example, remedies for transportation whistleblowers in the 9/11 law include possible punitive damages with a US$300,000 cap (Devine and Maaasarani 2011: 151–61). Recent laws also explicitly override any corporate non-disclosure agreements or company-financed and controlled arbitrations as a substitute for statutory rights and due process (Devine and Maassarani 2011: 160). Significantly, both often are a condition of employment. While in theory these laws apply to the international activities of multi-national US corporations, the Department of Labor has excluded extra-territorial coverage.[9]

The District of Columbia and 45 states also offer common law remedies in tort with jury trials through a 'public policy exception' to the traditional master-servant 'at will' doctrine of employment law. Remedies include punitive damages but not reinstatement or other equitable relief (Kohn 2011: 58). In addition to punitive damages, the primary advantage for this option is access to a jury trial in state court. In practice, however, the tort option has been under-utilized, and of little relevance to reduce the chilling effect on freedom of speech or public policy. The boundaries for protected activity are different for every state, and typically arbitrary and narrow for what constitutes protected activity. Further, since re-instatement is not possible as an equitable remedy, the only point of the lawsuit is money.

Bounty Statutes

The United States has also introduced whistleblower programs for corporate workers and government contractors which provide a profit when they successfully challenge fraud, waste or abuse. As discussed in detail by Faunce *et al.*, Chapter 16, some are mere 'bounty' statutes which authorize payments by the Internal Revenue Service, Securities Exchange Commission and Commodities Future Trading Corporation. The latter two were created as part of the Dodd-Frank Act of 2010 to overhaul financial regulation. Whistleblowers are eligible for rewards ranging from 10–30 per cent of government recoveries if an enforcement action leads to penalties of US$1 million or more.[10] However, the most effective US anti-corruption statute is a *qui tam* private attorney general law. This enables whistleblowers to file their own lawsuit on behalf of taxpayers to seek treble damage recoveries from fraud in government contracts and receive from 10–30 per cent of the recovery if they prevail. *Qui tam* is generally used by whistleblowers who are government contractors and is only available for federal employees in limited circumstances as a last resort.[11] The Department of Justice reviews all False Claims Act complaints and can take over the lawsuit if it decides that action is justified by the potential taxpayer benefits. The original whistleblower remains an intervenor.[12]

By way of evaluation, it can be argued that whistleblowers operating under these laws have made a difference, and that the False Claims Act is the United States' most effective anti-corruption law. In 1985, the year before it was revived and modernized, the Justice Department had unusual success in recovering US$26 million from fraud in government contracts. Since deputizing the whistleblowers, average annual recoveries have been over US$1 billion. However, the impact of laws has gone far beyond financial recoveries.[13]

Burdens of Proof

On paper, the WPA offers the broadest possible scope for protected speech, covering 'any' lawful disclosure challenging significant misconduct. The United States also has one of the world's most sympathetic legal burdens of proof: employees do not have to prove the hostility of retaliation, but only that a challenged adverse action was caused by their protected activity. Many statutes essentially utilize a relevance test since a *prima facie* case can be established merely by demonstrating with a preponderance of evidence that the protected activity was a 'contributing factor', or affected the personnel decision 'in any way'.[14] At that point, the burden of proof shifts to the employer, who must prove by 'clear and convincing evidence' that it would have taken the same action anyway in the absence of the protected activity. This is the highest burden in civil law, requiring 70–80 per cent of evidentiary proof (see McCauliffe 1982).[15]

Reality Behind Rights on Paper

More negatively, employee rights in the United States in practice have proved to be a shadow of those contained on paper. The Achilles heel has been weak due process compromised by lack of political independence. For federal employees, hostile judicial activism by the MSPB, and especially the Federal Circuit, have transformed the WPA into a Trojan horse. Government whistleblowers may spend tens or hundreds of thousands of dollars and endure years of mental stress to hammer the final nail in their own professional coffins at fora that have rubber-stamped approval for almost any harassment that has been legally challenged. We would argue that such rhetoric is justified by the track record of the Federal Circuit, which up until May 2012, was 3–226 against employees for decisions on the merits since 1994, when Congress last unanimously strengthened the WPA. From 2000–2010, the corresponding track record for final MSPB administrative decisions was 3–53 against (Devine 2012). The WPEA 2012, enacted unanimously after a 13-year campaign, attempts to restore the balance. In addition to normal appellate review, the new statute overturns virtually all the hostile Federal Circuit and MSPB rulings of the previous 18 years.[16] Some more of the ongoing practical challenges with any such system are discussed in more detail later in this book (Brown *et al.,* Chapter 19).

While there are exceptions with more recent statutes, traditionally state government employees' administrative remedies have been so narrow and weak that the laws have been little known and virtually irrelevant (Devine and Maassarani 2011: 193–5). Those whistleblowers primarily depended on constitutional claims under s. 42 USC 1983, where they had access to a jury trial. However, a 2006 Supreme Court decision, *Garcetti v Ceballos,*[17] cancelled First Amendment protection for speech connected with an employee's 'job duties', which removed free speech rights from challenges to nearly all government wrongdoing where the employee has first-hand knowledge or subject matter expertise.

Hostile judicial activism undermining statutory rights, in court and at administrative agencies, has proceeded through two themes. The first has been exceptions to protection for 'any' lawful, meritorious disclosure, despite unequivocal language and emphatic legislative history. The Federal Circuit precedents (recently cancelled by the WPEA 2012) had decreed that 'any' does not include to co-workers or supervisors without authority for corrective action;[18] about misconduct connected with job duties; about policies, even if illegal; about misconduct that is 'stale' or any misconduct previously raised by someone else. Perhaps the most extreme distortion was the Federal Circuit's overhaul of the merits test for protected speech: that the whistleblower disclose what she or he 'reasonably believes evidences' specified government misconduct. It translated this requirement to mean 'irrefragable proof'.[19]

Evaluating the effectiveness of corporate whistleblower rights is more difficult. Despite a wave of best practice statutes over the last decade, the laws applying to corporate whistleblowers are incoherent. Coverage is hit or miss, and no two of the 47 anti-retaliation statutes are identical. This incoherence extends to government contractors. Where there is fraud, any employee can expose it through the False Claims Act and be protected against retaliation.[20] However, until the passing of the National Defense Authorization Act (NDAA) in 2012, if the misconduct was anything beyond fraud, the only institutional channel for disclosures was the relevant agency's Office of Inspector General (OIG) under the Inspector General Act.[21] However, if the employee was paid out of funds from

President Obama's US$700 billion economic stimulus law, best practice rights provided for a jury trial. This involved WPA burdens of proof, compensatory damages and shields against gag orders or mandatory employer-controlled arbitrations that otherwise could supersede their rights.[22] If the contractor employee worked for a defense firm but was paid out of annual congressional appropriations, a jury trial was available but with only antiquated burdens of proof and no damages.[23] If the employee worked for a non-defense contractor, remedies were limited to an OIG investigation and recommendations to the agency head.[24] Since the NDAA 2012, defense contractor whistleblower rights have been permanently upgraded to match those in the stimulus law, which were also extended in a four-year pilot experiment to all government contractor employees. For civil service and contractor whistleblowers, the two statutes in December 2012 represent a comprehensive accountability make-over for federal spending.

For corporate employees, despite some encouraging recent laws, primitive rights are still the rule rather than the exception. Roughly 60 per cent of Department of Labor (DOL) corporate whistleblower cases allege retaliation for disclosing alleged violations of the Occupational Safety and Health Act (OSHA) (GAO 2010). The lack of due process hearings is only the tip of the iceberg for employee frustration with this law. Employees have no control of their cases because the DOL has sole discretion to decide whether to investigate and prosecute claims of retaliation under the OSHA, and for all practical purposes their rights are none of their business. Complainants are not allowed to know the outcome of the investigation of their allegations. If retaliation is held to have occurred, the Department of Labor may (but does not have to) file a lawsuit on behalf of the victim. If DOL chooses to remain passive, the vindicated whistleblower has no right to know why the government abandoned him or her.[25]

The primary modern corporate whistleblower law, the False Claims Act, is structured to lock in secrecy and is thus to some degree a conceptual oxymoron for a free speech statute. Employees who file False Claims Act cases gag themselves from discussing the misconduct. The case is under seal while the Justice Department reviews the evidence and decides whether to take it over (which can take years). The Department of Justice strictly enforces secrecy by opening criminal investigations of leaks. While repressive secrecy may not matter if the fraud merely involves money, it matters when it involves compliance with environmental or public health and safety laws, which is often the case. In those cases the seal could mean that citizens continue to get poisoned by pollution or harmed by product defects until the DOJ gets to the case.

However, a recent appellate court decision held that whistleblowers can disclose the facts of fraud affecting public health or safety before the seal is lifted.[26]

As with the WPA, the biggest problem has been political bias inherent in laws that primarily or exclusively have administrative remedies enforced by political appointees. This has been especially true at the Department of Labor, which enforces nearly all corporate whistleblower laws except the False Claims Act. For example, under Republican appointees DOL's Administrative Review Board (ARB) did not rule in favor of a Sarbanes-Oxley whistleblower until 2009, some seven years and 1,500 complaints after the law's enactment (Devine and Maassarani 2011: 166).[27] The ARB's track record of employee victories on the merits under corporate whistleblower laws improved from 19.75 per cent in 2009, before President Obama's team assumed the ARB majority, to 37.5 per cent during 2010 (Devine and Maassarani 2011: 183).

The overwhelming majority of unemployed whistleblowers cannot afford to act on their rights beyond preliminary OSHA investigations. Under both Republican and Democratic presidents from 1994 to 2008 the success rate was only 3.2 per cent (see Devine and Maassarani 2011). However, the causes transcend ideology. First, Congress has not meaningfully increased resources for OSHA's Office of Whistleblower Protection, despite the passage of 12 new laws providing coverage to some 65 million additional workers (DOL (US) 2012). Investigators are assigned up to 35 cases, when they only can properly serve a docket of six to eight at any one time. There is no time to investigate, and despite backlogs OSHA issued final rulings without any face-to-face interview in 46 per cent of cases (DOL (US) 2010). Secondly, whistleblower protection is given low priority in an agency whose primary responsibility is to detect and deal with workplace safety hazards. By contrast with advanced scientific training for workplace chemical threats, for example, OSHA investigators do not consistently receive even basic training in whistleblower laws. Nor are there any subject experts to help investigators assessing technical issues raised by whistleblowers. Not surprisingly, the Inspector General concluded that 80 per cent of OSHA investigations failed to comply with one or more standards in the agency's own *Whistleblower Investigations Manual* (DOL (US) 2010). Thirdly, the agency has a feudal organizational structure where regional offices effectively control their own enforcement. Whistleblower success rates combining settlements or favorable rulings have ranged from 14 per cent to 41 per cent, depending on the region (DOL (US) 2010).

Finally, it is conspicuous that most of what we know about the effectiveness of legal remedies is from individual case results, and as is typical for the legal system, chiefly those that are most prominent or notorious for the legal principles involved. Less is known about how many applicants seek to use the law or alternative remedies, but do not make it into reported cases; or to what extent the presence of legal remedies influences – or could influence – the way that organizations behave in respect of whistleblowers, in different situations.

UNITED KINGDOM

The sole purpose of the UK Public Interest Disclosure Act (PIDA) 1998, which applies to workers in both the public and private sector, is 'to protect individuals who make certain disclosures of information in the public interest'.[28] This legislation was the model for South Africa's Protected Disclosures Act 2000 and has been regarded as an exemplary piece of legislation in debates in other countries (Vandekerckhove 2006). Historically, the common law provided little of value to whistleblowers who suffered as a result of their actions. However, it did provide a rather uncertain public interest defense where an employer sought an injunction or damages on the grounds that confidential information had been disclosed (Lewis 2008). More recently, whistleblowers who suffer retaliation have been able to argue that an employer's actions or failure to protect him or her from victimization by others amounted to a breach of the implied duties of care or trust and confidence. In many ways, an action for damages for breach of contract (or negligence) in the civil courts is financially and logistically unattractive when compared with an employment tribunal claim under Part IVA of the Employment Rights Act (ERA) 1996. However, as we discuss below, workers relying on these provisions must show that they have fulfilled the technical requirements for making a protected disclosure and be able to pay tribunal fees.

The general law of unfair dismissal is available to whistleblowers, but this only applies to employees who have two years of service, and there is a statutory cap on the compensation that can be awarded, which is, however, due to be lowered in 2013. Where the employee fails to establish that a protected disclosure was the principal reason for dismissal, the employer may demonstrate that there was misconduct or 'some other substantial reason'. If a tribunal concludes that it was reasonable to dismiss in all the circumstances there will be no finding of unfairness.[29] In addition to Part IVA of the ERA 1996, sections 44 and 100 apply to those who suffer a detriment as a result of reporting specified safety failures. As in protected disclosure cases, no qualifying period of service is needed and unlimited compensation is available.

ERA 1996, Part IVA sets out the type of disclosure which can give rise to protection (a 'qualifying disclosure'); the circumstances in which a 'qualifying disclosure' will be protected (a 'protected disclosure'); and the workers to whom the protection applies. ERA 1996, section 43B(1) (as amended) defines a 'qualifying disclosure' as one which a worker reasonably believes is in the public interest and tends to show one or more of the following: (i) a criminal offence; (ii) a failure to comply with any legal obligation; (iii) a miscarriage of justice; (iv) danger to the health and safety of any individual (i.e., not necessarily a worker); (v) damage to the environment; (vi) the deliberate concealment of information tending to show any of the matters listed above. The 'public interest' test was inserted into the statute by the Enterprise and Regulatory Reform Act 2013 with effect from 25 June 2013. The obvious problem with this test is that it is not defined and workers will only learn after the event if a tribunal accepts the reasonableness of their view. ERA 1996, section 43A defines a 'protected disclosure' as a qualifying disclosure which is made to one of the designated recipients discussed below.

ERA 1996, section 43C(1) protects workers who make qualifying disclosures to their employer or to another person who is responsible for the matter disclosed. According to ERA 1996, section 43C(2), workers are to be treated as having made disclosures to their employer if they follow a procedure which the employer has authorized, even if the disclosure is actually made to someone else (for example, an independent person or organization). Workers who seek legal advice about concerns and reveal to their adviser the issues about which a disclosure may be made are protected by ERA 1996, section 43D. By virtue of ERA 1996, section 43E, workers in government-appointed organizations are protected if they make a disclosure to a Minister of the Crown rather than their legal employer. It is worth noting that the Minister, like other designated recipients under PIDA 1998, has no duty to take any action in relation to matters which may be disclosed. Nevertheless, those who have knowledge of potential wrongdoing may be held liable for culpable inaction under both the criminal and civil law, for example, in relation to health and safety matters or environmental issues.

Workers who make disclosures to a person (or class of persons) prescribed for the purpose by the Secretary of State are protected by ERA 1996, section 43F(1).[30] However, the worker must reasonably believe that (i) the matter falls within the remit of the prescribed person, and (ii) that the information and any allegation contained in it are substantially true. It should also be noted that if a concern is raised which is not within the remit of the recipient, that person is not obliged to refer it to the appropriate body. Significantly, while the legislation provides a worker with a broad range of prescribed persons to choose from, nobody is obliged to accept, investigate and deal with the matter. As regards the second requirement, it could be argued that society's interests may not be served if workers are deterred by the requirement to demonstrate their reasonable belief in the 'substantial truth' of information and allegations.

ERA 1996, section 43G, enables workers to make a protected disclosure to the media or other external recipients if the workers: (i) reasonably believe that the information and any allegation contained in it are substantially true; (ii) do not act for personal gain; (iii) have already disclosed substantially the same information to the employer or to a person prescribed under section 43F, unless they reasonably believe that they would be subject to a detriment for doing so, or that the employer would conceal or destroy the evidence if alerted; and (iv) act reasonably (for the matters to which regard will be had, see Lewis 2008). Disclosures about exceptionally serious failures are dealt with in ERA 1996, section 43H. In order to be protected, workers must fulfil the first three requirements of section 43G. In addition, the relevant failure must be of an exceptionally serious nature and it must be reasonable in all the circumstances to make the disclosure. It would defeat the object of catch-all section 43H if failures of an exceptionally serious nature were defined by statute. However, the effect is that these will be determined by employment tribunals and the courts on a case-by-case basis. Thus, as with the public interest test, workers will learn only after the event whether their disclosures were protected.

Employers are prevented by ERA 1996, section 43J from contracting out of the provisions in Part IVA. This section deals with 'gagging clauses' by invalidating a worker's agreement (whether contained in a contract or settlement of legal proceedings) not to make a protected disclosure. However, it would seem that a clause which prevented the disclosure of information about a type of wrongdoing which is not listed in ERA 1996, section 43B(1) (see above) would still be enforceable. For example, an express term could restrain disclosures about mismanagement but not unlawful maladministration. In 2013 much attention was focused on the use of gagging clauses in the health and social care sectors, but no reliable information about the extent of their use has emerged at the time of writing.

ERA 1996, section 47B(1) provides the right not to be subjected to any detriment 'on the ground that the worker has made a protected disclosure'. In *Fecitt v NHS Manchester*,[31] the Court of Appeal held that the protected disclosure must materially influence the employer's treatment of the whistleblower. In addition to personal liability, section 47B(1A) imposes vicarious liability when a worker is subjected to a detriment by a co-worker for making a protected disclosure and the employer did not take all reasonable steps to prevent this happening. Additionally, it is accepted that detriment suffered after employment has terminated will be actionable under ERA 1996, Part IVA.[32] ERA 1996, section 48(3) normally requires claims to be presented within three months of 'the date of the act or failure to act' or 'where that act or failure is part of a series of similar acts or failures, the last of them'.

According to ERA 1996, section 103A, it is automatically unfair to dismiss employees on the grounds that they have made a protected disclosure. Similarly, ERA 1996, section 105(6A) makes it unfair to select employees for redundancy if the reason for doing so is that they have made a protected disclosure. In both situations no qualifying period of service is required. As regards general exclusions and qualifications, it should be noted that ERA 1996, Part IVA applies to Crown employees who are not subject to a certificate exempting them on grounds of national security. However, it does not currently apply to the security services.

Interim relief is provided for in ERA 1996, sections 128 and 124(1A) and it allows unlimited compensation to be awarded for dismissal contrary to ERA 1996, sections 103A or 105(6A). However, ERA 1996, sections 49(6A) and 123(6A) allow an employment tribunal to reduce compensation for both detriment and dismissal by up to 25 per cent if a disclosure was not made in good faith. For several reasons, it can be argued that 'good faith' should not appear in whistleblowing legislation. As the judiciary have acknowledged, motives are notoriously difficult to identify and may well change in the process of reporting, for example, when an internal disclosure is ignored or results in the worker suffering reprisals (on motives see Roberts, Chapter 9).[33] It would seem that the likely effect of having a good faith test is a negative one: that some workers may simply choose not to report their suspicions about wrongdoing.

The Employment Appeals Tribunal (EAT) has taken the view that subjecting a whistleblower to a detriment should normally be regarded as a very serious breach of discrimination legislation. In *Vento v Chief Constable of West Yorkshire*, the Court of Appeal suggested that there should be three broad bands of compensation for injury to feelings in discrimination cases. The top band should normally be between UK£15,000 and UK£25,000. Thus, in the PIDA 1998 case of *Virgo Fidelis School v Boyle*, where a teacher who complained about the management of a voluntary aided school demonstrated that he suffered clinical depression largely as a result of the employer's treatment of him,

UK£25,000 was awarded for injury to feelings together with UK£10,000 aggravated damages. It is evident that large compensatory awards have been made by tribunals and that some settlements have also proved very costly for employers.[34]

Although it can be seen that the United Kingdom protects whistleblowers in a fairly wide range of circumstances, there are significant lacunae in both the protection and remedies afforded. Nevertheless, one alleged advantage of the UK industrial relations system is access to employment tribunals. In theory these utilize the expertise of specialist judges, managers and worker representatives and are speedy, cheap, accessible and informal. In practice, hearings have often become quite formal, especially where lawyers are engaged, and more costly with the introduction of both claim and hearing fees in 2013. Perhaps as a consequence, recently more interest has been shown in alternative dispute resolution (see Lewis 2013). According to the Employment Tribunal Service and the Department for Business, Innovation and Skills, in the most recent four years for which statistics are available, 8,461 applications were lodged under ERA 1996, Part IVA. Of the cases disposed of during this period, 43.7 per cent were settled after conciliation by the Advisory, Conciliation and Arbitration Service (ACAS); 31.2 per cent were withdrawn or settled privately; 5.9 per cent were successful at hearing; and 11.6 per cent were unsuccessful at hearing.

These figures, and other issues above, suggest several lines of enquiry for researchers. For example, how do ACAS conciliation officers go about their business; how many sacked workers were re-employed after lodging a claim; why are complainants more likely to lose than win at a hearing? In 2013, the Public Concern at Work (PCaW) report entitled *Whistleblowing: The Inside Story*, analyzed the experiences of 1,000 whistleblowers who used the charity's advice line. In addition, research is currently being conducted on how prescribed persons perform their role under the legislation.

AUSTRALIA

Australia provides interesting contrasts to both the United States and the United Kingdom, because in the 1990s it followed the United States in establishing civil remedies – even when, like the United Kingdom, it had an established and comprehensive employment protection system. As a result, it is perhaps not surprising that there is no evidence of stand-alone civil remedies being particularly effective (Dworkin and Brown 2013). Only very recently has federal law introduced a dual approach under the

Public Interest Disclosure Act 2013 (Cth), by bringing whistleblowing into the employment law system, as discussed below. The other major contrast with both the United States and United Kingdom is that to date, Australian legislation principally only protects public servants who blow the whistle, with few remedies available in the private sector.

Public Sector

While all jurisdictions in Australia now have whistleblowing statutes to facilitate and protect public interest disclosures by public employees, there are substantial differences in how these pieces of legislation afford protection.[35] For example, New South Wales provides protection to all public officials,[36] but the Commonwealth and Tasmania cover only those who have contracted with a public official or public body, and the employees of such contractors. Queensland provides differing levels of protection depending on whether the whistleblower is a public sector employee or a member of the public. In Queensland, a public sector employee and a member of the public are protected if they make a disclosure about physical risks to persons with disabilities, to the environment or about reprisals. Curiously, only public sector employees are protected if the disclosure pertains to official misconduct or maladministration that adversely affects a whistleblower's interests in a substantial and specific way.

Australian whistleblowing laws will only protect people where the subject matter of the disclosure is in the public interest. The content which is protected can be broadly divided into that which concerns the actions of public officials and that involving the activities of any person in the community. While each scheme is different, most disclosures concerning corruption or the malpractice of a public official will be protected. In most cases, until recently, the public interest disclosure was also only protected if the disclosure was made internally or to an authorized entity. Even though the New South Wales law also envisaged protected disclosures to the media as early as 1994, it was not until 2010 that Queensland and, subsequently, Western Australia and the Federal Government followed suit in adopting the 'three tiered' model described by Vandekerckhove (2010; see also Dworkin and Brown 2013).

As a consequence, the test of whether a disclosure is protected or not does not necessarily depend on its nature or whether it furthers the public interest. Despite the regulatory intention of encouraging disclosures about wrongdoing, some statutes allow disclosers to lose protection simply because the information was conveyed to the incorrect regulatory entity.[37] On the other hand, some jurisdictions provide a list of bodies that can receive reports of wrongdoing but do not immediately remove protection if a disclosure is made to the wrong entity. The Australian Capital Territory provides that where a person discloses to the wrong authority this disclosure will be protected where the 'person making the disclosure believes that the agency is a proper authority to receive the disclosure'.

Under the state laws, the typical remedial avenue is an entitlement to sue for damages in the general Supreme Court for any detrimental action, as if suing for a tort (such as personal injury). Only in Queensland did state employment law also expressly identify dismissal on the basis of having made a disclosure as a ground of action for unfair dismissal (see Brown, Latimer, McMillan and Wheeler 2008). Conspicuously, however, the new federal Public Interest Disclosure Act 2013 includes both a right to take civil action for detrimental action in the Federal Court, with no limit on damages; and access to the extensive general employment protection provisions under the Fair Work Act 2009 (Cth).[38]

Prior to these developments, the legislation above did relatively little to provide statutory remedies any better than those available under the common law. Employers have a common law duty to take reasonable steps to ensure that employees in their organization who blow the whistle are not bullied or victimized. This duty of care arises from either express or implied terms in contracts of employment. *Wheadon v State of New South Wales* provides a good example of how the tort of negligence protects workers. In this case Wheadon, who reported corrupt conduct to superiors, was victimized and developed a psychiatric illness. The New South Wales District Court found the police liable for failure to: give support and guidance to the plaintiff; provide the plaintiff with a system of protection (including active steps to prevent or stop harassment and persecution); properly investigate the plaintiff's allegations; and assure the plaintiff that he had done the right thing by reporting corruption. The employee was awarded AU$664,270 damages under the common law.[39] At the time, there was no statutory right to damages under the state's whistleblowing legislation.

However, even when such statutory remedies existed for public servants, they have not proved the most accessible, and have not been widely utilized. In fact, there is no known case of a successful outcome. A good example of the problem is the Bundaberg hospital scandal. In 2004, a nurse unit manager, Toni Hoffman, reported to Queensland Health management that Dr Patel was grossly incompetent and was carrying out operations he was not qualified to perform. Instead of investigating the complaints, hospital management covered up for Dr Patel, and engaged in various acts that the Queensland Public Hospitals Commission subsequently referred to the police (Davies 2005). Ultimately a court sentenced

Dr Patel to seven years in prison for the manslaughter of three patients; following an appeal court reversal, a retrial is pending. However, Hoffman received minimal compensation for her emotional suffering, damaged career and other losses until she commenced litigation in 2011. She did so not under the whistleblowing law, but general workplace health and safety legislation. Queensland Health settled Hoffman's claim for an undisclosed figure (*NewsMail* 2012), but it seems reasonable to conclude that whistleblowers who do not attract the same level of publicity may face more difficulty in obtaining a remedy through civil litigation.

Such cases point to problems flowing from the decision to create civil remedies about matters principally arising within the employment relationship, that were not coordinated with wider employment law. For example, if a worker bases their claim on breach of statutory duty then they may also face difficulties in establishing vicarious liability for victimization. In *Howard v State of Queensland*, the worker pleaded a breach of section 43 of the Whistleblower Protection Act 1994 (Qld). This claim was unsuccessful because a breach of that section was also a criminal act, and the employer could not be held vicariously liable for the criminal conduct of a worker where that behavior was inimical to the purposes of that person's employment. Statutory reform was undertaken in Queensland, and copied at the federal level, partly to address this lack of clarity about the relationship between criminal and civil liability.[40]

The other, likely more important barrier to accessing civil remedies, however, has been legal costs. Unlike most employment-related legislation, none of the state whistleblowing compensation schemes made any provision to protect the worker from exposure to the legal costs of their employer, should they lose. This fact alone is probably enough to explain the lack of litigation. Importantly, section 18 of the new federal Public Interest Disclosure Act 2013 (Cth) directly addresses this, for federal public servants, by providing a 'public interest' costs rule. Under this provision, where a whistleblower sues for civil damages in the Federal Court, then provided their claim is not assessed as legally vexatious and they conduct the litigation reasonably, they cannot be held liable for the respondent's costs; even though, if they make out their claim of detrimental action, the respondent may be obliged to pay the whistleblower's costs.

The main advantage of the new federal approach, however, is the express link between whistleblowing and general employment protection for federal employees. Australia's primary employment relations statute, for all public and private employment except some state government employment, is the Fair Work Act (FWA) 2009 (Cth). This legislation regulates the terms on which employment can be offered and terminated, trade union activities and various other matters relating to workplace relations. Historically, these provisions have not expressly protected whistleblowers. This meant employees who made public interest disclosures had to rely upon the unfair dismissal jurisdiction. Sections 22 and 22A of the Public Interest Disclosure Act 2013 (Cth) now provide as a matter of law that public interest disclosures are workplace rights for the purposes of Part 3–1 of the FWA 2009, protecting federal system employees from discrimination based upon their workplace rights. What constitutes unlawful 'adverse action' under Part 3–1 is widely defined and includes conduct such as dismissal, injuring a person in their employment, prejudicially altering the employee's position, and other conduct that may have an adverse impact upon an employee, either directly or indirectly (Harpur *et al.* 2012). The primary forum is not the general courts but, as in the United Kingdom, an informal specialist industrial relations tribunal, the Fair Work Commission.

It remains to be seen whether the employment approach will be more effective; and as yet, it still does not apply to state officials or to the private sector. However, notwithstanding other limitations with the scheme, it now provides public officials with access to the worker-friendly industrial relations jurisdiction in a way not before seen in Australia. As such, Brown has remarked that for the jurisdiction it creates, this statute will establish the 'most comprehensive protection regime for public sector whistleblowers in Australia'.[41]

Private Sector

By contrast to the public sector, other employees have limited statutory protection for whistleblowing. The main provisions dealing expressly with whistleblowing provide some protections only to disclosures relating to any breach of corporations law (which is otherwise undefined) under Part 9.4AAA of the Corporations Act 2001 (Cth). Introduced in 2004, these provisions are Australia's equivalent to the US Sarbanes-Oxley disclosure provisions, but are widely accepted as poorly framed, and irrelevant to the day-to-day practice of companies and their chief regulator (the Australian Securities and Investments Commission). In October 2009, the Assistant Treasurer issued an options paper for reform of the provisions, as part of a review conducted by the Federal Treasury and Attorney-General's Department (Attorney-General Department (Australia) 2009). However the review remained limited to compliance and enforcement of corporations law, rather than other regulatory breaches or types of wrongdoing in the private sector, and to date remains unconcluded.

The result is that remedies will only be available for most private sector whistleblowers who suffer adversely if they can show that they suffered a breach of a duty under general employment law. For example, the Federal Court of Australia has held that certain employment policies form part of the contract of employment.[42] This would include policies/procedures that enable employees to make internal or external disclosures about corruption, waste or other matters. Where such policies exist, in many cases employers will be contractually bound to comply with their internal company arrangements.

However, employees who seek a remedy through using the general law, negligence or breach of contract will incur substantial costs and delays. It is yet to be tested whether general protection is available under the FWA 2009, without the kind of explicit amendment now provided for federal public sector employees. Australia protects most employees against dismissals that are regarded as harsh, unjust or unreasonable. The FWA 2009 enables employees with a sufficient period of employment and who earn below a prescribed income to contest the fairness of their dismissal. In theory, if an employee is dismissed because they have blown the whistle then that dismissal can be held to be harsh, unjust or unreasonable and the employee will be able to receive compensation and potentially be reinstated. However, in practice whistleblowers face two main problems in trying to benefit from the unfair dismissal laws. First, employees confront evidential difficulties in establishing that their dismissal was because they blew the whistle and not for other reasons. If an employer argues that the fact the employee blew the whistle did not affect their decision to sack, employees will need to establish that the public interest disclosure was in fact the major factor. The second major barrier is that the reporting procedure the employee is required to follow is not defined in statute. Employees can blow the whistle internally or externally. Industrial relations laws will look at the employee's conduct and ascertain if the employer acted fairly. This means that it is unclear what whistleblowing will be protected and what disclosures would justify termination by an employer. As in the United Kingdom, above, it would seem that employers can effectively draw a distinction between dismissing for making a protected disclosure and terminating a person's employment for the manner in which they gathered evidence or conveyed their concerns.[43]

Beyond the new general protections found in the FWA 2009, the victimization provisions in Australia's anti-discrimination laws provide whistleblowers with minimal protection. In addition to federal legislation,[44] the Australian states have their own anti-discrimination statutes and tribunals. Every jurisdiction offers protection against victimization to people who propose to or actually raise a concern with their employer or the Human Rights Commission about a potential breach under the relevant laws. If a person is subjected to victimization, then this is an offence which attracts a maximum of six months' imprisonment. However, these victimization provisions are rarely, if ever, used. While the authorities can prosecute an employer for victimization, in practice the discrimination and victimization/harassment complaints are lodged by individual claimants.

The inclusion of anti-discrimination protection in a general industrial relations statute has significant implications when it comes to enforcement (Harpur *et al.* 2012). Generally, anti-discrimination laws are poorly enforced and attract low compensation awards. As a result of its enforcement mechanisms, the FWA 2009 has the potential to reverse this trend with respect to adverse action at the workplace.

Under FWA 2009, sections 365 and 367, employees can bring private suits for a breach of their workplace rights, but there is now an additional vehicle for enforcing anti-discrimination laws. Rather than treating discrimination as a predominately private affair, the FWA 2009 regards discrimination as a public concern and accordingly has empowered the Fair Work Ombudsman (FWO) to act as a state enforcer of workplace civil rights. The powers of the FWO include monitoring, inquiring into and investigating breaches and commencing prosecutions. The FWO has power to enter a workplace without any requirement that it suspects or believes that a breach has occurred. Once the FWO has detected unlawful adverse action and regards the breach as sufficient to warrant further steps, the FWO has two main options. First, is to accept an 'enforceable undertaking' from the employer. This is a written deed executed between an employer and the FWO in which the former admits wrongdoing; agrees to perform specific actions to remedy it; and commits to future compliance measures. If the undertaking is breached, the FWO retains the power to prosecute or obtain an order from the Federal Court forcing the employer to comply with the undertaking. The second option is to prosecute the employer in the Federal Court. Workers who are held to have been discriminated against under the FWA 2009 can obtain compensation and can also seek reinstatement if the adverse action has resulted in termination of employment. Perhaps most importantly, under section 539, employers found to have discriminated against employees by taking adverse action against them can be fined up to AU$33,000 for each act of discrimination.

While whistleblowing and victimization protection often has patchy enforcement, workplace health and safety victimization is taken more seriously.[45] Currently Australia's work health and safety laws are moving towards harmonization, and most states have adopted the Work Health and Safety Act. Under this legislation, a worker's duty of trust and confidence is subrogated to his or her right to raise health and safety concerns with their employer, another worker, a government inspector, a health and safety entry permit holder, health and safety representative or a member of a health and safety committee. Under Part 6 of the Work Health and Safety Act a person discriminates against a worker for raising a health and safety concern if they dismiss, fail to hire or detrimentally alter the position of a worker. Discriminating against a worker for raising a health and safety concern amounts to victimization punishable by a fine not exceeding AU$100,000 for each breach. The case of *Patrick Stevedoring Pty Ltd v Chasser*[46] provides an illustration of how protection operates. This arose out of a dispute about safe handling practices on a wharf. A unit manager suspended and threatened to dismiss a worker who raised a safety concern and refused to perform certain tasks. The worker, who was also the elected health and safety representative, complained that the staff had not been trained in the new procedure and that it had not been approved as required by the Occupational Health and Safety Act 2004 (Vic). The company was convicted for three acts of victimization and fined AU$180,000.

The Australian experience shows the advantages of strong research, but also large research gaps. As in the United States, little is known about the direct and indirect effectiveness of the available remedies, beyond high profile cases – and in Australia, the very small number and success rate of these has pointed to ineffectiveness. How the increased public sector protection impacts upon public integrity standards in Australia will now be a fertile ground for future research. However, highly comprehensive empirical research by world standards has already been conducted in the public sector (see Brown 2008; Roberts *et al.* 2011), which has been recognized by legislators and governments as directly useful and influential in devising the recent reforms.[47] By contrast, very little research has been undertaken into public interest whistleblowing in the private sector.

NEW ZEALAND

New Zealand protects both public servants and private sector employees who blow the whistle under the Protected Disclosures Act 2000 (NZ) (as amended by the Protected Disclosures Amendment Act 2009 (NZ)). Like the United Kingdom, the primary compensation mechanism is provided through the industrial relations statute, which is the Employment Relations Act 2000 (NZ). However, the relationship is unclear, in yet a different way again to that which it was in Australia, prior to the recent reforms.

Section 17(1)(b) of the Protected Disclosures Act provides that where an employee within the meaning of the Employment Relations Act 2000 claims to have suffered retaliatory action from his or her employer or former employer, 'they "may" have a personal grievance' for the purposes of the remedial provisions of the Employment Relations Act. As a result, the available remedies are limited to normal industrial circumstances, with no avenue for uncapped damages, in the manner of the United Kingdom or under the civil provisions of the federal Australian legislation. Moreover, owing to the use of the word 'may' in this context, there is uncertainty as to whether retaliatory action, even if proven, would automatically give rise to remedies.

As in Australia and the United Kingdom, New Zealand protects most employees against dismissals that are regarded as harsh, unjust or unreasonable. The Employment Relations Act 2000 (NZ) enables employees with a sufficient period of employment and who earn below a prescribed income to contest the fairness of their dismissal in an informal specialist industrial relations tribunal, the Employment Relations Authority. In theory, if an employee is dismissed because they have blown the whistle, even outside the Protected Disclosures Act, then that dismissal can be held to be harsh, unjust or unreasonable and the employee will be able to receive compensation and potentially be reinstated. However, in practice whistleblowers face the same problems in trying to benefit from the unfair dismissal laws.

The victimization provisions in New Zealand's anti-discrimination laws provide whistleblowers with minimal protection. Under the Human Rights Act 1993 (NZ), there is protection against victimization for people who propose to or actually raise a concern with their employer or the Human Rights Commission about a potential breach under the relevant laws. If a person is subjected to victimization, then this is an offense which attracts a maximum of six months' imprisonment. However, these victimization provisions are rarely, if ever, used. While the authorities can prosecute an employer for victimization, in practice the discrimination and victimization/harassment complaints are lodged by individual claimants.

CANADA

Despite Canada's international reputation as a leader in equality rights and protection of the individual, successive governments have denied protection for whistleblowers. Indeed, one statute currently provides the sole source of protection for Canadian government employees, who are the only whistleblowers that are covered. After decades of broken promises, in 2005 Canada finally enacted the Public Servants Disclosure Protection Act (PSDPA). Despite its enactment, to date the PSDPA has been a counter-productive exercise in frustration. The law cancels court access for traditional common law remedies in tort,[48] replacing them with an administrative remedy only available to certain government workers before a Public Service Integrity Commission and a Public Servants Disclosure Protection Tribunal. The Commissioners appointed to date have both been long-standing government insiders. So disgraced was the first Commissioner appointed under the newly passed PSDPA, that she was forced out after a blistering indictment by Canada's top government auditor which detailed a track record of bullying and incompetence. Counter-intuitive to a regime that supposedly promotes transparency and openness, the Tribunal's proceedings may be conducted in secret, without even a transcript being made available to the whistleblower filing suit (FAIR 2012).

The law does not cover corporate workers or government employees in military or national security fields and has a 60-day statute of limitations for filing reprisal claims (FAIR 2012). The Commission has no fact-finding powers for investigating reprisals. Arbitrary procedural loopholes exclude most of the situations in which retaliation occurs, and the Commission can apply wide-ranging devices (such as the existence of a grievance process) to cancel jurisdiction in any case (FAIR 2012). Attorney fees are not available for those who prevail (FAIR 2012). Like the US False Claims Act, whistleblowers filing retaliation claims are subject to a blanket gag order stopping all further communications on relevant misconduct (FAIR 2012). At least in the False Claims Act there is an excuse, i.e., law enforcement review of contractor fraud allegations, which is the point of the case. In Canada, the comprehensive gag is for a claim of retaliation for exercising free speech rights.

However, Canadian rights are not stagnant. Spurred by Canada's only public interest organization focused on whistleblowing rights, Federal Accountability and Reform Initiative (FAIR), a trend is emerging to ensure that anti-retaliation provisions comply with anti-discrimination, environmental and occupational safety laws and, most importantly, the

Canadian Charter of Rights and Freedoms. As a result of an effective and focused media campaign, FAIR has underscored the requirement that due process rights be consistent with that of the organic statute (Melnitzer 2012). It will be the task of researchers to investigate how far this is achieved in practice.

IMPLICATIONS FOR RESEARCH

In the light of the experience of the countries discussed above (and elsewhere) we suggest that researchers should consider the following matters. Inevitably, in striving to achieve adequate remedies, we will also be recommending that new rights should be established in some situations. A suitable starting point might be to evaluate the remedies currently provided by both public and private sector employers who have their own whistleblowing policies/procedures. Brown and Wheeler (2008: 312) highlighted the need for 'closer study of the forms of compensation available to employees who suffer adverse outcomes from reporting, including informal compensation', but no such research seems to have been conducted to date. If remedies by employers are found to provide effective alternatives to the legal process when retaliation occurs, it would lend weight to the argument that such procedures should be mandatory (see Moberly 2008). For example, the NZ Protected Disclosures Act 2000, which is not an ideal measure for a number of reasons, does impose a duty on both public and private sector organizations to have procedures.

It has been argued elsewhere (Lewis 2008) that it might be useful to designate union officials as recipients of concerns about wrongdoing. We therefore propose that the role of union and other workplace representatives should be assessed in the process of obtaining justice for whistleblowers. For example, could they be successful in dealing with complaints of retaliation and are they likely to secure the remedies sought by the victim? Disputes cannot always be resolved at the workplace, so it would seem sensible to investigate the efficacy of alternatives to adjudication. For example, how effective is conciliation without the pressure of a legal claim being lodged? Are there a sufficient number of competent specialist arbitrators and mediators in both the public and private sector? In what circumstances would employers and aggrieved whistleblowers be willing to engage in alternative dispute resolution? It may well be that independent,[49] alternative dispute resolution methods not only avoid crude win–lose situations and reduce expense, but they may also offer more constructive solutions to the practical problems involved.[50]

Assuming that it is desirable to have legal adjudication in place as a backstop, we feel that there is a strong argument for giving whistleblowers statutory employment protection rights and remedies. This could be achieved by extending existing anti-discrimination and unfair dismissal provisions and ensuring that detrimental treatment is covered whether it occurs before, during or after employment. Although some will argue that victimization in the recruitment process can easily be concealed, many countries already outlaw discrimination in all workplace situations on other prohibited grounds. Given that negative interference can occur at any stage of the whistleblowing process, the protected activity cannot just be the making of a disclosure,[51] but should cover people who are intending, preparing or attempting to make such a disclosure.[52] In addition, whistleblowers who fear detrimental action should be able to seek relocation,[53] and protection should be afforded to those providing supporting information, individuals closely associated with the whistleblower and people who are mistakenly perceived as whistleblowers.[54]

Thus, we would urge researchers to explore the feasibility of introducing rights that are exercisable at employment or industrial relations tribunals. We are aware that this would be a radical step in jurisdictions where such tribunals do not currently exist and in some countries it would involve recognizing that whistleblowing should be treated as another workplace discrimination issue (see Lewis 2005). At these tribunals people complaining of victimization should not have to prove that they raised their concern in the public interest, because this creates too much uncertainty for potential disclosers. Claimants should merely be required to demonstrate that they had reasonable grounds to believe that there had been qualifying wrongdoing (as defined in the relevant legislation) and that this had been reported to an appropriate person, as specified in the relevant statute. The burden might then be placed on the employer (or other defendant) to show that any retaliation was 'in no sense whatever' connected to the disclosure; this is the test used in some US statutes and in UK anti-discrimination cases.

Interim relief (including injunctions) should be available and successful litigants should be compensated in full for detriments suffered. Those who have been dismissed should be able to insist on reinstatement or re-engagement being ordered. Where the individual is not interested in re-employment or the employer fails to comply, compensation (including punitive damages) should be awarded. In deciding what legislative provisions are desirable it would be extremely valuable to know how successful the re-employment of whistleblowers has been in practice and to discover whether there is any evidence that strong civil law remedies deter people from retaliating against whistleblowers.

In addition to employers' liability for their own actions, we think it would send out a suitable message if people who victimize whistleblowers were personally exposed to actions for damages. Both as a matter of principle and to ensure that resources are available to meet successful claims, employers should be held vicariously liable for retaliatory actions taken by their staff (see also Spencer and Spencer, Chapter 17). Another matter that ought to be researched is the extent to which 'gagging' clauses are inserted into employment contracts and how often they are invoked. For instance, nearly all modern US corporate statutes that invalidate involuntary arbitrations also contain anti-gag clauses that invalidate those employment prerequisites.

For the rights mentioned above to be meaningful, generous time limits for claiming will be needed so that individuals take advice and prepare their case. Again, empirical research might shed some light on what might be a reasonable limit to impose and in what circumstances extensions might be needed. What is appropriate may well depend on what the individual is seeking. For example, it might be argued that shorter timescales are desirable where the individual is seeking to exercise an employment protection right, as opposed to claiming a reward (see below). Since few people can afford to bring legal proceedings if they are out of work, the thorny issues of legal aid and costs need to be addressed. Researchers need to establish the true costs of whistleblowing litigation and estimate the likely consequences of not making legal aid available.[55]

Moving away from an employment rights approach, we would urge that research is conducted into the efficacy and practicality of introducing rewards for whistleblowing.[56] Some employers already offer financial incentives and it is important to evaluate the success of such schemes. One of the reasons why a *qui tam* or reward system is popular is that it focuses attention on the wrongdoing (albeit financial) rather than on the connection between the disclosure of information and any retaliation suffered. In the United States, 'bounty' statutes and *qui tam* actions have been effective where the government has made savings and where fines have been imposed for fraud (see Faunce *et al.*, Chapter 16). There is much to be said for statutes that combine 'doing well' with 'doing good'. Whistleblowing and positive reinforcement traditionally have been oxymorons. What needs more exploration is whether and what type of statutory reward system will encourage people to report both financial and non-financial wrongdoing. For instance, is it preferable to offer administrative rewards (as under the US Dodd-Frank Act) or a *qui tam* system? Equally, we need to assess the potential negative implications of reward systems, for example, is there evidence that financial incentives encourage premature and/or false disclosures? Researchers may well conclude that it is desirable to have legislation which both offers protection to whistleblowers and provides rewards where savings can be calculated. The value of establishing national Public Interest Disclosure Agencies might also be investigated. Such bodies might be empowered to receive disclosures, arrange for their investigation by an appropriate authority, provide advisory and counseling services and protect whistleblowers from reprisals.[57]

Finally, it seems appropriate to call for researchers to assess generally the effectiveness of existing legislation.[58] For example, is there any evidence that anti-retaliation statutes deter people from victimizing whistleblowers or encourage those who would otherwise not report to do so? Do those who have experienced or anticipate detrimental action believe that their suffering has been or will be adequately compensated? It almost goes without saying that it would be easier to argue for a particular form of statutory intervention if empirical evidence was available about how and why current statutes work.

CONCLUSION

We have suggested several lines of inquiry for international research and we conclude by identifying four priority areas. First, we need to evaluate the remedies provided by employers in both the public and private sectors under internal whistleblowing arrangements. For example, are whistleblowers 'successfully' reinstated or re-engaged following a dismissal? Secondly, and related to this, would be a detailed investigation of the role of trade unions in the process of negotiating procedures and securing justice for whistleblowing members (Vandekerckhove and James 2013). Thirdly, given the costs and other difficulties in exercising legal rights, we think it critical that researchers examine the nature and extent of alternative dispute resolution in whistleblowing cases. Finally, in the light of the debate about the nature and role of financial incentives, it would be valuable to obtain data about the efficacy of both statutory and non-statutory schemes that offer rewards for whistleblowing.

NOTES

1. In the United States we have had the Whistleblower Protection Enhancement Act 2012; in Australia, the federal Public Interest Disclosure Act 2013 (Cth) became law in June 2013, and amendments to the UK legislation came into effect in the same month.
2. See e.g., *Heinisch v Germany* [2011] IRLR 922, where Art. 10 of the European Convention on Human Rights was successfully invoked.
3. P.L. 95–454, 92 Stat. 1111 (1978) (codified in scattered sections of 5 USC). Whistleblower protection is in 5 USC s. 2302(b)(8).
4. Pub. L. No. 101–12, 103 Stat. 16 (1989) (codified at 5 USC ss. 1201–1222 (1994, Supp. III 1997)).
5. 5 USC s. 2302(b)(8); 5 USC ss. 2302(b)(9)(A) and (B); 5 USC ss. 2302(b)(9)(C); 5 USC s. 2302(b)(9)(D); 5 USC ss. 1212 and 1214; 5 USC s. 7701; 5 USC s. 7703, respectively.
6. S. 743 (112th Cong., 2nd Sess.) s. 108.
7. 5 USC ss. 1214(a)(3) and 1221; 5 USC s. 7703(d).
8. 5 USC s. 7211; 42 USC ss. 5851(a)(2)(F) and (G); 15 USC s. 78 u–6; 15 USC s. 78u–6(h); 42 USC s. 2000e–3(a), respectively.
9. *Villanueva v Core Laboratories et al.*, ARB No. 09–108 (DOL ARB 22 December 2011).
10. 26 USC s. 7263; 7 USC s. 26(a)–(c) (Commodities Future Trading Corporation) and 15 USC s. 78u–6(a)–(c) (Securities and Exchange Commission).
11. 31 USC s. 3729 *et seq.* See *United States ex rel. Holmes v Consumers Ins. Group*, 318 F.3d 1199 (10th Cir. 2003).
12. 31 USC s. 3730(a)(c).
13. See www.taf.org/DoJ-fraud-stats-FY2011.pdf. For example, whistleblowers have been responsible for: the removal of a US prescription pain killer that had caused some 50,000 unnecessary heart attacks; the repair or cancellation of nuclear power facilities that were accidents waiting to happen owing to the substitution of automobile junkyard metal for nuclear grade steel; and exposure of 440 billion gallons of leaked radiation from the US nuclear waste site that had been concealed.
14. 5 USC s. 2302(b)(8); S. Rep. No. 100–413, 15–16 (1988); 5 USC ss. 1214(b)(4)(B)(i) (OSC litigation) and 1221(e)(1) (individual right of action); 135 Cong. Rec. 4509 (1989).
15. 5 USC ss. 1214(b)(4)(B)(ii) (OSC litigation) and 1221(e)(2) (individual right of action); S. Rep. No. 100–413, 15 (1988); 135 Cong. Rec. 5033 (1989).
16. WPEA, ss. 101–103. The statute also expands rights to challenge scientific censorship (s. 110) and agency gag orders (ss. 104 and 115); strengthens administrative due process (ss. 105 and 114); provides compensatory damages for employees who prevail (s. 107(b)); and strengthens the Office of Special Counsel's authority to defend the merit system through disciplinary prosecutions of those who retaliate (ss. 106–107); and friend of the court briefs backing whistleblowers in federal court appeals (s. 113).
17. 547 US 410 (2006).
18. *Horton v Navy*, 66 F.3d 279 (Fed. Cir. 1995).
19. *Willis v Department of the Interior*, 141 F.3d 1139 (Fed. Cir. 1998). This Federal Circuit WPA loophole pre-dated the Supreme Court's *Garcetti* decision, creating an analogous constitutional exception by eight years; *Lachance v White*, 194 F.3d 1378, 1381 (2006), *cert. denied*, 528 US 1153 (2000); *Watson v DOJ*, 64 F.3d 1524 (Fed. Cir. 1995). The court defined 'stale' as a 24-hour delay after the whistleblower was threatened with murder; *Meeuwissen v Interior*, 234 F.3d 9 (Fed. Cir. 2000);

Lachance v White, 174 F.3d 1378 (Fed. Cir. 1999). 'Irrefragable' means 'inconceivable, incontrovertible, undeniable, or incapable of being overthrown' (*New Webster's Comprehensive Dictionary* (1985)).

20. 31 USC s. 3730(h).
21. HR 4310 (112th Cong., 2nd Sess.); 5 USC app.
22. American Recovery and Reinvestment Act, PL 111–5, s. 1553.
23. 10 USC s. 2409.
24. 40 USC s. 265.
25. *Wood v Department of Labor*, 275 F.3d 107, 110 (D.C. Cir. 2001).
26. *ACLU v Holder*, No. 09–2086, slip op Fourth Circuit (slip op., 5 April 2011).
27. *Kalkunte v. DVI Financial Services,* ARB Nos. 05–139, 05–40 (27 February 2009).
28. It inserted a new Part IVA into the Employment Rights Act (ERA) 1996 and the references below are to the ERA 1996 as amended.
29. ERA 1996, s. 97.
30. The Schedule to the Public Interest Disclosure (Prescribed Persons) Order 1999/1549 (as amended) specifies the persons prescribed and the description of matters in respect of which they are prescribed. The Schedule includes such bodies as the Audit Commission, Commissioners of the Inland Revenue, Financial Services Authority, Health and Safety Executive and the Environment Agency.
31. [2012] IRLR 64.
32. See *Onyango v Berkeley* [2013] IRLR 338.
33. It is accepted that people motivated by ill-will are entitled to use the US False Claims Act 1986. See *Van Arsdale v International Game Technology*, 577 F.3d 989 (9th Cir. 2009). In *Street v Derbyshire Unemployed Workers Centre* [2004] IRLR 687, the Court of Appeal acknowledged that 'a failure or refusal by an employer to remedy a perceived failure of duty and/or injustice to a worker is often likely to engender in him an understandable resentment or antagonism that may grow if the matter is not remedied quickly'.
34. [2003] IRLR 102; [2004] IRLR 268 for the two cases. Regarding large compensatory awards, for example, in *Lingard v HM Prison Service* (ET 1802862/04), the claimant received UK£470,000 in compensation after being dismissed for reporting concerns that prisoners were being bullied. In *Fernandes v Netcom Consultants Ltd* (ET 2200060/00), Mr Fernandes was awarded UK£293,441 on the basis that the 58-year-old chief financial officer would not secure similar work in the future.
35. In historical order, the main whistleblowing legislation is the Whistleblower Protection Act 1993 (SA); Public Interest Disclosure Act 2010 (QLD, originally Whistleblower Protection Act 1994); Public Interest Disclosures Act 1994 (NSW, originally Protected Disclosures Act 1994); Public Interest Disclosure Act 2012 (ACT, originally 1994); Protected Disclosures Act 2012 (Vic., originally Whistleblowers Protection Act 2001 (Vic.)); Public Interest Disclosures Act 2002 (Tas.); Public Interest Disclosure Act 2003 (WA); Public Interest Disclosure Act (NT) (s. 1 explains the year should not be used when citing this Act); and the recent Public Interest Disclosure Act 2013 (Cth).
36. Public officials are defined to include people who are employed under the Public Sector Management Act 1988, employees of a state-owned corporation, a subsidiary of a state-owned corporation or a local government authority or any other individual having public official functions or acting in a public official capacity, whose conduct and activities may be investigated by a New South Wales public sector investigating authority.
37. For example, in New South Wales disclosure of corruption and disclosures concerning the activities of authorities must be made to the Independent Commission Against Corruption; disclosures concerning maladministration must be made to the Ombudsman; disclosures concerning serious and substantial waste must be made to

the Auditor-General; disclosures that show or tend to show corrupt conduct, maladministration or serious and substantial waste of public money must be made to a police officer or to the Police Integrity Commission; and disclosures concerning serious and substantial waste in local government must be made to the Director-General of the Department of Local Government.

38. See Public Interest Disclosure Act 2013 (Cth), ss. 13–18 and 22–22A.
39. *Wheadon v State of New South Wales*, unreported, District Court of New South Wales. See Brown, Latimer, McMillan and Wheeler 2008: 274.
40. [2000] QCA 223 (9 June 2000). See Brown et al. 2008. See also Public Interest Disclosure Act 2010 (Qld), ss. 42 and 43; Public Interest Disclosure Act 2013 (Cth), s. 19A.
41. See Media Release, 'Whistleblowing Bill a Historic Step: AJ Brown', Griffith University, 19 June 2013, available at http://app.griffith.edu.au/news/2013/06/19/whistleblowing-bill-a-historic-step; see also http://fairwhistleblower.ca/content/australian-national-whistleblowing-bill-historic-step.
42. *Goldman Sachs JB Were Services Pty Ltd v Nikolich* [2007] FCAFC 120.
43. See *Chrysostomou v Autohaus Classic BMW t/as lewTrivett Classic Pty Ltd* [2007] AIRC 869 and *Bolton School v Evans* [2007] IRLR 58.
44. For example, the Age Discrimination Act 2004 (Cth); the Disability Discrimination Act 1992 (Cth); the Racial Discrimination Act 1975 (Cth); the Sex Discrimination Act 1984 (Cth).
45. Occupational health and safety in New Zealand is regulated by the Health and Safety in Employment Act 2002 (NZ).
46. *Patrick Stevedoring Pty Ltd v Chasser* (Victorian WorkCover Authority) [2011] VSC 597.
47. See e.g., House of Representatives Standing Committee on Legal and Constitutional Affairs (Australia, 2009); Queensland Parliamentary Debates (Hansard) (Government Printer, Brisbane, 16 September 2010); Australian Government media release, 'Whistleblower Laws Passed', 26 June 2013, available at www.attorneygeneral.gov.au/Mediareleases/Pages/2013/Second%20quarter/26June2013-Whistleblowerlaws passed.aspx.
48. S.C. 2005, c. 46 (2005). For common law remedies in tort see s. 236 of the Public Service Modernization Act, S.C. 2003, c. 22.
49. The criteria for independence that are generally found in US labor management collective bargaining agreements are that the parties select the arbitrator by consensus, mutually agree on procedures and share the arbitrator's remuneration. By way of contrast, arbitrations financed and controlled by employers can be a fraudulent substitute for legal due process. US corporations often require employees to sign agreements as a job prerequisite that they will waive statutory rights for company controlled arbitrations. Recent whistleblower laws expressly invalidate those conditions of employment. See e.g., Federal Rail Safety Act, 49 USC s. 20109(h).
50. Section 15 of the Australian Public Interest Disclosure Act 2013 provides for a court to order that an apology should be made. Article 24 of the Act on the Protection of Public Interest Whistleblowers 2011 (Korea) facilitates the drawing up of 'reconciliation protocols' by the Anti-Corruption and Civil Rights Commission where 'disadvantageous measures' have been taken against whistleblowers.
51. The Employment Rights Act 1996 (UK) only protects those who have made a protected disclosure. By way of contrast, s. 8A of the Prevention of Corruption Act 2001 (Ireland) makes it an offense to penalize a person for 'giving notice of intention to communicate' an opinion.
52. The instance of people intending to make a disclosure is expressly covered by s. 15 of the Protected Disclosures Act 2010 (Jamaica). Article 22 of the Act on the Protection of Public Interest Whistleblowers 2011 (Korea), which provides for

requests to be made to the Anti-Corruption and Civil Rights Commission to prohibit 'disadvantageous measures' being taken at various stages, expressly mentions the process of collecting evidence.

53. This is provided, for example, in Public Interest Disclosure Act 1994 (ACT), s. 27, Whistleblower Protection Act 2010 (Malaysia), s. 19 and Public Interest Disclosure Act 2008 (NT), s. 18. Article 16 of the Act on the Protection of Public Interest Whistleblowers 2011 (Korea) goes further by providing for 'preferential consideration in personnel affairs'. Significantly, Whistleblower Act 2006 (Ghana), s. 17 and Whistleblower Protection Act 2010 (Uganda), s. 11 provide for state protection where the life or property of a whistleblower or their families are believed to be in danger. Article 13 of the Act on the Protection of Public Interest Whistleblowers 2011 (Korea) also provides for 'personal protection measures'.
54. Associative discrimination is also included in anti-discrimination statutes. For examples of legislative protection for third parties see Whistleblower Protection Act 2010 (Malaysia), s. 7, Whistleblower Protection Act 1993 (South Australia), s. 9(1) and Protected Disclosures Act 2000 (New Zealand), s. 19A. The last specifically covers people who 'volunteer supporting information'. Protecting people who are mistakenly perceived as whistleblowers would be consistent with the approach taken in anti-discrimination laws, for example, the Equality Act 2010 (UK).
55. Whistleblower Act 2006 (Ghana), s. 16 deals specifically with legal aid for whistleblowers and Act on the Protection of Public Interest Whistleblowers 2011 (Korea), art. 22 enables the Anti-Corruption and Civil Rights Commission to pay 'relief money' to cover a range of matters, including litigation expenses.
56. Whistleblower Act 2006 (Ghana), s. 20 created a Whistleblower Reward Fund and Act on the Protection of Public Interest Whistleblowers 2011 (Korea), art. 26 provides for resolutions to be made by a Reward Deliberation Board. Whistleblower Protection Act 2010 (Malaysia), s. 26 allows the enforcement agency to reward whistleblowers for disclosing improper conduct or reporting reprisals.
57. PDA 2000 (NZ), s. 6B requires an Ombudsman to provide information and guidance on a range of matters relating to how the legislation works. More specifically, where an allegation of unlawful reprisal is made to an authority in the Australian Capital Territory, it must supply the complainant with information about the protection and remedies available under the legislation. In South Africa, the relevant minister must issue 'practical guidelines which explain the provisions of this Act and all procedures which are available in terms of any law to employees who wish to report or otherwise remedy an impropriety'. All organs of state must give every employee a copy of these guidelines or must take 'reasonable steps to bring the relevant notice to the attention of every employee'.
58. The findings of a Whistleblowing Commission inquiry into the operation of UK whistleblowing legislation were published at the end of 2013. This Commission was established by the charity Public Concern at Work.

16. Because they have evidence: Globalizing financial incentives for corporate fraud whistleblowers

Tom Faunce, Kim Crow, Tony Nikolic and Frederick M. Morgan, Jr[*]

INTRODUCTION: THE NEED FOR AN EFFECTIVE GLOBAL ANTI-CORPORATE FRAUD SYSTEM

The power and size of supranational corporations in the global economy has increased their ability to strategically formulate, undertake and hide lucrative organizational corruption, bribery and fraud on the public purse (Faunce 2006). This chapter reviews the published state of research on financial incentives to individuals who have inside knowledge of corporate fraud and who come forward to regulators. Internal informants represent one of the most significant sources of evidence of corporate fraud. For this reason, this chapter will explore research on the nature and effectiveness of the financial incentives system for whistleblowers under the US False Claims Act, 31 USC (FCA), and examine whether it could provide a good governance model for more widespread international use.

More specifically, this chapter first presents an overview of the FCA and analyzes how its basic mechanisms have been implemented at the federal and state levels in the United States. It then compares those features of the FCA to jurisdictions outside the Unites States which similarly provide material incentives, assistance or compensation for informants (whether institutionally internal 'whistleblowers' or external 'bell-ringers', see Miceli, Dreyfus and Near, Chapter 3) about fraud on the public purse. It will highlight which features of the FCA system have emerged from the preceding analysis as crucial elements of that system's effectiveness. Finally, the chapter will explore international trade and investment agreements as mechanisms for globalizing an anti-fraud model drawing upon the essential features of the FCA.

OVERVIEW OF THE US FCA

The US FCA can be viewed as a relatively contemporary manifestation of an ancient common law concept. This collection of rules allowed individuals who had information relevant to crimes to initiate a suit on behalf on the King and, if successful, be financially rewarded by the state under a doctrine described by the Latin maxim *qui tam pro domino rege quam pro se ipso*, usually abbreviated to the words *qui tam* (Baird 1994). For example, English records from 695 AD show that King Whitred of Kent declared that rewards would be provided for persons who informed the King of people working during the Sabbath (Doyle 2009: 2). By the fourteenth century the English common law allowed such a citizen prosecutor of fraud on the public purse to receive 50 per cent of the recovery (Pitzer 1972).

This English common law concept of private enforcement of public rights was enshrined in ten of the 14 statutes passed by the first US Congress (*Stillwell v Hughes Helicopters*, 1989).[1] The concept was codified in the FCA in 1863, being enacted in response to Civil War suppliers who fraudulently sold substandard ammunitions, pack animals and other items to Union army purchasers (Haron *et al.* 2009). The FCA was substantially overhauled in 1986 and further amended in 2009 with bipartisan political support.

In 2009 Congress passed (and President Obama signed) the Fraud Enforcement and Recovery Act 2009 (FERA) to rectify interpretative ambiguities in the FCA that had allowed subcontractors and non-governmental entities to escape responsibility for proven frauds. The amendments focused on increasing whistleblower protections and government accountability, as well as expanding the breadth of the conduct covered by the Act. Today, the scope of the FCA extends to a wide range of prohibited conduct. In the words of the US Supreme Court, 'the [FCA] was intended to reach all types of fraud, without any qualification, that might result in financial loss to the Government'.[2]

Justifications for the FCA with *qui tam* enforcement procedures are generally based upon three principles: (1) the need to provide realistic incentives to informants (called 'relators') and their legal representatives for disclosure of fraudulent conduct; (2) the unwillingness of the Department of Justice (DOJ) to pursue and aggressively prosecute fraud cases; and (3) the limited enforcement resources available to the DOJ (Kovacic 1996, cited in Beck 2000: 563). While Congress recognized that the government did have capacity to detect fraud, it also recognized that it lacked the required level of intelligence offered by insiders in finding and punishing wrongdoers (Beck 2000: 563). The mission for the FCA and its *qui tam* provisions explicitly is to reward relators who bring fraudulent schemes to the attention of the government. Uncovering such activities is crucial to the public profile of the FCA and its deterrent effect (House of Representatives (US) 2009).

Applications of the FCA have been very broad. Defense contracting and the energy sector have been major areas of FCA litigation (Urbas *et al.* 2012: 113). It is estimated that in the United States as much as 10 per cent of general public health expenditure could be the result of fraud or anti-competitive behavior, in spite of regulatory measures in place (FBI 2007). In the health services and pharmaceuticals sectors, the FCA has been applied to the marketing of drug products for uses unapproved by government regulators, often accompanied by kickbacks to doctors to encourage such prescriptions (Harris 2009); knowingly or recklessly distributing adulterated or otherwise unsafe drug products (Wilson 2011); submitting inflated claims to government agencies for reimbursement (Voreacos 2012) and basing such claims on clinical trial research fraud (FDA 2002);[3] data suppression (Breggin 2006: 255) and selective publication of clinical trial outcomes (Turner *et al.* 2008: 252); international bribery (LaCroix 2011); scientific misconduct (Tavare 2012: 377); bias in drug trials (Rising *et al.* 2008: 1567); ghost-written literature in prominent journals promoting false benefits and risks (Healy and Cattell 2003: 22–7); as well as influencing prescribing practices (Healy 2006: 138).

Since the FCA's inception in the 1860s, relators (in the form of intra-organizational 'whistleblowers' and extra-organizational 'bell-ringers') encouraged by such mechanisms, have become its most versatile and valuable tool in uncovering fraudulent conduct by the private sector against the public purse. The Senate Judiciary Committee described the FCA as: '[O]ne of the most successful tools for combating waste and abuse in Government spending' and 'an extraordinary civil enforcement tool used to recover funds lost to fraud and abuse'.[4]

The basic mechanism utilized by the FCA (and its variations in related US federal and state statutes) is relatively simple. A relator with information on fraud against the government first convinces a large 'no-win no-fee' legal firm to represent him or her in the case (a law firm is not required, but an experienced lawyer can greatly assist a lay person with the process). That firm then draws upon its expertise in appropriately packaging the case for the relevant federal or state law enforcement officials. If those officials agree to proceed (or, if they don't, the informant and his legal team in most US jurisdictions can continue nonetheless), a *qui tam* action is filed under seal, and a 'disclosure statement' containing all the relevant and material facts is presented to the DOJ or the local state US attorney. The defendant does not learn about a pending *qui tam* action until the seal is lifted, at which time the complaint is provided to the defendant.[5] Following an investigation, if the government decides to intervene or join the case, it takes over the running of it. The individual who initially made the disclosure remains as relator to the proceedings. These provisions provide one the most important protective mechanisms for FCA informants.

One important aspect of the FCA model is that an action can be brought by anyone who has knowledge of fraud (as mentioned, whether a 'whistleblower' in the sense of an organizational member or a 'bell-ringer', that is, an extra-organizational informant), provided that it is not based on already publicly disclosed allegations or transactions in a criminal, civil or administrative hearing; in a congressional, administrative or Government Accountability Office report, hearing, audit or investigation; or from the news media.[6] These limitations are designed to avoid 'parasitic claims' by individuals who have made no material contribution to uncovering the fraud or providing the factual basis of the case.

In return for their efforts over what is usually many years, FCA relators (and their attorney working on a no-win no-fee basis) receive a share of the recovery ranging from 15 to 30 per cent (but averaging at the low end of that scale), as well as protection from retaliation. More specifically, when a *qui tam* action is successfully prosecuted, the relator is allowed a 15–25 per cent share of the (potentially) triple damages the government recovers if it intervenes through the DOJ; and between 25–30 per cent where the government does not.[7] A relator who is criminally convicted in connection with the fraud receives zero, and similarly, one who is found by the court to be a fraud 'planner and initiator' (rather than a 'perpetrator') may receive zero, though this is left to the court's discretion.[8] Related financial incentive systems exist in several federal and state programs in the United States.[9] As mentioned, a substantial proportion of a FCA relator's recovery goes to taxes and to his or her legal team; in the latter case, the large potential amounts encourage the largest law firms to sustain cases without income through many years of proceedings.

FCA actions often result in parallel criminal actions. For example, in the fiscal year 2011, 21 such criminal convictions were recorded, resulting in '$1.3 billion in criminal fines, forfeitures, restitution and disgorgement under the Food, Drug and Cosmetic Act (FDCA)' (DOJ 2012b). These criminal proceedings ensued due to a failure to comply with regulations under the FDCA which stipulate that all drugs must be approved by the Food and Drug Administration to ensure safety and efficacy for the public.[10]

Modes of financial incentives and compensation for informants vary under state versions of the FCA covering fraud on state governments. Under the Illinois False Claims Act, for example, funds recovered as a result of violations are managed by the state treasurer.[11] Section 175/8(a) creates a whistleblower and reward protection fund where all proceeds as a result of actions brought under this provision are deposited. Excluded from this are attorney's fees, expenses and costs recovered from a defendant who violates section 4 of the Act, which will not be considered part of the proceeds (section 175/8(a)). Section 175/8(b) expressly provides powers for the Illinois Attorney General to receive one-sixth of the recovered funds, with another one-sixth paid to state law enforcement authorities such as the police as a contribution to policing purposes. The remaining two-thirds are disbursed to *qui tam* plaintiffs and as otherwise specified under the Act (section 175/8(b)). Any remaining sums are deposited in the General Revenue Fund for Illinois (section 175/8(b)).

GLOBAL FRAUD INFORMANT INCENTIVES PROGRAMS

Many jurisdictions provide legislation designed to protect whistleblowers from retaliation (see Fasterling, Chapter 14 and Lewis, Devine and Harpur, Chapter 15). Occasionally such 'protections' coincide with the establishment of government funds to financially compensate them (Bowden 2005: 3). Yet, there has been a slow uptake of financial incentive programs for corporate 'whistleblowers' and 'bell-ringers' (Lobel 2009: 440; Cohn 2001: 469). These fraud informant financial incentive programs, to the extent that they exist in illustrative national laws in differing global regions, will now be briefly examined so as to establish a basis for comparison with the US FCA.[12]

United Kingdom, Australia and Canada

The United Kingdom, Australia and Canada share a common legal tradition that has recently begun to give greater recognition to the place of *qui tam* actions in fighting fraud on the public purse.

The United Kingdom's Employment Rights Act (ERA) 1996, as amended in 1998 by the Public Interest Disclosure Act (PIDA), provides that workers who can demonstrate that they have been penalized for making a protected disclosure under the ERA 1996 can pursue a cause of action for compensation.[13]

The ERA 1996 (as amended), section 47B(1) states: 'A worker has the right not to be subjected to any detriment by any act, or any deliberate failure to act, by his employer done on the ground that the worker has made a protected disclosure'. In the same section, the provision that the employee 'shall suffer no detriment in their employment as a result' creates a wide basis for financial compensation (Martin 2003: 1). Under section 124(4)(b), whistleblowers can also attain higher compensation awards when they can demonstrate that they have experienced retaliation by way of dismissal.

Yet, financial compensation under the ERA 1996 system is significantly different to the type and scale of potential awards under the US FCA system. More recently, the global financial market collapses and other health and safety events provided the impetus for the United Kingdom legislature to examine enhancing the effectiveness of whistleblower laws through incentive mechanisms (Pyper 2013). The UK Home Office Asset Recovery Action Plan, for example, noted the United Kingdom's interest in implementing *qui tam* style laws to enable the enlistment of private citizens to combat fraud more effectively (Home Office (UK) 2007: 34).

While no legislation was introduced, in March 2008 a UK Sub-Committee indicated that due to its successes in the United States, the United Kingdom could benefit from implementing a FCA-like program with *qui tam* provisions (Burchell 2008). The United Kingdom also currently has an anti-trust whistleblower rewards programs in place through the Office of Fair Trading (OFT). In 2008 the OFT began offering financial rewards to whistleblowers who disclosed information regarding cartel conduct (OFT 2010). Under this informant reward scheme, an individual may receive up to UK£100,000 for providing information on a cartel to the OFT.

The relative slowness with which the United Kingdom has taken up such provisions may be partially explained by a comment in the Home Office Action Recovery Plan: 'Clearly the *qui tam* provisions of FCA are embedded in a very different US historical, legal and cultural context. They would be a novel import into England and Wales' (Home Office (UK) 2007: 35). Such a critique appears to refer to the 'privatized' nature of law enforcement implicit in the FCA concept, the notion of a bounty for performing civic duties and the fear that the legal system will be overwhelmed with trouble-makers fabricating claims for financial gain.

Similar concerns have persisted in Australia. Currently in Australia there exists legislation aimed at protecting whistleblowers from reprisals, however, there are no statutes based on a *qui tam* type of financial reward provisions (Brown, Latimer, McMillan and Wheeler 2008). The prospect of introducing a version of the US FCA with *qui tam* provisions has been raised in government inquiries in Australia (House of Representatives Standing Committee (Australia) 2009: 83). But the same concerns about differing legal traditions have been expressed as in the United Kingdom (Feldman and Lobel 2009).

In terms of financial compensation, each Australian state varies regarding the compensation offered. For its first 16 years, the New South Wales regime did not allow proceedings for damages (Protected Disclosure Act 1994 (NSW); see Callahan *et al.* 2004: 879), a situation which only changed in 2010 (Public Interest Disclosures Act). In South Australia, reprisals can justify financial compensation as a tort under the Equal Opportunity Act 1984. In Queensland, whistleblower law provides for damages arising from injuries such as physical and psychological, health and career. Variations of remedies are available in the Australian Capital Territory in the Public Interest Disclosure Act 2012 (ACT); in Victoria in the Whistleblower Protection Act 2001, Protected Disclosures Act 2012 (Vic.); and in Tasmania in the Public Interest Disclosure Act 2002 (Tas.). All of these Acts provide for remedies under tort law, including exemplary damages in retaliation cases (Callahan *et al.* 2004: 879; Brown, Latimer, McMillan and Wheeler 2008).

The Commonwealth Fraud Control Guidelines (CFCG) indicate that litigation or criminal action may follow from breaches of the Public Service Act 1999, the Criminal Code, the Crimes Act 1914, the Competition and Consumer Act 2010 and the Financial Management and Accountability Act 1997, which in section 44(3) provides that public authorities are expected to act ethically and protect funds from being used for purposes not otherwise authorized (Osterhaus and Fagan 2009: 4). Nevertheless, whistleblowers are required, generally without the assistance of a 'no-win no-fee' legal team, to gather enough evidence to convince regulators to prosecute the defendant (Callahan *et al.* 2004: 7; Brown, Latimer, McMillan and Wheeler 2008). This presents obvious difficulties in the ability of a whisteblower to conduct a long and costly legal process against powerful public and private organizations (Ruhnka *et al.* 2000: 283).

In Canada in 2011, the Ontario Securities Commission (OSC) announced it was considering legislation to implement a program of financial incentives for people voluntarily providing original information to the OSC about marketplace misconduct. If the information resulted in successful enforcement and monetary sanctions of over CAN$1 million, the whistleblower would be eligible to receive between 10 and 30 per cent of the amounts recovered (Brown 2011).

Europe and the European Union

The European community has examined the prospects of enacting a version of the US FCA with *qui tam* provisions as a means of protecting revenue and expenditure of the European Union from corporate fraud (Riley 2003). At the national level, however, there has so far been little movement towards such schemes.

The legal basis for the European model was supported by Article 280(4) of the European Community (EC) Treaty. This treaty provides for the necessary adoption of measures combating fraud that otherwise may affect the financial interests of the EU (Riley 2003). The idea was to afford effective and equivalent protection to its Member States. The EU recognized that the US FCA provided significant advantages in terms of its capacity to deter and recover funds in the public's interests. The aim of this 'supra-national' legislation was to provide European Public Prosecutors (EPP) with equivalent power to conduct community wide investigations and enforcement to rein in fraud (Riley 2003). Yet the European FCA model is still to eventuate.

On 1 April 2010, the Hungarian competition authority (Gazdasági Versenyhivatal) introduced an informant financial rewards program under the Hungarian Competition Act (HCA) 2010. Article 79A(1) of the HCA 2010 relevantly provides (*inter alia*):

> [a] natural person who has disclosed to the Hungarian Competition Authority written evidence qualifying as indispensable for the establishment of an infringement, committed by competitors by means of agreements or concerted practices which infringe Article 11 or Article 81 of the EC Treaty and which directly or indirectly aimed at fixing purchase or selling prices, sharing of markets, including bid rigging, or at the allocation of production or sales quotas, shall be entitled to obtain informant reward.

Article 79A(3) of the HCA relevantly provides entitlements for whistleblowers to receive a reward of 1 per cent of the fine levied up to a maximum of Hungarian forints (HUF) 50 million or US$225,000. The Act also provides that 'in case more than one different natural person provide[s] indispensable evidence, each of them shall be entitled to [an] informant reward' but that '[o]ne person is entitled to receive [the] informant reward only one time'.[14] Article 79B(2), *inter alia*, provides the Competition Authority with powers to allow the whistleblower (informant) receiving the reward to be heard as a witness and to request that their personal details be managed confidentially. While the Act specifically allows a whistleblower to remain anonymous, it also warns the whistleblower that the confidential handling of their identity may have an effect on the probative value of the information provided.

Although no primary English language sources have been identified by the authors, secondary sources refer to the existence in Lithuania of a financial reward incentive scheme for persons disclosing 'valuable information' about crime in Lithuania (TIL 2009). Part A of the Transparency International Report on Lithuania mentions Government Resolution 75 that provides for a whistleblower to be rewarded 10 per cent of the value of damages paid for crime or the value of amounts recovered for criminal conduct, if a conviction for a crime carrying imprisonment as a penalty is recorded (TIL 2009: 5).

The Transparency International Report identifies numerous deficiencies with Resolution 75, including its application to convictions for a limited range of crimes, which generally excludes crimes of corruption but includes 'financial crimes and/or crimes against a standing economic order'; the unavailability of the reward mechanism if monies are unable to be recovered from the convicted person(s); the Resolution only states a maximum reward, thus the absence of a minimum payment offers no incentive to make disclosures; there is no mechanism for determining the value of the information, for example, if a recovery of money is based on information from multiple sources. Furthermore, there is no protection for whistleblowers from negative employment consequences (Osterhaus and Fagan 2009: 6). There are separate laws protecting whistleblowers in other respects, though not under dedicated whistleblower protection laws, and only utilizing a suite of legislation addressing disparate situations (Osterhaus and Fagan 2009: 7–8; see also Banisar 2006: 10–11).

The effectiveness of Resolution 75 is not ascertainable. There is no analysis or raw data concerning the payment of rewards pursuant to the Resolution, and Transparency International sources dated 2009 state that no such payments had been made at that time (Osterhaus and Fagan 2009: 18).

South Korea

The Korean Fair Trade Commission (KFTC) is empowered to adopt and enforce competition laws in Korea under the 2005 Monopoly Regulation and Fair Trade Act (MRFTA).[15] In 2010, 103 cartel cases were filed with the KFTC, of which 62 cases were successful in recovering an average of Korean won (KRW) 586 billion or a total of US$516 million, representing record fines for that year; a representative case involved collusion amongst oil refineries to restrict competition amongst petrol stations (Choi and Baek 2011: 1). KFTC is working closely with anti-fraud and antitrust regulators in Australia, the European Union, Japan and Germany to internationalize cooperation for multinational transactions (Choi and Baek 2011: 1).

India and Pakistan

The Central Vigilance Commissioner of India has recommended legislation creating financial incentives for anti-fraud whistleblowers based on the US False Claims Act model (Press Trust of India 2012).

In 2007, the Competition Commission of Pakistan (CCP) introduced a rewards program for whistleblowers (informants) to uncover cartel conduct/activity (Koury 2012: 1). The CCP is governed by the Competition Act 2010 and is part of a broader framework of Pakistan's anti-fraud policy to enhance and protect trade and competition. The revised Guidelines on the Reward Payment to Informants Scheme (CCP 2007) are issued pursuant to regulation 56 of the Competition Commission.[16]

The salient features provided for under the Guidelines involve the payment of rewards ranging from rupees (INR) 200,000 to 5 million (US$2,200 to US$55,000). The quantum of rewards depends upon a number of factors as relevantly provided for under the Guidelines (section 3(1)). The rewards are calculated and granted on the basis that the information provided by the whistleblower meets criteria which encompass the usefulness of the information; the seriousness of the cartel; the efforts made by the informant; and the level and nature of involvement by the whistleblower (section 3(2)). Further criteria involve the accuracy and verifiability of the information revealing the cartel conduct.[17]

The Pakistan model combines financial rewards with added protections that include that the 'identity of the whistleblower shall be kept secret unless he agrees to give evidence' (section 4). When the whistleblower has fulfilled the criteria set out in section 3 of the Guidelines, there are further provisions that direct the CCP to release the reward in a four-stage process under section 5. The four stages provide the CCP with power to release the payments based upon the validity and reliability of the information, and its use in the eventual findings of the illegality (section 5(i)–(iv)).

Ghana and Uganda

The Ghanaian Whistleblower Act, 2006 Act 720 appears to be the first African legislation to incorporate a reward scheme for good faith intra- or extra-organizational informants providing information to listed regulatory bodies on 'impropriety'. The Act defines 'impropriety' to include any past or likely to occur illegality, economic crime, miscarriage of justice, waste or mismanagement or misappropriation by a public institution, degradation of the environment, and the endangerment of the health or safety of an individual or community.

In recognition of Ghana's cultural mores, the list of bodies to report to include a chief, head or elder of the whistleblower's or bell-ringer's family and head of a 'recognized religious body', in addition to a range of government offices and institutions. The use of non-public bodies as recipients of disclosures gives rise to different confidentiality issues, since some such bodies are not subject to any statutory or contractual obligations of confidence. Accordingly the Act, in section 6(3), imposes heavy fines or not less than two years' imprisonment for conviction of a breach of a whistleblower's statutory right to confidentiality concerning the disclosure.

The Act confers on the pre-existing Commission on Human Rights and Administrative Justice (CHRAJ) the power to receive complaints of retaliatory conduct and to make orders that are 'just in the circumstances', including an order of a financial reward payment. For enforcement purposes, orders of the CHRAJ are given the same status as orders and judgments of Ghana's High Court. The Act also confers on whistleblowers a separate right of action to sue for damages, and to apply for police protection in specified circumstances.

The Ghanaian legislation is one of the few financial incentive systems for whistleblowers that utilizes a dedicated fund established under legislation: the Whistleblower Reward Fund. The Fund comprises the accumulation of voluntary contributions and amounts allocated by Parliament (including those recovered from fraudsters). Section 23 of the 2006 Act provides:

> A whistleblower who makes a disclosure that leads to the arrest and conviction of an accused person shall be rewarded with money from the Fund.

Section 24 provides:

> A whistleblower whose disclosure results in the recovery of an amount of money shall be rewarded from the Fund with:
>
> (a) 10 per cent of the amount of money recovered, or
> (b) the amount of money that the Attorney-General shall, in consultation with the Inspector-General of Police, determine.

It appears that sections 23 and 24 establish a right to financial reward, even if no money is recovered from fraudsters. The country profile for Ghana published in March 2012 on the Business Anti-Corruption Portal (2012) suggested that there have not been any rewards paid under the 2006 Whistleblower Act and the authors were unable to identify any detailed evaluation of the specific overall efficacy of the Act (Global Integrity Report 2009; Quaye and Coombs 2011; Ziem and Gyebi 2012).

The Ugandan Whistleblower Protection Act 2010 rewards informants on fraud with 5 per cent of the money recovered (section 19).

China, Taiwan and Nepal

Article 12 of the Taiwanese Anti-Corruption Informant Rewards and Protection Regulation declares the safety of informants and the punishment 'pursuant to the law' of those retaliating against informants (Ministry of Justice (Taiwan) 2005).

In 2008, China's Ministry of Finance, National Audit Office, Chinese Regulatory Commission, China Banking Regulatory Commission and China Insurance Regulatory Commission enacted the Basic Internal Control Norms for Enterprises. One tier below laws such as the Corporate Law and Securities Law enacted by the National People's Congress, article 43 prevents retaliation against whistleblowers but does not make clear if they are entitled to a cause of action against their retaliating employers.

In 2002, the Kingdom of Nepal enacted the Prevention of Corruption Act, 2059. The Act punishes a wide range of corrupt conduct involving public offices and government activities. Section 58 of the Act, entitled 'Provision relating to Rewards', provides:

> The investigating authority may give an appropriate reward to the person assisting it in connection with inquiries, investigation or collection of evidence in the offences punishable under this Act.

ASPECTS AND ADVANTAGES OF THE US FCA FOR A GLOBAL MODEL

The above brief survey arguably highlights how much more sophisticated the US FCA system is compared with other forms of financial incentives for informants on corporate fraud. With this perspective in mind, the potential advantages of the US FCA as a template for a global model of such laws can now be explored in greater detail.

Prevention of Spurious, Frivolous, Vindictive or Parasitic Claims

A common argument against whistleblower financial incentive programs is that they will motivate employees to fabricate claims, to initiate proceedings over matters that should involve the normal fulfilment of their duties, will reward complicity in corruption, or provide information already in the public domain (Callahan and Dworkin 1992: 274). Research, however, suggests that most whistleblowers disclose information chiefly for moral or ethical motives, such as furthering public safety or justice, and that this is not altered by schemes such as the FCA (Getnick and Skillen 2003; Kesselheim *et al.* 2010: 1834).

Nevertheless, there are a variety of robust mechanisms built into the FCA to reduce the likelihood of such events occurring (Howse and Daniels 1995). For example, the Attorney General investigates any allegations that involve violations contrary to the FCA[18] and, after filing the claim, the whistleblower must serve all documents and evidence upon the government *in camera*, which is to remain under seal for 60 days.[19] During this period the Attorney General has an opportunity to investigate and assess the probative value of the evidence before accepting or declining the matter. Indeed, a *qui tam* relator can bring the matter to court without the Attorney General's assistance. This is not prudent because the whistleblower (and his or her legal representative) risks paying his or her own costs and possibly the costs of the corporation if the matter is fabricated or frivolous.[20] Further, the 'first in time' FCA amendments prevent other insiders from bringing a similar action based on the same facts. This promotes a race to be first to disclose out of fear that others will bring forward the essential information and so reap both the financial rewards and accompanying immunity (Depoorter and De Mot 2006).

Frivolous claims present particular challenges to FCA law-makers because they increase costs associated with investigations by authorities (Orisini Broderick 2007: 962). Empirical research reveals that whilst the FCA *qui tam* provisions are not perfect and remain open to actions by frivolous litigants searching for monetary gains, the cost-benefit ratio of implementing FCA *qui tam* laws remains favourable, with a 95 per cent success rate in government supported *qui tam* cases (Wang 2007: 7). Moreover, the FCA investigation process does provide sufficient safeguards for investigators and the Attorney General to determine whether claims have merit prior to proceedings to hearing the matter in court (Orsini Broderick 2007: 963). The FCA system allows government prosecution costs to be reduced due to diminished investigation times and quality of evidence brought to trial (Scammell 2004: 71).

Opponents of *qui tam* suggest that the costs to the community are increased when the DOJ must investigate the high number of allegations that prove to be frivolous.[21] The available evidence suggests, however, that the returns from successful cases far exceed the costs that must be expended to weed out the frivolous claims (Alexion 2012: 404). For example, from 1987 to 2010 the government declined to intervene in 78 per cent of FCA cases because the DOJ did not believe that the case would succeed (Alexion 2012: 404), or otherwise determined that it should not intervene in the particular circumstances of the case (Grassley 2006).[22] Similar findings were made by Orsini Broderick (2007: 949), however the empirical research suggests that while 78 per cent of *qui tam* claims were dismissed, the 22 per cent that succeeded provided for a positive overall cost benefit recovery (Orsini Broderick 2007: 949).

Broad Definition of 'False Claims'

One of the strengths of the FCA system beyond those in the comparative financial incentive laws above is that it directly proscribes a wide variety of corporate activities in many sectors of society, including medical, hospital and financial services, pharmaceutical manufacture and distribution, as well as defense contracting. These include: (1) presenting a false claim; (2) making or using a false record or statement material to a false claim; (3) possessing property or money of the government and delivering less than all of it; (4) delivering a certified receipt with intent to defraud the government; (5) buying public property from a federal officer or employee, who may not lawfully sell it; (6) using a false record or statement material to an obligation to pay or transmit money or property to the government, or concealing or improperly avoiding or decreasing an obligation to pay or transmit money or property to the government; (7) conspiring to commit any such offense.[23] There is no requirement to prove specific intent to defraud under the FCA, and the standard of knowledge encompasses actual knowledge, deliberate ignorance and reckless disregard.[24]

Informants Supported by 'No-Win No-Fee' Legal Team with or without Regulator

It is the ability of relators to recover a reward for exposing fraudulent activity that distinguishes the US FCA from most other jurisdictions. Amongst the FCA's particular strengths are not just the large financial incentives available to relators, but how its numerous features robustly deal with two central reasons why people choose not to report fraud on the government: the belief that no improvement will result from the disclosure, and the fear that powerful forces will exact career, personality and family-destroying reprisals. The FCA significantly promotes the likelihood that genuine fraud on the government will be uncovered and dealt with. It does this, first, by allowing ordinary citizens who have inside knowledge of fraud to file lawsuits on behalf of taxpaying citizens as a whole. Secondly, in most forms of the legislation at federal and state levels, the *qui tam* provisions allow the 'relator' to continue with an action even if the relevant DOJ declines to assist,[25] although this type of action is far less successful.

Thirdly, the FCA system allows relators to be protected and assisted by their own 'no-win no-fee' lawyer, who in most instances will supplement the work and resources of government legal officials. The FCA's provisions ameliorate many of the logistical and resource problems for government regulators by allowing the whistleblower's private attorneys to share or assume the burden of investigating and litigating the case, and by providing the government with strong and often first-hand evidence of wrongdoing, thereby reducing its overall cost of such litigation (Scammell 2004: 71). In addition to the benefits of uncovering fraud on the government, *qui tam* laws serve the public and national interest by reducing litigation costs and deterring abuse, waste, corruption and fraud (Getnick and Skillen 1996).

Fourthly, a *qui tam* action is filed under seal, meaning that the defendant does not learn about a pending *qui tam* action until the seal is lifted. These provisions provide one of the most important protective mechanisms for FCA informants.

Encouraging Better Corporate Governance

Many of the countries listed above provide leniency programs encouraging organizations to implement internal compliance strategies (Aubert *et al.* 2005: 2). Another valuable feature of the FCA model is that it provides a more robust mechanism for a government to improve corporate governance and compliance.

One example is the implementation of Corporate Sentencing Guidelines which determine the penalties for corporations which have been charged with federal crimes. Corporations that have established internal accountability systems receive decreased fines and fewer sanctions than those that have not (Dworkin 2002: 464).

Further examples of FCA-induced improved corporate governance include government initiated 'Corporate Integrity Agreements' (CIAs). The use of such agreements to promote internal accountability mechanisms is illustrated by a 2012 FCA case involving GlaxoSmithKlein (GSK) and the US government. In a series of settlement agreements, GSK pleaded guilty to two charges of misbranding pharmaceuticals, one charge of failing to report safety data, and reached a compromise on a series of allegations made under the FCA. GSK accepted a criminal fine and forfeiture of US$1 billion for the three criminal charges and a further US$1.03 billion was paid under *qui tam* provisions for off-label promotion of pharmaceuticals and the payment of kickbacks to doctors (DOJ 2012a).

In addition to the monetary settlements, the US government and GSK also entered into a binding corporate integrity agreement (Department of Health and Human Services (US) 2012). The agreement imposed onerous requirements to mitigate the risk of future fraud. The requirements include the establishment of a corporate integrity structure within the existing organization. This structure includes a senior manager substantially dedicated to ensuring the integrity of GSK operations and overseen by a 'Compliance Committee'; the maintenance of an appropriate Code of Conduct; and a corporate 'Disclosure Program' enabling employees to confidentially report compliance breaches.

The corporate integrity agreement also specifies the monetary penalties that accrue for breaches of the agreement and, in the case of a 'material breach' (as defined for the CIA), for GSK to be excluded from participation in US federal health care programs. Exclusion would have the effect that GSK pharmaceuticals would not attract the Federal Government drug rebate, with the result that GSK would be priced out of the mainstream pharmaceuticals market. Although the agreement is primarily directed at GSK's US operations, Appendix D establishes a mirror integrity framework applicable to GSK's global operations. The integrity framework for GSK's global operations is not as onerous in detail as the main body of the agreement, yet, it constitutes a powerful risk mitigation tool for the US government, particularly given GSK's use of overseas manufacturing facilities.

Deterrent Effect

The FCA *qui tam* provisions appear to provide a substantial deterrent effect on potential wrongdoers (Stringer 1996, cited in Orsini Broderick 2007: 949). It has been argued that the 1986 amendments to the *qui tam* provisions of the FCA coincided with a 'significant increase' in the number of Fortune 500 companies adopting or updating organizational Codes of Conduct (Ruhnka *et al.* 2000). It is estimated that savings as a result of the deterrent effect from *qui tam* in the first ten years (1986 to 1996) ranged between US$35.6 billion and US$71.3 billion; whilst for the second ten-year period (1996 to 2006) these figures were estimated to have risen between US$105.1 billion and US$210.1 billion (Stringer 1996, cited in Orsini Broderick 2007: 981).

Provision for Triple Damages and Criminal Penalties

Offenders may be sued for triple damages, criminal penalties of up to US$11,000 per violation, costs, expenses and attorney's fees in a civil action brought either by the United States or by a *qui tam* relator (whistleblower) in the name of the United States.[26] Additional liability may also flow under the FCA from any retaliatory action taken against whistleblowers. Such provisions seem to be critical in creating an incentive for corporations to settle negotiations rather than take the risk of going to trial. As a result, rather than being necessarily punitive, they act in a greater proportion of cases as a mechanism to save the public substantial court costs.

Synergy between Federal and State FCAs

The FCA has been so successful in recovering money on a national scale that 30 states in the United States have implemented their own models. While these models vary, their purpose of combatting fraud and recovering funds lost to fraud is consistent. The growing number of states enacting their own versions of the FCA often results in the federal and state governments being linked as co-plaintiffs. Section 4(e) of FERA amends section 3732 of the FCA by clarifying that the seal does not preclude service or disclosure of such materials to the states. There are now 29 states and the District of Columbia with their own False Claims Acts covering fraud on state government programs, including the major states in terms of budget and population, New York, California, Texas and Florida.

Financial Compensation for Retaliation

Robust anti-retaliation protections are found in the FCA.[27] These provisions have proven successful in protecting the competing interests of individuals, companies and governments.

The FCA provides that any employee, contractor or agent who 'whistleblows' about fraud shall be entitled to all relief necessary to make him or her 'whole', if discharged, demoted, suspended, threatened, harassed or in any other manner discriminated against.[28] This is of particular importance given recent studies by Glazer and Glazer indicating that of some 41 whistleblowers, 28 struggled to find later employment (Glazer and Glazer 1989).

In the United States, most employees dismissed for whistleblowing can recover large damages under tort laws for 'firing in violation of public policy', including punitive damages for serious misconduct (Callahan and Dworkin, cited in Callahan *et al.* 2004: 879). Some states provide whistleblowers with a full range of compensatory remedies that include punitive damages, while other states provide variations to these laws that include limiting available remedies to reinstatement, economic loss through lost wages, benefits and attorney fees and costs (Callahan *et al.* 2004: 879).

Proven Effectiveness of the FCA

The proven success of the FCA model as an anti-fraud measure is one of the main features making it worthy of consideration for a global model. Since 1987, when whistleblowers initiated only 30 of the 373 new matters (8 per cent), there has been a substantial increase in recoveries from *qui tam* initiated matters (DOJ 2012b). In 2011, 762 new FCA matters were initiated, 84 per cent of which (638 cases) were initiated using the FCA's *qui tam* whistleblower provisions and yearly recovery is approaching US$9 billion (Taxpayers Against Fraud Education Fund 2011a, 2011b). The FCA model has facilitated the recovery of more than US$30 billion in defrauded US government funds in the past two decades (DOJ 2010, 2012b; see also Urbas *et al.* 2012: 113). Whistleblowers collectively received more than US$532 million in rewards from the recoveries collected in 2011 (DOJ 2012b).

The FCA has been very successful in providing an incentive that is cost effective (Howse and Daniels 1995: 526). It is estimated that US$15 is returned to the US treasury for every US$1 spent on FCA investigations and litigation (Meyer 2006; Laemmle-Weidenfeld 2013). Indeed, there has been a positive reception to recoveries under the FCA for the US taxpayer.

The US FCA has proven so successful that the concept of private citizen actions against government fraud is now branching into areas involving fraud against private corporations and the citizens they interact with. The Dodd-Frank Wall Street Reform and Consumer Protection Act signed into law on 21 July 2010 is a recent example. The reward provisions in section 922 of this legislation add a new section 21F to the Securities Exchange Act 1934 that allows the Securities and Exchange Commission (SEC) to award large bounties (10–30 per cent of any sanctions exceeding US$1 million including penalties, disgorgement and restitution) to informants (not government employees or auditors) who report securities and commodities fraud in areas such as debit cards, hedge funds and mortgages. These amendments accord whistleblowers a private right of action against retaliation by employers (for reinstatement, back pay and attorney's fees) provided that the whistleblower has reported externally to regulators. One important difference between Dodd-Frank and the FCA is that a Dodd-Frank whistleblower is not provided a right to bring a lawsuit on behalf of the public; instead, the whistleblower is dependent on the SEC to file charges and collect fines in order to fund any reward.

Amongst the touted reasons for the effectiveness of the FCA system is its potential to decentralize monitoring and uncover violations that would otherwise pass undetected or would only be detected without the insider's assistance at a high cost to enforcement agencies (Aubert *et al.* 2005: 2). The existence of a *qui tam* FCA system means that governments do not have to calculate expenditure on combating fraud and corruption chiefly on abstract calculations of likelihood of detection and punishment (Depoorter and De Mot 2006). It has been estimated that whistleblowing by individual *qui tam* relators is under-incentivized when it is inhibited by prospective government 'free-riding' and over-incentivized when it weakens the government's bargaining position or interests in wider enforcement issues (Depoorter and De Mot 2006).

USING TRADE AND INVESTMENT LAW TO IMPLEMENT A GLOBAL MODEL AGAINST CORPORATE FRAUD

Fraud by multi-national corporations (MNCs) is now one of the greatest threats to economic security, public health and environmental sustainability. Much of the political and economic power of MNCs is exercised through their influence on multilateral and bilateral trade negotiations (Faunce 2006). The World Trade Organization (WTO) arguably promotes an explicit agenda (through closed door 'liberalization' negotiations permitted by the General Agreement on Trade in Services) in facilitating increased control by private corporations that receive significant indirect and direct financial assistance from taxpayer funds (Faunce 2006).

As another example, the need of US banks to rapidly lend OPEC (Organization of the Petroleum Exporting Countries) petrodollars to finance interest repayments encouraged the World Bank and the International Monetary Fund (IMF) to loan vast sums to developing nations. To meet loan repayments these countries were then required by structural readjustment programs to compete with each other in trades of sugar, cotton, tobacco, forest timber and coffee that directly benefitted MNCs. The monies obtained often went to MNCs for armaments rather than education or public health services. Since 1987, the result has been that the IMF received US$2.4 billion more from Africa than it provided in finance, and by the end of 2002, the poorest nations in Africa had transferred US$167 billion to service First World creditors. This allowed those banks to make up to three times what was originally lent, as well as to finance takeovers by MNCs of Third World public infrastructure, such as telecommunications, 'old-photosynthesis' (oil, coal or natural gas based) electricity and fuel systems, as well as health care facilities. Over this time, developing nations' childhood and perinatal mortality increased as health systems collapsed and necessary professionals migrated. Regional and bilateral preferential trade agreements have become bridgeheads to drive pro-private corporate changes into domestic regulatory systems (Faunce 2006).

International trade and investment agreements almost unanimously permit anti-fraud measures, thus making them a fertile ground to implement a global FCA model. To highlight this, specific examples will now be given of how explicit such agreements are in supporting the right of nation states to implement robust anti-corporate fraud measures in the interest of free market competition.

In Europe, for example, Article 280 of the EC Treaty provides an explicit legal basis for operations by the Community and the Member States to combat fraud and other unlawful activities that are damaging to the Community's financial interests. Drawing upon this, the European Anti-Fraud Office (OLAF), in addition to carrying out investigations, is now responsible for devising and preparing legislation for the protection of the Community's financial interests and the fight against fraud.

The WTO's multilateral General Agreement on Trade in Services (GATS) provides in Article XIV (General Exceptions):

> Subject to the requirement that such measures are not applied in a manner which would constitute a means of arbitrary or unjustifiable discrimination between countries where like conditions prevail, or a disguised restriction on trade in services, nothing in this Agreement shall be construed to prevent the adoption or enforcement by any Member of measures:

(a) necessary to protect public morals or to maintain public order;
(b) necessary to protect human, animal or plant life or health;
(c) necessary to secure compliance with laws or regulations which are not inconsistent with the provisions of this Agreement including those relating to:
   (i) the prevention of deceptive and fraudulent practices.

The capacity to regulate against fraud and cooperate in the prevention of fraud are also common components of bilateral and preferential trade agreements. One illustrative example is the Australia–United States Free Trade Agreement (AUSFTA) which provides in Article 14.6 (Cross Border Consumer Protection):

> 2. The Parties recognize the existing mechanisms for cooperation in relation to consumer protection, including: …
>
> (b) the OECD Guidelines for Protecting Consumers from Fraudulent and Deceptive Commercial Practices Across Borders of 2003.
>
> 3. The Parties shall further strengthen cooperation and coordination among their respective agencies, including the US Federal Trade Commission (FTC) and the Australian Competition and Consumer Commission (ACCC) in areas of mutual concern, in particular fraudulent and deceptive commercial practices against consumers: …
>
> (b) in the development of coordinated strategies to combat fraudulent and deceptive commercial practices against consumers, both bilaterally and multilaterally.

Likewise, AUSFTA, Article 16.6 (Online Consumer Protection) provides:

> The Parties recognize the importance of maintaining and adopting transparent and effective measures to protect consumers from fraudulent and deceptive commercial practices when they engage in electronic commerce.

AUSFTA, Article 13.10 (Financial Services Exceptions) provides:

> 4. For greater certainty, nothing in this Chapter shall be construed to prevent the adoption or enforcement by a Party of measures necessary to secure compliance with laws or regulations that are not inconsistent with this Chapter, including those relating to the prevention of deceptive and fraudulent practices.

The fact that most trade and investment agreements expressly permit anti-fraud regulation suggests that representatives of nation states could implement a global financial incentive system for informants on corporate fraud (presumably based closely on the US FCA model) either through a specific multilateral treaty, by adding a specific chapter on the topic to existing multilateral, regional or bilateral trade and investment deals, or by simply convening a working group to draw up a model for national legislation.

The advantages of such a global system relate chiefly to more effective measures to deal with improper use of the global reach and political and economic power of MNCs. Given that the business models of such MNCs (including utilization of fraudulent practices) are likely to be essentially the same whichever national jurisdiction they operate in, it makes little sense for those practices to be strongly dealt with only in North America under the US FCA system, whilst essentially remaining undetected or ignored by regulators in the other countries in which they operate. In terms of effective law enforcement, prosecutors in differing nations will frequently encounter cases that will benefit from evidence obtained under coherent rules from multiple jurisdictions. Further, many of the large legal firms running FCA cases are now global in nature, meaning that lawyers in multiple jurisdictions are already familiar with the basic workings of the FCA. The model of governments outsourcing work to the private sector through consultancies, the use of litigation funding organizations, the spread of no-win no-fee litigation and the scale of fraud likely to be perpetrated by MNCs using similar methods in different jurisdictions, also support the establishment of a global model for financial rewards to informants on corporate fraud. Utilizing international trade and investment agreements to drive this public interest-oriented normative reform may begin the process of re-establishing their democratic legitimacy as normative instruments not primarily designed to advance the interests of MNCs.

CONCLUSION

This chapter has reviewed the published research on financial incentives for whistleblowers against corporate fraud. It has developed an argument that the US FCA encompasses many features that could be incorporated in a global anti-fraud system based on financial rewards for informants and has highlighted existing research concerning the numerous nations who have implemented such incentives and compensations, in some cases explicitly drawing from the US FCA model. There is certainly room for much more research here. This could, for example, include an investigation of why, despite recommendations by their own law reform bodies, many legal systems have been hesitant to incentivize informants of corporate fraud. A major gap in the existing literature is the absence of inter-jurisdictional research quantifying how much taxpayer funds are lost and recovered in different nations pursuant to their existing methods of discovering and prosecuting corporate fraud.

If this chapter has established at least a *prima facie* case for considering that some form of globalization of core features from the US FCA would be beneficial, then the question arises as to what implementation mechanism should be utilized. The most obvious such mechanism involves trade agreements: multilateral, regional and bilateral. The advantage of placing such a scheme in these agreements is that trade sanctions represent a powerful enforcement mechanism in a globalized economy. Furthermore and most importantly, almost all trade agreements explicitly permit ratifying nations to regulate strongly against fraudulent practices by corporations in their efforts to promote genuine market competition. Developing a trade-based global model for financial rewards for informants on corporate fraud may begin the slow process of re-democratizing the international trade and investment law normative regime.

NOTES

* The authors would like to acknowledge the research assistance of Sinead McKenna and Paul Hibberd. The lead author acknowledges the assistance provided to this research by an Australian Research Council Discovery Grant.

1. *United States ex rel. Stillwell v Hughes Helicopters*, 714 F.Supp. 1084, 1086 n.2 (C.D. Cal. 1989).
2. *United States v Neifert-White*, 390 US 228, 232 (1968).
3. FDA letter to R.L. Borison, personal communication, 26 November 2002; see also *United States v Maria Carmen Palazzo, MD., Ph.D., MMM* (2005) District Court Louisiana, Docket no. 05-266.
4. Senate Judiciary Committee, 23 March 2009.
5. 31 USC s. 3730(b).
6. 31 USC s. 3730(e)(4).
7. 31 USC s. 3730 (d)(1)–(2).
8. 31 USC s. 3730(d)(3).
9. See Insider Trading and Securities Fraud Enforcement Act (1988).
10. FDCA 21 USC s. 301.
11. 740 ILCS 175/1-175/8.
12. 31 USC ss. 3729–3733.
13. Employment Rights Act 1996, ss. 48(1)(a), 49, 103A, 124(1)(a).
14. Hungarian Competition Act 2010, art. 79A(3).
15. Monopoly Regulation and Fair Trade Act, Statutes of South Korea, Act No. 7796 (1961), 2005; see also Yun 2002: 3.
16. General Enforcement Regulations, 2007 (Revised Guidelines on the Reward Payment to Informants Scheme).
17. Guidelines, s. 3(3).
18. 31 USC s. 3730(a).
19. 31 USC s. 3730(2).
20. 31 USC. s. 3730(2).

21. 31 USC s. 3730(a).
22. Personal communication, 26 April 2012.
23. 31 USC s. 3729(a).
24. 31 USC s. 3729(b)(1).
25. 31 USC s. 3730(c).
26. 31 USC s. 3729(a).
27. 31 USC ss. 3729–3733.
28. 31 USC s. 3730(h).

17. When it all goes bad: Criminal remedies

Maureen Spencer and John Spencer

INTRODUCTION

Criminal law provides at best only partial protection to whistleblowers who are victimized for having spoken out. The measures that do exist are patchy and specific to particular situations. This chapter reviews criminal law provisions in a number of jurisdictions and considers how effective they have been in deterring and punishing the victimization of whistleblowers.

One of the earliest British whistleblower protection measures drew on criminal law. In the late 19th century, John Hood, an employee of the Cambrian railway company for over 20 years, had given devastating evidence to a House of Commons Select Committee about hours of work endured by railway workers. He was promptly dismissed. The directors of the company were summoned to the Bar of the House and told, 'A great principle has been infringed, the principle that evidence given before this house should be free and unrestrained'. The outcome was the Witnesses (Public Enquiries) Protection Act 1892, which is still in force today.[1] The relevant section reads as follows:

> Every person who commits any of the following acts, that is to say who threatens, or in any way punishes, damnifies or injures or attempts to punish, damnify or injure any person having given evidence upon any enquiry or on account of the evidence which he has given upon any such an enquiry shall, unless such evidence was given in bad faith, be guilty of a misdemeanour and be liable on conviction thereof to a maximum penalty of £100, or to a maximum imprisonment of three months.[2]

The statute also provides monetary compensation for the victims:

> any sum of money which [the court] may think reasonable, having regard to all the circumstances of the case, by way of satisfaction or compensation for loss of situation, wages, status, or other damnification or injuries suffered by the complainant through or by means of the offence may be awarded.[3]

Although more recent whistleblower protection laws often include remedies for whistleblowers who have suffered harm, most stop short of prescribing criminal sanctions to punish employer reprisals. Under UK law, to give one example, compensation provided for suffering whistleblowers is based on the system developed under discrimination law (see Lewis, Devine and Harpur, Chapter 15). Indeed, the suitability of criminalizing retaliation is not universally accepted. For example, the 2010 Council of Europe's Parliamentary Assembly Resolution on Whistleblower Protection does not refer to criminal sanctions to meet 'retaliatory measures' by employers.[4] By contrast, the Organisation for Security and Co-operation in Europe (OSCE) Review Report entitled *Strategic Approaches to Corruption Prevention* states: 'Those applying retaliatory measures against whistle-blowers should be held liable under criminal law' (OSCE 2012).

The extent of the availability of criminal law to protect whistleblowers is a matter of some doubt. The OSCE Report continues, 'In this sense most legislations, such as the Canadian Criminal Code, the Hungarian Criminal Code and the US Federal Criminal Code (as amended by the Sarbanes-Oxley Act) establish penalties for those imposing retaliatory measures on whistleblowers'.[5] Banisar (2011: 23), on the other hand, implies that 'most' is an exaggeration. He writes, 'A few countries have made it a criminal offense to retaliate against a whistle-blower'. Research confirms that few jurisdictions legislate for such criminal sanctions and that even where legislation is available, as in Australia and the United States, prosecutions are rarely applied.

As other chapters in this book have demonstrated (for example, Lewis, Brown and Moberly, Chapter 1 and Smith, Chapter 10), there is little doubt that those who blow the whistle are vulnerable to reprisals inflicted for making disclosures. They may win acclaim for the moral deed of disclosing wrongdoing and gain the internalized sense of wellbeing which comes from acting bravely and ethically. But in economic terms, their loss can be significant. Rapp (2012: 119) observes, 'whistleblowers gamble their entire accumulated human capital investment against various potential gains – to their firm and self – of blowing the whistle'.[6] The complex array of different ways of exacting reprisals against those who make disclosures inevitably means that it is difficult to find effective sanctions and methods of compensation.

The criminalization of whistleblowers themselves, in particular for making certain disclosures, is controversial. Some countries provide immunity from prosecution under certain circumstances, although rarely where the disclosure might threaten national security. The law attempts to address the difficulty of accommodating transparency and protecting national interests. Some commentators argue that a punitive approach to whistleblowers deters reporting and thus undermines the public interest.

As Moberly (2012b: 165) points out, 'The law should not permit illegal conduct to hide behind a veil of secrecy, even in the name of national security'.

This chapter reviews the availability of criminal sanctions, both those to protect victimized whistleblowers and those to punish dishonest, dangerous, reckless or frivolous reporting. It discusses their operation, rationale and efficacy and also reviews the implications for whistle-blowing research of the use of the criminal law.

CRIMINAL SANCTIONS FOR REPRISALS AGAINST WHISTLEBLOWERS

A handful of jurisdictions provide for criminal sanctions to protect whistleblowers against reprisals. In a few countries, employers who take reprisals against whistleblowers commit offenses which are contained within the general criminal code. Under the Mexican Criminal Code,[7] a crime of intimidation is committed when a civil servant, or a person acting on their behalf, uses physical violence or moral aggression to intimidate another person in order to prevent them from reporting, lodging a criminal complaint, or providing information concerning an alleged criminal act punishable by the laws of the Federal Criminal Law on Administrative Liability of Civil Servants. The Canadian Criminal Code has a similar provision.[8] It is an indictable offense for an employer, or a person acting on behalf of an employer, to take a disciplinary measure against an employee or to threaten to do so if the intent is either to compel the employee to abstain from providing information concerning an employment-related offense to a law enforcement officer or to retaliate against an employee who has provided such information. The penalty on conviction is imprisonment for a term not exceeding five years.[9] The Hungarian Criminal Code specifies that 'The person who takes a disadvantageous measure against the announcer because of an announcement of public concern, commits a misdemeanour, and shall be punishable with imprisonment of up to one year, labor in the public interest, or fine'.[10]

Specific anti-retaliation provisions creating criminal liability are included in the US, Australian and Ugandan whistleblowing legislation. Brown (2006: 37) writes, 'The criminalization of reprisals against whistleblowers has long been a cornerstone of [Australian] whistleblower protection. All but two jurisdictions, South Australia and the Commonwealth, have made it a criminal offense to threaten or undertake a reprisal because of the fact that a whistleblower has made, or might make, a public interest disclosure'. Writing four years later, Roberts and Brown (2010: 62) point out that 'Australian legislation routinely makes it a criminal offense for a person to undertake a reprisal against someone who has made a public interest disclosure'. The legislation varies somewhat between the jurisdictions (see Table 17.1), but to give a typical example, the Northern Territory Public Interest Disclosure Act 2008 (No. 38 of 2008) reads:

> *Offence to commit act of reprisal*
>
> A person commits an act of reprisal against another if the person causes, or threatens to cause, harm to another for a prohibited reason, that is because: (a) the other person or a third person: (i) has made or intends to make a public interest disclosure; or (ii) has complied with, or intends to comply with, a requirement imposed by a person acting in an official capacity; or (iii) has cooperated or intends to cooperate with a person acting in an official capacity; and (b) the person wants to obtain retribution for the disclosure, compliance or cooperation or, in the case of intended disclosure, compliance or cooperation, to discourage it.[11]

The maximum penalty is two years' imprisonment. In the Northern Territory, legislated criminal sanctions are in principle available against those who take action against not only the whistleblower, but also other internal witnesses, persons wrongly believed to be internal witnesses, and the family, friends or associates of internal witnesses.[12] By contrast, the New South Wales statute only outlaws reprisals taken directly against someone who has made a protected disclosure. The Victorian, Tasmanian and Northern Territory sections are ambiguous, but probably do outlaw reprisals against a third party. Brown argues that the best practice is to be found in the Queensland, ACT and Western Australia Acts. Prosecutions are at best rare (Brown 2006: 13; see also Trott 2004). Brown (2006: 13), nonetheless, makes the case for extending criminal sanctions and expresses surprise that the Commonwealth Parliamentary Committee omitted to recommend that reprisals should be made a criminal offense. For federal public workers, the Public Interest Disclosure Act 2013 (Australia), section 19, ultimately did so.

Table 17.1 Criminal anti-reprisal offenses in Australia (as of 2006)

Legislation	Detriment definition	Who can commit	Required extent of ground/ defense	Reverse onus of proof
1. SA 1993			Nil	
2. Qld 41, 42 1994	Sch. 6	42(1) a public officer	41(5) a substantial ground …, even if there is another ground	Nil
3. NSW 20 1994	20(2) not 'threat'	20(1). any person	20(1) substantially in reprisal	20(1A) it lies on the defendant to prove that detrimental action … was not substantially in reprisal for the person making a protected disclosure
4. ACT 25 (1) 1994	4	25(1) any person	25(2) It is defense … if it is established that the accused person – (a) had just and reasonable grounds for engaging in the conduct …; and (b) was engaging, or had engaged, in the conduct … before forming the belief that a person had made or may make a public interest disclosure	Nil
5. Cth (1) 1999			Nil	

Legislation		Detriment definition	Who can commit	Required extent of ground/ defense	Reverse onus of proof
6. Cth (2) Bill 2001–2002	22	3(1)	22(1) any person	22(2) as for ACT (1)	Nil
7. Vic. 2001	18	3(1)	18(1) any person	18(3) In determining whether a person takes detrimental action in reprisal it is irrelevant whether or not a reason referred to in sub-section (2) is the only or dominant reason as long as it is a substantial reason	Nil
8. Tas. 2002	19	3(1)	19(1) any person	19(3) as for Vic.	Nil
9. WA 2003	14	3(1)	14(1) any person	Nil	Nil
10. NT Bill 2005	18	4(1)	18(1) any person	18(3) A reason referred to in sub-section (2)(a) must be a substantial reason, but need not be the only or dominant reason for taking the reprisal	18(4) The defendant has the onus of proving: (a) the reprisal was not taken for reason referred to in sub-section (2)(a); or (b) if the reprisal was taken for a reason referred to in sub-section (2)(a) – the reason was not a substantial reason for taking the reprisal

Legislation		Detriment definition	Who can commit	Required extent of ground/ defense	Reverse onus of proof
11. ACT (2) Bill 2006	51 52	50	51(1), 52(1) any person	51(1)(b), 51(2)(b) intention of deterring 52(1)(b), 52(2)(b) intention of punishing	Nil

Note: Some legislation above was not enacted or has since been amended.

Source: Brown 2006: 37, Table 9.

The US Federal Sarbanes-Oxley Act (SOX) has been the subject of much academic comment, although more attention has been devoted to the civil rather than the criminal sanctions against reprisals established under section 1107.[13] The statute was passed in 2002 to try to restore confidence in US financial markets after the Enron scandal. Section 1107 imposes a fine and/or imprisonment of not more than ten years on anyone who knowingly, and with intent to retaliate, takes any action harmful to any person, including interference with the lawful employment or livelihood of any person, for providing to a law enforcement officer any truthful information relating to the commission of or possible commission of any federal offense.[14]

Academic comment is not universally supportive of the legislation. On the one hand, it has many enthusiasts. For example, Estlund (2005: 376) writes: 'Sarbanes-Oxley represents the gold standard in protection of employee whistleblowers, with both criminal sanctions and fully compensatory private civil remedies against reprisals'. Westman (2005: 146) outlines the ambitious scope of the statute, listing the many labor law statutes which create federal offenses covered by the SOX. He points out, 'In reviewing these partial lists, it is apparent that many employees who provide information to law enforcement officials could potentially fall within the protections of the criminal provisions of Sarbanes-Oxley, and that many companies and individual managers could face criminal prosecutions under Sarbones-Oxley'. Dworkin (2010: 38) explains that 'there is great potential for broad application to whistleblowing about non-securities issues'. She continues, 'also it applies to any company including non-profits, and individuals, not just the organization. It can also possibly apply to non-organization members since the language used is "any person"'.

On the other hand, others are critical, arguing that the provision is ill-advised and inoperable. Lechner and Sisco (2006: 85), while acknowledging that the inclusion of section 1107 'certainly reflects Congressional intent to aggressively ferret out criminal malfeasance … post-Enron', are sceptical about its effectiveness. They doubt its 'real value as a substantive prosecutorial tool' suggesting that 'it is arguably merely an extension of already existing obstruction of justice charges currently available under 18 USC 1150 (obstruction of criminal investigations) and 18 USC 1512 (tampering with witnesses, victims, or informants)'. The authors point out that the examples of other prosecutions involving corporate crime suggest that 'to get tough in the corporate sentencing arena often has the unintended result of creating more trials and less [*sic*] guilty pleas'. They cite four more specific criticisms (Lechner and Sisco 2006: 85). First, the potential defendants are widely drawn. The section applies to 'any person' so that 'employees who in the past were not subject to individual liability under other federal retaliation statutes now could face enormous fines and jail times for their workplace misconduct'. Small companies and third parties, 'regardless of their agency relationship with the employer' may also be liable for taking part in retaliation against whistleblowers. Secondly, since the term 'any federal offense' is not defined, the section 'may criminalize retaliatory conduct in seemingly unrelated contexts which in the past may have given rise to only civil liability'. They suggest that these include, for example, violations of discrimination law. Thirdly, if the term 'federal offense' is widely interpreted, complaints to employment-related agencies would be covered. Finally, prohibited conduct is also widely drawn, covering action 'harmful' to any person including 'interference with the lawful employment or livelihood of any person' (Lechner and Sisco 2006: 85). Arguably, harassment outside the workplace could be covered. Perhaps because of such statutory ambiguities, it seems that the Act, like the comparable Australian provisions, has not resulted in many prosecutions. Dworkin (2010: 39) points out that 'while this section has the potential to become the most important of all the SOX provisions in terms of whistleblowing, and could develop into a general whistleblower protection statute, so far it has not been broadly interpreted'.

Before assessing the strength of the practical and theoretical arguments for using specific sections in whistleblower legislation introducing criminal sanctions against those who exact reprisals, it is pertinent to assess how far protection is in any case provided by the general criminal law, in particular that relating to witness intimidation. Of course, not all whistleblowers become witnesses and some indeed prefer not to. Carr refers to the 2009 Report of the Council of Europe, *The Protection of Whistle-blowers*. It states that 'the notion of "whistleblower" should not be confused with or limited to that of a witness. A "whistleblower" will not necessarily wish to, or need to appear in a court of law, considering that "whistle-blowing measures" are designed to deter malpractice in the first place, or to remedy it at an early stage' (cited in Carr 2011: 106). Banisar, however, points out that 'There is some overlap between the two, often including a promise to keep the identity of the individual confidential'. He argues that witness protection is broader than safe-guarding whistleblowers. It involves people not in organizations and the focus is on the 'information not the person who made the disclosure' (Banisar 2011: 6). The latter may be bystanders.

Some whistleblowers, however, may be called as witnesses in criminal prosecutions of employers, managers or fellow employees. These may follow exposure of company or organizational wrongdoing. A major risk if the disclosers are called by the prosecution at trial is that they may lose their anonymity and thus lay themselves more open to reprisals. Most whistleblower legislation makes some provision for the protection of the identity of the whistleblower.[15] Some countries also impose criminal sanctions for disclosing the identity of the whistleblower. Under India's Public Interest Disclosure Bill, anyone who reveals the identity of the whistleblower faces a penalty of imprisonment and fine for revealing. In the event that they are called as witnesses, any anonymity they may have been able to safeguard previously will be threatened.

Intimidation of witnesses may amount to contempt of court and/or perverting the course of justice. In many jurisdictions, an employer or ex-employer who threatens reprisals against a witness will face contempt of court proceedings. This would have wide-ranging application to the sort of often secret threats which may be faced by whistleblowers. In common law systems the powers of the courts to punish for contempt are generally wider than those where civil law prevails.[16] The application of this in the employment relationship was expressed by Stephenson LJ in a criminal case, in which he stated:

> the exercise of a legal right to dismiss or to evict a person who has given evidence does not excuse interfering with the administration of justice by deterring persons who might wish to give evidence in other cases, or prevent such interference from being contempt.[17]

If the retaliation is taken or threatened after court proceedings are over, contempt may still apply.[18] Further indication of the scope of contempt proceedings in cases involving whistleblowers was given in the English courts in the decision in *Peach Grey v Sommers*.[19] The divisional court has power to punish contempt of an industrial tribunal in the same way as it can punish contempt of court.

A more specific criminal offense which could apply to threats against witnesses is perverting the course of justice. In a number of jurisdictions, including Canada, England, Hong Kong and Ireland, this is a common law offense, while in others such as Australia and New Zealand, there are statutory versions. In the United States, the offense is the more serious one of obstruction of justice.[20] Increasingly, however, and specifically in the wake of growing international recognition of the rights of victims of criminal offenses, a number of countries have made witness intimidation a specific criminal offense. Threatened whistleblowers could thus claim this additional protection. The Criminal Justice and Public Order Act 1994 in England and Wales created two new offenses, namely, intimidating a witness and harming or threatening to harm a witness.[21] It did not provide for compensation for such victims. The range of harmful acts includes financial harm to the person or property which arguably covers loss in an employment context. It is not clear whether these sections have been used in such a context because there are no reported cases on the issue and the numbers of convictions are included in the generic count of cases listed as 'perverting the course of justice'.

Changes to the law of evidence and criminal procedure in some jurisdictions have helped safeguard fearful witnesses. Whistleblowers could fall into the category of 'intimidated witnesses' and thus gain added protection at a criminal trial. For example, section 17 of the Youth Justice and Criminal Evidence Act 1999 (England and Wales), covers witnesses where the quality of the evidence is likely to be diminished by reason of the witnesses' fear or distress about testifying. Special Measures Directions allow various protections for frightened witnesses such as screening and evidence given by video link. In extreme cases, the identity of the witness may be kept secret.[22] Finally, the whistleblower witness may be helped by the gradual weakening of the rule against the admissibility of hearsay, including permitting documentary hearsay, and allowing hearsay evidence from witnesses who are in fear, including fear of financial loss.[23] These measures are pertinent particularly to adversarial court systems, but the law on hearsay is the subject of some relaxation in Europe also. The Grand Chamber of the European Court of Human Rights now holds that a conviction may be founded on hearsay evidence alone.[24]

There would be advantages for threatened whistleblower witnesses in using the above provisions in both general substantive criminal law and the adjectival law of criminal procedure and evidence. There is a growing body of jurisprudence on these provisions and thus the law in these matters would have a greater degree of potential certainty. However, the occasions on which these provisions would apply are likely to be rare, since witness protection is more generally associated with serious and violent crime rather than the sort of white collar corporate offenses on which the whistle is more likely to be blown. In fact, the law on witness protection which has been developed most robustly in England in recent years has itself been subject to criticism. It is argued that it has tended to sanctify victims and undermine the rights of the defendant. The accused employer is entitled to the presumption of innocence and to a hearing in open court facing witnesses who can be cross-examined. Of course, not all whistleblowers are pure. Spagnolo illustrates from an examination of anti-trust legislation that some whistleblowers have themselves engaged in undetected criminality. Following the tradition in the United States 'where prosecutorial discretion has always allowed for exchanges of leniency against evidence' they have in some cases obtained immunity in exchange for divulging breaches of the law (Spagnolo 2006: 7). Overall, however, official recommendations are that protection for whistleblowers should be extended in dedicated whistleblower legislation.

As the above account has shown, there is academic support for the use of specific criminal sanctions against those who victimize whistleblowers. In some instances, the need for criminal sanctions is asserted but not argued. In cases where reprisal has been proven sanctions could be considered, however, a review of the relevant literature on the role of criminal law reveals that there has been little sustained examination of the role of criminal sanctions. Moberly, for example, in his extensive recent review of the SOX, scarcely mentions section 1107 at all. He does, however, make pertinent points about the role of the judiciary in employment-related civil cases. For example, he argues that in the area of protection of whistleblowers, the nature of the administrative framework used may be just as important as the details of the legislation (Moberly 2012a). This argument could also be applied to criminal sanctions. Thus, from an analysis of commentary on the use of the civil law provisions it is possible to infer arguments for and against the efficacy of criminal sanctions.

Martin (2003) has drawn up a threefold typology as a model critique of whistleblower legislation. He cites 'sincere, symbolic, and cynical' explanations for the specific provisions, providing a useful model through which to examine whistleblower legislation and criminal sanctions in this instance. Taking 'sincerity' first, the heart of the argument would appear to be that whistleblowing is a public good and therefore the public, in the form of a state-initiated prosecution, should take action to defend those who are victimized as a result of their actions. There is much academic comment on the relevance of the motive of the whistleblower. Does he or she have to act out of altruism? This raises the question of whether the public good element in blowing the whistle should still prevail in view of the fact that the whistleblower may well have mixed motives. This question is dealt with further by Roberts, Chapter 9. Arguably, the whistleblower victim, no more than any other victim, does not have to be ethically pure in order to gain the protection of the criminal law against reprisals. This is in contrast with tortious remedies, where the degree of compensation may be determined by the nature of the actions and motives of the claimant. One argument in favor of using the criminal law to protect against reprisals is that society shows its condemnation of employer vindictiveness which, if allowed to prevail, would deprive the public of a supply of information.

The nature of the public good generated by whistleblowing draws on the analysis developed by Stiglitz (2002) of the risk posed to general well-being by such asymmetries in information, or supply of new knowledge. In social democracy, the common good also has wider connotations of collective benefits, accessible to all. As Marginson (2011: 417–18) points out, 'Though notions of inexhaustible national resources make less sense than they did, non-corporeal resources like knowledge are inexhaustible. In social democracy the common public goal is associated with democratic forms, openness, transparency, popular sovereignty and grass-roots agency'. However, he goes on suggest that not all would agree with this interpretation. Among doubtlessly equally sincere pro-market ideologues, criminal sanctions against employers, or even fellow employees for discriminating against whistleblowers, interfere with the freedom of the market, Smith's 'invisible hand'. The latter approach suggests that there should not be interference with the employer's freedom to operate. As Marginson puts it (2011: 418), 'the accumulation of profit, free from interference, drives the prosperity of all. Yet in socialist discourse the general benefit or public good is secured by statist regulations, the opposite of an under-regulated capitalist market'.

Sincerity is not a straightforward concept. This is clear from the extensive literature examining the value of the provisions protective of whistleblowers. Some oppose the legislation as interfering with the freedom of the market. Comment is more often directed to civil sanctions, but the points are of general application. Hansberry (2012: 197), citing the financial repercussions of fighting accusations, writes, 'The Dodd-Frank Act's whistleblower protections add to the burden on corporations in particular' (see Hansberry 2012: 30 for details of the Dodd-Frank Act). Fighting criminal charges over retaliation against those who made disclosures, on this argument, interferes with the generation of profit. Other arguments are put forward by some that the SOX amounts to ineffective legislation introduced for political motives in an atmosphere of moral panic. Romano (2005) argues that the complex relationship between alleged fraud, financial turmoil and legislation was obscured by the hasty implementation of the SOX. She doubts the sincerity of those who advocated legislation who, she says, were more influenced by 'electoral considerations' (Romano 2005: 1566). Rapp (2007) also questions the sincerity of the US provisions in the light of the overall objectives of the law. He suggests that the public good, which arguably is the motivating force for criminal sanctions, was not a major consideration since the Act privileges internal disclosures which can be covered up. He suggests that 'SOX evidences a general trend in federal law in favor of intra-organizational, or internal, whistleblowing. But in SOX this trend takes an acute form. SOX envisions whistleblowers as servants of shareholders, rather than servants of law enforcement officers or the public. Whether that is the best paradigm for whistleblowers is an open and debatable proposition' (Rapp 2007: 126).

Symbolism is a second justification for criminalizing victimization. Roberts and Brown (2010: 62) comment that while criminal provisions rarely result in successful prosecutions, they do carry important symbolic value by highlighting to organizations that reprisals are regarded very seriously by legislatures. Critical of the 'symbolic' arguments for criminalization, Martin (2003), however, points out that they may make for empty and misleading gestures or smokescreens. Romano (2005) is also scathing of symbolism. She is critical of the use of the criminal law generally in corporate governance, so her comment is not specifically directed at section 1107, but the argument can also be applied to this under-used section. She writes, 'the increased criminal sanctions fit more squarely with a characterization as symbolic politics' (Romano 2005: 1586). She cites the analysis made by Khanna who, she says, 'maintains that such laws satisfy Congress's need to react to a public outcry over corporate scandals at minimal cost to corporations. That is, the corporations prefer such legislation because, he contends, it deflects liability from individual officers to entities and avoids more detrimental forms of legislative responses such as facilitating private civil litigation' (Romano 2005: 1586, n. 396).

Khanna's argument is specific to the United States in that the notion of corporate criminal liability is more developed there than in other jurisdictions. However, again, the jurisprudential argument is of general application. Khanna (2004) suggests that the legislation has the effect of 'deflecting criminal liability away from managers and executives and onto corporations'. He points out that there was 'little corporate opposition to Sarbanes-Oxley compared to the opposition to moves to enhance corporate civil liability' (2004: 95, 115–16). Khanna concludes that the SOX adds to 'the already sprawling and ever-increasing area of corporate criminal liability' and that such legislation is not only ineffective as a deterrence to corporate crime but rather 'is a preferred response for corporate interests' when politicians need to assuage public anger over perceived wrongdoing (2004: 140). In other words, criminal justice provisions in this and other areas can be a substitute for deeper social and economic politics. In a perceptive analysis of the lobby for legal recognition of the rights of victims of crime generally, Roach refers to an unhealthy tendency to apply the criminal law as a panacea for serious social problems. He suggests that it is cheap politics (Roach 1999: 313). Thus the 'symbolic' argument often elides neatly into Martin's final category, cynicism.

The above review suggests that research is needed to derive a coherent theoretical analysis of the rationale for the use of anti-retaliation criminal provisions. Since there is a paucity of reported cases in any jurisdiction, it is equally difficult at present to uncover a consistent approach on the part of the judiciary. In his study of what he calls the US Supreme Court's 'Anti-Retaliation Principle', Moberly (2010: 377) comments, 'The Court's opinions appear untethered to any consistent judicial philosophy'. He suggests that, with the exception of *Garcetti v Ceballos* (2006),[25] the court is prompted in its decision-making in these civil claims by its obligation for law enforcement which includes witness protection. He writes, 'Employees must be protected from retaliation so that they will report illegal conduct. These employee reports will themselves aid law enforcement by alerting authorities to wrongdoing. As important, the threat of possible employee reports will deter employer violations in the first place' (Moberly 2010: 430). The author cites Westman who argued that 'judges do not like the idea that witnesses are going to be intimidated and that translates into the workplace' (cited in Moberly 2010: 420).

Unfortunately, there is insufficient evidence to see if privileging witness protection impacts on judges in employment cases under criminal law. It is not clear why prosecutions are not brought under section 1107 or under the Australian legislation; research is needed to discover if the cause is reluctance on the part of victims to report retaliation or reluctance on the part of the investigatory authorities to launch prosecutions. Moberly draws attention to the behavioral norms of the actors in the system. He suggests that 'individual players in the system, such as organizational supervisors, government administrators, and adjudicatory decision-makers impact whistleblowers as much as, if not more than, any formal legal provisions … we ought to spend as much effort determining who is involved in whistleblower protection as we do deciding what those protections should formally entail' (Moberly 2012a: 53–4). Given that even in civil cases the number of successful whistleblower claimants is small, it is arguable that potential prosecutions stall because of recognition that the judicial impetus to protect law enforcement, evidenced in civil cases according to Moberly, will be trumped by the more powerful judicial imperative in criminal cases to preserve the employer's right to manage.

Rapp (2007: 110, n. 110) asks the question: how far will judges be willing to impose stiff criminal sanctions in such situations? Thus, what Moberly (2010: 449) calls 'the chilling effect of retaliation' is arguably unlikely to be successfully defended by the criminal courts. He refers to the traditional purpose of labor law 'to address the imbalance in bargaining power between employees and employers'. He points out that 'legal protections must be balanced against the employer's countervailing interest in the flexibility and efficiency provided by the at-will-employment rule' (Moberly 2010: 381). However, the imbalance over the decades has been addressed almost entirely in civil law. In a criminal case there is no tangible redressing of the balance, since the aggrieved employee will not receive his or her job back or monetary compensation, only the satisfaction of a penalty of imprisonment or fine on the employer.

A deeper sociological question is how far there is majoritarian support for the extension of criminalization in this area of law. Parliamentary debates, trade union reaction and media commentary surrounding the introduction of criminal sanctions in the United States and Australia could usefully be researched to assess how far there is general acceptance of this attempt by the state to inculcate the arguably controversial new norm that taking reprisals against a whistleblower should be criminalized. The rushed nature of the US SOX Congressional debates might have had little effect in conditioning and preparing society to this new norm. The problem of changing prevailing social norms in preparing legislation is addressed by Kahan (2000). He outlines the 'sticky norms problem' by which he means that 'gentle nudges' might be better than 'hard shoves', since 'the prevalence of a social norm makes decisions-makers reluctant to carry out a law intended to change that norm'. He argues that the 'most effective regulatory strategy is moderate, not severe condemnation' (Kahan 2000: 644; on the question of social norms see also Posner 1996). In other words, was there recognition amongst both the general public and law enforcers of the value of making reprisals against whistleblowers a criminal offense?

Other more practical and procedural objections might explain the paucity of use of criminal sanctions. The experience of prosecuting corporate crime is that success is elusive. The rationale and the problems of applying criminal penalties to corporate misconduct are drawn out by Clarke (2005) in her study of the application of Part IV of the Trade Practices Act. Her analysis is helpful in assessing, by analogy, the potential for prosecuting employers who exact reprisals on their staff. The author outlines the 'key justifications' for criminal penalties for cartel wrongdoing and argues that they would act as a deterrent, their introduction ensuring fairness with other corporate crimes such as tax evasion and consistency with developing international best practice (Clarke 2005: 147–8). Moreover, she claims that the incidence of white collar crime is particularly affected by deterrence, in part because the offender has the time, inclination and resources to do a cost-benefit analysis. However, there are countervailing difficulties. She points in particular to the difficulty of proving intent and of evidence gathering: 'Concurrent civil and criminal prohibition also raises the problem of ensuring that any evidence gathered is done so in accordance with criminal standards where criminal prosecution is likely to be pursued' (Clarke 2005: 168).

Similarly, many jurisdictions find it difficult to successfully identify who to prosecute in corporations. Carr (2011: 106) also refers to the narrow interpretation in English law of the 'directing mind' test for finding companies liable for corruption and fraud. There are also many questions of definition and scope to be settled. Many of these apply to the whistleblowing legislation generally, not just the criminal sanctions. One issue concerns the question of whether the legislation criminalizing those who carry out reprisals should cover the indirect as well as the direct consequences of reprisal. How far are sanctions in criminal law appropriate for those who have suffered and may prefer a job offer after dismissal, a transfer to another post, comparable job positions and monetary compensation rather than the satisfaction of a criminal conviction of the person who victimized them?

Evidential difficulties in the legislation have been identified by Brown (2006: 36). He writes:

> it is notoriously difficult to prove that detrimental action has been taken because of a disclosure, rather than for some other reason. For example, has a whistleblower been harassed at work because of a disclosure, or because colleagues simply don't like him? Has he been dismissed by management

> because of a disclosure, or because he was incompetent? The lack of any known successful reprisal prosecution to date is often assumed to relate at least partly to this difficult burden.

A reprisal may take a very subtle form which does not constitute clear harm, let alone have the provable ingredients of a criminal offense. It may take the form of social pressures such as ostracising the whistleblower. Rapp (2007: 122) goes so far as to say that 'the law can do nothing, directly, to reduce the social pressures that impede whistleblowing'. He suggests that 'while SOX insulates a potential whistleblower from some of the more obvious methods of employment-related retaliation, it offers little or no hope of assuaging the other severe disincentives to whistleblowing such as fear of social ostracism or blacklisting' (Rapp 2007: 154).

One question is the difficulty of proof, whether the burden should be on the prosecution or on the defendant employer. In relation to civil actions, including discrimination, many statutes place the burden on the defendant employer. In relation to criminal offenses, however, the issue is complicated, because there may be a constitutional protection of the presumption of innocence. In England there are examples where, in prosecutions under health and safety legislation, the relevant statute has been interpreted to place the legal burden on the defendant employer. The experience of litigation in civil law countries also shows these problems are not easy to surmount. For example, in order to qualify for protection under the German Civil Code, a public servant has the burden of proving 'that his/her disclosure was legally permissible, that discrimination took place, and that retaliation happened because of his/her disclosure. This proof has proved to be almost impossible to provide as long as the employer has not explicitly mentioned this as the reason for termination' (OECD 2011: 24).[26] Another cause of vulnerability is that although the whistleblower in principle has the power of the state behind him, he or she is a witness for the prosecution and not a party to the proceedings and will not have access to legal aid. There is potentially an imbalance of power in a trial where the victimized employee may face a powerful and well-funded organization.

Other obstacles to extending criminal sanctions arise from cultural and historic factors in some countries, in part because of the historic privileging in law of the protection of property rights. As Callahan *et al.* (2004: 899) point out, 'reprisal for blowing the whistle is generally perceived as a private, not public, wrong in the United Kingdom and the US'. Other countries such as South Africa have a somewhat sceptical view of the value of whistleblowing. Uys reviews the relationship between whistleblowing and culture in South Africa, which affects, *inter alia*, the lack of importance attached to preventing reprisals. The author (2010: 121) comments that the emphasis on the concept of Ubuntu:

> places on the concrete principles of communal relations, harmony and consensus, and by implication loyalty to significant others, seems to preclude the generally individualistic act of whistleblowing where perceived organisational wrongdoing is exposed in the interest of the more abstract ideas of promoting the public interest.

A number of commentators advocate other methods of meeting reprisals than the criminal law. Rapp (2007) advocates increased used of the 'carrot' of 'bounties' and *qui tam* suits, while Moberly (2006) prefers a structural model in addition to the anti-retaliation model. Martin (2003: 120) is doubtful in fact if laws on whistleblowing are ever effective, pointing out that 'there are many subtle ways for employers to undermine employees without providing clear-cut evidence of reprisals'. Brown (2006: 36–8) cites empirical evidence on the difficulties of obtaining successful prosecutions of retaliating employers under Australian legislation. Lewis (2003: 332, 333) takes a similar stance:

> Making victimization a criminal offence sends out a useful message, but it is arguable that the availability of large damages awards will have a greater effect both on the willingness of people to speak out and on those contemplating the imposition of reprisals … Although it might be useful to make retaliation (by either an organisation or individual) a criminal offence, it is more important to make victimization a tort which attracts injunctive relief.

The South African Law Reform Commission (2004: para. 4.51) recommended against creating new offenses, stating that it would 'be likely to add to unnecessary tension to employment relationships and jeopardize good labor relations'. It also recommended that a better approach would be to improve remedies, give whistleblowers immunity, and create a duty of confidentiality. The point is that, arguably, the main objective in whistleblowing legislation must be to rectify the underlying harm to the public that has been revealed and not get preoccupied with satellite or secondary litigation or prosecutions aimed at protecting the messenger. Others also prefer a consequentialist rather than a deontological stance. As Rapp (2007: 116) puts it, 'Merely protecting whistleblowers should not be the only goal. Rather the goal should be to optimize the quantity and quality of information that whistleblowers bring to light about corporate malfeasance, and to do so in such a way that makes early intervention by public and private enforcement authorities feasible and effective'.

CRIMINAL SANCTIONS AGAINST WHISTLEBLOWERS

Criminal sanctions against whistleblowers fall into two groups in a number of jurisdictions. Several countries prescribe the prosecution of whistleblowers for giving false information and, more commonly, whistleblowers may face prosecution for breach of secrecy laws. Here it is relevant to distinguish whistleblowing from a duty to inform. Banisar points out, 'In much of the literature on anti-corruption, the positive – and often non-voluntary – duty of individuals to inform superiors or others of any wrongdoing that they discover is also described as whistleblowing. This is becoming especially common in areas such as civil service, banking and accounting'. The author points out that there may be criminal or other sanctions for the act of non-disclosure. He accepts that 'The functionality is similar – there is a disclosure and the person who made the disclosure requires some protection from sanctions that they may face'. However, he states that 'the motivation and the type of problems are different' (Banisar 2011: 5). Arguably, the conceptual difference between the two modes of disclosure is exaggerated and the imposition of a legal duty to disclose in a particular area may well follow from spontaneous self-motivated whistleblowing. For reasons of space, however, Banisar's typology will be followed here and the account below will concentrate on the conventional definition of whistleblowing.

A study prepared by the OECD in 2011, *G20 Anti-Corruption Action Plan, Action Point 7: Protection of Whistleblowers*, points out that whistleblower protection laws would normally not impose sanctions for misguided reporting, and protection would be afforded to disclosures that are made in honest error. However, in some jurisdictions whistleblowers may face specific charges if their allegations are unfounded.[27] Australia has the most comprehensive legislation in this area. Brown (2006: 21) writes:

> In all jurisdictions, it is a criminal offence to knowingly supply false or misleading information intending it to be acted on as a public interest disclosure. The provision that currently strikes the best balance is Queensland's, which provides that a person may not make a statement intending it to be acted on as a public interest disclosure and 'in the statement, or in the course of inquiries into the statement' intentionally give information that is 'false or misleading in a material particular'.

Brown (2006: 21) is critical of two jurisdictions for creating a much wider offense:

> Currently, the provisions in South Australia and Western Australia also create the problematic offence of 'being reckless about whether' information in an intended disclosure is false or misleading. Such recklessness is not only difficult to prove, but is a potential deterrent to whistleblowers, who might reasonably fear being exposed to such a prosecution if some aspect of their information proves incorrect.

IMMUNITY OF WHISTLEBLOWERS FOR UNFOUNDED CLAIMS

Few statutes provide immunity for whistleblowers from breaches of the general criminal law. The biggest exception is Australia (see Brown 2006: 35, Table 8). Some commentators have suggested that legislation should guarantee that those who disclose information in accordance with the correct procedures should be immune from civil and criminal liability. For example, Latimer (2006: 35) writes, 'Whistleblowers making protected disclosures should be relieved of civil and criminal liabilities so as to deter others from taking reprisals … There should be immunity for disclosure if the whistleblower believes on reasonable grounds that the information on fraud or misconduct was true, or that it may be true. False, misleading or frivolous reporting could be discouraged with penalties under the template'. Latimer and Brown (2008: 789) express the ideal provision very simply: 'Best practice should protect whistleblowers from civil and criminal liability if they make a protected disclosure, and they should be afforded absolute privilege'.

The most serious sanctions whistleblowers might face are prosecutions under official secrecy legislation. There are powerful arguments against a robust application of these laws in this context. The scholarship of open government provides a helpful analysis for the current criminalization of whistleblowers. Blanton (2003: 61), for example, identifies a shift over the last decade from the prevailing paradigm that security and public safety should be safeguarded by openness to a new 'secrecy theology'. He comments

> originally this paradigm had nothing to do with terrorism but came directly from the scientific method – tested hypotheses, complete actions, replicable results, peer review. The most articulate exponents of openness … were precisely the scientists who had developed the Bomb, and they argued not so much on behalf of democratic values, or civil rights and liberties, but on scientific efficiency, and national security.

The intellectual underpinnings of the paradigm of openness include the theory of information asymmetries expounded by Nobel Prize winner Stiglitz (2002). On this issue Australian academic Snell (2006: 300) writes, 'Freedom of information for Stiglitz serves as both a mechanism to offset information asymmetry and performs an instrumental role in that it leads to improvements in policy and decision making'.

As Moberly (2006: 1116) puts it, 'Employees have an information advantage over traditional corporate monitors because they have more complete knowledge regarding the inner workings of a large corporation'. Of course, the counter-argument against transparency is that of protecting national security. Research into the papers of reported cases where the arguments from national security claims have led to suppression of evidence at trial has revealed that the claims on occasion had no factual foundation (Spencer and Spencer 2010). Further research is recommended to establish the empirical basis of such claims made against whistleblowers.

Criminalizing Disclosures

Most countries impose criminal sanctions if employees disclose information concerning official secrets or national security. In the United States if a purported whistleblower makes a disclosure that is specifically ordered by law or Executive Order to be kept secret in the interest of national defense or the conduct of foreign affairs, the disclosure is prohibited by law and the individual will not be afforded whistleblower protection unless it is made to the agency's Inspector General or the Office of Special Counsel. Prosecution may follow. Many countries count on Official Secrets Acts, which prohibit the release of information obtained under government employment, as in the United Kingdom, under certain circumstances. In *R v Shayler* (2002) the House of Lords strengthened such legislation by stating that the Official Secrets Act 1989 did not have a public interest defense available to a Ministry of Defence's whistleblower. In Canada, public employees involved in national security cannot make a complaint to the Public Service Integrity Commissioner. In the United States, the 1999 Intelligence Community Whistleblower Protection Act only allows national security whistleblowing to the House and Senate Intelligence Committees and the agency's Inspector General, providing limited protection for intelligence employees. At least up until recently, there was no whistleblower protection in agencies like the CIA, Defense Intelligence Agency, Justice Department, Transportation Security Administration and the National Security Agency (POGO 2005).

Roberts and Brown (2010: 61) point out that 'while technically there is a clear distinction between whistleblowing and leaking, in practice the two are conflated in the public commentary. In Australia, South Africa, the US and United Kingdom, whistleblowers who are public employees have faced criminal investigation and prosecution even where there was arguably a clear public interest in their disclosures'. On the other hand, some Australian states have adopted more enlightened legislation.

South Africa's Protection of State Information Bill was passed by the National Assembly in April 2013, however at time of writing it was being reconsidered as President Zuma refused to sign it into law. Known as the 'Secrecy Bill', it may allow the possibility of sending whistleblowers and journalists to jail for up to 25 years. Radack and McClellan (2011) have drawn attention to the trend in the United States towards the criminalization of whistleblowing involving what are deemed to be security matters. They maintain that whistleblower protection in this area is a sham, since it exempts national security and intelligence officials, although they often have the most significant evidence of threats to security. Radack and McClellan (2011: 58) maintain that the administration is not protecting national security interests when it brings cases against whistleblowers who divulge information that is important to the public, sparks meaningful dialogue, or exposes fraud, waste, abuse, illegality or potential dangers to public health and safety.

There have been several notorious prosecutions (see, for example, the cases of Leibowitz and Drake, reported by Moberly 2012b: 77–8). A number of these involve revelations about torture. It is well established that since 9/11, the United States has regularly subjected prisoners to torture, but none of the torturers have been brought to justice. When he took office, President Obama proclaimed that it was time to 'look forward instead of looking backward' when it came to crimes committed in the course of the so-called war on terror. Some documents which included photographs of government employees and contractors who were involved in torture at Guantanamo Bay fell into the hands of defense lawyers. If the torturers were worried that they might be prosecuted, their fears were groundless. But an intensive investigation was set in train to discover the source of the disclosure. The result was the prosecution of a whistleblower, John Kiriakou. He was charged under the Espionage Act for having tipped off a journalist more than three years before. He also faced a charge of making a false statement because it was said that he had lied to the publications review board of the Central Intelligence Agency. Kiriakou was a long-serving CIA counter-terrorism operations officer serving in Pakistan, who later became senior investigator on the Senate Foreign Relations Committee, focusing on international terrorism, piracy and counter-narcotics. He ultimately pled guilty to violating the Intelligence Identities Protection Act for revealing the name of an undercover operative to a journalist. He received a sentence of 30 months in prison.

By far the most prominent recent whistleblower is Bradley (now Chelsea) Manning. He was held in solitary confinement in a military prison from June 2010, charged with having provided WikiLeaks with a video of American helicopter gunmen shooting unarmed Iraqi civilians and a huge cache of diplomatic cables and field reports from the wars in Iraq and Afghanistan. One of the initial charges against him was 'aiding the enemy', punishable by death. Manning, a private soldier, wanted to highlight 'how messed up the situation is'. He pled guilty to leaking thousands of classified documents to WikiLeaks and received a sentence of 35 years. WikiLeaks founder Julian Assange has been investigated by a secret grand jury in the United States and has taken refuge in the Ecuadorian Embassy to avoid extradition to Sweden on sex charges. He maintains that Sweden will send him to face trial in the United States; and that Manning's treatment, or mistreatment, may be part of an attempt to get him to implicate Assange.

Banisar (2011: 10) gives details of other prosecutions under the Secrets Act, even in the supposedly more open Danish society. He writes, 'In Denmark, intelligence official Major Frank Soehelm Grevil was convicted and sentenced to six months imprisonment in November 2004 for revealing to journalists documents stating that the government had no evidence that there were weapons of mass destruction in Iraq'. There is also the possibility of prosecutions for release of information under other laws such as those covering theft or trade secrets. Banisar (2011: 45) gives examples of whistleblower laws which override Secrecy Acts, but they are very limited.

Moberly (2012b: 54) argues that the line between whistleblowing and leaking is not clear and in a penetrating account of the prosecutions outlined above he concludes that, 'In short President Obama values secrecy over transparency and oversight when it comes to national security whistle-blowing and the law often reflects and supports his choice'. Moberly recommends that protected disclosures in this area should be made to Congress.

CONCLUSION

The question of criminal sanctions in whistleblower legislation is under-researched and under-theorized; there are therefore many fertile areas for empirical, theoretical and interdisciplinary research. Specifically, the difficulty of protecting wronged employees in law is well documented, and the blacklisting of whistleblowers has been a persistent feature in certain industries. This treatment of whistleblowers is not simply aberrant criminal behavior on the part of maverick employers, but arises in many cases from the power of big corporations, aided and protected by state officials, including the police, and more arrogantly aggressive in the wake of the reduction of trade union influence. A salutary episode in recent English industrial relations makes disturbing reading. The Information Commissioner in 2009 raided the offices of the Consulting Association. They discovered files on more than 3,200 people, the majority of whom were trade union members in the construction industry. The association was financed by 44 construction firms including Sir Robert McAlpine, Balfour Beatty and Taylor Woodrow, who would phone up the Association and check whether job applicants were on the blacklist. Among the victims were workers who had complained about violations of health and safety on building sites. It was clear that details about these 'trouble-makers' had often been supplied by the police. Large building companies routinely employ ex-police officers to ensure security, including the vetting of job applicants. Ian Kerr, who ran the Consulting Association, was fined UK£5,000 in 2009. His offense was simply a breach of the data protection laws.

The criminal law, particularly in the United States, is increasingly being used to prosecute whistleblowers whose actions allegedly threaten national security. By contrast, the criminalization of those who take reprisals against whistleblowers is rarely successful in those few jurisdictions where the criminal law is employed in this area. Legislation in this area thus may appear to be of symbolic rather than of practical value. Failures are, in part, due to limited state funding for prosecuting agencies and the consequential delay in collecting evidence and investigating allegations of victimization. This chapter has demonstrated that more research is needed to answer the following questions: Why has legislation making it a criminal offense to take reprisals against whistleblowers been introduced only in a limited number of jurisdictions? How often in those cases where such legislation is on the statute book are prosecutions mounted? How many result in convictions? What are the reasons for acquittals, if any? Other fertile lines of inquiry would include any problems of evidence gathering and proof and any cultural and social pressures inhibiting the use of the criminal law. Finally, research could do more to uncover the extent to which whistleblowers themselves might prefer monetary or other compensation, to the criminalization of those who have taken reprisals against them.

NOTES

1. *Daily Chronicle*, 3 March 1892.
2. Witnesses (Public Enquiries) Protection Act 1892, s. 2.
3. *Ibid.* s. 4.
4. Council of Europe Parliamentary Assembly Resolution 1729 (2010) on the Protection of Whistleblowers, art. 6.2.5.
5. OSCE 2012: 76.
6. See also Rapp 2012: 113 for examples of the range of reprisals and their perpetrators.
7. Federal Criminal Code, art. 219(I).
8. Canadian Criminal Code, 2004, c. 3, s. 6.
9. Canadian Criminal Code, 2004, s. 425.1.
10. Hungarian Criminal Code, art. 257 (Persecution of an Announcement of Public Concern).
11. Northern Territory Public Interest Disclosure Act 2008, No. 38, s. 15.
12. *Ibid.*
13. US Federal Sarbanes-Oxley Act 116 Stat. 745 (SOX).
14. *Ibid.* s. 1107.
15. See e.g., the US Whistleblower Protection Act, s. 1213(h).
16. See e.g., *Mulvaney* (1982) 4 Cr. App. R 106; *Pittendrigh* (1985) 7 Cr. App. R (S) 221; and *Maloney* (1986) 8 Cr. App. R (S) 123.
17. *R v Kellett* [1976] QB 372.
18. In *Attorney-General v Butterworth* [1963] 1 QB 696, the Court of Appeal held that victimizing a witness after he had given evidence amounted to contempt of court.
19. *Peach Grey Co. v Sommers* [1995] 2 All ER 513; [1995] ICR 549.
20. See 18 USC s. 1510.
21. Criminal Justice and Public Order Act 1994 (UK), s. 51. The act or threat must be intended to intimidate. These witness intimidation provisions apply to current investigations and harming or threatening to harm a witness applies after the trial has ended. The perpetrator must know or believe that the other person is helping or has helped an investigation, is a witness or potential witness, juror or potential juror. The perpetrator must have acted or threatened the prosecution to bring such a case. There is a presumption of intent unless the alleged harm or threat came more than a year after the conclusion of proceedings.
22. See Coroners and Justice Act 2009, ss. 86–96.
23. See Criminal Justice Act 2003. In the United States, the constitutional protection of the right to confrontation does not permit extensive exceptions to the rule against hearsay.
24. See *Al-Khawaja and Tahery v United Kingdom* (26766/05) [2011] ECHR 2127.
25. 547 US 410 (2006).
26. German Civil Code, art. 612a. Examples of the latter are the US WPA 5 USC ss. 1214(b)(2)(4) and 1221(e). South Africa's PDA (2000), s. 4(2)(a) states that any dismissal in breach (of s. 3) of the Act is deemed to be an automatically unfair dismissal.
27. See e.g., Whistleblower Protection Act 2010 (Uganda), s. 17; Prevention of Corruption Act 2001 (Ireland), s. 8A.

18. Whistleblower protection in international governmental organizations

Shelley Walden and Bea Edwards

INTRODUCTION

The role played by international governmental organizations (IGOs)[1] in global stability, development and finance has become increasingly important since the Second World War. IGOs, however, represent a formidable challenge to whistleblowers trying to report corruption, fraud, abuse of authority, gross mismanagement or a danger to public health and safety, without sacrificing their careers and reputations. Because they operate in a multinational environment, IGOs are not subject to the legal regime of any one member state in most types of disputes. They are especially insulated from external judicial review in labor disputes, and advances in whistleblower protection legislation at the national level do not, therefore, apply to their staff members.[2]

At the same time, these institutions escape the transparency mandates of their member states, and they are thus free to operate behind closed doors when significant policy and financial decisions must be taken.[3] Further, IGOs often influence policy in their borrowing member states and also control substantial amounts of funding in these countries.[4] Anti-corruption research generally plants a red flag of warning in territory like this: secrecy, power, global reach and money equal fertile ground for corruption. This set of circumstances defines the parameters of a unique set of problems for whistleblowers making disclosures at IGOs and seeking protection from retaliation.

James Wolfensohn first made corruption an issue at the World Bank in 1996, during an address to the Annual meetings.[5] Since then, much anti-corruption rhetoric has been heard from IGOs but concrete achievements on this front are few.[6] As a consequence of hearings held in 2004 by the US Senate, in which witnesses reported widespread corruption and diversion of public funds through the Multilateral Development Banks (MDBs), the US government began to advocate strong protections from retaliation for whistleblowers. In 2005, Congress passed the Foreign Operations, Export Financing and Related Programs Appropriations Act,

2006 (public law 109–102), which requires US executive directors at the MDBs to advocate for whistleblower protection policies that meet 'best practices in domestic laws and international conventions against corruption'. Since then, the IGOs have demonstrated a willingness to adopt anti-retaliation policies but a reluctance to implement them effectively. The data that do exist show an abysmal implementation record at several of these institutions.

Although IGOs rarely release implementation data, some of them have commissioned studies regarding the content of their whistleblower policies or the functioning of their internal justice systems through which employees contest violations of their rights.[7] However, since these studies are usually commissioned and funded by the institution, they cannot be seen as independent. Moreover, studies that are particularly critical may be withheld by the IGO and only made known to the public if they are disclosed by a whistleblower or cited in a subsequent report produced by the organization.[8]

Studies related to IGO internal justice systems and whistleblower policies have also been conducted by the US government, especially the US Government Accountability Office (GAO) (see, for example, GAO 1999, 2007). In addition, exposés by former employees have shed light on how IGO whistleblower policies are actually functioning (or, in many cases, *not* functioning, see, for example, Berkman 2008; Shaman 2009; Bolkovac and Lynn 2011; Balogun 2010). Finally, our non-profit organization, the Government Accountability Project (GAP), has released numerous studies related to IGO whistleblowing issues. These studies are, in many cases, based on information disclosed to us by IGO whistleblowers.

In 2004 GAP published 'Challenging the Culture of Secrecy: A Status Report on Freedom of Speech at the Multilateral Development Banks', a series of reports that evaluated whistleblower policies at the World Bank (WB), Inter-American Development Bank (IDB), Asian Development Bank (ADB) and European Bank for Reconstruction and Development (EBRD). Subsequently, all of these banks (with the exception of the EBRD) revised their policies.[9] In addition, GAP has conducted studies related to the internal justice systems of IGOs (see GAP 2007; Walden *et al.* 2011), investigative units (see Volcker *et al.* 2007) and substantive disclosures brought to us by whistleblowers.[10]

This chapter will examine the state of existing research on IGO whistleblower topics and identify areas in which additional studies are needed. It will describe whistleblower issues that are unique to IGOs; the current status of whistleblower protections at the Multilateral Development Banks and United Nations; and various pitfalls in the enforcement of IGOs whistleblower rights, including deficiencies in IGOs' internal systems for processing, investigating and adjudicating whistleblowers' retaliation claims. We argue that there is a need for IGOs to generate and publicly release data about their whistleblower protection records, in order to increase oversight and transparency. We also contend that there is a need for researchers to examine potential alternatives to the IGOs' fatally flawed internal justice systems, which often fail to provide just outcomes in whistleblower retaliation cases. These alternatives include, but are not limited to, the creation of a single tribunal system to be used by all IGOs, the provision of external arbitration in whistleblower cases, and the piercing of IGOs' sovereign immunities in labor disputes.

ISSUES THAT ARE UNIQUE TO THE IGOS

IGOs are multicultural in nature and are composed of employees from all over the world. Staff members tend to be well educated and affluent. For example, the World Bank director of diversity programs has described the ideal bank applicant as an articulate Ph.D in macro-economics from an elite university, able to speak multiple languages, with five years of experience in international development, a history of living abroad and working in teams, and an interest in other cultures (Edwards and Walden 2009: 20).

Once hired, employees enter a 'total institution'[11] that has a pervasive impact on their lives. These bureaucratic organizations have their own language (acronyms abound), rules and secretive cultures.[12] They also exert significant control over the personal lives of their employees, as most staff members are dependent on the institution for their immigration status. If employees' employment is terminated, they often lose not only their jobs, but also their visas and must return to their countries of origin. This dependence places staff members in positions of extreme vulnerability, should they decide to make disclosures that are embarrassing to the institution.

In the past eight years, GAP has represented whistleblowers from ten IGOs and 20 different countries.[13] We have found that the act of whistleblowing transcends cultures, and it appears that reprisal also transcends cultures and institutions.[14] Although the particular techniques of retaliation may vary from organization to organization, GAP has observed that many IGO managers will attempt to 'shoot the messenger' rather than address his or her substantive disclosures.

It is therefore not surprising that studies commissioned by IGOs consistently find that employees are afraid of speaking up when they witness wrongdoing. For example, a 2011 survey of 7,000 staff members at the Office of United Nations High Commissioner for Refugees (UNHCR) found that 70 per cent of respondents reported fear of speaking up – a dramatic increase from previous years (Wak-Woya 2012: 3–5). Given that the UNHCR is a human rights agency established to assist refugees, many of whom seek asylum in order to defend their rights to freedom of expression, these findings are particularly troubling. Similarly, a United Nations staff survey conducted by Deloitte Consulting LLP (2004: 60) found that 46 per cent of staff members felt unprotected from reprisal for reporting violations of the codes of conduct. Finally, a Review of Ethics, Conduct and Grievance Systems of the Inter-American Development Bank (IDB) conducted by Global Compliance found that of those IDB employees who observed misconduct, only 29.6 per cent reported it; according to Global Compliance the benchmark for other organizations is 41 per cent (Johnson *et al.* 2011: 5). This low reporting level exists despite the fact that 31.5 per cent of the IDB respondents reported observing misconduct within the last year, compared to Global Compliance's benchmark of 22 per cent.[15] The company that administered the IDB survey gave several theories for why IDB employees are reluctant to report misconduct:

> The consequences of retaliation, especially if it involves termination of employment, can be much greater at the IDB than at other organizations. Because many IDB staff members are on G–4 visas, if they lose their position they usually must leave the country within 30 to 60 days.
>
> IDB staff members' fear of retaliation may be heightened because there is a belief that the IDB's existing grievance mechanisms do not allow for fast and just relief if they were to face retaliation or other unfair treatment. For example, if an employee believes she has been terminated or suffered some adverse employment action unfairly or in retaliation for reporting misconduct, she generally must first bring her claim to a peer review panel called the Conciliation Committee. While the Conciliation Committee is often ineffective in resolving matters brought before it, the staff member must go through this process, which takes on average four to five months to complete. At the end of the process, the Conciliation Committee provides a recommendation to Management, which need not follow the recommendation. Only at this point can the staff member file a claim with the Administrative Tribunal, where a binding decision can be obtained …
>
> Even if the employee ultimately prevails, the Tribunal's ability to make the employee whole is limited by an 'either/or' approach to a rescission of Management's decision or monetary damages. Monetary damages are capped at two times the person's salary, three times in exceptional cases, without

> regard to what the actual damages may have been. Finally, the employee is not entitled to reimbursement for costs or attorney fees.[16] (Johnson *et al.* 2011: 5–6)

This statement is applicable to the majority of IGOs, although the details of the grievance process vary slightly from organization to organization. Moreover, IGOs enjoy extensive legal immunities that preclude staff members' access to most national courts in labor disputes.[17] If a whistleblower is subjected to retaliation after reporting corruption, fraud or misconduct, his or her only recourse is to an internal justice system designed and paid for by the organization. According to Arnold M. Zack, president of the Asian Development Bank Administrative Tribunal, some 20 IGOs have their own administrative tribunals and dozens of others use the administrative tribunals established by the United Nations or International Labour Organization (ILO) (Zack 2010a: 47).

Although the procedures vary among internal justice systems and tribunals, all tribunals are compromised by a structural conflict of interest. The institution is the defendant in any case brought before its own tribunal, at the same time that the tribunal is housed in, and funded by, the institution. This conflict is manifest in the myriad of pro-defendant biases built into the judicial procedures and operations.

There is also a lack of transparency, as many administrative tribunals require that all documents be sealed during the adjudication process; that discovery be limited to attorneys and plaintiffs; and that much of the process be conducted behind closed doors. Matthew Parish, a lawyer and scholar who worked in the legal department of the World Bank, observed 'No domestic court may order release of documents held by it [an IGO]. Thus, where a person does have a complaint about its operations, it is impossible to obtain access to its internal records to rebut flat denials of wrongdoing' (Parish 2010: 3). Additional shortcomings of IGO internal justice systems will be discussed in more depth below.[18]

PROGRESS AND CHALLENGES IN THE ADOPTION OF BEST PRACTICE WHISTLEBLOWER PROTECTIONS AT IGOS

In 2004, the US Senate Foreign Relations Committee held a hearing to spotlight fraud and corruption within the MDBs. During the hearing, Senator Richard Lugar (R–IN) cited experts who estimated that between US$26 and US$130 billion in loan money had been misappropriated over the lifetime of the World Bank alone (Senate Committee on Foreign Relations (US) 2004: 2).

Subsequently, the US government passed section 1505(a)(11) of the 2006 Foreign Operations, Export Financing and Related Programs Appropriations Act, which sets forth the policy of the United States towards whistleblower protection policies at the MDBs. As noted earlier, this legislation requires the US executive director at each MDB to advocate for the implementation of:

> Best practices in domestic laws and international conventions against corruption for whistleblower and witness disclosures and protections against retaliation for internal and lawful public disclosures by the bank's employees and others affected by such bank's operations who challenge illegality or other misconduct that could threaten the bank's mission, including: (1) best practices for legal burdens of proof; (2) access to independent adjudicative bodies, including external arbitration based on consensus selection and shared costs; and (3) results that eliminate the effects of proven retaliation.

Since that law was passed, most of the MDBs (and the United Nations) have adopted formal whistleblower protection policies. In 2005 the United Nations adopted a policy, followed by the African Development Bank (AFDB) in 2007, the World Bank in 2008 and the Asian Development Bank (ADB) in 2009. The Inter-American Development Bank (IDB), which had enacted a weak and ineffective whistleblower protection policy in 2003, strengthened it in 2010 and then amended it further in 2012.

But although the MDBs improved their policies, they still do not meet the criteria established in the 2006 Foreign Operations Act of the US government, although the United States pressured MDB management to adopt effective policies. To their credit, the banks' revised policies meet the first standard, which requires that internal and lawful public disclosures be protected. But they have not been as consistent in meeting the second standard, which requires shifting burdens of proof. The World Bank policy meets the shifting burdens of proof standard (Staff Rule 8.02, 3.01.a) as does the AFDB policy (Whistleblowing and Complaints Handling Policy: 6.67).[19] The ADB policy does not meet this standard (Administrative Order No. 2.10). The IDB policy adopted in 2012 (PE–328) includes a shifting burden of proof standard, but the policy has 'loopholes' that undermine its compliance with this standard.

The whistleblower protection policies are especially weak with respect to providing a whistleblower with relief that eliminates the effects of proven retaliation. Although the World Bank Administrative Tribunal (WBAT) may order a whistleblower reinstated, it is GAP's understanding that this had not been done by the WBAT since 1999 (in 2011, the WBAT ordered the reinstatement of a vindicated complainant, but rejected his claim that he was a whistleblower).[20] The ADB and IDB policies also fail to guarantee a vindicated whistleblower restoration to the employment status he or she enjoyed before making the contested disclosure and compensation for associated losses.

None of the MDBs meet the independent adjudicative body standard. The AFDB whistleblower protection policy includes a provision for Alternative Dispute Resolution (ADR), but anecdotal evidence suggests that the provision is not implemented. The World Bank provides access to nominally 'external' mediation, but the mediators must be selected from a roster of candidates formulated by the institution. The ADB also lacks external arbitration, though it does have a compulsory conciliation process in which a staff member is allowed to select a conciliator from a list appointed by the President. This required mediation is a step towards an ADR program, but lacks the necessary impartiality to be effective. As of December 2012, the IDB had no provision at all for access to an independent adjudicative body for whistleblowers, although it informed GAP that it planned to implement an informal and formal mediation system.

This failure to implement external arbitration is particularly troubling, given that numerous researchers have recommended that it be implemented at the MDBs. For example, in a report commissioned by the World Bank Group's management, CDR Associates (Moore and Wildau 2005: 38), recommended arbitration at the Bank if the 'impartiality of the Appeals Committee or the Tribunal cannot be internally guaranteed, if issues raised involve either senior management or members of the Board or its committees, or if confidentiality or disclosure issues are at stake'. Similarly, Robert Vaughn, a legal scholar at the Washington College of Law at American University, prepared a report for the Bank in which he recommended external arbitration in whistleblower cases and described a potential model that included consensus selection and shared costs (Vaughn 2005: 31). Also, Arnold Zack (2010b: 40) recommended that the adjudicative step prior to the AT allow for arbitration.

DONOR COUNTRY MANDATES AND THE NEED FOR RESEARCH ON WHISTLEBLOWER PROTECTION

Because the headquarters of the World Bank, the IDB and the United Nations are located in the United States, and because the United States makes substantial contributions to IGOs headquartered in other countries, its concerns with respect to staff rules on corruption and fraud have a particular weight. The US government received an opportunity to influence these regulations when the MDBs came to the Congress with requests for increased general funding in the wake of the 2008–2009 financial collapse. In 2010, the MDBs' authorities requested General Capital Increases (GCIs) from donor governments, and the US government was asked to contribute tens of billions of dollars in new funding to these institutions. In December 2011, US President Barack Obama signed into law the 2012 Consolidated Appropriations Act, which authorized these increases for the AFDB, IDB and World Bank.[21] The legislation requires the US Treasury Department (per section 7082) to submit semi-annual progress reports to the Congressional Committee on Appropriations documenting the extent to which the World Bank, AFDB and IDB are making 'substantial progress' towards 'implementing best practices for the protection of whistleblowers from retaliation, including best practices for legal burdens of proof, access to independent adjudicative bodies, results that eliminate the effects of retaliation, and statutes of limitation for reporting retaliation'.[22]

The reporting requirement by the US Department of Treasury is crucial to ensuring that the MDBs actually *implement* the whistleblower protection policies they adopt. At present, the MDBs do not release data directly to the public regarding the implementation of their policies, but anecdotal evidence suggests that the policies are not effectively applied.[23] With the recently authorized GCIs, opportunities to divert loan and project funds and commit fraud will multiply. Given the lack of transparency surrounding the financial operations of all of these institutions, strong whistleblower protections are crucial to ensuring that economic crimes are detected and that the billions of taxpayer dollars flowing into the MDBs are spent appropriately.

In November 2012, the US Department of the Treasury issued two reports that contain information about the whistleblower protection records of four MDBs. The reports include information about the number of whistleblower retaliation allegations received by the offices responsible for processing such claims at each institution. They show that from 2009 through July 2012 the applicable office at the World Bank received 26 retaliation claims (none of which were vindicated by that office) and the ADB office received seven (three of which were vindicated, one through mediation and one through a rare court decision in a member country, DOT (US) 2012b: 10–13). From 2007–2011, the ADB received five requests for whistleblower protection, but did not find retaliation in any of these cases (DOT (US) 2012a: 2). From 2009–2011 the IDB Ethics Office received four requests for protection from retaliation and determined that there had been no retaliation in three of them (DOT (US) 2012b: 13). Three complainants subsequently appealed their cases to the IDB Administrative Tribunal: the Bank resolved one case to the constructive satisfaction of the complainant outside the judicial process; in the second case, the whistleblower received substantial compensation but was not reinstated; and the third case is still pending nearly three years after the whistleblower reported retaliation.[24] This record, while sparse, indicates that meritorious claims are not hospitably received at the Ethics Office. This same problem appears to exist at the World Bank, as its tribunal received 13 retaliation cases, (presumably half of those rejected by the Bank's Office of Ethics and Business Conduct) and found in favor of six applicants.

While the Treasury Department report released data that had not previously been made available to the public, additional information is needed to obtain a more accurate picture of each organization's implementation record. For example, the report mentions that the World Bank Administrative Tribunal found in favor of six complaining staff members, but does not mention whether their retaliation claims were substantiated. Often, such cases involve not only allegations of retaliation, but also allegations of due process violations, and in GAP's experience, the WBAT has been hesitant to substantiate retaliation, even in cases in which it sided with the applicant on other claims. These data would also be more meaningful if they indicated whether the relief received by whistleblowers who prevail is comprehensive and covered the consequences of reprisal. This would include information about whether vindicated whistleblowers who requested reinstatement were, in fact, reinstated. To assess progress in the implementation of the policy, it would also be useful to know whether:

(1) the Ethics Office or channel for reporting retaliation has been adequately staffed and funded;
(2) staff members at the respective MDBs ascribe credibility, confidentiality and reliability to the Office;
(3) staff members whose retaliation complaints are substantiated on a preliminary basis and who requested interim protection from retaliation received it;
(4) Staff Associations at each organization have confidence in the adequacy of the policies and the effectiveness of enforcement;
(5) individuals have been held accountable for reprisal against whistleblowers.

Such data are crucial to determining the effectiveness of an IGO's whistleblower protection policy. Additional research in this area would therefore be useful, both for policy and for legal reasons.

Although the Treasury Department's report contained data about the implementation record at each MDB, the banks themselves have not released this information to the public. In this regard, the MDBs lag far behind the United Nations. The UN Ethics Office has released annual activities reports since its establishment in 2006. While discouraging, these data are nonetheless available, and they are crucial to designing strategies that will improve policy implementation. According to the UN Ethics Office's Annual Activities Reports from 2006–2012, 343 protection-against-retaliation inquiries had been received since the office's launch in 2006. The Office completed a preliminary review in 87 of these cases and found a *prima facie* case of retaliation in only nine. After further review, the Ethics Office found in favor of only one whistleblower.[25] Thus, the statistics show that 99 per cent of UN personnel who have sought protection under the whistleblower protection policy were not shielded from retaliation. While these data do not reveal the dynamics that produced such skewed results for complainants, they do clearly demonstrate that the whistleblower protection system at the United Nations is in need of reform. They also provide quantifiable annual benchmarks, so that progress made on the implementation of the whistleblower policy can be easily tracked. For example, by reviewing all of the reports, one can see that in 2011, under a new director, the record of the Ethics Office in protecting whistleblowers improved, as there were three *prima facie* findings issued by the office that year and one case that was ultimately substantiated (versus five *prima facie* cases total from 2006–2010, with apparently no ultimate substantiation of retaliation allegations).

Thus, the lack of public annual reports that document the implementation of the whistleblower protection policies at the MDBs is a crucial deficit from an operational perspective. Any office tasked with protecting whistleblowers must collect such information in order to produce a credible governance audit. Data collection and publication of this nature would be a simple, quantitative, objective exercise. In the absence of annual benchmarks, it is not clear that any change, whether positive or negative, can be accurately assessed and reported during the review period established by the 2012 Consolidated Appropriations Act. Without this information, the US government cannot accurately and objectively determine whether the banks are implementing their whistleblower policies, as required by US law. One could in fact argue that continuing disbursements to the MDBs are unlawful. The data released to date by the Treasury Department strongly suggest that the banks are not making substantial progress toward implementation. Very few cases are vindicated and in some of the MDBs (such as the IDB) few cases are brought forward. A researcher would therefore suspect that: (a) either little corruption exists in IDB projects (a claim that management itself is unlikely to support); or (b) the word is out among the staff that the policy is not an effective protection. That is why it is crucial that staff perceptions and the other measures outlined above be incorporated into the Treasury Department's assessment and into any subsequent research conducted in this area.

PITFALLS IN THE ENFORCEMENT OF IGO WHISTLEBLOWER RIGHTS

Unfortunately, at many IGOs whistleblower rights are largely symbolic. Employees risk retaliation believing they have genuine protection, when in fact there are no real protections in place for them. Those assessing, investigating and responding to a complaint are frequently compromised by institutional conflicts of interest[26] and cannot issue impartial decisions without endangering their own careers. Investigative offices and the departments to which whistleblowers make disclosures usually report to the executive heads of international organizations, who are, formally, also the defendants in complaints of institutional retaliation.

Channels for Reporting Misconduct

IGOs tend to have numerous avenues through which an employee can make a protected disclosure. For example, at the United Nations, disclosures are protected if they are made by UN civilian personnel to the Office of Internal Oversight Services (OIOS), which operates a hotline for reporting waste, fraud, mismanagement and other misconduct. Disclosures are also protected if they are made to the Assistant Secretary-General for Human Resources, the head of department or office concerned or the focal point appointed to receive reports of sexual exploitation and abuse.[27] At the United Nations and most of the MDBs, external reports that meet specific criteria are also protected.

Although potential whistleblowers at the United Nations have numerous channels through which to make a disclosure, recent research by GAP has found that employees in the peacekeeping missions are often reluctant to use those channels. In 2012, GAP spoke with whistleblowers from eight different UN peacekeeping missions. Interviewers found that although UN employees in the field were generally aware of available channels for reporting misconduct, virtually all respondents believed that UN employees are afraid to speak up when they have information about potential misconduct in a peacekeeping mission.

Respondents gave several reasons why UN employees may be afraid to report misconduct in the field. Several respondents raised concerns about the inability of local focal points to protect the whistleblower's identity. Some staff members said that they believed that the report would go nowhere and nothing would be done to correct the corruption. GAP heard repeatedly that those reporting misconduct in the field are likely to become the targets of retaliation. Also, the UN whistleblower protection policy does not formally protect victims, peacekeepers or UN police officers, even though they are on the front-lines and are therefore more likely to witness sexual exploitation, abuse and other crimes or misconduct committed in the peacekeeping missions (Edwards and Walden 2012: 29–34). GAP's report made numerous suggestions for addressing these shortcomings in the United Nations' whistleblower protection policy and procedures.

Investigative Bodies

Many people interviewed for GAP's 'Tipping the Scales' study also raised concerns about the bodies that would investigate their disclosures. Respondents reported that UN investigative bodies lacked independence, investigated cases inadequately, dropped cases without providing an explanation, delayed investigations, and failed to investigate certain cases, including ones involving abuse of authority by senior officials. With respect to the peacekeeping missions, respondents in the study raised additional concerns about the number of distinct investigative bodies that exist within the missions and the lack of clarity regarding the jurisdiction of each (Edwards and Walden 2012: 25–6).

Whistleblowers at other IGOs have also raised concerns about the failure of their respective organization to effectively investigate their disclosures. This happened, for example, at the World Bank in 2007. In March of that year, a whistleblower submitted a complaint to the Bank's investigative body, the Department of Institutional Integrity (INT), requesting an investigation into allegations of corruption in the World Bank-funded Municipal Development Project in Yerevan, Armenia. The whistleblower produced evidence showing that the General Director of the Yerevan Water and Sewerage Company (YWSC) in the capital and the international representative of the Italian company contracted to manage and modernize the YWSC were the same person. As a result of this conflict of interest, project objectives were changed without authorization, substandard materials were used, performance standards were lowered, and works to be completed were never undertaken, among other things. Five months later, INT informed the whistleblower that the case was ranked 'medium priority'. A review of INT procedures conducted by an independent panel chaired by Paul Volcker (2007: 16) subsequently revealed that: 'INT periodically reviews the "medium" priority cases in the event that additional evidence develops to warrant a higher ranking, but normally these cases are not otherwise investigated'.

Therefore, in effect, a claim of corruption supported by compelling evidence, involving substantial amounts of financing, compromising a vital service to a country capital, and implicating a highly placed World Bank staff member, was unlikely to be investigated. More importantly perhaps, INT appeared to be in a legal position that allowed the department to block any investigation proposed by the national authorities affected. In the absence of a credible, timely investigation by the World Bank, GAP was compelled to conduct its own investigation and to release a report detailing the findings (see GAP 2008a).

Indeed, shortcomings in IGO investigative bodies, which often examine both the whistleblower's substantive disclosures and his or her retaliation complaints, are well documented, both in studies funded by these institutions (see, for example, UNJIU 2006; Girodo 2007; Grimstad 2007; Wynes and Zahran 2011) as well as in administrative tribunal judgments and independent reports. For example, in 2006 and 2007, GAP received a series of disclosures from World Bank whistleblowers about widespread abuses at INT. Based on these disclosures, GAP subsequently released a study that documented multiple short- and long-term problems, including a conflict of interest for the department director; routine breaches of confidentiality during ongoing investigations between 2005 and 2007; the department's failure to comply with an authorized audit; the suppression of an investigative report for political reasons; and a failure to investigate serious allegations of fraud raised by a whistleblower. This report was released one week prior to a World Bank panel's own review.[28] The panel's report also raised a series of red flags about INT, but was less critical than GAP's study. Subsequent retaliation cases heard at the World Bank Administrative Tribunal revealed the manner in which the internal panel's report was tainted by a lack of confidentiality for the witnesses interviewed and widespread retaliation against these witnesses, which explains the discrepancies between the two studies (WBAT 2009: para. 45). Taken together, these reports and the related WBAT decisions showed that separation between the president's office and INT is permeable and can be penetrated when convenient.

GAP has also observed that IGO investigations often focus on the whistleblower, rather than on the substantive disclosures or concerns about retaliation that he or she raises. For example, in speaking with UN civilian personnel in the peacekeeping missions, GAP found that:

> A serious concern, raised by both staff association representatives and whistleblowers, was the tendency of the organization to investigate the whistleblower rather than the person against whom allegations of wrongdoing have been made. This punitive practice is certainly not confined to the UN, but it is serious indeed. The chilling effect of investigating the whistleblower rather than his/her disclosure may eliminate all willingness to report misconduct for years. As one whistleblower from a peacekeeping mission stated, 'the trend seems to be that if you make a complaint [in this mission] they find you guilty no matter what'. A staff representative thought that this was particularly the case when the wrongdoer was at a higher-level than the person who reported misconduct. Yet another staff representative reported that s/he had seen cases of 'ping-pong' retaliation in a peacekeeping mission, in which someone reported something in good faith, but the report was not substantiated and the person whom they complained about tried to get the whistleblower investigated in retaliation for the report. (Edwards and Walden 2012: 34)

Whistleblower James Wasserstrom's case demonstrates the lengths to which retaliators at an IGO will go to discredit a whistleblower. After Wasserstrom reported corruption concerns involving the UN Mission in Kosovo (UNMIK) to senior officials, he was subjected to criminal and administrative investigations based on trumped up charges. UNMIK Border Police arrested Wasserstrom at the Kosovo border and UNMIK Financial Crimes police conducted an illegal and warrantless search of his home and car and unlawfully seized his property. Wasserstrom's post was abolished, his office was closed, 'Wanted' style posters bearing his photograph were placed at the gates of all UNMIK premises, and crime scene tape was placed across his office door. UNMIK also leaked defamatory information about the investigations to local and international media, in an attempt to damage Wasserstrom's reputation. The criminal investigation ended quickly with no charges, but the administrative investigation dragged on for almost a year before finally clearing Wasserstrom of any wrongdoing.

Such retaliatory investigations are not unique to UN peacekeeping whistleblowers. Indeed, it is truly remarkable to see the lengths to which specific UN agencies will go in order to retaliate against a whistleblower who has made a particularly embarrassing disclosure. For example, Artjon Shkurtaj, a United Nations Development Programme (UNDP) whistleblower, was subjected to a retaliatory investigation that tarnished his reputation after he raised concerns about certain financial and administrative aspects of UNDP's operations in the Democratic People's Republic of Korea (DPRK). The issues that Shkurtaj raised related to the use of hard currency, local staff hiring and project monitoring were ultimately substantiated. In the meantime, Shkurtaj's appointment was rescinded and the UN Department of Safety and Security was directed to include his photo in an array of pictures used to bar 'threatening' individuals from UN grounds and facilities. Shkurtaj requested protection against retaliation from the UN Ethics Office, which opined that he was a whistleblower. In response, then UNDP Administrator Kemal Dervis declared that the UN Ethics Office had no jurisdiction over whistleblower complaints involving its staff members and blocked the Ethics Office from concluding its review. UNDP then created its own whistleblower protection policy and Ethics Office, but decided that the procedures established in that policy would not apply in Shkurtaj's case.[29]

In addition, IGOs frequently fail to grant whistleblowers due process rights during an investigation[30] and tend to withhold the results of investigations, even when the information contained in those reports could influence the outcome of the whistleblower's case. Wasserstrom, for example, ultimately filed a claim with the United Nations Dispute Tribunal[31] and, in doing so, requested a copy of the OIOS report that investigated his retaliation claims. Although the judge ordered the UN Secretary-General to provide Wasserstrom with a copy of this report, the Secretary-General repeatedly ignored orders to produce it. Eventually, the presiding judge herself had to turn the document over to Wasserstrom after the Secretary-General failed to do so. To this day, the United Nations has yet to release OIOS' separate investigative report into internal corruption in UMIK, which Wasserstrom risked his career to help expose.

Channels for Reporting Retaliation

When an IGO whistleblower wants to request protection from retaliation, he or she usually approaches a designated person, assigned to review such complaints. The UN Secretariat, Funds Programs and Specialized Agencies, the World Bank and the IDB have Ethics Offices that receive such complaints, whereas retaliation complaints at the ADB and the AFDB are submitted directly to investigative bodies. Where Ethics Offices exist, anecdotal evidence suggests that they lack sufficient institutional independence to act impartially. To ensure objectivity, a credible ethics officer must be recruited externally by an objective and representative committee. Candidates must have legal training in the field, and occupy a secure position that allows the incumbent to protect the confidentiality of complainants while insulating the officer from harassment or dismissal. Ethics Offices must be adequately staffed with similarly secure and trained officers. Above all, ethics personnel must be shielded from internal pressure and retaliation themselves.

Many of the IGO Ethics Offices fail to meet these standards. According to a report by the UN Joint Inspection Unit, an independent oversight body mandated to conduct system-wide evaluations and investigations:

> The Inspectors found there was a strongly held perception throughout the United Nations System of a pervasive culture of secrecy in the decision-making processes of the organizations and little or no accountability. Against this background, there was little staff buy-in to the ethics function, which was viewed merely as a management device that did nothing to address the underlying problems. (Wynes and Zahran 2010: 11)

Staff representatives throughout the system expressed 'deep mistrust concerning the recruitment and selection of the heads of ethics offices' (Wynes and Zahran 2010: 9). JIU also found that, with the exception of the UN Secretariat and UNESCO, all of the Funds and Programs had hired internal candidates to direct their Ethics Office, many of whom lacked a professional background in ethics. According to the JIU report, some of the larger Specialized Agencies, such as the International Labour Organization (ILO), showed 'a lack of commitment to the ethics function' and 'conflicts of interest, both real and perceived' in their Ethics Offices (Wynes and Zahran 2010: 8).

Even IGO Ethics Offices that have a professional, qualified director may lack a commitment to protecting whistleblowers. For example, the UN Secretariat Ethics Office, which has historically been headed by a qualified, external candidate, has failed to protect 99 per cent of UN personnel who have filed protection-against-retaliation inquiries, including whistleblower James Wasserstrom. In 2007, Wasserstrom approached the Ethics Office to request protection from retaliation. The Office found that there was a *prima facie* case of retaliation, meaning that the case passed its initial burden of proof hurdle and proceeded to the next stage. But after an investigation by OIOS, the Ethics Office decided that Wasserstrom was not retaliated against and it failed to provide him with relief. Wasserstrom appealed this decision to the UN Dispute Tribunal, which issued a scathing review of the Ethics Office and OIOS. The judge wrote that the Ethics Office 'clearly violated the Applicant's right to a fair and competent consideration of the facts' and that 'as an institution charged with the responsibility of uncovering acts of retaliation the effectiveness of the Ethics Office leaves much to be desired'. The judge concluded that it was:

> difficult to envisage a worse case of insensitive, highhanded and arbitrary treatment in breach of the fundamental principles of the Universal Declaration of Human Rights, including arts. 1, 3, 6, 7, 8 and 9. The failures of the Ethics Office to recognize such gross violations calls seriously into question its suitability and effectiveness as a body charged with the duty … to assist the Secretary-General in ensuring that all staff members observe and perform their functions consistent with the highest standards of integrity required by the Charter of the United Nations. (UNDT 2013: 17)

But despite this finding, the judge awarded Wasserstrom only US$65,000, which was only 2 per cent of his claimed losses and damages. This relief was far from comprehensive, given that Wasserstrom incurred significant losses in wages, benefits and pension, and was subjected to mental distress, defamation, damage to his professional reputation and violations of his due process rights, in retaliation for his whistleblowing. In May 2013, Wasserstrom appealed the decision to the United Nations Appeals Tribunal.

Grievance Mechanisms

If a whistleblower at an IGO is not satisfied with the decision of the Ethics Office regarding a retaliation claim, he or she can usually appeal the decision through the organization's internal grievance mechanisms, as Wasserstrom did. Typically, the first step in the internal grievance process is to challenge a specific administrative decision before a committee of peers. However, most staff members on such panels lack expertise and training in personnel matters and in legal and judicial disputes. All staff members have an institutional conflict of interest when serving on these panels. According to a US GAO study, for example, World Bank employees expressed concern that 'panel members may not be entirely immune from worry about how their decisions on controversial grievances will be regarded by senior Bank management' (GAO 1999: 8). Similarly, in his study about the World Bank's Conflict Resolution System, Graham Scott (2006: 39) wrote that it 'is not easy to see how the President [of the Bank] can practically give a committee of staff the right to overrule decisions of his and of those to whom he has delegated powers'. An independent panel of experts (the Redesign Panel) that reviewed the United Nation's former justice system noted the difficulties experienced by volunteer staff members when confronting the responsibility for evaluating cases. Specifically, the Redesign Panel (2006: 15) wrote: '[W]ith the increase in fixed-term contracts relative to permanent contracts, there is a growing concern on the part of staff about the independence of both bodies'.

Not only do such peer review mechanisms lack independence, they also tend to deny applicants basic rights such as the right to an attorney, an oral hearing and to call or cross-examine witnesses, and impose strict confidentiality requirements (see, for example, Walden *et al.* 2011). Moreover, peer review decisions are often recommendations only and can be rejected out of hand by management.

In response to such shortcomings, the UN Redesign Panel recommended that the United Nations create a new two-tiered justice system that would replace the peer review system with a 'decentralized first-instance adjudicatory body that issues binding decisions that either party can appeal' to an Appeals Tribunal (Redesign Panel 2006: 6). In both the first instance and in an appeal, judicial bodies would be staffed by professional judges, appointed by the General Assembly, with the power to make binding decisions (Redesign Panel 2006: 17). Many of the Panel's recommendations were approved by the UN General Assembly and a new, formalized system of justice, based on a Dispute Tribunal and an Appeals Tribunal, was established on 1 July 2009. But peer review systems remain in place at some of the MDBs and UN agencies.

The next and final avenue for redress after a peer review process (or a hearing before an internal tribunal like the UN Dispute Tribunal) is an administrative tribunal. As previously mentioned, serious legal concerns have been raised about the independence of such tribunals. According to Matthew Parish (2010: 7), intergovernmental organizations have 'no impartial adjudicative body to apply or enforce' laws. He notes that, when confronted with a staff member's grievance:

> The customary response by international organizations is that domestic courts are inappropriate venues because the national law of the place where the employee is employed is inapplicable; the only applicable law is the 'international law of the civil service'. This branch of law is remarkable because it does not exist. It has few sources, no statutes, refuses to draw even upon the most elementary principles of human rights law, and is created entirely by the organization against which it is sought to be enforced.

Numerous studies have identified shortcomings in these administrative tribunals. Most notably, the UN Redesign Panel (2006: 4) found that the organization's (pre-2009) justice system was 'neither professional nor independent', was 'extremely slow, under-resourced, inefficient and, thus, ultimately ineffective' and failed 'to meet many basic standards of due process established in international human rights instruments'. Although the United Nations has since abolished that system and replaced it with a new one, many of these critiques are applicable to the existing administrative tribunals in place at other IGOs. Also, some of these critiques still apply to the new UN system, especially the claim that it is under-resourced.[32]

In general, IGO tribunals are characterized by delays, a lack of independence and an 'either/or' approach that gives management the final say in cases in which a terminated whistleblower requests reinstatement. Senior management is frequently influential in the appointment of judges, and in most IGO tribunals, discovery is limited, witnesses may be vetoed (and subjected to retaliation), oral hearings are not routine, and no appeal process is provided. As noted by attorneys Thad Guyer and Nikolas Peterson, the judges on these tribunals are also clearly reluctant to:

> Make findings of fact that a staff member has been the victim of whistleblower retaliation by his or her supervisors. The tribunal judges do not like to rule that a named manager is a retaliator. Instead, these tribunals prefer to find alternative less professionally impugning legal grounds upon which to grant relief to the whistleblower. If the whistleblower can attain full relief by a finding of 'abuse of discretion' or violation of 'due process,' that will more likely be the basis of relief adopted by the tribunal. (Guyer and Peterson 2013: 21)

Ultimately, IGOs often lack the necessary capacity, impartiality or willingness to provide an effective system for adjudicating whistleblowers' retaliation claims. As the World Bank's Independent Advisory Board (IAB), which makes recommendations to the Bank regarding governance and anti-corruption issues, wrote in its 2012 Annual Report:

> It is not possible for the Bank to run a judicial system. It does not have the legal basis to do so, or the sovereign power to enforce it. Its investigative arm, INT, has no coercive power to gather evidence in a way which would be required for a fully judicial system. The World Bank is not a law enforcement agency, it is not a judicial body, nor is it a sovereign state. It is a lending and development institution. (IAB: 2013: 8)

Although the IAB was referring to issues with the Bank's sanctions regime, rather than to its internal justice system for employment grievances *per se*, one could argue that these concerns are equally applicable to the latter.

ISSUES THAT REQUIRE FURTHER RESEARCH

There is an urgent need for quantitative data about the implementation of the whistleblower protections at the MDBs, as described above.[33] In addition to this crucial research, there are several other areas that researchers interested in whistleblower protections at IGOs may want to explore.

(1) Why do initial retaliation complaints tend to originate in the office responsible for oversight?

In 2009, the Bank's Independent Evaluation Group (IEG) released a Review of International Development Association (IDA) Internal Controls that found weaknesses in the Bank's ability to address fraud and corruption risks. It also found that staff members in INT reported fear of reprisal more than the staff of any other unit. Evidence strongly suggests that this fear of reprisal by investigators transcends IGOs. Indeed, a pattern has been observed showing that the offices responsible for evaluating and investigating whistleblower disclosures, as well as corruption and fraud, often produce the first whistleblowers after a whistleblower protection policy is adopted. This pattern has been observed at the Inter-American Development Bank, the United Nations Secretariat and the UNHCR. Experience indicates that as the whistleblower protection measures established at these institutions become better known and staff members come forward with disclosures, institutional resistance to anti-corruption reforms comes to bear on these departments first, resulting in retaliation, though more research is needed in this area.[34]

(2) The role of Staff Associations

Staff Associations at the IGOs have a key role to play in protecting whistleblowers. In GAP's experience, most IGO Staff Association representatives are extremely supportive of whistleblowers and advocate for stronger whistleblower protections at their respective organizations.[35] Nevertheless, in practice Staff Associations lack the mechanisms and authority necessary to assist a whistleblower effectively. At most IGOs, Staff Associations do not have standing to bring claims before the internal justice system and cannot file a class action on behalf of a group of staff members.

The UN Redesign Panel recommended that Staff Associations be granted the right to file cases before the UN internal tribunal 'to enforce the Staff Rules and Regulations and related administrative instructions or on behalf of a particular class of its members affected by a particular administrative decision'. The experts concluded that 'staff members are sometimes reluctant to enter the formal justice system for fear of reprisals', and that 'it is considered necessary to give staff associations an independent right to bring action to enforce the Staff Rules and Regulations. This is consistent with the jurisprudence of ILOAT [ILO Administrative Tribunal] and will help promote accountability. The right of a staff association to bring a class or representative action will promote efficiency in the judicial process' (Redesign Panel 2006: 18). Unfortunately, this recommendation was not adopted by the United Nations when it launched its new justice system in 2009.

Staff Associations could therefore greatly benefit from research regarding the impact of their standing before internal administrative tribunals. Such research could focus on the rights of unions to file class actions, both under national and international law.

(3) Administrative tribunal decisions and immunities require judicial review

According to Edward Flaherty (2007: 3), there is a need for more data and judicial review of the decisions taken by IGO administrative tribunals:

> Much of the commentary has taken a theoretical approach, discussing possible merits and disadvantages of the internal legal protection systems, and potential cases where problems could arise. Part of the reason for this approach is the difficulty, particularly on the part of staff members and their counsel, in obtaining detailed information regarding the functioning of the tribunals and cases they adjudicate. In fact, one could reasonably describe the nature of these legal protection systems as being in many ways secretive. There is extremely limited judicial review of the internal mechanisms, and even more troubling, more limited access [*sic*] national or international courts which can be availed by litigants to address their deficiencies.

Several scholars have predicted that the immunities of IGOs will be increasingly challenged in national courts in the years to come. According to former WBAT Executive Secretary Nassib Ziadé (2007, cited in Zack 2010a: 55), 'the involvement of national courts is now a real and even more pressing challenge to the immunity of organizations and underscores the risks that those organizations take if they neglect the independence of their tribunals'. Similarly, August Reinisch and Ulf Andreas Weber (2004: 109, 110) identified a 'recent judicial trend emphasizing the absolute character of the fundamental rights guarantee of access to the courts which overrides potential immunity defences' and stated that 'taking these fundamental rights deficits seriously may lead national courts, as well as the ECtHR [European Court of Human Rights], to reassess their readiness to accept an unqualified immunity from suit of defendant international organizations'.

Additional research in this area could help to resolve the issue of whistleblower rights and legal immunities at the IGOs. The international community lacks a comprehensive meta-analysis of the application and justification of sovereign immunities in labor disputes across national legal systems. A literature review of relevant cases and arguments would address this deficit in the research.

(4) Alternatives to the existing tribunals

Studies commissioned by the IGOs tend, with the exception of the UN Redesign Panel, to focus on reforms to the existing administrative tribunals, rather than exploring the possibility of abolishing them. In contrast, Arnold Zack (2010a: 56) has suggested that IGOs consider 'procedures for enhanced cooperation and coordination, and perhaps consolidation'.

When CDR Associates reviewed the World Bank's Conflict Resolution System it too recommended that the Bank:

> Explore the creation of a tribunal for use by multiple international organizations. A very 'out of the box' idea suggested by a few interviewees was for the Bank to join with other international institutions that either have tribunals or are establishing them, to create an international tribunal that would serve the needs of multiple institutions. Existing panels could be merged to provide a broader panel of judges, an integrated international panel could contribute to a body of international employment law that could be applied across organizations and significant costs savings could be realized by the involved institutions. There would, however, no doubt be significant hurdles involved in either merging or dissolving existing tribunals. (Moore and Wildau 2005: 38)[36]

Thus, research that examines the costs, benefits, drawbacks and feasibility of such consolidation, as well as potential models for its implementation, is imperative.

There is also a need for research that examines the benefits and potential pitfalls of providing an external arbitration option for IGO whistleblower claims. Although US law requires the US executive directors to the MDBs to advocate for external arbitration based on consensus selection and shared costs, the MDBs have yet to implement it and their lawyers routinely oppose the idea. Unfortunately, some MDB Staff Associations have also been hesitant to support even an arbitration option, for reasons not entirely understood. But in GAP's experience, whistleblowers themselves have been overwhelmingly supportive of the idea, especially when they perceive the process as being impartial enough to result in a just outcome. But at this juncture, it is unlikely that any IGO will provide this option unless scholars present impartial, compelling research that demonstrates the benefits of doing so.

CONCLUSION

Focused research in a number of specific areas related to whistleblowing at the IGOs is a significant need. First, there is a lack of research on the impact that multiculturalism has played on whistleblowing in these institutions. While this deficit is not, perhaps, the most crucial one for advancing whistleblowers' rights, it could provide fundamental insights into the nature of whistleblowing at the IGOs. Secondly, while numerous descriptive studies exist that set out the content of IGO whistleblower protection policies, little is known about the actual implementation and effectiveness of these provisions. Although the US Department of the Treasury recently issued data about the MDBs' implementation records, additional information is still needed to adequately evaluate the effectiveness of each policy. Without additional information, such as data about whether the relief received by the whistleblowers (including interim relief) was comprehensive and whether individuals have been held accountable for reprisal against whistleblowers, it is difficult to assess the effectiveness of whistleblowing as an anti-corruption measure at IGOs.

In order to address the research deficits, it is now essential that IGOs themselves annually release data relevant to the implementation of the policies they adopted. These data could be used to compare the implementation of policies across institutions and to design potential reform strategies for adoption at IGOs with poor enforcement records. The grievance procedures and the rules of engagement before administrative tribunals, including the standing of Staff Associations to file claims on behalf of a group of members, should also be examined. Finally, research that explores the benefits and drawbacks of various alternatives to IGO administrative tribunals, including external arbitration, the piercing of IGO's immunities, and the consolidation of existing tribunals and/or investigative bodies into a single over-arching body, could potentially provide a new model of justice at the IGOs. Such models have the potential not only to better protect whistleblowers' rights, but also the labor rights of all staff members.

NOTES

1. In the category of IGOs we include those studied by the Government Accountability Project (GAP): the United Nations (Secretariat), the World Bank, the Inter-American Development Bank, the Asian Development Bank and the African Development Bank. Some of the issues discussed in this chapter are common to all IGOs, and others are particular to the multilateral development banks (MDBs). Issues confined to the MDBs are identified as such.
2. In the United States, where the United Nations, the World Bank, the International Monetary Fund and the Inter-American Development Bank are headquartered, legal immunities in labor disputes are robust. The relevant legal decision is *Mendaro v World Bank*, 717 F.2d 610 (1983). In other jurisdictions, however, some experts report that the immunities of the IGOs are eroding. For more information on this topic see Reinisch (2008).
3. The immunities of the IGOs shield them from the reach of 'Freedom of Information' and 'Right to Know' legislation in member states, in most cases.
4. Although most IGOs are prohibited by charter from interfering in the political affairs of member states, in practice the MDBs frequently attach overtly political conditions to loans and grants. Borrowing countries risk losing access to approved funds if they fail to meet these political requirements.
5. 'At the beginning of the Wolfensohn Presidency, corruption was rarely mentioned in international development circles. In 1996 Wolfensohn gave a groundbreaking "cancer of corruption" speech to the World Bank/IMF annual meeting, citing corruption as a major burden for the poor in developing countries. Corruption is now widely recognized as a major impediment to development that must be tackled aggressively.' See 'James D. Wolfensohn and the World Bank', available at http://go.worldbank.org/G6QRI22RQ0.
6. See the report of the Independent Evaluation Group on the Governance and Anti-Corruption Program at the World Bank. 'World Bank Country-Level Engagement on Governance and Anticorruption: An Evaluation of the 2007 Strategy and Implementation Plan', available at http://ieg.worldbankgroup.org/content/dam/ieg/gac/gac_eval.pdf.
7. Examples of studies commissioned by the World Bank include: Grievances Process Review Committee, *Reforming the World Bank Group's Internal Conflict Resolution System* (1998); CDR Associates, *Assessment of the Functioning and Performance of World Bank Mechanisms, Offices and Services for the Resolution of Personnel Complaints and Grievances* (2005); Robert Vaughn, *Report on the World Bank's Whistleblower Procedures* (2005); and Graham Scott, *World Bank Group Conflict Resolution System: Some Issues and Recommendations* (2006). The Inter-American Development Bank commissioned Global Compliance, *Review of the Ethics, Conduct and Grievance Systems of the Inter-American Development Bank* (2011). The 2006 Report of the Redesign Panel of the United Nations System of Administration of Justice (A/61/205), which found that the United Nations' internal justice system failed to meet human rights standards and should be abolished and replaced from scratch, is generally seen as impartial. The UN Joint Inspection Unit has also conducted a study on whistleblower protections throughout the United Nations entitled *Ethics in the United Nations System* (JIU/REP/2010/3, 2010).

8. The World Bank, in particular, has commissioned numerous studies that have not been released to the public. For example, it failed to release a *Report on the World Bank's Whistleblower Procedures* prepared by Robert Vaughn (2005). Nine months after the World Bank received the Vaughn report, it was still refusing to publicly release it, so GAP posted a leaked copy of it on our website.
9. Updated copies and evaluations of these policies are available on GAP's website (www.whistleblower.org).
10. See GAP (2008a); GAP (2008b); Edwards and Walden (2009); *Financial Times* (2009); GAP (2009); GAP (2010).
11. 'Total institution' is a term coined by sociologist Erving Goffman that defines a place of work (and often of residence) where similarly situated people lead a life isolated from the outside world. We refer to the IGOs as total institutions because they tend to have their own cultures, expectations and privileges that set their staff members apart from the surrounding environment.
12. Former World Bank employee Steve Berkman, for example, has described the Bank as an environment 'where obfuscation and hypocrisy seem to be the primary modus operandi' (2008: 15) and where 'truth, honesty, accountability and professional integrity are gradually filtered out as information rises up through the bureaucracy' (2008: 226).
13. GAP has represented whistleblowers from Somalia, Vietnam, Uruguay, El Salvador, Sri Lanka, Ethiopia, the United States, Cameroon, South Korea, Albania, United Kingdom, Paraguay, Pakistan, Canada, Belgium, Argentina, India, Kosovo, Spain and Denmark. Their cases have been filed at the World Bank, IDB, ADB, AFDB, UNDSS, UNDP, WFP, UNHCR, UNHABITAT and IMF.
14. There is a lack of research on the impact that multiculturalism has played on whistleblowing in these institutions. However, some research has been done on broader diversity issues. For example, GAP's 2009 report on *Racial Discrimination at the World Bank* found evidence of racial discrimination against black professional grade employees at the World Bank, especially black Americans (Edwards and Walden 2009). GAP's 2009 *IDB, Poverty and Racial Discrimination* study found that there was a lack of IDB projects and loans designed to address the needs of Afro-Latinos and Indigenous peoples and that these populations were grossly under-represented in the Bank's staff.
15. Global Compliance includes these 'benchmarks' in its study, but does not provide a source for them nor explain the methodology used to determine them.
16. In response to this report, the IDB is currently considering changes to its grievance mechanisms.
17. There are a few exceptions to this. For example, the World Bank's immunities were successfully challenged in Bangladesh by a former Bank employee (Ismet Zerin Khan). In this case, the judge ruled that the 'provision of immunity is in contradiction with the Constitution of Bangladesh'.
18. See section entitled 'Pitfalls in the Enforcement of IGO Whistleblower Rights'.
19. The United Nations Secretariat whistleblower policy (ST/SGB/2005/21, s. 4) is particularly strong in this regard. However, the United Nations has not always enforced this aspect of its policy. For example, in the case of *Artjon Skurtaj v United Nations Development Programme*, despite clear evidence of the misapplication of the burden of proof in favor of the institution, the plaintiff (Skurtaj) did not receive relief on this specific issue through the judicial mechanism. See www.whistleblower.org/blog/31-2010/720-un-tribunal-awards-compensation-to-long-suffering-undp-whistle blower for more information. See also *Wasserstrom v Secretary-General of the United Nations,* Judgment UNDT/2012/92, available at www.whistleblower.org/blog/42-2012/2102-un-tribunal-issues-important-decision-for-whistleblowers.

20. See Case 448, available at http://lnweb90.worldbank.org/crn/wbt/wbtwebsite.nsf/%28resultsweb%29/747BFCD689EE1874852578B200722E5C. For more information about this case, see Behar (2012).
21. The ADB's GCI was authorized in April 2011 through Public Law 112–10. Section 2126(c)(3) of that law contains similar (though not identical) requirements regarding the Treasury's reporting obligation about the implementation of the ADB's whistleblower protection policy.
22. According to GAP's best practices list, which was developed by reviewing whistleblower policies around the world, six months is the minimum functional statute of limitations for whistleblowers to become aware of or act on their rights. One year statutes of limitations are consistent with common law rights and are preferable. The AFDB, IDB and World Bank do not meet the minimum six month standard. The World Bank has a 120 day statute of limitations, the AFDB has a 90 day statute and the IDB has a three business day statute for reporting misconduct and a 90 day statute for filing a formal retaliation grievance with the Bank's internal justice system.
23. See e.g., *Ada Piazze v Inter-American Development Bank*, Inter-American Development Bank Administrative Tribunal, Judgment Case no. 73 (2011), available at www.whistleblower.org/storage/documents/Judgment_73.pdf. Ms Piazze, who was recognized as a whistleblower, was awarded compensation, but was not reinstated. In a Partial Dissent, Judge Guilherme Caputo Bastos wrote: 'The whistleblower protection dictated in the aforementioned rule will be rendered useless for future cases. Staff members will think twice before reporting wrongdoing because despite the fact that the Ethics Committee ultimately found that the person accused of misconduct was guilty as charged, Management did nothing to protect the whistleblower' (at 24–5).
24. This sentence is based on GAP's personal knowledge of each case, and not on the Treasury Report itself, as that report contained somewhat misleading information about some of these cases. For more information, see www.whistleblower.org/blog/42-2012/2446-new-reports-contain-statistics-regarding-whistleblower-cases-at-the-multilateral-development-banks.
25. For more information on this statistic, see www.whistleblower.org/blog/42-2012/2158-gap-responds-to-critique-of-united-nations-ethics-office-statistic and the 2012 UN Ethics Office Activities Report (A/67/306) 14–15, available at www.un.org/Docs/journal/asp/ws.asp?m=A/67/306.
26. For example, at the United Nations Development Programme (UNDP), those who process whistleblower retaliation complaints consult with Human Resources, even though that department has a conflict of interest, as retaliation often occurs as an administrative action that is implemented by HR.
27. ST/SGB/2005/21 (2005) 2. According to the UN Ethics Office, some UN whistleblowers have requested protection from retaliation after making their disclosures to their supervisor. Unfortunately, such disclosures are not currently covered by the UN whistleblower protection policy. In contrast, some IGOs, including the World Bank, do protect disclosures made by a whistleblower to their line management.
28. GAP objected to Volcker's appointment to head the panel as an independent evaluator, as his professional connections placed him too close to former INT staff members subsequently employed by a corporate intelligence gathering firm (Diligence, LLC) that had a contractual relationship to INT.
29. In the Skurtaj case, the UNDP Administrator then appointed his own ad hoc panel to investigate. In naming this panel, however, Dervis held no consultations to ensure objectivity or competence. Moreover, even before the panel began its work, Dervis announced to the press that the panel would conclude that Shkurtaj was not a whistleblower. Although Shkurtaj was not supposed to be the subject of the

investigation, the Panel's final report attacked his character, competence, conduct and veracity. UNDP released the report publicly without informing Shkurtaj about the critical findings or giving him an opportunity to respond. The Panel's Terms of Reference required that the report's findings be transmitted to the director of the UN Ethics Office. After reviewing the report, the director recommended that UNDP compensate Shkurtaj for having violated his rights. UNDP refused to compensate Shkurtaj, forcing him to appeal to the UN's internal administrative tribunals: the lower UN Dispute Tribunal (UNDT) and the higher UN Appeals Tribunal (UNAT). Years later, both the UNDT and UNAT ruled in Shkurtaj's favor on this issue, although UNAT reduced the compensation award. The US Senate Permanent Subcommittee on Investigations and Committee on Homeland Security and Governmental Affairs subsequently found that 'by preventing access to its audits and not submitting to the jurisdiction of the UN Ethics Office, UNDP impeded reasonable oversight and undermined its whistleblower protections' (Senate Permanent Subcommittee (US) 2008: 1).

30. For example, whistleblowers are frequently denied the right to have an attorney accompany them to an interview.
31. Case No. UNDT/NY/2009/044.
32. For more information about the new justice system, see MacFarquhar (2010) and Otis and Reiter (2011).
33. See section entitled 'Donor Country Mandates and the Need for Research on Whistleblower Protection'.
34. GAP has observed and documented this pattern extensively. The most striking evidence is available through the World Bank Administrative Tribunal website, Decisions 408–423, available at http://web.worldbank.org/external/default/main?pagePK=7333373&contentMDK=22956444.
35. There are some exceptions to this, as occasionally Staff Association leaders will use their position as a stepping stone for a subsequent promotion within the organization. When this occurs, the leaders tend to be less supportive of whistleblowers and avoid confrontations with management.
36. IGOs could also consider merging their investigative units, potentially resulting in decreased costs and increased independence and accountability. This possibility was considered by the UN Joint Inspection Unit (JIU) in 2011. Specifically, JIU recommended that 'the Secretary-General, under the auspices of CEB, should set up an inter-agency task force that will develop options for establishing a single consolidated United Nations system Investigation Unit by the end of December 2013 for presentation to the legislative bodies' (Wynes and Zahran 2011: 25).

19. Whistleblower support in practice: Towards an integrated research model

*A.J. Brown, Daniel P. Meyer, Chris Wheeler and Jason Zuckerman**

INTRODUCTION

A pervasive theme of this book is how empirical research into whistleblowing has focused to date on primarily two things. First, researchers and policy makers have sought to know the patterns of whistleblowing in organizations: how much is there, who does it, when and why they do it, and what appears to happen as a result, primarily to the whistleblower themselves. As sketched in Parts II and III of the book, however, this research is now turning towards a more complete understanding not simply of whistleblowing, but of the role it plays in governance and political life, including how managers, organizations and institutions respond, and what happens in terms of other outcomes, including measures of impact and effectiveness.

Secondly, efforts to protect whistleblowers since the 1970s have been spearheaded by legal reforms aimed at removing legal barriers and bases for retaliation, incentivizing whistleblowing, compensating whistleblowers for career and life damage, and regulating for institutions to recognize and respond more effectively to whistleblowing within their governance systems. As documented by the previous chapters in this Part, however, knowledge about the effectiveness of these legal approaches has been fragmented, anecdotal and limited, rather than integrated and systematic. It has tended to involve comparative legal and institutional research, and case-based research, rather than detailed empirical evidence of how these legal and organizational systems are actually performing in practice.

This chapter takes stock of what we know about the practicalities of whistleblower protection, in two countries (the United States and Australia) with a reasonable history of both types of research, as well as the policy and law reform that underpins them. As detailed by Lewis, Devine and Harpur (Chapter 15), Faunce *et al.* (Chapter 16), and elsewhere (e.g., Dworkin and Brown 2013), whistleblowing laws in these countries have a related history. In both, there is a common policy objective: that more whistleblowers should be protected from reprisals or detrimental outcomes than currently appears to be the case. But what do we know about the results of protection efforts, at a practical level within institutions? What gaps in knowledge are there, and how could these be filled?

To answer these queries, the first section of the chapter reviews the situation for the US federal public sector; while the second section reviews the situation for the Australian public sector. We look at the basic approach to whistleblower protection in the relevant jurisdiction(s), the requirements and roles of key agencies, the degree of knowledge generated by official monitoring, and the other available research. In the third section, we analyze common and contrasting themes and issues, identifying five particular challenges which might inform the development of a more systematic, integrated approach to gauging the effectiveness of whistleblower protection, before proceeding to conclusions about possible improvements to oversight and research.

We do not examine whistleblower protection in the private sectors in these jurisdictions, not least due to much larger contrasts in regulatory environment in the two countries. There are, as yet, few meaningful statutory whistleblower protection obligations upon companies and non-government organizations in Australia, as against the United States; instead, non-government employees in Australia have the benefit of a higher level of general, overall employment protection than in the United States. Where we are aware of research on the practicalities of whistleblower protection in the private sector, we nevertheless refer to it. We also focus specifically on protection, even though this is just one of three common objectives of whistleblowing legislation, alongside encouragement and facilitation of whistleblowing, and ensuring that effective action is taken in response to disclosures. While all three are important, there is evidence that many organizations are far better at institutionalizing improved disclosure channels and investigative responses, than they are at institutionalizing whistleblower support and protection. Further, as the institutional or 'structural' model of whistleblowing regulation develops, and the importance of whistleblowers as information sources becomes increasingly recognized in management and regulation, organizational and regulatory responsibilities for whistleblower protection increase. As described by Fasterling (Chapter 14), the 'deputization' of insiders as part of organizational monitoring and disclosure systems, whether as a 'complementary' or a 'residual' measure to other mechanisms for detecting wrongdoing, carries with it the need to not only harmonize these systems, but also to ensure that organizations and regulators are effectively fulfilling their protection obligations towards the individuals so 'deputized'.

As will be seen, there are also two main ways of understanding whistleblower 'protection'. In both countries, protection has been dominated by an 'anti-retaliation' approach, based on creating and enforcing criminal, civil and employment sanctions against reprisals or other detrimental action. However, unless these sanctions and remedies are so effective and readily available that they have a pervasive deterrent effect on all organizations, they remain largely reactive: it is only the whistleblower who has suffered detriment, and is able to successfully prosecute or sue for relief, or have their complaint taken up by those in authority, who is 'protected' (or more accurately, compensated in some way for damage suffered). By contrast, requirements for agencies to respond more effectively to disclosures from the outset, especially the bulk made internally, carry assumptions that management should prevent or minimize such damage in the first place – in other words, also provide protection in a more proactive or preventative sense. The same is true of oversight or regulatory agencies.

These 'anti-retaliation' and 'institutional' approaches are not separate. Whether or not agencies seriously embrace the need for a proactive whistleblower protection approach depends in part on the risks and costs of enforcement action should they fail in those responsibilities, and remedial action is taken by or on behalf of a whistleblower. As concluded by Lewis, Devine and Harpur (Chapter 15), civil and employment remedies thus 'remain the backbone of achieving more effective whistleblowing regimes'. However, the ultimate test of success in whistleblower protection is not how many applications for compensation succeed – which, after all, is an indicator of levels of proven reprisals, or failures in whistleblower protection, rather than success. Instead, the ultimate test is how effectively protection rights and obligations 'translate into the practices and behaviors of organizations, which really means the behavior of managers, individually and collectively, who control organizations' (Vandekerckhove *et al.*, Chapter 2).

For those who doubt that detrimental outcomes for whistleblowers can ever be prevented or significantly minimized, then a reactive understanding of 'protection' remains the solution. However, for those who hope for organizational and regulatory systems to develop in ways that properly value the role of whistleblowing, then understanding those systems and collecting other information which may indicate their relative success or failure, becomes a new and high priority.

PRACTICALITIES OF US WHISTLEBLOWER PROTECTION

Basic Approach

While aspects of Congressionally-sanctioned whistleblowing date to as early as the American Continental Congress (1778), the current legal framework for whistleblower protection in the US federal government, introduced previously by Lewis, Devine and Harpur (Chapter 15), developed in the wake of the Watergate scandal. The modern US pattern of legislation protecting whistleblowers followed from well publicized allegations of retaliation by federal government agencies against employees who had blown the whistle on wasteful defense spending, and revelations of partisan political coercion in the federal government. As a result, the Civil Service Reform Act of 1978 (CSRA) sought to ensure that '[e]mployees are … protected against arbitrary action, personal favoritism, and from partisan political coercion'.[1] To achieve those goals, Congress identified merit system principles and prohibited personnel practices designed to ensure, among other things, protection of whistleblowers.[2] The Senate report accompanying the CSRA reveals that Congress was especially concerned with protecting whistleblowers from retaliation:

> In the vast federal bureaucracy it is not difficult to conceal wrongdoing provided that no one summons the courage to disclose the truth. Whenever misdeeds take place in a federal agency, there are employees who know that it has occurred, and who are outraged by it. What is needed is a means to assure them that they will not suffer if they help uncover and correct administrative abuses. What is needed is a means to protect the Pentagon employee who discloses billions of dollars in cost overruns, the GSA employee who discloses widespread fraud, and the nuclear engineer who questions the safety of certain nuclear plants. These conscientious civil servants deserve statutory protection rather than bureaucratic harassment and intimidation.[3]

The system was further upgraded. By departmental regulation, US federal employees organized for the collection of intelligence had official language protecting intelligence oversight sources as early as 1982. Then, under the Whistleblower Protection Act of 1989 (WPA),[4] and by Executive Order, all public employees working under the President of the United States have been required to report corruption, that is, blow the whistle.[5] This mandate reinforces the implicit need to protect those complying with the President's Executive Order. And in 1994, Congress tasked federal agency heads with a clear duty to prevent prohibited personnel practices against whistleblowers, and to ensure that agency employees are informed of the rights and remedies available to them under the civil service laws.[6]

The primary strategy for meeting this need across the public sector is education of civil service managers about what constitute prohibited personnel practices in response to whistleblowing, and how to avoid these. One vehicle is the lessons provided by judicial outcomes in favor of aggrieved whistleblowers, although amendments under the Whistleblower Protection Enhancement Act (WPEA) of 2012 reflect difficulties in this process (see Chapter 15).[7] Another vehicle is the lessons provided by the outcomes of retaliation complaints dealt with by the core oversight agencies for US government whistleblower protection, the Office of Special Counsel (OSC) and Merit Systems Protection Board (MSPB), as well as by Inspectors General (IGs) operating in and alongside agencies themselves. Under the Notification and Federal Employee Anti-discrimination and Retaliation Act of 2002 (No FEAR Act) and the WPEA, there are also sector-wide requirements upon agencies to educate their employees about anti-discrimination and whistleblower protection laws.

Beyond these requirements, and guidelines for agencies regarding how to conduct whistleblower reprisal investigations, there are, at best, minimal administrative due process requirements for whistleblower protection. Outside the case law available through the decisions of the US MSPB, for example, there are no public sector or wider industry corporate governance standards that include specific advice as to how whistleblowers should be supported. Rather, agencies must learn from their own mistakes, or those of other agencies, and develop their own management systems to avoid the errors thrown up by proven cases of retaliation or mismanagement. Further, when whistleblower protection obligations are lodged in institutional structures which, by law, require independence and neutrality, there are legal limits to practices which may be seen as advocacy for an individual. These issues have a significant influence on the extent of whistleblower protection in practice.

Institutionalizing Protection: Core Agencies

The Office of Special Counsel (OSC) is the independent federal investigative and prosecutorial agency with the primary mission of safeguarding the merit system by protecting federal employees and applicants from prohibited personnel practices, especially reprisal for whistleblowing. It also provides an independent, secure channel for disclosure and resolution of wrongdoing in federal agencies.[8] The OSC investigates allegations of reprisal and is authorized to seek corrective action to make a whistleblower whole and to initiate disciplinary action against civilian government officials who commit prohibited personnel practices. Originally established as part of the MSPB under the 1978 reforms, in 1989 the OSC became an independent agency in the Executive Branch. The Special Counsel, the head of the OSC, is appointed by the President, with advice and consent from the Senate.[9] Unlike most agency heads, the Special Counsel does not serve at the pleasure of the President. By statute, the Special Counsel serves a five-year term and 'may be removed by the President only for inefficiency, neglect of duty, or malfeasance in office'. The WPA also broadened the OSC's authority and clarified that the OSC's primary role is to protect employees, especially whistleblowers, from prohibited personnel practices.

The Special Counsel has broad powers, including the authority to compel witness testimony under oath; obtain documents; bring petitions for corrective action; file a complaint or make recommendations for disciplinary action; receive, review and, where appropriate, forward disclosures to the Attorney General or an agency head; take depositions and receive evidence. The Special Counsel is also authorized to seek to delay or stay an adverse personnel action pending an OSC investigation where the OSC has reasonable grounds to believe that the action is the result of a prohibited personnel practice.[10]

The OSC conducts preliminary investigations into about 3,000 complaints per year, more than half of which allege whistleblower reprisal. Where further investigation is warranted, the complainant and agency are offered the opportunity to try to resolve the matter through mediation. Investigations of a reprisal complaint include obtaining and reviewing pertinent records and interviewing witnesses under oath. Where the OSC determines that there are reasonable grounds to believe that a prohibited personnel practice has occurred and the matter has not been resolved, the OSC sends a report to the agency head setting forth its findings and recommending corrective action.[11] In most cases, the agency agrees to implement the OSC's recommendations. If an agency declines to take corrective or disciplinary action, the OSC can file a petition for action at the MSPB and the parties then try the case on the merits before an MSPB Administrative Law Judge who can order corrective and disciplinary action.[12] The MSPB thus remains crucial to whistleblower protection, as the independent, quasi-judicial agency in the Executive branch serving as the overall guardian of federal merit systems, primarily by adjudicating these individual employee appeals (MSPB 2010).

Corrective action is the priority focus for the OSC, in line with Congress' intent that while disciplining those who commit prohibited personnel practices may help accomplish the goal, 'the protection of individuals who are the subject of prohibited personnel practices remains the paramount consideration'.[13] There are a wide range of 'make whole' remedies available designed to place the whistleblower in the position they would be in had the agency not retaliated. Such relief can include reinstatement, back pay (lost wages), medical costs, compensatory damages, and any other reasonable and foreseeable consequential charges, along with attorneys' fees.

The OSC is also authorized to seek disciplinary action against an employee who has retaliated against a whistleblower.[14] Disciplinary action is important to deter retaliation and can send a strong signal to managers or agency officials at every level that they can be held accountable for retaliating against a whistleblower.

Finally, the OSC itself serves as a secure channel for federal workers to disclose information about violations of laws, rules or regulations, gross mismanagement or waste of funds, abuse of authority, and substantial and specific dangers to the public health and safety. Upon receipt of a disclosure, if there is a substantial likelihood that the information discloses one or more of those five categories of wrongdoing,[15] the OSC refers it to the head of an agency for an investigation, and the agency must investigate the allegations and submit a written report to the OSC on the agency's findings. Absent the whistleblower's consent, the OSC does not disclose the identity of the whistleblower with limited exception.[16] The OSC reviews agency reports for statutory compliance and reasonableness, and affords the whistleblower an opportunity to review and comment, before transmitting the report to the President and the congressional committees with oversight responsibility for the agency, as well as posting the report on its website, along with the whistleblower's comments. Since the OSC's core mission is protection of the whistleblower against retaliation, its role as a disclosure channel assists in securing greater protection at the agency level, given that agencies are fully conscious that the OSC is not only interested in the response to the disclosure, but will be well placed to establish if reprisals (or further reprisals) have occurred since its referral.[17]

Enabling Functions: US Agencies and Inspectors-General

While the OSC and MSPB play core roles in whistleblower protection, their functions and actions are also aimed at influencing what occurs at the agency level, and thus depend on how much agencies and governments generally are willing and able to respond, as well as to learn from findings, recommendations and decisions in individual cases. Securing protection thus also relies on agencies themselves, and particularly their Offices of Inspector General. These were also established under statutes such the Inspector General Act (IGA) of 1978 and the National Security Act (NSA) of 1947, as amended. The IGA was part of the post-Watergate reforms of the 1970s and 1980s, as well as reaction to Defense procurement fraud scandals of the late Cold War. The NSA was amended in 2010 to provide for a presidentially appointed, Senate confirmed independent Inspector General of the Intelligence Community.[18] The IGA and NSA Inspector General provisions are broadly similar.

As amended, the IGA includes a provision permitting, but not necessarily requiring, statutory Inspectors General the ability to protect their whistleblowers.[19] This reflects the fact that, with respect to such source protection through whistleblower protection provisions, Inspectors General do not come to the activity as lead actors. Their core functions are the conduct of audits, investigation of violations of law and performance of evaluations in and over their agency or portfolio. Whistleblower or source protection is an enabling, not a core, function – one that supports completion of the core function. This is in contrast to the OSC and MSPB, for whom source protection is the *raison d'etre*. Inspectors General accordingly approach source protection as a functional task that enables a larger core mission. This places inherent restraints on their role. Whistleblowers in need of protection need to assess whether the institutional goals of an Inspector General align with her or his personal goal in protection. A Congressional staff member seeking to find protection for a source needs to assess the ability of an Inspector General to protect the Congressional source in light of the committee's relative need to protect the flow of information in its investigation. And Inspectors General need to be clear about the limits of what they provide, and the manner in which their source protection advances their mission.

Nevertheless, overall, whistleblower protection by an Inspector General can be seen as a 'force multiplier' for the Office of Special Counsel, one that is in the interest of an Office of the Inspector General mindful of its need to protect the sources of its audits, investigations, inspections and evaluations. Agency heads frequently task their Offices of Inspector General with the responsibility for investigating disclosures referred by the OSC. Supervisors and managers find themselves in no different position when facing an investigation by the OSC, or an Office of Inspector General. The criminal and administrative investigative powers of Inspectors General can be extensive, meaning that a relatively high level of agency performance can be generated by a motivated and well-disciplined investigative team working under the administrative investigative protocol available to, for instance, the Office of the Inspector

General for the US Department of Defense (CIGIE 2011). As an Inspector General's process is *inquisitorial* rather than *adjudicative*, the information needed to establish whether unfair action has been taken against a whistleblower is available without discovery, and the objections or defense of agency representative counsel. Electronic mail must be produced; hard drives may be seized; other employees may disclose to a hotline in support of a reprised-against complainant. At the Defense Department's Office of the Inspector General, administrative investigators also have access to the power of subpoena, and can draw on the expertise of other criminal investigators, auditors and analysts within the Office.

The US Department of Defense Office of the Inspector General provides an example of immense jurisdiction, as it has the power to review and make findings over the activities of all Defense Department personnel (civilian and military), no matter what level of seniority. The office is created by statute, and reports jointly to *both* the US Secretary of Defense and the US Congress. The three Military Services (US Army, US Navy and US Marine Corps, and the US Air Force) as well as the Joint Commands, defense agencies and defense components, all fall under the Inspector General's jurisdiction. This includes the intelligence personnel serving in the Defense Intelligence Agency, the National Geospatial-Intelligence Agency, the National Reconnaissance Office and the National Security Agency, jurisdiction which is shared with the Inspector General of the Intelligence Community.[20] Some of the Inspector General's jurisdiction is obligatory, as in the protection of whistleblowers serving in uniform. Under the Military Whistleblower Protection Act of 1989, as amended, the Inspector General reviews, and decides whether to investigate all allegations of whistleblower reprisal against military members of the uniformed services.[21] These complaints are docketed through the Department of Defense hotline, which assesses the initial contact and forwards actionable allegations to the appropriate investigating authority.[22] The Inspector General also has discretion to undertake whistleblower or source protection of civilian appropriated-fund employees, outside the intelligence community. Given that the US Department of Defense employs approximately 3.2 million people, including 700,000 civilians; manages territory of about 30 million acres; and has an annual financial outlay almost equal to the Kingdom of Belgium, overseeing the US Defense Department is comparable to doing the same for a good-sized nation state.

Investigation reports from Inspectors General are forwarded to a command or agency component capable of providing remedial and corrective action, as detailed in the report's 'recommendations'.[23] The same general process also applies to the discretionary investigations conducted into alleged reprisal against civilian appropriated-fund employees. Notwithstanding their powerful role, therefore, one perceived weakness of source protection by Inspectors General is their inability to issue a corrective order requiring remedial or disciplinary action. By relying on a command component (or civilian equivalent) to take action in response to the report, this system of protection creates a 'disposition' problem for Inspectors General. Having made a finding, an Inspector General may not receive cooperation from the local authority. The local authority may ignore the violation of law, rule or regulation found by the Inspector General.

This leaves the system lacking in perceived equal protection of the law, as the decision of whether to correct the mischief created by the supervisor or manager is dependent on the relative level of corruption within the department which employs the complainant. Some Military Services and defense agencies or components may have more enlightened or proactive leadership than others. Or, hypothetically, a Flag officer coming up for promotion (another 'star') may be more sensitive to corrective action in response to an Inspector General's report of investigation than one anticipating retirement, who may be more responsive than a political employee enjoying the support of the White House or a member of the Senior Executive Service unconcerned by promotion or political support. And, indeed, a letter of interest from a Chair or Ranking Member of a committee of jurisdiction within the United States Congress may be the deciding factor as to whether a whistleblower is vindicated. Despite presumptions of the equal protection of the law, the equalizing function of the United States' federal judicial branch is thus denied, in many respects, to the government's own whistleblowers. Instead, executive branch leadership has to find substitutes inside 'the Administrative State', or so-called 'fourth branch' of government.

Ultimately, therefore, the management systems of agencies are crucial not only to whether remedial or disciplinary recommendations will be heeded, but whether managers respond appropriately in the first place when disclosures arise. Under US law, a supervisor or manager properly and proficiently adhering to the Office of Personnel Management's rules for managing federal employees, or the Department of Defense's regulations regarding military members, will do well in a subsequent investigation. It is the managerial slouch that undoes his or her administrative defense, by failing to deal with issues or generate the documentation that will, incidentally, be the proof they are not a reprisor.

However, as noted earlier, there are few administrative requirements or sources of guidance for how agencies should embed whistleblower protection in these management systems. The primary requirements are ones of awareness raising. For example, the No FEAR Act imposes specific duties on agencies to educate their employees about anti-discrimination and whistleblower protection laws. An agency must (1) provide annual notice to employees, former employees and applicants for federal employment concerning the rights and remedies applicable to them; (2) at least every two years, provide training to its employees, including managers, regarding these rights and remedies; (3) submit an annual report setting forth information about the agency's efforts to improve compliance with the employment discrimination and whistleblower protection laws; and (4) post quarterly on its public website summary statistical data pertaining to EEO complaints filed with the agency.[24] In addition, the Whistleblower Protection Enhancement Act imposes a general outreach or training requirement for a Whistleblower Protection Ombudsman in offices of Inspectors General, who 'shall educate agency employees... about prohibitions on retaliation for protected disclosures; and... [educate employees] who have made or are contemplating making a protected disclosure about the rights and remedies against retaliation for protected disclosures'.[25] Many supervisors and managers recognize these training requirements as a positive workforce requirement.

Beyond this, while the Council of Inspectors General does publish generalized standards for its members, specific best practices and model procedures to guide agencies in the requirements of whistleblower support do not exist across the executive branch. In effect, each agency or agency component is on their own as to how much effort they put into either preventing detrimental outcomes, or remedying them if they occur. Executive branch department heads do have the ability to protect sources below the level of a statute, but agencies' approaches will be determined by whether they choose to have policies and procedures for supporting employees and heading off retaliation or other avoidable detrimental outcomes. In the US Defense Department, a comprehensive system of directives, instructions and regulations are managed by the Washington Headquarters Service (WHS) in order to implement administration policy decisions and enable Congressional statutes. An example of source protection provided solely by agency regulation would include Department of Defense Regulations 1540.20, Procedures 14 and 15. This regulation governs the conduct of intelligence oversight (I/O). In the reporting of suspicious activities by US intelligence and counter-intelligence personnel under Procedure 15, whistleblower protection is provided under Procedure 14.[26] A source in an I/O investigation alleging that he or she has been reprised against will find their allegations docketed through a hotline, forwarded probably to an Inspector General, and subject to the specific policies and procedures in effect in that Inspector General's office. So the limitations on the protection of I/O sources are, in effect, the same as the limitations on Inspectors General themselves.

This challenge is compounded by two further issues. First, federal employees may be covered by the plethora of whistleblower protections contained in a wide variety of regulatory statutes, each with its own standard of proof, either explicit or implicit, and falling within distinct and discreet systems of decision-making. These decision-making paradigms may have different means of reporting the finding of reprisal, and will also have differing systems of imposing correction action, both remedial and disciplinary. Accordingly, the first question asked by administrative investigators is 'what category does the complainant employee fall within, and what statutory authority provides the source protection she or he is providing through his or her complaint?'. The end result is a legislative patchwork known more often for its 'holes' than its quality of global seamless whistleblower protection.

Secondly, as noted earlier, whistleblower protection obligations are lodged in institutional structures which, by law, require independence and neutrality. Even though the act of whistleblowing is neither a 'management' nor a 'labor' action, support for a whistleblower which amounts to advocacy for 'labor' (or 'management') could be a violation of law by a public employee. The fine line between neutrality and advocacy can be seen in something as innocuous as employee education. Federal agencies have used their Inspectors General to promote whistleblowing and protect whistleblowers, but IGs cannot undertake 'management' functions without compromising their need to be independent of the department's management. If an IG performs such training, how could an inspection team from that office respond, say, to a Congressional request to inspect that training as a management function at some point in the future. So IGs can only act as subject matter experts (SMEs) and may simply assist management as it executes a training plan and documents compliance for them to inspect later. In the same way that judicial fora or law enforcement agencies find themselves with limitations in protecting sources as whistleblowers, so too do agencies.

Oversight and Monitoring

There is no specific framework for monitoring which federal agencies do or do not have procedures for preventing retaliatory actions or decisions, or the adequacy of those procedures. As noted, the major requirement is that federal agency heads must inform their workforce about the rights and remedies available to them under the whistleblower protection and prohibited personnel practice provisions of the WPA and WPEA, and, for the US intelligence community, Presidential Policy Directive No. 19.[27] Apart from investigating reprisal complaints, the OSC assists agency heads in fulfilling their duty to prevent prohibited personnel practices (PPPs) by offering training in each of the areas within the OSC's jurisdiction. In addition, since 2002, the OSC has offered a voluntary certification program under which the OSC will certify an agency's compliance with this duty if its meets five requirements for informing its workforce about their rights and remedies: (1) placing informational posters at agency facilities; (2) providing information about PPPs and the WPA to new employees as part of the orientation process; (3) providing information to current employees about PPPs and the WPA; (4) training supervisors on PPPs and the WPA, at least once every three years; and (5) creating a computer link from the agency's website to the OSC's website (OSC 2012: 35).

This certification program is voluntary. Other than the initial certification and/or recertification, the OSC does not have the resources to monitor agencies to determine compliance. However, at the onset of the certification process, the OSC works with agencies (if, for example, there are issues with conforming documentation or training materials) to help agencies become certified. The certification program provides a means to encourage agencies to follow their statutory requirements to inform their staff. While there is no enforcement mechanism to ensure, for instance, that agencies are providing information on the WPA to all new employees, if an agency obtains certification or attempts to recertify, it must provide to the OSC all the information it provides to its workforce.

There is also no published information on the training agencies provide to employees. For certification, the OSC only requires that supervisors be trained, although some agencies opt to train both supervisors and staff level employees. This ensures that supervisors (those individuals who could engage in any of the prohibited personnel practices) be prioritized for training, both as an education tool and to deter potential wrongdoing. Targeting supervisors for more in-depth training is also a more realistic goal, given the many thousands of employees larger agencies employ. The OSC encourages, whenever possible, in-person training and makes available experienced OSC trainers. For instance, the Office of Personnel Management hosted a filmed web-based training (all agencies invited) where the OSC conducted webinar training for thousands of federal employees and managers across the United States.

Research on Agency System Performance

Surprisingly, perhaps, for such a large and important system, there is very little research into the effectiveness of federal whistleblower protection laws or of the specific strategies being used by agencies to manage their whistleblowers. The most comprehensive research going in this direction has been conducted by the MSPB, which also carries out its responsibilities through merit systems studies. Following up on a survey of more than 13,000 federal employees in 1992, the MSPB surveyed more than 40,000 randomly sampled federal employees on their experiences of wrongdoing and whistleblowing in 2010 (MSPB 2011). This showed that while the percentage of employees who perceived any wrongdoing had decreased, perceptions of retaliation against those who blow the whistle remained a serious concern; and that while training for employees about the protections available to whistleblowers had improved since 1992, there were still far too many employees who had not received this information.

The MSPB research confirmed the importance of agency systems for protecting employees, by documenting (like other research) that most whistleblowers are less concerned with the personal consequences for themselves, than 'whether the agency will act on a report of wrongdoing' (MSPB 2011: i). Consequently, it is the system which must protect whistleblowers, because their reporting behavior is usually motivated by higher concerns. The research also highlighted that where that had occurred, positive improvements appeared related to improvements in management culture and systems. For example, the percentage of respondents who were identified as the source of a wrongdoing report without experiencing any unpleasantness increased from 37 per cent in 1992 to 44 per cent in 2010, with the greatest change being in the perception (down from 36 per cent to 28 per cent) that someone above the respondent's supervisor was unhappy with the respondent for having reported the problem (MSPB 2011: 10). The MSPB consequently urged agencies to create cultures in which employees believe that they will not be shunned or punished for reporting wrongdoing, but instead will be supported or praised (MSPB 2011: ii). However, US research so far does not extend to any comparative evaluation of which agencies are achieving better outcomes in these respects than others; nor whether these different outcomes relate to specific differences in their cultures, practices or systems. For example, there is (as yet) no analysis of whether those agencies who have been certified by the OSC as compliant with their education requirements are achieving better outcomes than those who have not sought certification. Nor is there analysis of what elements of their disclosure management systems may bear upon their outcomes.

Research in the private sector confirms the salience of these issues, while as yet also only scratching the surface of what practices and procedures separate those organizations with better whistleblower protection results from those with worse. The Ethics Resource Center's 2009 National Business Ethics Survey (NBES), one of a longitudinal series, surveyed a representative, random national sample of 2,852 private sector employees and found that respondents' decisions to report wrongdoing directly to their own supervisor, as against higher management, were positively related to their perception of the strength of the ethical culture and climate of their particular organization. In other words, it seemed 'likely that employees in weak cultures report to higher management because they are seeking the safety of the organizational structure and resources which higher management are perceived to represent' (ERC 2010c: 16). The nine lessons extracted by ERC researchers included the need for supervisors at all levels to be trained to 'communicate their openness to receiving reports; to listen to, document, and follow up on reports that are made, and avoid behavior that could be perceived as retaliation against reporters' (ERC 2010c: 21). However, exactly *how* more managers in particular organizations succeed in avoiding such behavior, or what systems organizations might put in place to prevent or detect its early stages, remains unclear.

In further analysis of results regarding retaliation, ERC researchers conclude that it is possible and necessary for managers to be 'mindful of groups that are more likely to feel retaliated against', and 'take extra steps to make sure that these employees are safeguarded from punishment for reporting and, just as importantly, that they do not feel vulnerable to retaliation', as well as for everyone who is likely to receive reports, especially supervisors, to be trained to 'follow up with reporters in an appropriate manner and to be mindful of how unrelated actions might be misinterpreted by an employee who is feeling uncertain and exposed after deciding to report' (ERC 2010b: 16). The importance of procedural fairness and justice in the disclosure management process has also been analyzed in a separate survey of 612 individuals who used hotlines to report wrongdoing in five companies (ERC 2013). However, in-depth, comparative study of what works and what does not in different agencies or organizations is rare. One of the notable exceptions remains the International Business Ethics Institute's 'Creating a Non-Retaliatory Workplace' project, to analyze 'the cutting edge strategies that companies can use to prevent retaliation against whistleblowers' and create a safe environment where employees can raise concerns about misconduct (Heard and Miller 2006; see Miceli *et al.* 2008: 195–6). However, any standard research model that could help agencies or oversight bodies identify the relative strengths and weaknesses in different agency efforts, in a more systematic and comparative way, is yet to be developed.

PRACTICALITIES OF AUSTRALIAN WHISTLEBLOWER PROTECTION

Basic Approach

How do Australian whistleblower protection systems compare with the US federal public sector? Are there equivalent research needs, and are these being met? Here the total Australian public sector will be considered, state and federal, for a number of reasons: Australia's much smaller population makes it logical to consider a larger scope of activity, especially when the largest public agencies are at the state rather than federal level; and it was at state level, in the 1990s, that Australian governments first embraced dedicated legislative schemes to protect whistleblowers, with the federal parliament only finally enacting equivalent federal legislation under the Public Interest Disclosure Act 2013 (Cth) (see Brown, Latimer, McMillan and Wheeler 2008; Brown 2013; Lewis, Devine and Harpur, Chapter 15).

Australia's legislation came in response to a mixture of major corruption scandals and a desire in all jurisdictions to strengthen integrity systems against such breakdowns. For example, Queensland's Whistleblower Protection Act 1994 followed similar findings by the Fitzgerald Commission of Inquiry into police and political corruption, as those reached in the United States in response to Watergate:

> Honest public officials are the major potential source of the information needed to reduce public maladministration and misconduct. They will continue to be unwilling to come forward until they are confident that they will not be prejudiced … There is an urgent need … for legislation which prohibits any person from penalising any other person for making accurate public statements about misconduct, inefficiency or other problems within public instrumentalities. (Fitzgerald 1989: 134; see Brown 2009)

While the legislation copied US precedent by focusing on anti-retaliation remedies for detriment suffered by whistleblowers, it was also overlaid on a stronger history of pre-existing merit and public sector management legislation, as well as a recently enlarged number of independent integrity agencies, such as Ombudsman's offices and anti-corruption commissions. Therefore, while the approach was similar in some respects, it also differed in two major respects, by adopting a more 'institutional' or 'structural' approach to whistleblowing (Dworkin and Brown 2013). First, it was assumed that public agencies could and should be able to make strong efforts to protect whistleblowers within 'the system', rather than relying on criminal and civil remedies for damage after the event. Accordingly, Australian whistleblowing laws have tended to include requirements for public agencies and managers to have whistleblower protection procedures, with these becoming more significant over time. Secondly, it was assumed, until recently, that this could be done without the need for any additional 'core' independent agency specializing in whistleblower protection, on the model of the US OSC.

Institutionalizing Protection: Core Agencies

This more limited role of core agencies is typified by the Queensland (Qld) and New South Wales (NSW) systems. Rather than a separate agency providing a fresh channel for whistleblower disclosures, existing independent agencies were made conduits for disclosures, for example, Ombudsmen for serious and substantial maladministration, and anti-corruption bodies for official misconduct or corrupt conduct.[28] In Queensland, it was recommended that no single agency should be the point of receipt, referral and coordination for all public interest disclosures (EARC 1991: 122–5), with each public agency instead made responsible for receiving public interest disclosures about the conduct of its officers, managing the disclosure process and taking steps to protect its officers from reprisals.

As the same time, it was recommended in Queensland that one existing agency (the anti-corruption body, now the Crime and Misconduct Commission (CMC)) should act as a general oversight agency, with power to oversee agency whistleblowing systems and procedures (EARC 1991: A11–17). However, not even this recommendation was taken up for many years. The government was required to prepare an annual report on the Act's administration,[29] but in the first 15 years, such a report was rarely if ever made (Brown 2009). While the anti-corruption body was given some limited roles to seek injunctions or take civil action in defense of whistleblowers, these remedies were used only once in Queensland and twice in NSW.[30] As outlined earlier (Lewis, Devine and Harpur, Chapter 15), unlike in the United States, there have been few actions under whistleblowing legislation for civil compensation for damage caused by detrimental action. Indeed, in NSW there was no facility for such compensation, until amendments in 2010.[31]

In all states reprisals were also made criminal, but no particular agency was given special responsibility for investigating and prosecuting such offenses. To date, in all the Australian jurisdictions where there is whistleblowing legislation, there have only been five prosecutions for the criminal offense of detrimental action in reprisal, all in NSW, and all of which failed.[32] No known formal disciplinary action has been taken in response to alleged detrimental action, and in only one case has an anti-corruption body been known to make an allegation of detrimental action the subject of a formal investigation.[33] This track record is likely explained by a mix of two factors: the much greater difficulty of proving retaliation to a criminal standard of proof, especially when most detrimental action is low level, employment-based and within the control of managers; and the lack of a clear, independent mandate on any agency to pursue such cases (see also Spencer and Spencer, Chapter 17).

Overall, the criminal, disciplinary and compensation remedies in whistleblowing legislation have thus proved to be largely theoretical deterrents. This history raises important research questions as to whether this is because *ex post facto* remedies are seen as being of limited use, in any event, since they only become available after damage has been done or threatened; or because the remedies have been poorly designed; or whether it is the lack of clear responsibilities for enforcing the remedies (see Smith and Brown 2008; Brown, Latimer, McMillan and Wheeler 2008; Brown 2013). Given evidence that many Australian whistleblowers do suffer the same kinds of unfair detrimental outcomes as in the United States, there has been much criticism of a lack of a stronger central agency role in defending whistleblowers (e.g., De Maria 1999). Research also points to basic deficiencies in the scheme; for example, some Australian integrity agencies' history of referring whistleblower complaints and reprisals back to the agencies concerned, in the same manner as any normal public complaint, without consent or even prior warning of this procedure to whistleblowers (Annakin 2011). This practice stands in contrast to the roles and responsibilities of the OSC, as well as the practices of other integrity agencies in Australia, and has only recently been explicitly addressed, for the first time, in Australia's new federal whistleblowing legislation.[34]

Over time, Australian laws have been strengthened to require a central agency to more thoroughly monitor the protections being afforded by individual agencies, in a bid to make whistleblowing work. This began with new legislation in Victoria (2001) and Western Australia (2003), with Queensland and NSW both eventually updated in this way in 2010. Stronger oversight was also recommended at the federal level (House of Representatives Standing Committee (Australia) 2009) and became basic to the new federal Public Interest Disclosure Act in 2013. A potentially strong oversight regime is thus now embedded in all Australian jurisdictions, apart from South Australia. This regime is based on a belief that oversight agencies can perform their most useful roles in relation to providing advice to agencies about support and protection of whistleblowers, encouraging cultural change and capacity building within organizations, and auditing and monitoring the provision of support and protection by agencies, as discussed further below.

As yet, there is little movement towards a stronger, interventionist protection role for core agencies. Only in the small Northern Territory government are the oversight agency's functions focused mostly, let alone solely on whistleblower investigations and protections;[35] and only in the Australian Capital Territory (ACT), also small, has the oversight agency (public service commission) been given an explicit function to 'ensure just outcomes for people who make public interest disclosures, including by preventing and remedying the effect of detrimental action against people because of disclosures'.[36] In general, there is a continuing view that oversight or regulatory agencies are not in a good position to support or protect whistleblowers within the workplace, other than on the rare occasions where full confidentiality is both practical and appropriate; nor to manage the workplace fallout of disclosures. Nevertheless, more systematic oversight necessarily carries the potential for a core agency to help conciliate or resolve ongoing disputes between whistleblowers and their agencies, including the fairness of treatment in individual cases. Moreover, allegations are also still likely to default to a core or independent agency if they concern agency heads or other senior staff, or require more complex investigations involving more extensive investigatory powers, or require investigation into whether an agency has failed to properly manage disclosures or protect whistleblowers. Such functions require an oversight agency to investigate and assess whether agencies have taken effective steps to prevent, acknowledge or remedy unfairness, in individual cases, and thus may require an agency to express opinions or to initiate actions in defense of whistleblowers. In important respects, therefore, a more active protection role cannot be separated from the new, stronger monitoring role.

Enabling Functions: Ethical and Professional Standards Branches

Given the focus on agency level protection, explained above, the distribution of responsibility for whistleblower support in Australia is quite different to the United States. For legislative protections to work, functional units within agencies who are responsible for corporate integrity, internal audit, ethical and professional standards, and complaint investigation and resolution, play a more significant role. In general, there is no overall equivalent to US Inspectors General. At Australian federal government level, this title does have some use, but is not supported by a general statute, and in the three main instances, it describes quite different institutions.[37] More typically, in both federal and state agencies, internal integrity functions fall to internal audit, professional standards and ethical standards units or branches embedded in corporate governance areas.

While US Inspectors General do not come to whistleblower protection activity as lead actors, Australian public agencies must internalize this function if it is to work at all. Therefore, in addition to processes for facilitating and investigating disclosures, agencies must have active systems for supporting whistleblowers. From an early stage, all jurisdictions except South Australia (now the oldest and most out-of-date law) have legislated that every agency 'must establish reasonable procedures to protect its officers from reprisals that are, or may be, taken against them by the entity or other officers of the entity' (Queensland).[38]

From the outset, this approach has required a focus on preventing reprisals and detrimental action, in addition to offering remedies once detriment is suffered. Over time it has developed from general to more specific requirements, in line with the strengthening of monitoring and oversight. Recent legislation tends to detail the obligations on organizations to recognize and manage disclosures, which must be set out in agency procedures that are consistent with jurisdictional standards, stipulated in turn by the lead oversight agency.[39] Since 2003, a basic framework for support has been set out in an Australian Standard for organization level whistleblower protection programs within the corporate governance of any organization, public or private (Australian Standard 8004–2003). The most detailed guide for many years was the NSW Ombudsman's Public Interest Disclosure Manual, which in 2010 was given a statutory but non-binding basis, and revised into a detailed, online manual of guidelines (NSW Ombudsman 2013). The guidelines range from required statements of management commitment to specific models of internal reporter support. This revised approach, which has been followed by other jurisdictions, was informed by a considerable body of collaborative research, discussed further below. The new federal Public Interest Disclosure Act (PIDA) requires all federal agencies to have 'procedures for facilitating and dealing with public interest disclosures relating to the agency', which must comply with standards set by the principal oversight agency, the Commonwealth Ombudsman.[40]

Some laws not only impose requirements for procedures, but a direct statutory responsibility on agency heads to take 'reasonable steps ... to protect public officials who belong to the agency from detriment, or threats of detriment' relating to disclosures.[41] How these translate into the employment and performance conditions of senior managers is another question. However, building on the reformed Queensland (2010) and ACT (2012) laws, protection obligations under the new federal law commence with an internal disclosure to any manager who directly supervises the whistleblower, in addition to designated 'disclosure officers' or external agencies.[42] The two most recent laws, the ACT and new federal law, make reprisal prevention obligations even more explicit by requiring that procedures include processes for 'assessing risks that reprisals may be taken' against persons who make disclosures.[43] Under this new standard, the responsibility to protect whistleblowers becomes an even more proactive requirement, internalized in management.

Oversight and Monitoring

For the reasons outlined, whistleblower protection in the Australian public sector relies on systematic oversight of agencies' efforts to implement the above requirements. Whereas in the United States the primary statutory requirement is for agencies to inform their staff of their legal rights, under the Australian regimes this is simply one of around 20 key procedural requirements (see, for example, NSW Ombudsman 2013: 'Guideline A3: Awareness and Training'). While training is still important, as are requirements for agency heads to ensure that their staff are aware of the contents of their agency policies and the protections available,[44] agencies are overseen and monitored in respect of all key procedural requirements.

Who performs this oversight? The Australian decision not to task new agencies has meant decisions about which existing integrity agencies are best to carry out this function. Although it was originally recommended in Queensland that the new anti-corruption body should do so, only one Australian jurisdiction, Victoria, has recently given the oversight function to that kind of agency.[45] A primary reason for not doing so has been that the scheme must be made to work for disclosures about a range of wrongdoing types, and not simply corrupt or serious misconduct which is the focus of anti-corruption bodies. Therefore oversight functions have tended to fall to either the Ombudsman (currently NSW, Queensland, Tasmania, and the federal government; formerly Victoria) or a Public Sector Standards or Public Service Commission (currently Western Australia and ACT; formerly Queensland). Questions remain about the best arrangements. Public management agencies should theoretically be able to help embed whistleblower protection in good workplace relations, but may also be focused on workforce needs, and insufficiently independent of government. Ombudsmen may have the necessary independence and oversight powers, but may struggle to devote sufficient resources to their whistleblowing functions when also responsible for large volumes of public and citizen complaints.

Oversight roles vary subtly between jurisdictions. Typically, the guidelines, standards and/or codes published by the oversight agency are binding on agencies, whose internal protection procedures must be consistent.[46] In some cases, the oversight agency must also directly review and approve the procedures.[47] Agencies must either publish statistics annually on the use of the procedures, or report statistics to the oversight agency who then publishes annually.[48] The oversight agency usually has explicit responsibility to monitor, audit or review compliance and implementation in all agencies; in NSW and Western Australia, this is at least once every 12 months.[49] Where not explicit, the responsibility to monitor and report is implicit. Often the agency (especially if an Ombudsman) has an explicit power to receive and investigate individual complaints about failures in agency practice, in addition to reviewing procedures and practices in general.[50] In other cases, the ability to follow through in individual cases is implicit in a power to review not just the procedures, but their 'implementation', with no restriction on the recommendations that might be made.[51] In two cases (Queensland and ACT), the agency has explicit power to review how an agency handles either 'public interest disclosures generally, or particular public interest disclosures'.[52]

Research on Agency System Performance

Apart from research based on anecdotal case histories and self-selected samples (see Brown and Donkin 2008: 13), systematic research into the effectiveness of whistleblower protection dates from an early survey of NSW public officials focusing on awareness and attitudes of new legislative protections (Zipparo 1999a, 1999b). As in the United States, the first systematic empirical data on perceived levels of wrongdoing and actual reporting in the public sector, from the early 2000s, came from official government surveys, such as the State of the Service Surveys conducted at federal level by the Australian Public Service Commission (see, for example, APSC 2004, 2005). Conducted more frequently than the US MSPB surveys, these surveys provide a longitudinal barometer of perceptions of wrongdoing and preparedness to report. However, they also provide less depth than the US MSPB surveys, as they cover many more issues than simply whistleblowing, and do not collect detailed evidence of impacts, outcomes or the relative effectiveness of agency protection efforts.

To fill this gap, government integrity agencies and university researchers have thus engaged in at least one major collaborative research project, 'Whistling While They Work' (WWTW), aimed at collecting evidence of how protection systems are actually performing. As mentioned in several other chapters in this volume (Chapters 2, 8, 9, 10, 12, 13), this research collected evidence of the contents of the whistleblowing procedures of 304 federal, state and local agencies, from four different Australian jurisdictions; assessed the written procedures of 175 of those agencies; surveyed random samples of employees in 118 of those agencies (n = 7,763); and in a further selection of 15 'case study' agencies, surveyed a further 1,150 employees, and interviewed 92 employees (see Brown, Latimer, McMillan and Wheeler 2008; Roberts *et al.* 2011).

Like the later MSPB research, the WWTW surveys confirmed the importance of agency systems for protecting employees by documenting that most whistleblowers are less concerned with personal outcomes than whether the agency will listen and take action (Wortley *et al.* 2008). As mentioned earlier, the findings also revealed great variation and patchiness between agencies, and to some extent between jurisdictions, in the quality of written policies, and in key outcomes from the whistleblowing process. While some of the agencies studied could boast that less than 10 per cent of employees who observed serious wrongdoing did nothing about it, in at least one organization in each of the four jurisdictions the 'inaction rate' was more than 55 per cent of staff in the same position, i.e., who neither reported the wrongdoing nor took any other action, in circumstances where no one else had reported it (see also Olsen, Chapter 8). Similarly, in some agencies, the proportion of whistleblowers that claimed mistreatment fell close to zero, but in others, upwards of 46 per cent claimed to have been mistreated directly by management of the agency.

Especially striking from the research was that, notwithstanding the legislative focus on agency level protection described above, only 54 per cent of agencies studied indicated that they had systems for providing 'active management support' to whistleblowers who reported wrongdoing. In only 11 per cent of agencies were the procedures supported by a formal program. Consistently with this, only a small fraction of whistleblowers were being correctly identified as protected, with high levels of under-reporting and under-implementation of the schemes in most agencies (see Brown and Olsen 2008b). These findings had a direct impact on the upgrading of legislative requirements and oversight arrangements since 2008, described above.

More positively, the research also provided departure points for identifying better practices for agencies. Comparative analysis across jurisdictions and agencies showed that notwithstanding weaknesses in implementation, agencies who were taking their whistleblower protection responsibilities more seriously were achieving better outcomes than agencies who were not (Roberts 2008). Consistently with the US private sector research findings, the answers to more effective protection appear to lie not only in better legislative requirements and oversight, but in the context and management culture of different organizations, as well as capacity building as to how, at a practical level, key whistleblower protection problems can be solved. Consequently, the research confirmed that there is no 'one size fits all' for a whistleblower support program, but that programs can and should be designed around six common principles: systematic; proactive; informed; tailored; collaborative; and accountable (Brown and Olsen 2008b). Crucial within them is the need for agencies to have identified senior staff who can act as mentors to whistleblowers and people who are the subject of disclosures (see NSW Ombudsman 2013: Guideline D1).

Most usefully, the research enabled direct comparison of the different procedures and systems of different agencies; in particular, the 15 case study agencies analyzed in greatest depth. Table 19.1 sets out an overview of how the empirical data was used to generate an aggregate ranking of agency performance, using a combination of assessments and indicators, in order to identify those agencies (marked by letters) whose systems and procedures appeared to be working, relative to others.

The results and rankings in Table 19.1 were validated in workshops with agency representatives, and used to extract a mix of best practices and procedures reflecting the cumulative experience of what appeared to be working across the agencies, especially those ranked highly (for the resulting guide, see Roberts *et al.* 2011). By generating data on key measures which could then be broken down to enable comparisons between jurisdictions and agencies, this research thus served as both a means of measuring the performance of individual agencies, for the purposes of enforcement and capacity building, and as a means of

Table 19.1 'Whistling While They Work', Australia: Ranking of case study agency performance

	Agency rankings														
Agency Code Letter	B	A	M	P	N	E	C	F	D	O	L	G	K	H	I
Procedures comprehensiveness	2	1	10	8	12	3	15	6	14	5	11	13	4	7	9
Indicators (employee survey results):															
1. Attitudes to reporting (% all staff)	2	1	9	12	6	3	10	5	4	11	14	13	8	15	7
2. Awareness of legislation (% all staff)	4	2	1	7	3	6	11	13	5	8	9	10	15	14	12
3. Awareness of policies (% all staff)	5	1	2	10	6	3	4	7	9	12	8	13	15	14	11
4. Whistleblowing propensity (% all staff)	3	1	2	6	8	4	5	7	9	10	13	11	14	15	12
5. Trust in organizational response to reported wrongdoing (% all staff)	3	2	4	1	11	7	12	8	15	6	5	9	13	10	14
6. Inaction rate in response to perceived wrongdoing (% staff who observed serious wrongdoing)	1	13	6	4	7	14	8	5	10	12	3	9	11	2	15
7. Knowledge of whether report investigated (% staff who reported wrongdoing)	7	5	9	1	2	4	11	12	3	6	13	10	8	15	14
8. Perceived treatment by management following report (% staff who reported wrongdoing)	1	6	7	3	5	11	2	9	14	10	13	4	8	12	15
(Sum of ranks)	(26)	(31)	(40)	(44)	(48)	(52)	(63)	(66)	(69)	(75)	(78)	(79)	(92)	(97)	(100)
Overall performance ranking	**1**	**2**	**3**	**4**	**5**	**6**	**7**	**8**	**9**	**10**	**11**	**12**	**13**	**14**	**15**

Source: Roberts *et al.* 2011: 117

identifying potential better practices from which under-performing agencies could learn. Whereas previously very little was known about how agencies were seeking to implement their responsibilities, this research approach showed that it is indeed possible to systematically scratch the surface of such mysteries.

SYSTEMIC INSTITUTIONAL AND RESEARCH LESSONS

Basic Approach: The 'Indicator' Challenge

How do we know when some efforts to protect whistleblowers are working, relative to others, in order to then pursue better organizational and regulatory systems in support of the role of whistleblowing? Notwithstanding differences in the context, approaches and available information regarding whistleblowing in the United States and Australian public sectors, the above accounts suggest five areas, or issues, which research can and should address in order to help inform public policy and regulatory practice, not only in the US and Australia, but potentially more broadly.

First, even though the basic approach in each country has evolved in a different direction, research and practice in both countries are pointing to a common need for agreed measures of what constitutes success in whistleblower protection. Moreover, it is clear that these measures should transcend the specific requirements imposed by legislation, given that legislation can be seen as only providing a skeletal or partial framework on which whistleblowing management and protection hangs. On either view of the 'protection' starting point, the complexities of securing just outcomes for whistleblowers are such that legislation alone is inherently unable to address them. This challenge has been set out in the United States by the MSPB (2011: 1):

> The law is remedial – it provides some redress for retaliation. However, to achieve the purpose of the law – encouraging employees to make disclosures – the Government must do more than just provide legal protections against retaliation. Individual agencies must also create cultures that persuade employees that their whistleblowing will make a positive difference towards preventing wrongdoing.

It flows that the main legislated strategy for implementing protection in the United States – the education of supervisors and employees about whistleblowers' remedial rights – is just one part of the protection jigsaw in practice. Both countries show the difficulty of legislative approaches that assume that detrimental action suffered by whistleblowers will be easily amenable to criminal, disciplinary and/or compensatory remedies, in such a way as to make these an effective deterrent and foster better managed workplaces. In practice, certainly in Australia, it is rare to discover blatant actions taken by colleagues or management that can be categorized as detrimental action in reprisal (e.g., dismissal, unjustified disciplinary action, demotion, or clear examples of harassment or discrimination), even with reformed legal thresholds and remedies. Detrimental action is more usually conduct that can be described as 'flying below the radar' or 'leaving no finger prints', or action that is justified in the circumstances but becomes inseparable from a retaliation complaint through poor handling of the disclosure process or the underlying wrongdoing, poor documentation, poor risk management, poor communication, or poor recognition of the impacts of any of these on a whistleblower, even when no retaliation is intended.

At the same time, the ineffectiveness of remedial measures in Australia to date, even compared to the United States, shows Australia has its own legislative gaps. At least until recently, the lack of viable remedies is a likely key contributor to the often poor and patchy implementation of agency level protections. Accordingly, the relative lack of case law and reported official interventions is itself another indicator of relative lack of success. Such information in the United States shows that it is possible, even if arduous and sometimes pyrrhic, for whistleblowers to access their rights at least some of the time. In Australia, most of the time, the legal reality has been that whistleblowers are unable to enforce the rights intended to be bestowed by legislation.

From both perspectives, the question becomes, what are the best indicators of relative success and failure in whistleblower support? Not only understanding the key elements of protection systems, but accurately collecting agreed information which may indicate their relative success or failure, becomes the new and high priority. Focused at the agency level, the Australian research approach summarized at Table 19.1 shows that a range of research-based indicators are possible, but debate is needed as to the relative weight that should be attached to each, as well as whether other indicators might have greater value. Moreover, missing from the equation is any indicator of how many whistleblowers who have sought, or should be entitled, to access their legal remedies have actually been able to do so. Given the experience of both systems to date, there is scope and need for the development of a discrete set of indicators against which relative success and failure can be empirically judged.

Core Agency Roles: The 'Intervention' Challenge

Although the US and Australian approaches differ dramatically in the roles given to core or oversight agencies, there is again a common informational need: when is it that a core agency should use its limited resources to intervene to secure a particular whistleblower protection outcome, in individual cases? How should a core agency identify and prioritize such cases? Is it enough, as in the US situation, that potentially deserving cases are usually only identifiable after damage has already been done, and complaints or litigation are filed? Would better outcomes be achieved in more cases if early warnings were in place, by which the core agency became aware of cases that were more likely to be mismanaged by an agency, and was able to intervene in a lower key, lower cost way to influence the management response; or help strengthen the hand of the relevant Inspector General in pursuing a preventative outcome?

The same questions apply to Australian core agencies, given that, as outlined, their oversight roles still make them the final fall-back and dispute resolution point, in cases where agency handling proves inadequate or conflict becomes unmanageable. Indeed, the more pro-active, reprisal prevention approach pursued by Australian legislatures calls for a conscious strategy under which cases that agencies are unlikely to readily manage and resolve by themselves are identified earlier rather than later, so that independent assistance might be used to help contain a problem that is otherwise set to become intractable. With similar intention, a range of Australian integrity legislation puts in place 'mandatory reporting' systems, whereby public agencies must notify particular integrity agencies, such as anti-corruption bodies, as soon as there is reasonable suspicion that a relevant case has arisen, so that protocols can be triggered regarding the best response to the particular case. In some cases, Australian legislation, including the new federal Public Interest Disclosure Act, requires the oversight agency to be notified by agencies in 'real time' about disclosures, at early key stages of the process.[53]

With this information goes an oversight agency responsibility not simply to monitor, but to ensure effective implementation of the protection regime at the agency level. Therefore, even under the Australian model, the core agency has a role in not only promoting and requiring best practice agency whistleblowing programs, but in 'real time' coordination and quality assurance with regard to investigations and decision-making affecting whistleblower welfare. Empirical research shows it is possible to identify risk factors to help flag which cases are higher priority for monitoring and early intervention (Brown and Olsen 2008a). Research has therefore a role to play in helping maximize effective core agency roles, in both contexts.

Agency Management of Disclosures: The 'Triage' and 'Broker' Challenges

Thirdly and fourthly, in both contexts, the practicalities of agency level whistleblower support rely on two sets of decision-making capacities that are far removed from the historical presumptions of whistleblowing legislation. Public interest whistleblowing is generally accepted as a 'pro-social' activity (see Chapters 1 and 9), recognized as having special value because of the relative accuracy of inside information about wrongdoing, as well as the frequent courage of whistleblowers. From this, it is easy to assume that all whistleblowers are employees of high competence and professionalism, who are largely disinterested third parties not directly involved in the circumstances of their disclosures, motivated to help the organization or by the general public interest. Legislation also tends to assume that whistleblowers, and others such as managers affected by disclosures, are rational actors, with a high understanding of organizational and political processes, as well as capacity to weigh risks and plan considered responses to challenges. This has led in turn to the assumption that the primary barrier to people reporting wrongdoing is rational risk aversion, i.e., a fear that they will not be protected.

In practice, research indicates that whistleblowers come in all shapes and sizes; and that in a majority of cases where protection obligations apply, few or none of these assumptions may be true. In particular, whistleblowing may be relatively unplanned or motivated by a range of reactions to conflicts within an organization, including self-protective or defensive reactions (see Roberts, Chapter 9). The parties to a disclosure often do not act or react rationally – the circumstances of a disclosure can raise strong emotional reactions on the part of the whistleblower, who is often personally directly affected by the alleged wrongdoing in some way, as well as the subject(s) of the disclosure and/or the managers who receive the disclosure or are responsible for acting on it. The institutional and legislative objectives of acting on a whistleblowing matter may or may not align with the whistleblower's personal objectives. And utility concerns, or whether or not anyone is listening or interested in taking action to address the possible wrongdoing, are now established by research as the primary concerns influencing employees' decisions whether to blow the whistle, over and above risks of reprisal or considerations about levels of protection.

These realities alter and increase, rather than reduce, agencies' obligations to take a preventative, active management approach to whistleblower support. However, this poses two further challenges, with little known so far about agencies' relative capacities to meet them, or how they are currently being dealt with. The first of these is how frontline managers and case officers separate out the different motives and issues involved in typical, complex whistleblowing incidents, and then initiate appropriate actions, and coordinate those actions, including responses to assessments of reprisal risk. We call this the 'triage' challenge. Meeting it rests upon capacities for crisis management and conflict resolution. It also rests upon strategies of informational control, given that the responses to disclosures often require a high degree of confidentiality. The whistleblower and any subject(s) of the disclosure have limited information as to what is happening, and will make various assumptions. If people don't know what 'government' is doing in relation to an issue, the standard default position is to assume that nothing is happening, that whatever is being done is ineffective or in some other way 'wrong', or that there is a 'cover up'. Similarly, if substantiation of the disclosure becomes the critical factor in whether or not the whistleblower feels they are being protected and supported in these processes, then whistleblowers are more likely to become obsessed with the need for vindication.

Therefore, these initial decision-making processes are crucial to whether whistleblowing incidents are set on a positive or negative path. The fact that they must be made in a highly emotional situation, with limited information, in which key participants are not likely to be acting rationally, only increases the dimensions of the challenge. Disclosures need to be dealt with by staff who are properly resourced, trained, experienced and motivated to deal with this challenge, including the functions of managing and supporting the whistleblower and not simply the conduct of fair and thorough investigations. Moreover, agencies need to have risk assessment processes in place, and be careful and pragmatic with their strategies to provide confidentiality, or alternatively to implement a proactive approach to the protection of reporters (see NSW Ombudsman 2013: PID Guideline, C7).

The 'broker' challenge adds a further layer of complexity to these capacities. A whistleblower may be taken seriously by front-line managers, case officers or Inspectors General, but as noted earlier in respect of the US system, senior management may have difficulty understanding and following through on why protection is needed and in the best interests of the agency. In these situations, institutional pressures and even reprisal risks may be focused onto the 'brokers' (those who are investigating or managing disclosures) as much or more than onto the whistleblower themselves.

Research in both countries points to the most important driver of organizational responses being the attitude of the CEO and senior management towards internal disclosures and the people who make them, not legislative obligations. If there is a negative attitude, legislation alone will not be sufficiently effective to encourage disclosures or protect the people who make them. In any organization, there are a range of reasons why senior management may be less than supportive of disclosures and the people who make them, including issues of:

- *rationalisation*: that in the circumstances the conduct is not so serious as to warrant a formal process;
- *perception*: perceptions about the validity or accuracy of information in a disclosure being influenced by the perceived motive of the whistleblower (e.g., disaffected employee = perceived malice = low validity);
- *loyalty*: taking action on a disclosure being seen as being disloyal to colleagues generally or friends in particular, or to the organization as a whole;
- *complicity*: the recipient of the report, or persons above them, are either involved in the wrongdoing or have turned a blind eye to it in the past;
- *personality*: unwillingness to 'rock the boat' or take risks;
- *futility*: that no good purpose is served by taking action because nothing will come of it in the end;
- *fear*: that taking action on a disclosure will not be supported by other management or by political leaders, or their career will suffer;
- *reputation*: the expectation that the disclosure will have a significant impact on their own reputation, or the reputations of others or of the agency or government as a whole, to an extent that outweighs the whistleblower's claims or interests.

Some basic implications include the need for internal disclosures to be dealt with by staff who are not part of the work unit to which the disclosure relates, and who can report directly to the CEO or Deputy CEO, as well as to outside agencies. However, these factors can still conspire to mean that despite strong theoretical whistleblower protections, management can remain unsympathetic in practice to dealing with a disclosure or supporting a whistleblower – against advice about the wisest course of action from those tasked with organizational integrity functions, or even to the detriment of those 'brokers'. In the United

States, this is compounded by the requirements for independence and neutrality, dictating that support for a whistleblower must stop short of advocacy for 'labor' against 'management', or risk violating the law. How organizations deal with these challenges becomes determinative of the overall response and whether unfair detriment is suffered. Unless resolved internally within the organization, these conflicts will play out in conflict with core agencies, in court or in the public domain. However, little is known about how different organizations currently resolve these challenges, in better or worse ways. Both become important foci for better information gathering and research.

Oversight and Monitoring: The 'Performance' Challenge

The above issues combine to make clear the difference between evaluating agency compliance with protection obligations on paper (for example, by ensuring that mandated training or procedures are in place and being followed), and evaluating the effectiveness of agencies' whistleblower protection strategies, by establishing whether those procedures are actually working. A compliance approach is doubly difficult because research and common sense indicate there is no one fixed way of protecting whistleblowers in practice, and no single set of requirements or procedures against which compliance can be simply systematically checked. Support systems must be tailored to organizational circumstances, and even then must remain flexible and adaptive, given that it is nigh impossible to set out whistleblower support and protection rules that can be effective in every circumstance. Instead, the starting point for improved protection is a recognition that the management of whistleblowing and protection of whistleblowers is more an art than a science. There is no simple formula or set of rules that will work every time, or even most of the time, even though certain processes and approaches can be effective.

An evidence-based policy process is needed in both contexts, therefore, which allows the indicators and information on how agencies are meeting the above challenges, to be linked with information on whether good outcomes are being achieved. By good outcomes, we mean not just the identification and correction of wrongdoing as identified by disclosures, important as this is, but also whether:

- appropriate action is being seen within the organization as having been taken on disclosures;
- confidentiality has been maintained as to the identity of the reporter, where this is possible and appropriate;

- assessments of disclosures are seen as professional and objective;
- the handling of disclosures (including investigation techniques) are seen within the organization as being fair; and
- investigation and support outcomes are being seen to be reasonable in the circumstances (which might include allegations being found to be unsubstantiated or even knowingly false).

This information is crucial to determining whether agency approaches are performing and meeting statutory objectives, irrespective of how those approaches are structured or embedded in procedures. If agencies are genuinely striving for better outcomes, then information about the extent to which these outcomes are being achieved is also a key asset for the management of the agency. Since it is clear that retaliation is more likely to occur, and not be properly addressed, in an environment where whistleblowing and whistleblowers are viewed negatively, one of the key ways to help develop a more positive attitude within an agency (if not the public sector as a whole) is by demonstrating that good outcomes can flow from disclosures.

CONCLUSIONS: INFORMATION NEEDS AND RESEARCH IMPLICATIONS

This chapter has reviewed the limited research that exists into the take-up and performance of organizational strategies for protecting whistle-blowers, in the US and Australian public sectors. It highlights that even though the countries have taken different approaches, they face common issues when it comes to reliance on agency level whistleblower protection efforts, supported by core agency interventions and oversight. Fundamental information needs are common. The chapter has also highlighted that even countries with relatively long histories of dedicated statutory regimes for whistleblower protection lack systematic frameworks for collecting the information needed to effectively evaluate the performance of those regimes, and the agency systems that hang from them.

Elsewhere, a strong case is identified for empirical research into whistleblowing to shift from studying whistleblower behavior, to studying how managers respond to whistleblowing (Moberly, Chapter 12; Vandekerckhove, Brown and Tsahuridu, Chapter 13). Similarly, this chapter shows the strong need for the study of whistleblower protection efforts to shift beyond comparative legal studies or attempts to identify good and bad features of whistleblowing laws and procedures, in the abstract, to also include hard data on how the systems established under those laws are operating in practice. Australian research has led the way, so far, as might be expected under laws predicated more strongly on agency level prevention and protection efforts, rather than on external or legal enforcement of rights to remedies. In such an environment, it is only by collecting information regarding what is going on inside organizations that any systematic picture of the effectiveness of whistleblowing regimes can be formed. However, so far this research has been 'one off' rather than ongoing; with official longitudinal data gathering generally limited to levels of perceived wrongdoing, levels of reporting and basic measures of outcomes for whistleblowers, rather than more comprehensive data on the effectiveness of whistleblower protection.

From this, the chapter identifies five particular challenges which might inform the development of a more systematic, integrated approach to gauging the effectiveness of whistleblower protection in practice. Meeting these information needs would not only solve significant research questions, but provide information to assist with regulatory oversight and, indeed, assist the management of agencies themselves. First, there is demonstrated benefit in having agreed sets of indicators regarding success or failure in whistleblower protection, for comparison between organizations and jurisdictions. Secondly, there is a need for information which will enable those whistleblowing cases to be more easily identified, where central intervention or oversight is more likely to be needed than others. Thirdly, there is a lack of information on whether and how managers in different organizations are conducting the complex 'triage' processes at and soon after the point of receiving disclosures, which are crucial to the effective management of whistleblowing in practice, as against an often idealized and unrealistic theory.

Fourthly, there is a similar lack of information about how different organizations are dealing with the 'brokering' challenges which may be determinative of whether an organization ultimately supports or abandons a whistleblower, and which hinge less on the relationship between whistleblowers and management, and more on the roles and challenges facing those integrity practitioners within organizations whose functions are to influence senior management decision-making about the right and wrong ways to respond to individual disclosures. Finally, there is a need for research on the key outcomes from whistleblowing, again to enable comparison between organizations and jurisdictions as to potential best practices, but also as an input into meaningful regulatory oversight, given the need for diversity and adaptiveness in whistleblower protection procedures.

Together, these challenges point to a more integrated research model for identifying which agencies or strategies are achieving greater effectiveness in whistleblower protection. This research model would be especially useful if incorporated in official mechanisms for monitoring and overseeing agency efforts, and comparing legislative regimes as a whole. By comparing approaches to the practicalities of whistleblower protection in each country, therefore, it has been possible to identify a set of research priorities which can help generate the information needed to better evaluate whistleblower protection efforts even under quite different institutional arrangements and conditions. It is hoped that such a model could be the beginning of a more useful comparative approach, within and between jurisdictions, for the more efficient identification of best practice in the ways that organizations manage whistleblowing.

NOTES

* This chapter should not be construed as legal advice, a legal opinion or a statement of policy or official position of the US Office of Special Counsel, US Intelligence Community Inspector General, ODNI or NSW Ombudsman. The material includes a summary of some areas of law, and constitutes outreach to whistleblowing stakeholders by the Intelligence Community Whistleblowing and Source Protection program, and others, but does not purport to exhaust its subject. The chapter does not create, and shall not be construed as creating, any right or benefit, substantive or procedural, enforceable at law by any person against the NSW Government or the United States, its agencies, its officers or employees, or any other person.

1. S. Rep. No. 95–969, 19 (1978), reprinted in USCCAN 2723, 2741 (1978). Civil Service Reform Act of 1978 (CSRA), 13 October 1978, Pub. L. No. 95–454, 92. See also Fong 1991: 1017–18.
2. The nine merit system principles are set forth at 5 USC s. 2301(b) and include: '(9) Employees should be protected against reprisal for the lawful disclosure of information which the employees reasonably believe evidences: (A) a violation of any law, rule, or regulation, or (B) mismanagement, a gross waste of funds, an abuse of authority, or a substantial and specific danger to public health or safety'. The 13 prohibited personnel practices are set forth at 5 USC s. 2302(b).
3. S. Rep. No. 95–969, 8 (1978).
4. See Pub. L. No. 101–12, s. 2 (1989).
5. Executive Order 12674 (12 April 1989) (as modified by EO 12731). See s. 101(k).
6. This requirement is codified at 5 USC s. 2302(c).
7. And the provisions in the Whistleblower Protection Enhancement Act closing loopholes to establishing protected whistleblowing under the WPA will likely increase the percentage of whistleblowers who prevail under the WPA.
8. The OSC also enforces the Hatch Act provisions on permissible and impermissible political activity by government employees and protects the employment and reemployment rights of military veterans and reservists under the Uniformed Services Employment and Reemployment Rights Act.
9. 5 USC s. 1211(b). See Pub. L. No. 101–12, 103 Stat. 32 (1989).
10. See 5 USC s. 1214(b)(1)(A)(i).

11. See 5 USC s. 1214(b)(2)(B).
12. See 5 U.C s. 1214(b)(2)(D). In addition, an employee can pursue an individual right of action appeal at the MSPB if the OSC declines to pursue the claim or does not act on the case within 120 days of filing with the OSC: see 5 USC s. 1221. An employee pursuing a significant adverse action at the MSPB can also assert whistleblower reprisal as an affirmative defense.
13. See Pub. L. No. 101–12, s. 2 (1989).
14. See 5 USC s. 1215. Disciplinary action includes removal, reduction in grade, debarment from federal employment for a period not to exceed five years, suspension, reprimand, a US$1,000 civil penalty, or a combination of such actions.
15. See 5 USC s. 1213.
16. The OSC can disclose the identity of a whistleblower where it 'determines that the disclosure of the individual's identity is necessary because of an imminent danger to public health or safety or imminent violation of any criminal law'. 5 USC s. 1213(h).
17. The OSC's annual reports contain summaries of major cases showing how the OSC's provision of a safe channel for whistleblower disclosures helps to regularly rein in waste, fraud, abuse, illegality and threats to public health and safety that pose the very real risk of catastrophic harm to the public, and huge remedial and liability costs for the government: see www.osc.gov.
18. See Public Law 111–259, codified at 50 USC 3033.
19. 5 USC Appx C, ss. 7(a), (c). In addition, amendments to the Inspector General Act created a misnamed intelligence community whistleblower protection program which does not provide general protection for members of the Defense intelligence and counter-intelligence community.
20. The NSA creates shared jurisdiction for both the Department of Defense IG and the Intelligence Community IG over whistleblower complaints made by intelligence personnel in the Defense Department. See 50 USC s. 3033. However, under the Obama administration's Presidential Policy Directive No. 19, 'Protecting Whistleblowers with Access to Classified Information', only the Intelligence Community IG has appellate authority to review, at his or her discretion, the findings of whistleblower cases conducted by other Inspectors General, such as the Department of Defense's Inspector General, with partial jurisdiction over the Intelligence Community.
21. 10 USC s. 1034.
22. Defense Department Instruction 7050.01, 'Defense Hotline' (17 December 2007).
23. Defense Department Directive 7050.06, 'Military Whistleblower Protection' (23 July 2007).
24. See Public Law 107–174, codified at 5 USC 2301 note; 'Questions and Answers: No FEAR Act', available at www.eeoc.gov/eeoc/statistics/nofear/qanda.cfm.
25. 5 USC App. S. 3.
26. See Department of Defense Regulation 5240.1–R, 'Procedures governing the activities of DoD intelligence components that affect United States persons' (December 1982), see Procedure 14: Employee Conduct and Procedure 15: Identifying, Investigating, and Reporting Questionable Activities.
27. 5 USC s. 2302(c). Under PPD–19, the Director of National Intelligence is responsible for educating the IC workforce on its whistleblowing rights and responsibilities. The Intelligence Community IG is providing subject matter expertise on this educational process through the ED-ICW&SP.
28. See Whistleblowers Protection Act 1994 (Qld) (now Public Interest Disclosure Act 2010), and Protected Disclosures Act 1994 (NSW) (since 2010, Public Interest Disclosures Act 1994).
29. Whistleblowers Protection Act 1994 (Qld), s. 31.

30. Taken out in mid-1990s in Queensland by the CMC to protect a Council CEO; and in NSW, in early 2012 by the Mayor of Cessnock Council to restrain the council from terminating the contract of the General Manager (see www.caselaw.nsw.gov.au/action/pjudg?jgmtid=159872); and an injunction to protect the General Manager of Ryde Council who had made a disclosure to the Independent Commission Against Corruption (see www.caselaw.nsw.gov.au/action/pjudg?jgmtid=161326, www.caselaw.nsw. gov.au/action/pjudg?jgmtid=160637).
31. Public Interest Disclosures Act 1994 (NSW), s. 20A, as inserted in 2010.
32. All five prosecutions took place in NSW and were for offenses under either the Protected Disclosures Act 1994 (NSW) (as it was then called) or the protected allegation provisions of the Police Act (NSW).
33. The NSW Commission Against Corruption's Operation Magnus (April 2011), which made findings of corruption conduct against the General Manager of Burwood Council. However, despite the ICAC's recommendation that criminal charges be laid against the General Manager for two offenses of detrimental action contrary to the Protected Disclosures Act 1994 (now the Public Interest Disclosures Act 1994), the Director of Public Prosecutions advised against prosecution: see www.icac.nsw.gov.au/investigations/past-investigations/article/3856.
34. See Public Interest Disclosure Act 2013 (Cth), s. 44(1).
35. Public Interest Disclosure Act 2008 (NT).
36. Public Interest Disclosure Act 2012 (ACT), s. 28(d).
37. In the Department of Defense, it is another title for the central major internal investigations unit (especially dealing with fraud control); in Taxation, it describes a semi-independent monitoring and assurance body; and the Inspector General of Intelligence and Security is an independent statutory agency overseeing complaints and integrity matters regarding national intelligence agencies, equivalent to an Ombudsman and anti-corruption body for those agencies.
38. Whistleblowers Protection Act 1994 (Qld), s. 44.
39. See Public Interest Disclosure Act 2002 (Tas.), ss. 38(1)(c), 60; Public Interest Disclosure Act 2003 (WA), ss. 20, 21, 23(2); Public Interest Disclosure Act 2008 (NT), s. 47; Public Interest Disclosure Act 2010 (Qld), ss. 28, 49, 60; Public Interest Disclosure Act 2012 (ACT), ss. 28, 33; Protected Disclosure Act 2012 (Vic.), ss. 55(2), 57–61.
40. Public Interest Disclosure Act 2013 (Cth), ss. 59(1) and 74.
41. See e.g., Public Interest Disclosure Act 2013 (Cth), s. 59(3)(a).
42. Public Interest Disclosure Act 2013 (Cth), ss. 26, 34, 60A.
43. See Public Interest Disclosure Act 2012 (ACT), s. 33(2); Public Interest Disclosure Act 2013 (Cth), s. 59(1).
44. Public Interest Disclosures Act 1994 (NSW) (as amended 2010), s. 6E(1)(b). The new federal PIDA requires agency heads to 'take reasonable steps' to ensure that all officials in their agency know the identity of all 'authorized officers' responsible for making the Act work in that agency: PIDA, s. 59(3)(b) and (c).
45. Protected Disclosure Act 2012 (Vic.), ss. 55, 57–61, 67. Prior to this reform, the oversight agency was Victoria's State Ombudsman: see Whistleblower Protection Act 2001.
46. Although the NSW Ombudsman's guidelines are theoretically non-binding, agencies must have policies and report to the Ombudsman on their operations, with the Ombudsman required to conduct monitoring and audit reports 'on the exercise of functions … and compliance' with the Act, covering all agencies at least once every 12 months: Public Interest Disclosures Act 1994 (NSW) (as amended 2010), ss. 6B, 6C, 6CA, 6D.
47. Public Interest Disclosure Act 2012 (ACT), ss. 32 and 33.

48. See e.g., Public Interest Disclosure Act 2013 (Cth), s. 76; cf. Public Interest Disclosure Act 2002 (Tas.), ss. 84 and 86.
49. Public Interest Disclosure Act 2003 (WA), ss. 19 and 20.
50. See e.g., Public Interest Disclosure Act 2013 (Cth), Consequential Amendments, Ombudsman Act 1976 (Cth), s. 5A; Public Interest Disclosure Act 2013 (Cth), notes at ss. 42, 46 and 58.
51. Public Interest Disclosure Act 2002 (Tas.), s. 62; Protected Disclosure Act 2012 (Vic.), s. 60(2).
52. Public Interest Disclosure Act 2010 (Qld), s. 59(b); Public Interest Disclosure Act 2012 (ACT), s. 28.
53. See Public Interest Disclosure Act 2013 (Cth), ss. 44(1A), 48(1), 50A.

PART IV

CONCLUSIONS

20. Research that whistleblowers want – and what they need

*Brian Martin**

INTRODUCTION

In 2011, I received this email:

> I am a whistleblower who has been forced into the state industrial commission to fight for a workers' compensation claim that was denied in February 2010. I represented myself after having legal representation who dropped my case in the review stage as they believed I didn't have a chance of winning … Can you suggest any type of help?

Then there was this one:

> As a whistleblower being put through the wringer, and this has occurred over a long period of time now, I think you can appreciate the nature and lack of information contained in this email … I'm scared. If I may, I'm a professional investigator of over 20 years experience. I'm amazed, though probably shouldn't be, that I've tabled evidence that is being ignored, including by national and international bodies. Though as I'm sure you appreciate, ain't I coppin' it as a result?

And this one:

> I am a former nurse, and I am contacting you in the hope that you will be able to give me advice regarding some whistle blowing that I have undertaken … I have decided to write a book about my experiences and am writing to you in the hope that you could advise me or give me the name of a lawyer who would be able to advise me as to the scope, boundaries and limitations of what can be published.[1]

These are samples of the dozens of unsolicited queries about whistleblowing and dissent I receive each year from individuals previously unknown to me. I try to provide helpful information and advice. It would be especially good if this information and advice were based on research. Unfortunately, there is not all that much research directly targeted at what whistleblowers want and need to know.

The topic of this chapter is research helpful to whistleblowers. I begin by outlining my experiences as a whistleblower adviser and describing some of the insights this role provides. Then I discuss what whistleblowers really need: practical skills and insights into the ways organizations and society operate. Next is an outline of the ways that research can help whistleblowers. Finally, I list a variety of research areas that I think are highly relevant to whistleblowers. These offer a research agenda oriented to those on the front line.[2]

INSIGHTS FROM ADVISING WHISTLEBLOWERS

A lot of what I cover in this chapter derives from my experiences advising whistleblowers, so it will be useful to describe the context. I'm a long-standing office bearer in Whistleblowers Australia (WBA), a volunteer national group that provides information, advice and contacts for whistleblowers. WBA was set up in 1991 and developed a profile for its advocacy and support (Martin 2004). Those who know about WBA pass the word to others, and that leads to people contacting me.

Another reason why people contact me is my website, which contains a large number of articles and other documents about dissent and whistleblowing. Some people having trouble at work start searching the Web for information and come across my site. Increasingly, enquirers say they are reading my book *The Whistleblower's Handbook* (Martin 1999, free online).

Having talked to whistleblowers regularly for 20 years, and researching the topic of dissent for a decade before that, I've heard from people from a wide range of occupations and circumstances. There are lots of public servants (government employees), teachers, police and military personnel. Because I'm an academic, a lot of academic and student enquirers are referred to me. There are also people working in private companies, churches, Aboriginal organizations and even women's groups. No sort of group seems to be exempt from these problems.

Despite this enormous diversity of occupations, and an associated diversity of political and personal viewpoints, there is a remarkable similarity in the experiences reported. The common denominator is speaking out or doing something threatening to a powerful individual or group. Reprisals are standard, and follow a fairly routine pattern of escalation. Another thing strikingly predictable is the failure of official channels. At least 90 per cent of enquirers have already blown the whistle and suffered reprisals. Many of them have gone to some external agency like an ombudsman or an anti-corruption commission. Some have approached half a dozen different agencies. In case after case, they report receiving little or no assistance, or at least not enough.

I am well aware that those who contact me are not typical. After all, if an agency provided ample protection and support to people, they would not be contacting me. So there is a systematic bias in the sample of people from which I draw generalizations. There is no obvious way to compensate for this bias. Suffice it to say that there are a lot of people who believe they are suffering reprisals at work and who are seeking information and support.

Although the sorts of people who contact me are not a representative sample of people who speak out at work, they do seem representative of those who contact WBA and other such organizations. I've talked to others in WBA who receive enquiries and their experiences are much the same as mine. When I read accounts by and about whistleblowers from the media and from researchers, everything is compatible with what I've observed (e.g., De Maria 1999; Glazer and Glazer 1989; Hunt 1995, 1998).

The people who contact me are not necessarily ones with high profile cases. When cases are reported in the media, they seldom involve people I've talked to, and often no one in WBA has talked to them. A few international cases come my way, especially because within WBA I'm the contact for international liaison. So far as I can tell, the dynamics of cases seem much the same in different countries, though the risks and reprisals are much more serious in some countries.

Over time, there have been some changes. Decades ago, most contact was by telephone or the post. WBA's branch in the state of New South Wales held weekly 'caring and sharing' meetings, and week after week new people would show up: face-to-face contact was an important feature of whistleblower support. When any of us received a call or a letter, we posted out a packet of leaflets and articles.

With the rise of e-mail and the Web in the 1990s, this pattern gradually changed. Today, the majority of contact is initially via e-mail: it is obvious that people are scouring the Web to learn about whistleblowing, sometimes reading lots of material, and then contacting us if they have specific queries. Sometimes I do not even know what country an e-mail enquirer is living in, especially when they are cautious about giving out personal information. The Web has internationalized the provision of information for whistleblowers, though only to the extent of availability of material in relevant languages. With the uptake of e-mail and the Web, there has been less demand for face-to-face meetings which, in New South Wales, are now held on an ad hoc basis rather than every week.

Another noticeable change over the past couple of decades concerns the respectability of being called a whistleblower. In the 1990s, it was common for callers to say they did not want to be called whistleblowers: they considered it a derogatory term. They would say, 'I was just doing my job'. However, media coverage and whistleblower legislation seems to have increased the status of being a whistleblower, so that now the term seems as often to be a badge of honor as an unwelcome label.

Some callers remain anonymous and give only a few details about their situation. Others launch into an exhaustive (and exhausting) blow-by-blow account of their experiences (see Alford 2001). Some who make contact by e-mail remain anonymous; others send huge files giving enough material for a book. Gradually, through hearing stories and reading reams of documents, a sense emerges about what seems to be a genuine, or at least typical, case of whistleblowing, in which there seems to be some unfairness or other problem involved, and the person who raised concerns about it is being unfairly treated. The core issues of some cases can be identified by studying them in depth; furthermore, their complexity becomes apparent.

With this background of study and experience, it becomes possible to sense whether a caller has a genuine case. In WBA, our policy is not to try to judge whether someone is 'really' a whistleblower, because the process of assessing someone's case can be a further experience of invalidation and humiliation, adding to the trauma they have already experienced. Nevertheless, it is often quite apparent that some cases do not fit the standard picture.

At the boundary with whistleblowing lies a host of people with a spectrum of related issues and concerns, and many of these people contact anyone who will listen:

- people who have been bullied at work. Some are bullied as a reprisal for speaking out (Martin and Peña 2012), but others are bullied for other reasons, for example for being a member of a minority group or just a convenient target for their harasser. They might be considered whistleblowers in a very general sense when they speak out about their treatment;
- people in family disputes, for example, fathers bitter about child access arrangements following divorce;
- people with personal grievances. They might not get along with a co-worker, or get into disputes with their boss, or believe they are being unfairly treated. In many such cases, it is plausible to suspect that the person with the grievance may be the source of the problem;

- people sued for defamation or threatened with legal action. Some of them spoke out about some problem (they best fit the usual description of whistleblowers), but others were expressing their views about an individual, a business, or whatever, and someone is trying to shut them up;
- people who believe they are under surveillance or the target of a conspiracy. Some of these individuals seem to be deluded, for example, when they believe government agencies are beaming radiation at them to control their thoughts, even though there is no good reason why the government would have the slightest interest in their activities.

These are some of the prime categories of people presenting with problems in what might be called the penumbra of whistleblowing: only occasionally do their situations fit conventional definitions of whistle-blowing, yet there are some commonalities between their experiences and problems and those of whistleblowers.[3] One implication is that research on whistleblowing should be coordinated with research on problems people raise that do not fit into the formal category of whistleblowing.

Gaining insights about whistleblowing by talking to whistleblowers has both weaknesses and strengths. Some obvious weaknesses are that the sample is unrepresentative and is biased towards serious cases in which formal processes have not resolved the matter; many of the cases are unverified; only one side of the story is heard and the sample is dominated by people who are vocal, whereas other serious problems may go unheard. Another problem is that whistleblowing in the private sector is under-represented, perhaps because formal protection is minimal, so those who speak out seldom have procedural grounds for contesting adverse actions and therefore do not seek outside assistance. Fortunately, some of these weaknesses can be addressed by studying survey and other research that gives a feel for typical patterns (Brown 2008; Miceli *et al.* 2008) and allows the anecdotal cases to be put in context, often as falling at the extreme end of the spectrum.

The advantage of talking to whistleblowers is the fact that it allows one to acquire a vivid feeling for the incredibly powerful adverse effects of reprisals, for the interminable and complex nature of most cases, and for the tortuousness of official channels and the ways they fall short for all too many whistleblowers (for an examination of whistleblowing and suffering see Smith, Chapter 10). One of the most valuable insights from talking to many whistleblowers is a strong sense of the usual things that happen, which seem remarkably similar and mostly independent of occupation or circumstances. These advantages provide a useful basis for commenting on research that is or would be useful to whistleblowers.[4]

One of the most common refrains is that whistleblowers want protection and justice. A very large number of them are desperately searching for validation, which they hope to achieve by finding a champion, such as a lawyer or a crusading agency, that will fix the problem they spoke out about and restore their reputation and their position. At the same time, their stories and available research suggest that this is a forlorn hope: very few whistleblowers who have suffered serious reprisals receive formal vindication and fewer still are restored to their previous jobs and careers. Even less likely is that the problems they spoke out about are fixed and wrongdoers subject to any significant penalties. My conclusion is that whistleblowers know what they want but what they want is often not achievable, and hence what they really need, in the face of an unyielding reality, is something else.

WHAT DO WHISTLEBLOWERS REALLY NEED?

My assumption is that in dealing with problems in organizations and society, those who want to bring about change need skills. Relying on internal procedures or an outside agency is uncertain at best, especially when top figures in an organization are part of the problem. Workers, when they speak out about such problems, seldom bring about significant organizational change. About the most they can hope for is some protection against reprisals, or perhaps a generous compensation payment. There are exceptions, but not as many as most people imagine, because quite a few of the rare cases of whistleblowers who make a difference are trumpeted in the media. Just because a few whistleblowers win the compensation lottery does not mean the lottery provides good odds.

As has often been remarked, many whistleblowers are conscientious workers who believe the system works. That is why they speak out when they see a problem: they believe that managers will agree to look into the problem and, if it is confirmed, take steps to address it. So they are shocked to the core when they come under attack.

There is another sort of worker whose experiences are much different but seldom receives much attention: the shrewd, strategic worker who understands how the organization works, realizes the risks in speaking out and hence proceeds in a different way. Such a worker is akin to an activist in a social movement, working strategically to bring about change rather than assuming that revealing a problem is sufficient to cause it to be fixed.[5]

Collecting Information

A standard piece of advice for whistleblowers is to collect lots of information about the problem. This sounds straightforward, and in some aspects it is, as for instance saving documents and e-mails. It might also involve soliciting signed statements, sending messages that confirm interpretations, listening in on conversations and, in some cases, making covert recordings.

Part of being effective in collecting information is knowing what is useful and what is not.[6] It involves knowing whether to use formal information gathering methods such as accessing personnel files held by the organization or using freedom of information requests. Another dimension is being trusted by co-workers who have their own special access to information and are willing to pass on some of it.

Writing Accounts

Having lots of information is a good start, but to make an effective case, it is nearly always valuable to be able to develop a succinct summary of the issues. When approaching potential supporters or outlets, whether co-workers, outside agencies, journalists or social media, it is vital to be able to describe the issues in a persuasive way. Too many whistleblowers rely on long-winded verbal accounts of their experiences that confuse and exhaust rather than inform listeners. Too many provide piles of documents without providing a convenient summary or even a sequence of events.

The skills involved here are ones of extracting central issues, namely, ones that inform and resonate with others, and mustering evidence and arguments in a way that is understandable to the audience. This usually requires some capacity to see a situation as others might, namely, to step back from the intensely personal and emotional close-up view.[7] Incidentally, writing about one's case can be therapeutic (Pennebaker 1997). An alternative or supplement to writing one's own story is finding someone who is willing to do it.

Understanding Organizational Dynamics

As well as collecting information about the problem, it is valuable to learn how the organization works: who has connections; what networks exist; what practices are standard; how people get things done; what sort of measures are taken against those who challenge the status quo (Bolman and Deal 2000; Schrijvers 2004). It is helpful to find experienced workers who can provide stories of what has happened in the past.

Building Support

It is vital to find potential allies to help bring about change. This might involve gently raising issues and, without giving away too much, finding out who might be sympathetic to a change effort. Sometimes allies are internal, such as co-workers or union officials; sometimes they are external, such as activist groups or journalists. The point is to find allies and make a common cause. Five people taking action is far more effective than acting alone, and 50 people acting is, in many organizations, the beginning of a mass movement.

Sociologist Deena Weinstein (1979) has likened bureaucracies (the standard organizational form, especially for large organizations) to authoritarian states.[8] In an authoritarian state, there is little or no freedom of speech, no free elections, no independent opposition parties and sometimes no freedom of assembly. These same features apply in bureaucracies. People can speak to each other in private, but speaking out critically of management is a likely road to dismissal. Top bureaucrats are not elected; there are seldom opposition movements. The implication is that a whistleblower in an organization is analogous to a lone dissident in a repressive state: the most likely scenario is reprisals, such as arrest, without having any noticeable effect on the power of the state or its policies.

Authoritarian states can be challenged, most effectively by people power, namely, mass action without using violence (Ackerman and DuVall 2000). The analogy in an organization is gaining widespread support for change and then taking collective action, for example, simply not obeying policies, working to rule and calling in sick. An individual taking such action has little chance of survival but with enough participation the power is enormous. There are guides to building support against repressive regimes (Sharp 2010; War Resisters' International 2009), but nothing well-known for building support within an organization.

Unions and professional associations can provide a collective voice against management and potentially can be valuable allies for whistleblowers. Informal feedback on the role of unions and professional associations gives a mixed picture: in some cases they are outstanding advocates for whistleblowers, but in other instances provide no assistance or, even worse, help the other side.

Generating Publicity

In many cases, publicity is a whistleblower's most powerful tool.[9] Publicity takes the issue out of the closed circle of perpetrators and bystanders, appealing to others who have no personal stake in it. Outsiders, if anything, have a stake in exposing and dealing with corruption and hazards to the public. Publicity holds the potential of bringing in powerful outside forces to challenge perpetrators. It can also encourage others on the inside to break ranks.

However, few whistleblowers know much about generating publicity. To be effective, they need to know how the mass media operate: what sorts of information and angles are most likely to interest journalists; how to approach and interact with journalists; how to manage an ongoing relationship; what to expect after media coverage; and how to use media coverage in ongoing struggles.

There are some traps for whistleblowers, including journalists more interested in sensationalism than balanced reporting; journalists who break implied confidentiality; and editors who decide to attack the whistleblower. Learning about the risks, and weighing them against opportunities, is important for being effective in using the media.

Whistleblowers no longer need to be reliant on mass media for publicity: they can make their own by setting up websites, making contributions to blogs and sending out e-mails and tweets. There is an entire skill set in using social media for impact, getting out information, winning allies and putting opponents on the back foot.

As well as the open use of media for publicity, it is also possible to do this while remaining anonymous. It is possible to be an anonymous informant to a journalist, to leak documents either to a journalist or an online site like WikiLeaks, and to anonymously set up websites and send e-mails. Special skills are needed for such an operation, including making sure documents and revelations reveal no traces of one's identity; performing all significant activities offsite so that checks on a work computer or e-mail address reveal nothing; and using methods to hide one's electronic identity.[10]

In pre-Internet days, there were cases in which dissident employees produced newsletters commenting on workplace activities, exposing problematical actions or policies. This involved writing the text, laying it out in newsletter format, printing it and distributing it to co-workers – all anonymously. This sort of undercover commentator role is now possible in a more direct electronic fashion, by using websites and anonymous remailers, but with the proviso that electronic methods of tracking down individuals are now more sophisticated. There is an evolutionary path from *samizdat* (dissident writing in the former Soviet Union, often copied by hand or typed) to current day distribution of information unwelcome to managers. This indicates again the parallels between bureaucracies and authoritarian states: challengers need to know how to dissent and survive.

Self-understanding

Organizational activists, to be effective, need to understand themselves: their goals, capacities, strengths and vulnerabilities. It is surprising how many whistleblowers have not thought through their goals: when I ask them; they may be nonplussed or express an entirely unrealistic hope of getting their job back and having justice done for all the wrongdoers. Figuring out sensible goals involves understanding one's own place in the world and realistically assessing what can be done.

Whistleblowers need to know what they are good at, so they can deploy their strengths. They also need to know their own weaknesses and vulnerabilities. It is not wise to launch a court process that could take years when financial or emotional weaknesses will undermine the effort later on. Self-understanding includes knowing one's social skills; a related form of understanding involves figuring out what others think and are likely to do. Mounting a publicity campaign, for example, depends on judging what will be effective in convincing others. Knowing whether one has a sterling reputation or is seen as self-centered and self-interested can help in planning campaigns.

Self-understanding is difficult to develop even for those who live uncomplicated lives. A worker who challenges the status quo and suffers reprisals is typically subject to all sorts of reactions that have seldom been experienced before, often undermining the worker's previous self-image and making self-understanding more difficult. Obtaining sensitive feedback from counsellors or wise friends – and, even better, other whistleblowers – can help in developing a better sense of one's own capacities, thoughts and behaviors.

I have described six areas in which people can develop skills that will better enable them to bring about organizational change with a lower risk of suffering reprisals. These can be used to stimulate ideas about research helpful to whistleblowers. But first it will be useful to outline avenues by which research can help whistleblowers.

HOW RESEARCH CAN BENEFIT WHISTLEBLOWERS

Research of various sorts can benefit whistleblowers, most obviously research directly on whistleblowing, but also research that gives insights into the operation of organizations or into how to develop skills. Here I will describe several avenues by which research can benefit whistle-blowers.

It is important to point out that whistleblowing research is not necessarily designed to assist whistleblowers. It often has wider goals, such as challenging patterns of corruption, improving the functioning of organizations or avoiding public health disasters. Whistleblowing is often seen as a means to alert society to problems that need addressing: protecting or validating whistleblowers then becomes a means to an end, rather than the end itself. Because my focus here is on whistleblowers and their travails, I look at ways research can benefit them, while acknowledging that in many cases wider goals can and should take precedence.

Indirect Effect 1

Whistleblowing research can have an impact on policy relevant to whistleblowers, most obviously on whistleblower laws, and also on related laws and policies on access to information, compensation for unfair dismissal, and media shield laws, as well as internal organization policies. Whistleblower researchers seem far more likely to have an impact on laws and policies than whistleblowers themselves. For example, in Australia, quite a few state governments introduced whistle-blower laws without any consultation with whistleblower groups.

Researchers are more likely to be consulted or have their findings taken into account because they have higher status, as credentialed experts, and are seen as more independent. It is reasonable to presume that whistleblowing research is more likely to have an impact on laws and policies when it involves government agencies as stakeholders or co-investigators, when it has a high profile (including media coverage) and when it resonates with the orientations and ethos of policy makers. It is possible that sometimes research will provide a justification for a policy that was desired anyway, but even in such cases the research may affect policy in small ways: policy makers, in using research to justify their actions, may adopt some elements of the research agenda.

Indirect Effect 2

Whistleblowing research occasionally gains a public profile, sometimes due to effective promotion and sometimes due to enterprising journalists. Publicly visible whistleblowing research can have effects on several audiences. Policy makers are more likely to be aware of it and possibly take it into account; members of the public are more likely to be aware of whistleblowing and think it is worthwhile; potential whistleblowers may be emboldened; and whistleblowers may gain some credibility. Most of this assumes the research is supportive of whistleblowing.

There is far more media coverage of individual whistleblowers than there is of whistleblowing research. Nevertheless, publicity about whistleblowing research gives extra credibility to whistleblowing via the status of research and of the researchers. Researchers are commonly seen as independent and respectable, based on their achievements: if they are taking whistleblowing seriously, this implies others should too.

Indirect Effect 3

When research findings are popularized, for example, described in media stories, some readers may learn from them. For example, if researchers say that laws are too weak, potential whistleblowers may decide to rely less on legal protection, and perhaps not blow the whistle at all. If researchers say many workers are afraid to report on wrongdoing, potential whistleblowers may gain a new appreciation of what is going on at their workplaces.

Popularization of research findings can occur in many ways, for example, through media releases, media stories, websites, blogs and word of mouth. The key process here is that someone explains the findings in a way that is accessible and understandable to the general public.

Direct Effect

It is possible for whistleblowers to read research papers and in this way be influenced by their research content. No one has studied how often this happens, but it is probably only rarely.

Most research, including whistleblowing research, is written for peers, namely, other researchers, and is seldom appealing to others. There is a tension for researchers in writing: which audiences are more important?

Writing in typical academic style has the best prospect of gaining scholarly recognition, but it reduces accessibility to others. Writing popular articles, for example, for newspapers and blogs, gets the message out to wider audiences but potentially at the expense of scholarly credibility. Doing both means more work.

Information for Whistleblowers

No one seems to have studied how workers go searching for information about whistleblowing. Based on anecdotal evidence, it is plausible to assume that two routes are common: searching the Web and obtaining links from others. Some just stick 'whistleblowing' into a search engine and proceed until they find something useful. Others, who have told co-workers, family or friends about their difficulties, receive from one of them some suggested links. Another likely route is seeing stories in the media. Other routes to information are probably less common, such as seeing posters, receiving leaflets, attending talks and attending classes.

Also little studied is what sort of information whistleblowers find most useful. It is plausible that important factors are accessibility, especially free online access, readability, practical orientation and content relevant to understanding and strategic choice and, even better, the possibility of personal support and advice. Most research papers do not rate highly by these criteria: they are most commonly only available through subscription databases or academic libraries, are not written for a general readership, are oriented to research findings rather than practical purposes, and do not look at strategic choice. Few researchers offer to provide advice to individuals. If this assessment is correct, it suggests research is more likely to benefit whistleblowers indirectly than directly.

Possible Risks

I have been assuming that whistleblowing research is always advantageous to whistleblowers, but in some cases it is possible that harm may be greater than benefits. Some research projects require a fair bit of time and input from whistleblowers, for example, extensive interviewing or provision of documents. If there is no benefit to whistleblowers – as may be true with some student projects – then time is wasted: any research project has opportunity costs. On the other hand, whistleblowers might appreciate that others are interested in their stories.

A potential disadvantage is that attention is diverted from important issues to less significant ones. Another risk is that whistleblowers might think that research is going to help them directly and promptly, whereas the benefits are modest, indirect and diffuse.

In some cases, research may put whistleblowers at risk, for example, by revealing their identity to employers or prosecutors. This is most likely to occur when whistleblowing itself is most dangerous, for example, when it involves the military or organized crime or occurs in a repressive regime.

To my knowledge, no one has studied or even commented on the hazards of whistleblowing research for whistleblowers, which suggests the risks are probably small, with time wasting being the most likely problem. Even so, the risks should be taken seriously because even just one or two negative experiences can poison opportunities for subsequent researchers.

RESEARCH TOPICS FOR WHISTLEBLOWERS

Putting 'whistleblowing' into Google Scholar gives an indication of the sorts of research available and what is most highly cited, which includes whistleblower laws, surveys of workers, organizational climate, conditions favouring whistleblowing, benefits, predictors, definitions, impacts, models and policies. It would be valuable for someone to do a review of the field, giving an assessment of the research done so far.

My interest here is slightly different, less about what researchers think is worth studying and more about what sorts of research would be useful to whistleblowers. Because this topic has received so little systematic attention, my aim is to stimulate thinking rather than reach definitive conclusions. Here, I list a range of potential research topics that I think would be useful to whistleblowers, focusing on content that seems to have been neglected by researchers so far. For findings to be useful to whistleblowers, in most cases they would need to be written in a readable fashion and made freely available, either directly by the researchers or indirectly via popularizations.

Psychology of Attackers

Whistleblowers need to understand the psychology of others around them, especially those who initiate reprisals, who join mobbing attacks and who sit passively as observers. What do whistleblower opponents think? How do they justify their behavior?

Many whistleblowers say, afterwards, 'I was naive'. By this they mean they had no idea that bosses and co-workers would respond in the unsympathetic, harsh and unrelenting way they did. Researchers have spent more time looking at the psychology of whistleblowers than at the psychology of managers and co-workers confronted by whistleblowing.

The most useful study along these lines is Robert Jackall's book *Moral Mazes* (1988). Jackall gained access to corporations as an anthropologist, observing the mores of organizational culture. He witnessed the treatment of two individuals who tried to challenge official policy, and captured the thinking of those on the 'other side'. More investigation along these lines would be immensely valuable to whistleblowers.[11] Potentially relevant is the study of the psychology of managers who are perceived as abusive (Crawshaw 2007).

Anti-ostracism Skills

Whistleblowers are often ostracized: formerly friendly co-workers turn away. Walking through the office and having lunch can become traumatic rites. Ordinary collegial relationships become problematical. Many whistleblowers do not understand why this is happening. Even when they do, they usually find it very difficult to live with.

There is some research on ostracism (Williams 2001), but not much is oriented to strategies to deal with it. Simple insights would aid survival.

I know one individual who, even after he had made a formal complaint about bias in hiring, implicating a small clique, was able to continue cordial interactions with his erstwhile colleagues. By doing this, he was able to collect valuable information for his further efforts. Significantly, he was an anthropologist, perhaps suggesting that skills in interacting with an alien and potentially hostile culture may be useful.

Winning over Bystanders

Whistleblowers usually have little hope of convincing their opponents, especially when the opponents have a personal stake in corrupt or dangerous practices. However, there is hope to win over those with less invested in such practices – those who are commonly called bystanders. Co-workers may support the whistleblower in principle but be afraid to become involved because they might suffer reprisals. Other co-workers are just too busy with their jobs to become involved. Some avoid any sort of conflict.

Some whistleblowers are able to win over bystanders, through personal skills or perhaps by good luck. Relevant skills include knowing who is most likely to be sympathetic, how to approach individuals and figuring out the potential role of each individual. There is a large amount of research on persuasion (Cialdini 1984; Rushkoff 2000) but little on how persuasive techniques can be selected, adapted and learned by whistleblowers.

Assessing Threats

Many whistleblowers suffer reprisals, a process that is well documented (and discussed by Smith in Chapter 10). What is not so well studied is the seriousness of threats, whether explicit or perceived. A threat (of being reprimanded, dismissed, sued or assaulted) can itself be a reprisal, but there is also the question of the actual risk that a threat will be realized. For example, a potential whistleblower or a bystander might be worried that saying anything will jeopardize promotion prospects. Is this a genuine fear? A boss might threaten dismissal or legal action. Is the risk serious or is the threat a bluff or even just idle chatter in a moment of annoyance?

The seriousness of threats depends sensitively on the circumstances, including the psychology of the person making an explicit threat. Even so, facts and figures can help to assess risk. For example, it would be useful to know how often employees are threatened with being sued and how many legal actions are actually initiated.

Exemplary Stories

Stories about individual whistleblowers are a mainstay in writing in the field, especially more popular genres. Stories are highly educational: they vividly portray scenarios with which readers or viewers can empathize and sometimes identify. Stories help validate a whistleblower's experience which is otherwise inexplicable to others and sometimes to the whistleblower.

However, there is a systematic bias in the stories available. They are mostly about dramatic cases, in which the stakes are high and the whistleblower righteous (and right). Prominent stories are biased towards outcomes that vindicate the whistleblower, even when wrongdoers sometimes escape justice. This is apparent in Hollywood treatments such as *Serpico, Karen Silkwood, The Insider, Erin Brockovich* and *The Whistleblower,* and highly publicized cases such as Sharron Watkins of Enron.

Researchers could do more to supplement the stories available with ones that are more typical of whistleblower experiences. These could be hypothetical, using survey data to compose a series of exemplary stories, or chosen from actual cases as typifying common but neglected trajectories. Especially important in stories are the lessons based on what was done along the way and how things might have been done better, based on information about successes and failures.

Enforcing Whistleblower Laws

Many whistleblower laws look good on paper but are less satisfactory in practice. Researchers have examined the laws in some depth but have devoted less attention to enforcement. This might involve studies of how discretion is exercised by authorities; how courts interpret laws; how employers are able to avoid or nullify the intent of the laws; and how advocates can push along reluctant or overloaded agencies. Vaughn (2012) provides the best treatment of these issues yet available.

Challenging Disincentives to Speaking Out

Defamation law, official secrets acts, corporate non-disclosure rules, privacy laws and non-disclosure clauses in legal settlements are some of the formal means that can discourage employees from speaking out, because they are afraid they might be hit with legal sanctions and even criminal prosecution. Research is needed on dealing with these disincentives. One solution is to reform the rules, for example to change draconian defamation laws, but this is usually a long-term prospect requiring political rather than research skills. Another option is to improve understanding of how these disincentives can operate, the likelihood that they will actually be used and the ways they can be sidestepped or challenged. For example, if employees understand that publicity about their claims is likely to reduce the risk that they will be met with a defamation action or some other charge, they can modify their plans accordingly (Gray and Martin 2006). Likewise, if employers know that employees might respond to threats by seeking publicity, they might adopt a different stance. If researchers show the damaging effects of disincentives for speaking out, this can help discredit these methods and encourage more employees to challenge them.

Choice Criteria

In pragmatic terms, whistleblowers need to know what to do. A few always know exactly what they should or must do, but many agonize over their choices. Whistleblower advisers often spell out the sorts of choices available, sometimes expanding awareness of options. But even knowing about a variety of options, there is still the question of making a decision.

Research would be useful to whistleblowers if it articulated or clarified the criteria that are most likely to aid whistleblowers in choosing options that advance their goals – assuming they have accurately understood their own goals. Some possible criteria might relate to effectiveness in bringing about change, short-term versus long-term gains, and surviving in the job versus creating a new career.

Emotional Survival

It is well known that many whistleblowers suffer extreme stress, sometimes leading to psychological problems that may continue for years afterwards (Lennane 1993). Being able to endure stress, or even thrive on it, is a valuable attribute or skill in such circumstances. There is a body of writing about emotional resilience that is relevant (Maddi and Khoshaba 2005). More research on the specific skills for resilience against reprisals in the workplace would be highly valuable to whistleblowers.

Families and Friends

Whistleblowers greatly benefit from having family members, friends, co-workers, counsellors and others who are available to listen and offer guidance and support. Researchers and writers often look at whistleblowing from the point of view of whistleblowers but only infrequently from the point of view of families, friends and other potential supporters. Insights for these supporters would be valuable, for example, on understanding what whistleblowers are going through and how they are likely to respond; on interventions that are most likely to be useful; and on the advantages and risks of becoming more directly involved in the struggle. Many of these insights for supporters can be taken directly from counselling practice, but others may need to be developed to apply specifically to the situation of whistleblowers.

Degradation Rituals

A degradation ritual or degradation ceremony is a process by which authorities take action to lower a person's status (Garfinkel 1956). Formal rituals include reprimands, investigations and referring people to psychiatrists. Informal rituals include tirades from the boss and condemnations at staff meetings. Degradation rituals are regularly used against whistleblowers, sending a signal to any witnesses about the unacceptability of the target and the target's actions.

Degradation rituals are intended to shame targets, and many targets are indeed shamed: they feel humiliated. Such rituals are powerful tools of control. There is a fair bit of research on degradation rituals (Thérèse and Martin 2010), but hardly any on how to resist. Some options are to refuse to participate (for example, by walking out of meetings, if necessary by claiming illness), to describe and expose what is happening thus reducing the ritual's power, and developing psychological defenses that reduce the power of the ritual to cause shame.

What Processes Work?

Whistleblowers need information about which laws, agencies and other official processes actually work, or when they are most likely to. Specifics provide the most telling evidence, such as that 74 out of 75 appeals to a court by whistleblowers were unsuccessful (Devine 2004: 85) or that ten out of 15 approaches to an agency resulted in an investigation. These sorts of figures help whistleblowers to make more informed judgments about their course of action. (They are still subject to over-optimism, often based on a whistleblower's assumption that 'my case is different, because I know I'm right', not grasping that previous whistleblowers felt exactly the same way.)[12] This sort of specific information is highly useful to whistleblowers to whom it directly applies, but not all that useful to others.

Next most useful are generalizations about avenues, agencies or laws, such as that hotlines hardly ever work or that the False Claims Act is the most promising avenue for having an impact. An excellent example of this sort of information is *The Whistleblower's Survival Guide* (Devine 1997; see also Devine and Maassarani 2011), about half of which contains commentary about specific US laws and agencies. This sort of information is useful to many whistleblowers in the United States, though it gradually gets out of date and has limited value in other countries.

Of more general value is information on the signs of effective processes, agencies and laws, namely, the sorts of things to look for when deciding whether to pursue or accept mediation, whether to use internal grievance procedures, which external agencies to approach or which legal mechanisms to use. Potentially useful signs might be outcomes of previous cases,[13] openness about outcomes, prompt responses to queries, and favourable comment from whistleblower advisers. Researchers could, for example, correlate various signs with actual outcomes in order to generate a guide to choosing the most promising options.

Dealing with the Media

Publicity is often a powerful tool for whistleblowers, yet few of them know much about how the media operate. Some whistleblowers learn through their own interactions with journalists and editors, but this can be restricted to particular circumstances.

Whistleblowers need to know whether it is worthwhile contacting journalists in the first place and, if so, which ones and how to go about it. Therefore, it would be useful to study how journalists and editors respond to whistleblowers and to their stories, including assessments of different ways of making contact with journalists, providing information and framing their stories.

Changing Organizational Cultures

Blowing the whistle is one way to try to bring about a change in actions and policies. Another approach is to try to change the culture in an organization, so that problems are less likely to arise and addressing them is more accepted. An example is introducing into a hospital a system for routinely reporting adverse incidents, without fault being attributed to those who make reports (Freestone *et al.* 2006). The result of bedding down such a system is a culture of openness and learning from mistakes, replacing the more common culture of hiding mistakes. With such a system, the need for whistleblowing is greatly reduced.

The question is, then, how can such a change be brought about? Organizational researchers have examined change processes extensively, but usually from the point of view of high performance rather than addressing the sorts of issues that confront whistleblowers. The sort of research that would most help potential whistleblowers would say, in effect, rather than speaking out immediately, here are some options for bringing about change in the longer term, and here is some information about how an individual can determine whether such change is possible and, if so, how to contribute to it.

How to Leak

Leaking is the unauthorized disclosure of information. It can be a method of whistleblowing, typically without the leaker's identity being revealed. Arguably, anonymous whistleblowing via leaking is often more effective than revealing one's identity in making disclosures: this type of leaker is far less likely to suffer reprisals, is able to remain in the job and continue to collect information and leak it, and normally contacts outside groups that are likely to have an impact. Leaking is most commonly done to the media or action groups, such as environmental campaigners, which are more likely to take the information to receptive audiences, including the general public, whereas the audience for open disclosures is most commonly bosses, human resources staff and outside agencies such as ombudsmen.

There are disadvantages to anonymous leaking. One is that leakers do not carry the moral authority of an open whistleblower. Another is that witch-hunts for leakers can cause fear in a workplace and sometimes lead to reprisals against innocent parties.

The phenomenon of WikiLeaks has triggered a huge media interest, but this should not obscure the reality that leaking has been occurring for decades and that most leaking will continue to be by traditional methods of passing documents to individual journalists or activists. There is only a little research on leaking (Flynn 2006) and a limited amount of writing about how to do it effectively (Hager and Burton 1999: 240–7; POGO 2002: 9–16). This area is wide open for investigation.

Citizen Action against Corruption

Most research on corruption looks at what can be done by governments and corporations. The potential role of citizens has been neglected. Yet there is evidence that citizen action, through forms of non-violent action or people power such as rallies, mass petitions, coordinated symbolic actions and committees to monitor projects, can have a major effect (Beyerle 2011; Beyerle and Hassan 2009).

Whistleblowers can play an important role in assisting citizen movements against corruption, by providing information directly to campaigners and by making principled public stands that inspire opposition to corrupt practices. However, there is little research on citizen action against corruption and none focusing on the most useful contributions by whistleblowers as part of such action. There are many possible topics to investigate, such as how to organize a citizens' group; how to maintain momentum; how to interact with official agencies; and how to follow up on promised reforms. Research on the connection between whistleblowing and citizen action against corruption can usefully draw on research from three areas: whistleblowing, non-violent action and corruption.

CONCLUSION

Apparently there are no studies specifically investigating what sorts of research projects are most useful to whistleblowers. In this absence, I have presented preliminary ideas drawing on my experience hearing from and advising whistleblowers, in conjunction with recommendations from other whistleblower advisers. Whistleblowers often initially seek advice on specific steps in taking legal or other formal action, but in practice this is usually late in the process, after they have suffered reprisals. To use a health/disease analogy, whistleblowers are seeking a cure or palliative care for an auto-immune disease that has afflicted them, namely, an organization that has turned against its own antibodies – whistleblowers being analogous to antibodies fighting organizational pathology. After the auto-immune reaction has begun, it is extremely difficult to bring the organization back to health. Far better is prevention, which can be by the antibodies (the whistleblowers) being much more informed and strategically savvy against both the organizational disease and the auto-immune reprisals.

Research is seldom directly useful to whistleblowers: research papers and books are usually oriented to other researchers, not to actual or potential whistleblowers. However, research can have an indirect effect via popularizations and via impacts on policy and practice and on public attitudes. Furthermore, whistleblowers are not the only beneficiaries from whistleblowing research, which can be used to inform policy and to foster healthier organizational cultures. It is not sensible to orient all whistleblowing research to whistleblowers. Still, the emphasis is tilted too far in the other direction, towards formal procedures to deal with disclosures, with little research that can give guidance to whistleblowers and, more generally, organizational activists.

I have outlined a series of possible research areas that I think would help workers increase their understanding and improve their skills for surviving and bringing about change, and surviving in the face of opposition. The common feature of these research areas is that they do not rely on agencies, laws or management initiatives: they are oriented to practical knowledge and skills. An empowered workforce, along with an empowered citizenry, is a potent challenge to corruption and, more widely, to other organizational pathologies such as bullying and disregard of the public interest.

When I receive an e-mail or phone call from a whistleblower, I would like to be able to refer them to practical, accessible advice. And I would like to know there is solid research backing up that advice.

NOTES

* I thank Jeff Ruch and Guido Strack for their contributions and for their separate comments to me, and the editors for many helpful suggestions.

1. These extracts from e-mails have been edited, including the removal and altering of identifying information.
2. I sent a draft of this chapter to several whistleblower advisers for comment. Two of them provided comments: Jeff Ruch, executive director of Public Employees for Environmental Responsibility, a US organization; and Guido Strack, of Whistleblower-Network Germany. Their comments are given below.
3. Guido Strack comments: Up to here I can completely confirm your statements from my experience answering the hotline of Whistleblower-Network Germany. I had always thought that getting so many enquiries far from the classical definition of whistleblowing was due to the fact that there is no German equivalent to the word whistleblowing; we use the English language word, although not many Germans know it. Yet you confirm that this phenomenon occurs also where the word whistleblowing is more widely known.
4. Jeff Ruch is Executive Director of Public Employees for Environmental Responsibility (PEER), an important US private non-profit watchdog organization that 'protects the government employees who protect our environment'. He provided the following comments in response to a draft of this chapter, saying they illustrate the perspective of 'an advocate rather than a researcher'.
    1. On social acceptance of whistleblowing, we are seeing a greater social expectation that there *should* be whistleblowers. So, when a particularly horrendous scandal involving a long-standing abuse finally surfaces, our media ask, 'Where were the whistleblowers? Why didn't someone report this years ago?'.
    2. The vast majority of people we see at PEER are not facing reprisal for blowing the whistle; they face retaliation for simply doing their jobs too well or on a sensitive subject. This is often the case with scientists, who in many cases have been doing research on a subject for years if not decades. Suddenly, due to a shift in political winds or an outside circumstance (such as an environmental lawsuit citing the scientist's data), these specialists through no conscious act are transformed from Golden Boy to Public Enemy #1. I think some attention should be paid to folks treated like whistleblowers but who, on the basis of the content of their information, are merely institutionally inconvenient.
    3. In addition to the mindset of bureaucratic retaliation, some note should be taken of organization tolerance or promotion of such behavior. When retaliators are protecting the agency or its agenda, as is often the case, they are then promoted. Conversely, retaliators rarely suffer negative career consequence, regardless of the outcome of the whistleblower's 'case'. Thus, it may be far too narrow to look at a retaliator's mindset outside the context of the organizational power dynamics which, in my view, are the driving force behind organized actions to quash dissent.
    4. In our experience, people take career risks in order to accomplish change, either stopping what they perceive to be a bad thing or bringing about or rescuing a good result. In many instances, these conscientious folks would willingly sacrifice their career to produce the change they seek, because they see it as transcending them. The motivation of the whistleblower in seeking the social or environmental benefit deserves more attention. In that same vein, whistleblower litigation (which we do a fair amount) is of limited benefit. Even if the whistleblower 'wins' and is restored, the judicial forum can only redress the personal injury and has no power to address the underlying dysfunction that

triggered blowing the whistle in the first place. In some instances, the winner is restored to an even more hostile and screwed up situation.

5. Finally, to follow that train of thought, our organization is rooted in how much change for the good can be accomplished by harnessing the insights of these inside experts. In our experience, a lot of the progress we see comes only because someone sought outside helped to turn the internal course of events. Our website is full of examples. Since PEER is completely 'intake-driven', every legal victory is rooted in an employee activist.

   P.S. If you visit our website, you will note that we counsel a 'deliver the message and not the messenger' approach, embodied by the underwear we sell (boxer shorts with an Undercover Activist legend across the rear and our logo on the leg). The guidance document we provide intakes is called *The Art of Anonymous Activism* (POGO 2002). This approach allows the activist to concentrate on bringing about change and living to tell the tale.

5. Guido Strack comments: Why don't you call this a superhero? What you describe in the following sections seems to expect people to have a combination of skills that few have and even fewer can acquire when they are already in a whistleblowing and reprisal situation.
6. Guido Strack comments: Often you only know too late. And as different future contacts might ask for different pieces of information, it is better to collect anything you can get hold of that could possibly be useful. Then comes the task of assembling and sorting information in a way so you can find specific items when you need them.
7. Guido Strack comments: Which again is a very hard task. And don't forget a good summary presents what readers want to know and what they are able to digest, so normally you will need several different summaries depending on the person you want to contact, with different lengths for initial and for later more intense contact.
8. Guido Strack comments: Most people recognize the realities of authoritarian states, whereas in the case of bureaucracies, outsiders and even some insiders believe that they are what they claim to be – following the rule of law and rational arguments – while in reality they just follow personal influence and power rules.
9. Guido Strack comments: I am quite sceptical. To be effective, publicity needs to attract attention by others who are powerful enough to achieve change, but attention is a very limited and precious resource that nobody wants to waste. Whistleblowers and their messages are competing with many experienced and well respected players who know how to win the attention of others and who are able to offer something in exchange. So why should a whistleblower win?
10. Guido Strack comments: The more specific a case is, the more difficult it will be for a whistleblower to pass the message without identifying their identity by its content. Statistics show that nearly all whistleblowers report internally first: for them, the possibility of anonymity is almost gone. But can they be blamed for giving internal means a chance first?
11. In 1999, I applied for a research grant to study how managers, employees and whistleblowers responded to key decision points in whistleblowing stories, with a research design aimed at overcoming some of the obstacles Jackall faced in gaining access to organizations: see www.bmartin.cc/others/ARC/ARC2000.pdf. The application was unsuccessful.
12. Guido Strack comments: This is a key problem also with bystanders. Everybody believes the system is working until there is no other choice than accepting that it doesn't. So how should a whistleblower convince others who have not gone through a change of perspective and do not want to hear that the system is flawed?

13. Guido Strack comments: This would be an important message also for businesses wanting to install whistleblower hotlines – provided they want them to be used.

21. Strategic issues in whistleblowing research

Wim Vandekerckhove, A.J. Brown, Richard Moberly and David Lewis

Our plan for this research handbook was always to provide researchers and policy makers with a comprehensive overview of existing knowledge, but also to discuss what further and new research is needed to inform decision-making about whistleblowing around the world. Accordingly, when we invited our contributors into the project, we did so with the intention of presenting these stocktakes and analyses under three parts. In Part I Research Fundamentals, we have assembled chapters on the core topics whose definition and conceptualization is basic to all whistleblowing research, and which remain important to all researchers. Part II Organizational Culture and Responsiveness puts research into its context, dealing with issues of research design and existing evidence. This becomes crucial if applied research is to have validity and relevance, especially as the nature of whistleblowing as an organizational and political process has become more central than the individual characteristics of whistleblowers. In Part III Research in Action, we have assembled chapters that discuss research on the nature and use of policies and legislation to protect whistleblowers, including the major needs, gaps and opportunities that lie at this level of applied research.

Each chapter offered a systematic review of how research into a particular aspect of whistleblowing has evolved, as well as the current state of knowledge about it. However, every chapter went beyond presenting the status quo and identified the new research avenues opening up from the recent interplay between research and practice. These new avenues emphasize the strategic importance research can have in the coming decade for the practice of whistleblowing. Put simply, the strategic goal for researchers and practitioners should be to make whistleblowing successful. This means both making it safe to blow the whistle as well as ensuring that whistleblowing is effective in stopping wrongdoing. This applies to all stages in the process, whether it is internal whistleblowing, or disclosing externally to a regulator, or to the media, and for all stakeholders: whistleblowers, recipients of whistleblower concerns, those managing organizations, regulatory agencies and the public.

Previous research successfully put whistleblowing on the public and political agenda and removed some common misconceptions about who whistleblowers are and why they choose to raise their concerns. The next generation of research is expected to turn its attention further away from trying to profile the whistleblower to focusing on the wrongdoing, what works and does not work in terms of whistleblowing policies and procedures, and the contexts in which these are implemented. Hence, the strategy is to engage in pragmatic as well as fundamental research, supporting conceptual, empirical and policy work that can promote safer and more effective whistleblowing. This can be achieved by bringing about a common understanding about specific aspects of whistleblowing among the various stakeholders, such as advice givers, support providers, investigators, judges, managers and policy makers.

Accordingly, the chapters in the Handbook offer contributions towards that next generation research on four dimensions which are important to recognize, if whistleblowing research is to evolve in the more coherent, useful and even powerful ways that we envisage. These dimensions, which we consider in turn, involve: new conceptual delineations, new theoretical developments, new research methods, and new departures for policy and practice.

NEW CONCEPTUAL DELINEATIONS

In the age of intensifying globalization, it is not surprising that key new delineations developed in this book stem from new technologies that can be used by whistleblowers, such as online channels or social media. Chapter 11 (Bosua *et al.*) discussed the advantages and risks of the new technology-enhanced whistleblowing from a journalist's perspective. Related to this is the new distinction made in Chapter 3 (Miceli, Dreyfus and Near) between whistleblowing and bell-ringing, which is based on rapid changes in information acquisition, reporting channels, the openness of communication and motives for reporting. More broadly, technological change now makes both types of disclosure easier, and more necessary the type of more comprehensive, consistent empirical research across organizations and countries that is recommended below.

Several chapters included a fresh look at the way research treats the motives of those who report. Chapter 5 (Leys and Vandekerckhove) avoided this issue by developing a typology of whistleblowing duties based on expanding the principal-agent perspective beyond private business to include all types of organizations. However, Chapter 9 (Roberts) confronted the problem head-on, pointing out that, through a review of conceptualizations of motivation in whistleblowing research, even self-interested whistleblowing often has a public interest dimension. Chapter 16 (Faunce *et al.*) linked to this research by discussing the similarities and differences in reward schemes, *qui tam* provisions and antitrust instruments. The same chapter offered illustrations drawn from various parts of the world and linked these to concepts like 'false claims' and 'corporate governance'.

However, this focus on organizations, subject to national regulation, should be read together with Chapter 18 (Walden and Edwards), which pointed out that, while many high profile whistleblowing cases involve international governmental organizations (IGOs), these are mainly forgotten in research. The authors suggested that this might be because IGOs are not subject to the legal regime of any one member state. They make suggestions about how this research gap could be filled by outlining specific issues and challenges for whistleblowing in these important organizations. So too, as Chapter 16 mentioned, it is the increasingly transnational basis of business that can render corporations relatively immune to regulation at the national level, and whistleblowing policy responses need to take this into account.

Chapter 10 (Smith) offered a typology of whistleblower suffering, and discussed its incidence and causes. The important conceptual development here is that the author doubts that a clear line can be drawn between objective and subjective suffering. Highly relevant to any detriments experienced by whistleblowers are the remedies that are available to them. Chapter 15 (Lewis, Devine and Harpur) discussed constitutional, statutory, common law, administrative and contractual remedies for whistleblowers, and linked these with corresponding strategies for encouraging and compensating whistleblowing. In addition, the authors make a case for employment remedies (e.g., alternative dispute resolution) rather than legal ones.

If the next generation of whistleblowing research is going to focus on the wrongdoing rather than the whistleblower, then the review in Chapter 4 (Skivenes and Trygstad) of the various notions of wrongdoing in whistleblowing research is fundamental to future work. This chapter examined findings on individual and contextual variables related to wrongdoing. It also distinguished formal from informal wrongdoing and explained how the perspectives of industrial relations and law conceptualize wrongdoing. But the wrongdoing whistleblowers initially raise a concern about can become compounded by organizational wrongdoing in responding to this disclosure. In relation to that, Chapter 17 (Spencer and Spencer) developed rationales for criminal sanctions for reprisals against whistleblowers and discussed the 'national security' argument for criminalizing whistleblowing that involves classified or confidential information.

NEW THEORETICAL DEVELOPMENTS

In terms of the new theoretical developments suggested or called for in this book, Chapter 14 (Fasterling) outlined an important agenda for comparative legal research. The author based such a program on two public policy objectives that have their parallel in what we understand successful whistleblowing to be: guaranteeing the rights of the whistleblower (safe whistleblowing), and preventing and detecting violations of law and dangers to health and safety (effective whistleblowing). Related to this, Chapter 15 (Lewis, Devine and Harpur) called for research into the feasibility of introducing rights that are exercisable at employment or industrial tribunals, as well as research into the efficacy and practicality of rewarding whistleblowing. For the reasons just mentioned, Chapter 18 (Walden and Edwards) called for research on the operationalization of whistleblowing policies in international governmental organizations, developing theories that link resources, attitudes of recipients, remedies and alternatives.

These suggestions for new, more coordinated research streams make a similar point to that made in Chapter 19 (Brown *et al.*), that there is a paucity of research into what actually works and what does not in relation to the protection of whistleblowers. Although whistleblowing research has come a long way, we still need research into laws and procedures that can deliver a body of knowledge which identifies the key issues in the implementation of effective whistleblowing policies. These needs are not just pragmatic; they require review of the theoretical underpinnings that drive research, such as, for example, simple dichotomies of reporting versus silence in response to perceived wrongdoing. This point, made powerfully in Chapter 7 (Loyens and Maesschalck), is addressed by the new approach described in Chapter 8 (Olsen) for calibrating research which not only operationalizes theories of reporting, but also theories of inaction.

Chapter 12 (Moberly) reviewed existing whistleblowing theories to develop predictions about the behavior of whistleblowing recipients. This led the author to call for research on training managers in this role, as well as research on the responses of various external agencies. Similarly, Chapter 17 (Spencer and Spencer) argued that theories are needed to research the use of criminal sanctions in dealing with retaliation and, more precisely, how these link directly or indirectly to successful whistleblowing. Chapter 13 (Vandekerckhove, Brown and Tsahuridu) takes these needs and propositions one step further by developing a framework, propositions and variables for exploring manager responses to whistleblowing, using Ajzen's theory of planned behavior.

Other chapters also invoked Ajzen's theory. Chapter 6 (Bjørkelo and Bye) suggested it is well suited to the study of intended and actual whistleblowing in relation to each other. The authors showed how previous whistleblowing research could be used to operationalize the 'norm' element in that theory. In Chapter 7 (Loyens and Maesschalck), Ajzen's theory was also suggested as a viable framework to identify causal mechanisms to link context with the 'locus of control' characteristic. This chapter also suggested a broadening of the scope of whistleblowing research from a power perspective. In particular, in addition to moving to a report-silence continuum as noted above, they call for researchers to use explanatory complexity to generate asymmetrical explanations for speaking and silence, as people might have very different reasons for speaking than for remaining silent. Chapter 10 (Smith) argued we should allow more ambiguity in the ontological status of whistleblower suffering in our research.

Whistleblowing never happens in a moral vacuum. The theoretical contributions acknowledge this (e.g., the suggested use of Ajzen's theory of planned behavior), and Chapter 2 (Vandekerckhove *et al.*) explicitly focused on the relationship between whistleblowing and cultural norms. The chapter advocated researching societal cultures and whistleblowing from perspectives other than that of Hofstede, and offered Schwartz as an alternative. Chapter 2 also argued for an international comparison of political rather than societal cultures, and suggested that progress in whistleblowing research could be attained by looking for universal similarities rather than differences.

RESEARCH METHODS

The new research avenues suggested in this Handbook also come with a stocktake on past methods, and advice on new methodological requirements. The next generation of whistleblowing research will have to work with different types of data sets. This will involve researchers gathering material in different places and from new actors, and having to use more sophisticated variables and analysis. For example, when measuring attitudes to whistleblowing, researchers must always distinguish between internal and external whistleblowing (Chapter 2). Chapters 4, 8 and 9 all point out the limitations of current survey descriptions of types of wrongdoing. These chapters also demonstrate that what the wrongdoing was, and why the whistle was blown (motivation) should be pursued as quite separate questions. Chapter 10 (Smith) then argued for treating 'types of suffering' as a nominal variable rather than a continuous or ordinal one.

It goes without saying that whistleblowers themselves remain a vitally important group of research participants. However, future research will face the methodological challenges of both needing to give voice to their experience (e.g., Chapter 10), and analyzing in greater depth the full spectrum of behavior, including not only all those who have blown the whistle, but those who have the intention to do so and haven't done so yet, and those who indicate they do not intend to raise their concern. This would facilitate research into the relationship between actual and intended whistleblowing (Chapter 6) as well as the determinants of both reporting and silent individuals and other forms of speaking up (Chapter 8). Chapter 8 (Olsen) also reviews the many variables which need to be studied in a more consistent way, through common, comparative research designs, if the limitations of existing, non-comparable studies are to be overcome.

These examples of new participants, new data sets and new variables will need to be taken into account in research design in order to focus attention away from individual characteristics and towards contextual factors. Chapter 2 (Vandekerckhove *et al.*) called for cross-national studies testing how national cultures differ in relation to the contextual factors influencing whistleblowing rather than just the individual ones. Chapter 7 (Loyens and Maesschalck), suggested ethnographic research and narrative approaches would be best suited to take into account contextual factors. These allow for in-depth research into decision-making about whistleblowing and can also be used for process-tracing explanations of successful whistleblowing. A broadening of research scope to include more context is also needed in legal research. Chapter 14 (Fasterling) made the case for avoiding superficiality in comparing legislation. For example, when evaluating whistleblower protection one should not just look at the anti-retaliation provisions in whistleblowing laws. We also need to take into account the general level of employment protection provided in the particular jurisdiction, as well as the evidential constraints involved in bringing a claim.

One obvious challenge researchers will need to face in order to create the new data sets, locate the appropriate participants, and utilize the variables called for in the chapters above, is that of analyzing contemporary examples of successful whistleblowing. Other than anecdotally, how will researchers know about it and, if it did become public knowledge, what incentive would whistleblowers and non-whistleblowers, recipients, managers and other stakeholders have to cooperate in the examination of such cases? Subsequent historical analysis creates problems of accessing persons and documents, accurate recall, and so on. Here, quantitative research methods such as surveys can take us a long way, but still only so far. The use of qualitative methods such as those emphasized by Chapter 7 (Loyens and Maesschalck) and demonstrated by Chapter 9 (Roberts) will remain especially important, but also face these particular challenges.

POLICY AND PRACTICE

As already indicated, while engaged with applying new conceptualizations, theories and methods to whistleblowing research, many if not most chapters remained focused on the utility of this for policy change and practice. This is also not the only purpose, or potential purpose of research. As Chapter 20 (Martin) powerfully reminds us, research is vital for those purposes, but should also be devoted to helping to directly equip employees with the knowledge which will help increase the chances of their whistleblowing being successful. It provides a salutary reminder of a fact to be remembered by all whistleblowing researchers, even when snowed under with mountains of empirical data: research participants are not just numbers, but people.

So too, whistleblowing does not take place in isolation from organizational, industrial relations and political contexts, and so too many chapters showed how employers, unions, advocacy groups, national governments and international bodies can all gain from whistleblowing research that provides evidence on which to base laws and practices. Miceli, Dreyfus and Near in Chapter 3 suggest the development of definitions, because current definitions do not seem to satisfy all the needs in public debate and public policy. Chapter 8 (Olsen) brings together the conceptual and methodological challenges in many chapters, by demonstrating why and how empirical research on reporting and inaction levels can be made more useful for managers and regulators. This is obviously important for linking research to practice, but future research will also have to include those policy makers or policy 'operators'.

Chapters 12 and 13 pointed out the need for rich data on the roles played by recipients of whistleblowing concerns in determining whether they are effectively dealt with. This can be read alongside Chapter 19, where the authors discuss the need for research indicators which can be used to evaluate and rank the performance of different organizations in relation to successful whistleblowing. Importantly, this is not just for theoretical purposes – it is specifically so that regulatory oversight of whistleblowing regimes can be made effective, providing the performance information needed to ensure implementation of whistleblowing laws, and positive developments in organizational culture and leadership. Chapters 14–17, dealing with legal responses, emphasize why this is necessary. With legal recognition and regulation of whistleblowing likely to continue to expand, these chapters in themselves will contribute directly to policy and practice, through their more effective comparison of the content and purposes of different legal strategies. But as public and policy recognition of whistleblowing grows, it will be research that helps better determine whether there is improvement in the conditions for the reporting of wrongdoing at the 'coalface' of organizational life, and what should be done about it, which will become the most valuable of all. Ultimately, all the chapters in the book combine to support that ultimate, applied purpose.

CONCLUSION

This Handbook shows that whistleblowing research has made significant progress over the last three decades, and that it has impacted on public understanding of whistleblowers and on public policies, legislation, procedures and even organizational practices. We hope that the chapters above have offered enough pointers so that they can become a catalyst for another decade of research progress on whistleblowing. Inevitably, this will depend to a large degree on the availability of funds. Historically, researchers have faced difficulties in persuading potential sponsors that: conducting and reporting on hypothetical vignettes is valuable; actual whistleblowers and their employers will be willing to cooperate in studies; and that researchers have the appropriate expertise to carry out inter-disciplinary research. We hope that the scale and depth of applied and collaborative research in many of the chapters, together with the increasingly effective use that researchers have made in making sense of official data collected by others, will continue to dispel these barriers, and see an increasing share of research resources devoted to this strategic field. We call on research funding agencies and potential sponsors to support credible proposals for empirical research whenever they can.

Across these issues, it also clear that the promises offered by further research are owed in no small part to the degree of inter-disciplinarity being achieved in the whistleblowing research community. It might be argued that early research suffered from a lack of inter-disciplinarity, with lawyers looking at the law but little else, including any evidence as to whether or not it was working; while social scientists looked at behaviors but not necessarily the legal context, and so on. In assembling this Handbook, not only was it apparent that we would need to draw authors from a variety of backgrounds, but that the best whistleblowing research is now highly inter-disciplinary. Not only do the chapters come from authors spread across law, management, psychology, media studies, public policy, criminology and philosophy, but very often individual chapters are written by authors that mix these backgrounds. In addition, at least four co-authors are not employed as scholars at all, but are practitioners engaged on the front-line of whistleblower management and protection. This kind of collaboration is now key not only to the conduct of the research, but also to maximizing its impact.

It is beyond doubt that the first 30 years of whistleblowing research has had a positive impact on public opinion, policy making and organizational practices around whistleblowing. However, this process has been slow. Research definitely has an influence, but researchers need to show perseverance. It is our firm belief that the avenues for exploration and new demands for evidence set out in this volume can contribute to further improvements for whistleblowers and the detection and correction of wrongdoing. We hope that researchers will continue with the same perseverance over the next 30 years, and expect that if they do, even more timely and influential impacts will be their rewards.

Bibliography

AASW (Australian Association of Social Workers) 2010. 'AASW Code of Ethics 2010', available at www.aasw.asn.au/publications/ethics-and-standards

ABC (Australian Broadcasting Corporation) 2013. 'Cover Up', ABC Television Four Corners, 30 September. Producers Nick McKenzie and Bentley Dean, available at www.abc.net.au/4corners/stories/2013/09/30/3857148.htm

ACFE (Association of Certified Fraud Examiners) 2008. *Report to the Nation on Occupational Fraud and Abuse*. Austin, available at www.acfe.com/uploadedFiles/ACFE_Website/Content/2008-rttn.pdf

ACFE (Association of Certified Fraud Examiners) 2012. *Report to the Nations on Occupational Fraud and Abuse: 2012 Global Fraud Study*. Austin, TX: available at www.acfe.com/uploadedFiles/ACFE_Website/Content/rttn/2012-report-to-nations.pdf

Ackerman, P. and J. DuVall 2000. *A Force More Powerful: A Century of Nonviolent Conflict*. New York: St Martin's Press

Adam, P. 2010. 'Sur la liberté pour le salarié de dénouncer des faits répréhensibles' *Revue de Jurisprudence Sociale* 3(10): 187–97

ADB (Asian Development Bank) 2009. 'Whistleblower and Witness Protection', Administrative Order No. 2.10, 11 December, available at www.adb.org/sites/default/files/AO2-10.pdf

Adler, N.J. 1983. 'Cross-Cultural Management Research: The Ostriche and the Trend' *Academy of Management Review* 8(2): 226–32

African Development Bank Group 2007. 'Whistleblowing and Complaints Handling Policy' (January), available at www.afdb.org/fileadmin/uploads/afdb/Documents/Policy-Documents/18136242-EN-WHISTLE-BLOWING-POLICY-FINAL-FINAL-WKF.PDF

Agalgatti, B. and S. Krishna 2004. *Business Ethics (Concepts and Practices)*, 4th edn. Pune: Nirali Prakashan

Aguinis, H. 2013 *Performance Management*, 3rd edn. Upper Saddle River, NJ: Pearson Prentice Hall

Ajzen, I. 1991. 'The Theory of Planned Behavior' *Organizational Behavior and Human Decision Processes* (December) 50(2): 179–211

Alain, M. and M. Grégoire 2008. 'Can Ethics Survive the Shock of the Job? Quebec's Police Recruits Confront Reality' *Policing and Society: An International Journal of Research and Policy* 18(2): 169–89

Alexion, C.M. 2012. 'Open the Door, not the Floodgates: Controlling *Qui Tam* Litigation under the False Claims Act' *Washington and Lee Law Review* (Winter) 69(1): 365–408

Alford, C.F. 2001. *Whistleblowers: Broken Lives and Organizational Power*. Ithaca, NY: Cornell University Press

Alford, C.F. 2007. 'Whistle-Blower Narratives: the Experience of Choiceless Choice' *Social Research* (Spring) 74(1): 223–48

Alper, A. 2012. 'Whistleblower Tips Trickle into U.S. Futures Register' *Thomson Reuters News and Insight*, 19 September

AMA (American Medical Association) 2001. 'AMA's Code of Medical Ethics', available at www.ama-assn.org/ama/pub/physician-resources/medical-ethics/code-medical-ethics.page

Anderson, R.M., R. Perucci, D. Schendel and L. Trachtman 1980. *Divided Loyalties: Whistleblowing at BART*. West Lafayette, IN: Purdue University Press

Annakin, L. 2011. 'In the Public Interest or Out of Desperation? The Experience of Australian Whistleblowers Reporting to Accountability Agencies', Unpublished Ph.D Thesis, University of Sydney, Sydney

Anon. 2002. 'The Financial Collapse of Enron- art 3: Hearing Before the Subcommittee on Oversight and Investigations of the Committee on Energy and Commerce House of Representatives', 107th Congress, 2nd session, available at www.gpo.gov/fdsys/pkg/CHRG-107hhrg77991/pdf/CHRG-107hhrg77991.pdf

APA (American Psychiatric Association) 2010. 'The Principles of Medical Ethics', available at www.psych.org/practice/ethics/resources-standards/ethics

Applebaum, E. and J. Schmitt 2009. 'Low Wage Work in High Income Countries: Labor Market Institutions and Business Strategy in the US and Europe' *Human Relations* (December) 62(12): 1907–34

APSC (Australian Public Service Commission) 2004. *State of the Service Report 2003–2004*. Commonwealth of Australia, Canberra, available at https://resources.apsc.gov.au/pre2005/SOSR0304.pdf

APSC (Australian Public Service Commission) 2005. *State of the Service Employee Survey Results 2004–2005*. Commonwealth of Australia, Canberra, available at https://resources.apsc.gov.au/pre2005/ESR0405.pdf

APSC (Australian Public Service Commission) 2006. *State of the Service Employee Survey Results 2005–2006*. Commonwealth of Australia, Canberra, available at https://resources.apsc.gov.au/2006/ESR0506.pdf

APSC (Australian Public Service Commission) 2007. *State of the Service Employee Survey Results 2006–2007*. Commonwealth of Australia, Canberra, available at https://resources.apsc.gov.au/2007/ESR0607.pdf

APSC (Australian Public Service Commission) 2009. *State of the Service Employee Survey Results 2008–2009*. Commonwealth of Australia, Canberra, available at https://resources.apsc.gov.au/2009/ESR0809.pdf

APSC (Australian Public Service Commission) 2010. *State of the Service Employee Survey Results 2009–2010*. Commonwealth of Australia, Canberra, available at https://resources.apsc.gov.au/2010/ESR0910.pdf

APSC (Australian Public Service Commission) 2011. *Employee Survey Results: State of the Service Series 2010–2011*. Commonwealth of Australia, Canberra, available at https://resources.apsc.gov.au/2011/ESR1011.pdf

Armour, N. 2011. 'Penn State's Mike McQueary Might be Protected as Whistle-Blower as Scandal Fallout Continues', *Detroit Free Press* (online), 11 November, available at www.freep.com/article/20111111/SPORTS08/111111008/Penn-State-s-Mike-McQueary-might-protected-whistle-blower-scandal-fallout-continues

Arvis, J.F. and R.E. Berenbeim 2003. *Fighting Corruption in East Asia: Solutions from the Private Sector*. Washington, DC: International Bank for Reconstruction and Development/World Bank

Assange, J. 2010. 'The Truth will Always Win', *The Australian*, 7 December, available at http://blogs.theaustralian.news.com.au/mediadiary/index.php/theaustralian/comments/julian1/

Attorney-General Department (Australia) 2009. *Improving Protections for Corporate Whistleblowers: Options Paper*. Canberra: Australian Government (October)

Attorney-General Department (Australia) 2011. 'Commonwealth Fraud Control Guidelines I and III'. Canberra: Australian Government, available at www.ag.gov.au/CrimeAndCorruption/FraudControl/Pages/CommonwealthFraudControlGuidelines.aspx

Aubert, C., P. Rey and W.E. Kovacic 2005. 'The Impact of Leniency and Whistleblowing Programs on Cartels' (21 June), available at http://idei.fr/doc/by/rey/leniency.pdf

Augoustinos, M. and I. Walker 1999. *Social Cognition: An Integrated Introduction*. London: Sage

Australian Standard 8004 2003. *Whistleblower Protection Programs for Entities*. Sydney: Standards Australia International

Avila, J. 2012. '70 Percent of Ground Beef at Supermarkets Contains "Pink Slime"', *ABCNews.go.com*, 7 March, available at http://abcnews.go.com/blogs/headlines/2012/03/70-percent-of-ground-beef-at-supermarkets-contains-pink-slime/

Baird, E.C. III 1994. 'The Use of *Qui Tam* Actions to Enforce Federal Grazing Permits' *Washington University Law Quarterly* 72: 1407–34

Balogun, M.J. 2010. *Headhunting for World Peace: An Inside View of UN Employment Law and Practices.* Baltimore, MD: Publish America

Bandura, A. 1990. 'Mechanisms of Moral Disengagement' in W. Reich (ed.), *Origins of Terrorism: Psychologies, Ideologies, Theologies, States of Mind.* Cambridge: Cambridge University Press, 161–91

Bandura, A. 2002. 'Social Cognitive Theory in Cultural Context' *Applied Psychology: An International Review* (April) 51(2): 269–90

Banisar, D. 2006. 'Whistleblowing: International Standards and Developments', paper prepared for the First International Conference on Corruption and Transparency: Debating the Frontiers between State, Market and Society, Mexico City, 23–25 March, available at www.corrupcion.unam.mx/documentos/investigaciones/banisar_paper.pdf

Banisar, D. 2011. 'Whistleblowing: International Standards and Developments' in I.E. Sandoval (ed.), *Corruption and Transparency: Debating the Frontiers between State, Market and Society.* Washington, DC: World Bank, Institute for Social Research, Unam, available at SSRN, http://ssrn.com/abstract=1753180

Barnett, T.R. 1992. 'A Preliminary Investigation of the Relationship between Selected Organizational Characteristics and External Whistleblowing by Employees' *Journal of Business Ethics* 11(12): 949–59

Barnett, T.R., D.S. Cochran and G.S. Taylor 1993. 'The Internal Disclosure Policies of Private-Sector Employers: An Initial Look at Their Relationship to Employee Whistleblowing' *Journal of Business Ethics* (February) 12(2): 127–36

Barry, B. 2007. 'The Cringing and the Craven: Freedom of Expression in, Around, and Beyond the Workplace' *Business Ethics Quarterly* (April) 17(2): 263–96

Bashir, S., H.R. Khattak, A. Hanif and S.N. Chohan 2011. 'Whistle-Blowing in Public Sector Organizations: Evidence from Pakistan' *American Review of Public Administration* (May) 41(3): 285–96

Baucus, M. and T.M. Dworkin 1994. 'Wrongful Firing in Violation of Public Policy: Who Gets Fired and Why' *Employee Responsibilities and Rights Journal* (September) 7(3): 191–206

Bauer, M. 1996. 'The Narrative Interview: Comments on a Technique for Qualitative Data Collection' (October), available at www.lse.ac.uk/methodology/pdf/QualPapers/Bauer-NARRAT1SS.pdf

Bayer, A.E., D.C. Strickland and T.D. Miethe 1992. *Quality of Life in Virginia.* Charlottesville, VA: Center for Survey Research

BBC News 2009. 'Madoff Whistle-Blower Attacks SEC', 5 February, available at http://news.bbc.co.uk/1/hi/business/7871253.stm

Beck, J.A. 2000. 'The False Claims Act and the English Eradication of *Qui Tam* Legislation' *North Carolina Law Review* 78: 539–642

Behar, R. 2012. 'Whistle Stop' *Forbes*, 25 July, available at www.forbes.com/global/2012/0806/companies-people-world-bank-kim-wistle-stop.html

Ben-Yehuda, N. 2001. *Betrayals and Treason: Violations of Trust and Loyalty.* Boulder: CO: Westview Press

Benkler, Y. 2011. 'A Free Irresponsible Press: WikiLeaks and the Battle over the Soul of the Networked Fourth Estate' *Harvard Civil Rights–Civil Liberties Law Review* 46: 311–97

Bennett, A. 2010. 'Process Tracing and Counterfactual Analysis', PowerPoint presentation 'Process Tracing' in Module 16, IQMR (Institute for Qualitative and Multi-Method Research), Syracuse, 14–25 June

Benson, G. 1992. 'Codes of Ethics, Whistleblowing and Managerial Auditing' *Managerial Auditing Journal* 7(2): 37–40

Berkman, S. 2008. *The World Bank and the Gods of Lending*. Sterling, VA: Kumarian Press

Berry, B. 2004. 'Organizational Culture: A Framework and Strategies for Facilitating Employee Whistleblowing' *Employee Responsibilities and Rights Journal* (March) 16(1): 1–11

Berthelsen, M., A. Skogstad, L.J. Hauge, M.B. Nielsen and S. Einarsen 2008. *Mobbing og utstøting i arbeidslivet: Resultater fra en lands-representativ og longitudinell undersøkelse [Bullying and Exclusion from Working Life: Results from a National Representative and Longitudinal Study].* Bergen: University of Bergen

Berthold, A. 2010. *Whistleblowing in der Rechtsprechung des Bundesarbeitsgerichts* [*Whistleblowing in the Jurisprudence of the German Federal Labor Court*]. Frankfurt: Peter Lang

Bertram, C.N. and L.A. Pate 2005. 'Sarbanes-Oxley: A New Whistle Stop for Whistleblowers' *Labour Lawyer* (Summer) 21(1): 19–36

Beyerle, S. 2011. 'Civil Resistance and the Corruption-Violence Nexus' *Journal of Sociology and Social Welfare* (June) 38(2): 53–78

Beyerle, S. and A. Hassan 2009. 'Popular Resistance Against Corruption in Turkey and Egypt' in M.J. Stephan (ed.), *Civilian Jihad: Nonviolent Struggle, Democratization, and Governance in the Middle East.* New York: Palgrave Macmillan, ch. 18, 265–79

Bjørkelo, B. 2010. 'Whistleblowing at Work: Antecedents and Consequences', Unpublished Ph.D Thesis, University of Bergen, Bergen

Bjørkelo, B., S. Einarsen and S.B. Matthiesen 2010. 'Predicting Proactive Behaviour at Work: Exploring the Role' *Journal of Occupational and Organisational Psychology* (June) 83(2): 371–93

Bjørkelo, B., S. Einarsen, M.B. Nielsen and S.B. Matthiesen 2011. 'Silence is Golden? Characteristics and Experiences of Self-Reported

Whistleblowers' *European Journal of Work and Organizational Psychology* 20(2): 206–38

Bjørkelo, B. and S. Matthiesen 2011. 'Preventing and Dealing with Retaliation Against Whistleblowers' in D.B. Lewis and W. Vandekerckhove (eds), *Whistleblowing and Democratic Vision*. London: International Whistleblowing Research Network, 127–40

Bjørkelo, B., W. Ryberg, S.B. Matthiesen and S. Einarsen 2008. 'When You Talk and Talk and Nobody Listens: A Mixed Method Case Study of Whistleblowing and its Consequences' *International Journal of Organisational Behavior* 13(2): 18–40

Blackburn, M.S. 1988. 'Employee Dissent: The Choice of Voice Versus Silence', Dissertation, University of Tennessee, Knoxville

Blanton, T.S. 2003. 'National Security and Open Government in the United States: Beyond the Balancing Test' in *National Security and Open Government: Striking the Right Balance*. New York: Campbell Public Affairs Institute, 33–74, available at www1.maxwell.syr.edu/uploadedFiles/campbell/events/NSOG.pdfhttp://www.statewatch.org/news/2003/oct/deirdrec.pdf

Bok, S. 1981. 'Blowing the Whistle' in J.L. Fleishman, L. Liebman and M.H. Moore (eds), *Public Duties: The Moral Obligations of Government Officials*. Cambridge, MA: Harvard University Press, ch. 8, 204–20

Bolkovac, K. with C. Lynn 2011. *The Whistleblower: Sex Trafficking, Military Contractors, and One Woman's Fight for Justice*. New York: Palgrave Macmillan

Bolman, L.G. and T.E. Deal 2000. *Escape from Cluelessness: A Guide for the Organizationally Challenged*. New York: Amacom

Borrie, G. 1996. 'Blowing the Whistle: Business Ethics and Accountability' *Political Quarterly* (April) 67(2): 141–50

Botero, I.C. and L. Van Dyne 2009. 'Employee Voice Behavior: Interactive Effects of LMX and Power Distance in the United States and Colombia' *Management Communication Quarterly* 23(1): 84–104

Bouville, M. 2008. 'Whistle-Blowing and Morality' *Journal of Business Ethics* (September) 81(3): 579–85

Bowden, P. 2005. 'A Comparative Analysis of Whistleblower Protection', paper prepared for the Australian Association for Professional and Applied Ethics 12th Annual Conference, Adelaide, 28–30 September, available at http://w3.unisa.edu.au/hawkeinstitute/gig/aapae05/documents/bowden-whistleblower.pdf

Bowden, P. and V. Smythe 2010. 'Ethics, Good Governance and Whistleblowing' in S. Young (ed.), *Contemporary Issues in International Corporate Governance*. Melbourne: Tilde University Press, ch. 7

BP (British Petroleum) 2012. 'Code of Conduct', available at www.bp.com/liveassets/bp_internet/globalbp/STAGING/global_assets/downloads/C/Code_of_Conduct_2011.pdf

Brabeck, M. 1984. 'Ethical Characteristics of Whistle Blowers' *Journal of Research in Personality* (March) 18(1): 41–53

Bradburn, N.M. 1983. 'Response Effects' in P.H. Rossi, J.D. Wright and A.B. Anderson (eds), *Handbook of Survey Research*. New York: Academic Press, 289–328

Braxton, J.M. and A.E. Bayer 1996. 'Personal Experiences of Research Misconduct and the Response of Individual Academic Scientists' *Science, Technology, and Human Values* (April) 21(2): 198–213

Breggin, P.R. 2006. 'Drug Company Suppressed Data on Paroxetine-Induced Stimulation: Implications for Violence and Suicide' *Ethical Human Psychology and Psychiatry* (Fall) 8(3): 255–63

Brewer, G.A. 1996. *Incidence of Whistleblowing in the Public and Private Sectors*. Athens, GA: Department of Political Science, University of Georgia

Brewer, G.A. and S.C. Selden 1998. 'Whistle Blowers in the Federal Civil Service: New Evidence of the Public Service Ethic' *Journal of Public Administration Research and Theory* 8(3): 413–40

Brewster, C., R. Croucher, G. Wood and M. Brookes 2007. 'Collective and Individual Voice: Convergence in Europe?' *International Journal of Human Resource Management* 18(7): 1246–62

Brief, A.P. and S.J. Motowidlo 1986. 'Prosocial Organizational Behaviors' *Academy of Management Review* (October) 11(4): 710–25

Bristol Royal Infirmary Inquiry 2001. *Learning from Bristol: the Report of the Public Inquiry into Children's Heart Surgery at The Bristol Royal Infirmary 1984–1995*. Command Paper (CM 5207, 18 July), available at http://webarchive.nationalarchives.gov.uk/+/www.dh.gov.uk/en/Publicationsandstatistics/Publications/PublicationsPolicyAndGuidance/DH_4005620

Brock, J. 1999. 'Full and Fair Resolution of Whistleblower Issues: The Hanford Joint Council for Resolving Employee Concerns, a Pilot ADR Approach' *Administrative Law Review* 51(2): 497–529

Brody, R.G., J.M. Coulter and S. Lin 1999. 'The Effect of National Culture on Whistle-Blowing Perceptions' *Teaching Business Ethics* 3(4): 383–98

Brody, R.G., J.M. Coulter and P.H. Mihalek 1998. 'Whistle-Blowing: A Cross-Cultural Comparison of Ethical Perceptions of U.S. and Japanese Accounting Students' *American Business Review* 16(2): 14–21

Brown, A.J. 2006. *Public Interest Disclosure Legislation in Australia: Towards the Next Generation, an Issues Paper*. Commonwealth

Ombudsman, NSW Ombudsman, Queensland Ombudsman (November), available at www.griffith.edu.au/__data/assets/pdf_file/0015/151314/full-paper.pdf

Brown, A.J. (ed.) 2008. *Whistleblowing in the Australian Public Sector: Enhancing the Theory and Practice of Internal Witness Management in Public Sector Organisations*. Canberra: ANU E-Press, available at http://epress.anu.edu.au/anzsog/whistleblowing/pdf_instructions.html

Brown, A.J. 2009. 'Returning the Sunshine to the Sunshine State: Priorities for Whistleblowing Law Reform in Queensland' *Griffith Law Review* 18(3): 666–89

Brown, J. 2011a. 'Combatting the Whistleblower Bounty' *Canadian Lawyer Magazine*, 19 December, available at www.canadianlawyermag.com/3973/combating-the-whistleblower-bounty.html?print=1&tmpl =component

Brown, A.J. 2011b. 'Weeding out WikiLeaks (and Why it Won't Work): Legislative Recognition of Public Whistleblowing in Australia' *Global Media Journal* (Australian edn) 5(1): 1–12

Brown, A.J. 2013. 'Towards "Ideal" Whistleblowing Legislation? Some Lessons from Recent Australian Experience' *E-Journal of International and Comparative Labour Studies* (September/October) 2(3): 153–82

Brown, A.J. and M. Donkin 2008. 'Introduction' in A.J. Brown (ed.), *Whistleblowing in the Australian Public Sector: Enhancing the Theory and Practice of Internal Witness Management in Public Sector Organizations*. Canberra: ANU E-Press, 1–24

Brown, A.J., S. Dreyfus, S. O'Grady and R. Sheales 2012. 'Australia Not an "Anti-Dobbing Culture": World Online Whistleblowing Survey Stage 1 Results Release' (Griffith University and University of Melbourne), available at http://www.griffith.edu.au/business-government/centre-governance-public-policy/publications/whistleblowing

Brown, A.J., W. Vandekerckhove and S. Dreyfus 2014. 'The Relationship between Transparency, Whistleblowing, and Public Trust' in P. Ala'I and R. Vaughn (eds), *Research Handbook on Transparency*. Cheltenham: Edward Elgar

Brown, A.J., P. Latimer, J. McMillan and C. Wheeler 2008. 'Best-Practice Whistleblowing Legislation for the Public Sector: The Key Principles' in A.J. Brown (ed.), *Whistleblowing in the Australian Public Sector: Enhancing the Theory and Practice of Internal Witness Management in Public Sector Organizations*. Canberra: ANU E-Press, ch. 11, 261–88, available at http://epress.anu.edu.au/anzsog/whistleblowing/pdf_instructions.html

Brown, A.J., D. Magendanz and C.M. Leary 2004. 'Speaking Up: Creating Positive Reporting Climates in the Queensland Public Sector' (Crime and Misconduct Commission, Brisbane) *Building Capacity* 6: 1–11

Brown, A.J., E. Mazurski and J. Olsen 2008. 'The Incidence and Significance of Whistleblowing' in A.J. Brown (ed.), *Whistleblowing in the Australian Public Sector: Enhancing the Theory and Practice of Internal Witness Management in Public Sector Organisations*. Canberra: ANU E-Press, ch. 2, 25–52

Brown, A.J. and J. Olsen 2008a. 'Whistleblower Mistreatment: Identifying the Risks' in A.J. Brown (ed.), *Whistleblowing in the Australian Public Sector: Enhancing the Theory and Practice of Internal Witness Management in Public Sector Organisations*. Canberra: ANU E Press, ch. 6, 137–61.

Brown, A.J. and J. Olsen 2008b. 'Internal Witness Support: the Unmet Challenge' in A.J. Brown (ed.), *Whistleblowing in the Australian Public Sector: Enhancing the Theory and Practice of Internal Witness Management in Public Sector Organisations*. Canberra: ANU E-Press, ch. 9, 203–32

Brown, A.J. and C. Wheeler 2008. 'Project Findings: An Agenda for Action' in A.J. Brown (ed.), *Whistleblowing in the Australian Public Sector: Enhancing the Theory and Practice of Internal Witness Management in Public Sector Organisations*. Canberra: ANU E-Press, ch. 12, 289–312

Brown, M. and L. Trevino 2006. 'Ethical Leadership: A Review and Future Directions' *Leadership Quarterly* 17(6): 595–616

Bryman, A. 2001. *Social Research Methods*. Oxford: Oxford University Press

Bull, N., T. Riise and B.E. Moen 2002. 'Work-Related Injuries and Occupational Health and Safety Factors in Smaller Enterprises: A Prospective Study' *Occupational Medicine* 52(2): 70–4

Burchell, A.M. 2008. 'Letter from Mr A. M Burchell to Sub-Committee E (Law and Institutions)' (3 March), available at www.publications.parliament.uk/pa/ld200708/ldselect/ldeucom/150/150we02.htm

Burke, R.J. and C.L. Cooper (eds) 2013. *Voice and Whistleblowing in Organizations* Cheltenham: Edward Elgar

Burton, B.K. and J.P. Near 1995. 'Estimating the Incidence of Wrongdoing and Whistleblowing: Results of a Study Using Randomized Response Technique' *Journal of Business Ethics* (January) 14(1): 17–30

Business Anti-Corruption Portal 2012. 'Public Anti-Corruption Initiatives', Ghana Country Profile, available at www.business-anti-corruption.com/country-profiles/sub-saharan-africa/ghana/initiatives/public-anti-corruption-initiatives/

Calas, M.B. and L. Smircich 1999. 'Past Postmodernism? Reflections and Tentative Directions' *Academy of Management Review* (October) 24(4): 649–72

Calderone, M. 2010. 'Some News Outlets Stop Calling Wikileaks a "Whistle-Blower"', (6 December), available at http://news.yahoo.com/blogs/cutline/news-outlets-stop-calling-wikileaks-whistle-blower.html

Calderone, M. 2011. 'NY Times Considers Creating an "EZ Pass Lane for Leakers"' (25 January), available at http://news.yahoo.com/blogs/cutline/ny-times-considers-creating-ez-pass-lane-leakers-20110125-053811-988.html

Callahan, E.S. and J. Collins 1992. 'Employee Attitudes Toward Whistleblowing: Management and Public Policy Implications' *Journal of Business Ethics* (December) 11(12): 939–48

Callahan, E.S. and T.M. Dworkin 1992. 'Do Good and Get Rich: Financial Incentives for Whistleblowing and the False Claims Act' *Villanova Law Review* 37: 273–366

Callahan, E.S. and T.M. Dworkin 1994. 'Who Blows the Whistle to the Media, and Why: Organizational Characteristics of Media Whistleblowers' *American Business Law Journal* (September) 32(2): 151–84

Callahan, E.S. and T.M. Dworkin 2000. 'State of State Whistleblower Protection' *American Business Law Journal* (September) 38(1): 99–175

Callahan E.S., T.M. Dworkin and D. Lewis 2004. 'Whistleblowing: Australian, UK, and US Approaches to Disclosure in the Public Interest' *Virginia Journal of International Law* 44(3): 879–912

Calland, R. and G. Dehn (eds) 2004a. *Whistleblowing Around the World: Law, Culture and Practice*. Capetown: ODAC and PCaW in partnership with the British Council

Calland, R. and G. Dehn 2004b. 'Introduction: Whistleblowing Around the World: The State of the Art' in R. Calland and G. Dehn (eds), *Whistleblowing Around the World: Law, Culture and Practice*. Capetown: ODAC and PCaW in partnership with the British Council, 2–20

Campbell, E.G., S. Regan, R.L. Gruen, T.G. Ferris, S.R. Rao, P.D. Cleary and D. Blumenthal 2007. 'Professionalism in Medicine: Results of a National Survey of Physicians' *Annals of Internal Medicine* (December) 147(11): 795–802

Carr, I. 2011. 'The UK Bribery Act 2010, Business Integrity and Whistleblowers' in D.B. Lewis and W. Vandekerckhove (eds), *Whistleblowing and Democratic Values*. London: International Whistleblowing Research Network, 102–14

Carr, I. and D. Lewis 2010. 'Combating Corruption through Employment Law and Whistleblower Protection' *Industrial Law Journal* (March) 39(1): 52–81

Carroll, A.B. 1979. 'A Three-Dimensional Conceptual Model of Corporate Social Performance' *Academy of Management Review* (October) 4(4): 497–505

Carson, T.L., M.E. Verdu and R.E. Wokutch 2008. 'Whistle-Blowing for Profit: An Ethical Analysis of the Federal Claims Act' *Journal of Business Ethics* (February) 77(3): 361–76

Caryl, C. 2011. 'Why WikiLeaks Changes Everything' *New York Review of Books*, 13 January, available at www.nybooks.com/articles/archives/2011/jan/13/why-WikiLeaks-changes-everything/?pagination=false&printpage=true

Castells, M. 1996. *The Information Age: Economy, Society and Culture*, vol. I, *The Rise of the Network Society*. Oxford: Blackwell

Catania, J.A., H. Turner, R.C. Pierce, E. Golden, C. Stocking, D. Binson and K. Mast 1993. 'Response Bias in Surveys of AIDS-related Sexual Behaviour' in D.G. Ostrow and R.C. Kessler (eds), *Methodological Issues in AIDS Behavioural Research*. New York: Plenum Press, ch. 6, 133–62

Cavanagh, G.F., D. Moberg and M. Velasquez 1981. 'The Ethics of Organizational Politics' *Academy of Management Review* (July) 6(3): 363–74

Cavico, F.J. 2004. 'Private Sector Whistleblowing and the Employment-at-Will Doctrine: A Comparative Legal, Ethical, and Pragmatic Analysis' *South Texas Law Review* 45: 543–645

CCP (Competition Commission of Pakistan) 2007. 'Revised Guidelines on Reward Payment to Informants Scheme', available at www.cc.gov.pk/images/Downloads/reward_paymentannexure_ii.pdf

Chambers, A. 1995. 'Whistleblowing and the Internal Auditor' *Business Ethics: A European Review* (October) 4(4): 192–8

Cherry, J. 2006. 'The Impact of Normative Influence and Locus of Control on Ethical Judgments and Intentions: A Cross-Cultural Comparison' *Journal of Business Ethics* (October) 68(2): 113–32

Chiaburu, D.S., C. Farh and L.V. Dyne 2013. 'Supervisory Epistemic, Ideological, and Existential Responses to Voice' in R. Burke and C. Cooper (eds), *Voice and Whistleblowing in Organizations*. Cheltenham: Edward Elgar: 224–253

Child, J. 1981. 'Culture, Contingency and Capitalism in the Cross-National Study of Organizations' in L.L. Cummings and B.M. Staw (eds), *Research in Organizational Behavior*. Oxford: JAI Press, 303–56

Chiu, R.K. 2003. 'Ethical Judgment and Whistleblowing Intention: Examining the Moderating Role of Locus of Control' *Journal of Business Ethics* (March) 43(1–2): 65–74

Choi, J.H and D. Baek 2011. 'South Korea: A Firm Stance' *International Financial Law Review*, 1 October, available at www.iflr.com/Article/2919312/South-Korea-A-firm-stance.html. Also available at www.shinkim.com/upload_files/data/CompSKorea2011.pdf

Chung, J. and G.S. Monroe 2003. 'Exploring Social Desirability Bias' *Journal of Business Ethics* 44(4): 291–302

Cialdini, R.B. 1984. *Influence: How and Why People Agree to Things*. New York: Morrow

CIGIE (Council of Inspectors General for Integrity and Efficiency) 2011. *Quality Standards for Investigations* (Washington DC, 15 November), available at www.ignet.gov/pande/standards/invstds2011.pdf

Clairmont, A. 2011. 'Indecent Disclosures: Whistleblower Ethics, Consequentialism, and Wikileaks' in *Sewanee Senior Philosophy Essays*. Sewanee, GA: University of the South, 1–31

Clarke, J. 2005. 'Criminal Penalties for Contraventions of Part IV of the Trade Practices Act' *Deakin Law Review* 10(1): 141–76

Clegg, S. 1990. *Modern Organizations: Organization Studies in the Postmodern World*. London: Sage

Clegg, S. 1994. 'Power Relations and the Constitution of the Resistant Subject' in J. Jermier, D. Knights and W. Nord (eds), *Resistance and Power in Organizations*. London: Routledge, ch. 9, 274 –325

CMC (Crime and Misconduct Commission, Australia) 2010. *The Ethical Perceptions and Attitudes of Queensland Police Service Recruits and First Year Constables: 1995–2008*. Brisbane, Qld: CMC (November)

Cobb, A.T., C. Stephens and G. Watson 2001. 'Beyond Structure: The Role of Social Accounts in Ideal Control' *Human Relations* (September) 54(9): 1123–53

COER (Council of Europe Resolution) 2010. 'Resolution 1729 (2010): The Protection of "Whistle-Blowers"' (29 April), accompanies Recommendation 1916 of the same name, available at http://assembly.coe.int/Main.asp?link=/Documents/AdoptedText/ta10/EREC1916.htm and http://assembly.coe.int/Main.asp?link=/Documents/AdoptedText/ta10/ERES1729.htm

Cohn, M. 2001. 'Fuzzy Legality in Regulation: The Legislative Mandate Revisited' *Journal of Law and Policy* (October) 23(4): 469–97

Coleman, E.G. 2011. 'Anonymous: From the Lulz to Collective Action' in *The New Everyday: A Mediacommons Project* (6 April), available at http://mediacommons.futureofthebook.org/tne/pieces/anonymous-lulz-collective-action

Collinson, D. 1994. 'Strategies of Resistance: Power, Knowledge and Subjectivity in the Workplace' in J. Jermier, D. Knights and W. Nord (eds), *Resistance and Power in Organizations*. London: Routledge, ch. 1, 25–68

Commissioner for Public Employment 2007. *Workplace Perspectives: Survey Report 2006*. Government of South Australia, available at http://intra.sa.gov.au/Policies/cpe/docs/Workplace/2006%20Workplace_Perspectives_Survey_Report.pdf

Cooper, J. 2012. 'Noble Cause Corruption as a Consequence of Role Conflict in the Police Organisation' *Policing and Society: An International Journal of Research and Policy* 22(2): 169–84

Cooper, T.L. 2006. *The Responsible Administrator: An Approach to Ethics for the Administrative Role*, 5th edn. San Francisco, CA: Jossey Bass

Cooper, T.L. and N. Wright (eds) 1992. *Exemplary Public Administrators: Character and Leadership in Government*. San Francisco, CA: Jossey-Bass

Cortina, L. and V. Magley 2003. 'Raising Voice, Risking Retaliation: Events Following Interpersonal Mistreatment in the Workplace' *Journal of Occupational Health Psychology* 8(4): 247–65

Crawshaw, L. 2007. *Taming the Abrasive Manager: How to End Unnecessary Roughness in the Workplace*. San Francisco, CA: Jossey-Bass

Cronqvist, L. 2003. 'Presentation of TOSMANA: Adding Multi-Value Variables and Visual Aids to QCA', paper prepared for COMPASS Launching Conference, Louvain-La-Neuve and Leuven, 16–17 September

Cullen, D. 1990. *The Public Inquiry into the Piper Alpha Disaster* (Department of Energy, CM 1301). London: HMSO

Culp, D. 1995. 'Whistleblowers: Corporate Anarchists or Heroes? Towards a Judicial Perspective' *Hofstra Labor Law Journal* 13: 109–38

Curtis, M.B. 2006. 'Whistleblower Mechanisms: A Study of the Perceptions of "Users" and "Responders"', paper sponsored by the Dallas Chapter of the Institute of Internal Auditors (April)

Curtis, M.B. and E.Z. Taylor. 2009. 'Whistleblowing in Public Accounting: Influence of Identity Disclosure, Situational Context, and Personal Characteristics' *Accounting and the Public Interest* (December) 9(1): 191–220

Dale, M.C. 2010. 'APNewsBreak: IRS Awards $4.5M to Whistleblower' (8 April), available at http://newss-business.blogspot.com.au/2011/04/apnewsbreak-irs-awards-45m-to.html

Daniels, R.J. and R. Morck (eds) 1995. *Corporate Decision-Making in Canada*. Calgary: University of Calgary Press

Daugareilh, I. 2008. 'Corporate Norms on Corporate Social Responsibility and International Norms' in *Governance, International Law and Corporate Social Responsibility*, IILS (International Institute for Labour Studies) Research Series 116 Monograph. Geneva: International Labour Office, 63–78

Davies, G. 2005. *Queensland Public Hospitals Commission of Inquiry Final Report*. Brisbane: Queensland Public Hospitals Commission of Inquiry

Davis, A.J. and E. Konishi 2007. 'Whistleblowing in Japan' *Nursing Ethics* (March) 14(2): 194–202

Davis, M. 1989. 'Avoiding the Tragedy of Whistleblowing' *Business and Professional Ethics Journal* (Winter) 8(4): 3–19

Dawson, S. 2000. 'Whistleblowing and Public Policy', paper prepared for the Australasian Political Studies Association Conference, Canberra, 4–6 October

De Graaf, G. 2010. 'A Report on Reporting: Why Peers Report Integrity and Law Violations in Public Organizations' *Public Administration Review* (September/October) 70(5): 767–79

De Maria, W. 1994. *Wounded Warriors*. Brisbane: Department of Social Work and Social Policy, University of Queensland

De Maria, W. 1999. *Deadly Disclosures: Whistleblowing and the Ethical Meltdown of Australia*. Adelaide: Wakefield Press

De Maria, W. and C. Jan 1997. 'Eating its Own: The Whistleblower's Organization in Vendetta Mode' *Australian Journal of Social Issues* (February) 32(1): 37–59

De Schepper, M. 2009. 'Setting the Right Incentives for Whistleblowers', European Master in Law and Economics, available at www.emle.org/_data/Marten_De_Schepper_-_Setting_the_Right_Incentives_for_Whistle blowers.pdf

Della Porta, D. and A. Vannucci 2012. *The Hidden Order of Corruption: An Institutional Approach*. Farnham: Ashgate

Deloitte Consulting LLP 2004. *United Nations Organizational Integrity Survey: Final Report*, available at www.whistleblower.org/storage/documents/UN_Integrity_Survey.pdf

Dempster, Q. 1997. *Whistleblowers*. Sydney: ABC Books

Denzin, N.K. 1978. *The Research Act: A Theoretical Introduction to Sociological Methods*. New York: McGraw-Hill

Department of Health and Aging (Australia) 2013. 'About the PBS', available at www.pbs.gov.au/info/about-the-pbs#What_is_the_PBS

Department of Health and Human Services (US) 2012. 'Corporate Integrity Agreement between the Office of Inspector General of the Department of Health and Human Services and GlaxoSmithKline LLC' (28 June), available at https://oig.hhs.gov/fraud/cia/agreements/GlaxoSmithKline_LLC_06282012.pdf

Depoorter, B. and J. De Mot 2006. 'Whistle Blowing: An Economic Analysis of the False Claims Act' *Supreme Court Economic Review* 14: 135–62

Detert, J.R., V.L. Sweitzer and L.K. Treviño 2008. 'Moral Disengagement in Ethical Decision Making: A Study of Antecedents and Outcomes' *Journal of Applied Psychology* 93(2): 374–91

Devillé, A., E. Jaspaert and M. Swyngedouw 2007. *Inferentie via kwalitatief onderzoek. Methode en analyse [Inference through Qualitative Research. Method and Analysis]*. Leuven: Instituut voor Sociaal en Politiek Opinieonderzoek (KU Leuven)

Devine, T. 1997. *The Whistleblower's Survival Guide: Courage Without Martyrdom*. Washington, DC: Fund for Constitutional Government

Devine, T. 2004. 'Whistleblowing in the United States: The Gap Between Vision and Lessons Learned' in R. Calland and G. Dehn (eds), *Whistleblowing Around the World*. Cape Town: Open Democracy Advice Centre, 74–100

Devine, T. 2012a. 'Jury Trials and the Whistleblower Protection Act: Talking Points', available at www.whistleblower.org/ on request

Devine, T. 2012b. 'Federal Circuit Whistleblower Decisions Since Passage of the 1994 Amendments' (2 July), available at www.openthegovernment.org/sites/default/files/Federal_Circuit_digest.pdf

Devine, T. and D. Aplin 1988. 'Whistleblower Protection: the Gap Between the Law and Reality' *Howard Law Review*, 31: 223–39

Devine, T. and T. Maassarani 2011. *The Corporate Whistleblower's Survival Guide*. San Francisco, CA: Berrett-Koehler

Di Lorenzo, V. 2007. 'Business Ethics: Law as a Determinant of Business Conduct' *Journal of Business Ethics* (March) 71(3): 275–99

DOJ (Department of Justice, US) 2010. 'Department of Justice Recovers $3 Billion in False Claims Cases in Fiscal Year 2010' (Office of Public Affairs, Washington, DC, 22 November), available at www.justice.gov/opa/pr/2010/November/10-civ-1335.html

DOJ (Department of Justice, US) 2011. 'Fraud Statistics Overview: October 1, 1987–September 30, 2011' (Civil Division, 7 December), available at www.justice.gov/civil/docs_forms/C-FRAUDS_FCA_Statistics.pdf

DOJ (Department of Justice, US) 2012a. 'GlaxoSmithKline to Plead Guilty and Pay $3 Billion to Resolve Fraud Allegations and Failure to Report Safety Data', Office of Public Affairs Press Release, 2 July, available at www.justice.gov/opa/pr/2012/July/12-civ-842.html

DOJ (Department of Justice, US) 2012b. 'Fraud Statistics Overview: October 1, 1987–September 30, 2012' (Civil Division, 7 December), available at www.justice.gov/civil/docs_forms/C-FRAUDS_FCA_Statistics.pdf

DOL (Department of Labor, US) 2010. *Complainants Did Not Always Receive Appropriate Protection under the Whistleblower Protection Program*, Office of Inspector General Report no. 02–10–202–10–105

DOL (Department of Labor, US) 2012. *Federally Operated Whistleblower Program Costs*, Office of Inspector General Report no. 22–12–014–10–105

Donkin, M., R. Smith and A.J. Brown 2008. 'How Do Officials Report? Internal and External Whistleblowing' in A.J. Brown (ed.), *Whistleblowing in the Australian Public Sector: Enhancing the Theory and Practice of Internal Witness Management in Public Sector Organizations*. Canberra: ANU E-Press, ch. 4, 83–108

Doran, K.B. 2001. 'Methodological Issues in Cross-Cultural Research: Lessons Learned in a Study of Chinese and North American Consumers' *Asia Pacific Advances in Consumer Research* 4: 239–42

DOT (Department of the Treasury, US) 2012a. *Report on Asian Development Bank Reform Progress* (21 November), available at www.treasury.gov/resource-center/international/development-banks/Documents/2012%2011%2021%201400%20AsDB%20GCI%20Report%20_posting%20version.pdf

DOT (Department of the Treasury, US) 2012b. *Report on MDB Reform Commitments* (November 21), available at www.treasury.gov/resource-center/international/development-banks/Documents/2012%2011%2021%201400%20GCI%20Report_posting%20version.pdf

Doyle, C. 2009. '*Qui Tam*: The False Claims Act and Related Federal Statutes' (Congressional Research Service, 6 August), available at www.fas.org/sgp/crs/misc/R40785.pdf

Dozier, J.B. 1988. 'Is Whistle-Blowing Helping Behavior?: A Laboratory Study of Team Members' Reporting of an Unethical Team Leader', Dissertation, Ohio State University, Colombus, OH

Dozier, J.B. and M.P. Miceli 1985. 'Potential Predictors of Whistle-Blowing: A Prosocial Behavior Perspective' *Academy of Management Review* (October) 10(4): 823–36

Dreyfus, S. and A.J. Brown 2013. 'Traitors, Troublemakers or Trailblazers? Preliminary Analysis from the World Online Whistleblowing

Survey on Public Attitudes to Whistleblowing', paper prepared for the International Whistleblowing Research Network Conference, University of Middlesex, London, 20–21 July

Dreyfus, S., R. Lederman, A.J. Brown, S. Milton, M. Miceli, R. Bosua, A. Clausen and J. Schanzle 2013. 'Human Sources: The Journalist and the Whistleblower in the Digital Era' in S. Tanner and N. Richardson (eds), *Journalism Research and Investigation in a Digital World*. Oxford: Oxford University Press, ch. 4

Dussuyer, I., S. Mumford and G. Sullivan 2011. 'Reporting Corrupt Practices in the Public Interest: Innovative Approaches to Whistleblowing' in A. Graycar and R. Smith (eds), *Handbook of Global Research and Practice in Corruption*. Cheltenham: Edward Elgar, ch. 23, 429–62

Dworkin, T.M. 2002. 'Whistleblowing, MNCs, and Peace' *Vanderbilt Journal of Transitional Law* 35: 457–86

Dworkin, T.M. 2007 'Sox and Whistleblowing' *Michigan Law Review* (June) 105(8): 1757–80

Dworkin, T.M. 2010. 'US Whistleblowing: A Decade of Progress?' in D.B. Lewis (ed.), *A Global Approach to Public Interest Disclosure: What Can We Learn from Existing Whistleblowing Legislation and Research?*. Cheltenham: Edward Elgar, ch. 4, 36–55

Dworkin, T.M. and M. Baucus 1998. 'Internal vs. External Whistleblowers: A Comparison of Whistleblowing Processes' *Journal of Business Ethics* (September) 17(12): 1281–98

Dworkin, T.M. and A.J. Brown 2013. 'The Money or the Media? Lessons from Contrasting Developments in US and Australian Whistleblowing Laws' *Seattle Journal of Social Justice* 11(2): 653–713

Dworkin, T.M. and E.S. Callahan 1991. 'Internal Whistleblowing: Protecting the Interests of the Employee, the Organization, and Society' *American Business Law Journal* (June) 29(2): 267–308

Dworkin, T.M. and J.P. Near 1987. 'Whistle-Blowing Statutes: Are They Working?' *American Business Law Journal* 25(2): 241–64

Dworkin, T.M. and J.P. Near 1997. 'A Better Statutory Approach to Whistle-Blowing' *Business Ethics Quarterly* 7(1): 1–16

Dyck, A., A. Morse and L. Zingales 2010. 'Who Blows the Whistle on Corporate Fraud?' *Journal of Finance* (December) 65(6): 2213–53

EARC (Electoral and Administrative Review Commission) 1991. *Report on Protection of Whistleblowers*. Brisbane: Queensland Government (October)

Earley, P.C. 2006. 'Leading Cultural Research in the Future: A Matter of Paradigms and Taste' *Journal of International Business Studies*, Three

Lenses on the Multinational Enterprise: Politics, Corruption and Corporate Social Responsibility (November) 37(6): 922–31

EC (European Commission) 2004. 'Staff Regulations of Officials of the European Communities', available at http://ec.europa.eu/civil_service/docs/toc100_en.pdf

EC (European Commission) 2011. 'Proposal for a Regulation of the European Parliament and of the Council on Insider Dealing and Market Manipulation (Market Abuse) of 20.10.2011' COM(2011)651 final, available at http://ec.europa.eu/prelex/liste_resultats.cfm?CL=en&PCP=21&ReqId=9&CB1=MARKT

Edmonds, S. and C. Rowley 2011. 'Rescind President Obama's "Transparency Award" Now', *The Guardian* (online), 14 June, available at www.guardian.co.uk/commentisfree/cifamerica/2011/jun/14/rescind-barack-obama-obama-transparency-award/print

Edwards, B. and S. Walden 2009. 'Racial Discrimination at the World Bank: A Review of the Treatment of Black Employees in Recruitment, Retention and Justice Decisions' GAP (Government Accountability Project), Washington, DC, 9 June), available at www.whistleblower.org/storage/documents/RDWB.pdf

Edwards, B. and S. Walden 2012. 'Tipping the Scales: Is the United Nations Justice System Promoting Accountability in the Peacekeeping Missions or Undermining it?' GAP (Government Accountability Project), Washington, DC, 9 September), available at www.whistleblower.org/storage/documents/FinalFinalTippingTheScales.pdf

Edwards, M. 2008. 'The Conceptualisation and Measurement of Whistleblowing: A New Way Forward' in M. Wilson (ed.), *Proceedings of the 22nd ANZAM Conference 2008: Managing in the Pacific Century*, Auckland, 2–5 December, 1–15

Ellis, S. and S. Arieli 1999. 'Predicting Intentions to Report Adminstrative and Disciplinary Infractions: Applying the Reasoned Action Model' *Human Relations* (July) 52(7): 947–67

Elliston, F.A. 1982. 'Anonymity and Whistleblowing' *Journal of Business Ethics* (August) 1(3): 167–77

ERC (Ethics Resource Center) 1999. *1994 Ethics in American Business Survey*. Arlington: ERC, available at www.ethics.org/resource/1994-ethics-american-business-survey

ERC (Ethics Resource Center) 2003. 'Office of Government Ethics of Puerto Rico Releases Survey on Employee Ethics', ERC Media Release, 27 October

ERC (Ethics Resource Center) 2007a. *National Government Ethics Survey: An Inside View of Public Sector Ethics*. Arlington: ERC

ERC (Ethics Resource Center) 2007b. *National Business Ethics Survey: An Inside View of Private Sector Ethics*. Arlington: ERC

ERC (Ethics Resource Center) 2008. *National Nonprofit Ethics Survey: An Inside View of Nonprofit Sector Ethics*. Arlington: ERC

ERC (Ethics Resource Center) 2009. *2009 National Business Ethics Survey: Ethics in the Recession*. Arlington: ERC

ERC (Ethics Resource Center) 2010a. *Blowing the Whistle on Workplace Misconduct*. Arlington: ERC (December), available at www.ethics.org/files/u5/WhistleblowerWP.pdf

ERC (Ethics Resource Center) 2010b. *Retaliation: The Cost to Your Company and its Employees*, Supplemental Research Brief. Arlington: ERC, available at www.ethics.org/files/u5/Retaliation.pdf

ERC (Ethics Resource Center) 2010c. *Reporting: Who's Telling You What You Need to Know, Who Isn't, and What You Can Do About It*, Supplemental Research Brief. Arlington: ERC, available at www.ethics.org/files/u5/Reporting.pdf

ERC (Ethics Resource Center) 2011. *National Business Ethics Survey 2011: Workplace Ethics in Transition*. Arlington: ERC

ERC (Ethics Resource Center) 2012a. *Just What is a Whistleblower?*. Arlington: ERC (31 May), available at http://ethics.org/news/2011 nbes-reporting?utm_source=NBES+

ERC (Ethics Resource Center) 2012b. *National Business Ethics Survey of Fortune 500 Employees: An Investigation into the State of Ethics at America's Most Powerful Companies*. Arlington: ERC

ERC (Ethics Resource Center) 2012c. *Inside the Mind of a Whistleblower*, Supplemental Report of the 2011 National Business Ethics Survey. Arlington: ERC

ERC (Ethics Resource Center) 2012d. *Retaliation: When Whistleblowers Become Victims*, Supplemental Report of the 2011 National Business Ethics Survey. Arlington: ERC

ERC (Ethics Resource Center) 2012e. *2011 National Business Ethics Survey: Workplace Ethics in Transition*. Arlington: ERC

ERC (Ethics Resource Center) 2013. *Encouraging Employee Reporting through Procedural Justice*. Arlington: ERC (May), available at www.ethics.org/files/u5/procedural-justice.pdf

Estlund, C. 2005. 'Rebuilding the Law of the Workplace in an Era of Self-Regulation' *Columbia Law Review* (March) 105(2): 319–404

Evans, A.J. 2008. 'Dealing with Dissent: Whistleblowing, Egalitarianism, and the Republic of the Firm' *Innovation: European Journal of Social Sciences* 21(3): 267–79

FAIR (Federal Accountability Initiative for Reform) 2012. 'What's Wrong with Canada's Federal Whistleblower Legislation', available at http://fairwhistleblower.ca/psdpa/psdpa_critique.html
Fang, T. 2003. 'A Critique of Hofstede's Fifth National Culture Dimension' *International Journal of Cross Cultural Management* 3(3): 347–68
Farrell, D. 1983. 'Exit, Voice, Loyalty and Neglect as Responses to Job Dissatisfaction: A Multidimensional Scaling Study' *Academy of Management Journal* (December) 26(4): 596–607
Farrell, D. and J.C. Petersen 1982. 'Patterns of Political Behavior in Organizations' *Academy of Management Review* (July) 7(3): 403–12
Fasterling, B. and D.B. Lewis 2014. 'Leaks, Legislation and the Freedom of Speech: How Can the Law Effectively Promote Public Interest Whistleblowing' *International Labour Review*, postprint
Faunce, T.A. 2006. 'Global Intellectual Property Protection of "Innovative" Pharmaceuticals: Challenges for Bioethics and Health Law' in B. Bennett and G.F. Tomossy (eds), *Globalisation and Health: Challenges for Health Law and Bioethics*. Dordrecht: Springer, 87–108
Faunce, T.A. 2011 'Will International Trade Law Promote or Inhibit Global Artificial Photosynthesis?' *Asian Journal of WTO and International Health Law and Policy* 6: 313–47
Faunce, T.A., G. Urbas and L. Skillen 2011. 'Implementing US-Style Anti-Fraud Laws in the Australian Pharmaceutical and Health Care Industries' *Medical Journal of Australia* (May) 194(9): 474–8
Faunce, T.A., G. Urbas, L. Skillen and M. Smith 2010. 'Recovering Fraudulent Claims for Australian Federal Expenditure on Pharmaceuticals and Medical Devices' *Journal of Law and Medicine* (December) 18(2): 302–15
Faunce, T.A. and T. Vines 2008. 'Change Culture to Encourage Whistleblowing' (Civil Liberties Australia, 24 September), available at www.cla.asn.au/0805/index.php/articles/articles/change-culture-encourage-whistleblowing
FBI (Federal Bureau of Investigation) 2007. *Financial Crimes Report to the Public: October 1, 2006–September 30, 2006*, available at www.fbi.gov/stats-services/publications/fcs_report2007
FDA (Food and Drug Administration) 2002. 'Proposal to Debar: Notice of Opportunity for Hearing', Letter to Dr Richard L. Borison, Docket No. 00N–1530, Department of Health and Human Services, US (26 November), available at www.fda.gov/ohrms/dockets/dailys/02/Dec02/121902/00n-1530.pdf
Feldman, Y. and O. Lobel 2009. 'The Incentives Matrix: The Comparative Effectiveness of Rewards, Liabilities, Duties and Protections for

Reporting Illegality', available at http://law.haifa.ac.il/LawAndMarkets/Papers/FeldmanLobel.pdf

Feldman, Y. and O. Lobel 2011. 'Individuals as Enforcers: The Design of Employee Reporting Systems' in C. Parker and V. Lehmann Nelson (eds), *Explaining Compliance: Business Responses to Regulation*. Cheltenham: Edward Elgar, ch. 12, 263–84

Fifth Report of the Shipman Inquiry 2004. *Safeguarding Patients: Lessons from the Past, Proposals for the Future*, vol. 1 (CM 6394, London, December), available at www.archive2.official-documents.co.uk/document/cm63/6394/

Financial Times 2009. 'Corrupt Privatization Does Not Deter IMF Lending to Sri Lanka', 9 August, available at www.sundaytimes.lk/090809/FinancialTimes/ft307.html

Fishbein, M. and I. Ajzen 2010. *Predicting and Changing Behavior: The Reasoned Action Approach*. New York: Psychology Press

Fitzgerald, G.E. 1989. *Report of the Commission of Inquiry into Possible Illegal Activities and Associated Police Misconduct* (Fitzgerald Report). Queensland Government Printer, available at www.cmc.qld.gov.au/about-us/our-organisation/our-background/fitzgerald-inquiry

Flaherty, E. 2007. 'Legal Protection for Staff in International Organisations: A Practitioner's View', paper prepared for the Conference on Accountability for Human Rights Violations by International Organizations, Brussels, 16–17 March, available at http://securitymanagementinitiative.org/index.php?option=com_docman&task=doc_download&gid=414&Itemid=32&lang=fr

Fleischer, H. and K.U. Schmolke 2012. *Financial Incentives for Whistleblowers in European Capital Markets Law? Legal Policy Considerations on the Reform of the Market Abuse Regime*, ECGI–Law Working Paper No. 189/2012, available at SSRN: http://ssrn.com/abstract=2124678, also available at http://dx.doi.org/10.2139/ssrn.2124678

Fleming, P. 2005. 'Kindergarten Cop: Paternalism and Resistance in a High-Commitment Workplace' *Journal of Management Studies* (November) 42(7): 1469–89

Flynn, K. 2006. 'Covert Disclosures: Unauthorized Leaking, Public Officials and the Public Sphere' *Journalism Studies* 7(2): 256–73

Fong, B.D. 1991. 'Whistleblower Protection and the Office of Special Counsel: the Development of Reprisal Law in the 1980s' *American University Law Review* 40: 1015–63

Foucault, M. 1977. *Discipline and Punish*. London: Allen & Unwin

Foucault, M. 1980. 'Truth and Power' in C. Gordon (ed.), *Power/Knowledge: Selected Interviews and Other Writings 1972–1977*. Brighton: Harvester Press, ch. 6, 109–33

Fredin, A.J. 2011. 'The Effects of Anticipated Regret on the Whistleblowing Decision' *Ethics and Behavior* 21(5): 404–27

Freestone, L., S.N. Bolsin, M. Colson, A. Patrick and B. Creati 2006. 'Voluntary Incident Reporting by Anaesthetic Trainees in an Australian Hospital' *International Journal for Quality in Health Care* (December) 18(6): 452–7

French, J.R.P. and B.H. Raven 1959. 'The Bases of Social Power' in D. Cartwright (ed.), *Studies in Social Power*. Ann Arbor, MI: Institute for Social Research, University of Michigan, ch. 9, 150–67

Gabriel, Y. 1999. 'Beyond Happy Families: A Critical Reevaluation of the Control-Resistance-Identity Triangle' *Human Relations* (February) 52(2): 179–203

Gabriel, Y. 2004. 'The Glass Cage: Flexible Work, Fragmented Consumption, Fragile Selves' in J.C. Alexander, G.T. Marx and C.L. Williams (eds), *Self, Social Structure and Beliefs*. Berkeley, CA: University of California Press, ch. 4, 57–76

Gabriel, Y. 2008. 'Spectacles of Resistance and Resistance of Spectacles' *Management Communication Quarterly* (February) 21(3): 310–26

Gallagher, R. 2012. 'Skype Won't Say Whether it Can Eavesdrop on Your Conversations' (20 July), available at www.slate.com/blogs/future_tense/2012/07/20/skype_won_t_comment_on_whether_it_can_now_eavesdrop_on_conversations_.html

Gallie, D. (ed.) 2007. *Employment Regimes and the Quality of Work*. Oxford: Oxford University Press

GAO (General Accountability Office, US) 1999. *World Bank Status of Grievance Process Reform, Report to Congressional Committees*. Washington, DC, GAO (13 May), available at www.gao.gov/archive/1999/ns99096.pdf

GAO (General Accountability Office, US) 2007. 'Progress on Management Reform Efforts has Varied' (14 November), available at http://gao.gov/products/GAO-08-84

GAO (General Accountability Office, US) 2010. *Sustained Management Attention Needed to Address Longstanding Program Weakness*, Report 10–722 (17 August), available at www.gao.gov/products/GAO-10-722

GAP (Government Accountability Project, US) 2007. 'OSLA Proposal for the United Nations' (8 November), available at www.whistleblower.org/storage/documents/OSLAReport.pdf

GAP (Government Accountability Project, US) 2008a. 'Plundering the Yerevan Water Utility', Executive Summary, available at www.whistleblower.org/storage/documents/PlunderingtheYerevanWaterUtility.pdf

GAP (Government Accountability Project, US) 2008b. 'Privatization and Corruption: the World Bank and Azerbaijan' (8 August), available at www.whistleblower.org/storage/documents/Privatization_and_Corruption.pdf

GAP (Government Accountability Project, US) 2009. 'The IDB, Poverty and Racial Discrimination' (27 October), available at www.whistleblower.org/storage/documents/IDBPRDExecSummary.pdf

GAP (Government Accountability Project, US) 2010. 'Lack of Security for World Bank Staff and Consultants' (15 March), available at www.whistleblower.org/storage/documents/Lackofsecurityforworldbankstaff3.15.10.pdf

Garfinkel, H. 1956. 'Conditions of Successful Degradation Ceremonies' *American Journal of Sociology* (March) 61(5): 420–4

Gartrell, N., J. Herman, S. Olarte, M. Feldstein and R. Localio 1987. 'Reporting Practices of Psychiatrists Who Knew of Sexual Misconduct by Colleagues' *American Journal of Orthopsychiatry* (April) 57(2): 287–95

Geertz, C. 1973. *The Interpretation of Cultures*. New York: Fontana

George, A.L. and A. Bennett 2005. *Case Studies and Theory Development in the Social Sciences*. Cambridge, MA: MIT Press

Getnick, N.V. and L.A. Skillen 1996. 'The *Qui Tam*: Arming the Citizenry to Fight Fraud' *New York Law Journal*, Outside Counsel, 22 October, available at www.getnicklaw.com/media/article_06.html

Getnick, N.V. and L.A. Skillen 2003. *The Fundamentals of Qui Tam*, International Association of Defense Counsel Mid-Year Meeting (meeting papers) (February), available at www.getnicklaw.com/media/article_13.html

Gillam, C. 2012. 'Scientist Who Coined "Pink Slime" Reluctant Whistleblower' (24 March), available at http://mobile.reuters.com/article/idUSBRE82N0AG20120324?irpc=932

Girodo, Michael 2007. *A Culture Review of the Investigations Division of OIOS*, Consultant Report (13 July), available at www.innercitypress.com/oiosrev2.pdf

Glazer, M.P. and P.M. Glazer 1989. *The Whistleblowers: Exposing Corruption in Government and Industry*. New York: Basic Books

Global Integrity Report 2009. 'Ghana: 2009', available at http://report.globalintegrity.org/Ghana/2009/

Goldschmidt, J. and Anonymous 2008. 'The Necessity of Dishonesty: Police Deviance, "Making the Case", and the Public Good' *Policing and Society: An International Journal of Research and Policy* 18(2): 113–35

Gong, T. 2000. 'Whistleblowing: What Does it Mean in China?' *International Journal of Public Administration* 23(11): 1899–1923

Gorta, A. and S. Forell 1995. 'Layers of Decision: Linking Social Definitions of Corruption and Willingness to Take Action' *Crime, Law and Social Change* 23(4): 315–43

Gottschalk, P. and S. Holgersson 2011. 'Whistle-Blowing in the Police' *Police Practice and Research* 12(5): 397–409

Gouveia, V.V. and M. Ros 2000. 'Hofstede and Schwartz's Models for Classifying Individualism at the Cultural Level: Their Relation to Macro-Social and Macro-Economic Variables' *Psicothema* 12(1): 25–33

Gowen, S. 2011. 'Grand Jury Timeline: What Happened at Penn State?' *OC Register*, 8 and 11 November

Grace, D. and S. Cohen 1998. 'Whistleblowing' in *Business Ethics: Australian Problems and Cases*, 2nd edn. Melbourne: Oxford University Press, ch. 9

Graham, J.W. 1986. 'Principled Organizational Dissent: A Theoretical Essay' in B.M. Staw and L.L. Cummings (eds), *Research in Organizational Behavior*. Greenwich: JAI Press, ch. 1, 1–52

Grant, C. 2002. 'Whistle Blowers: Saints of Secular Culture' *Journal of Business Ethics* (September) 39(4): 391–9

Grassley, C.E. 2006. 'Correspondence to Federal Department of Health and Human Services and Attorney-General in his Capacity as Chair of the US Senate Committee on Finance' (26 April), available at www.ncsl.org/Portals/1/documents/health/GrassleyLtr.pdf

Gray, T. and B. Martin 2006. 'Defamation and the Art of Backfire' *Deakin Law Review* 11(2): 115–36

Grimstad, E. 2007. *Review of the OIOS Investigations Division, United Nations*, Final Report (26 June), available at www.innercitypress.com/oiosrev1.pdf

Gundlach, M.J., S.C. Douglas and M.J. Martinko 2003. 'The Decision to Blow the Whistle: A Social Information Processing Framework' *Academy of Management Review* (January) 28(1): 107–23

Guyer, T. and N. Peterson 2013. 'The Current State of Whistleblower Law in Europe: A Report by the Government Accountability Project', paper prepared for the American Bar Association Section of Labor and

Employment Law International Labor and Employment Law Committee, Rome, 5–9 May, available at www.whistleblower.org/storage/documents/TheCurrentStateofWhistleblowerLawinEurope.pdf

Ha, M. 2008. 'Whistleblower Reward Program Reaches New Record', *Korea Times*, South Korea, 12 September, available at www.koreatimes.co.kr/www/news/nation/2010/03/116_35849.html

Hagen, I.M. 2010. *The Powerful Minority: Employee Board Level Representative Between Corporate Industrial Relations*, Fafo-Report 02, available at www.fafo.no/pub/rapp/20146/index.html

Hagen, I.M. and S.C. Trygstad 2008. *Models and Dilemmas: Transferring Corporate Governance to Public Sector*, Fafo-Report 24, available at www.fafo.no/pub/rapp/20066/index.html

Hager, N. and B. Burton 1999. *Secrets and Lies: The Anatomy of an Anti-Environmental PR Campaign*. New Zealand: Craig Potton Publishing

Hall, P. 2013. 'Penn State Asks Judge to Throw Out Mike Mcqueary Whistle-Blower Suit', *The Morning Call* (Lehigh Valley's Newspaper), 15 January, available at http://articles.mcall.com/2013-01-15/sports/mc-penn-state-mcqueary-lawsuit-dismiss-20130115_1_curley-and-schultz-mike-mcqueary-vice-president-gary-schultz

Hall, P.A. and D. Soskice (eds) 2001. *Varieties of Capitalism: the Institutional Foundations of Comparative Advantage*. Oxford: Oxford University Press

Hammersley, M. and P. Atkinson 1995. *Ethnography: Principles in Practice*. London: Routledge

Hansberry, H. 2012. 'In Spite of its Good Intentions, the Dodd-Frank Act has Created an FCPA Monster' *Journal of Criminal Law and Criminology* (Winter) 102(1): 195–226

Haron, D.L., M.V. Dordeski and L.D. Lahmann 2009. 'Bad Mules: A Primer on the Federal and Michigan False Claims Acts' *Michigan Bar Journal*, 28 November, 22–5, available at www.michbar.org/journal/pdf/pdf4article1590.pdf

Harpur, P., B. French and R. Bales 2012. 'Australia's Fair Work Act and the Transformation of Workplace Disability Discrimination Law' *Wisconsin Law Review*, 6 February, available at SSRN: http://ssrn.com/abstract=2000187

Harris, G. 2009. 'Pfizer Pays $2.3 Billion to Settle Marketing Case', *New York Times*, Washington, 2 September, available at www.nytimes.com/2009/09/03/business/03health.html

Harris, G. and D. Wilson 2010. 'Glaxo Pays $750 Million for Sale of Bad Products', *New York Times*, New York, 26 October, available at www.nytimes.com/2010/10/27/business/27drug.html?pagewanted=all

Harrison, G.L and J.L. McKinnon 1999. 'Cross-Cultural Research in Management Control Systems Design: A Review of the Current State' *Accounting, Organizations and Society* (July) 24(5–6): 438–506

Hartmann, M. 2013. 'Ahead of his Sentencing, Bradley Manning Says, "I'm Sorry I Hurt the United States"', *New York Times*, 15 August, available at http://nymag.com/daily/intelligencer/2013/08/bradley-manning-im-sorry-i-hurt-the-us.html

Hassard, J. 1994. 'Postmodern Organizational Analysis: Toward a Conceptual Framework' *Journal of Management Studies* (May) 31(3): 303–24

Hassink, H., M. de Vries and L. Bollen 2007. 'A Content Analysis of Whistleblowing Policies of Leading European Companies' *Journal of Business Ethics* (September) 75(1): 25–44

Healy, D. 2006. 'Manufacturing Consensus' *Culture, Medicine and Psychiatry* (June) 30(2): 135–56

Healy, D. and D. Cattell. 2003. 'Interface Between Authorship, Industry and Science in the Domain of Therapeutics' *British Journal of Psychiatry* 183: 22–7

Heard, E. and W. Miller 2006. 'Creating an Open and Non-Retaliatory Workplace' *International Business Ethics Review* (Summer) 1–7

Hedin, U.-C. and S.-A. Månsson 2012. 'Whistleblowing Processes in Swedish Public Organisations: Complaints and Consequences' *European Journal of Social Work* 15(2): 151–67

Hedström, P. and R. Swedberg 1998. *Social Mechanisms: An Analytical Approach to Social Theory*. Cambridge: Cambridge University Press

Henderson, M.U. 2008. *Women Whistleblowers in the Workplace*. St Paul, MN: University of St Thomas and ProQuest

Henik, E. 2008. 'Mad as Hell or Scared Stiff? The Effects of Value Conflict and Emotions on Potential Whistle-Blowers', Unpublished Ph.D Thesis, University of California, Berkeley, CA, available at http://ezproxy.csu.edu.au/login?url=http://proquest.umi.com/pqdweb?did=1607090331&Fmt=7&clientId=20957&RQT=309&VName=PQD

Hess, D. 2007. 'A Business Ethics Perspective on Sarbanes Oxley and the Organizational Sentencing Guidelines' *Michigan Law Review* (June) 105(8): 1781–1816

Hofstede, G. 1980. *Culture's Consequences: International Differences in Work-Related Values*. London: Sage Publications

Hofstede, G. 1991. *Cultures and Organizations: Software of the Mind*. London: McGraw-Hill

Hofstede, G. 2002. 'Dimensions Do Not Exist: A Reply to Brendan McSweeney' *Human Relations* 55(11): 1–7

Hofstede, G., G.J. Hofstede and M. Minkov 2010. *Cultures and Organizations: Software of the Mind*. New York: McGraw-Hill

Hollings, J. 2011. 'The Informed Commitment Model: Best Practice for Journalists Engaging with Reluctant, Vulnerable Sources and Whistle-Blowers' *Pacific Journalism Review* (May) 17(1): 67–89

Home Office (UK) 2007. *Asset Recovery Action Plan: A Consultation Document* (May), available at www.lccsa.org.uk/assets/documents/consultation/asset-recovery-consultation.pdf

Hopman, P. and E. van Leeuwen 2009. 'Who Do We Inform? The Role of Status and Target in Intergroup Whistleblowing' *Group Processes and Intergroup Relations* (September) 12(5): 605–18

House of Representatives (US) 2009. *False Claims Act Correction Act of 2009*, House Report 111–97 (United States Government Printing Office, 5 May), available at www.gpo.gov/fdsys/pkg/CRPT-111hrpt97/html/CRPT-111hrpt97.htm

House of Representatives Standing Committee on Legal and Constitutional Affairs (Australia) 2009. *Whistleblower Protection: A Comprehensive Scheme for the Commonwealth Public Sector, Report of the Inquiry into Whistleblowing Protection within the Australian Government Public Sector* (Commonwealth of Australia, February), available at http://fraud.govspace.gov.au/files/2010/12/Whistleblower-protection-House-of-Representatives.pdf

Howse, R. and R.J. Daniels 1995. 'Rewarding Whistleblowers: The Costs and Benefits of an Incentive-Based Compliance Strategy' in R.J. Daniels and R. Morck (eds), *Corporate Decision-Making in Canada*. Calgary: University of Calgary Press, 525–50

Huberts, L., T. Lamboo and M. Punch 2003. 'Police Integrity in the Netherlands and the United States: Awareness and Alertness' *Police Practice and Research* 4(3): 217–32

Human Rights and Equal Opportunity Commission 2004. *20 Years On: The Challenges Continue: Sexual Harassment in the Australian Workplace*. Sydney, NSW: HREOC

Hunt, G. (ed.) 1995. *Whistleblowing in the Health Service: Accountability, Law and Professional Practice*. London: Edward Arnold

Hunt, G. (ed.) 1998. *Whistleblowing in the Social Services: Public Accountability and Professional Practice*. London: Hodder Arnold

Hunton, J.E. and J.M. Rose 2011. 'Effects of Anonymous Whistle-Blowing and Perceived Reputation Threats on Investigations of Whistle-Blowing Allegations by Audit Committee Members' *Journal of Management Studies* (January) 48(1): 75–98

Hwang, D., B. Staley, Y.T. Chen and J.S. Lan 2008. 'Confucian Culture and Whistle-Blowing by Professional Accountants: An Exploratory Study' *Managerial Auditing Journal* 23(5): 504–26

IAB (Independent Advisory Board, World Bank) 2013. *2012 Annual Report* (February), available at http://siteresources.worldbank.org/PROJECTS/Resources/40940-1244163232994/IAB-2012AnnualReport.pdf

IFAC (International Federation of Accountants) 2012. *International Ethics Standards Board for Accountants: Responding to a Suspected Illegal Act*, Exposure Draft and Consultation Papers, available at www.ifac.org/publications-resources/responding-suspected-illegal-act

International Association of Whistle Blowers 2011. 'Doctors United Demand Integrity in Medicine! America Needs H.R. 2472' (15 September), available at http://whistleblowersupporter.typepad.com/my_weblog/2011/09/iaw-press-release-america-needs-jr-2472.html

Ipsos Reid 2013. 'Four in Ten (42%) Employed Canadians have Observed Some Form of Workplace Misconduct; One in Five (17%) Cite Witnessing Privacy Violations' (Toronto, Canada, July), available at www.ipsos-na.com/news-polls/pressrelease.aspx?id=6187

Irish-Qhobosheane, J. 2007. *Gentlemen or Villains, Thugs or Heroes? The Social Economy of Organised Crime in South Africa*. South African Institute of International Affairs

IRS (Internal Revenue Service, US) 2012. 'Whistleblower: Informant Award', available at www.irs.gov/uac/Whistleblower-Informant-Award

Jackall, R. 1988. *Moral Mazes: the World of Corporate Managers*. New York: Oxford University Press

Jackson, D., K. Peters, S. Andrew, M. Edenborough, E. Halcomb, L. Luck *et al.* 2010. 'Understanding Whistleblowing: Qualitative Insights from Nurse Whistleblowers' *Journal of Advanced Nursing* (October) 66(10): 2194–2201

Jensen, J.V. 1987. 'Ethical Tension Points in Whistleblowing' *Journal of Business Ethics* (May) 6(4): 321–8

Jermier, J.M., D. Knights and W.R. Nord 1994. *Resistance and Power in Organizations*. London: Routledge

Jo, M., J.E. Nelson and P. Kiecker 1997. 'A Model for Controlling Social Desirability Bias by Direct and Indirect Questioning' *Marketing Letters* (October) 8(4): 429–37

Johnson, M., S. Reich, D. Henry and A. Baker 2011. *Review of the Ethics, Conduct and Grievance Systems of the Inter-American Development Bank*, Review by Global Compliance (16 May), available at http://idbdocs.iadb.org/wsdocs/getdocument.aspx?docnum=36474237

Johnson, R.A. 2003. *Whistleblowing: When it Works – and Why*. Boulder, CO: Lynne Rienner Publishers

Jones, G.E. and M.J. Kavanagh 1996. 'An Experimental Examination of the Effects of Individual and Situational Factors on Unethical Behavioral Intentions in the Workplace' *Journal of Business Ethics* (May) 15(5): 511–23

Jos, P.H., M.E. Tompkins and S.W. Hays 1989. 'In Praise of Difficult People: A Portrait of the Committed Whistleblower' *Public Administration Review* 49(6): 552–61

Jubb, P.B. 1999. 'Whistleblowing: A Restrictive Definition and Interpretation' *Journal of Business Ethics* (August) 21(1): 77–94

Kahan, D.M. 2000. *Gentle Nudges vs. Hard Shoves: Solving the Sticky Norms Problem*, Faculty Scholarship Series Paper 108, available at http://digitalcommons.law.yale.edu/fss_papers/108

Kaplan, E. 2001. 'The International Emergence of Legal Protections for Whistleblowers' *Journal of Public Inquiry* (Fall/Winter) 37–42

Kaplan, S.E., K.R. Pope and J.A. Samuels 2010. 'The Effect of Social Confrontation on Individuals' Intentions to Internally Report Fraud' *Behavioral Research in Accounting* (Fall) 22(2): 51–67

Kaptein, M. 2011. 'From Inaction to External Whistleblowing: The Influence of the Ethical Culture of Organizations on Employees Responses to Observed Wrongdoing' *Journal of Business Ethics* (February) 98(3): 513–30

Keenan, J.P. 1988. 'Communication Climate, Whistleblowing, and the First-Level Manager: A Preliminary Study' *Annual Meeting of the Academy of Management Best Paper Proceedings* (Washington, DC, August) 247–51

Keenan, J.P. 1990. 'Upper-level Managers and Whistleblowing: Determinants of Perceptions of Company Encouragement and Information about Where to Blow the Whistle' *Journal of Business and Psychology* (Winter) 5(2): 223–35

Keenan, J.P. 1995. 'Whistleblowing and the First-Level Manager: Determinants of Feeling Obliged to Blow the Whistle' *Journal of Social Behavior and Personality* (September) 10(3): 571–84

Keenan, J.P. 2000. 'Blowing the Whistle on Less Serious Forms of Fraud: A Study of Executives and Managers' *Employee Responsibilities and Rights Journal* (December) 12(4): 199–217

Keenan, J.P. 2002a. 'Comparing Indian and American Managers on Whistle-Blowing' *Employee Responsibilities and Rights Journal* 14(2–3): 79–89

Keenan, J.P. 2002b. 'Whistleblowing: A Study of Managerial Differences' *Employee Responsibilities and Rights Journal* 14(1):17–32

Keenan, J.P. 2007. 'Comparing Chinese and American Managers on Whistleblowing' *Employee Responsibilities and Rights Journal* (June) 19(2): 85–94

Keenan, J.P. and D.A. McLain 1992. 'Whistleblowing: A Conceptualization and Model' *Academy of Management Best Papers Proceedings* (Las Vegas, NV, 10–12 August) 350–2

Keenan, J.P. and R.L. Sims 1995. 'The Organizational and Intrapersonal Influences on Whistleblowing', paper prepared for the National Academy of Management Meeting, Social Issues in Management Division, Vancouver, Canada

Keil, M., A. Tiwana, R. Sainsbury and S. Sneha 2010. 'Toward a Theory of Whistleblowing Intentions: A Benefit-to-Cost Differential Perspective' *Decision Sciences* (November) 41(4): 787–812

Kelley, L. and R. Worthley 1981. 'The Role of Culture in Comparative Management: A Cross-Cultural Perspective' *Academy of Management Journal* (March) 24(1): 164–73

Kelton, E. 2012. 'Fraud Shouldn't be So Rewarding' *Forbes*, 2 April, available at www.forbes.com/sites/erikakelton/2012/04/02/fraud-shouldnt-be-so-rewarding/

Kennedy, K. 2012a. 'Drugmakers have Paid $8 Billion in Fraud Fines', *USA Today*, Washington, 6 March, available at www.usatoday.com/news/washington/story/2012-03-05/health-drugmakers-fraud-fines/53372792/1

Kennedy, K. 2012b. 'Whistle-Blowers Key in Health Care Fraud Fight', *USA Today*, Washington, 23 February, available at www.usatoday.com/news/washington/story/2012-02-22/health-care-fraud-whistleblowers/53212468/1

Kesselheim, A.S, D.M. Studdert and M.M. Mello 2010. 'Whistle-Blowers' Experiences in Fraud Litigation against Pharmaceutical Companies' *New England Journal of Medicine* (16 May) 362: 1832–39

Khanna, V. 2004. 'Corporate Crime Legislation: A Political Economy Analysis' *Washington University Law Quarterly* 82(95): 95–142

Kilmann, R.H., L.A. O'Hara and J.P. Strauss 2013. 'Developing and Validating a Quantitative Measure of Organizational Courage' in R. Burke and C. Cooper (eds), *Voice and Whistleblowing in Organizations*. Cheltenham: Edward Elgar: 311–342

King, E. 2012. 'Skype, Please Act like the Responsible Global Citizen You Claim to Be' (27 July), available at www.privacyinternational.org/blog/skype-please-act-like-the-responsible-global-citizen-you-claim-to-be

King, G. 1997. 'The Effects of Interpersonal Closeness and Issue Seriousness on Blowing the Whistle' *Journal of Business Communication* (October) 34(4): 419–36

King, G. 1999. 'The Implications of an Organization's Structure on Whistleblowing' *Journal of Business Ethics* (July) 20(4): 315–26

Klockars, C.B., S.K. Ivkovich, W.E. Harver and M.R. Haberfield 2000. 'The Measurement of Police Integrity' in *National Institute of Justice Research in Brief* (US) 1–11, available at www.ncjrs.gov/pdffiles1/nij/181465.pdf

Knapp, D.E., R.H. Faley, S.E. Ekeberg and C.L.Z. Dubois 1997. 'Determinants of Target Responses to Sexual Harassment: A Conceptual Framework' *Academy of Management Review* (July) 22(3): 687–729

Kohn, S.M. 2011. *The Whistleblower's Handbook: A Step-by-Step Guide to Doing What's Right and Protecting Yourself.* Guildford: Lyons Press

Kohn, S.M. and M.D. Kohn 1986. 'An Overview of Federal and State Whistle Blower Protections' *Antioch Law Journal* 4: 99–152

Kölbel, R. 2008. 'Zur Wirtschaftsstrafrechtlichen Institutionalisierung des Whistleblowing' ['On the Institutionalization of Whistleblowing under Criminal Economic Law'] *Juristenzeitung (JZ)* 23: 1134–41

Koury, M. 2012. 'Making it Easier to Whistle While You Work' (16 February), Law 360, Portfolio Media, available at www.constantinecannon.com/pdf_etc/kouryart02162012.pdf

Kovacic, W.E. 1996. 'Whistleblower Bounty Lawsuits as Monitoring Devices in Government Contracting' *Loyola Los Angeles Law Review* 29: 1799–1858

KPMG 2010. *Fraud and Misconduct Survey 2010: Australia and New Zealand*, available at www.kpmg.com/AU/en/IssuesAndInsights/ArticlesPublications/Fraud-Survey/Documents/Fraud-and-Misconduct-Survey-2010.pdf

Kunda, G. 1991. 'Ritual and the Management of Corporate Culture: A Critical Perspective', paper prepared for Eighth International Standing Conference on Organizational Symbolism, Copenhagen, June

LaCroix, K.M. 2011. 'Big Pharma Bribery Probe Gains Momentum, Spurs Civil Litigation', *D & O Diary*, 5 May, available at www.dandodiary.com/2011/05/articles/foreign-corrupt-practices-act/big-pharma-bribery-probe-gains-momentum-spurs-civil-litigation/

Laemmle-Weidenfeld, L. 2013. 'Coronia: After a Decade of Windfall Verdicts and Settlements in Off-Label FCA/FDCA Cases, the Second Circuit has Changed the Landscape', *JD Supra Law News* (April), www.jdsupra.com/legalnews/false-claims-act-focus-april-2013-17988/

Lamb, T.M. 2009. *Whistleblowers: A Study of Employee Decision-Making*. Minneapolis, MN: Capella University

Larkin, P.J., B.D. de Casterlé and P. Schotsmans 2007. 'Multilingual Translation Issues in Qualitative Research: Reflections on a Metaphorical Process' *Qualitative Health Research* (April) 17(4): 468–76

Latané, B. and J.M. Darley 1970. *The Unresponsive Bystander: Why Doesn't He Help?*. New York: Appleton-Century Crofts

Latimer, P. 2006. 'Heroes or Traitors?' *Monash Business Review* (April) 2(1): 34–5

Latimer, P. and A.J. Brown 2008. 'Whistleblower Laws: International Best Practice' *UNSW Law Journal* 31(3): 766–94

Leborgne-Ingelaere, C. 2011. 'Dénoncer son employeur n'est pas, en soi, un motif de licenciement' ['To Tell on Your Employer is Not, in Itself, a Reason for Dismissal'] *La Semaine Juridique Social* (January) 25(4): 1028–32

Lechner, J.P. and P.M. Sisco 2006. 'Sarbanes-Oxley Criminal Whistleblower Provisions and the Workplace: More than Just Securities Fraud' *Florida Bar Journal* (June) 80(6): 85–8

Lennane, K.J. 1993. 'Whistleblowing: A Health Issue' *British Medical Journal* (September) 307(6905): 667–70

Levine, A. 2011. 'Whistleblowing as Treated in Jewish Law' in M. Arszutowicz and W.W. Gasparski (eds), *Whistleblowing: In Defense of Proper Action*, vol. 18. New Brunswick: Transaction Publishers, 69–82

Lewis, D.B. 2003. 'Whistleblowing Statutes in Australia: Is it Time for a New Agenda?' *Deakin Law Review* 8(2): 318–34

Lewis, D.B. 2005. 'Providing Rights for Whistleblowers: Would an Anti-Discrimination Model be More Effective?' *Industrial Law Journal* (September) 34(3): 239–52

Lewis, D.B. 2006. 'The Contents of Whistleblowing/Confidential Reporting Procedures in the UK: Some Lessons from Empirical Research' *Employee Relations* 28(1): 76–86

Lewis, D.B. 2008. 'Ten Years of Public Interest Disclosure Legislation in the UK: Are Whistleblowers Adequately Protected?' *Journal of Business Ethics* (October) 82(2): 497–507

Lewis, D.B. (ed.) 2010. *A Global Approach to Public Interest Disclosure: What Can We Learn from Existing Whistleblowing Legislation and Research?*. Cheltenham: Edward Elgar

Lewis, D.B. 2011a. 'Whistleblowing in a Changing Legal Climate: Is it Time to Revisit our Approach to Trust and Loyalty at the Workplace?' *Business Ethics: A European Review* (January) 20(1): 71–87

Lewis, D.B. 2011b. 'Whistleblowing and Data Protection Principles: Is the Road to Reconciliation Really that Rocky?' *European Journal of Information Technology* (January) 2(1): 1–15

Lewis, D.B. 2013. 'Resolving Whistleblowing Disputes in the Public Interest: Is Tribunal Adjudication the Best that Can be Offered?' *Industrial Law Journal* 42: 35–53

Lewis, D.B. with M. Kender 2010. *A Survey of Whistleblowing/Confidential Reporting Procedures in the UK Top 250 FTSE Firms* (SAI Global and Middlesex University, October), available at www2.gre.ac.uk/__data/assets/pdf_file/0004/578461/Lewis-and-Kender.pdf

Lewis, D.B. and S.C. Trygstad 2009. 'Protecting Whistleblowers in Norway and the UK: A Case of Mix and Match?' *International Journal of Law and Management* 51(6): 374–88

Lewis, D.B. and W. Vandekerckhove (eds) 2011. *Whistleblowing and Democratic Values*. London: International Whistleblowing Research Network

Lim, L. and P. Firkola 2000. 'Methodological Issues in Cross-Cultural Management Research: Problems, Solutions, and Proposals' *Asia Pacific Journal of Management* (April) 17(1): 133–54

Lindblom, L. 2007. 'Dissolving the Moral Dilemma of Whistleblowing' *Journal of Business Ethics* (December) 76(4): 413–26

Liyanarachchi, G.A. and R. Adler 2011. 'Accountants' Whistle-Blowing Intentions: the Impact of Retaliation, Age, and Gender' *Australian Accounting Review* (June) 21(2): 167–82

Lobel, O. 2009. 'Citizenship, Organizational Citizenship and the Laws of Overlapping Obligations' *California Law Review* 97: 433–500, available at www.californialawreview.org/assets/pdfs/97-2/09Apr_Lobel.pdf

Lovink, G. and P. Riemens 2010. 'Twelve Theses on WikiLeaks' *Eurozine*, Frankfurter Rundschau, available at www.eurozine.com/articles/2010-12-07-lovinkriemens-en.html

Loyens, K. 2012a. *Integrity Secured: Understanding Ethical Decision Making among Street-Level Bureaucrats in the Belgian Labor Inspection and Federal Police*. Leuven: KU Leuven

Loyens, K. 2012b. 'Towards a Custom-Made Whistleblowing Policy: Using Grid-Group Cultural Theory to Match Policy Measures to Different Styles of Peer Reporting' *Journal of Business Ethics* (May) 114(2): 239–49

Loyens, K. 2013. 'Why Police Officers and Labour Inspectors (Do Not) Blow the Whistle: A Grid Group Cultural Theory Perspective' *Policing: An International Journal of Police Strategies and Management* 36(1): 27–50

Lubalin, J.S. and J.L. Matheson 1999. 'The Fallout: What Happens to Whistleblowers and Those Accused but Exonerated of Scientific Misconduct?' *Science and Engineering Ethics* 5(2): 229–50

Ludlow, P. 2010. 'WikiLeaks and Hacktivivist Culture', *The Nation*, 15 September, available at www.thenation.com/article/154780/wikileaks-and-hacktivist-culture#axzz2e5XyWU3D

Ma, S. 2008. 'The Dual Nature of Anti-Corruption Agencies in China' *Crime, Law and Society* (March) 49(2): 153–65

Maas, P. 1973. *Serpico*: London: Bantam Books

MacFarquhar, N. 2010. 'Review Panel Judges See a Culture of UN Secrecy', *New York Times*, 16 June, available at www.nytimes.com/2010/06/17/world/17nations.html?pagewanted=all&_r=0

MacNab, B., R. Brislin, R. Worthley, B.L. Galperin, S. Jenner, T.R. Lituchy, J. MacLean, G.M. Aguilera, E. Ravlin, J.H. Tiessen, D. Bess and M.F. Turcotte 2007a. 'Culture and Ethics Management: Whistle-Blowing and Internal Reporting within a NAFTA Country Context' *International Journal of Cross Cultural Management* (April) 7(1): 5–28

MacNab, B., R. Worthley, R. Brislin, B. Galperin and T. Lituchy 2007b. 'National Homogeneity v. Regional Specificity: An Examination of the Canadian Cultural Mosaic and Whistle-Blowing' *Canadian Journal of Regional Science* (Summer) 30(2): 293–312

Madar, C. 2012. *The Passion of Bradley Manning: The Story Behind the Wikileaks Whistleblower*. London: OR Books

Maddi, S.R. and D.M. Khoshaba 2005. *Resilience at Work: How to Succeed No Matter What Life Throws at You*. New York: Amacom

Mahoney, J. and K. Thelen 2010. *Explaining Institutional Change: Ambiguity, Agency, and Power*. Cambridge: Cambridge University Press

Malek, J. 2010. 'To Tell or Not to Tell? The Ethical Dilemma of the Would-be Whistleblower' *Accountability in Research: Policies and Quality Assurance* 17(3): 115–29

Malin, M.H. 1983. 'Protecting the Whistleblower from Retaliatory Discharge' *University of Michigan Journal of Law Reform* (February) 16(2): 277–318

Manning, R., M. Levine and A. Collins 2008. 'The Legacy of the 38 Witnesses and the Importance of Getting History Right' *American Psychologist* (September) 63(6): 562–3

Mansbach, A. 2011. 'Whistleblowing as Fearless Speech: The Radical Democratic Effects of Late Modern Parrhesia' in *Whistleblowing and Democratic Values*, D.B. Lewis and W. Vandekerckhove (eds). London: International Whistleblowing Research Network, 12–26

Manz, C., V. Anand, M. Joshi and K. Manz 2008. 'Emerging Paradoxes in Executive Leadership: A Theoretical Interpretation of the Tensions

Between Corruption and Virtuous Values' *Leadership Quarterly* (June) 19(3): 385–92

Marcoux, A.M. 2003. 'A Fiduciary Argument Against Stakeholder Theory' *Business Ethics Quarterly* (January) 13(1): 1–24

Marginson, S. 2011. 'Higher Education and Public Good' *Higher Education Quarterly* (October) 65(4): 411–33

Marnburg, E. 2001. 'The Questionable Use of Moral Development Theory in Studies of Business Ethics: Discussion and Empirical Findings' *Journal of Business Ethics* (August) 32(4): 275–83

Marshall, S. 2012. 'Bradley Manning Defense Seeks Dismissal of Charges', *ABC OTUS News*, 15 March, available at http://abcnews.go.com/blogs/politics/2012/03/bradley-manning-defense-seeks-dismissal-of-charges/

Martens, L.T. and A. Crowell 2006. 'Whistleblowing: A Global Perspective' in K. Rao (ed.), *Whistleblowing: An Introduction*. Hyderabad: Lemag Books, Magnus School of Business

Martin, B. 1997. *Suppression Stories.* Wollongong: Fund for Intellectual Dissent

Martin, B. 1999. *The Whistleblower's Handbook: How to be an Effective Resister*. Sydney: Envirobook

Martin, B. 2003. 'Illusions of Whistleblower Protections' *University of Technology Sydney Law Review* 5: 119–30

Martin, B. 2004. 'Australia: Whistleblowers Australia' in R. Calland and G. Dehn (eds), *Whistleblowing around the World: Law, Culture and Practice*. Cape Town: Open Democracy Advice Centre, 194–8

Martin, B. and F. Peña 2012. 'Mobbing and Suppression: Footprints of their Relationships' *Social Medicine* 6(4): 217–25

Martin, B. and W. Rifkin 2004. 'The Dynamics of Employee Dissent: Whistleblowers and Organizational Dissent Jiu-Jitsu' *Public Organization Review* (September) 4(3): 221–38

Maslin, J. 2012. 'The Secret Lives of Dangerous Hackers', *New York Times*, 3 May, available at www.nytimes.com/2012/06/01/books/we-are-anonymous-by-parmy-olson.html

Mayntz, R. 2004. 'Mechanisms in the Analysis of Social Macro-Phenomena' *Philosophy of the Social Sciences* (June) 34(2): 237–59

Mazerolle, P. and A.J. Brown 2008. 'Support for Whistleblowing Among Managers: Exploring Job Satisfaction and Awareness of Obligations' in A.J. Brown (ed.), *Whistleblowing in the Australian Public Sector: Enhancing the Theory and Practice of Internal Witness Management in Public Sector Organizations*. Canberra: ANU E-Press, ch. 7, 165–80

Mazerolle, P. and P. Cassematis 2010. 'Whistling While You Work: Lessons to be Learned from the Pan-Australian Research' in D.B.

Lewis (ed.), *A Global Approach to Public Interest Disclosure: What Can We Learn from Existing Whistleblowing Legislation and Research?* Cheltenham: Edward Elgar, ch. 9, 128–58

McCauliffe, C.M.A. 1982. 'Burdens of Proof: Degrees of Belief, Quanta of Evidence, or Constitutional Guarantees?' *Vanderbilt Law Rev*iew 35: 1293–1336

McDonald, G. 2000. 'Cross-Cultural Methodological Issues in Ethical Research' *Journal of Business Ethics* 27(1): 89–104

McLain, D.A. and J.P. Keenan 1999. 'Risk, Information, and the Decision about Response to Wrongdoing in an Organization' *Journal of Business Ethics* (April) 19(3): 255–71

McSweeney, B. 2002. 'Hofstede's Model of National Cultural Differences and their Consequences: A Triumph of Faith – A Failure of Analysis' *Human Relations* (January) 55(1): 89–118

Meinert, D. 2012. 'Retaliation Claims are Greatest Legal Risk', SHRM (Society for Human Resource Management) (7 March), available at (SHRM members only) www.shrm.org/LegalIssues/FederalResources/Pages/RetaliationClaimsRisk.aspx

Melnitzer, J. 2012. 'Canada Ramps up Whistleblower Enforcement' (15 August), available at http://fairwhistleblower.ca/content/canada-ramps-whistleblower-enforcement

Mendelsohn, J. 2009. 'Calling the Boss or Calling the Press: A Comparison of American and British Responses to Internal and External Whistleblowing' *Washington University Global Studies Law Review* 8: 723–45

Mesmer-Magnus, J. and C. Viswesvaran 2005. 'Whistleblowing in Organizations: An Examination of the Correlates of Whistleblowing Intentions, Actions, and Retaliation' *Journal of Business Ethics* (December) 62(3): 277–97

Meyer, J.A. 2006. 'Fighting Medicare Fraud: More Bang for the Federal Buck', paper prepared for the Taxpayers Against Fraud Education Fund (July), available at www.taf.org/FCA-2006report.pdf

Miceli, M.P., J.B. Dozier and J.P. Near 1991. 'Blowing the Whistle on Data Fudging: A Controlled Field Experiment' *Journal of Applied Social Pscyhology* (February) 21(4): 271–95

Miceli, M.P. and J.P. Near 1984. 'The Relationships among Beliefs, Organizational Position, and Whistle-Blowing Status: A Discriminant Analysis' *Academy of Management Journal* (December) 27(4): 687–705

Miceli, M.P and J.P. Near 1985. 'Characteristics of Organizational Climate and Perceived Wrongdoing Associated with Whistle-Blowing Decisions' *Personnel Psychology* (September) 38(3): 525–44

Miceli, M.P. and J.P. Near 1988. 'Individual and Situational Correlates of Whistle-Blowing' *Personnel Psychology* 41(2): 267–81

Miceli, M.P. and J.P. Near 1989. 'The Incidence of Wrongdoing, Whistle-Blowing, and Retaliation: Results of a Naturally Occurring Field Experiment' *Employee Responsibilities and Rights Journal* (June) 2(2): 91–108

Miceli, M.P. and J.P. Near 1992. *Blowing the Whistle: The Organizational and Legal Implications for Companies and Employees*. New York: Lexington

Miceli, M.P. and J.P. Near 1994. 'Relationship among Value Congruence, Perceived Victimization, and Retaliation Against Whistle-Blowers' *Journal of Management* 20(4): 773–94

Miceli, M.P. and J.P. Near 1997. 'Whistle-Blowing as Anti-Social Behavior' in R. Giacalone and J. Greenberg (eds), *Antisocial Behavior in Organizations*. Thousand Oaks, CA: SAGE, ch. 7, 130–49

Miceli, M.P. and J.P. Near 2002. 'What Makes Whistle-Blowers Effective? Three Field Studies' *Human Relations* (April) 55(4): 455–79

Miceli, M.P. and J.P. Near 2005. 'Standing Up or Standing By: What Predicts Blowing the Whistle on Organisational Wrongdoing?' *Research in Personnel and Human Resource Management* 24: 95–136

Miceli, M.P. and J.P. Near 2006. 'How Can One Person Make a Difference? Understanding Whistle-Blowing Effectiveness' in M.J. Epstein and K.O. Hanson (eds), *The Accountable Corporation*, vol. 4. Westport: Praeger, 295–324

Miceli, M.P. and J.P. Near 2010. 'When Do Observers of Organizational Wrongdoing Step Up? Recent US Research on the Factors Associated with Whistleblowing' in D.B. Lewis (ed), *A Global Approach to Public Interest Disclosure: What Can We Learn from Existing Whistleblowing Legislation and Research?*. Cheltenham: Edward Elgar, ch. 6, 74–90

Miceli, M.P. and J.P. Near 2013. 'An International Comparison of the Incidence of Public Sector Whistle-Blowing and the Prediction of Retaliation: Australia, Norway, and the US' *Australian Journal of Public Administration* (December) 72(4): 433–46

Miceli, M.P., J.P. Near and T.M. Dworkin 2008. *Whistle-Blowing in Organizations*. New York: Routledge

Miceli, M.P., J.P. Near and T.M. Dworkin 2009. 'A Word to the Wise: How Managers and Policy-Makers Can Encourage Employees to Report Wrongdoing' *Journal of Business Ethics* (May) 86(3): 379–96

Miceli, M.P., J.P. Near, M.T. Rehg and J.R. Van Scotter 2012. 'Predicting Employee Reactions to Perceived Organizational Wrongdoing: Demoralization, Justice, Proactive Personality, and Whistle-Blowing' *Human Relations* (August) 65(8): 923–54

Miceli, M.P., J.P. Near and C.R. Schwenk 1991. 'Who Blows the Whistle and Why?' *Industrial and Labor Relations Review* (October) 45: 113–30

Miceli, M.P., M. Rehg, J.P. Near and K.C. Ryan 1999. 'Can Laws Protect Whistle-Blowers? Results of a Naturally Occurring Field Experiment' *Work and Occupations* (February) 26(1): 129–51

Miceli, M.P., J.R. Van Scotter, J.P. Near and M.T. Rehg 2001. 'Individual Differences and Whistle-Blowing' *Annual Meeting of the Academy of Management: Best Paper Proceedings*. Washington, DC (August)

Miethe, T.D. 1999. *Whistle-Blowing at Work: Tough Choices in Exposing Fraud, Waste and Abuse on the Job*. Boulder, CO: Westview Press

Miethe, T.D. and Rothschild, J. 1995. 'Whistleblowing and the Control of Organizational Misconduct' *Sociological Inquiry* 64(3): 322–47

Miller, W., A. Grodeland and T. Koshechkina 2001. *A Culture of Corruption?: Coping with Government in Post-Communist Europe*. Budapest: Central European University Press

Ministry of Justice (Taiwan) 2005. 'The Anti-Corruption Rewards and Protection Regulation', available at (English) http://mojlaw.moj.gov.tw/LawContentE.aspx?id=FL010647

Ministry of Labor and Inclusion (Norway) 2006. *Changes in the WEA (Om lov om endringer i arbeidsmiljøloven (varsling)), (Arbeids-og inkluderingsdepartementet),* White Paper no. 84/Ot.prp. nr. 84. 2005–2006

Moberly, R.E. 2006. 'Sarbanes-Oxley's Structural Model to Encourage Corporate Whistleblowers' *Brigham Young University Law Review* 2006(5): 1107–80

Moberly, R.E. 2007. 'Unfulfilled Expectations: An Empirical Analysis of Why Sarbanes-Oxley Whistleblowers Rarely Win' *William and Mary Law Review* 49: 65–155

Moberly, R.E. 2008. 'Protecting Whistleblowers by Contract' *Colorado Law Review* 79: 975–1042

Moberly, R.E. 2010. 'The Supreme Court's Antiretaliation Principle' *Case Western Reserve Law Review* 61(2): 375–452

Moberly, R.E. 2012a. 'Sarbanes-Oxley's Whistleblower Provisions: Ten Years Later' *South Carolina Law Review* 64(1): 1–54

Moberly, R.E. 2012b. 'Whistleblowers and the Obama Presidency: The National Security Dilemma' *Employee Rights and Employment Policy Journal* 16(1): 51–141

Moberly, R.E. and L.E. Wylie 2011. 'An Empirical Study of Whistleblower Policies in United States Corporate Codes of Ethics' in D.B. Lewis and W. Vandekerckhove (eds), *Whistleblowing and Democratic Values*. London: International Whistleblowing Research Network, 27–55

Monsen, P.-Y. 2008. *Muldvarp i Siemens. En dokumentar* [*Mole in Siemens. A Whistleblower's Story*]. Oslo: Spartacus

Moore, C. 2008. 'Moral Disengagement in Processes of Organizational Corruption' *Journal of Business Ethics* (June) 80(1): 129–39

Moore, C.W. and S.T. Wildau 2005. *Assessment of the Functioning and Performance of World Bank Mechanisms, Offices and Services for the Resolution of Personnel Complaints and Grievances* (CDR Associates, 30 June)

Moore, L. and E. McAuliffe 2010. 'Is Inadequate Response to Whistleblowing Perpetuating a Culture of Silence in Hospitals?' *Clinical Governance: An International Journal* 15(3): 166–78

Morvan, P. 2009. 'A Comparison of the Freedom of Speech of Workers in French and American Law' *Indiana Law Journal* (Summer) 84(3): 1015–46

Moscovici, S. 1976. *Social Influence and Social Change*. London: Academic Press

MSPB (Merit Systems Protection Board) 1981. *Whistleblowing and the Federal Employee: Blowing the Whistle on Fraud, Waste, and Mismanagement*. Washington, DC: US Government Printing Office (October)

MSPB (Merit Systems Protection Board) 1984. *Blowing the Whistle in the Federal Government: A Comparative Analysis of 1980 and 1983 Survey Findings*. Washington DC: US Government Printing Office

MSPB (Merit Systems Protection Board) 1993. *Whistleblowing in the Federal Government: An Update, A Report to the President and the Congress of the United States by the Merit Systems Protection Board.* Washington DC: US Government Printing Office (October), available at www.mspb.gov/netsearch/viewdocs.aspx?docnumber=253699&version=253986&application=ACROBAT

MSPB (Merit Systems Protection Board) 2010. *Whistleblower Protection for Federal Employees, A Report to the President and the Congress of the United States by the US Merit Systems Protection Board.* Washington DC: US Government Printing Office (December), available at www.mspb.gov/netsearch/viewdocs.aspx?docnumber=557972&version=559604&application=ACROBAT

MSPB (Merit Systems Protection Board) 2011. *Blowing the Whistle: Barriers to Federal Employees Making Disclosures, A Report to the President and the Congress of the United States by the US Merit*

Systems Protection Board. Washington DC: US Government Printing Office (November), available at www.usda.gov/oig/webdocs/Blowing_The_Whistle.pdf

Myers, A. 2004. 'Whistleblowing: the UK Experience' in R. Calland and G. Dehn (eds), *Whistleblowing Around the World: Law, Culture and Practice*. South Africa: ODAC and PCaW in partnership with the British Council, 101–18

Nader, R., P.J. Petkas and K. Blackwell (eds) 1972. *Whistle Blowing: The Report of the Conference on Professional Responsibility*. New York: Grossman

National Accountability Ordinance (Pakistan) 2007. Ordinance No. XVIII of 1999 (September), available at http://whistleblowers.nonprofitsoapbox.com/storage/whistleblowers/documents/pakistan/nao%20-%201999.pdf

Nayir D.Z. and C. Herzig 2012. 'Value Orientations as Determinants of Preference for External and Anonymous Whistleblowing' *Journal of Business Ethics* (May) 107(2): 197–213

Near, J.P., T.M. Dworkin and M.P. Miceli 1993. 'Explaining the Whistle-Blowing Process: Suggestions from Power Theory and Justice Theory' *Organization Science* (August) 4(3): 393–411

Near, J.P. and T.C. Jensen 1983. 'The Whistleblowing Process: Retaliation and Perceived Effectiveness' *Work and Occupations* (February) 10(1): 3–28

Near, J.P. and M.P. Miceli 1985. 'Organizational Dissidence: the Case of Whistle-Blowing' *Journal of Business Ethics* (February) 4(1): 1–16

Near, J.P. and M.P. Miceli 1986. 'Retaliation against Whistle-Blowers: Predictors and Effects' *Journal of Applied Psychology* 71(1): 137–45

Near, J.P. and M.P. Miceli 1988. *The Internal Auditor's Ultimate Responsibility: The Reporting of Sensitive Issues*. Altamonte Springs, FL: Institute of Internal Auditors Research Foundation

Near, J. P. and M.P. Miceli 1991. 'How to Succeed as a Whistle-Blower: Predictors of Effective Whistle-Blowing', Unpublished working paper, Indiana University, Bloomington, IN

Near, J.P. and M.P. Miceli 1995. 'Effective-Whistle Blowing' *Academy of Management Review* (July) 20(3): 679–708

Near, J.P. and M.P. Miceli 1996. 'Whistle-blowing: Myth and Reality' *Journal of Management* (June) 22(3): 507–26

Near, J.P. and M.P. Miceli 2008. 'Wrongdoing, Whistle-Blowing, and Retaliation in the U.S. Government: What Have Researchers Learned from the Merit Protection Board (MSPB) Survey Results?' *Review of Public Personnel Administration* (September) 28(3): 263–81

Near, J.P., M. Rehg, J. Van Scotter and M.P. Miceli 2004. 'Does Type of Wrongdoing Affect the Whistle-Blowing Process?' *Business Ethics Quarterly* (April) 14(2): 219–42

Negandhi, A.R. 1974. 'Cross-Cultural Management Studies: Too Many Conclusions, Not Enough Conceptualization' *Management International Review* 14(6): 59–67

Negandhi, A.R. 1983. 'Cross-Cultural Management Research: Trends and Future Directions' *Journal of International Business Studies* (Autumn) 14(2): 17–28

The Network 2013. *2013 Corporate Governance and Compliance Hotline Benchmarking Report: An Expanded Analysis of Enterprise Incident Reporting Activity* (August), available at www.whistleblowing.com.au/wp-content/uploads/2013/09/2013-TNW-Corporate-Governance-and-Compliance-Hotline-Benchmarking-Report.pdf

New Zealand Herald 2012. 'Recording Shows ACC Claims False – Pullar', 30 April, available at www.nzherald.co.nz/politics/news/article.cfm?c_id=280&objectid=10802396

NewsMail 2012. 'Toni Wants a Slice of Quiet', 9 March, available at www.news-mail.com.au/news/patel-whistleblower-toni-hoffman-compensation/1299811/

Nielsen, M.B., J. Hetland, S.B. Matthiesen and S. Einasren 2012. 'Longitudinal Relationships Between Workplace Bullying and Psychological Distress' *Scandinavian Journal of Work, Environment and Health* 38(1): 38–46

NSW Ombudsman 2012. *Oversight of the Public Interest Disclosures Act 1994: Annual Report 2011–2012* (Sydney, Australia, 29 November), available at www.ombo.nsw.gov.au/news-and-publications/publications/annual-reports/public-interest-disclosures/public-interest-disclosures-annual-report

NSW Ombudsman 2013. 'Public Interest Disclosure Guidelines', available at www.ombo.nsw.gov.au/news-and-publications/publications/guidelines/public-interest-disclosures

Oakes, L. 2010. *On the Record: Politics, Politicans and Power*. Sydney: Hachette Australia

O'Brien, A. 2013. 'Bradley Manning's Full Statement: A Transcription of the Soldier's Statement, Read in Court, Explaining Why He Leaked State Secrets to Wikileaks', *Salon*, 2 March, available at www.salon.com/2013/03/01/bradley_mannings_full_statement/

O'Day, R. 1974. 'Intimidation Rituals: Reactions to Reform' *Journal of Applied Behavioral Science* (July) 10(3): 373–86

OECD (Organisation for Economic Co-operation and Development) 2011. 'G20 Anti-Corruption Action Plan. Action Point 7: Protection of Whistleblowers', available at www.oecd.org/general/48972967.pdf

OFT (Office of Fair Trading, UK) 2010. 'Rewards for Information about Cartels', available at www.oft.gov.uk/OFTwork/competition-act-and-cartels/cartels/rewards#.UftYql1-8-U

Oh, L.B. and H.H. Teo 2010. 'To Blow or Not to Blow: An Experimental Study on the Intention to Whistleblow on Software Piracy' *Journal of Organizational Computing and Electronic Commerce* 20(4): 347–69

Ohnishi, K., Y. Hayama, A. Asai and S. Kosugi 2008. 'The Process of Whistleblowing in a Japanese Psychiatric Hospital' *Nursing Ethics* (September) 15(5): 631–42

Omtzigt, P. 2009. *The Protection of 'Whistle-Blowers', Report by the Committee on Legal Affairs and Human Rights*, Document 12006 (14 September), available at http://assembly.coe.int/ASP/Doc/XrefViewHTML.asp?FileID=12302&Language=EN

OPSSC (Office of the Public Sector Standards Commissioner) 2010. *State of the Sector Report 2010* (Western Australia, November), available at www.publicsector.wa.gov.au/sites/default/files/documents/state_of_the_sector_report_2010.pdf

Orr, L. 1981. 'Is Whistleblowing the Same as Informing?' *Business and Society Review* (Fall) 39: 4–17

Orsini Broderick, C. 2007. '*Qui Tam* Provisions and the Public Interest: An Empirical Analysis' *Columbia Law Review* (May) 107(4): 949–1001

OSC (Office of Special Counsel) 2012. *Annual Report 2012*. Washington, DC: OSC, available at www.osc.gov/RR_AnnualReportsToCongress.htm

OSCE (Organisation for Security and Co-operation in Europe) 2012. *Strategic Approaches to Corruption Prevention in the OSCE Region*, Review Report published for the concluding meeting of 20th OSCE Economic and Environmental Forum 'Promoting Security and Stability through Good Governance', Prague, 12–14 September, available at www.osce.org/eea/93468

Osterhaus, A. and C. Fagan 2009. *Alternative to Silence: Whistleblower Protection in 10 European Countries, Report for Transparency International* (15 November), available at http://fairwhistleblower.ca/files/fair/docs/ti/Alternative_to_silence_whistleblower_protection.pdf

Otis, L. and E.H. Reiter 2011. 'The Reform of the United Nations Administration of Justice System: the United Nations Appeals Tribunal After One Year' *Law and Practice of International Courts and Tribunals* 10(3): 405–28

PACE (Parliamentary Assembly of the Council of Europe) 2009. *The Protection of Whistleblowers, Report of the Committee on Legal Affairs and Human Rights*, Document 12006 (14 September), available at http://assembly.coe.int/ASP/Doc/XrefViewHTML.asp?FileID=12302&Language=EN

Padraic, S. 2005. *Sympathy for the Devil: Confessions of a Corrupt Police Officer*. Sydney: ABC Books

Pagnattaro, M.A. and E.R. Peirce 2008. 'Between a Rock and a Hard Place: the Conflict Between US Corporate Codes of Conduct and European Privacy and Work Laws' *Berkeley Journal of Employment and Labor Law* 28(2): 375–428

Parish, M. 2010. 'An Essay on the Accountability of International Organizations' *International Organizations Law Review* 7(2), available at http://ssrn.com/abstract=1651784

Park, H. and J. Blenkinsopp 2009. 'Whistleblowing as Planned Behavior: A Survey of South Korean Police Officers' *Journal of Business Ethics* (April) 85(4): 545–56

Park, H., J. Blenkinsopp, M. Kemal Oktem and U. Omurgonulsen 2008. 'Cultural Orientation and Attitudes Toward Different Forms of Whistleblowing: A Comparison of South Korea, Turkey, and the UK' *Journal of Business Ethics* (November) 82(4): 929–39

Park, H., M.T. Rehg and D. Lee 2005. 'The Influence of Confucian Ethics and Collectivism on Whistleblowing Intentions: A Study of South Korean Public Employees' *Journal of Business Ethics* (June) 58(4): 387–403

Parker, D. 2012. 'Pullar did Nothing Criminal – Police', 5 June, available at www.3news.co.nz/Pullar-did-nothing-criminal–police/tabid/1607/articleID/256751/Default.aspx

Parker, M. 1992. 'Post-Modern Organizations or Postmodern Theory?' *Organization Studies* 13: 1–17

Parmerlee, M.A., J.P. Near and T.C. Jensen 1982. 'Correlates of Whistle-Blowers Perceptions of Organizational Retaliation' *Administrative Science Quarterly* (March) 27(1): 17–34

Passman, E.H and B.J. Schwartz 2005. 'In the Name of Security, Insecurity: the Trend to Diminish Federal Employees' Rights' *Labor Lawyer* (Summer) 21(1): 57–80

Patapan, H., J. Wanna and P. Weller (eds) 2005. *Westminster Legacies: Democracy and Responsible Government in Asia and the Pacific*. Sydney: University of New South Wales Press

Patel, C. 2003. 'Some Cross-cultural Evidence on Whistle-blowing as an Internal Control Mechanism' *Journal of International Accounting Research* (Fall) 2(1): 69–96

Pawson, R. and N. Tilley 1997. *Realistic Evaluation*. London: Sage

PCaW (Public Concern at Work) 2007. *Rewarding Whistleblowers as Good Citizens: Response to the Home Office Consultation* (30 November), available at www.pcaw.org.uk/files/Rewarding%20whistleblowers%20as%20good%20citizens.pdf

PCaW (Public Concern at Work) 2010. *Where's Whistleblowing Now? 10 Years of Legal Protection for Whistleblowers*. London: Public Concern at Work, available at www.pcaw.org.uk/files/PIDA_10year_Final_PDF.pdf

PCaW (Public Concern at Work) 2013. 'Whistleblowing: the Inside Story', Research Project, Public Concern at Work and University of Greenwich, London, available at www.pcaw.org.uk/files/Whistleblowing%20-%20the%20inside%20story%20FINAL.pdf

Peek, L., M. Roxas, G. Peek, Y. Robichaud, B.E. Covarriubas Salazar and J.N. Barragan Codina 2007. 'NAFTA Students' Whistle-Blowing Perceptions: A Case of Sexual Harassment' *Journal of Business Ethics* (September) 74(3): 219–31

Pelletier, K. 2012. 'Perceptions of and Reactions to Leader Toxicity: Do Leader-Follower Relationships and Identification with Victim Matter?' *Leadership Quarterly* (June) 23(3): 412–24

Pemberton, S., S. Tombs, M. Chan and L. Seal 2012. 'Whistleblowing, Organizational Harm and the Self Regulating Organization' *Policy and Politics* (April) 40(2): 263–79

Pennebaker, J.W. 1997. *Opening Up: The Healing Power of Expressing Emotions*. New York: Guilford

Penner, L.A., J.F. Dovidio, J.A. Piliavin and D.A. Schroeder 2005. 'Prosocial Behavior: Multilevel Perspectives' *Annual Review of Psychology* 56: 365–92

Pershing, J.L. 2003. 'To Snitch or Not to Snitch? Applying the Concept of Neutralization Techniques to the Enforcement of Occupational Misconduct' *Sociological Perspectives* (Summer) 46(2): 149–78

Peters, C. and T. Branch (eds) 1972. *Blowing the Whistle: Dissent in the Public Interest*. New York: Praeger

Peters, K., L. Luck, M. Hutchinson, L. Wilkes, S. Andrew and D. Jackson 2011. 'The Emotional Sequelae of Whistleblowing: Findings from a Qualitative Study' *Journal of Clinical Nursing* (October) 20(19–20): 2907–14

Pfeffer, J. and G.R. Salancik 1978. *The External Control of Organizations*. New York: Harper and Row

Pitzer, D.D. 1972. 'The *Qui Tam* Doctrine: A Comparative Analysis of its Application in the United States and the British Commonwealth' *Texas International Law Journal* 7(3): 415–40

POGO (Project on Government Oversight) 2002. *The Art of Anonymous Activism: Serving the Public while Surviving Public Service*. Washington, DC: Government Accountability Project/Public Employees for Environmental Responsibility

POGO (Project on Government Oversight) 2005. *Homeland and National Security Whistleblower Protections: The Unfinished Agenda* (Washington, DC, 28 April), available at http://fairwhistleblower.ca/files/fair/docs/gap/2008-06%20GAP_conference/Panel%202/TAB%2015.pdf

Posner, E. 1996. 'Law, Economics and Inefficient Norms' *University of Pennsylvania Law Review* (May) 144(5): 1697–1744

Press Trust of India 2012. 'Government Working on False Claims Law, Says CVC', Hyderabad, 8 July, available at www.indianexpress.com/news/government-working-on-false-claims-law-says-cvc/971639/

Price Waterhouse Coopers 2007. *Economic Crime: People, Culture and Controls*, Fourth Biennial Economic Crime Survey, Martin Luther University, Economy and Crime Research Centre, Saxony Anhalt, available at www.pwc.com/gx/en/economic-crime-survey/pdf/pwc_2007gecs.pdf

PRLOG 2012. 'Samsung's American Whistleblower Tells His Story', Press Release Distribution, available at www.prlog.org/11982859-samsungs-american-whistleblower-tells-his-story.html

PSC (Public Service Commission, NSW) 2012. *People Matter Employee Survey 2012: Main Findings Report*. Sydney: New South Wales Government

Pyper, D. 2013. *Whistleblowing: The Public Interest Disclosure Act of 1998*, 8 Library of the House of Commons, Standard note SN00248 (last updated 29 November), available at www.parliament.uk/briefing-papers/SN00248.pdf

Quaye, R. and H. Coombs 2011. 'The Implementation of Anti-Money Laundering, Terrorist Finance and Corruption Laws in Ghana' *International Journal of Government Financial Management* 11(2): 50–9

Radack, J. and K. McClellan 2011. 'The Criminalization of Whistleblowing' *Labor and Employment Law Forum* 2(1): 57–77

Ragin, C.C. 1987. *The Comparative Method: Moving Beyond Qualitative and Quantitative Strategies*. Berkeley, CA: University of California Press

Ragin, C.C. 1999. 'Using Qualitative Comparative Analysis to Study Causal Complexity' *Health Services Research* (December) 34(5): 1225–39

Randall, D.M. and F.M. Fernandes 1991. 'The Social Desirability Response Bias in Ethics Research' *Journal of Business Ethics* (November) 10(11): 805–17

Rapp, G.C. 2007. 'Beyond Protection: Invigorating Incentives for Sarbanes-Oxley Corporate and Securities Fraud Whistleblowers' *Boston University Law Review* 87: 91–156

Rapp, G.C. 2012. 'Mutiny by the Bounties? The Attempt to Reform Wall Street by the New Whistleblower Provisions of the Dodd-Frank Act' *Brigham Young University Law Review* 2012(1): 73–152

Redesign Panel (UN) 2006. *Report of the Redesign Panel on the United Nations System of Administration of Justice, A/61/205*, United Nations General Assembly (28 July), available at www.un.org/ga/president/62/issues/resolutions/a-61-205.pdf

Rehg, M.T., M.P. Miceli, J.P. Near and J.R. Van Scotter 2004. 'Predicting Retaliation Against Whistle-Blowers: Outcomes of Power Relationships within Organizations' *Academy of Management Proceedings*, Meeting Abstract Supplement (August) E1–E6

Rehg, M.T., M.P. Miceli, J.P. Near and J.R. Van Scotter 2008. 'Antecedents and Outcomes of Retaliation Against Whistleblowers: Gender Differences and Power Relationships' *Organization Science* (March/April) 19(2): 221–40

Reinisch, A. 2008. 'The Immunity of International Organizations and the Jurisdiction of Their Administrative Tribunals' *Chinese Journal of International Law* 7(2): 285–306

Reinisch, A. and U.A. Weber 2004. 'In the Shadow of Waite and Kennedy: The Jurisdictional Immunity of International Organizations, the Individual's Right of Access to the Courts and Administrative Tribunals as Alternative Means of Dispute Settlement' *International Organizations Law Review* 1: 59–110, available at http://zsu-schmelz.univie.ac.at/fileadmin/user_upload/int_beziehungen/Personal/Publikationen_Reinisch/waite_kennedy_iolr_2004.pdf

Rest, J.R., D. Narvaez, S.J. Thoma and M.J. Bebeau 2000. 'A Neo-Kohlbergian Approach to Morality Research' *Journal of Moral Education* 29(4): 381–95

Rest, J.R., S.J. Thomas, D. Narvaez and M.J. Bebeau 1997. 'Alchemy and Beyond: Indexing the Defining Issues Test' *Journal of Educational Psychology* (September) 89(3): 498–507

Rettig, C.P. 2012. 'The IRS Whistleblower Program: Making Money the Old Fashioned Way!' *Journal of Tax Practice and Procedure* (April/May) 21–9

Richardson, B.K. and J. McGlynn 2011. 'Rabid Fans, Death Threats, and Dysfunctional Stakeholders: The Influence of Organisational and Industry Contexts on Whistle-Blowing Cases' *Management Communication Quarterly* (February) 25(1): 121–50

Rieble, V. and B. Wiebauer 2010. 'Meinungskampf im Betrieb' ['Battle of Opinions at the Workplace'] *Zeitschrift für Arbeitsrecht* (ZFA) 41(1): 63–160

Rihoux, B. 2006. 'Qualitative Comparative Analysis (QCA) and Related Systematic Comparative Methods: Recent Advances and Remaining Challenges for Social Science Research' *International Sociology* (September) 21(5): 679–706

Riley, A. 2003. *The Civil False Claims Act: Using Lincoln's Law to Protect the European Community Budget*, CEPS (Centre for European Policy Studies) Policy Brief 43 (December), available at http://aei.pitt.edu/1943/1/PB43.pdf

Rising, K., P. Bacchetti and L. Bero 2008. 'Reporting Bias in Drug Trials Submitted to the Food and Drug Administration: Review of Publication and Presentation' *PLOS Medicine* (November) 5(11): 1561–70

Roach, K. 1999. *Due Process and Victim's Rights: The New Law and Politics of Criminal Justice.* Toronto: University of Toronto Press

Roberts, P. 2008. 'Evaluating Agency Responses: The Comprehensiveness and Impact of Whistleblowing Procedures' in A.J. Brown (ed.), *Whistleblowing in the Australian Public Sector: Enhancing the Theory and Practice of Internal Witness Management in Public Sector Organisations*. Canberra: ANU E-Press, ch. 10, 233–60

Roberts, P. 2012. 'Whistleblowing and Conflict', paper prepared for the Whistleblowing: Law, Compliance and the Public Interest Conference, Seattle Law School, 23–24 March

Roberts, P. and A.J. Brown 2010. 'The Australian Legislative Experience' in D.B. Lewis (ed.), *A Global Approach to Public Interest Disclosure: What Can We Learn from Existing Whistleblowing Legislation and Research?*. Cheltenham: Edward Elgar, ch. 5, 56–73

Roberts, P., A.J. Brown and J. Olsen 2011. *Whistling While They Work: A Good Practice Guide for Managing Internal Reporting of Wrongdoing in Public Sector Organisations*. Canberra: ANU E-Press, available at http://epress.anu.edu.au/whistling_citation.html

Rohde-Liebenau, B. 2006. 'Whistleblowing Rules: Best Practice – Assessment and Revision of Rules Existing in EU Institutions', paper prepared for the Budgetary Support Unit, IPOL/D/CONT/ST/2005 (12 May)

Romano R. 2005. 'The Sarbanes-Oxley Act and the Making of Quack Corporate Governance' *Yale Law Journal* 114: 1521–1611

Rossouw, D. 2004. *Developing Business Ethics as an Academic Field.* Johannesburg: Ben Africa

Rothschild, J. 2008. 'Freedom of Speech Denied, Dignity Assaulted: What the Whistleblowers Experience in the US' *Current Sociology* (November) 56(6): 884–903

Rothschild, J. and T.D. Miethe 1994. 'Whistleblowing as Resistance in Modern Work Organizations: the Politics of Revealing Organizational Deception and Abuse' in J. Jermier, D. Knights and W. Nord (eds), *Resistance and Power in Organizations*. London: Routledge, 252–73

Rothschild, J. and T.D. Miethe 1999a. 'Whistle-blower Disclosures and Management Retaliation: the Battle to Control Information about Organization Corruption' *Work and Occupations* (February) 26(1): 107–28

Rothschild, J. and T.D. Miethe 1999b. 'Disclosing Misconduct in Work Organizations: An Empirical Analysis of the Situational Factors that Foster Whistleblowing' in Randy Hodson (ed.), *Deviance in the Workplace*, vol. 8, Research in the Sociology of Work series. Bingley: Emerald Group Publishing, 211–27

Rothwell, G.R. and J.N. Baldwin 2007a. 'Whistle-blowing and the Code of Silence in Police Agencies' *Crime and Delinquency* (October) 53(4): 605–32

Rothwell, G.R. and J.N. Baldwin 2007b. 'Ethical Climate Theory, Whistle-Blowing, and the Code of Silence in Police Agencies in the State of Georgia' *Journal of Business Ethics* (February) 70(4): 341–61

Rotter, J.B. 1966. 'Generalized Expectancies for Internal vs. External Control of Reinforcement' *Psychological Monographs* 80: 1–18

Ruhnka, J.C., E.J. Gac and H. Boerstler 2000. '*Qui Tam* Claims: Threat to Voluntary Compliance Programs in Health Care Organizations' *Journal of Health Politics, Policy and Law* 25(2): 283–308

Rushkoff, D. 2000. *Coercion: The Persuasion Professionals and Why We Listen to What They Say*. London: Little, Brown

Ryan, A.M., D. Chan, R.E. Ployhart and L.A. Slade 1999. 'Employee Attitude Surveys in a Multinational Organization: Considering Language and Culture in Assessing Measurement Equivalence' *Personnel Psychology* (March) 52(1): 37–58

Sawyer, K. 2004. 'Courage Without Mateship', paper prepared for the National Conference of Whistleblowers Australia, Melbourne, 28 November, available at www.bmartin.cc/dissent/documents/Sawyer04.pdf

Scammell, H. 2004. *Giant Killers*. New York: Grove Press

Schaffer, B.S. and C.M. Riordan 2003. 'A Review of Cross-Cultural Methodologies for Organizational Research: A Best-Practices Approach' *Organizational Research Methods* (April) 6(2): 169–215

Schrijvers, J.P.M. 2004. *The Way of the Rat: A Survival Guide to Office Politics*. London: Cyan

Schultz, J.J., D.A. Johnson, D. Morris and S. Dyrnes 1993. 'An Investigation of the Reporting of Questionable Acts in an International Setting' *Journal of Accounting Research* 31: 75–103

Schwartz, S.H. 1994. 'Are there Universal Aspects in the Structure and Contents of Human Values?' *Journal of Social Issues* (Winter) 50(4): 19–45

Schwartz, S.H. and A. Bardi 2001. 'Value Hierarchies across Cultures: Taking a Similarities Perspective' *Journal of Cross-Cultural Psychology* (May) 32(3): 268–90

Scott, G. 2006. *World Bank Group Conflict Resolution System: Some Issues and Recommendations: A Report on Reviewing the Findings and Implementing Recommendations in Various Reports on the Conflict Resolution System and Some Related Functions Within the World Bank Group*, Report prepared for the World Bank Group

Scott, W.R. 1995. *Institutions and Organizations*. Thousand Oaks, CA: Sage Publications

Seabright, P. 2010. *The Company of Strangers: A Natural History of Economic Life*, revised edn. Princeton, NJ: Princeton University Press

SEC (Securities and Exchange Commission, US) 2011. 'Implementation of the Whistleblower Provisions of Section 21F of the Securities Exchange Act of 1934', 17 CFR Parts 240 and 249, Release No. 34–64545, File No. S7–33–10, RIN 3235–AK78, available at www.sec.gov/rules/final/2011/34-64545.pdf

SEC (Securities and Exchange Commission, US) 2012. 'SEC Issues First Whistleblower Program Award', Press Release, 21 August, available at www.sec.gov/News/PressRelease/Detail/PressRelease/1365171483972#.UnnNtYx–Uk

Seifert, D.L., J.T. Sweeney, J. Joireman and J.M. Thornton 2010. 'The Influence of Organizational Justice on Accountant Whistleblowing' *Accounting, Organisations and Society* (October) 35(7): 707–17

Senate (Australia) 1994. *In the Public Interest, Report of the Senate Select Committee on Public Interest Whistleblowing*. Canberra: Parliament House

Senate Committee on Foreign Relations (US) 2004. 'Combating Corruption in the Multilateral Development Banks (Part I)', Hearing before the Committee on Foreign Relations, Second Session, S. HRG. 108–734, Washington, DC, 13 May, available at www.gpo.gov/fdsys/pkg/CHRG-108shrg21394/html/CHRG-108shrg21394.htm

Senate Judiciary Committee (US) 2009. *Senate Report 111–010 Fraud Enforcement and Recovery Act of 2009*, 111th Congress 2009–2010, available at http://thomas.loc.gov/cgi-bin/cpquery/?&dbname=cp111&sid=cp11123vD4&refer=&r_n=sr010.111&item=&sel=TOC_17601&

Senate Permanent Subcommittee on Investigations and Committee on Homeland Security and Governmental Affairs (US) 2008. *United Nations Development Program: A Case Study of North Korea*, Staff Report, US Senate, 24 January, available at http://web.undp.org/dprk/docs/UNDP-senate-report.pdf

Shaman, D.I. 2009. *The World Bank Unveiled: Inside the Revolutionary Struggle for Transparency*. Chicago, IL: Parkhurst Brothers Publishers

Shapiro, J. 2011. 'Calls for More Reporting of Suspected Child Abuse', *NPR.org Morning Edition*, 21 December, available at www.npr.org/2011/12/21/143841832/calls-for-more-reporting-of-suspected-child-abuse

Sharp, G. 2010. *From Dictatorship to Democracy: A Conceptual Framework for Liberation,* 4th edn. East Boston, MA: Albert Einstein Institution

Sheen, B. Sir 1987. *MV Herald of Free Enterprise: Report of Court No. 8074 Formal Investigation*. London: HMSO for Department of Transport (September), available at www.maib.gov.uk/cms_resources.cfm?file=/hoffefinal.pdf

Sims, R.L. and J.P. Keenan 1998. 'Predictors of External Whistleblowing: Organizational and Intrapersonal Variables' *Journal of Business Ethics* (March) 17(4): 411–21

Sims, R.L. and J.P. Keenan 1999. 'A Cross-Cultural Comparison of Managers' Whistleblowing Tendencies' *International Journal of Value-Based Management* 12(2): 137–51

Singer, M., S. Mitchell and J. Turner 1998. 'Consideration of Moral Intensity in Ethicality Judgements: Its Relationship with Whistle-Blowing and Need-For-Cognition' *Journal of Business Ethics* (April) 17(5): 527–41

Sinzdak, G. 2008. 'An Analysis of Current Whistleblower Laws: Defending a More Flexible Approach to Reporting Requirements' *California Law Review* 96(6): 1633–68

Skivenes, M. and S.C. Trygstad 2010a. 'When Whistle-Blowing Works: the Norwegian Case' *Human Relations* (July) 63(7): 1071–97

Skivenes, M. and S.C. Trygstad 2010b. 'Loyalty and Whistleblowing in Norway: How Roles Come into Play' in D.B. Lewis (ed.), *A Global Approach to Public Interest Disclosure: What Can We Learn from Existing Whistleblowing Legislation and Research?*. Cheltenham: Edward Elgar, ch. 7, 91–108

Skivenes, M. and S.C. Trygstad 2012. *Openness, Expression and Whistleblowing* [*Åpenhet, ytring og varsling*]. Oslo: Gyldendal Akademisk

Slavin, R.E. 1986. 'Best-Evidence Synthesis: An Alternative to Meta-Analytic and Traditional Reviews' *Educational Researcher* (November) 15(9): 5–11

Sledge, M. 2012. 'Bradley Manning Lawyer Charges Obama with Hypocrisy over Whistleblower Protection', 4 December, available at www.huffingtonpost.com/2012/12/04/bradley-manning-obama-whistle blower_n_2238383.html

Smith, M. 2011. 'Is Skype a Security Risk that Endangers Your Privacy?', *Network World*, 25 March, available at www.networkworld.com/community/blog/skype-security-risk-endangers-your-privacy

Smith, R. 2001. *Australian Political Culture*. Frenchs Forest: Pearson Education

Smith, R. 2010. 'The Role of Whistle-Blowing in Governing Well: Evidence from the Australian Public Sector' *American Review of Public Administration* (November) 40(6): 704–21

Smith, R. and A.J. Brown 2008. 'The Good, the Bad and the Ugly: Whistleblowing Outcomes' in A.J. Brown (ed.), *Whistleblowing in the Australian Public Sector: Enhancing the Theory and Practice of Internal Witness Management in Public Sector Organisations*. Canberra: ANU E-Press, 109–36

Snell, R. 2006 'Freedom of Information Practices' *Agenda* 13(4): 291–307

Solano, F. and B.H. Kleiner 2003. 'Understanding and Preventing Workplace Retaliation' *Management Research News*, 26(2–4): 206–11

South African Law Reform Commission 2004. *Protected Disclosures*, Discussion Paper 107 (June), available at http://salawreform.justice.gov.za/dpapers/dp107.pdf

Spagnolo, G. 2006. 'Leniency and Whistleblowers in Antitrust' in P. Buccirossi (ed.), *Handbook of Antitrust Economics*. Cambridge, MA: MIT Press, ch. 7, 259–304

Spencer, J. and M. Spencer 2001. 'Witness Protection and the Integrity of the Criminal Trial', paper prepared for the Conference on Modern Criminal Investigation, Organized Crime and Human Rights, Durban, South Africa, 3–7 December

Spencer, M. and J. Spencer 2010. 'Coping with *Conway v. Rimmer* [1968] AC 910: How Civil Servants Control Access to Justice' *Journal of Law and Society* (September) 37(3): 387–411

Stableford, D. 2011. 'Murdochleaks, a WikiLeaks-Style Site for News Corp. Whistleblowers, Goes Live', *The Cutline*, 25 July, available at http://news.yahoo.com/blogs/cutline/murdochleaks-wikileaks-style-news-corp-whistleblowers-goes-live-201343504.html

Stansbury, J.M. and B. Victor 2009. 'Whistle-blowing among Young Employees: A Life-Course Perspective' *Journal of Business Ethics* (March) 85(3): 281–99

Starkey, P. 1998. *Whistleblowing Behavior: The Impact of Situational and Personality Variables*. Oxford, MS: University of Mississippi

Statoil 2011. 'Ethics Code of Conduct', available at www.statoil.com/en/About/EthicsValues/Downloads/Ethics%20code%20of%20conduct.pdf

Steel, D. 2004. 'Social Mechanisms and Causal Inference' *Philosophy of the Social Sciences* (March) 34(1): 55–78

Sterling, T. 2002. *The Enron Scandal*. New York: Nova Science Publishers

Stiglitz, J. 2002. 'Information and the Change in the Paradigm in Economics' *American Economic Review* (June) 92(3): 460–501

Stonefrost, M. 1990. *Encouraging Citizenship: Report of the Commission on Citizenship*. London: HMSO

Strack, G. 2011. 'Whistleblowing in Germany' in M. Arszutowicz and W.W. Gasparski (eds), *Whistleblowing: In Defense of Proper Action*, vol. 18. New Brunswick, NJ: Transaction Publishers, 109–24

Stringer, W.L. 1996. *The 1986 False Claims Act Amendments: An Assessment of Economic Impact*. Washington, DC: Taxpayers Against Fraud/False Claims Act Legal Center

Sturdy, A. 1998. 'Customer Care in a Consumer Society: Smiling and Sometimes Meaning It?' *Organization* (February) 5(1): 27–53

Su, S.H., C. Kan and H.L. Yang 2010. 'Cross-Cultural Difference and Accounting Ethics: An Empirical Study for Accounting Students' *International Journal of Organizational Innovation* 2(3): 161–85

Sumanth, J.J., D.M. Mayer and V.S. Kay 2011. 'Why Good Guys Finish Last: the Role of Justification Motives, Cognition, and Emotion in Predicting Retaliation Against Whistleblowers' *Organizational Psychology Review* (May) 1(2): 165–84

Swanepoel, D. 2011. *The State of Whistleblowing in South Africa: An Analysis of Public Opinion*, Report prepared for ODAC (Open Democracy Advice Centre). Pinegowrie, SA: Ipsos Markinor Research (December)

Sydney Morning Herald 2013. 'Anonymous Hackers Jailed over PayPal Attack', 25 January, available at www.smh.com.au/it-pro/security-it/anonymous-hackers-jailed-over-paypal-attack-20130124-2damw.html

Tavakoli, A., J.P. Keenan and B. Crnjak-Karanovic 2003. 'Culture and Whistleblowing: An Empirical Study of Croatian and United States Managers Utilizing Hofstede's Cultural Dimensions' *Journal of Business Ethics* (March) 43(1–2): 49–64

Tavare, A. 2012. 'Scientific Misconduct is Worryingly Prevalent in the UK, Shows BMJ Survey' *British Medical Journal* (January) 344: 377

Taxpayers Against Fraud Education Fund 2011a. 'False Claims Act Update and Alert' (Washington, DC, 15 December), available at www.taf.org/whistle334.htm

Taxpayers Against Fraud Education Fund 2011b. 'FY 2011 False Claims Act Settlements', *Major False Claims Act Cases Resolved in Fiscal Year 2011* (8 July), available at www.taf.org/total2011.htm

Taxpayers Against Fraud Education Fund 2012. 'False Claims Act Story', available at www.taf.org/

Taylor, S. and P.A. Todd 1995. 'Understanding Information Technology Usage: A Test of Competing Models' *Information Systems Research* (June) 6(2): 144–76

Teo, H.D. and D. Caspersz 2011. 'Dissenting Discourse: Exploring Alternatives to the Whistleblowing/Silence Dichotomy' *Journal of Business Ethics* (December) 104(2): 237–49

Therapeutic Goods Administration (Australia) 2011. 'Compliance with Ministerial and Default Standards' (Department of Health and Aging, Australian Government, 21 February), available at www.tga.gov.au/industry/compliance-with-standards.htm

Thérèse, S. and B. Martin 2010. 'Shame, Scientist! Degradation Rituals in Science' *Prometheus* 28(2): 97–110

Thoroughgood, C., A. Padilla, S. Hunter and B. Tate 2012. 'The Susceptible Circle: A Taxonomy of Followers Associated with Destructive Leadership' *Leadership Quarterly* (October) 23(5): 897–917

Thurmond, V.A. 2001. 'The Point of Triangulation' *Journal of Nursing Scholarship* (September) 33(3): 253–8

TI (Transparency International) 2009. 'Recommended Draft Principles for Whistleblowing Legislation', available at www.opendemocracy.org.za/wp-content/uploads/2011/05/Recommended-draft-principles-for-whistleblowing-legislation-Nov-09-doc.pdf

TIL (Transparency International Lithuania) 2009. *Whistleblower Protection Assessment: Country Report/Lithuania/2009*, available at www.transparency.lt/new/images/lithuania_whistleblower_protection_assessment_2009.pdf

Tippett, E.C. 2006. 'The Promise of Compelled Whistleblowing: What the Corporate Governance Provisions of Sarbanes Oxley Mean for Employment Law', available at http://ssrn.com/abstract=930226

Tourangeau, R., L.J. Rips and K. Rasinski 2000. *The Psychology of Survey Response*. Cambridge: Cambridge University Press

Triandis, H.C. 1995. *Individualism and Collectivism*. Boulder, CO: Westview Press

Triandis, H.C. 1996. 'The Psychological Measurement of Cultural Syndromes' *American Psychologist* (April) 51(4): 407–15

Triandis, H.C. and M.J. Gelfland 1998. 'Converging Measurement of Horizontal and Vertical Individualism and Collectivism' *Journal of Personality and Social Psychology* (January) 74(1): 118–28

Trongmateerut, P. and J.T. Sweeney 2013. 'The Influence of Subjective Norms on Whistle-Blowing: A Cross-Cultural Investigation' *Journal of Business Ethics* (February) 112(3): 437–51

Trott, K. 2004. 'The Australian Perspective' in R. Calland and G. Dehn (eds), *Whistleblowing Around the World: Law, Culture and Practice*. Cape Town: ODAC, 119–42

Truelson, J.A. 2001. 'Whistleblower Protection and the Judiciary' in T.L. Cooper (ed.), *Handbook of Administrative Ethics*, 2nd revised edn. New York: Marcel Dekker, ch. 20, 407–28

Trygstad, S.C. 2010. 'With a Right to Blow the Whistle … But, Does it Help, and is it Wise?' ['Med rett til å varsle … men hjelper det, og er det lurt?'] *Fafo-rapport* 18 (Oslo), available at www.fafo.no/pub/rapp/20162/index.html

Tsahuridu, E.E. 2011. 'Whistleblowing Management is Risk Management' in D.B. Lewis and W. Vandekerckhove (eds), *Whistleblowing and Democratic Values*. London: International Whistleblowing Research Network, 56–69

Tsahuridu, E.E. and W. Vandekerckhove 2008. 'Organisational Whistleblowing Policies: Making Employees Responsible or Liable?' *Journal of Business Ethics* (September) 82(1): 107–18

Tsui, A.S., S.S. Nifadkar and A.Y. Ou 2007. 'Cross-National, Cross-Cultural Organizational Behavior Research: Advances, Gaps, and Recommendations' *Journal of Management* (June) 33(3): 426–78

Tucker, D. 1995. 'Whistleblowing Without Tears: the Exposure of Brisbane's King George Square Car Park Fraud' *Australian Journal of Public Administration* (December) 54(4): 475–82

Tucker, N. 2007. 'Taking a Whack Against Comcast', *Washington Post*, 18 October, available at www.washingtonpost.com/wp-dyn/content/article/2007/10/17/AR2007101702359_2.html

Turner, E.H., A.M. Matthews, E. Linardatos, R.A. Tell and R. Rosenthal 2008. 'Selective Publication of Antidepressant Trials and its Influence on Apparent Efficacy' *New England Journal of Medicine* (17 January), 358: 252–60

UNJIU (United Nations Joint Inspection Unit) 2006. 'Oversight Lacunae in the United Nations System', available at www.unjiu.org/en/reports-notes/archive/JIU_REP_2006_2_English.pdf

Urbas, G., T. Faunce, L.A. Skillen and M. Smith 2012. 'Responding to Fraud in the Australian Health and Pharmaceuticals and Medical Devices Sectors: A Proposal for Reform' *World Review of Business Research* 2(2): 109–19

Uys, T. 2000. 'The Politicisation of Whistleblowers: A Case Study' *Business Ethics: A European Review* (October) 9(4): 259–67

Uys, T. 2002. 'Students, Sex and Aids: A Methodological Controversy' *Society in Transition* 33(3): 382–402

Uys, T. 2008. 'Rational Loyalty and Whistleblowing: the South African Context' *Current Sociology* (November) 56(6): 904–21

Uys, T. 2010. 'Speaking Truth to Power: the Whistleblower as Organizational Citizen in South Africa' in D.B. Lewis (ed.), *A Global Approach to Public Interest Disclosure: What Can We Learn from Existing Whistleblowing Legislation and Research?*. Cheltenham: Edward Elgar, ch. 8, 109–27

Van den Hende, R. 2004. 'Jiang Yanyong and SARS' in R. Calland and G. Dehn (eds), *Whistleblowing Around the World: Law, Culture and Practice*. Cape Town: Open Democracy Advice Centre/Public Concern at Work

Van der Wal, Z. 2008. *Value Solidity: Differences, Similarities and Conflicts between the Organizational Values of Government and Business*. Amsterdam: VU University

Vandekerckhove, W. 2006. *Whistleblowing and Organizational Social Reponsibility: A Global Assessment.* Aldershot: Ashgate

Vandekerckhove, W. 2010. 'European Whistleblowing Policies: Tiers or Tears?' in D.B. Lewis (ed.), *A Global Approach to Public Interest Disclosure: What Can We Learn from Existing Whistleblowing Legislation and Research?*. Cheltenham: Edward Elgar, ch. 3, 15–35

Vandekerckhove, W. 2012. *UK Public Attitudes to Whistleblowing*, Working Paper. London: University of Greenwich (15 November), available at http://ssrn.com/abstract=2176193

Vandekerckhove, W. and M.S.R. Commers 2004. 'Whistle Blowing and Rational Loyalty' *Journal of Business Ethics* (August) 53(1–2): 225–33

Vandekerckhove, W. and C. James 2013. 'Blowing the Whistle on the Union: How Successful is It?' *E-Journal of International and Comparative Labour Studies* (September/October) 2(3): 66–93

Vandekerckhove, W. and S. Langenberg 2012. 'Can We Organize Courage? Implications of Foucault's Parrhesia' *Electronic Journal of Business Ethics and Organization Studies* 17(2): 35–44

Vandekerckhove, W. and D.B. Lewis 2012. 'The Content of Whistleblowing Procedures: A Critical Review of Recent Official Guidelines' *Journal of Business Ethics* (June) 108(2): 253–64

Vandekerckhove, W. and E.E. Tsahuridu 2010. 'Risky Rescues and the Duty to Blow the Whistle' *Journal of Business Ethics* (December) 97(3): 365–80

Vaughn, R.G. 1999. 'State Whistleblower Statutes and the Future of Whistleblowers Protection' *Administrative Law Review* 51(2): 581–625

Vaughn, R.G. 2005. *Report on the World Bank's Whistleblower Procedures*, Report commissioned by the World Bank (New York, 30 April), available at www.whistleblower.org/storage/documents/Vaughn_Report.pdf

Vaughn, R.G. 2012. *The Successes and Failures of Whistleblower Laws*. Cheltenham: Edward Elgar

Vermaas, J., R. van der Linden, T. Serail and A. Klomps 2001. *De weg van de klokkenluider: keuzes en dilemma's. Onderzoek naar de klokkenluidersproblematiek in Nederland* [*The Way of the Whistleblower: Choices and Dilemmas. Research on Whistleblowing in the Netherlands*]. Tilburg: IVA

Victor, B. and J.B. Cullen 1988. 'The Organizational Bases of Ethical Work Climates' *Administrative Science Quarterly* (March) 33(1): 101–25

Victor, B., L.K. Trevino and C.L. Shapiro 1993. 'Peer Reporting of Unethical Behavior: the Influence of Justice Evaluations and Social Context Factors' *Journal of Business Ethics* (April) 12(4): 253–63

Vinten, G. 1994. *Whistleblowing: Subversion or Corporate Citizenship*. London: Paul Chapman

Volcker, P., G. Gaviria, J. Githongo, B.W. Heineman, Jr, W. van Gerven and J. Vereker 2007. *Independent Panel Review of the World Bank Group Department of Institutional Integrity*. Washington, DC: World Bank Group (13 September), available at http://siteresources.worldbank.org/NEWS/Resources/Volcker_Report_Sept._12,_for_website_FINAL.pdf

Voreacos, D. 2012. 'Mylan to Pay $57 Million to Settle Drug Overpricing Claims', *Bloomberg News*, 29 February, available at www.bloomberg.com/news/2012-02-28/mylan-to-pay-57-million-to-settle-drug-overpricing-claims-1-.html

Wahl-Jorgensen K. and J. Hunt 2012. 'Journalism, Accountability and the Possibilities for Structural Critique: A Case Study of Coverage of Whistleblowing' *Journalism* (May) 13(4): 399–416

Wak-Woya, B. 2012. 'Fear of Speaking Up: Perception or Reality' *Dialogue: The UNHCR Staff Magazine* (published by the Staff Council) (March) 3–5

Wald, M. and D.W. Wolf 1985. 'Recent Developments in the Law of Employment at Will' *Labor Lawyer* (Summer) 1(3): 533–82

Walden, S., J. Cavallo and B. Edwards 2011. 'How the World Bank's Peer Review Services Deny Staff the Right to a Fair Hearing' (12 August), available at www.whistleblower.org/storage/Peer_Review_Services_Final_August_12.pdf

Walters, K. 1975. 'Your Employees' Right to Blow the Whistle' *Harvard Business Review* 53(4): 26–34

Wang, Y. 2010. 'Is a Whistleblower Incentive Program Right for Canada?' (3 December), available at http://accounting.uwaterloo.ca/ethics/estey/Submission%206%20-%20Wang-1.pdf

War Resisters' International 2009. *Handbook for Nonviolent Campaigns*. London: War Resisters' International, available at www.wri-irg.org/pubs/NonviolenceHandbook

Warren, D.E. 2003. 'Constructive and Destructive Deviance in Organizations' *Academy of Management Review* (October) 28(4): 622–32

Waytz, A., J. Dungan and L. Young 2013. 'The Whistleblower's Dilemma and the Fairness–Loyalty Tradeoff' *Journal of Experimental Social Psychology* (November) 49(6): 1027–33

WBAT (World Bank) 2008. 'Staff Rule 08.02: Protections and Procedures for Reporting Misconduct (Whistleblowing)', available at http://siteresources.worldbank.org/INTSTAFFMANUAL/Resources/StaffManual_WB_web.pdf

Weber, M. 1947. *The Theory of Social and Economic Organization*. New York: Free Press

Weber, M. 1978. *Economy and Society*, G. Roth and C. Wittich (trans.). Berkeley, CA: University of California Press

Weber, P.J. and R. Satter 2012. 'Leaked Emails Shine Rare Light on Stratfor', *Yahoo News*, 28 February, available at http://news.yahoo.com/leaked-emails-shine-rare-light-stratfor-080701186.html

Webley, S. and P. Dryden 2005. *Ethics at Work: A National Survey*. London: Institute of Business Ethics (June)

Webley, S. and A. Werner 2008. *Employee Views of Ethics at Work: The 2008 National Survey*. London: Institute of Business Ethics (April)

Weinstein, D. 1979. *Bureaucratic Opposition: Challenging Abuses at the Workplace*. New York: Pergamon

Wenger, N.S., S.G. Korenman, R. Berk and H. Liu 1999. 'Reporting Unethical Research Behavior' *Evaluation Review* (October) 23(5): 553–70

Westman, D.P. 2005. 'The Significance of the Sarbanes-Oxley Whistleblower Provisions' *Labor Lawyer* (Fall) 21(2): 141–55

Westmarland, L. 2006. 'Police Ethics and Integrity: Breaking the Blue Code of Silence' *Policing and Society: An International Journal of Research and Policy* 15(2): 145–65

Whitton, H. 1995. 'Ethics and Principled Dissent in the Queensland Public Sector: A Response to the Queensland Whistleblower Study' *Australian Journal of Public Administration* (December) 54(4): 455–61

Williams, K.D. 2001. *Ostracism: The Power of Silence.* New York: Guilford

Williamson, D. 2002. 'Forward from a Critique of Hofstede's Model of National Culture' *Human Relations* 55(11): 1373–95

Wilson, D. 2011. 'Glaxo Settles Cases with US for $3 Billion', *New York Times*, 3 November, available at www.nytimes.com/2011/11/04/business/glaxo-to-pay-3-billion-in-avandia-settlement.html

Wise, T.D. 1995. *An Analysis of Factors Proposed to Affect the Decision to Blow the Whistle on Unethical Acts.* Ruston, LA: Louisiana Tech University

Worth, M. 2013. *Whistleblowing in Europe: Legal Protections for Whistleblower in the EU*, Report for Transparency International, Berlin (November), available at www.transparency.org/whatwedo/pub/whistleblowing_in_europe_legal_protections_for_whistleblowers_in_the_eu

Wortley, R., P. Cassematis and M. Donkin 2008. 'Who Blows the Whistle, Who Doesn't and Why?' in A.J. Brown (ed.), *Whistleblowing in the Australian Public Sector: Enhancing the Theory and Practice of Internal Witness Management in Public Sector Organizations.* Canberra: ANU E-Press, ch. 3, 53–82

Wright, E. 2005. *Approaches to Class Analysis.* Cambridge: Cambridge University Press

Wulczyn, F., D. Daro, J. Fluke, S. Feldman, C. Glodek and K. Lifanda 2010. *Adapting a Systems Approach to Child Protection: Key Concepts and Considerations.* New York: UNICEF (United Nations Children's Fund)

Wynes, D. and M. Zahran 2010. *Ethics in the United Nations System.* Geneva: Joint Inspection Unit, United Nations, available at www.unjiu.org/en/reports-notes/archive/Ethics%20in%20the%20United%20Nations%20system.pdf

Wynes, D. and M. Zahran 2011. *The Investigation Function in the United Nations System.* Geneva: Joint Inspection Unit, United Nations, available at www.unjiu.org/en/reports-notes/JIU%20Products/JIU_REP_2011_7.pdf

Yeganeh, H., S. Zhan and E.V.M. Chrysostome 2004. 'A Critical Review of Epistemological and Methodological Issues in Cross-Cultural Research' *Journal of Comparative International Management* 7(2): 66–86

Yun, Sai Ree 2002. *Antitrust Law in Korea* (Social Science Research Network, 25 June), available at http://papers.ssrn.com/sol3/papers.cfm?abstract_id=445042

Zack, A.M. 2010a. 'Developing Standards of Workplace Justice within International Organizations' (Harvard Law) *American Society of International Law International Organizations Interest Group Review* (Summer) 44–57, available at www.law.harvard.edu/programs/lwp/people/staffPapers/zack/2010%20Zack%20Developing%20Standards%20of%20Workplace%20Justice.pdf

Zack, A.M. 2010b. 'Some Thoughts on the Step Before: Speech Delivered on Feb. 22, 2010 at the Celebration of the 30th Anniversary World Bank Administrative Tribunal' (Harvard Law) *American Society of International Law International Organizations Interest Group Review* (Summer) 37–43, available at www.law.harvard.edu/programs/lwp/people/staffPapers/zack/International%20Organizations%20Interest%20Group%20Review%20-%202010%20Issue.pdf

Zeller, R.A. 1993. 'Combining Qualitative and Quantitative Techniques to Develop Culturally Sensitive Measures' in D.G. Ostrow and R.C. Kessler (eds), *Methodological Issues in AIDS Behavioral Research.* New York: Plenum Press

Zhang, J., R. Chiu and L.Q. Wei 2009a. 'On Whistleblowing Judgment and Intention: the Roles of Positive Mood and Organizational Ethical Culture' *Journal of Managerial Psychology* 24(7–8), 627–49

Zhang, J., R. Chiu and L. Wei 2009b. 'Decision-Making Process of Internal Whistleblowing Behavior in China: Empirical Evidence and Implications' *Journal of Business Ethics* (April) 88(1): 25–41

Zhuang, J., S. Thomas and D.L. Miller 2005. 'Examining Culture's Effect on Whistle-Blowing and Peer Reporting' *Business and Society* (December) 44(4): 462–86

Ziadé, N. 2007. 'The Independence of International Administrative Tribunals', paper prepared for the 25th Anniversary Celebration of the World Bank Administrative Tribunal, 27 March

Ziem, J. and E. Gyebi 2012. 'Boss Dissects Whistleblower Law, Points out Challenges', *Savannah News*, 8 June, available at http://savannahnewsblogspotcom.blogspot.com.au/2012/06/nr-chraj-boss-dissects-whistleblower.html

Zipparo, L. 1999a. 'Encouraging Public Sector Employees to Report Workplace Corruption' *Australian Journal of Public Administration* (June) 58(2): 83–93

Zipparo, L. 1999b. 'Factors which Deter Public Officials from Reporting Corruption' *Crime, Law and Social Change* 30(3): 273–87

Zweigert, K. and H. Kötz 1998. *An Introduction to Comparative Law*, 3rd revised edn, Tony Weir (trans.). Oxford: Clarendon Press

Index